Baedeker

Switzerland

Hints for using this Guide

Following the tradition established by Karl Baedeker in 1844, sights of particular interest, outstanding buildings, works of art, etc., as well as good hotels and restaurants are denoted by stars as follows: especially worth attention ★, outstanding ★★.

To make it easier to locate the various places listed in the "A to Z" section of the Guide, their co-ordinates on the large country map are shown in red at the head of each entry: e.g., Berne H 7.

Coloured lines down the right-hand side of the page are an aid to finding the main heading in the Guide: blue stands for Facts and Figures (Nature, Culture, History, etc.), red for the "A to Z" section, and yellow indicates Practical Information.

Only a selection of hotels and restaurants can be given; no reflection is implied therefore on establishments not included.

In a time of rapid change it is difficult to ensure that all the information given is entirely accurate and up-to-date, and the possibility of error can never be entirely eliminated.

Although the publishers can accept no responsibility for inaccuracies and omissions, they are constantly endeavouring to improve the quality of their Guides and are therefore always grateful for criticisms, corrections and suggestions for improvement.

Preface

This Pocket Guide to Switzerland is one of the new generation of Baedeker guides.

These guides are designed to meet the needs of the modern traveller. They are quick and easy to consult, with the principal sights described in alphabetical order and useful details shown in the margin.

Each guide is divided into three parts. The first gives a general account of the country, its geography, climate, flora and fauna, population, prominent personalities and so on; in the second part the principal sights are described, and the third part contains a variety of practical information designed to help visitors to find their way about and make the most of their stay. For the reader's convenience this practical information, like the main part of the guide, is arranged in alphabetical order.

The new guides are abundantly illustrated and contain a series of specially drawn plans. In a pocket at the back of the book is a large road map, and each entry in the main part of

Massive 500 year-old castle in Sargans and beautiful mountain walk in Valais

the guide gives the co-ordinates of the square on the map in which the place concerned can be found. Users of this guide, therefore, will have no difficulty in finding the places they wish to visit.

Contents

Rütli Oath and

"The hat shall be regarded as highly as its wearer". The tyrannical ruler named Gessler issued this absurd proclamation more than 700 years ago. According to the legend passed down to us by Friedrich Schiller, instead of complying and showing the hat the same degree of reverence as its owner, representatives of the three original forest cantons of Schwyz, Uri and Unterwalden met in August 1291 at the Urner See and agreed to form the "Perpetual Alliance" and to strive for justice and their traditional rights. The "Rütli Oath", the "Apple Shoots" and "Death to the Tyrant", led by the national hero William

Tell, are further stages in a development which finally led to the founding of the Swiss Confederation.

Grüezi, bonjour, buon di, buongiorno . . . these can all be heard today in the four national languages of German, French, Italian and Romansch when somebody wishes to say "good-day" in this region between Basle, Lake Constance, Geneva and Chiasso. The country itself, lying in the very heart of Europe, is just as varied as the people and their languages. There are snow-covered mountains reaching

The Jungfrau Region
The Eiger and the Mönch

he Apple Shoots

heights of 4000m/13,000ft and more, flower-covered mountain meadows, gardens of palm-trees in the south, lakes and rivers together with colourful flora and fauna. The people are steeped in tradition and festivals, and enjoy such legendary entertainments as yodelling, the blowing of Alpine horns, country dancing, shooting and wrestling; jazz, rock and blues festivals and music weeks meet the needs of those more interested in contemporary forms of amusement. Visitors can see numerous examples of ancient buildings and memorials dating from the Roman, Romanesque, Gothic and

Baroque periods, preserved villages and towns, as well as hypermodern architecture. There are more than 700 museums of varying size covering every conceivable subject, including some world-famous art collections, especially those covering the 19th and 20th centuries.

However, Switzerland is much more than history, nature and culture. This Baedeker guide also touches on such subjects as the democracy of the Confederation, its traditional neutrality, and its wealth.

Zurich
the unofficial capital of Switzerland

Valais
a carved treasure in Ernen church

Facts and Figures

Introduction

For long one of the world's great tourist countries, Switzerland contains within a relatively small area an extraordinary abundance of natural beauties and interesting attractions, and at the same time, in spite of the country's varied geographical pattern and the differences in language, religion and way of life among its inhabitants, offers an admirable example of unity in diversity. The 4000m/13,000ft peaks of the High Alps and the lesser summits of the Pre-Alpine regions began to attract the first modern tourists – mainly British – during the 19th c. Since then Switzerland has developed into a Mecca for visitors of every nationality and every age and condition, who find here accommodation to suit every taste from modest to luxurious, modern tourist facilities and a hospitable welcome.

General

Switzerland

Location

Situated in the south of Central Europe, Switzerland is mainly a mountainous country. Its landlocked position, with no direct access to the sea and once a commercial disadvantage, is compensated for by its location in the very centre of the Alps and thus in the centre of Europe itself. As the crow flies, some 250km/150 miles separate the southern tip of Switzerland from the nearest sea-port of Genoa. The rail journey from Lucerne in central Switzerland to Genoa is 430km/270 miles and culminates in the Gotthard Tunnel 1156m/3800ft above sea level. The trip by water between Geneva and the mouth of the Rhône measures some 640km/400 miles, and the rail journey 510km/320 miles, as it winds its way over a 375m/1230ft difference in altitude. The Rhine is the only route to the sea for ships, representing a voyage of 800km/500 miles from Basle to Rotterdam. Switzerland's northernmost point lies 47° 48′ 35″ north at Oberbargen in the canton of Schaffhausen, and its southernmost at Chiasso in the canton of Ticino, at 45° 49′ 8″ north. Thus, its maximum distance from north to south is about 220km/140 miles. From west to east, between Chancy near Geneva (5° 57′ 24″ east) and the easternmost peak of the Grisons at Piz Chavalatsch (10° 29′ 36″ east) the country measures over 348km/215 miles. The local time difference is 18 minutes and nine seconds.

Area

With an area of 41,293.2sq.km/15,943sq.miles, the country is about the same size as the Netherlands (41,160sq.km/15,892sq.miles), larger than Belgium (30,514sq.km/11,781sq.miles), but rather smaller than Denmark (43,069sq.km/16,629sq.miles), and about a sixth of the size of the United Kingdom (244,000sq.km/94,208sq.miles).

Switzerland has a common frontier with five neighbouring countries. The total length of its frontiers is 1881.5km/1169 miles – 363km/226 miles with the German Federal Republic, 165km/103 miles with Austria, 41km/25 miles with Liechtenstein, 741km/460 miles with Italy and 572km/355 miles with France.

◀ *Over the Julier pass into the Engadine*

Switzerland is made up of three geographical regions of different size – the Alps (some 60% of the total area), the Mittelland (30%) and the Jura (10%). Of the total area 46% is occupied by meadowland and pasture, 25% by forest and 6% by arable land. Thus 77% of the country's area has been brought into productive use and is densely populated; the remaining 23% is unproductive land in the mountains, but these empty regions provide magnificent recreation areas for holidaymakers and nature-lovers.

Geography and Geology

Geographical divisions

Geographically Switzerland is made up of three very dissimilar parts. The south-eastern half of the country consists of the Alps; to the north-west are the Jura mountains, and between these two mountain regions is the lower-lying Mittelland, extending from Lake Geneva in the south-west – where the Jura beyond the rift valley of the Rhône abuts on the Alpine chain – to Lake Constance in the north-east, beyond which lies the German Alpine foreland region. The total area of the country is divided fairly equally between the Jura and Mittelland on the one hand and the Alps on the other – one half well cultivated and densely inhabited, the other offering the grandeur and beauty of the high mountains.

Jura

The Swiss Jura extends in long rolling crests and much-weathered ridges from the south-west, around Geneva, where it adjoins the similarly formed and oriented chains of the French Pre-Alpine region, to Schaffhausen in the north-east, where Randen (912m/2992ft) and the volcanic Hegau form a transition to the Swabian Jura.

The limestone chains of the Jura reach their highest points in Swiss territory – Mont Tendre, 1679m/5509ft, and La Dôle, 1677m/5502ft – and fall steeply down to the Mittelland. Between the Lac de Neuchâtel

Geographical Regions of Switzerland

Schaffhausen · Basel · Winterthur · Delémont · Aarau · Zürich · St. Gallen · Olten · Solothurn · Zug · LIECHTENSTEIN · Neuchâtel · Biel/Bienne · Luzern · Glarus · **BERN** · Schwyz · Fribourg · Thun · Altdorf · Chur · Yverdon · Interlaken · Davos · Lausanne · St. Moritz · Montreux · Brig · Genève · Sion · Locarno · Bellinzona · Martigny · Zermatt · Lugano · © *Baedeker*

___ Approximate boundaries of regions

Jura 10%
Mittelland 30%
Alpen 60%

A solitary farm on the Jura plateaux

and the Doubs valley near Besançon there are some twenty successive chains, their highest points rising only slightly above the uniform ridges in the form of gently rounded hills. The chains are frequently cut by gorges (known as "Klus", from the Latin claudere = to close or cut off), through which the river flowing down a longitudinal valley finds its way into the next valley, continuing through further gorges until it emerges from the mountains. Here the slopes covered with beautiful forests and the summits with pastureland and scrub open up to reveal in their light-coloured bands of rock the folding to which the strata have been subjected (most strikingly seen in the Val Moutier and the Gorges de Court).

From the west the Burgundian Jura, flatter but still wave-like in form, advances into Swiss territory in the plateaux of La-Chaux-de-Fonds and the Franches Montagnes and is known as the Jura plateau. A weak build-up of synclines coupled with marked erosion produced the sandstone plateaux of the Franches Montagnes, creased with wooded ridges (resistant layers of friable limestone) and flat hollows. The long gorge of the Doubs river, which here forms the frontier, flows between steep wooded rock walls 400m/1300ft below the edges of the plateau, is particularly beautiful. Jura plateau

Between Basle and Brugg the Jura, only a few hundred metres high, forms tabular plateaux. In the Oligocene Age the unfolded Mesozoic strata were broken down into numerous ice floes, pierced by deep valleys, some widened by erosion, which now frequently serve as important mountain roads. Jura table

Mittelland

The Swiss Mittelland (about 400–800m/1312–2625ft), which rises gradually from the Jura to the foot of the Alps, belongs to the Molasse Molasse

11

The principal Mountains, Lakes and Rivers

Trough i.e., the accumulation basin which was filled by the Alpine rivers with detritus during the Alpine folding in the Tertiary Age. This resulted in a number of flat sediment layers being deposited on the crystalline mountain floor. A fresh-water lake was left by the arm of the sea which reached from South Germany to Lyons during the time of the Alpine folding; it later became part of the sea again, only to silt up and end up as a lake once more. As a result, the Molasse displays the following structure: lower sea, lower fresh-water, upper sea and upper fresh-water Molasse. The detritus deposited by the Alpine rivers in the foothills led to the formation of pockets of debris and deltas, where initially heavy boulders and gravel were deposited, followed by sand and finally clay materials. With the help of mainly chalky binding materials this rubble became compressed into new layers of stone, which together reach a massiveness of almost 3000m/10,000ft. Near the Alps the conglomerate "nagelfluh" was formed, sand became sandstone and mud produced a marl mixture. Through these conglomerates the same rivers later cut their way once more, widening and deepening their channels to form valleys. The hills between them are remnants of the older rocks which have resisted erosion. The Tertiary rocks, however, are covered almost everywhere with a mantle of pasture and arable land, peatbogs and lakes, with small areas of woodland on the hills.

In the western part of the Mittelland the heights have a gently rounded tabular form ("le plateau suisse"), like, for example, Mont Jorat (932m/3058ft) above Lausanne. To the east they are mostly in the form of long and fairly uniform ridges, the flanks of which have been worn smooth by the glaciers of the last Ice Age, such as the Pfannenstiel (853m/2799ft) near Zurich and the Lindenburg (881m/2891ft) in the Aargau. The Napf group, built up by the original rivers Rhine and Aare, (1411m/4629ft) and the Toss hills (Hörnli, 1136m/3727ft) lay outside the glaciated area and were exposed to continual erosion by running water; in consequence, they now show a much-dissected pattern of alternating ridges and furrows.

The final Alpine folding movement affected the neighbouring foreland region, thrusting the Helvetian layers over the southernmost

Molasse strata, which in turn became buried by or were folded into the Alps. The rounded peaks of the Molasse which were thus forced upwards have since been largely eroded away, however. Some remnants of these folds, however, survive in the nagelfluh beds which can be seen rising towards the north on the Rigi (1800m/5900ft), Rossberg (1584m/5197ft) and Speer (1954m/6411ft). From the summits of these rocky heights there is a view over the intervening uplands to the distant chains of the Jura.

During the various Ice Ages the Molasse surfaces were almost com- **Moraines** pletely covered by the moraines of the Alpine glaciers. Many side and end moraines remain in the form of high, long-shaped hills. The wide valley areas around Winterthur, Zurich, Burgdorf, Berne and Geneva are traversed by moraines left by the last great Ice Age, which lasted until about 10,000 B.C. These moraines appear mostly as undulations across the valleys or along the hillsides and frequently bounding the lower ends of lakes. With its variety of landscape pattern the Mittelland is a region of great attraction, even on cloudy days when the view of the Alps is cut off.

The Mittelland is the most densely settled part of Switzerland, with almost all its larger towns and more than three-quarters of its total population. However, it is also a highly developed agricultural region.

Alps

Even though 58% of the country lies in the centre of the Alps it in fact accounts for only one-seventh of their total area. The longitudinal valleys of the Rhône and young Rhine, together with the transverse valleys of the Reuss and Ticino, divide the mountainous backbone of Europe into a north-eastern chain (Alpstein–Toggenburg, the Glarus,

The towering Churfirsten

13

Geography and Geology

Schwyz and eastern Uri Alps), the north-west Alps (western Urn, Unterwalden, Berne, Fribourg, Vri Vaud Alps) and the southern Alps (Valais, Ticino and Grisons Alps). The average height of these young folded mountains is about 1700m/5600ft; some one hundred peaks reach 4000m/13,000ft or more. The highest point in Switzerland is the Dufour Peak in the Monta Rosa massif (Valais canton), which is 4634m/15,209ft above sea level.

The formation of the mountains

The formation of the Alpine range commenced in the Palaeolozic Age, about 300 million years ago. When molten granite flowed upwards during the Carboniferous period and solidified as cooled magma into granite, this produced a mountain in Hercynian form. Today, largely hidden under later layers of stone, the central massifs which pushed up during the formation of the Alps (e.g. Aiguilles-Rouges and Mont Blanc massif in Lower Valais, the Aare and Gotthard massif in the central Alps) still bear witness to this ancient crystalline base. In the Mesozoic Age, when the sea covered everything and eroded the "original Alps", a long-reaching valley was created. Over a period of some 160 million years its bottom became covered by material swept in by the rivers and limestone and dolomite accumulated in the peaks and troughs thus formed. The Helvetian section of the trough included the northern coastal region, the central ocean area was embraced by the Pennines and the southern coastal strip by the eastern and southern Alps. In the Chalk Age, towards the end of the Mesozoic period, the coastal floe in the southern Tethys moved northwards, probably as a result of strong undercurrents: the formation of the mountain range had begun.

Due to the resistance from the northern mainland mass there was a folding, elevation and shifting of the sediment from the Pennine region to the Helvetian deposit area. As the land surface arched upwards horizontal folds extended even further and covered other stone masses over a large area, thus producing the characteristic tabular construction found in many parts of the Alps. The Mesozoic sediments, originally extending over 500km/300 miles from north to south, became forced together and on top of one another in various phases until they ended up as mountains 150km/90 miles in width. The result was an extremely complex system of layers and inversions. Constant weather erosion acted against the formation of the mountains, thus making geological relationships even more difficult to diagnose in many places. The erosion also reduced the strain on the subsoil, so that in the central Alps isostatic equilibrium movements resulted in the crystalline base piercing the surface in some places. As the granite and gneiss masses pushed upwards they formed the Central Massif. The Helvetian deposits which were also involved in the formation of the mountains became stratified and their brow pushed up against the Molasse foothills.

Magnificent scenery

The Alps, which from a distance appear to be a uniform chain, are in fact deeply indented by many valleys, terrasses, passes, chains and corridors, indicating that they were formed by Pleistocene glacier masses. On the north side of the mountain mass are the Pre-Alps, long limestone chains which in many places rise above the Mittelland in sheer rock walls. Running parallel to one another, they are broken up by wide, deep valleys extending down from the High Alps (for example, at Montreux, Thun, Lucerne, Rapperswil and Rorschach-Bregenz).

Even the Pre-Alps offer magnificent scenery, with light grey limestone peaks rearing above green upland pastures and dark pine forests. In spite of much erosion and weathering the violent folding of the strata still reveals the gigantic wave-like structure of the rock formations which follow one another in close succession northwards – particularly impressive in the Säntis ridges (2504m/8216ft) and Pilatus (Tomlishorn, 2132m/6995ft). Elsewhere massive limestone mountains

Monte Rosa massif, Grenz and Gorner glaciers in the background

tower up, such as Tödi (3614m/11,858ft), Selbsanft (3026m/9928ft) and Glärnisch (Bächistock, 2915m/9564ft) which enclose the canton of Glarus. To the south of the Pre-Alps, forming a magnificent backdrop, are the glaciated summits of the High Alps, which slope down on the south, almost without transition, to the North Italian plain. On this side there are no limestone Alps preceding the main massif of ancient rocks.

The Alpine world of Switzerland is brought within reach by a dense network of roads and railways. Nature has created a pattern of valleys which provide access to the mountains and make possible the extension of human settlement to considerable altitudes. The valleys extend far into the mountains on a fairly gentle gradient. The fall of the rivers is sufficient, however, to enable them when the water level is high to bring down great quantities of rock debris which cover the whole floor of the valleys. The sides of the valleys are cut by deep gorges and gullies, filled after heavy rain by rushing mountain streams which also carry down quantities of weathered rock and debris, surging over their banks and any man-made barriers. The hillsides below these gullies, formed by the destructive force of nature, are indebted to nature also for their fertility.

The Alpine valleys were given their characteristic form during the Ice Age. Perhaps 20,000 years ago they were filled with great seas of ice reaching almost to the summit ridges of the mountains. and under the pressure of the ice the rock debris which had been carried down on the floor of the valleys took on a more or less pronounced U shape. Above the steep sides of these trough valleys are found terraces which are probably the remains of earlier valley floors (e.g. the Lauterbrunnen valley and Lake Uri). The side valleys were less deeply indented than the main ones, since the glaciers they contained were smaller, and in consequence their floors lie high above the main valley. The streams

Ice Age formation

15

flowing down these "hanging valleys" tumble over the edge in the form of waterfalls (Giétro, in the Valais Alps; Giessbach near Brienz; Trümmelbach and Staubbach, Lauterbrunnen; Reichenbach, near Meiringen; falls in the Ticino valleys) or emerge from a dark enclosed gorge (Trient gorge, Valais; Medel gorge, Disentis). The floor of the main valley does not fall in a regular gradient but in stages or "steps". The drop between one step and another may be no more than a few metres, but is usually several hundred metres. The head of the valley is frequently a cirque enclosed by high rock walls.

Lakes

Almost all the larger Alpine valleys have lakes near the foot of the mountain. Essentially, these are merely elongated basins within the valley, such as the 38km/24 miles long Lake Lucerne which is a section of the Reuss valley. The bottom of the lake frequently goes down almost to sea-level and, in some cases, to considerably below sea-level as in Lake Maggiore. Smaller lakes are found right up to the highest stages in the valleys; sometimes, as on the Engstligenalp, they have been filled up by rock and soil and are now pastureland. The lakes were originally formed either by glacier action during the Ice Age or by a sinking of the mountain mass after the formation of the valleys which reversed the gradient at the mouth of a valley, thus damming the river and creating a lake.

The Swiss lakes, like the mountains, have become popular holiday areas, providing visitors during the warm periods of the year with bases from which they can make excursions into the mountains, the Mittelland and the towns; bathing is possible in most Swiss lakes. Switzerland has a total of 1484 natural lakes, the two largest of which, Lake Geneva and Lake Constance, are shared respectively with France and with Germany and Austria. In addition there are 44 man-made lakes, created for the purpose of producing hydro-electric power, which contribute to the beauty of the landscape in many areas. The largest of these is the Sihlsee in the canton of Schwyz (11sq.km/

Vierwaldstätter See: Basin of the prehistoric Reuss glacier

4sq.miles), while the Grande-Dixence dam in the canton of Valais is the highest gravity dam in the world (285m/935ft).

Switzerland has none of the plateau-like high mountains found, for example, in Scandinavia. The various valley systems, each usually meeting on the summit ridge with a corresponding system on the other side, are separated by sharp ridges of variegated profile. The main rock mass is broken up by Kare – corries formed on the flanks of the ridge by small glaciers – into jagged arêtes and rugged towers and pinnacles. Where two corries meet on opposite sides of the ridge they form a breach in the summit line (Lücke, Joch, Furka, Fuorcia) between the towering peaks on either side.

High mountains

Most of the high peaks are pyramids of crystalline rock with sharply defined edges, their varying form reflected in a variety of designations such as Horn, Stock, Dent, Aiguille, Piz, Becca, Poncione, etc. The rugged forms of the mountains are shaped not only by the action of rain and snow but by the daily variation in temperature, which has a particularly destructive effect at the highest altitudes. During the day the rock is heated by the sun and then sharply chilled during the night. In consequence the St Gotthard group, for example, is riven by deep clefts, and many ridges and summits are formed only of loosely bedded blocks, buttresses and tabular formations.

The differences in height between individual peaks in a group appear greater from below than they are in reality: there are only a few giant peaks which stand out from the rest, dominating the landscape. From a high viewpoint, on the other hand, hundreds of peaks fit together into a total picture: at these altitudes the view extends to distances at which differences in height of a few hundred metres are of little significance. Only the very highest peaks, including Mont Blanc, Monta Rosa, the Weisshorn, the Finsteraarhorn and Bernina, rise commandingly above the mass of mountains which appear to sink down from these few giants.

The geographical centre of the Swiss Alps is the St Gotthard massif, the water-tower of Europe, with the sources of the Rhine, the Rhône, the Reuss and the Ticino. The highest peaks in the Alps, however, are to be found in Valais, the Bernese Oberland and Grisons.

The numerous passes in the Alps have since time immemorial provided means of passage through the mountains. During the Ice Age the sea of ice reached up to heights of over 2000m/6560ft in the interior of the Alps, and consequently the glaciers were able in places to gouge out a passage over the summit ridges and to enlarge it into a broad saddle. The ice-smoothed ridges of rock, the little lakes of clear dark water and the jagged peaks, unaffected by ice action, which rise above them give the St Gotthard, Bernina, Grimsel and other passes an atmosphere of Arctic desolation.

Alpine passes

Many of the Alpine passes have a long history, which in some cases goes back to Roman times. The San Bernardino pass (Chur-Bellinzona) is almost always open throughout the winter. A drive over one of the great Alpine passes in good weather is a tremendous experience; and with the excellently maintained pass roads day trips are possible over many passes. In winter (November to May or June) many passes are closed. The Swiss Alps can be traversed from east to west by way of the Oberalp and Furka passes, via Andermatt; and the journey from Chur into Valais takes only a few hours, either by road or by rail.

The original sea of ice which many millennia ago covered the whole of the Mittelland and filled the Alpine valleys almost to the summit ridge of the mountains has left behind it about 140 glaciers, some of them steadily retreating, others still growing. The total area of all the Swiss glaciers is 1556sq.km/601sq.miles. The three largest are in Valais – the Aletsch glacier (area 117.5sq.km/45sq.miles, length 23.6km/15 miles –

Glaciers

Glacial giant: The Rhône glacier

the longest in Europe), the Gorner glacier at Zermatt (area 63.7sq.km/25sq.miles, length 14.5km/9 miles) and the Fiesch glacier (area 39sq.km/15sq.miles, length 14.7km/9 miles). The great majority of glaciers, however, are no more than a few dozen square kilometres in area.

At altitudes approaching 3000m/10,000ft and above the snow is largely permanent, since in the low air temperatures prevailing at these altitudes there is little melting. The layers of new snow change into the thinner but more compact layers, called "firn" or "névé", which in turn, under the weight of successive annual falls, becomes granular – but still stratified – glacier ice. The snow-line (the lower boundary of perpetual snow) lies between 3200 and 2500m/10,500 and 8200ft. The firn accumulates particularly at the heads of the highest valleys, where hundreds of metres of firn and ice may build up, forming the origin of the glaciers in the proper sense.

Particularly characteristic of Switzerland are the "valley glaciers", some of which extend over several "steps" in the valley and may reach down almost to the 1000m/3300ft mark (Lower Grindelwald Glacier). Most of these glaciers, however, end at heights of between 1500 and 2000m/5000 and 6500ft, although they reach down to more than 1000m/3300ft below the snow-line.

More numerous than the valley glaciers, however, are the "mountainside glaciers" or "corrie glaciers" (Hanggletscher, Kargletscher) – glaciers clinging to the feared upper slopes, occupying hollows in the mountainside which are known as "corries" (Kare). On warm summer days parts of these overhanging glaciers frequently break off and thunder down into the valley in the form of avalanches.

Variations in the rate of movement in the glaciers (the central part having the fastest pace, up to 200m/660ft a year) lead to the formation of crevasses, which open and close according to the pulling action or the pressure of the ice. At the steeper places the glacier is broken up by large deep transverse crevasses which transform it into a chaos of vertical ice walls and towers, known by the Savoyard term "sérac". Where the bed of the glacier becomes wider, on the other hand, longitudinal crevasses open up. Wide glaciers of this kind may bear the designation of Eismeer ("sea of ice") and are usually flanked by lateral crevasses formed by friction against the sides of the valley, which frequently impede access to or return from the glacier. The rock debris which falls into the crevasses is carried down with the stones from the firn area to the melting tip of the glacier, where it emerges together with the ground moraine, material abraded by the movement of the glacier and splintered fragments of the rock bed. Still more rock debris is carried down by the moraines proper which run down the edges, and often also the middle, of the glacier. All this detritus eventually forms the horseshoe-shaped terminal moraine or is carried farther down by the melt water.

Snow is also carried down from the mountains by avalanches. In winter these take the form of dry "dust avalanches" generated by wind; in spring come the real avalanches, in which compact masses of ice break away and hurtle down into the valley. In the steep-sided transverse valleys of the Reuss and the Aare and in the Valais Alps great masses of avalanche snow can still be seen on the valley floor in summer, covered with stones and reddish earth and with foaming mountain streams running through them in a tunnel. The protective measures taken against avalanches (barriers, walls, lines of posts, belts of trees) can be seen particularly in the Upper Valais, in the Bedretto valley, on the St Gotthard railway and on the Albula railway at Bergün.

Avalanches

The main Swiss rivers – the Rhine, the Rhône, the Aare, the Reuss and the Ticino – rise in the St Gotthard area. The catchment areas of Swiss rivers are as follows: Rhine 36,494sq.km/14,090sq.miles (of which 8531sq.km/3294sq.miles are outside Switzerland), Rhône 10,403 sq.km/4017sq.miles (3456sq.km/1334sq.miles), Inn 2150sq.km/ 830sq.miles (358sq.km/138sq.miles), Ticino 1616sq.km/624sq.miles, Poschiavino 238sq.km/92sq.miles.

Watersheds

67.7% of Swiss waters drain into the Atlantic, 27.9% into the Mediterranean and 4.4% into the Black Sea. The mean annual flow of the Rhine at Basle is 1026cu.m/36,228cu.ft per second.

The unique panorama of the Swiss Alps is shaped by two dozen peaks over 4000m/13,000ft, all first climbed between 1811 (Jungfrau, 4158m/13,642ft) and 1865 (Matterhorn, 4478m/14,692ft), and some 70 mountains rising to over 3000m/10,000ft. With three fifths of its area occupied by mountains, Switzerland ranks as Europe's "No. 2 Alpine state", first place being taken by Austria, where the Alps cover more than two-thirds of the country.

Climate

Taken as a whole, the populated areas of Switzerland have a cool, temperate and always humid climate; the higher mountainous regions, however, display many variations including icy climates. Broadly there are three climatic zones: in the northern side of the Alps (Jura and Mittelland), the inner Alpine region and the southern foot of the Alps.

The climates experienced in the above regions are illustrated on page 20 by means of climatic diagrams of various places showing the annual range of temperature, precipitation and periods of sunshine (reading from left to right; J = January, D = December). The blue rain/snowfall columns show the precipitation (in mm) per month, as shown on the blue scale at the side. Temperatures are shown as an orange-red band.

Climatic diagrams

Eight regional climate stations in Switzerland

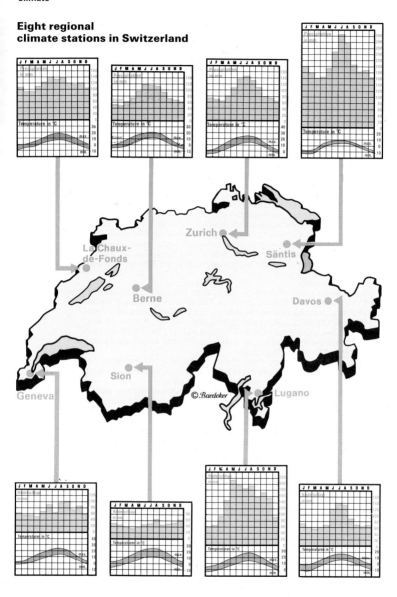

Explanations in text

Drawn by Prof. Dr. Wolfgang Hassenpflug

The upper edge corresponds to the average maximum day temperature, the lower the average minimum night temperature. The corresponding temperature figures can be read off the red scale at the side.

For the Jura region the climatic values for La-Chaux-de-Fonds have been chosen, for the Mittelland those of Berne, Geneva and Zurich, whilst for the inner Alpine region Säntis (climate in the upper mountains), Davos (mountain climate) and Sion (dry climate of the inner Alps) have been used, together with the climatic values of Lugano to illustrate the southern foot of the Alps.

North side of the Alps
(Climatic stations: Berne, La-Chaux-de-Fonds, Geneva, Zurich)

On the north side of the Alps the prevailing westerly winds bring with them moist Atlantic air masses. Forced upwards by the Jura mountains, they cool down and produce cloud formations and heavy rain. As the air masses flow down to the Mittelland the air warms up again, becomes drier and there is less rain and cloud. As they proceed further across the Alps the air masses climb once more, resulting in increased cloud and precipitation in the higher regions of the Mittelland near to the Alps.

The annual rainfall in the Jura is between 1500 and 2000mm/60 and 80in., in the Mittelland where it adjoins in the east between 800 and 1000mm/32 and 40in., and 1000 and 1500mm/40 and 60in. in the higher Mittelland. On average the rainfall on the north side of the Alps is 1200mm/48in. spread over 140 days in the year.

From the edges of the mountains to the inner parts the temperatures fall and the precipitation increases (from over 1200mm/48in. per annum at the edges to more than 2000mm/80in. in the upper regions). While the January temperatures on the east side (Neuchâtel) remain above freezing point and vine-growing is possible, the high trough valleys are extremely cold in winter (temperature reversal). The lowest temperatures in Switzerland are normally found in a basin filled with cold air in the Neuchâtel Jura – not in the Alps.

Jura

The western and north-eastern parts of the Mittelland lie within the rain shadow of the Jura and the Black Forest (Geneva: 852mm/34in. over 104 days in the year, Zurich: 1136mm/45in. over 134 days in the year).

Mittelland

The periods of winter sunshine enjoyed on the north side of the Alps are conspicuously short in comparison with the inner and southern Alps (Zurich 37 hours in December and 46 hours in January). The valley bottoms are then drowned under a deep sea of mist and suffer lower temperatures than the sunny uplands above the cloud cover (temperature reversal/inversion). Near the edge of the Alps the blankets of mist often lift for days on end, so this is a more pleasant place to stay.

Periods of sunshine

A particular feature of the Alpine climate is the "föhn". This occurs mainly in spring and autumn, when a depression north of the Alps sucks air from a summit ridge south of the Alps. These comparatively moist and foggy air masses cool off as they ascend the southern side, forming clouds and heavy rain (as happens on the Jura when the wind blows from the west). Because of the warmth released by condensation the air cools only slightly as it rises, but its temperature is raised by 1° C for every 100m/328ft as it descends the northern side. Accompanied by squalls and storms, it then falls down into the valleys as an increasingly warm, dry and cloud-free wind. The edge of the cloud dispersal, the so-called "föhn wall", remains stationary above the central Alps, while to the north appears a band of blue sky, the "föhn window". The stronger the föhn the deeper it penetrates into the

Föhn

valleys and the Alpine foothills. Often it affects only the upper Mittelland (for example, in the canton of Appenzell), and the valleys remain under cold masses of air. The föhn is at its strongest in the "föhn lanes", that is in the great Rhône, Reuss or Rhine valleys leading out of the Alps; for example, it is felt in Altdorf on 64 days in the year.

The effects of the föhn are many: it increases the average temperatures (Altdorf has a January temperature almost 2° higher than Winterthur, which is at the same altitude but on the other side of the mountain); it encourages the ripening of the fruit in the fields (warms the grapes); it melts the snow, as much on some days as it would take the sun 14 days to do; it causes a lot of damage through storms and spreading fire, especially in villages of timber construction. Not least is its effect on the well-being of the human body. For example, during föhn weather conditions, there are increases in migraine attacks, blood circulation problems and extreme changes in mood.

Inner Alps (Climatic stations: Säntis, Davos, Sion)

Overall, the Alps show marked differences in climate between north and south. As a result the inner Alpine valleys, especially the upper ones, being higher and protected on all sides, have a unique climatic character, quite different from that of the outer valleys and lowlands.

Temperatures and precipitation

Generally, as you go higher the temperature falls by 0.5° C per 100m/328ft, but by less in winter, or even the other way round where temperature reversal prevails. Humidity, cloud and rainfall, on the other hand, increase with altitude, while the deep valleys are very dry. The wettest region in all Switzerland (the peaks around Mönchsgrat and Monte Rosa, with an annual rainfall of up to 4100mm/160in.) lies scarcely 40km/25 miles from the driest (Visp in Valais, with only 529mm/21in.).

The proportion of the precipitation which falls as snow also increases the higher you go (Lugano 5%, Davos 40%, Säntis 72% and, at heights above 3,500m/11,500ft, 100% of the annual fall). Falls of fresh snow total 5m/16ft in Davos and as much as 19m/62ft in Säntis. At an altitude of 700m/2300ft the snow remains for three months, whilst at 1800m/6000ft it remains for eight and at 2500m/8200ft for more than ten months. At above 2800m/9200ft in the northern Alps and 3300m/10,800ft in the southern Alps the snow remains all through the year.

It is true, of course, that less falls in the valleys and basins of the inner Alps than in the northern foothills, but nevertheless the night temperatures there, especially when there is a blanket of snow, drop well below freezing point and in fact reach temperatures normally experienced only in the peak regions. The intervening slopes are less cold, so the main health resorts lie on mountain terraces and midway up the slopes.

Periods of sunshine

In winter there is a minimum of cloud and rain or snow, with long periods of sunshine, at a time when the lowlands are often completely overcast. Heat and ultra-violet rays noticeably increase, as the air is very dry.

Winds

Wind speeds remain low. In summer the sun and heat from the upper sides of the valleys give rise to a valley wind which blows up the slopes and causes clouds to form above the peaks during the morning. During the evenings and nights, on the other hand, the cooled masses of air roll downhill towards the valleys in the form of a mountain wind, while the clouds disappear above the peaks. Generally, the valley wind is characteristically stronger than the mountain wind. The strength of the wind is clearly demonstrated in, for example, Valais, by the clumps of trees bent over to point up the mountainsides (wind deformity).

Because of their climatic attractions and therapeutic benefits the inner Swiss Alps are particularly suitable for health cures, especially in winter. The different combinations of climate to be found in the many spas means there is an excellent choice to meet individual therapeutic needs. The climatic diagram for Davos, for instance, shows a marked increase in hours of sunshine from February to March, so that although there will be sharp frosts at night and low air temperatures by day you can still count on getting a tan in the warm sunshine.

Therapeutic factors

Southern foot of the Alps (Climatic station: Lugano)

The southern foot of the Alps (Ticino) lies in the lee of the prevailing north-westerly winds. This is where the air masses, which brought rain and snow to the northern side of the Alps and to the central heights, make their way downhill again, resulting in reduced precipitation and cloud. In particular, the period of winter sunshine is greater than anywhere else in the country, even more than in Davos, and is exceeded only on some peaks such as on the Säntis. The predominantly mild, sunny and mist-free winter produces vegetation some of which has an almost Mediterranean look about it, even though the heat and aridity typical of the Mediterranean climate are lacking. In summer, six to seven days in each of the months of July and August are sultry. The nights, however, are always pleasantly cool and the fresh lake breezes on sunny days and the cool north winds ensure a pleasant atmosphere.

Temperatures and periods of sunshine

The fall of rain and snow at the southern foot of the Alps is about one-third higher than that on the northern side of the Alps (1800mm/72in. per annum instead of 1200mm/48in.), with the greatest amounts falling in summer. Conversely, however, the number of hours and days when it rains or snows is smaller in the south than in the north (Lugano 107, Zurich 134 days per annum). In fact, a large part takes the form of intensive, thundery showers lasting only a short time. As a result, the summer months with the heaviest rainfall are also those blessed with the longest periods of sunshine. When there is a föhn in the northern Alps there is heavy rain on the southern foot of the mountains.

Precipitation

Flora and Fauna

The plants of Switzerland are abundant and varied. From the subtropical warmth of Lake Lugano to the snow-clad regions of the High Alps, the country has areas belonging to every zone of plant life in Europe. Particularly notable for its variety of form and splendour of colour is the Alpine flora, which contrives to exist and to flourish in the most rigorous climatic conditions, with temperatures which may rise to 40° C (104° F) during the day and freeze hard when the rocks cool down at night. Among the species are rhododendron, gentian, Alpine pansy, primula, globe-flower, silver thistle, soldanella, martagon lily, Alpine aster, and in the rockier regions edelweiss, Alpine poppy, glacier buttercup and a variety of saxifrages.

Of Switzerland's more than 3000 flowering plants and ferns 160 are fully or partially protected by law. A federal law provides for the protection of plants and their habitat, but the executive regulations are the responsibility of the cantons, since the plants vary from area to area. Fully protected plants may not be picked or uprooted; in the case of partially protected plants picking is permitted within reasonable limits, but such plants or flowers may not be sold or supplied commercially.

Protected Plants

Flora and Fauna

Fauna

The animal life of Switzerland is very similar to that of other Central European countries. The country's stock of game includes some 110,000 roe deer, 70,000 chamois, 20,000 red deer, 9000 ibex and 100 recently established sika deer from Asia. Stocks of pheasants, hares and partridges are released every year. Marmots are to be found all over the Alps.

Protected Animals

Among the species protected by federal law are: hedgehog, beaver, brown bear, otter, wild cat, lynx, ibex, black grouse, capercaillie, hazel hen, eagles, falcons, owls, nutcracker, jackdaw, Alpine chough, turtle-doves and rock doves, swans, curlew, black-tailed godwit, sandpipers, rails (except the coot), snow finch and numerous less common species.

Shooting and Fishing

Regulations on shooting and fishing vary from canton to canton. More than half the cantons issue individual shooting licences (some 20,000 of which are in force); the others lease particular areas to shooting clubs.

Height Zones

The height limits for plants, animals and human settlement vary according to climatic conditions. In the northern Alps vines are grown in certain areas up to 550m/1800ft, and above this is the zone of deciduous forest, which in these areas can be regarded also as the highest level of agricultural use of the land. In favourable situations the beech grows at levels of 1500m/5000ft or over; and this is also the height reached by permanent human settlements, mostly small villages, which are more commonly found on the sheltered fringes of the valley floor than on hillsides or hill terraces. The growing of corn, which was once practised in these areas with rather meagre results, was almost completely abandoned in the 19th c. In consequence, increased attention has been given to the flower-spangled pastures and the fruit-trees which grow at heights up to 900m/3000ft.

Alpine marmots

The next zone, some 1300 to 1700 or 1800m/4300 to 5600 or 6000ft, is dominated by coniferous forest, with patches of mountain pasture, which is cut in summer, in the clearings. Deciduous trees are represented by the beautiful maples which grow around the log huts and barns of the mountain-dwellers.

At altitudes between 1600 and 1700m/5250 and 5600ft the dense forest ceases, and only the sturdiest spruces and stone pines survive in proud isolation. The last outposts of the forest are alders and mountain pines. The lower-growing plants flourish in the summer warmth of the soil, the tough short-stemmed species form a vigorous mantle of turf. This is the real "Alp", the mountain pasture to which the stock is brought in summer and on which the herdsmen have their characteristic huts.

Higher still there are only meagre strips of grass between the areas of scree and the rocky crags. Then the patches of firn and the remains of avalanches become increasingly numerous, and between 2800 and 3000m/9200 and 9850ft the snow-line is reached. Even in the zone of perpetual snow, however, plant life does not completely disappear. The glacier buttercup is found at heights of over 3000m/9850ft, and even on the high tops lichens cover the sunny rock faces with their patterns of colour.

In Valais and the Engadine all these various zones reach unusually high, owing to the favoured climate of these areas as a result of the upthrust of the mountain masses and to the warm and dry conditions in their sheltered valleys. In these areas there are still cornfields as well as pastureland, and, exceptionally, rye and potatoes are grown as high as 1900m/6200ft (Chandolin).

In Ticino vines are grown on stone and timber frames up to a height of some 600m/2000ft, and early flowering almonds and peaches and chestnuts are cultivated up to 1000m/3300ft. Above this is a zone of spruce, larch and stone pine; then, as on the north side of the Alps, the mountain pastures begin at 1800m/6000ft and the snow at 2800m/9200ft.

The Swiss National Park, in the canton of Grisons, is a federal plant and animal reserve with an area of 159sq.km/61sq.miles.

Swiss National Park

Population

The historical development of Switzerland, during which influences from the neighbouring areas of German, French and Italian culture mingled with survivals from the Roman and pre-Roman periods, is reflected in the composition and characteristics of its population.

General

At the present time the country has over 6.85 million inhabitants, with an annual growth rate of 0.6%; some 18% of the resident population are foreigners.

The overall population density is 166 per sq.km/430 per sq.mile. In accordance with the nature of the countryside, however, the population is spread unevenly across the country. The most densely populated part is the Mittelland (250 per sq.km/648 per sq.mile), where the cantons of Zug, Nidwalden and Ticino have shown the most marked growth during the past decade, whereas the cantons of Basel-Land, Neuchâtel and Schaffhausen have suffered the greatest reductions. These changes arise from the recession on the one hand, coupled with a general trend towards moving out of the cities and into the surrounding countryside. The root causes of this phenomenon, the very opposite of the classical flight from the land found elsewhere, lie in the tendency for more and more service industries (banks, insurance companies and office buildings) to move out of the towns and cities, together with a radical increase in land prices and the growing noise of

Population Density and Spread

Languages of Switzerland

Schaffhausen · Basel · Winterthur · Olten · Aarau · Zürich · St. Gallen · Delémont · Solothurn · Zug · LIECHTEN-STEIN · Biel/Bienne · Luzern · Glarus · Neuchâtel · Schwyz · Chur · Davos · **BERN** · Fribourg · Altdorf · Yverdon · Thun · Lausanne · Interlaken · St. Moritz · Montreux · Brig · Genève · Sion · Locarno Bellinzona · Martigny · Zermatt · © *Baedeker* · Lugano

German
French
Italian
Romansh

—— Linguistic boundaries

traffic in the city centres. Although the large cities remain fairly big (Zurich 342,000 inhabitants, Basle 169,000, Geneva 165,000, Berne 134,400), more than 60% the total population lives in "new towns" or urban regions (more than 10,000 inhabitants). In the Alpine regions, for obvious geographical reasons, the density is very low (about 30 per sq.km/78 to the sq.mile).

Foreigners

Since population growth has not kept pace with economic development Switzerland has had to bring in foreign labour, mainly from Italy and Spain. A big increase in their numbers produced a fear in the seventies of "swamping", leading to a tightening of the regulations governing immigration and the granting of citizenship. The law relating to foreigners passed in 1980 created a new legal concept in Swiss foreign policy, together with changes in the periods in which seasonal workers may stay in the country. In 1981 the so-called Mitenand-Initiative, which had as its aim an improvement in the position of foreigners working in Switzerland, suffered defeat after a referendum set up for the purpose. In April 1987 a fresh referendum approved the revision of the law governing asylum and foreigners.

Language

A striking indication of the heterogenous population structure is the multilingual character of the country. Some three-quarters of the Swiss speak German, a fifth French, 4% Italian and 1% Romansch or Rhaeto-Romanic. All four languages are recognised for official purposes throughout the country.

"Swiss German" (Schwyzerdütsch)

Although in schools and in correspondence in the German-speaking parts of the country standard German is used, with the occasional form peculiar to Switzerland, the spoken language is a quite distinctive tongue, Schwyzerdütsch or Swiss German, derived from the old Alemannic (West Germanic) language and diversified into a series of local and regional dialects. The use of Schwyzerdütsch is deliberately cultivated, and on radio and television, and even in the political and military fields, it is strongly preferred to standard German at every level including the highest.

The Swiss forms of French (in western Switzerland or Suisse Romande) and Italian (in the canton of Ticino and some valleys in Grisons) differ only slightly – mainly in intonation – from standard French and Italian. A notable feature of Swiss French (as of Belgian and Canadian French) is the divergent formation of certain numbers (70 = septante instead of soixante-dix, 80 = huitante or octante instead of quatre-vingts, 90 = nonante instead of quatre-vingt-dix).

French, Italian

Rhaeto-Romanic, a language derived from Vulgar Latin which is spoken in a number of dialectal forms in Grisons, has also been officially recognised since 1938 as an independent language. The main dialects of Romansch are Surselvian, Sutselvian, Surmeirian and the forms spoken in Unterhalbstein, Oberhalbstein, Oberengadin and Unterengadin (the Upper and Lower Engadine).Closely related to these dialects are the Ladin and Friulian spoken in South Tirol. The general written language of Rumantsh Grischun, developed in 1982 by Prof. H. Schmid, represents a compromise between the main idioms of Surselvian, Ladin and Surmeirian.

Rhaeto-Romanic or Romansch

Another result of differing development in the various parts of the country is the diverse pattern of religious belief. Today 44% of the population are Protestants (protesting the special form of Protestantism established by Zwingli and Calvin) and 48% Roman Catholics. 0.3% belong to the Old Catholic Church of Christ, the same number as those of the Jewish faith.

Religious beliefs

Government and Society

The official (Latin) designation of the Swiss Confederation is Confoederatio Helvetica: hence the letters CH to be seen on Swiss cars and in Swiss post codes.

Confoederatio Helvetica (Swiss Confederation)

The name of the country (in German "Schweiz", French "Suisse", Italian "Svizzera", Romansch "Svizera") comes from the canton of Schwyz, and was originally applied only to central or inner Switzerland, i.e. the three cantons of Uri, Schwyz and Unterwalden, which laid the foundations of the Confederation when they formed a perpetual alliance on the Rütli meadow by Lake Lucerne in 1291. From the 14th to the 16th c., as the number of cantons joining the alliance increased, the term confederation (Eidgenossenschaft) was preferred; but in the end the designation of Schweiz or Switzerland became generally accepted. The official name of the state, Swiss Confederation, combines both forms.

The Swiss National Flag depicts a white cross on a red ground: the arms of the cross are of equal length, each arm being one-sixth longer than it is broad.

Swiss Flag

Reversing the colours produces the flag of the Red Cross, the organisation which came into being in 1863–66 as a result of the efforts of Henri Dunant.

It may at first appear surprising to an outsider that a state which has developed out of a medley of different ethnic groups should have become the very symbol of stability and harmony; but on closer observation it will be seen that the Swiss communes, the cantons and the Confederation as a whole owe their democratic strength to this very diversity and to the preservation of a federal structure which has eschewed the centralisation of authority. An essential element in Swiss attitudes, too, is the proverbial neutrality of Switzerland, stemming from the Peace of Paris of November 1815.

Federal Constitution

Extensive rights of self-government, practical participation in the reaching of political decisions and the basic human rights and freedoms are the foundations of Swiss democracy.

Switzerland
Swiss
Confederation

Suisse
Svizzera
Svizera

**Confoederatio
Helvetica**
(CH)

LIECHTEN-
STEIN

Boundaries
of Cantons

Confédération Helvétique
Confederazione Helvetica
Confederaziun Svizera

© Baedeker

Area and Population

Cantons		Area in sq. km (sq. miles)	Popu-lation (1991)	Cantons		Area in sq. km (sq. miles)	Popu-lation (1991)
AG	Aargau	1405 (542)	496,200		Unterwalden:		
AR	Appenzell-Ausserhoden	243 (94)	51,400	**NW**	Nidwalden	276 (107)	32,600
AI	Appenzell-Innerrhoden	172 (66)	13,500	**OW**	Obwalden	491 (190)	28,800
				SG	St Gallen	2041 (788)	420,200
BL	Basel-Land	518 (200)	248,488	**SH**	Schaffhausen	298 (115)	71,600
BS	Basel-Stadt	37 (14)	191,700	**SZ**	Schwyz	908 (351)	110,500
BE	Berne	5961 (2300)	938,121	**SO**	Solothurn	791 (305)	226,600
FR	Fribourg	1670 (645)	207,700	**TG**	Thurgau	1013 (391)	205,900
GE	Geneva	282 (109)	375,900	**TI**	Ticino	2811 (1085)	286,700
GL	Glarus	685 (264)	37,600	**UR**	Uri	1076 (415)	33,600
GR	Grisons	7106 (2744)	170,400	**VS**	Valais	5226 (2018)	248,300
JU	Jura	837 (323)	65,600	**VD**	Vaud	3219 (1243)	583,600
LU	Lucerne	1492 (576)	319,500	**ZG**	Zug	239 (92)	84,900
NE	Neuchâtel	797 (308)	160,600	**ZH**	Zurich	1729 (668)	1,150,500
				CH	**Swiss Confederation**	41,293 (15,943)	6,750,600

The Cantons of the Swiss Confederation

Aargau (AG)
Canton since 1803
Capital: Aarau

Appenzell-Ausserrhoden (AR)
Half-canton since 1513
Capital: Herisau

Appenzell-Innerrhoden (AI)
Half-canton since 1513
Capital: Appenzell

Basel-Land (BL)
Half-canton since 1501
Capital: Liestal

Basel-Stadt (BS)
Half-canton since 1501
Capital: Basle

Berne (BE)
Canton since 1353
Capital: Berne

Fribourg (FR)
Canton since 1481
Capital: Fribourg

Geneva (GE)
Canton since 1815
Capital: Geneva

Glarus (GL)
Canton since 1352
Capital: Glarus

Grisons (GR)
Canton since 1803
Capital: Chur

Jura (JU)
Canton since 1979
Capital: Delémont

Lucerne (LU)
Canton since 1332
Capital: Lucerne

Neuchâtel (NE)
Canton since 1815
Capital: Neuchâtel

Nidwalden (NW)
Half-canton since 1291
Capital: Stans

Obwalden (OW)
Half-canton since 1291
Capital: Sarnen

St Gallen (SG)
Canton since 1803
Capital: St Gallen

Schaffhausen (SH)
Canton since 1501
Capital: Schaffhausen

Schwyz (SZ)
Canton since 1291
Capital: Schwyz

Solothurn (SO)
Canton since 1481
Capital: Solothurn

Thurgau (TG)
Canton since 1803
Capital: Frauenfeld

Ticino (TI)
Canton since 1803
Capital: Bellinzona

Uri (UR)
Canton since 1291
Capital: Altdorf

Valais (VS)
Canton since 1815
Capital: Sion

Vaud (VD)
Canton since 1803
Capital: Lausanne

Zug (ZG)
Canton since 1352
Capital: Zug

Zurich (ZH)
Canton since 1351
Capital: Zurich

Unterwalden

Government and Society

The federal constitution of 1848 converted the previous federation of states into a single federal state with a common postal service, army, legislature and judiciary and without any customs or commercial barriers. The new form of union was then approved by all the then existing cantons.

Communes

The smallest unit in the administrative structure is the Commune, of which there are over 3000. They are independent bodies which settle their own budgets and fix their own taxes. The communal or municipal councils are directly elected, usually for a four-year term.

Cantons

Since Jan. 1st 1979 Switzerland has had 26 cantons (20 full cantons and six half-cantons: see page 29), whose independence is enshrined in the constitution. They are real states with their own constitutions, legislatures, executives and judiciaries. Legislative power rests with the people or with a parliament elected by them (Great Council, Cantonal Council, Provincial Council). The cantonal executive is known as the Governing Council, the Smaller Council, the State Council or the Permanent Committee.

In the cantons of Appenzell, Glarus and Unterwalden the cantonal assembly ("Landesgemeinde") of local citizens still meets frequently in the open air to exercise the votes enjoyed by each participant.

The coats-of arms of the individual cantons can be seen, for example, on car licence-plates and cyclists' tax-discs.

Federal Assembly (Legislative)

The Swiss cantons are incorporated in the "Confederation", which has a two-chamber legislature, the Federal Assembly, French, consisting of the National Council, which represents the people, and the Council of States composed of representatives of the cantons. The 200 seats in the National Council are distributed among the cantons in proportion to population, with a minimum of one seat for each canton or half-canton. Each full canton sends two and each half-canton one member to the Council of States. The decisions of the Federal Assembly come

Landsgemeinde (local parliament) in Glarus

into effect only after both chambers have approved them by a majority vote.

Executive power is in the hands of the Federal Council consisting of seven members elected by a joint meeting of both chambers of the Federal Assembly for a four-year term. In the selection of members attention is paid to the interests of linguistic, ethnic and geographical minorities. No canton may have more than one member of the Council.

Federal Council (Executive)

The Federal President is chosen from the ranks of the Federal Council and holds office for a year, during which he continues to be responsible for his ministerial department. The Federal Council renders an account of its activity annually to the Federal Assembly.

Federal President

Every Swiss elector (from the age of 18) is entitled to participate in the affairs of his commune by virtue of the basic rights guaranteed by the constitution — equality before the law, freedom of conscience and religious belief, freedom of establishment, freedom of the press, freedom of association and freedom of trade.

Basic Rights

The people of Switzerland can exert an important degree of influence on national policy through the mechanisms of the "initiative" and the "referendum". An amendment in the constitution can be effected by an initiative of at least 100,000 votes. At least 50,000 voters or eight cantons can demand the approval of a federal law passed by both chambers or of generally binding federal decisions by means of a plebiscite (known as a facultative referendum). Any change in the constitution must be approved by a majority of the people and the Council of States (obligatory referendum).

The federal army is a militia based on universal military service between the ages of 20 and 50. After serving their time members of the forces keep their equipment (including weapons) at home and must take part in periodic shooting practice and put in an annual period of training. There is no provision for performing civilian service in place of military service.

Defence of the Realm

A relic of earlier centuries when many Swiss took service with other states is the Swiss Guard, which still serves as the Papal guard in the Vatican City in Rome.

Swiss Guard

Numerous international organisations have their headquarters in neutral Switzerland. Although, following a referendum in 1986, the country is not a member of the main United Nations Organisation, it does belong to almost all the important independent subsidiary organisations of UNO. For example, the following bodies have their headquarters in Geneva: the Food and Agriculture Organisation (FAO), the General Agreement on Tariffs and Trade (GATT), the International Labour Organisation (ILO), the World Health Organisation (WHO), the United Nations Educational, Scientific and Cultural Organisation (UNESCO), the United Nations Industrial Development Organisation and numerous UNO sub-bodies (UNICEF, United Nations Development Programme, United Nations Environmental Programme, etc.). Switzerland is also a member of the European Free Trade Association (EFTA), the Council of Europe and the Organisation for Economic Cooperation and Development (OECD). Since 1977 Switzerland has had a free trade agreement with the European Union (EU).

International organisations

Geneva is also the seat of the International Committee of the Red Cross, the members of which are all Swiss citizens. This institution is responsible for upholding the four Geneva Conventions, promotes humanitarian international law and organises help in the event of natural catastrophes.

Education and Science

General

"Head, heart and hand" were the three elements identified by the Swiss educationalist Johann Heinrich Pestalozzi (1746–1827) as requiring training; and the objectives which he set out so clearly not only influenced the development of the Swiss school system but also aroused wide international interest – forming the basis, for example, of Wilhelm von Humboldt's reform of the Prussian educational system in 1810. Johann Wolfgang von Goethe, who visited Switzerland three times, expressed the view that this was where "thought based on sound common-sense" originated.

During the early medieval period the main centres of education and culture were the episcopal sees (Sion, Chur, Geneva, Lausanne, Basle, Konstanz, now in Germany) from the 6th c. onwards, followed later by the monastic houses (St Maurice, St Gallen: Reichenau, in Germany). At the height of the Middle Ages the cultural importance of the towns increased. Powerful new impulses came from the Councils of Constance (1414–18) and Basle (1431–39). Basle was also the centre of Swiss humanism, and Erasmus was active here between 1521 and 1529. The humanists were the first to show an awareness of national identity. The Reformers Ulrich Zwingli (1484–1531) in Zurich and Jean Calvin (1509–64) in Geneva gave fresh stimulus to intellectual and religious life in Switzerland. Later the Enlightenment directed the main currents of thought, in Switzerland as in other countries, towards the exact sciences.

School System

Education was slow in reaching the broad mass of the population. In the early days it was in the hands of the Church, and the ability to read and write was until the High Middle Ages a privilege reserved for a small élite. The need for a wide expansion of basic education came to the fore only at the Reformation and Counter-Reformation, with the vigorous new impulses which they gave to human thought. Then, in the 18th and 19th centuries, the Swiss educational systems advanced and developed under the influence of Jean-Jacques Rousseau (1712–78) and the great educationalist Johann Heinrich Pestalozzi.

The Swiss constitution of 1848 assigns the main responsibility for education to the cantons, which share it with the communes. A constitutional amendment making education a joint responsibility of the Confederation and the cantons was rejected by a national referendum in 1972. Only vocational training falls within the competence of the Confederation.

Switzerland also has some 350 private and boarding schools, many of them with an international reputation. Some of these – like some of the Swiss universities – run special holiday courses for both Swiss and foreign students.

Universities

Higher education is also, in general, the responsibility of the cantons. The Confederation is responsible only for the Federal Colleges of Technology in Zurich (opened 1855) and Lausanne (opened in 1853 as a private college for road and civil engineers and taken over by the Confederation in 1968). There are cantonal universities at Basle (founded 1460), Berne (1834), Fribourg (1889), Geneva (1873), Lausanne (1890), Neuchâtel (1909) and Zurich (1833), together with the School of Economic and Social Sciences in St Gallen (1899). There is also a private Theological Faculty (1878) in Lucerne.

The massive increase in student numbers has strained the resources of the cantons responsible for universities, and has led these cantons to put forward claims for federal aid and for contributions from other cantons related to the number of students from those cantons. In addition to the universities there are numbers of technical colleges throughout the country. The total number of students at Swiss higher

University of Zurich . . .   *. . . University of Geneva*

educational establishments during the 1993/94 winter term was 91,037.

As the OECD noted in a report, expenditure on research in Switzerland is well above the international average. There is a well-established division of function between public and private agencies, with the state accepting responsibility for the running of academic institutions, while the main costs of research (some 70% of the total), particularly in the natural sciences, are borne by the private sector. The state is thus unable to exert any major influence on research and development. Here, as in other fields of Swiss life, the trend towards decentralisation can be observed.

Research and Development

1901	Henri Dunant	Nobel Peace Prize
1902	Elie Ducommun	Nobel Peace Prize
1902	Albert Gobat	Nobel Peace Prize
1909	Theodor Kocher	Medicine
1913	Alfred Werner	Chemistry
1919	Carl Spitteler	Literature
1920	Charles-Eduard Guillaume	Physics
1937	Paul Karrer	Chemistry
1939	Leopold Ružička	Chemistry
1945	Wolfgang Pauli	Physics
1946	Hermann Hesse	Literature
1948	Paul Müller	Medicine
1949	Walter Rudolf Hess	Medicine
1950	Tadeusz Reichstein	Medicine
1975	Vladimir Prelog	Chemistry
1978	Werner Arber	Medicine
1986	Heinrich Rohrer	Physics
1987	Karl Alexander Müller	Physics

Swiss Nobel Prize Winners

Economy

General

Switzerland is poorly supplied with minerals and raw materials, and accordingly was compelled from an early stage to turn to the processing industries, commerce and the services sector. The market is characterised by a wide range of products, the result of decentralisation, high quality products and widely distributed capital wealth.

The country possessed some 3.48 million wage-earners in 1992 (of whom 26% were foreigners, including seasonal workers and international commuters), over 64% being in the service industries. While the number of new jobs in the service sector has continued to increase since the seventies, those in manufacturing industry and agriculture have fallen, just as in other European countries. Only 5.4% still work in agriculture. Barely 30% continue in industry, but additional automation, transferring production to more cost-favourable countries and structural streamlining all lead to a relative reduction in the numbers of industrial workers in absolute terms. In 1992 the Gross National Product increased to 352,745 million Swiss francs, a nominal increase of 2.1% compared with the previous year. The number of unemployed, which in 1984 stood at 35,100, the highest since the thirties, increased by April 1994 to 177,500, equal to 4.9% of the work force.

Industry

In spite of the difficulty of communication in this mountainous land – a handicap for a country so heavily dependent on imports – Switzerland's principal source of income is industry, which employs 30% of the working population and accounts for around 35.3% of the GNP (1992). This industry, however, mainly medium and small firms with high quality, individual products, is distributed all over the country, with none of the industrial concentrations found in Britain, Germany or Belgium. Even industrial focal points like Basle, St. Gallen, Zurich, Winterthur and La Chaux-de-Fonds are poles apart from the traditional idea of dirty and pollution-ridden factory towns. However, the fact that risks to the environment exist here too was demonstrated by two serious chemical accidents which occurred recently in the Basle area, at the firms of Sandoz and Ciba-Geigy, causing contamination to the Rhine as far as the North Sea.

In comparison with other European countries Swiss industry operates under most unfavourable conditions. The country's land-locked situation increases freight costs; the high living standard calls for high wages; and production costs are higher because of the lack of local raw materials and fuels. Faced with these difficulties, Swiss industry must compete in foreign markets not by offering lower prices but by the quality of its products. Economically, Switzerland is one of the group of Western European industrial countries which depends essentially on exchanging its finished products for raw materials and foodstuffs from other countries.

The main branches of industry are the highly developed and highly export-orientated chemicals and pharmaceuticals (concentrated mainly in the Basle area), engineering and armaments (Zurich, Winterthur, Oerlikon, Schaffhausen, Baden, Geneva), metalworking, instruments and apparatus, leather, plastics and textiles, the graphic trades and foodstuffs.

Modern Swiss watch designs

The traditional watchmaking industry (concentrated in La Chaux-de-Fonds) is also of great importance. In spite of its quartz technology, the tremendous growth in digital electronics meant that, at the end of the seventies, the Swiss watch industry found itself in serious competition with foreign suppliers (especially Japan). Changes in manufacturing methods (e.g., fully-automatic production based on the modular construction system) and new projects such as the "Swatch" made by the SMH Group (Société Suisse de Microélectronique et d'Horlogerie) have meant that sales figures have markedly increased again since the

Industrial area of the High Rhine, near Basle

middle of the eighties. Switzerland now produces some 132 million watches, clocks and parts each year, equivalent to 16% of the world's watch and clock production and putting it in third place behind Japan and Hong Kong.

Industrial products account for some four-fifths of Switzerland's total exports. The largest industrial firms include Nestlés (foodstuffs) in Cham and Vevey, Ciba-Geigy (chemicals and pharmaceuticals), Roche (chemicals and pharmaceuticals) and Sandoz (chemicals and pharmaceuticals) in Basle, Brown Boveri (electrical engineering) in Baden, Alusuisse (metalworking) in Chippis and Zurich, Sulzer (engineering) in Winterthur, Oerlikon-Bührle (engineering, armaments) and Jacobs (foodstuffs) in Zurich and Holderbank (cement) in Glarus.

In the field of energy Switzerland is again almost wholly dependent on imports. Electric power is an exception: some 62% of electrical energy comes from nearly 450 hydro-electric power stations, some 39% in the country's five nuclear power stations and only 2% from oil-fuelled thermal power stations. Roughly a third of the output is available for export. Alternative sources of energy come from a large number of solar-energy installations, electrical heat pumps, wind-generators and bio-gas plants. A national referendum taken in the spring of 1988 agreed to restrict the use of nuclear energy.

Energy

The services sector continues to grow in importance. Catering for the Swiss desire for material security, the country boasts an established insurance industry formed of companies which enjoy an international reputation and obtain the bulk of their premium income from abroad.

Particular mention must be made of the many, newly-formed service institutions in the administrative sphere which – partly in close collaboration with industry, partly fully independently – offer highly complex financial plans for building, production and organisational projects.

Services sector

35

Economy

The biggest insurance companies in Switzerland include the Zurich, the Swiss Re, Vita, Helvetia Personal Accident and Pensions Company (Helvetia Unfall und Rentonanstalt) in Zurich, Winterthur Insurance and Winterthur Life in Winterthur, Basle Insurance, Basle Life and Patria Life in Basle.

The biggest commercial firms in the Transport and Services sectors are: PTT (postal and communications services) in Berne, Danzas (haulage) in Basle, Kühne & Nagel (haulage) in Pfäffikon, SBB (railways) with its headquarters in Berne, Swissair (air services) in Zurich, Panalpina (haulage) in Binningen, Wienerwald Schweiz (hotels and restaurants) in Feuisberg, Publicitas (press advertising) in Lausanne, Kuoni (travel agency) in Zurich and Adia Interim (temporary employment agency) in Lausanne.

Commerce and Trade

The industrial and services sector form the framework for trade and commerce which, given the high level of imports and exports, also plays a very important part in the economy. The balance of trade is still in deficit, but exports have shown a marked expansion since 1985 (mainly consumer durables such as watches, aircraft, medical instruments and apparatus, machinery for paper-making and printing, yarns and textiles) mainly as the result of increased demand from the United States and the EU countries.

The biggest commercial companies include Migros (foodstuffs and non-food goods) in Zurich, Co-op (foodstuffs and non-food goods) in Basle, AMAG (motor vehicles) and Jelmoli (chain of department stores) in Zurich, Usego (foodstuffs and non-food goods) in Egerkingen, Globus (chain of department stores) and Siber Hegner (international trading company) in Zurich, Shell Switzerland (petroleum products) in Zurich, Denner (foodstuffs) in Zurich as well as VOLG (products for use in agriculture) in Winterthur.

Banking

The country's world-wide trading connections and stable currency, combined with the strict confidentiality maintained by the banks, have

Swiss Banking company in Basle

Upland cattle on the Julier Pass

given banking a dominant position in Switzerland. In addition to the "big five", which are concerned mainly with commercial and credit companies, investment administration and trade in securities, precious metals and foreign currencies, the cantonal banks also play a major role, with a quarter of the total volume of business; there are also regional, local and private banks.

The largest Swiss banks are: Schweizerischer Bankverein in Basle, Schweizerische Bankgesellschaft, Schweizerische Kreditanstalt and Zürcher Kantonalbank in Zurich, Schweizerische Volksbank and Kantonalbank von Bern in Berne, Banque Cantonale Vaudoise in Lausanne, Luzerner Kantonalbank in Lucerne, St Gallische Kantonalbank in St Gallen and Crédit Foncier Vaudois in Lausanne.

Within the total economic picture, agriculture is of comparatively small importance (3% of the GNP). The mountain regions are unfavourable to the development of agriculture, with only a small proportion of usable land, so that reasonably intensive cultivation is possible only in the Alpine foreland. Nevertheless, Switzerland contrives to produce more than half of its requirements of foodstuffs. In spite of government measures to help agriculture the drift from the land gives rise to problems.

Agriculture

More than a quarter of the total area of the country is unproductive. A further quarter is covered by forest, 70% of which is publicly owned, pastureland occupies around 46%, with only 6% of the country's area devoted to arable farming. These proportions are mainly a reflection of climatic conditions, which are favourable to the growth of meadow-land and pasture. Most of the farm holdings are small: only some 30% are larger than 25 acres/10 hectares. Stock-farming is the most impor-

Tourist Regions of Switzerland

Schematic boundaries of tourist regions

1 Grisons	7 Jura-Fribourg-Neuchâtel
2 Eastern Switzerland and Liechtenstein	8 Lake Geneva
3 Zurich	9 Valais
4 Central Switzerland	10 Ticino
5 North-western Switzerland	11 Bernese Mittelland
6 Bernese Oberland	12 Geneva

37

tant branch of agriculture, and Swiss breeds of cattle are sought after in many countries in the world.

The principal type of agricultural produce is milk, and Swiss cheeses (Emmental, Gruyère, etc.) take first place in the country's exports of foodstuffs. Wheat, barley, oats, maize, sugar-beet and potatoes are being grown in increasing quantities. Vines grow in the sunniest and mildest parts of Switzerland – Valais, southern Ticino, on Lake Geneva and the Lac de Neuchâtel and in the transverse valley of the Rhine.

Tourism

Since the end of the 19th c. the tourist trade has been one of Switzerland's major sources of income, and latterly its importance in the economy as a whole has steadily increased, with 300,000 people now being employed, directly or indirectly, in the industry. In recent years the decrease in purchasing power of the dollar has led to a fall in the number of tourists from the USA, and this became even more marked in 1991 as a result of the Gulf War. Adverse world economic conditions and the civil war in the former Yugoslavia also had an adverse effect on tourism in that year. In 1992, however, income from tourism reached the record figure of 21,800 million Swiss francs. Although in 1993 the number of visitors decreased by 2.5% to some 75 million, the prospects are nevertheless very good. Today German tourists account for 45.6% of the total, followed by those from Holland, Britain, USA, France, Belgium and Italy.

On the Rütli meadow, scene of the foundation of the Confederation ▶

History

Stone Age

Finds of Palaeolithic material in caves (e.g. below the Ebenalp in the canton of Appenzell and at the Schweizerbild crag in the canton of Schaffhausen) point to the presence of primaeval hunters in Switzerland during the Ice Age. In the Neolithic period the commonest form of settlement was the lake village built on piles, first identified in Lake Zurich in 1853.

Bronze and Iron Ages

In the Bronze Age (c. 2500–800 B.C.) and Early Iron Age the area of human settlement expands, and cultural links are established with the neighbouring regions to the north and east.

400–58 B.C.

About 400 B.C. the Celts advance into Switzerland from the west. The period takes its name from a Celtic island stronghold discovered at La Tène, near Neuchâtel. The Helvetii, a Celtic tribe, seek to move into southern France, but are defeated and driven back by Julius Caesar at Bibracte in Burgundy (58 B.C.).

15 B.C. to A.D. 455

The Romans' campaigns of conquest over the Alps (first roads over the passes) are completed with the subjugation of Rhaetia, in the western Alpine region, in 15 B.C. There follows a period of peaceful colonisation under Roman rule, which comes to an end only about A.D. 455 with the incursion of the Alemanii into northern Switzerland and the settlement of the Burgundians (who soon become Romanised) in western Switzerland.

(Roman Remains in Switzerland: see map on page 41.)

5th–9th c.

About the turn of the 5th and 6th centuries the Alemanii and Burgundians are conquered by the Franks. Switzerland now becomes part of the Frankish kingdom and, under Charlemagne, of the Holy Roman Empire. After the fall of the Frankish Empire the noble families of Zähringen, Habsburg, Kyburg and Savoy establish separate domains which seek to achieve independence.

1098

Count Berthold of Zähringen is granted the imperial protectorate (Reichsvogtei) of Zurich.

1218

After the death of the last of the Zähringen family, Berthold V, the Zähringen possessions fall to the Counts of Kyburg. Berne, Zurich and Solothurn become free Imperial cities.

1231

Uri, an area of importance through its situation on the St Gotthard route, is granted "immediacy" (Reichsunmittelbarkeit: self-government in direct subordination to the Emperor) by Henry, son of the Emperor Frederick II.

1240

Schwyz is also granted immediacy by the Emperor Frederick II.

1264–91

Count Rudolf III of Habsburg (German Emperor from 1273) wins power over large parts of Switzerland. Strict rule by governors from outside the area.

1291

After Rudolf's death the forest cantons of Uri, Schwyz and Unterwalden form the "Perpetual Alliance" which is the germ of the Confederation. By the "Rütli Oath" they promise mutual assistance in the struggle for their traditional rights and against the dynastic policy of

The Romans in Helvetia

Roman remains
in Switzerland

1 Geneva *(Genava)*: Town walls, villa; museum
2 Nyon *(Noviodunum*: Columns; museum
3 Ste-Croix: Roman road
4 Baumes: Columns, altar
5 Yverdon *(Eburodunum)*: Fort; museum
6 Orbe *(Urba)*: Mosaics
7 Ursins: Temple
8 Ferreyres: Kilns
9 Lausanne *(Lousonna)*: Mosiac pavement, remains of fortifications; museum
10 Moudon *(Minnodunum)*: Inscriptions
11 St-Saphorin: Remains of walls, milestone with inscription
12 Massongex *(Tarnaiae)*: Mosiac pavement, inscriptions
13 St-Maurice *(Acaunum)*: Milestone, gateway; museum
14 Martigny *(Octodurum)*: Theatre, milestone, remains of columns
15 Great St Bernard *(Summus Poeninus)*: Temple, Roman road; museum
16 Avenches *(Aventicum)*: Theatre, temple, remains of town
17 Fribourg: Mosaic pavement; museum
18 Sion *(Sedunum)*: Milestone, inscriptions; museum
19 Pierre Pertuis *(Petra Pertusa)*: Rock gateway with inscription
20 Studen *(Petinesca)*: Temples, gate tower
21 Berne: Theatre, temples, remains of town; museum
22 Solothurn *(Salodurum)*: Fort; museum, lapidarium
23 Schauenburgerflüe: Temple
24 Liestal: Aqueduct; museum
25 Munzach: Villa, mosaics
26 Augst *(Augusta Raurica)*: Remains of town; museum
27 Kaiseraugst *(Castrum Rauracense)*: Fort

28 Hauenstein: Roman road
29 Pfärichgraben: Watch-tower
30 Bürkli: Remains of fortifications
31 Stelli: Watch-tower
32 Wittnau: Remains of fortifications
33 Olten: Villa, fortifications; museum
34 Zofingen: Mosaic pavement
35 Bözberg: Roman road
36 Schwaderloch: Watch-towers
37 Brugg: Fort; museum
38 Windisch *(Vindonissa)*: Theatre, military camp, aquaduct
39 Lenzburg: Theatre
40 Sarmenstorf: Villa
41 Wettingen: Inscription
42 Baden *(Aquae Helveticae)*: Baths; museum
43 Koblenz: Watch-tower, inscriptions
44 Zurzach *(Tenedo)*: Fort, inscriptions; museum
45 Rümikon: Watch-tower
46 Weiach: Remains of fortifications
47 Schleitheim-Salzbrunnen *(Juliomagus)*: Bath; museum
48 Seeb: Villa
49 Zurich *(Turicum)*: Remains of fortifications; museum
50 Stein am Rhein: Fort; museum
51 Stuetheien: Villa
52 Pfyn *(Ad Fines)*: Fort
53 Winterthur *(Vitudurum)*: Fort, temple, inscriptions; museum
54 Irgenhausen: Fort
55 Ufenau: Temple
56 Arbon *(Arbor Felix)*: Fort; museum
57 Stralegg: Watch-tower
58 Filzbach: Watch-tower
59 Sargans:Villa
60 Julier (Guglia) pass: Remains of columns
61 Stabio: Altar

the Habsburgs, with the object of maintaining the self-government and independent jurisdiction of the rural communities and towns and achieving the status immediacy. When the Habsburgs try to bring Switzerland back under Austrian rule in 1439 the Confederation breaks free of the Empire.

History leading up to the Perpetual Alliance	The meeting on the Rütli, Wilhelm Tell's great feat and the destruction of the castles of Zwing-Uri, Sarnen, etc. are vividly described in the "Federal Chronicle" of Obwalden – an account which is probably based on historical facts, though we possess it only in a much revised version of about 1470. Later chroniclers, in particular Ägidius Tschudi of Glarus (c. 1570), who did not possess the text of the 1291 alliance, erroneously dated the rising to the reign of King Albrecht (1307–08). Schiller's play "Wilhelm Tell" (1804) was based on Tschudi's account.
1315	The forest cantons defeat the Habsburg forces in the Battle of Morgarten, south of the Ägerisee (Nov. 15th). Renewal of the Perpetual Alliance at Brunnen (Dec. 9th).
1332–53	The Confederation is enlarged to eight members by the admission of the Habsburg territory of Lucerne in 1332, the Imperial city of Zurich in 1351, Glarus and Zug in 1352 and the Imperial city of Berne in 1353. Tension with Austria leads to further fighting.
1367–1471	Formation of the "Three Leagues" in Rhaetia. To defend themselves against oppression by the nobility the common people form a series of alliances – the "League of God's House" (1367), in which the lead is taken by the Chur church; the "Upper League" or "Grey League" (1395, renewed at Truns in 1424); and the "League of the Ten Jurisdictions" (1436). In 1471, at Vazerol, they become the "Three Perpetual Leagues".
1386	Victory of the Confederates at Sempach over Duke Leopold III of Austria, who is killed in the battle (July 9th). Sacrificial death of Arnold von Winkelried ("A road to freedom").
1388	Defeat of the Austrians at Näfels in the canton of Glarus.
1394	In the "Twenty Years' Peace" Austria renounces its claims to sovereignty over the forest cantons of Lucerne, Glarus and Zug.
1403–74	By adroit tactics the Confederation gains additional territories, some of them (Appenzell, Aargau, Thurgau and a number of places between the Walensee and Lake Constance) as "associated territories" which are not admitted to the Confederation but form defensive alliances with it.
	Valais breaks away from Savoy and becomes an associated territory. The Confederation acquires influence in Upper Ticino. St Gallen, Schaffhausen and Mulhouse in Alsace ask for the Confederation's protection.
1436–50	In the "Old Zurich War", which arises out of a conflict between Zurich and Schwyz, the Confederation once again finds itself involved in a confrontation with Austria, which now seeks the support of France. On Aug. 26th 1444 the Confederates are defeated at St Jakob an der Birs by an army of French mercenaries (the "Armagnacs"), but defeat the Austrians at Ragaz in 1446. Under a peace treaty in 1450 they retain possession of the territories they hold.
1474	Peace with Austria (March), which once again recognises the territories held by the Confederates. Alliance between the Confederates and

Louis XI of France (Oct.). Both agreements are directed against Charles the Bold of Burgundy, who is seeking to encircle the Confederates in the Black Forest and Upper Rhine area and in Vaud.

The treaty with France is the first agreement for the provision of Swiss mercenary troops to a foreign power – the beginning of a practice which later, in the Milanese campaigns, leads to Swiss fighting Swiss.

Burgundian War, in which the Confederation fights on the side of Austria against Charles the Bold. Charles marches on Berne, but is defeated by the Swiss at Grandson (Mar. 2nd 1476) and Murten (June 22nd 1476) and is killed in the Battle of Nancy on Jan. 15th 1477. Swiss mercenaries fighting for Duke René of Lorraine play a considerable part in this victory. Berne and Fribourg acquire territory in Vaud. | 1476–77

At the Battle of Giornico by the Ticino river the Confederates defeat the Milanese, who renounce their claim to the Livine valley. | 1478

Fribourg and Solothurn are admitted into the Confederation. | 1481

Grisons enters into a loose association with the Confederation. | 1497/98

Swabian War, in which the Confederation and Grisons are allied against Austria and the Swabian League. In the Calven defile, near Taufers, a Grisons force of 6000 men defeats an Austrian army of 12,000 (May 22nd). Victory of the Confederates over the Swabian League at Dornach (July 22nd). In the Peace of Basle (Sept. 22nd) the Confederation in effect breaks free of the Holy Roman Empire. | 1499

Basle and Schaffhausen join the Confederation. | 1501
  After the admission of Appenzell in 1513 the composition of the Confederation, which now has 13 members, remains unchanged until 1798.

Milanese campaigns. The Confederates, originally involved only as mercenaries (with Swiss fighting against Swiss), later take part in the campaigns as an independent power. After the victory won by François I of France at Marignano (Sept. 13th–14th 1515) the Swiss are left in an untenable position and give up mercenary service. The Confederates assert their possession of Ticino, and Grisons holds on to the Valtellina, conquered by them in 1512, retaining it until 1797. | 1500–15

Peace with France (Nov. 29th). The Confederates thereafter abandon their role as a belligerent power and declare their complete neutrality. | 1516

Ulrich Zwingli (born 1484 in Wildhaus, killed at the Battle of Kappel in 1531) begins his reforming work as priest at Great Minster in Zurich. | 1519

The Reformation is adopted in Zurich, Schaffhausen, St Gallen, Basle, Berne and Grisons; the four forest cantons, Zug, Fribourg, Solothurn and Valais remain Catholic. | 1523–28

The First Kappel War, arising out of religious conflicts, ends in a peace favourable to the Reformed faith. | 1529

Second Kappel War. Defeat and death of Zwingli in the Battle of Kappel, north of Zug, against the original (Catholic) cantons (Oct. 11th). The peace treaty gives each territory the right to choose its own faith. | 1531

Berne is appealed to for help by Geneva, under threat from Savoy. The Bernese conquer the Savoyard territory of Vaud and impose the Reformed faith. The Confederation thus attains approximately the same area as present-day Switzerland. | 1536

History

The theologian Jean Calvin (1509–64), having fled from Paris, pursues his work as a Reformer in Geneva. The town becomes the great centre of Calvinism, which then spreads to France, the Netherlands, Brandenburg, Hungary, Britain and North America. (The French term "Huguenot" is a corruption of "Eidgenosse" or "Confederate".)

1548–86   The Counter-Reformation and the exacerbation of religious differences lead to an internal split within the Confederation. Ludwig Pfyffer (1524–94) makes Lucerne the centre of the Catholic territories.

1618–48   Switzerland remains neutral in the Thirty Years' War. Only Grisons, disturbed by party strife, is involved in the conflict, since the strategic importance of the Alpine passes within its territory draws Austrian and Spanish forces and a French army commanded by the Duc de Rohan into the area. Thanks to the bold efforts of Colonel Georg Jenatsch (1596–1659); however, the country succeeds in regaining its independence. In the Peace of Westphalia Switzerland is recognised as a European State.

18th century   The patchwork of separate units that makes up the Confederation remains, politically and constitutionally, in the pattern achieved at the time of the Milanese campaigns. The lack of any all-embracing state authority is reflected in the continuing religious, party-political and social tensions. At the same time, however, there is a flowering of intellectual life, linked with that of the neighbouring countries of France and Germany (Haller, Bodmer, Breitinger, Lavater, Pestalozzi, Rousseau, etc.).

1790–97   The influence of the French Revolution makes itself felt; uprisings against aristocratic and patrician rule. Loss of the Valtellina (1797).

1798   France occupies the whole of Switzerland, dissolves the old Confederation and establishes the Helvetian Republic, a unified state on the French model. Geneva, the Jura and the former free Imperial city of Mulhouse (in Swiss hands since 1515) are annexed to France.

1803   Under the Mediation Acts (mainly the work of Napoleon) Switzerland again becomes a confederation of equal cantons, now nineteen in number, with the addition of Aargau, St Gallen, Grisons, Ticino, Thurgau and Vaud to the previous thirteen. Geneva and Valais remain French. Napoleon constructs the road over the Simplon pass.

1813   Dissolution of the Medication Acts following the fall of Napoleon.

1814–15   At the Congress of Vienna the number of cantons is increased to 22 by the addition of Geneva, Valais and Neuchâtel. Under the Bundesvertrag (Federal Agreement) a new constitution is introduced: the 22 cantons are now recognised as sovereign bodies (Aug. 1815).
    Peace of Paris (Nov. 1815): the perpetual neutrality of Switzerland is guaranteed. Customs-free zones established on the frontiers of Geneva.

1830–39   A Liberal Movement ("Regeneration") in many cantons and attempt to achieve a liberal revision of the federation; this fails in the face of conservative opposition.

1845   The Catholic and conservative cantons of Lucerne, Uri, Schwyz, Unterwalden, Zug, Fribourg and Valais form a separate federation, the Sonderbund.

1847   Sonderbund War, which soon ends, after no serious fighting, in the defeat of the Sonderbund.

Adoption, by national referendum, of a new federal constitution: the federation of states becomes one Federal State.	1848
Geneva Convention. On the initiative of Henri Dunant (1828–1910) an international agreement on the conduct of war on land is signed in Geneva (Aug. 22nd: formation of Red Cross).	1864
Switzerland remains neutral in the Franco-Prussian War.	1870
Revision of the federal constitution to increase both the unity of the Confederation and the independence of the cantons. The federal government is assigned responsibility for foreign policy, the army and economic affairs (currency, railways, postal services) and partial responsibility for justice.	1874
On the outbreak of the First World War the Swiss army is mobilised, but the country's neutrality is fully preserved. During the war Switzerland takes in wounded and sick prisoners of war from both sides.	1914–18
First meeting of the League of Nations in Geneva (May 15th). Switzerland becomes a member of the League after a national referendum (May 18th).	1920
During the Second World War Switzerland again remains neutral, but gives aid to those of any nation who need it.	1939–45
Switzerland becomes a member of UNESCO.	1948
Switzerland becomes a member of the Organisation for European Economic Cooperation (OEEC).	1950
Switzerland joins the European Free Trade Association (EFTA).	1960
Switzerland becomes the 17th member of the Council of Europe.	1963
Women are granted the right to vote and stand for election in federal elections.	1971
Switzerland signs a free trade agreement with the European Community (EC).	1972
Regional referenda on the establishment of a new canton of Jura.	1974–75
Economic agreement with the Soviet Union (Jan. 12th). The formation of the new canton of Jura is approved in a national referendum (Sept. 24th).	1978
The new canton of Jura becomes a member of the Confederation as the République et Canton du Jura (Jan. 1st).	1979
A national referendum rejects a proposal for the separation of church and state. Queen Elisabeth II becomes the first British Head of State to visit Switzerland (May). On Sept. 5th the new 16.3km/10 mile long road tunnel through the St Gotthard is opened to traffic.	1980
In a referendum a majority votes for a constitutional measure by which the equality of men and women will be legally established.	1981
Demolition of the Autonomous Youth Centre (AJZ) in Zurich (Mar. 20th). The Foreigners Law, aimed at improving the standing of foreign citizens, is rejected by referendum (June 6th).	1982
Pope John Paul II makes a pastoral visit to Switzerland June 11th–17th. By a plebiscite the Principality of Liechtenstein becomes the last country in Europe to give women the vote. Although Franz Joseph II remains the titular head of the Principality, the business of government	1984

is transferred in August to his son, Hans Adam. On Oct. 2nd a woman is elected for the first time to the Federal Government of Switzerland.

1985 Following a referendum, tolls are introduced for motorways (highways) in Switzerland. The meeting of the US President Reagan and the Soviet Party Chief Gorbachev in Geneva (Nov. 19th–21st) creates world-wide interest.

1986 Following a referendum (Mar. 16th) 75% of the electors vote against Switzerland's joining UNO. Chemical accidents in the Ciba-Geigy and Sandoz firms lead to pollution of the Rhine and the air near Basle and in the adjoining area. The National Council resists sanctions against South Africa (mid-Dec.).

1987 The revision of the laws concerning refugees and foreigners is approved in a referendum (Apr. 5th).

1988 Parliament resolves in May to build no more nuclear power stations in Switzerland. Introduction of the concept of "Rail and Bus 2000" which proposes a thorough modernisation of Swiss railways and public transport. In June the government in Berne approves a budget of some 55 million Swiss francs to celebrate in 1991 the 700th anniversary of the Swiss Confederation.

1989 Immediate resignation of the cabinet member Elisabeth Kopp following a breach of the Official Secrets Act (Jan. 12th).
Federal President Delamuraz confirms before the European Parliament Switzerland's readiness to assist in the reconstruction of Europe.
The planned construction of the Kaiseraugst nuclear power station near Basle is turned down by both houses of parliament. Women in Appenzell-Ausserrhoden receive the right to vote in cantonal elections (Apr.). Although, in a referendum in Nov., a majority of the people were against the abolition of the Swiss army, one third were in favour.

1990 By a majority of three to one, the National Council votes against a ban on further use of nuclear energy (Feb.). The voting age is lowered from 20 to 18 years of age.

1991 The 700th anniversary celebrations of the founding of the Confederation in 1291 open on January 11th in the courtyard of the Castello Grande in Bellinzona (Ticino).
In a referendum, 63·6% of the votes are in favour of building the New Trans-Alpine Railway (NEAT); it will comprise two rail tunnels through the Gotthard (49.3km/30½ miles) and the Lötschberg (28km/17 miles), estimated cost between £7 and 14,000 million/US$ 10 and 20,000 million. As a result most of north–south freight traffic, which is expected to double following the finalising of the European internal market, will go by rail instead of by road. Women vote for the first time in the Appenzell-Inerrhoden municipality (April).
The conservative right-wing splinter parties, especially the Auto Party, gain 42.6% of the votes in the Swiss parliamentary elections. In spite of a renewed absolute majority, the FDP (Liberal Democrats), CVP (Christian Democrats), SPS (Social Democrats) and SVP (Swiss Popular Party) suffer considerable losses.

1992 In a referendum the majority vote against joining the European Economic Union.

1994 In further referendums the Swiss people decline to participate in UN military interventions and approve the Anti-Racial Agreement adopted by UNO in 1965. On December 9th the Swiss artist, sculptor and architect Max Bill dies.

Art and Culture

Cultural Life and Museums

Switzerland is a turn-table of lively cultural exchange. Foreign artists have always come to the country to live and work, while at the same time the Swiss have made important contributions to the international art scene with artists such as Paul Klee, Alberto Giacometti, Le Corbusier or Jean-Luc Godard.

The fullness and variety of Swiss cultural life is largely the product of the four different languages found in the country – not to mention the numerous dialects – each of which has its own important cultural spheres. Added to this is the fact that while the cantons are mainly responsible for overall cultural policy, the local communes, each with its own peculiarities, have developed a considerable degree of cultural autonomy. The Federation aims mainly at a balance between the regions, preserving the landscape (nature reserves), historical monuments and other testimonials to Swiss culture, as well as promoting the arts.

The "Pro Helvetia" foundation set up in Zurich in 1939 is devoted to protecting Swiss culture within the country and spreading its name abroad.

Cultural collections are displayed in over 700 museums large and small throughout the country. The most important include the Swiss National Museum in Zurich and the art museums in Basle, Berne, Geneva and Zurich. The world's major collection of marginal art ("Art Brut") is to be found in Lausanne, while large numbers of visitors are attracted to the Fondation Gianadda in Martigny, which embraces a culture centre, an archaeological museum and a collection of vintage cars. Modern art is represented at the Museum of Contemporary Art in Basle, the Hallen für Neue Kunst in Schaffhausen, and in the museums of Berne, Zurich, Solothurn, Aargau, St Gallen and Winterthur. Those interested in post-1945 photography will find their needs met in museums in Winterthur and Lausanne (Musée de l'Elysée). Private enterprise must be thanked for some superbly equipped collections, such as the Oskar Reinhart exhibition "Am Römerholz" in Winterthur, the Abegg Foundation in Riggisberg and the Rietberg Museum in Zurich, the William Tell Museum in Bürglen (canton of Uri), the Ballenberg Open Air Museum near Brienz (canton of Berne) and in the Gotthard Museum in the St Gotthard Pass. Technorama in Winterthur and the International Clock and Watch Museum in La-Chaux-de-Fonds are examples of museums devoted to science and technology. Also especially worthy of mention are the Swiss Musical Automata Museum in Seewen (canton of Solothurn), the Postal, Telegraph and Telephone Museum in Berne, and the Swiss Transport Museum in Lucerne, the largest of its kind in Europe. Local collections of domestic and regional history are also gaining in importance in all parts of the country.

Most museums are described under the corresponding heading in the A to Z section of this guide; further information can be found under "Museums" in the Practical Information section. The Association of Swiss Museums (Verband der Museen der Schweiz; publishers Friedrich Reinhardt Verlag, Basle) produce comprehensive information in their "Swiss Museum Guides". For items of specialised interest the Swiss Historical Art Company (Schweizerische Gesellschaft für Kunstgeschichte) issues monographs.

Cultural Life

Museums

History of Art

General   The history of Swiss culture is as varied and manifold as the landscape of Switzerland. This region of passage, this land of four languages, has been open at all times to influences from the wider world, and it is not surprising, therefore, to find that its art and architecture in particular show affinities with those of the neighbouring countries of Germany, Austria, France and Italy. But these creative impulses operated in both directions, with architects from Ticino and the Italian-speaking Grisons making a major contribution to the development of Baroque architecture in Rome and South Germany in the 16th and 17th c., and Austrian and South German architects creating the finest Baroque buildings in Switzerland in the 17th and 18th c.

Accordingly Switzerland's numerous works of art and architecture show no distinctively national style; and the federal structure influenced by the linguistic and ethnic differences, the absence of any princely houses to act as patrons, and other factors; all these inhibited the development of any major national centre of artistic creation.

The art and culture of Switzerland are predominantly centred on the commune, the valley or the region. With few exceptions (Ferdinand Hodler) Swiss artists of international reputation have established their fame outside Switzerland, for example the Ticinese architects Francesco Borromini and Carlo Maderna (who designed the nave of St Peter's in Rome), Alberto Giacometti and Le Corbusier, who opened up new dimensions of sculpture and architecture while working in Rome, and Othmar Ammann, the engineer who built the George Washington Bridge in New York.

Stone Age   Implements and animal bones dating from the Palaeolithic period were found in the Wildkirchli cave on the Ebenalp, and the prehistoric material in the excellent All Saints Museum in Schaffhausen points to occupation during the Ice Age.

The Neolithic period (c. 3000 B.C.) is represented in Switzerland by traces of the Cortaillod culture and Michelsberg culture (belonging to the Western European cultural sphere), probably left by a Pre-Indo-European population which already practised arable and stock farming (tulip-shaped cups, mostly black undecorated ware).

Bronze and Iron   In the Bronze Age (from c. 2500 B.C.) the Alpine regions, paricularly in
Ages   Grisons, were settled up to altitudes of 2000m/6500ft. In sheltered situations on the shores of lakes (e.g. Lake Zurich) pile-dwellings have been found. In the Bronze Age and Early Iron Age (the Hallstatt culture) there is evidence of cultural links with the regions to the north and east. The Iron Age inhabitants of Grisons and Ticino were the Rhaetians, while central Switzerland was settled from about 450 B.C. by Celts.

They developed the Late Iron Age La Tène culture (c. 450–50 B.C.), named after the site at Lac de Neuchâtel. The characteristic feature of La Tène art is its ornament, partly vegetable and partly abstract and showing strong Etruscan influence. Highly stylised human and animal heads are also found.

In the Late La Tène period art degenerated completely and the decoration of plane surfaces was abandoned.

Roman   In 15 B.C. the Romans completed their conquest of Rhaetia. Thereafter
Occupation   major Roman settlements were established, particularly in western Switzerland.

Avenches (*Aventicum*): The town flourished in the 1st and 2nd c. A.D. but was destroyed by the Alemanni in 260. Considerable remains survive – a theatre seating 10,000, fragments of the 6km/4 mile circuit of walls, the forum baths, the Corinthian column known as the "Cigognier". Artifacts can be seen in the local museum.

Remains of Roman settlement in Nyon . . .   . . . and in Avenches

Lausanne (*Lousonna*): Bust of Marcus Aurelius in the Archaeological Museum.

Nyon (*Noviodunum*): Columns in the Bourg-de-Rive park.

Geneva (*Genava*).

St Maurice (*Acaunum*).

Martigny (*Octodurum*): Remains of a Roman amphitheatre.

Sion (*Sedunum*).

Windisch (*Vindonissa*): Roman camp and remains of an amphitheatre seating 10,000. Rich collection of material in Vindonissa Museum, Brugg.

Kaiseraugst (*Augusta Raurica*): Large theatre and remains of several temples, a basilica and an amphitheatre. Roman museum and domestic animal park.

Notable remains of Roman pass roads can be seen on the Julier (Guglia), Septimer (Sett), Splügen and Great St Bernard passes.

With the beginning of the Great Migrations the Alemanni penetrated into northern Switzerland in 455, and the Burgundians, who became Romanised at a very early stage, settled in the south-west (linguistic boundary between French and German). By 534 the Franks had conquered the whole country.

The Great Migrations

During the medieval period the French-, German- and Italian-speaking parts of Switzerland pursued their separate development, influenced respectively by France, Germany and Italy but nevertheless retaining a certain cultural independence.

Middle Ages

Christianity now became the main cultural force, particularly in Valais and Grisons.

Examples of pre-Carolingian architecture can be seen in a number of places, particularly at St-Maurice, Disentis (a Benedictine abbey founded about 720 by St Sigisbert) and Chur (8th c. crypt in the 12th c. church of St Lucius; St Martin's church, 8th c.).

The Carolingian
Period

The Carolingian Period

The Carolingian period is represented by an abundance of buildings, including the choir of St John's church at Moutier (Grisons). The church, originally founded in 780, was rebuilt in Late Gothic style at the end of the 15th c. It is notable for its frescoes, some of them revealed only about 1950 (now in the National Museum, Zurich), which give some impression of what the original abbey church of St Gallen must have been like.

Also of the Carolingian period are the octagonal baptistery of Riva San Vitale on Lake Lugano; parts of the Augustinian abbey of St-Maurice in Valais, the oldest monastic house in Switzerland, founded about 515 (4th c. chapel, devastated by the Saracens about 940; famous treasury, with Merovingian works of art including reliquaries, an Oriental ewer enamelled in gold and a Roman vessel of sardonyx; 11th c. Romanesque tower); and St Martin's church at Zillis (Early Romanesque nave and tower, Late Gothic choir; unique painted ceiling of 1140, a magnificent example of very early figural painting).

The Benedictine abbey of Einsiedeln was founded in 934 on the site of the hermitage of St Meinrad (murdered in 861). The library contains very beautiful illuminated manuscripts.

Abbey of St
Gallen

The Benedictine abbey of St Gallen was founded by St Othmar on the site of a hermitage established by the Irish missionary monk St Gall or Gallus about 612. In the 9th c. it rose to considerable economic prosperity and enjoyed a great cultural flowering (dissolved 1805). Its school and library made it one of the leading intellectual centres of the Alpine region (Ekkehart, Notker Balbulus, Notker Labeo).

About 820 the famous plan of the abbey of St Gallen (now in the abbey library at St Gallen) was drawn up. This shows the detailed layout of a medieval monastic establishment with a double-choired church and a complete range of conventual buildings. The plan is not to scale, and probably represents the proposed layout for the 9th c. abbey, none of which has survived.

Church of St-Pierre-de-Clages *Benedictine Abbey of Payerne*

The abbey library, with its magnificent interior architecture, contains a rich store of valuable manuscripts and incunabula (ivory book-covers by Tutilo, c. 900; "Psalterium Aureum", 9th c.; Folchard Psalter, c. 860–70; "Casus Monasterii Sancti Galli", by Ekkehart IV, 11th c.; 13th c. manuscript B of "Nibelungenlied", etc.).

Romanesque

The Benedictine abbey on the island of Reichenau, founded in 724, was one of the leading cultural centres of the early medieval period from the 9th to the 11th c. (miniatures, wall-painting), the influence of which was particulary strong in northern Switzerland. A notable establishment in this area was the Benedictine abbey of All Saints at Schaffhausen. The minster (1087–1150), a pillared basilica with a single tower, a flat roof and (since its restoration) a sparsely decorated interior, is an outstanding example of Romanesque architecture (12th c. cloister with elegant arcades). All saints was a daughter house of the Cluniac abbey of Hirsau in the Black Forest.

Of the Benedictine abbey of Muri (Aargau), founded by the Habsburgs in 1027 (dissolved 1841, largely destroyed by fire in 1859), parts of the east and west ends and the Romanesque three-aisled crypt survive. The "Acta Murensia" are informative on the early period of the abbey, and a Middle High German Easter play has also been preserved.

About the year 1000 a small Romanesque church showing Lombard influence, with fine frescoes, was built at Spiez; and the churches at Amsoldingen and Romainmôtier also date from the 10th to the 11th c. The church of St-Pierre-de-Clages (11th–12th c.), in Valais, is one of the finest Romanesque churches in Switzerland.

The Benedictine abbey of Engelberg in the canton of Obwalden, founded about 1120 (church and conventual buildings rebuilt by Kaspar Moosbrugger in 1730–37 after a fire), became noted in the time of Abbot Frowin (1143–78) for its scriptorium and school of painters. The abbey library (open to men only) contains valuable illuminated manuscripts, incunabula and miniatures.

Also of the 12th c. are the two fine Romanesque churches of Giornico, San Nicolao (three-aisled crypt) and Santa Maria di Castello, and part of the Château of Neuchâtel (west wing). The Grossmünster in Zurich was built between the 11th and 13th c. (fine double crypt of 1100; nave stripped of its interior decoration at the Reformation).

Other examples of Romanesque architecture are the 11th c. three-aisled pillared basilican church (fine porch) of the Benedictine abbey of Payerne (founded during the Cluniac reform movement of the 10th c., dissolved in 1536); the 12th c. church of St-Jean, a pillared basilica with Carolingian work in the nave and a Gothic choir, in the picturesque little town of Grandson; the 12th c. collegiate church and the Tour de la Reine Berthe, a relic of the Church of St-Martin, in St-Imier; and the Cistercian abbey of Hauterive (Fribourg), showing Burgundian influence, which was founded by Guillaume de Glâne about 1138 and dissolved in 1848 (the church in Romanesque-Gothic transitional style, c. 1160; Romanesque cloister; fine stained glass of 1332).

Other examples of the Romanesque-Gothic transitional style of the 12th and 13th c. are the Cathedral of Chur (crypt 6th and 12th c.); the five-aisled minster of Basle, which dates in its oldest parts from the 9th c. and was replaced at the end of the 12th c. by a new structure mingling the most varied influences with earlier Ottonian architectural traditions (remodelled in Gothic style 1356; richly carved Romanesque capitals; remains of Late Romanesque pavements and frescoes; Late Gothic choir-stalls of the late 14th c.); and the church of the former Cistercian abbey of Kappel on the River Albis (13th–14th c.).

Impressive examples of Romanesque sculpture can be seen in the Grossmünster of Zurich (seated figure of Charlemagne in crypt; copy

Romanesque
Sculpture

on south tower). Notable also are the richly varied capitals in the choir of the church of Notre-Dame de Valère (12th–13th c.) in Sion, which is built on Roman foundations. The famous St Gallus doorway in the minster in Basle (originally on the west front, now in the north transept: 1170–1200), the earliest major figured doorway in German-speaking territory, has rich sculptured decoration, including figures of the Four Evangelists and the Wise and Foolish Virgins and representations of Christ as Judge of the world and the Last Judgment in the tympanum. It appears to have been based on Italian and Provençal models, like the south doorway of the conventional church (12th–13th c.) in the little town of St-Ursanne.

The National Museum in Zurich has a large collection of Romanesque sculpture in wood.

Gothic

During the Gothic period the art and architecture of the towns begins to develop, although the appeal of the buildings of this period frequently lies in their picturesque effect rather than in their architectural quality.

Throughout the 15th c. Switzerland remained open to influences from outside the country. Only Basle, with its University (founded in 1460), evolved a distinctive intellectual culture of its own. The altar by Konrad Witz in Geneva (1444), with the first representation of the mountains as seen by the artist, marks the beginning of landscape painting.

The political successes of the Confederates in the Burgundian wars also created the basis for a distinctively Swiss development of art and architecture. Each town now took on a character of its own, building the town halls, gates and fortifications still to be seen in Murten, Romont, Solothurn, Schaffhausen and many other towns. The finest urban ensembles which have survived from this period are Berne and Fribourg, the charm of which is enhanced by their situation on peninsulas rising high above the river valleys.

Gothic Church
Building

Notable among the Gothic churches is the church of the Cistercian abbey of Wettingen, founded in 1227 and dissolved in 1841 (richly carved choir-stalls of 1604; fine 16th–17th c. stained glass in cloister). To this period also belongs the cathedral of Notre-Dame in Lausanne (dedicated by Pope Gregory X in 1275), in Early Burgundian Gothic style, with five towers, fine sculptured decoration in the Apostles' Choir (13th c.) and on the main doorway (16th c.) and a rose window containing beautiful 13th c. stained glass. The cathedral of St-Pierre in Geneva, built between the 12th and 14th c. and a Protestant church since the Reformation, has notable capitals in the Romanesque-Gothic transitional style and beautiful Late Gothic choir-stalls.

The minster in Basle was rebuilt in Gothic style in 1356 after an earthquake. The west front, between St George's tower (1428) and St Martin's tower (1500), is decorated with magnificent 13th c. sculpture, including a figure of the Emperor Henry II holding a model of the church. The double cloister, built on Romanesque foundations, dates from the 15th c. The Rathaus of Basle, in Late Burgundian Gothic style with a brightly painted façade and arcades, was built between 1504 and 1521. The parish church of Winterthur was built between 1264 and 1515, though the towers date only from the 17th and 18th c.

The cathedral of St Nicholas in Fribourg dates from the 14th and 15th c. and has magnificent sculpture of that period above the principal doorway (Apostles; the Angelic Salutation; Last Judgment in tympanum); it contains a beautiful choir screen and choir-stalls, stained glass and a famous organ.

The Late Gothic minster of Berne, a three-aisled pillared basilica without transepts, was begun in 1421 to the design of the Ulm architect M. Ensinger. The richly decorated west doorway has a Last Judgment, with numerous figures, in the tympanum. The side walls are embel-

Murten: Medieval town moat in the Törfliplatz

lished with frescoes of 1501 (restored); the nave and choir have reticulated vaulting with fine roof bosses bearing coats of arms; choir-stalls (1523) in Renaissance style; beautiful stained glass by Hans Acker (1441–50).

The Rathaus of Berne was built in 1406–16 in Late Burgundian Gothic style. The clock tower with its astronomical clock of 1530 dates from the 15th century, but has undergone much subsequent rebuilding. Also of great interest are the old streets and lanes of Berne with their charming fountains, including the Banner-Carrier fountain of 1542 and the Ogre fountain of 1540.

The cathedral of Notre-Dame-du-Glarier in Sion was rebuilt in the 15th c.; it contains fine Gothic tombs. The beautiful Gothic parish church of Moudon has fine choir-stalls of 1502, and the town also possesses three castles, the Tour de Broye (12th c.), the Château de Rochefort (1595) and the Château de Billens (1677).

Other buildings showing the influence of French models are the Gothic castles of western Switzerland – at Champvent (a massive 13th c. stronghold), Grandson (Vufflens-le-Château, one of the most imposing castles in Switzerland, 14th–15th c.), Lucens (a massive structure of the 15th–16th c., with a 13th c. round tower, now the Conan Doyle Museum) and Chillon, near Monyteux (founded in the 9th or 10th c., present structure 13th c.; rock-cut dungeons, large church, court hall, living quarters, etc.: cf. Byron's poem "The Prisoner of Chillon").

At Sion is the ruined Château de Tourbillon, once an episcopal stronghold (built 1294, burned down 1788).

The only structures in southern Switzerland which can be compared with these massive fortresses are the three castles of Bellinzona, built in their present form by the Dukes of Milan in the 15th c. and in 1503 given the names of the three original cantons of Uri, Schwyz and

Gothic Castles

Gothic castle of Vufflens-le-Château

Unterwalden. In German Switzerland the castles are on a considerably more modest scale, for example the Habsburg (*c.* 1020), ancestral seat of the Austrian Imperial House, or the Kyburg, which first appears in the records in the 11th century (restored 1925).

The finest examples of Gothic sculpture are to be seen in the cathedrals of Lausanne and Fribourg and in the Collegiate Church of Notre-Dame-de-Valère in Sion, a three-aisled pillared basilica of the 12th–13th c. with its original interior furnishings, a carved wood altar of the 16th c. and a 15th c. organ still in working order. In the collegiate church in Neuchâtel is the tomb of the Counts of Neuchâtel (1372) with its fifteen painted effigies, the most magnificent funerary monument in Switzerland.

Gothic Sculpture

The beautiful stained glass produced in Switzerland during this period has unfortunately survived only in a very small number of examples – e.g. in the minster in Berne, the choir of the Gothic conventual church of Königsfelden (14th c.) and the cloister of the Cistercian abbey of Wettingen. A secular form of stained glass is represented by the "Schweizerscheiben" (stained glass panels) in the National Museum in Zurich.

Stained Glass

After the defeat of Charles the Bold of Burgundy the enhanced political standing of the Confederation was matched by a greater degree of independence in art and architecture. The towns now increased in importance, and secular building played a much more prominent part in comparison with religious building. These developments coincided with the coming of the Renaissance to Switzerland.

Renaissance

The architecture of this period can be seen at Murten, with its completely preserved circuit of walls, its timber wall-walk, its arcades and

◄ *Neuchâtel: Monumental tomb of the Counts of Neuchâtel*

its picturesque fountains; at Romont, also with handsome walls and towers; at Solothurn; and in Fribourg, Berne, Lucerne and Schaffhausen.

Decorative Arts

The decorative arts flourished during this period, which has left some beautifully decorated interiors – e.g. in the house built by Georg Supersaxo in Sion in 1505 (panelled banqueting hall with carved and painted ceiling), the richly appointed palace built for Colonel Freuler in Näfels in 1642–47 (panelled rooms, Winterthur stoves: now the Glarus Cantonal Museum) and the Ital-Reding house in Schwyz, and above all in the canton of Grisons.

Many churches were equipped with new choir-stalls and pulpits at this period, for example at Muri, Wettingen and Beromünster.

15th and 16th c. Painting

The painting of the 15th and 16th c. ranks as one of the high points of Swiss art. A particularly notable figure who worked at Basle in the first half of the 15th c. was Konrad Witz (1400–44), one of the great masters of Late Gothic painting. He broke away from the "soft" style and became the first artist to depict real landscapes (Lake Geneva) and was the founder of Swiss landscape painting ("St Christopher" c. 1435; altar of 1444 in Museum of Art and History, Geneva). Of his 20 surviving panel-paintings thirteen belong to the Basle "Mirror of Salvation" altar (c. 1435).

Urs Graf (1485–1527), who also worked as a goldsmith, depicts the life of the landsknechts (mercenary soldiers), which he knew from personal observation, in vigorous and often overcharged drawings and woodcuts (Museum of Art, Basle).

Niklaus Manuel, known as Deutsch (1484–1530), was a draughtsman of exceptional quality who also depicted scenes from the life of the landsknechts in a rather Mannerist style, as well as altarpieces, mythological pictures and frescoes.

Hans Leu the Younger (1490–1531) was another of the early Swiss landscape-painters, showing affinities with the work of the Danube

"St Peter's Catch" by Konrad Witz

school. Hans Asper (1499–1571) was another painter who also produced woodcuts.

Jost Amman (1539–91), who worked mainly in Nuremberg, produced an extraordinary number of woodcuts covering the whole range of subject-matter then in vogue (historical, military and hunting scenes; armorials; illustrations to rhymes by Hans Sachs).

Tobias Stimmer (1539–84) was one of the leading Swiss painters of the Late Renaissance (portraits; vividly coloured paintings on the façade of the Haus zum Ritter in Schaffhausen (1485), the originals of which are now in All Saints Museum).

Hans Fries (1465–1520), working mainly in Basle, Fribourg and Berne, is known principally for his altarpieces, painted in glowing colours. The Berne and Zurich Masters of the Carnation also devoted themselves mainly to religious themes.

Hans Holbein the Younger (1497–1543), a native of Augsburg, worked for many years in Basle (Public Art Collection, Basle). In scale and variety his output can be compared only with that of Dürer, and as a portrait-painter he is unequalled. Most of his wall-paintings have unfortunately been lost. His woodcuts are also of the highest quality ("Dance of Death", c. 1525).

Bernardino Luini painted frescoes in the church of Santa Maria degli Angioli in Lugano in 1529. The cathedral of San Lorenzo in that town, with a marble façade of about 1515, is an early example of Renaissance architecture in Ticino.

After the end of the Thirty Years' War there was a great burst of building activity – mainly by the Catholic Church, then concentrating all its resources on the Counter-Reformation, but also by princes and great nobles.

Baroque

During the Baroque period no huge and imposing secular buildings were erected in Switzerland, but mainly fine town houses and small country houses, particularly around Berne, Basle, Geneva, Solothurn and Fribourg. Almost all the house fronts in Berne were rebuilt at this time.

Protestant churches built during this period included a number of small country churches, the Church of the Holy Ghost in French baroque style, in the Bubenbergplatz in Berne (1726–29), the Temple de la Fusterie in Geneva and the temple in Neuchâtel. The parish church in Yverdon was built in 1755–57 (the Town Hall in 1769–73), a beautiful church at Morges in 1776.

Protestant Church Building

The Catholic Church did a great deal of building in the first half of the 18th c., and most of the monastic houses were rebuilt or altered. In contrast to protestant building, however, it followed Italian rather than French models: Cathedral of St Ursen, Solothurn (1763–73) and Jesuit churches in Solothurn (1680–89) and Lucerne (1666–77; Rococo interior 1750).

Catholic Church Building

The South German type of Baroque hall-church is also found, for example in the church (built 1705, with a sumptuous interior) of the Benedictine abbey of Rheinau (founded in the 9th c., dissolved in 1862).

From the 1680s onwards three families of architects belonging to the Vorarlberg school – the Beers, the Thumbs and the Moosbruggers – developed an indigenous form of Baroque which displaced the Italian style. Several generations of these families worked in Switzerland. Peter Thumb (1681–1766) and Johann Michael Beer built the three-aisled hall-church of St Gallen (1755–66), and Peter Thumb was also responsible for the famous abbey library at St Gallen (1758–61), which already shows strong Rococo influence. The principal work of Kaspar Moosbrugger (1656–1723) was the rebuilding of the abbey and church of Einsiedeln (1704–23), a masterpiece of Baroque form and boldly

Vorarlberg School of Architecture

contrasting spatial sequences. The interior of the church was the work of two Bavarian brothers, Cosmos Damian and Egid Quirin Asam, who had been trained in Rome but cast off the influence of Roman Baroque and created theatrical architectural forms which sought to achieve an indissoluble unity between space, light, colour and plastic and architectural movement.

The Ticinese architects Carlo Maderna or Maderno (1556–1629: nave of St Peter's, Rome) and Carlo Fontana (1624–1714) were among the great masters of the Roman Baroque.

18th c. Painting

Although in the first half of the 18th c. sculpture, painting and decorative art were completely subordinate to architecture, towards the end of the century they achieved a greater degree of independence.

The poet and painter Salomon Gessner (1730–88) illustrated his famous "Idylls" with delicately etched vignettes, and painted small gouaches and water-colours which depicted mythological scenes and landscapes.

Jean-Etienne Liotard (1720–89), who worked in many different countries, produced charming pastels.

Anton Gaff (1736–1813) was exclusively a portrait painter, notable particularly for his likenesses of leading intellectual figures of the day (Bodmer, Bürger, Gellert, Lessing, Schiller, Wieland, etc.).

Johann Heinrich Füssli (1741–1825), known in Britain as Henry Fuseli, worked first in Italy and later became Keeper of the Royal Academy in London. He specialised in the dramatically Baroque and the fantastically horrific ("The Nightmare").

Neo-Classicism

The Neo-Classical period is represented in Swiss architecture by handsome mansions built for the wealthy middle classes (e.g. Talacker, Zurich), the church at Heiden and the Town Hall of Altdorf (1805–08).

An important Neo-Classical painter was Angelica Kauffman (1741–1807), most of whose work was on mythological, allegorical and religious themes. She was a prominent member of the group of German artists working in Rome and produced a famous portrait of Goethe. Johann August Nahl the Younger, a pupil of the German artist J. H. Tischbein, painted mythological and historical pictures.

Historicism

During the second half of the 19th c. the Swiss government commissioned a number of major buildings, including the massive Bundeshaus in Berne, in the style known as Historicism or Neo-Renaissance, with the Bundesterrasse rising 164ft/50m above the Aare on its huge retaining walls, the Swiss National Museum in Zurich and various administrative buildings, railway stations, etc.

19th c. Painting

The painting of this period was of higher quality than its architecture. Among painters working in French Switzerland were Alexandre Calame (1810–64), noted for his paintings of the mountains, François Diday (1802–77) and Barthélemy Menn (1815–93); in German Switzerland Albert Anker (1831–1910), Frank Buchser (1828–90), Max Buri (1868–1915), Hans Sandreuter (1850–1901: sgraffito work, stained glass, water-colours) and the etcher Albert Welti (1862–1912: stained glass in Bundeshaus, Berne, 1901–03).

A painter who exerted wide influence was Arnold Böcklin (1827–1901), who alternated between the two extremes of gay joie de vivre and profound melancholy ("Island of the Dead").

Giovanni Segantini (1858–99), a native of Trento, painted the mountains of the Upper Engadine (Segantini Museum, St Moritz), but also produced pictures of symbolic content ("The Dead Mothers").

Ferdinand Hodler (1835–1918) gave fresh impulses to painting, developing beyond the naturalism of the late 19th c. and setting up in sharp opposition to Impressionism. His monumental murals, "Retreat of the Swiss after the Battle of Marignano" and "Departure of the Jena

Students, 1813", gave fresh direction to historical painting (National Museum, Zurich; Museum of Art, Berne; Museum of Art and History, Geneva).

The Lausanne-born painter and graphic artist Félix Vallotton (1865–1925) worked mainly in Paris (landscapes; Art Nouveau).

In the middle of the First World War the Dadaist movement was launched in Zurich, where the pacifist Hugo Ball opened the Cabaret Voltaire in 1916 as a meeting-place for Dadaists.

20th c. Painting

Cuno Amiet (1868–1961) was influenced by the Impressionists and Neo-Impressionists, and also by Gauguin. Other notable painters of this period were René Auberjonois (1872–1957), Augusto Giacometti (1877–1947), Heinrich Altherr (1878–1947), Alfred Heinrich Pellegrini (1881–1958) and Hans Erni (b. 1909).

The painter and graphic artist Paul Klee (1879–1940), who had affinities with the Surrealists and was a member of the "Blauer Reiter" group, worked at the Bauhaus in Weimar, Dessau and Düsseldorf. His pictures, usually of small size and endearing themes, often have a droll humour and an enigmatic charm ("The Twittering Machine").

Among sculptors of this period are Carl Burckhardt (1876–1928: "Amazon", 1923), Hermann Haller (1880–1950) and Alexander Zschokke (b. 1894).

20th c. Sculpture

Alberto Giacometti (1901–66) sets his figures, lean and emaciated, in empty space, thus emphasising their loneliness and vulnerability ("L'Homme qui marche"). After 1930 he became associated with the Surrealist movement.

Jean Tinguely (1925–91) has produced major works in the field of kinetic sculpture ("meta-mechanisms" and "machine sculpture" such as the huge "Heureka" in Zürichhorn Park) and self-destroying sculpture ("La Vittoria", a golden phallus over 26ft/8m high). A museum named after him was opened in Basle in 1991.

The massive sculptures of Bernhard Luginbühl (b. 1929) in iron and wood and his strange pieces of machinery also convey the concept of the hypertechnical age *ad absurdum* ("C-figure", 1960).

Among leading Swiss architects of the 20th c. are Karl Moser (1860–1936): St Anthony's Church, Basle, 1927, Adolf Wasserfallen (b. 1920) and Jean-Claude Steinegger (b. 1930). Max Bill (1908–94) was one of the pioneers of modern architecture in Switzerland; he was also a sculptor, producing abstract plastic works.

20th c. Architecture

The architect who left his mark on the century, however, was Le Corbusier (Charles-Edouard Jeanneret, 1887–1965). Trained under Josef Hoffmann and Peter Behrens, he established a new style of housing and a new pattern of urban living in his "unité d'habitation", a form of residential accommodation which went beyond the normal functions of a house, which he criticised as a mere "machine for living in". Almost all his work was done abroad: in Switzerland there are the Immeuble Clarté in Geneva (1930–32) and the Centre Le Corbusier in Zurich (1966).

Modern architecture in Switzerland finds expression mainly in churches and schools, but also in offices and industrial buildings with glass and steel being the main building materials.

In Dornach stands the Goetheanum II, built in 1924–28. Mario Botta (b. 1943), an architect who has gained a reputation extending far beyond the borders of Switzerland, designed the Banco del Gottardo and the Palazzo Ransila in Lugano and the Jean-Tinguely Museum in Basle (opening planned for 1996). Other interesting new museum buildings include the "Slice of Melon" in Baden (historical museum designed in 1992 by Katharina and Wilfrid Steib), the Kirchner Museum in Davos (1992, Annette Gigon and Mike Guyer), and the Hans Josephson Museum in Giornico (1992, Peter Märkli).

In Switzerland there are also some attractive buildings designed by contemporary foreign architects. For example, Frank Gehry, a Californian born in 1929, drew up the plans for the Vitra Head Office in Birsfelden, a suburb of Basle (1994), and for the Vitra Design Museum (1989) in the little town of Weil am Rhein on the German border. The fire station in the grounds is the work of the London-based Iraqi architect Zaha Hadid. In the west of Biel and in Fribourg the Parisian architect Jean Nouvel (b. 1945) designed buildings for the Cartier Group. In 1994 a referendum found in favour of a proposed culture and congress centre to be built by Nouvel in Lucerne by the year 2000. The Spaniard Santiago Calatrava designed the entrance hall to Lucerne railway station (1991) and the new station in Zurich-Stadelhofen (also 1991). There are plans to build a new museum in Riehen (near Basle) by Renzo Piano (b. 1937); it is intended to house the collection of modern art formed by the Beyelers, who own a gallery in Basle.

Modern Trends in Art

Of the artists active in Switzerland since the Second World War, representing a variety of trends which run parallel to and influence one another, only a brief selection can be mentioned. Wilfried Moser (b. 1914) produces collages, assemblages and sculpture intended for walking and climbing on. André Thomkins (1930–85: "holograms"), a strikingly original draughtsman, shows affinities with surrealism. Roland Werro (b. 1926) creates coloured objects, monochrome bas-reliefs and mobile sculpture. Christian Megert (b. 1936) loves mirror constructions and light-kinetic objects, as does Christian Herdeg (b. 1952: "light sculpture"). Karl Gerstner (b. 1930) creates "colour sound", pictures with gradations of colour in exactly calculated degrees. Fritz Glarner works in the field of "relational painting". Franz Gertsch (b. 1930, originally belonging to the "peinture naïve" school, is the only Swiss Hyper-Realist. Peter Travaglini (b. 1927) is a Pop artist ("Zip-Fastener", 1970), as is Urs Lüthi (b. 1947). Gérald Minkoff (b.

Hipped-roof farmhouse near Berne

1937) produces video tapes, and Alex Sadowsky experiments with Surrealist and metaphysical films.

Modern Swiss graphic art also has considerable achievements to its credit, and Switzerland occupies one of the leading places in the field of commercial art and advertising. Notable among contemporary graphic artists is Celestino Piatti (b. 1922), best known for his expressive book-covers.

Modern Graphic Art

The Buildings of Switzerland

Swiss domestic buildings show a carefully cherished individuality of style, with differences and contrasts not only between town and country but also between different parts of the country. Common to all Swiss, however, is the idea that in building a family home they are building for more than one generation, so that the house must be a substantial and durable structure.

Swiss towns and villages are notable for their trim and well-kept appearance, and flowers are much in evidence in squares, on fountains and on houses. Town halls and other public buildings, and private houses as well, match the country's high standard of living, and are almost invariably well maintained and cared for.

Many buildings have paintings, either old or modern, on their façades – a practice which was originally a great speciality of the Engadine. In eastern Switzerland projecting oriel windows have long been a popular feature. Many Swiss towns and villages offer attractive pictures of streets and lanes and sometimes whole quarters built in uniform style. The picturesque little town of Stein am Rhein with its old painted façades is particularly notable in this respect.

Barn with "mice stones" on roof, Valais

Typical façade in Obertoggenburg

Trim wooden houses in Urnäsch/Appenzell-Ausserrhoden

The strong sense of local awareness found in the small Swiss communities means that there is wide support for the conservation of their architectural heritage. Perhaps the most distinctive contribution made by Switzerland to European architecture is its varied range of farmhouses and other rural houses, differing widely from region to region. Local styles are determined by climatic conditions and local needs, but also by a firm attachment to comfort and cosiness. Local differences are reflected principally in the disposition of the masses, the distribution of the living and working quarters and the roof structure.

The Open-Air Museum of Rural Life at Ballenberg, near Brienz, is designed to show the variety of house types by selected examples.

Rural House Types

Travellers in the 17th c. were already remarking on the handsome houses of the Swiss peasants and the degree of comfort – extraordinarily high by the standards of the day – which they enjoyed. The independent Swiss of today still show a great pride in them.

Every part of Switzerland, indeed almost every valley, has its own distinctive type of house. It is only possible, therefore, to mention the most important types out of this wide range.

Appenzell

In the Appenzell region, with its relatively high rainfall, the house and farm buildings are brought together under a single roof. The fronts of the houses, built of timber, are frequently broken by continuous rows of windows.

North-eastern Switzerland

In north-eastern Switzerland, a region of deciduous forests, the houses are predominantly half-timbered, with whitewashed panels in the interstices of the framing.

Jura

In the Jura the houses are massive stone-built structures, broad-based, with saddle roofs which frequently come far down over the walls.

Around Berne and in the Emmental the houses are predominantly of timber, with deep hipped roofs and the barn usually adjoins the living quarters.

Berne, Emmental

In the Bernese Oberland, as in other mountain regions with large coniferous forests, the "log-cabin" method of building is preferred, the walls being constructed of horizontally laid tree-trunks. The house is separate from the farm-buildings and can thus achieve considerable architectural dignity.

Bernese Oberland

Characteristic of Valais are its timber-built houses of several storeys with flat gables and stone-built kitchen premises, and its store-houses built on piles, with flat stones at the top of the piles to keep rodents out.
    In the area of Lake Geneva the rear of the house, with deep eaves, faces on to the street.

Valais and Lake Geneva

The houses of the Engadine differ sharply from those of other parts of Switzerland, showing both Germanic and Latin influence. The timber core of the house is surrounded by masonry walls, with sgraffito decoration on the façade (see "Switzerland from A to Z": Engadine).

Engadine

In Ticino the houses are very similar to those found over the frontier in Italy. The walls are of undressed stone, the roof (which projects only slightly over the walls) of stone slabs.

Ticino

Literature

The earliest literary activity in Switzerland dates back to the Carolingian period, when the abbey of St Gallen (founded in 613) was a centre of intellectual life. Notable figures who worked at St Gallen were Notker Balbulus (c. 840–912), whose "Gesta Karoli Magni" is one of the

Earliest Literary Works

William Tell statue

J. J. Rousseau: "Back to Nature"

finest narrative works of the Middle Ages, and the historian Ekkehart (c. 980–1060).

The period of chivalry is reflected in the works of the epic poet Hartmann von Aue (c. 1200) and the minnesingers Johannes Hadlaub of Zurich (first half of the 14th c.) and Otau de Grandson.

In the age of humanism Aegidius (Gilg) Tschudi (1505–72) of Glarus wrote his "Helvetian Chronicle", which became a standard work. Economic themes and contemporary criticism were the hallmarks of the works of the doctor Paracelsus (1493–1541). Some leading figures of the Reformation, including Ulrich Zwingli (1484–1531) were also writers of some note.

18th century

Swiss literature reached its full development, however, only in the 18th c. The Bernese poet, doctor and scientist Albrecht von Haller (1708–77) wrote a poem, "Die Alpen", contrasting the beauty of the mountains and the natural life of the mountain people with the unhealthy life of the towns. The Geneva-born Jean Jacques Rousseau (1712–78), who spent most of his life in France, was one of the great revolutionary influences of his day, preaching a "return to nature" and preparing the way for the French Revolution with his doctrine of liberty and equality of men. His ideas on politics, education and literature were equally fertile in stimulation, and influenced both the German "Sturm und Drang" period of the 1770s and the French Romantic movement of 50 years later.

Johann Jakob Bodmer (1698–1783) and Johann Jakob Breitinger (1701–76), both of Zurich, ran a moral and aesthetic weekly "Discourse der Mahlern" ("Discourses of the Painters") which influenced the development of German literature. Other Zurich writers whose reputation extended beyond the bounds of Switzerland were the lyric-poet, etcher and landscape painter Salomon Gessner (1730–88), Johann Caspar Lavater (1741–1801) and Heinrich Pestalozzi (1746–1827). Johannes von Müller (1752–1809) of Schaffhausen wrote a "History of the Swiss Confederation", which gave Schiller the inspiration for his play "Wilhelm Tell". Ulrich Bräker (1735–98) also achieved some reputation abroad with his autobiography "Life History and Natural Adventures of the Poor Man in Toggenburg".

Western Switzerland produced three of its notable writers during this period in Germaine de Staël-Holstein (1766–1817), born in Paris but descended from an old Geneva family, who became one of the forerunners of the French Romantic movement under the name of Mme de Staël; Benjamin Constant de Rebecque (1767–1830) of Lausanne; and Léonard de Sismondi (1773–1842) of Geneva. From Italian Switzerland there was Francesco Soave (1743–1806).

19th century

In the 19th c., under the influence of the Romantic movement, national and regional themes came increasingly to the fore.

Jeremias Gotthelf (Albert Bitzius, 1797–1854), a native of Murten who became pastor of Lützelflüh, takes a high place in Swiss literature with his simple but profoundly human stories of peasant life in Emmental.

The writings of Gottfried Keller (1819–90) and Conrad Ferdinand Meyer (1825–98), both of Zurich, are an enduring contribution to literature in the German language.

Johanna Spyri (1827–1901), best known for her children's stories ("Heidi"), also wrote short stories and novels on regional themes.

The literature of Rhaeto-Romanic Switzerland began with Conradin de Flugi about 1845. The most notable Romansch writer is Giachen Casper Muoth (1844–1906), known principally as an epic poet but also of importance as a lyric poet and philogist.

20th century

The first generation of 20th c. writers must include the names of Robert Walser (1878–1956), a master of the inward approach, and Albin

Zollinger (1895–1941). The latter found a great admirer in Max Frisch (b. 1911 in Zurich), whose novels and tales are grouped around the Swiss theme. He has made important contributions to literature worldwide, as has the author Friedrich Dürrenmatt of Berne (b. 1921), whose works for the stage have gained him a reputation extending far beyond the frontiers of Switzerland. Plays such as "Andorra" and "Biedermann und die Brandstifter" ("The Fire-Raisers") by Max Frisch and Dürrenmatt's "Der Besuch der alten Dame" ("The Visit") and "Die Physiker" ("The Physicists") and novels such as Frisch's "Stiller" and "Mein Name sei Gantenbein" occupy a high place in contemporary German Literature.

Carl Jakob Burckhardt of Basle (1891–1974) made a considerable contribution to international understanding by his work as an art historian and essayist.

Carl Spitteler (1845–1924) from Liestal, as an innovator of epic poems and author of psychological novels, was awarded the Nobel Prize for Literature in 1919.

The outstanding writers in French and Italian were respectively Charles Ferdinand Ramuz (1878–1947), whose prose on the Vaud region was the first in the local dialect to gain true recognition and who collaborated with the composer Igor Stravinsky in writing the "Histoire du Soldat", and Francesco Chiesa (1871–1973), of Sagno (near Chiasso), who established his place in Italian literature in spite of the fact that his work was deeply rooted in his native Ticino.

The writer and art-historian Piero Bianconi (b. 1899) produces impressive descriptions of the wild mountains of Ticino.

A number of younger writers, including Otto F. Walter (b. 1928), Adolf Muschg (b. 1934), Hugo Loetscher (b. 1929), Peter Bichsel (b. 1935), Beat Brechbühl (b. 1939), Urs Widmer (b. 1938), Gerold Spät (b. 1939) and E. Y. Meyer (actually Peter Meyer, b. 1946) concern themselves with the problems of contemporary life, usually from a critical point of view. Hansjörg Schneider (b. 1938) and Manfred Schwarz (b. 1932) have made their mark as dramatists while Jürg Federspiel (b. 1931) writes tales and novels.

The literature of French Switzerland concerns itself less with social and political problems, and concentrates more on inner conflicts. The masters of this "inwardness" include Gustave Roud from the Vaud region (1897–1977), whose influence can be seen in the work of Philippe Jaccottet (b. 1925).

Jacques Chessex (b. 1934), from French-speaking Switzerland, won the French Prix Goncourt in 1973 for his novel "L'Ogre", and Georges Boorgeaud (b. 1914) was awarded the Prix Renaudot in 1974. While the work of Maurice Chappaz (b. 1916) shows a new and unique vitality, Georges Haldas (b. 1918) is one of the most relentless analytical thinkers of his time. Important essayists include Gonzague de Reynold (1880–1970) from Fribourg and the non-conformist Denis de Rougemont (1906–85).

Of the literary critics, special mention must be made of Jean Starobinski (b. 1920) and Marcel Raymond (1897–1981).

Among the main female literary figures hailing from French-speaking Switzerland are Monique Saint-Hélier (actually Betty Briod, née Ymann, 1895–1955), Cathérine Colomb (actually Marie-Louise Reymond, 1893–1965), S. Corinna Bille (1912–79), Alice Rivaz (b. 1901), Yvette Z'Graggen (b. 1920) and Anne Cunéo (b. 1936).

In Grisons literature in the Romansch language, which has tended not to spread far because of the small area involved, has made a considerable breakthrough in the 20th c. The most important writers from this part of Switzerland include the traditionalist Peider Lansel (1863–1943) from the Engadine, Alexander Lozza (1880–1953), whose lyrics are closely linked to folklore and nature, the master story-teller Gion Fontana (1897–1935) and Cia Biert (b. 1920) from the Münster valley, with his humorous tales. Andri Peer (b. 1921) is the originator of the contemporary Engadine lyric. Of the more modern writers mention must also be made of Gian Belsch (b. 1913), Tista Murk (b. 1915) and Gion Depiazes (b. 1918).

In recent years literature in dialect has developed with fresh vigour in every part of Switzerland.

Foreign authors

Switzerland has given asylum to many foreign writers subject to persecution in their own countries on political or racial grounds. The most prominent of the German authors who found a home in Switzerland during the Nazi period were Thomas Mann and Carl Zuckmayer. More recently writers and scientists from the Eastern bloc have found a refuge in Switzerland, notably Alexander Solzhenitsyn from the Soviet Union and Ota Šik from Czechoslovakia.

Theatre

Switzerland's theatrical life can trace its origins back to the 10th c. religious plays performed in the German language. Towards the end of the 19th c. the popular theatre received a special boost. Some of the patriotic festival productions introduced at that time, such as the popular William Tell plays in Altdorf and Interlaken, are still regularly enacted today.

The "Great World Theatre" by Calderón de la Barca, held every 10 years in Einsiedeln (next one in 2005) has become famous far beyond Switzerland itself.

Every 25 years since the end of the 18th c. the "Fête des Vignerons" takes place in French Switzerland (last one was in 1977), to give thanks to the farmers and wine-producers.

The performances by the "Théâtre du Jorat", which was founded in 1908 in Mézières near Lausanne, also form a part of the true popular theatre.

Playhouses

Internationally famous are Switzerland's great playhouses in Basle, Berne, Geneva and Zurich. A considerable contribution to the establishment of these came from the large number of German authors, playwrights and directors who were obliged to emigrate to Switzerland before and during the Second World War, such as Bertolt Brecht.

The contemporary theatre, which for a long time was dominated by the works of Max Frisch and Friedrich Dürrenmatt, has received fresh creative impulses from "Living Theatre" and "Open Theatre".

Small theatres

Although the bulk of state subsidies goes to the larger theatres the number of small playhouses and experimental theatres is continually growing. The most successful of these are in the German-speaking regions, especially the theatre on the Hechtplatz in Zurich, the Zähringer workshop-theatre and the Gaskessel Youth and Culture Centre in Bern, the "Kulturtäter" and Théâtre de Poche in Biel, the Fauteuil ("Armchair") and Zum Teufel ("To the Devil") theatres in Basle, the basement theatre by the Müller Gate in St Gallen, the Little Theatre on the Bundesplatz in Lucerne, the Upper Valais Basement Theatre in Brig and La Claque and Spatz & Co. in Baden.

In French-speaking Switzerland the Compagnie des Faux-Nez in Lausanne, founded in 1948, and the Centre Dramatique Romand have made a name for themselves. Swiss and foreign plays are included in the programme of the Théâtre de Carouge, Théâtre de l'Atelier and Nouveau Théâtre in Geneva, while the Théâtre Populaire Romand is above all else a popular theatre which involves the audience, and therefore often performs at schools.

Cabaret and Mime Artists

Swiss cabaret artists of note are Elsi Attenhofer, Voli Geiler, Walter Morath, Franz Hohler and "Emil" Steinberger; Bernard Haller from western Switzerland is working successfully in Paris.

Mention should also be made of the world-famous artiste and clown Grock (real name Adrian Wettach, 1880–1959), the pantomimes of the "Mummenschanz" group, the solo artistes Kaspar Fischer and Dimitri, the "clown of Ascona", who also founded the theatre and school of acting in Verscio in the canton of Ticino.

Music

An independent school of Swiss music first came to the fore in the 19th c. The names of the composers of this period, however, have largely fallen into oblivion.

In the early 20th c. the belated Romantic Othmar Schoeck (1886–1957) was a composer of some quality, and Willy Burkhard (1900–55) – not to be confused with Paul Burkhard (1911–77), the composer of musicals – made a name for himself.

Contemporary Music

The leading Swiss composer is Arthur Honegger (1892–1955), who was born in France, lived for many years as one of the principal members of the Groupe des Six and died there. Among his chief works are five symphonies (including the "Symphonie Liturgique" and "Deliciae Basilenses"), a number of symphonic poems ("Pacific 231", "Rugby"), the scenic oratorios "Judith", "Jeanne d'Arc au Bûcher" and "Le Roi David", and an impressive Christmas cantata, with a final section in which Christmas carols in various European languages are skilfully mingled.

Frank Martin (1890–1974), a native of Geneva, was also an exponent of 12-tone music (dodecaphony), and taught for some years at the Cologne Academy of Music. In addition to symphonic music (Concerto for seven wind instruments, strings and drums) he also composed much choral and chamber music.

Another contemporary composer of more than regional significance is Heinrich Sutermeister (b. 1910), whose opera "Titus Feuerfuchs" received its first performance during the Brussels Exhibition of 1958. Volkmar Andreae (1879–1962), who was conductor of the orchestra of the Tonhalle-Gesellschaft from 1906–49, wrote operas and choral works as well as orchestral and chamber music. Rolf Liebermann (b. 1910), from Zurich, was for many years manager of the Hamburg State Opera and until 1980 Director-General of the Paris Opéra. As a composer he works mainly in the 12-tone technique. The Bernese opera, ballet and instrumental composer Gottfried von Einem (b. 1918) has put to music works by Büchner, Kafka and Dürrenmatt, among others. The world-famous oboist Heinz Holliger (b. 1939) has also made a name for himself as an avant-garde composer.

Although Switzerland is a relatively small country, it has a remarkable number of good opera companies, orchestras, conductors and soloists. The Zurich Opera is one of the largest and finest opera-houses in German-speaking territory, and the Grand Théâtre in Geneva and the Municipal Theatre in Basle also enjoy a considerable reputation.

Opera Houses

The best-known orchestras in Switzerland are the Orchestre de la Suisse Romande, the Tonhalle-Orchester of Zurich, the Basle Symphony Orchestra, as well as the chamber orchestras of Basle, Zurich and Lausanne, the Camerata of Berne and the Festival Strings of Lucerne.

Orchestras, Conductors and Instrumentalists

Swiss conductors of international reputation include Ernest Ansermet, Paul Sacher, Edmond de Stoutz, August Wenzinger, Silvio Varviso, René Klopfenstein, Charles Dutoit, Armin Jordan, Michel Corboz and Robert Denzler (1892–1972); among instrumentalists there are Heinz Holliger (oboe), Ursula Holliger (harp), Peter-Lukas Graf and Aurèle Nicolet (flute) and Karl Engel and Adrian Aeschbacher (piano).

In addition, many musicians from countries all over the world have made Switzerland their home, among them Paul Kletzki (1900–73), Andor Foldes and Nikita Magaloff. During the 19th and 20th c., too, many composers took advantage of Swiss tolerance and generosity in cultural matters and came to live in Switzerland in order to escape the censorship or persecution to which they were exposed in their own country (Wagner, Stravinsky, Hindemith, etc.).

Light Music and Jazz

In the fields of light music and jazz a considerable number of individual performers and groups have achieved reputations outside Switzerland, such as Teddy Staufer, Cedric Dumont, Hazy Osterwald, George Gruntz, Pierre Favre Franco and Flavio Ambrosetti, the Tremble Kids Jazz Group, Vico Torriani and Pepe Lienhard. Internationally popular, too, are the annual jazz festivals in Montreux and Willisau, as well as the folk and rock festival in Nyon.

Folk Music

The folk music of the Alpine regions – yodelling, Kuhreigen (round dances), dance tunes such as the ländler, etc. – is popular and performed with committed enthusiasm throughout the whole of Switzerland.

Films

The critical differences in Swiss films lie in their basic themes. While the German-speaking contributions are mainly documentaries, the emphasis in French-speaking Switzerland has always been on feature films. It was in the latter sphere that many of the great film-makers, such as Claude Goretta, Michel Soutter, Jean-Jacques Lagrange, Jean-Luc Godard (who worked almost solely in France) and Alain Tanner, who was honoured in Cannes for his film "Années lumière", experienced their first successes. International recognition was also found by such films as Yves Yersin's "Les Petites Fugues", "It Happened in Broad Daylight", the filming of Dürrenmatt's "The Promise" with Gert Fröbe and Heinz Rühmann, "The Boat is Full" by Markus Imhof, which impressively describes the refugee problem during the Second World War, "A Swiss named Nötzli" and "The Swissmaker", a best-seller by Rolf Lyssy, which analyses the typical Swiss man in a humorous manner. Other well-known Swiss film-makers of the modern generation are Daniel Schmid, Jacqueline Veuve, Francis Reusser, Richard Dingo and Kurt Gloor.

Folklore

General

Present-day Switzerland is still rich in traditional celebrations which have been lovingly nurtured over the centuries. Relics of pagan times are very apparent in numerous customs relating to late winter and Shrove Tuesday. The people really "go to town" with religious feasts and processions. The Swiss national pride is clearly demonstrated in the old, traditional communal elections, the Rütli shoots and other popular events. In addition there are many specifically Swiss sports which have developed from competitive games held among the farming communities.

New Year and Shrove Tuesday Customs

On New Year's Eve, especially in the German-speaking region, figures disguised in fancy costumes parade through the streets, symbolising the end of the Old Year and the time of darkness.

Well into Lent, indeed right up to the beginning of spring, the numerous Shrove Tuesday customs continue the symbolic battle between winter and spring. Atavistic fertility rites and pagan natural beliefs are

Engadine . . .   *. . . Appenzell costumes*

reflected in the numerous masks worn by wild characters named according to the region they hail from, such as "Butzi", "Wildma", "Bärzeli" or "Roitschäggädä".

Well-known is the "Baseler Fasnacht", which begins at four in the morning on the Monday after Ash Wednesday with the "Morgen-straich" (morning stroll) and lasts until the following Thursday. Before daybreak the various Shrovetide carnival guilds, known as "cliques", parade through the old town, accompanied by loud music played on pipes and drums. This is followed on the Monday afternoon by the official parade, in which the masked members of the individual cliques wear their own unique costumes. They are accompanied by floats on which various satirical scenes are performed. The noisy celebrations continue on the Tuesday, when the "Guggenmusiken" parade with drums and wind-instruments. The time-difference between this and the German "Karneval" is explained by the fact that the Swiss shrove-tide follows the Julian Calendar.

Another old spring custom is the "Eieraufleset" (picking up the eggs), in which the egg is a fertility symbol representing the victory of spring over winter.

Swiss traditions are rich in processions. In Ticino, the region strongly influenced by Roman culture, Holy Week processions are held in many towns, sometimes (such as in Mendrisio) depicting representation of scenes from the Passion.

Processions

At the beginning of April in the canton of Glarus the "Näfelser Fahrt", in which the Capucin monks take part, is held to remind the people of Glarus of their victory over the Austrians on April 9th 1388. The "Stoos Pilgrimage" in Appenzell has similar origins. In many places in the canton of Lucerne around Ascension Day the so-called "Ascension Ride" is celebrated, a procession which harks back to pre-Christian traditions for the blessing of the fields. The most beautiful and impres-sive processions take place at the time of the Feast of Corpus Christi in

Schwingen: Swiss wrestling

those regions with a mainly Roman Catholic population and on such occasions beautiful traditional costumes are worn.

Historical Festivals

There are a vast number of historical festivals reflecting the Swiss love of freedom and willingness to bear arms when necessary. Magnificent parades in historical costume commemorate the battles of Morgarten (1315), Sempach (1386), Näfels (1388; see above), Murten (1476) and Dornach (1499). Many are the festivities held by rifle clubs and military celebrations such as the "Rütli shooting contest" in Uri, the "Zurich Boys' Shoot", the "Thun Shoot", the "Women's Shoot" in the canton of Lucerne and others. Perhaps the best-known historical celebration is the "Geneva Escalade", which commemorates the successful repulsion of an attack by the Savoyards in 1602.

Communal Assemblies

A living testimonial to the way the Swiss view democracy is found in the communal assemblies (landsgemeinde), at which the representatives of the citizens are elected by public vote.

National Day

The Swiss National Day, celebrated throughout the country with torchlight processions, fireworks and shooting contests, is August 1st. This "Bundesfeier" revives memories of the year 1291, when the representatives of the three "original cantons" of Schwyz, Uri and Unterwalden swore the "Rütli Oath", promising mutual assistance in their struggle for their traditional rights, thus laying the foundations of the Confederation. In 1991 there was a big programme of festivities to mark the 700th Jubilee.

Sports

There are three sports which are specifically Swiss, known respectively as "Schwingen", "Hornussen" and "Steinstossen". Schwingen is a kind of wrestling, in which each combatant grasps the other's short trousers made of strong twill and tries to throw him to the ground. In Hornussen the batting side tries to hit a kind of puck about the size of a man's hand, as far as possible with the "Hornuss", a flexible club nearly 2m/6½ft long with a hardwood head. The "Abtuer" (fielders),

Cattle coming down from Alpine pasture

armed with big wooden shingles, try to catch the Hornuss before it hits the ground. In Steinstossen the object is to hurl a stone weighing 83½kg/184lb as far as possible. The record is about 3½m/11½ft.

Yodelling plays a major role in folk music. Most Swiss yodelling is improvised without an established format, unlike that practised in Upper Bavaria or Austria. Yodelling was a traditional method of communicating from one Alpine pasture to another, and this was also the original function of the alphorn made from the hollowed-out trunk of a mountain pine, usually about 3½m/11½ft. long. The characteristically soft sound carries a surprisingly long way. The accordion ("Schwyzörgeli" or "Handörgeli", with a chromatic keyboard) is widely played. Flag-wavers ("Fahnenschwinger") often accompany the bands playing folk-music.

Farming traditions are also reflected in many customs, especially in the Alpine festivals. In early summer the "Alpaufzug" (Alpine Parade) celebrates the move of cattle up to the mountain pastures. A similar custom, especially in the canton of Valais, is the "Kuhkampf" (cow fight), in which cows fight for positions within the herd. The victor is the leader for the coming year. When summer ends the cheese produced on the mountain pasture is distributed to the individual farmers, who draw lots to decide how it is to be allocated.

In autumn many vintage and grape festivals are held in the wine-producing regions. This is also the season of markets, the best known of which are the onion markets in Berne and Biel.

The Swiss people's favourite card game is "Jass", played with 36 cards in four colours.

Local crafts also flourish in the form of rural paintings, embroidery, wood-carving and hand-weaving.

Folk Music

Alpine Festivals

Winter Festivities, Markets.

Jass

Local Crafts

71

Recommended Routes

The following suggested routes are intended to inspire the motorist to discover Switzerland while still allowing scope for individual planning.

The routes have been selected to include the main towns and places of interest. Not all the places described in this guide can be reached without making a detour, and this section should, where applicable, be read in conjunction with the suggested excursions and round trips described under the major headings in the "Switzerland A to Z" section.

The suggested routes can be easily followed on the map which accompanies this guide, thereby facilitating detailed planning.

Places and regions listed in the "A to Z" section are printed in **bold type**.

Towns, places, regions, rivers, etc. and sights mentioned can be found in the index at the end of this guide, so they can be easily located.

The distances in brackets following the titles of the routes are approximate and relate to direct routes. Distances for the longer recommended alternatives or detours are also given.

Western Switzerland

1: From Basle to Lake Geneva (about 250km/155 miles)

Route

The route leads from **Basle**, lying close to the French and German frontiers, southwards through the charming Birs valley via **Delémont** and Moutier to the bilingual town of **Biel/Bienne** by the lake of the same name. The journey continues parallel to the vineyards on the lower slopes of the **Jura Mountains** on the banks of the lake, to **Neuchâtel**, where the tombs of the Counts of Neuchâtel can be seen in the collegiate church.

Detour

Visitors are highly recommended to make a detour from here to the little medieval town of **Murten** (33km/20½ miles), with its splendidly preserved encircling wall, narrow old streets and romantic arbours. About 8km/5 miles south lies Avenches, once the Roman capital of Helvetia.

The route continues along the west bank of the Lac de Neuchâtel and through tiny villages to Grandson, with its interesting Romanesque Church of St Jean-Baptists. **Yverdon-les-Bains**, capital of northern Vaud, is situated at the south-west end of the Lac de Neuchâtel. The lively town of **Lausanne** lies on **Lake Geneva**, on terraces rising above the lake; its cathedral is one of Switzerland's major Gothic edifices.

Continue along the west bank by way of **Nyon** to the elegant and cosmopolitan city of **Geneva** (in French Genève; in German Genf), the headquarters of the United Nations. The Corniche de Lavaux runs from Lausanne along the east bank of the lake via **Vevey** and the chic town of **Montreux** to the Château de Chillon, rendered famous by Lord Byron and Victor Hugo.

On the way to the St Gotthard ▶

Recommended Routes

Alternative route Alternatively, the visitor can elect to drive from **Delémont** to **Lake Geneva** through the beautiful **Jura Mountains**, the traditional centre of the Swiss watch and clock industry which is superbly documented in the International Watches and Clocks Museum in **La Chaux-de-Fonds** (for details of this stretch see A to Z, Jura Mountains).

North Switzerland

2: From Basle to Zurich (85km/53 miles)

Route This route begins in the "regio" of **Basle** on the Swiss–German border. Attractive excursions in the region include Arlesheim (7km/4½ miles), with its Baroque cathedral and Silbermann organ, the original Cat Museum in Riehen (6km/4 miles), the Monterverdi Car Collection in Binningen (2km/1¼ miles), and the Goetheanum designed by Rudolf Steiner in Dornach (9km/6 miles).

Proceeding parallel to the Hochrhein (High Rhine) beyond Basle the route first comes to Augusta Raurica, the oldest Roman colony on **The Rhine**. The drive continues through picturesque little lakeside towns to Stein, and thence in a southerly direction to the Argau spa town of **Baden** and on the N1 to **Zurich**, the country's major business and cultural centre. A wide variety of excursions can be made around the magnificent **Lake Zurich**.

3: From Solothurn to Winterthur (130km/80 miles)

Route This route commences in the splendid Baroque town of **Solothurn** and continues northwards to **Olten** on the Aare, from where a detour should be planned to **Zofingen** (15km/9 miles), founded by the Counts of Froburg, with its well-preserved historical town centre. Having returned to Olten, travel along the Aare until the old town of **Aarau** on a rocky plateau above the river comes into view. The next stop is the charming town of **Baden**. From here follow the Limmat as far as **Zurich**, the largest city in Switzerland on **Lake Zurich**, which can be crossed near **Rapperswil**. Those interested in aviation will wish to visit the Dübendorf Aviation Museum, before continuing in a north-easterly direction to **Winterthur**, the second largest town in the canton, lying in a broad valley in the foothills of the Alps.

Central Switzerland

4: From Lucerne to Airolo via St Gotthard (120km/75 miles)

Route In the very heart of Switzerland lies the fjord-like landscape of the **Vierwaldstätter See**. This was the scene of the traditional "Cradle of the Confederation" on the Rütli meadows at Seelisberg and it was here that the William Tell legend was created. At the north-western end of the lake with its many bays lies the cantonal capital **Lucerne**, the focus of the tourist industry. Its town emblem, the "Kapellbrücke" (Chapel Bridge), is one of the country's oldest wooden bridges.

Detour If time allows, a detour should be made to the Sempacher See (15km/9½ miles), not far from the battlefield where, in 1386, the Swiss Confederates won their legendary victory over the Austrians. Particularly attractive, too, is a trip on the Pilatus cog-wheel railway, 10km/6 miles to the south, with information boards along the way providing geological information on the history of the region.

Back in Lucerne, the route continues along the south bank (for details of this stretch see A to Z, Vierwaldstätter See) to the holiday resort of Beckenried, where the Seelisberg Tunnel provides a quick link to the Urner See and **Altdorf**, the scene of the famous shooting of the apple by William Tell from his son's head. Continuing upstream along the Reuss river the visitor will soon pass Wassen. From here the Susten road branches off; this is part of the beautiful 100km/62 mile-long Circuit of Three Passes, starting from **Andermatt** (for details of this stretch see A to Z, Andermatt). This includes the Furka road, with a view of the impressive Rhône glacier, and Grimsel pass, a winding road used since Roman times and a pleasing challenge to keen motorists. Nature in the raw is displayed by the Schöllenenschlucht, a granite gorge running eastwards from Andermatt to the Oberalp pass and to **Disentis/Mustèr** (30km/19 miles), which boasts the oldest Benedictine abbey in Switzerland.

From Andermatt there is now a choice between driving through the St Gotthard Tunnel (toll), the longest road tunnel in Europe, or taking a winding stretch of the **St Gotthard** Pass to the River Ticino in the Valle Leventina near Airolo, and the town of **Ticino** with its Mediterranean-type vegetation (for details of this stretch see A to Z, St Gotthard).

5: From Lucerne around the Vierwaldstätter See to Einsiedeln
(80km/50 miles)

From **Lucerne**, the route follows the northern shore of the **Vierwald-**   Route
stätter See via **Küssnacht am Rigi** where, according to legend, William Tell slayed the Habsburg governor Gessler in the Hohle Gasse. After enjoying a magnificent view over the lake, continue by way of Weggis and Vitznau along the **Rigi**; here there are some of the most famous views in Switzerland (accessible along three mountain roads – for details see A to Z, Vierwäldstatter See). Near **Brunnen** lies the beginning of the Urner See, along which runs the main road with a magnificent panoramic view southwards in the direction of St Gotthard. The route continues north-eastwards to **Schwyz** which lies under the towering twin horns of the Mythen.

From the town from which the whole of Switzerland gets its name   Detour
visitors are recommended to make a detour south-eastwards to Höl-loch (about 16km/10 miles), a giant cave system in the Starzlenbach valley (guided tour lasts about 2 hours).
    After returning to Schwyz proceed north to Biberbrugg and then turn south-east to **Einsiedeln**. The twin-towered Benedictine Abbey of Maria Einsiedeln is the finest example of Vorarlberg Baroque architecture in Switzerland.

An alternative route leaves the **Vierwaldstätter See** near **Küssnacht**   **Alternative**
am Rigi and continues by way of Arth along the Zuger See to **Zug**, with   **route**
its old town dotted with splendid residences.

In Baar, 10km/6 miles to the north, it is worth making a detour to the   Detour
impressive Höllgrotten (7km/4½ miles), caves with massive dripstone formations. In Wädenswil, which boasts an original Mustard Museum, the route reaches **Lake Zurich** and leaves it again at the south-east near Wollerau and continues via Biberbrugg to the Baroque pilgrimage destination of **Einsiedeln**.

Bernese Oberland

6: From Berne to Aigle in the Rhône Valley (120km/75 miles)

Route

The route starts in the tranquil city of **Berne**, the capital of Switzerland, with its romantic lanes, arcades and arbours, a magnificent Late Gothic minster, superb fountains designed by the great Hans Gieng, and the Swiss Parliament Buildings.

Detour

There is a wonderful detour via Burgdorf into the 50km/30 mile-long **Emmental** (Emme valley). The valley is famous not only for its cheese but also for its "homely" villages and farmhouses decorated with wooden carvings and colourful epigrams.

After returning to Berne, follow the N12 south-westwards to **Fribourg**, one of Switzerland's most beautiful medieval towns situated on a peninsula of the Saane. Bulle is in the heart of the **Gruyère** district, where the tasty cheese of that name is produced (model cheese-dairy). The pretty old town of Gruyères, once the capital of an Alpine county, lies high up on a green ridge of hills above the Saane. In Château d'Oex turn off south on to the N11.

Detour

Skiing enthusiasts will need no introduction to the Col du Pillon, but those with no interest in the sport will still enjoy the journey to it eastwards from Le Sepey by way of Les Diablerets (15km/9½ miles). Ascent is by way of a 5km/3 mile-long cable railway up the fascinating glacial slopes of Les Diablerets (for details see A to Z, St Maurice).

After this detour, again follow the N11 eastwards from Le Sepey to **Aigle** in the **Rhône Valley**, from where the journey continues either into the canton of **Valais** (see A to Z, Valais Alps) or to **Lake Geneva**.

Alternative route

There is an alternative route from **Berne** via the N16 to **Thun**, charmingly situated on **Lake Thun**. Turn off here onto the N11 into the **Simmental**. Characteristic of this Bernese farming area are the handsome timber houses and the herds of Simmentaler cattle (for details of this stretch see A to Z, Simmental).

Detour

At Saanen it is worth making a detour to the chic winter sports resort of **Gstaad** (3km/2 miles south), the venue for international tennis championships and the Menuhin Festival.

Beyond Saanen is the village of Rougemont, with its important Early Romanesque church. Finally, a delightful stretch of the N11 passes through Château d'Oex and thence to the **Rhône Valley** at Aigle.

7: From Berne to Andermatt via Interlaken (125km/78 miles)

Route

Leave the beautiful Swiss capital of **Berne** on the N6 and proceed along the River Aare to **Thun**. Around **Lake Thun** there are numerous places of interest to the visitor. In order to reach the traffic junction of **Interlaken** the driver has a choice between the northern bank with Schloss Oberhofen (feudal castle) and the Beatushöhlen (St Beatus' Caves), or the expressway along the southern bank via Spiez, with the massive Schloss Spiez, a medieval castle by the lake.

Detour

Excursions to the glaciers and peaks of the **Jungfrau** region will provide an unforgettable experience. Either drive into the **Lauterbrunnen Valley** (12km/7½ miles), on the west flank of which lies the winter sports resort of **Mürren** (access by cable railway), or alternatively turn off at Zweilütschinen to the charming village of **Grindelwald** (20km/12½ miles), the setting-out point for tours to the Eiger, Mönch and Jungfrau. The trip with Europe's highest cogwheel railway lasts about 50 minutes and goes under the north wall of the Eiger and by way of the Eismeer to the Jungfrauhoch (for details of this stretch see A to Z, Jungfrau).

To the east of Interlaken stretches **Lake Brienz** (see A to Z. Lake Thun and Lake Brienz), into which the Giessbach Falls plunge from a height of over 300m/1000ft. Visitors are strongly recommended to include a visit to the magnificent Ballenberg Open Air Museum at the eastern end of the lake, which displays traditional buildings and domestic cultures from all regions of Switzerland. Then follow the Aare to **Meiringen**, the site of a Sherlock Holmes Museum, not far from the Reichenbach Falls and the Aare Gorge. The road winds its way steeply up through the Hasli valley to the Grimsel reservoir which is reminiscent of the fjords of northern Europe. Continuing down to Gletsch the breathtaking panorama of the Rhône glacier opens up on the Furka road, which finally enters **Andermatt**, at the junction of four major Alpine roads.

Valais

8: From Lake Geneva through the Rhône Valley to Brig
(120km/75 miles)

This route begins on the east bank of **Lake Geneva** near **Montreux**. On a small rocky island south of the town lies the fairy-tale castle of Chillon, which Lord Byron immortalised in his poem "The Prisoner of Chillon" in 1816. A few miles further on the **Rhône Valley** opens up; drive initially to **Aigle**, where the castle surrounded by vineyards houses a Wine Museum. The next stop is **St Maurice**, the abbey church of which boasts one of the most valuable collections of medieval goldsmiths' work. **Martigny**, with the famous Fondation Pierre Giannadda, lies on the great bend in the Rhône where the N21 continues to the **Great St Bernard**. The route now runs parallel to the Rhône, passing close by the notable Romanesque Church of St-Pierre-de-Clages (see A to Z. Sion), and on to **Sion**, dominated by the mighty Château de Tourbillon and the collegiate church of Notre-Dame-de-Valère. **Route**

There is a worthwhile detour northwards up to **Crans-Montana** (27km/17 miles), especially for golfers and skiers. Southwards there is also a recommended tour into the romantic Val d'Hérens, where heavy falls of glacial debris in the Pleistocene period have produced bizarre pyramidal shapes. **Detour**

By way of St Leonhard, which possesses the largest underground lake in Europe, the visitor will finally pass through vine-covered slopes to the little old town of **Sierre**, near the boundary of the German and French-speaking regions in the **Rhône Valley**.

Poets have been inspired by the beauty of the Val d'Anniviers which branches off to the south. Note particularly the typical old Valais wooden houses and storehouses with their characteristic stone "mouse dishes". **Detour**

Further upstream along the Rhône lies Leuk, 16km/10 miles beyond the much-visited spa town of **Leukerbad/Loèche-les-Bains**, from which eight wooden ladders once formed the only link with the mountain village of Albinen (today there is a motor road from Leuk, 10km/6 miles).

At Gampel the **Lötschental** branches off to the north. This valley has some beautiful old wooden houses in the traditional Valais style and the Lötschberg tunnel (through which cars are transported by rail).

The route continues through the flat **Rhône Valley** to Visp, the setting-out point southwards to the Mattertal and Saastal in the **Valais Alps**.

Recommended Routes

Detour   At Stalden (7km/4½ miles south) the road forks west to Täsch
(23km/14½ miles) and from there the railway leads to the car-free
winter sports resort of Zermatt, at the foot of the magnificent Matterhorn, the "mountain of mountains", as the Swiss say; continue east
through the **Saas Valley** to Saas Fee (19km/12 miles), beautifully situated between the Fee glacier and the peaks of the Mischabel group.

After returning to Visp, again drive along the Rhône as far as **Brig**,
with its Baroque "Stockalpenschloss". The town is an important junction of the great pass route over the Simplon and through the wild
Gondo gorge to Italy, over the Furka to **Andermatt**, and the Nufenen
pass into **Ticino**.

Detour   Between Brig and Gletsch the route crosses the charming countryside
of Goms with its typical dark Valais wooden buildings. Beyond Mörel
the Aletsch glacier (see A to Z, Brig) is a unique feature. The magnificent view of the greatest glacier in the Alps can be enjoyed from the
Moosfluh (chairlift) and the Eggishorn (funicular).

Ticino

9: From Airolo to Bellinzona (60km/37 miles)

Route   Passing through the shortest north–south link in the Alps, the **St Gotthard**, the visitor will arrive in the canton of **Ticino** near Airolo in the
Valle Leventina. The route follows the River Ticino through the old
village of Giornico with the important Romanesque Church of San
Nicolao, to Biasca (for details of this stretch see A to Z, St Gotthard).
Lined by vineyards, Spanish chestnuts and other Mediterranean vegetation, the road then passes through the wide Ticino valley, now known
as the "Riviera", to **Bellinzona**. The chief town of the region is dominated by three massive fortresses dating from the time of the Counts
of Visconti from Milan.

Detour   East of Bellinzona the Val Mesolcina, the site of Mesocco (35km/22
miles) and the impressive castle ruins of Misox, forms the link with the
San Bernardino Pass and the canton of **Grisons**.

There are beautiful excursions to be made near **Lake Maggiore** to the
west of Bellinzona and **Lake Lugano** to the south.

10: From Locarno to Lugano via Bellinzona (45km/28 miles)

Route   The old Ticenese town of **Locarno**, at the north end of **Lake Maggiore**,
enjoys a life style shaped by its mild climate and southern atmosphere.

In a bay 3km/2 miles to the west lies the picturesque little town of
Ascona. If time permits a trip to the charming valleys in the area is
strongly recommended. Narrow roads lead to small, colourful mountain villages in the Val Verzasca, Val Maggia and Val Centovalli, with
shady chestnut forests and clear mountain brooks.

Proceeding eastwards from Locarno the route follows the River
Ticino to the cantonal capital of **Bellinzona**, famous for its magnificent
castles. Now turn south on the N13, which leads via Lugano and
through the Mendrisiotto as far as Chiasso on the Swiss–Italian border
(for details of this stretch see A to Z, Lake Lugano). Between San
Salvatore and Monte Brè lies the pleasantly luxurious town of **Lugano**,
the most enchanting town in Ticino. There are some magnificent
excursions to be made on and around **Lake Lugano** by boat or car; for
example, to the Art Collection in the Villa Favorita in the Castagnola
district of the town, to the picturesque old fishing villages of Gandria
and Morcote, or to Melide, where visitors can see a display of "Switzerland in miniature".

Grisons

11: From Chur over the San Bernardino Pass to Bellinzona
(115km/72 miles)

The route starts in **Chur**, the oldest urban settlement in Switzerland. **Route**
The cathedral, forming part of the Bishop's Court, possesses the most
beautiful of all Swiss Late Gothic carved altars. Continue upstream
parallel to the **Rhine** a far as Rhäzüns, then proceed in a southerly
direction and cross the wildly romantic Domleschg to Thusis, passing
numerous medieval castles and ruins. The road then enters the Via
Mala, a wild gorge once impassable but now served by a very beautiful
road; the N13 then leads on to Zillis. The unique wooden roof of
the village Church of St Martin dates from the 12th c. and consists of
153 individual square panels depicting Biblical themes. Beyond the
neighbouring township of Andeer it is well worth visiting the imposing
Rofla gorge on the Rhine (for details of this stretch see A to Z, The
Rhine). Then continue via Splügen thorugh the Hinterrhein valley
up to the **San Bernardino Pass**, the fastest link, negotiable all the
year round, between **Grisons** and the Ticinese cantonal capital of
Bellinzona.

12: From Chur to St Moritz (80km/50 miles)

The setting-out point for this route is **Chur**, capital of the Grisons **Route**
canton, and at one time the see of the bishops with the status of princes
of the Empire. The route then continues southwards on the N3 through
the popular holiday resorts of **Lenzerheide-Valbella** to Tiefencastel at
the northern end of the **Oberhalbstein/Sursés** valley. The Julier pass
then leads up to the winter sports resort of Savognin and then on past
the Lai de Marmorera (an artificial lake) to the Julier pass, with the
preserved stumps of two Roman columns (for details see A to Z,
Oberhalbstein/Sursés). Just before reaching the **Engadine** valley at
Silverplana there is a magnificent view of the **Bernina Pass**.

From here the N3 leads westwards along the surfer's paradise of the **Detour**
Silverplaner See and the Silser See at the foot of Piz Corvatsch to
the Maloja pass, from where 13 sharp bends in the road have to be
negotiated on the way down to the **Val Bregaglia**, a wild and romantic
gorge.
    East of Silvaplana continue to the world-famous and chic winter
sports resort of **St Moritz**. The old village is almost urban in character
with its huge luxury hotels. The spa facilities of St Moritz Bad lie in the
bottom of the valley by the lake of the same name.

13: From St Moritz to Bad Ragaz via Davos (115km/71½ miles)

This stretch starts in **St Moritz**, the world-famous spa and winter sports **Route**
resort in the Upper Engadine, where the N29 continues southwards via
Pontresina and **Bernina** to Tirano in Italy. From St Moritz travel through
the broad Inn valley in a north-westerly direction to Zernez, the major
setting-out point for visits to the **Swiss National Park**. A short transverse valley then leads to the little village of Susch.

From here the charming Lower Engadine pass leads along the south- **Detours**
ern foothills of the mighty Silvretta group of mountains and through
the ever narrower and more heavily wooded Inn valley to **Bad Scuol/**

Schuls-Tarasp-Vulpera. En route, two detours can be recommended, going up to the romantic mountain villages of Guarda and Ardez, where many artistically decorated old Engadine farmhouses, circular fountains and churches have been preserved (for details see A to Z, Engadine).

After returning to Susch, take the Flüela pass to the well-known health resort of **Davos**, internationally renowned for its beneficial climate. To the north-east, in the broad valley of the Prättigau, lies the popular health resort of **Klosters**. Parallel to the River Landquart the route continues on the N28 to where the Landquart enters the **Rhine**. Here, turn north to **Bad Ragaz**, one of the leading Swiss spa resorts, at the mouth of the Tamina gorge.

North-east Switzerland

14: From Bad Ragaz to Altdorf via Glarus (120km/75 miles)

Route
From the popular health resort of **Bad Ragaz**, whose thermal springs rise in the Tamina gorge, this route takes us to Sargans, dominated by an imposing medieval castle, and then on to Walenstadt at the eastern end of the the **Walensee**. With a beautiful view of the steep rocky faces of the Churfirsten chain follow the road along the south bank, with its forests of chestnuts and its vineyards on the slopes, as far as Weesen, where the N17 turns south into the Linthal in the canton of **Glarus**. The Cantonal Museum housed in the magnificent Freulerpalast in Näfels contains some interesting collections. To the south, at the foot of the Glärnisch, lies the interesting cantonal capital of **Glarus**.

Detour
It is well worth making a detour from there into the idyllic Klöntal to the west.

From Glarus the panoramic N17 continues westwards via Linthtal and the Klausen pass and ends at **Altdorf** on the **Vierwaldstätter See**.

15: From Bad Ragaz to St Gallen (70km/43 miles)

Route
This route begins in the spa town of **Bad Ragaz**, and then continues on the N13 north-westwards via the principality of **Liechtenstein** to Werdenberg. This little medieval picture-book town, preserved as an historical monument, with its lovingly restored old wooden houses, town wall and gates now forms part of Buchs. The N13 continues along the Rhine valley via Oberriet to Altstätten, in the **Appenzell** region.

Detour
A favourite excursion destination near Appenzell is the Säntis, the highest peak in the Alpstein massif. From the peak there are fantastic views of the Vorarlberg, Grison, Glarus and Uri Alps and across Lake Constance (for details see A to Z, Appenzell).

After returning to Appenzell, drive via Gais and Teufen to **St Gallen**, the capital of the canton of the same name. The Benedictine Abbey houses the famous Abbey Library, with many valuable manuscripts and illuminated books.

Alternative route
Alternatively, beyond Werdenberg the 75km/47 miles stretch through the varied countryside of the **Toggenburg** region can be chosen. Passing through the popular health resort of Unterwasser, lying in a beautiful sheltered setting between the Säntis chain and the Churfirsten, continue through the green Alpine high valley of Obertoggenburg to Neu-St Johann. The former Benedictine abbey boasts a fine Baroque church.

The trip up the Säntis by cable railway will be found very rewarding. Detour
From Neu-St Johann it is 12km/7 miles to the lower station at Schwägalp (for details see A to Z, Toggenburg).

Romantic arbours and proud old arcaded houses can be seen in
Lichtensteig, the principal town in the Toggenburg region on the right
bank of the Thur. Here the N8 branches off to the east and leads via
Herisau to **St Gallen**, the commercial hub of North-eastern
Switzerland.

16: From St Gallen to Schaffhausen (72km/45 miles)

St Gallen, the cantonal capital with its famous Abbey Library, is the   Route
starting point of this route. Some 27km/17 miles to the west Wil, once a
summer residence of the Prince-Abbots of St Gallen, is a beautiful old
town. From here continue along the N7 to the little town of Wängi and
then northwards to Frauenfeld, where the castle high above the River
Murg now houses the **Thurgau** Cantonal Museum. Via Gisenhard the
N14, which becomes the N13 beyond Diessenhofen, leads to **Schaffhausen**, on the north bank of the **Rhine**. Surrounded by vineyards, on a
hill above the capital, stands Kastell Munot, an imposing circular structure designed in accordance with Dürer's principles of fortification. The
Rhine Falls (Rheinfall) in nearby Neuhausen are Europe's mightiest
falls.

A charming alternative route is that from **St Gallen** along **Lake Con-**   **Alternative**
stance and the **Rhine** to **Schaffhausen**. Begin by driving in a north-   **route**
westerly direction to the old port of **Rorschach** on the southernmost
bay of **Lake Constance** (Obersee). After passing Arbon continue to the
lakeside resort of Romanshorn, where the Swiss lake steamers are
based. The southern route of the Upper Swabian Baroque road forms
the next part of the route to Kreuzlingen, sister city to the German town
of Constance (Konstanz) opposite. On the south bank of the Untersee
we then pass Schloss Arenenberg, which houses a Napoleonic
Museum, and then continue to the little town of Steckborn, with its
picturesque timbered houses, and thence to **Stein am Rhein**. The
historical old town, beautifully preserved, has some fine residences
decorated with frescoes. Passing along the south bank of the Rhine, the
N13 finally reaches **Schaffhausen**.

An excursion to the mighty **Rhine Falls** is highly recommended. Here
the waters of the High Rhine cascade down over a ledge of Jurassic
limestone 150m/492ft across and up to 22m/52ft high.

Switzerland A to Z

Aarau K 4

Canton: Aargau (AG)
Altitude: 388m/1273ft
Population: 16,000

Aarau, capital of the canton of Aargau since 1803, lies on the River Aare under the southern slopes of the Jura. With Late Gothic houses dating from the period of Kyburg rule, their street fronts colourfully remodelled in Baroque style, it is known as the "town of gables and gardens". In addition to its role as an administrative and cultural centre it also has a variety of industry (manufacture of instruments, iron and steel works, optical industry, bell-casting).

Situation and general

Founded about 1240 by the Counts of Kyburg, Aarau soon passed into the hands of the Habsburgs. In 1415 it came under Bernese rule, and in 1798 became for six months capital of the Helvetian Republic. In the 18th c. the Swiss national gymnastic, shooting and singing associations were founded or held their first meetings in Aarau.

History

Sights

The well-preserved old town, built on a prominent rocky hill above the Aare, has many gabled houses with carved decoration (ornamental and figured) on the roofs and painted shingle fronts. The Rore tower (1240) is the oldest part of the Rathaus (Town Hall), which was enlarged about 1520 and remodelled in Baroque style in 1762. The Late Gothic parish church (Stadtkirche: Protestant), a pillared basilica, was built in 1471–78. Both these buildings are in the Halde, the best preserved old street in the canton, with houses ranging in date from the 16th to the 19th c. Here, too, is the Upper Tower (Oberer Turm, 1270). Its clock dates from 1532 and still strikes daily. On the south side of the tower is the painting "Dance of Death" by Felix Hoffman.

The Schlössli was originally a castle keep (11th c.). The Grossrats-gebäude, seat of the cantonal parliament, is the finest Neo-Classical building in Aargau (1826–28). From the new bridge over the Aare (Neue Aarebrücke,1949) there is a fine view of the old town. Also of interest are the Municipal Museum (Stadtmuseum Alt-Aarau) in the castle (open: Wed., Sat. and Sun.) and the Art Gallery (Swiss paintings, drawings and sculpture 1750 to the present day; closed Mon.), as well as the Aargau Museum of Nature (closed Mon.).

Aarau: Fountain of Justice

Surroundings

Good walking in the Aare valley, the Jura and Mittelland hills. In the wooded Roggenhausen valley are a wildlife park and a nature trail, and in Schachen an interesting aviary.

10km/6 miles north-east on road 5 lies Wildegg (357m/1171ft), at the foot of the Kestenberg, with saline springs containing iodine (water available only bottled). Above the town to the north (1.5km/1 mile by road) stands the imposing Schloss Wildegg (438m/1438ft: 12th and 17th c.; now open to the

Schloss Wildegg

◄ *Parish church of St Stephen in Tiefencastel*

public as a museum). The Schaerer-Citterio Weapon Collection and the Erlach House have been open to visitors since 1988. The latter was built by Albrecht von Effinger in 1825 in Biedermeier (early Victorian) style for his half-sister Sophie von Erlach-von Effinger.

On the left bank of the Aare, a little way downstream, is Schloss Wildenstein, now an old people's home.

Bad Schinznach

5.5km/3 miles farther downstream we come to Bad Schinznach (355m/1165ft), an elegant spa established in 1694 (closed in winter), with sulphurous water (34° C–93° F) which is effective in the treatment of rheumatism and metabolic disorders; beautiful park (restaurant) and golf course.

Habsburg ruins

Beyond Bad Schinznach, on the left, a steep narrow road ascends (2.5km/2 miles) to the ruins of the Habsburg (513m/1683ft: inn), on the Wülpelsberg. The castle, built about 1020 was in the 12th and 13th c. the seat of the Counts of Habsburg, one of whom, Rudolf III, was elected King of Germany in 1273 and thus became the founder of the Imperial dynasty of Habsburg. From the 24m/79ft-high tower there are superb views. The castle can also be reached from Brugg (see p. 109) on a steep and not very good road (3.5km/2 miles).

Lenzburg

East of Aarau by way of Buchs is Lenzburg (400m/1312ft), a little town of 7000 inhabitants well known for its food-preserving factories (particularly fruit preserves). Above the old town with its unspoiled 17th and 18th c. houses rises the Burgberg (512m/1680ft: road to top) crowned by the large Schloss Lenzburg (11th–16th c.), now the property of the town of Lenzburg and the canton of Aargau (cantonal historical museum, open: Apr.–Oct., Tues.–Sun. 9.30am–noon, 1.30–5pm). To the west on the Staufberg (520m/1706ft: view), is a Gothic pilgrimage church with 15th c. stained glass.

★Schloss Lenzburg

To the west of the motorway access road are the foundations of a Roman theatre of the 1st c. A.D. discovered in 1964 and restored in 1970–72.

Aarau: the Old Town   *Lenzburg Castle*

8km/5 miles north-east on the Baden road, in the old country church of Wohlenschwil, is the Swiss Country Museum (Bauernmuseum: house types, costumes, weapons).

Adelboden   H 9

Canton Bern (BE)
Altitude: 1400m/4600ft
Population: 3500

The village of Adelboden, a popular altitude and winter sports resort in the Bernese Oberland, lies in a sheltered situation on the west side of the Engstligen valley at the end of a road from Lake Thun. Along the east side of the wide valley with its scatter of huts rises the Lohner chain; to the south is the Wildstrubel.

Situation and townscape

This attractive mountain village is famed for its scenic beauty, its many charming old farmhouses, and its hotels and chalets scattered about on sunny terraces. On the south wall of the church (1433) is a late 15th c. painting of the Last Judgment.

Via Hahnenmoos up the Laveygrat (2254m/7395ft: 3½ hours, not particularly difficult); via Schermtanne up the Albristhorn (2765m/9072ft: 5½ hours, for experienced climbers only); from the Engstligenalp in 5½–6 hours, with guide, up the Wildstrubel (the east peak, Grosstrubel, 3253m/10,673ft), with magnificent views (west peak climbed from Lenk in the Simmental); from the Engstligenalp by way of the Engstligenrat to the Gemmi pass (4–5 hours, with guide: see p. 259)

Climbs

Good downhill runs from the Fleckli (1862m/6109ft: two lifts from Boden), on the Engstligenalp (1940m/6365ft: three lifts; accessible by cableway); from the Kuonisbergli (1731m/5679ft; two lifts from Boden); from the

Winter sports

85

Schwanfeldspitz (2029m/6659ft; lift; accessible by cableway); from the Luegli (2080m/6824ft) and from Lavey (2200m/7220ft; chair-lift from Geils) and on the Hahnenmoos (1957m/6421ft: lifts from the Simmental; combined "ski pass" with Lenk; accessible by cableway from Geilsmäder). Also ski-jumping, cross-country skiing, skating (rink with artificial ice) and curling (indoor and outdoor rinks).

Surroundings

Schwanfeldspitz   There are about 200km/125 miles of signposted walks. A chair-lift, 1268m/4160ft long, ascends in 8½ minutes to the Tschentenalp, on the east side of the Schwanfeldspitz (2029m/6657ft: restaurant), from which there are magnificent views of the Lohner and Wildstrubel. A road runs 3.5km/2 miles west up the Allenbach valley to the Schermtanne inn.

Engstligenalp   A narrow road branches off the road to Frutigen (on right, after the second bend), runs south up the Engstligen valley and passes through Boden to the hamlet of Unter dem Berg, at the Lower Engstligen Falls (6km/4 miles), from which a cableway takes us up past the Upper Engstligen Falls to the Engstligenalp (1940m/6365ft: Berghaus Bärtschi, 15b. Berghotel Oester, 40b.), a former lake basin at the foot of the Wildstrubel. A bus runs southwest up the Gilbach valley to Geils. Cableway from Geilsmäder (1707m/5601ft) to the Hahnenmoos pass (1957m/6421ft: Berghotel 15b.). Chair-lift 1650m/5414ft long from Geils to the Laveygrat (2200m/7218ft) and a chair-lift from Geils to Luegli (2080m/6824ft), both operating only in winter. From Hahnenmoos it is a 45 minutes' descent to the Bühlberg restaurant (1660m/5446ft), from which a road leads down (6km/4 miles, with steep bends) to Lenk in the Simmental (see entry), or alternatively along the valley by cableway.

Aigle   F 10

Canton: Vaud/Waadt (VD)
Altitude: 420m/1378ft
Population: 6500

Situation   The small town of Aigle is situated in the Chablais on the banks of the Rhône, surrounded by the well-known vineyards of the Vaud Fendant.

History   The history of Aigle goes back to the Bronze Age. Ruled by Savoy from 1076, this small market town was conquered by Berne in 1476 and remained in its possession until the independence of Vaud was declared in 1798.

Sights

A stroll through the Fontaine quarter and the picturesque Rue Jerusalem with its old houses connected by covered arcades is to be recommended. The main shopping street is the Rue du Bourg (pedestrianised). Other attractions include the market square, the medieval church of St Jacques, where the reformer G. Farel (1489–1565) once preached his sermons, and the old clock tower.

★ Schloss Aigle,   Renowned as one of the most important castle sites in Switzerland the
Viticultural   12th c. Schloss Aigle, surrounded by vineyards, towers above the town.
Museum   This former residence of the Bernese provincial governors served as the district prison until 1972 and today houses an important viticultural museum (open: Apr.–June, Sept., Oct., closed Mon.; July–Aug. daily).

Surroundings of   11km/7½ miles through the Ormonttal, at the foot of the Mont d'Or and
Aigle   the Tours-d'Aï lies Le Sepey (979m/3213ft). A road leads on further to

Aigle Castle, framed by vineyards

Wine-press in the Museum of Viniculture

Leysin (6km/4 miles south-west, 1263–1500m/4145–4923ft), a popular holi- **Leysin**
day and health resort (including treatment for respiratory problems). From
here there is a fantastic panorama view, taking in the Savoy and Bernese
Alps, the Vaud and Valais mountains, a part of the Mont Blanc chain, the
Dents-du-Midi massif and the mountains around Lake Geneva. There is
also a rail link between Aigle and Leysin. From Leysin there are cable
railways up to the Bernenspitze (2037m/6685ft) and the Tour de Mayen
(2326m/7634ft).

Altdorf

Canton: Uri (UR)
Altitude: 458m/1519ft. Population: 8200

Altdorf, capital of the canton of Uri, a little town with a long and eventful **Situation**
history, lies 3km/2 miles south of the outflow of the Reuss into Lake Uri in a
wide plain at the mouth of the Schächen valley; it is the starting-point of the
road over the Klausen pass. It is here that William Tell is supposed to have
shot at the apple on his son's head.

The parish is believed to have been established in the 10th c., although its **History**
first appearance in the records is only in 1223. After the struggle to shake off
Habsburg rule the place acquired political and economic importance as
capital of the territory of Uri, which until 1439 was self-governing in direct
subordination to the Emperor.

Sights

In front of the Rathaus (Town Hall, 1805–08) and a medieval tower house **★Tell**
is the Tell Monument (by Richard Kissling, 1895). To the east is the Tell **Monument**

Altdorf: William Tell Monument

Schloss a Pro, on Lake Uri

Theatre (1925), in which Schiller's "Wilhelm Tell" is performed by Altdorf townspeople. Also of interest are the parish church of St Martin (rebuilt 1801–10), the Uri Historical Museum (founded 1892), the Suvorov house and the Capuchin friary.

The Historical Museum, (Gotthardstrasse 18), founded in 1892, contains a cultural collection from the Canton of Uri (wooden sculpture, altars, embroidery from the 15th–18th c., costumes; closed Mon.).

Surroundings

Bürglen

3km/2 miles away on the road to the Klausen pass is Bürglen (552m/1811ft: pop. 3600), one of the oldest settlements in Uri, built on detritus deposited by the Schächenbach, which here flows into the Reuss. Parish church (1684), with Romanesque crypt and substructure of the tower. Bürglen is supposed to have been the home of the mythical William Tell, whom Schiller's plays made the greatest figure in Swiss legend. The Tell chapel (1582) is said to occupy the site of Tell's house, and a stone cross beside the bridge marks the spot where Tell is traditionally believed to have been drowned while rescuing a child from the Schächenbach in his later years. There is a Tell Museum in a Romanesque tower adjoining the church.

Attinghausen

1.5km/1 mile south of Altdorf, on the left bank of the Reuss, is Attinghausen (469m/1539ft; pop. 1200), with the remains of a castle in which Freiherr von Attinghausen, who features in Schiller's play, died in 1321.

★Schloss a Pro

From Altdorf a road runs via Seedorf (437m/1434ft) at the south-west tip of Lake Uri. At the end of the village, directly on the lake, stands the pinnacled Schloss a Pro, which was built for the Knight Jacob (1556–60) of the same name. Nowadays the castle houses the Uri Mineral Museum (slide shows).

★Urirostock

From Isleten to the delightfully situated village of Isenthal (10km/6 miles: 778m/2553ft; pop. 600), the starting-point for the ascent of the Urirostock (2932m/9620ft; 6–7 hours, with guide; cableways).

14km/9 miles south by way of Erstfeld (475m/1558ft: station on the St Gotthard line) is Amsteg (552m/1811ft), a beautifully situated village and summer holiday resort at the mouth of the Maderanertal, here spanned by a 53m/174ft-high viaduct carrying the St Gotthard railway; cableway (1440m/4725ft long: 7 minutes) up the Arniberg (1392m/4567ft).

Amsteg

A road to the left leads into the Maderanertal, one of the most beautiful of the Alpine valleys, watered by the rushing Kärstelenbach. A steep mountain road, with many bends, climbs (4km/2 miles) to Bristen (797m/2615ft), from which there is a cableway to the Golzernsee (1410m/4626ft) and a rough track which leads in 2½ hours up to the magnificently situated Hotel Schweizer Alpenclub (1354m/4442ft), a good base for climbers and hillwalkers (e.g. to the Oberalpstock, (3330m/10,926ft); 8–9 hours, with guide).

★Maderanertal

Andermatt

N 9

Canton: Uri (UR)
Altitude: 1444m/4713ft
Population: 1600

Andermatt lies in the wide Urseren valley at the junction of four important Alpine roads, which with the exception of the access road from the Reuss valley are closed for between four and six months in the year. The old village has developed into an ideal base for walkers and climbers and a popular winter sports resort.

Situation

The Urseren valley was settled from the Valais, and the oldest parts of Andermatt and Hospental still show Valaisian features. The people of the valley were long subject to the authority of Disentis abbey, but achieved independence in 1382, with their own constitution and their own amman (chief magistrate) and the village is still a separate district within the canton of Uri.

History

View of the road from Andermatt to the Oberalp Pass

Sights

The Baroque church of St Peter and Paul dates from 1695 (Rococo interior). On the mountainside is the little 13th c. church of St Columban (dedicated to the Irish monastery saint). In the Schönbächler House, with rare Rococo paintings of 1786, is the Uri Valley Museum (domestic culture). From the Mariahilf chapel, above the village to the south, there are far-ranging views of the Bäzberg (2550m/8367ft), the Furka pass, with the Muttenhorn (3103m/10,181ft), and the Badus (2931m/9617ft).

Surroundings

Urschner
Höhenweg

The five-hour walk along the Urschner Höhenweg from Andermatt to Tiefenbach is recommended.

Gemstock

There is a cableway up to the Gemstock (2963m/9721ft; length 4036m/13,240ft; height difference 1525m/5003ft; time 12 minutes; magnificent views).

★Devil's Bridge

Road 2 runs north up the wide Ursren valley (Bear Hunters' Valley), a massive Alpine trough flanked by high mountains, some of them snow-capped, and by scree-covered slopes, and watered by the streams feed the Reuss. The road crosses the Devil's Bridge (Teufelsbrücke 1402m/4600ft), built in 1955–56, which spans the Reuss at a waterfall 30m/98ft high. The bridge, 86m/282ft long, inherited its name from an old 15th c. bridle-path bridge at the same spot. A stone cross 12m/39ft high commemorates the fighting in September 1799, when General Suvorov's Russians, coming from the St Gotthard pass, defeated the French force which attempted to bar their way. To the right, on the old road, is the Teufelsbrücke restaurant.

The road passes through the Teufelswand ("Devil's Wall") in a short tunnel, and leaving a parking place (fine views) and five sharp bends (Schöllenen restaurant) returns to the right bank of the river of the Spänngi bridge (1234m/4049ft).

★Schöllenen
gorge

It then enters the Schöllenen (probably from Latin "scala"=ladder), a wild gorge enclosed between precipitous granite walls, and after another four sharp bends (fine views) crosses to the left bank again on the Vordere Brücke. Thereafter it crosses the Göschenen-Reuss and continues to wind sharply downhill on the St Gotthard road to the village of Göschenen.

Göschenen

Göschenen (1115m/3658ft) is magnificently situated at the junction of the Göschenen-Reuss with the Reuss, which issues from the Schöllenen gorge. It lies near the north entrance to the 15km/9 miles long St Gotthard tunnel (see p.373) and has a large railway station. The builder of the tunnel, Louis Favre, died of a stroke in the tunnel in 1879, shortly before its completion, and is buried in Göschenen churchyard.

★Göschenen
valley

To the west an attractive road ascends the beautiful Göschenen valley to a reservoir on the Göschener Alp (9.5km/6 miles). 7km/4 miles from Göschenen, on the right is the Göschener Alp inn (1715m/5627ft), and 2.5km/2 miles beyond this, in a magnificent mountain setting, the Dammagletscher inn (1795m/5889ft) with a large parking place. Above the inn, from a reservoir (75 million cu.m/2648 million cu.ft), there is a superb view of the Dammastock and its glacier. The Göschenen Alp is the starting-point of a variety of rewarding climbs: to the Lochberg (3088m/10,132ft: 4½ hours, with guide), the Dammastock (3633m/11,920ft: 6½ hours, with guide), the Susterhorn (3503m/11,497ft: 6½ hours, with guide).

The road continues down the bare mountainside and once again crosses to the right bank on the Schöni Bridge (981m/3219ft). Below, on the right, lies the Teufelstein ("Devil's Stone"), a massive boulder which was moved 127m/417ft upstream in 1973, during the construction of the St Gotthard road tunnel. The road passes the village of Wattingen (920m/3019ft) and crosses to the left bank of the Reuss, with the Rienzenstock (2964m/9725ft) on the right and the magnificent Dammafirn (névé) on the left.

5km/3 miles from Göschenen we reach Wassen (934m/3064ft), a beautifully situated village at the junction with the road over the Furka pass. From the terrace in front of the church (1734), which stands on higher ground, there are superb views of the valley in both directions.

Wassen

★★ Circuit of three passes

This circuit (a round trip from Wassen) of the Susten, Grimsel and Furka passes offers a breathtaking experience, combining splendid Alpine scenery with the tremendous technical achievements of the road engineers.

The newest of the three roads, the boldly engineered Susten road (No. 11), built between 1938 and 1946, runs up from Wassen through the wildly beautiful Meiental, goes over the Susten pass in a tunnel (2224m/7297ft) just under the summit and descends the Gadmen valley, passing close to the Stein glacier, to Innertkirchen, where it leaves the magnificence of this high Alpine valley for a gentler landscape of pastureland and orchards.

★ Susten road

The Grimsel road (No. 6), built in 1891–94, which links the Bernese Oberland with Upper Valais (the Upper Rhône valley) and the Furka, starts from Innertkirchen (626m/2054ft), in a beautiful setting of forest and Alpine meadows, and runs up the attractive Hasli valley. Above Guttannen this becomes narrower and wilder, until at Handegg the trees disappear altogether and the road continues to climb through a bare rocky wilderness, past massive dams and narrow fjord-like reservoirs. From the Grimsel pass

★ Grimsel road

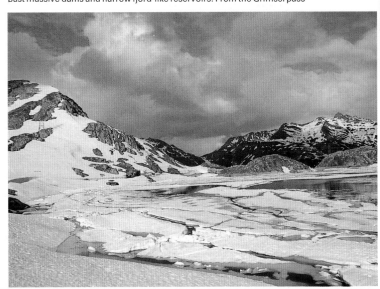

An artistic impression: the Totensee (dead lake) on the Grimsel Pass

(2165m/7013ft), the lowest of the three passes, the road runs down, with many hairpin bends, to Gletsch (1763m/5784ft), in the Upper Rhône valley.

★ Furka road

From here the Furka road (No. 19), built in 1864–66, leads up through the bare upper reaches of the valley, passes immediately under the Rhône glacier and continues up to the Furka pass (2431m/7976ft), the highest point on the trip. It then continues down into the Urseren valley through scenery of a different type, with rugged mountains of uncompromising bulk.

All three roads are well built and excellently engineered, particularly the Susten road (minimum width 6m/20ft, well-cambered bends, maximum gradient 8%). The Grimsel road, with its many bends, has been modernised (4–7m/13–23ft wide, maximum gradient 9%). The Furka road (improved 1960–63; 4–8m/13–26ft wide) is the steepest of the three (10%); the stiffest gradients are mostly on the bends, and in the thinner air at this altitude they make particularly heavy demands on the engine of a car. The round trip involves an ascent of some 3600m/11,812ft with about 60 sharp bends. Motorists who are unused to Alpine driving should exercise particular care. All three passes are usually open from mid June to mid October (emergency telephones).

★ Susten road

The Susten road, branching off the St Gotthard road at Wassen, runs uphill at a moderate gradient, with an attractive view of Wassen church to the rear. In 0.5km/¼ mile it winds its way through two tunnels, between which is another view of Wassen. The road then crosses the gorge of the Meienreuss on a high concrete bridge, from where there is a view of Titlis (3239m/10,627ft) ahead. At the Leggistein tunnel on the St Gotthard railway the road takes a left-hand turn, beyond which one has a view of the Fleckistock (3420m/11,221ft) and Stücklistock (3309m/10,857ft). Soon after this it goes through a third tunnel and runs high up on the mountainside above the gorge of the Meienreuss, with a panorama of the valley. After a total of 5.5km/3 miles the road comes to the group of houses and the church at Meien (1300m/4265ft), beautifully situated at a point where the valley

Meiental

opens out. Beyond this point, in the upper reaches of the Meiental, an area of Alpine pasture enclosed by steep mountain walls, the road continues uphill on a moderate gradient above the left bank of the Meienreuss; from here one can see the jagged peaks of the Wendenhorn and Fünffingerstöcke at the head of the valley. In another 3km/2 miles a road goes off on the left and runs down into the valley to the hamlet of Färnigen, on the old bridlepath to the Susten pass.

8.5km/5 miles farther on, at Gorezmettlen, the road crosses the stream flowing down the Kleinalp valley from the Kleiner Spannort and then climbs higher up the slopes of the Meiental, now wild and desolate, with a view of the summit of the pass and the Sustenhorn, with the Rüttifirn and Kalchtalfirn. The Sustenstübli inn is passed on the right of the road. Beyond this, to the left, there is a magnificent panorama, looking backwards down the valley; ahead to the left, is the summit of the pass, from which the jagged crest of the Fünffingerstöcke extends to the right towards the Wendenhorn (3023m/9918ft) and Grassen (2946m/9666ft). Then follow two

★ Susten pass

bends and a short tunnel leading up to the Susten pass (2259m/7412ft), under which the road passes in a tunnel 325m/1066ft long (alt. 2224m/7297ft). Just beyond the far end of the tunnel are a large parking place and a small lake, from which there is a rewarding climb (5 minutes) to the summit of the pass (restaurant), the boundary between the cantons of Uri and Berne, with views of the imposing chain of mountains north of the Meiental (highest point Titlis, 3239m/10,627ft), the group formed by the Gewichtenhorn (3425m/11,327ft) and the Tierberge (3444m/11,300ft) rearing up above the Stein glacier, the Himmelrank gorge and, in the background, the tunnels on the Susten road and the Gadmerfluh.

Beyond the pass the road – still scenically and technically magnificent but now showing more variety of scenery – runs down in two sharp bends, offering superb close-up views of the Stein glacier and its drainage lake immediately below. It then passes through the Himmelrank gorge, with seven tunnels or arches in the rock, and takes a left-hand bend down to the Hotel Steingletscher (1866m/6122ft), on the Alp Stein. From here there is first a road (3km/2 miles) to the Steinlimmi glacier (summer skiing centre), and then a footpath (20 minutes) to the mighty Stein glacier, also a climb of 7 hours (with guide) to the summit of the Sustenhorn (3503m/11,497ft: superb views). From the Steingletscher Hotel the road descends the Wendental on the stony slopes of the Gschletterwald, through wild and rugged scenery, passing through five tunnels and under a sheer rock face, with a backward view of the Sustenhorn, of which there is a further glimpse after a left-hand bend. It then continues to wind its way down, with continually changing prospects of the Tierberge and Gewichtenhorn to the south and the precipitous walls of the Wendenstöcke and Gadmerfluh to the north. In another 5km/3 miles it crosses a stream, and soon after this traverses another tunnel into a left-hand bend (turning-place), and through three more tunnels and round two bends to the Wendenwasser bridge over the stream of the same name. It then continues down the Gadmental, the valley of the Gadmer Wasser. The scenery becomes gentler, with fresh green pastureland and woods of maple and stone pine. Ahead can be seen the Wetterhorn (3701m/12,143ft).

★Himmelrank

★Stein glacier

Gadmen (1207m/3960ft) is a straggling little village in a picturesque situation under the steep rock faces of the Gadmerfluh.

Gadmen

The road continues downhill on a gentle gradient, passes through a tunnel, crosses the gorge of the Gadmer Wasser on the high Schwendi bridge and winds its way down to the mouth of the Trift valley, from where one can see the Trift glacier. It then comes back to the right bank of the Gadmer Wasser and comes into the commune of Nessental (930m/3051ft) which gives its name to the lower part of the valley where fruit-trees abound. The road then runs down on a uniform easy gradient to Mühletal (837m/2746ft), at the mouth of the Gental, a valley running down from the Engstlenalp (toll road 11.5km/7 miles); the stream is crossed on the Ross-weidli Bridge. Then on to Wiler (4.5km/3 miles: 740m/2428ft). Beyond this point there is another fine view of the mountains, after which the road winds down into the wide valley of the Aare and arrives at Innertkirchen (626m/2054ft), a holiday resort surrounded by lush Alpine meadows.

Innertkirchen

From Innertkirchen the road to the Grimsel goes gradually uphill in the wooded and steadily narrower Oberhaslital above the right bank of the Aare, with beautiful vistas of the mountains ahead. In another 2.5km/2 miles, beyond the huts on the Aussere Urweid (716m/2349ft), a narrow stretch of road above the gorge-like valley bears left around a wall of rock and passes through the short Zuben tunnel, under a waterfall, into the Innere Urweid (760m/2494ft: inn). 1km/½ mile farther on the road runs through another short tunnel in a rocky spur of the Tönende Fluh, after which the valley opens out a little. At the hamlet of Boden (876m/2874ft) the road crosses the river and winds its way up the wooded mountainside, with four hairpin bends, to Guttannen (1060m/3478ft), the last village in the Oberhaslital, under the precipitous Ritzlihorn (3282m/10,768ft), which every year sends its dreaded avalanches tumbling down into the Spreitlaui valley. The crystal museum at Wirzen in Guttanen has examples of crystals from the Hasli valley and other regions of Switzerland.

Guttannen

★Grimsel road

The Grimsel road proper, which begins at Guttanen, follows a fairly straight and gentle course up the valley for a kilometre or so, begins to climb more steeply through the forest and crosses the river on the Tschingel bridge

(1140m/3740ft). It then passes rugged black crags and massive accumulations of debris which bear witness to the violence of the avalanches and the rushing torrents, returns by the Schwarzbrunnen bridge to the left bank (1217m/3993ft) and continues around the rocky bulk of the Stäubender.

The compensation reservoir of the Handegg I hydro-electric station is passed on the left (1309m/4295ft). Then two sharp bends carry the road up through a further stretch of forest to the Handegg (Handeck) saddle, 150m/492ft higher up. From a wider length of road there is a view of the

★Handegg falls Handegg falls, in which the grey-green waters of the Aare mingle with the silvery Aerlenbach, emerging below the road, and plunge into the chasm 46m/151ft below. Soon after this, off the road to the right, is the Hotel Handeck (1404m/4607ft). From here a cableway (for industrial use only) ascends the east side of the valley to the Gelmersee (1849m/6067ft), an artificial lake formed by a dam 35m/115ft high. The Grimsel road follows the valley bottom, strewn with boulders, and then winds its way, with sharp bends, up the granite mountainside, worn smooth by the glaciers, to the Kunzentännlen Alp (1616m/5302ft), where the last firs disappear, giving place to dwarf pines and rhododendrons. To the right, below, is the Handegg I hydro-electric station with its lake; to the left, higher up, the Gerstin glacier; straight ahead the dam of the Räterichsboden reservoir, up to which the road now winds its way (one hairpin bend). Above, to the right, is

Räterichsboden
reservoir
the Räterichsboden reservoir (1767m/5798ft), which the road skirts, with a view of the Grimselsee dam; near the end of the lake it passes through a short tunnel. The road then climbs again (to the right, below, a fine view of the Räterichsboden lake), and after two hairpin bends at the massive

★Grimmelsee Seeuferegg dam, reaches the Grimselsee (1909m/6263ft), a fjord-like lake extending for 5.5km/3 miles to the Unteraar glacier (nature reserve). A road on the right (0.8km/½ mile) leads by way of the Seeuferegg dam (325m/1155ft long, up to 42m/138ft high) to the Grimsel hospice (hotel and restaurant, 1960m/6431ft on the Granite ridge of Nollen, with a view of the Spitallamm (258m/846ft long, up to 114m/374ft high) and a magnificent

The Grimsel road and lake

view over the lake of the Zinkenstock, the Finsteraarhorn and the Agassizhorn. There is a rewarding walk from the hotel (2–3 hours) to the Unteraar glacier.

In 1974, when opening up the entrance to the Oberaar–Grimsel power-station deep under the Grimelsee, the Gerstenegg crystal cavern was discovered (guided tours from Meiringe (see entry) by prior arrangement; tel. (036) 71 43 22).

Gerstenegg
crystal cavern

The Oberhasli hydro-electric scheme (1925–54) comprises four separate power stations. The Handegg I station (90,000kW), built in 1925–32, uses the water of the Grimselsee (100 million cu.m/3531 million cu.ft), formed by the Seeuferegg and Spitallamm dams, which is carried in a 5km/3 mile-long tunnel to a subsidiary reservoir, the Gelmersee (13 million cu.m/459 million cu.ft) and the power station 540m/1772ft below. The Innertkirchen station (192,000kW) uses water from Handegg I, which is conveyed to it in a tunnel 10km/6 miles long. The Handegg II station (60,000kW), built in 1947–50, obtains its water from the Räterichsboden lake (27 million cu.m/953 million cu.ft) and the small Gauli reservoir in the Upper Urbach valley. The power station (underground) is at Handegg. The Oberaar station (31,000kW), built in 1950–54, uses water from the Oberaarsee, formed by a dam 525m/1723ft long and 105m/345ft high; the underground power station is between the Grimselsee and Räterichsboden. An expansion of the power station is planned for the 90s, with the construction of a new dam.

★Oberhasli
power stations

From the Seeuferegg dam the Grimsel road skirts the east end of the Grimselsee and then climbs on a moderate gradient (four sharp bends), with magnificent views to the rear (Grosser Schreckhorn, to the west, 4080m/13,386ft). 3.5km/2 miles farther on is the Grimsel pass (2165m/7103ft; Hotel Grimselblick, 80b.), on the boundary between the cantons of Berne and Valais, with beautiful views of the Valais Alps, particularly the Gries glacier. Rewarding climb (2½ hours) of the Kleines Siedelhorn (2768m/9082ft; fine panorama). From the top of the pass a beautiful but narrow private road (alternating one-way traffic) runs 6km/4 miles west to the Oberaarsee (58 million cu.m/2048 million cu.ft), with a car park and the Berghaus Oberaar (hotel and restaurant, 12b., camp-site; 2340m/7678ft). A little farther on, to the right, are the Hotel Grimselpass Höhe (30b.) and the Totensee (2144m/7034ft), whose name ("Lake of the Dead") commemorates the bitter fighting here between Austrian and French forces in 1799. Various crystals from the region are exhibited in the crystal cavern at Grimsel.

★Grimsel pass

★Kleines
Siedelhorn

The road descends the steep slope of the Meienwang in six sharp bends, with views of the Rhône glacier and the windings of the Furka road: to the left the Galenstock and Dammastock, to the south-east the Pizzo Rotondo. It then comes to the hotel centre of Gletsch (1763m/5784ft) at the lower end of the debris-covered valley, which a century ago was blanketed for more than half its area by the Rhône glacier.

Gletsch

★Furka road

In Gletsch the Furka road crosses the Rhône and then climbs (three sharp bends) up the south side of the valley and follows the slope. At the head of the valley the road crosses the narrow-gauge Furka railway. This was closed in 1981 but is gradually being brought back into use (as far as Tiefenbach since 1992, to Furka since 1993, to Gletsch from 1996 and to Oberwald from 1998; for information tel. (044) 6 80 25). Since 1982 a basic tunnel (15.4km/9½ miles long) replaced this section of the line from Lake Geneva through the Rhône and Rhine valleys to Lake Constance. The road then crosses the Muttbach bridge and climbs steeply (five hairpin bends) up the north side of the valley, with beautiful views of the Rhône glacier and of Gletsch far below. In 7.5km/4½ miles the car park of the Belvedere restaurant (2272m/7454ft), is reached. From here it is only a few minutes'

View of the Rhône glacier and Rhône valley

★Rhône glacier

walk to the Rhône glacier, between the Grosses Furkahorn (3169m/ 10,400ft) and the Gerstenhörner (3184m/10,447ft), which hangs over the side of the valley in a formidable cataract of ice (charge for access: interesting artificial cave hewn from the glacier).

The road continues to climb (two steep bends), with a magnificent view of the Rhône glacier to the rear, and to the right, above the Gratschlucht glacier, of the Grosses Muttenhorn (3099m/10,171ft). In 2.5km/2 miles the road reaches the Furka pass (2431m/7976ft). The Furka ("Fork") is a saddle, falling steeply away on each side, between the Kleines Furkahorn (3026m/ 9928ft; 2 hours north) and the Blauberg (2757m/9046ft; 1½ hours south), both offering easy and rewarding climbs. It forms the boundary between the cantons of Valais and Uri and affords magnificent views, extending north-east to the Urseren valley and the Oberalp pass and west to the Bernese Alps (Finsteraarhorn) and the Valais Alps (Weisshorn). Rewarding climb, to the north, of the Galenstock (3583m/11,756ft; 5 hours, with guide), which commands extensive views.

★Furka pass

Furka art

Since 1983 the Swiss art exhibitor Marc Hostettler has invited artists to show their "Furka art" on the Furka pass every spring. Nature determines the end of the event, the first snow being the signal to dismantle the exhibition. Among the artists who have shown work here are James Lee Byars, Per Kirkeby, Daniel Buren, Jenny Holzer and Ian Hamilton Finlay.

Hotel Furkablick

500m/1641ft farther on is the Hotel Furkablick (39b.) recently renovated by the Dutch architect Rem Koolhaas. The road then continues downhill, high up on the bare north face of the Garschental, a valley constantly threatened by avalanches, with the Furka-Reuss flowing down below. Views of the Siedeln glacier and the sharp pinnacles of the Bielenhorn (2947m/9669ft). Then by way of the Tiefentobel gorge (to the left a waterfall) to the Hotel Tiefenbach (2109m/6920ft; 20 b.). 1.5km/1 mile farther on at the Ebnetenalp (1995m/6548ft), where the road takes a sharp bend to the right, there are magnificent views of the Urseren valley and the Wyttenwasser valley, which now opens up to the south, with Piz Lucendro (2964m/9725ft). Now down the rounded slopes of Fuchsegg (nine sharp bends) to the valley bottom and the little village of Realp (1547m/5076ft), the name of which is derived from "riva alpa" (riva,"stream"; alpa,"mountain pasture"). To the south-east is Pizzo Rotondo (3192m/10,473ft; 8 hours, with guide), the highest peak in the St Gotthard group.

Realp

★Pizzo Rotondo

The road now follows a level and almost straight course to Andermatt down the wide Urseren valley, between the river Furka-Reuss and the Furka railway, which is crossed in another 8km/5 miles. From this point the road becomes narrower. Ahead can be seen the square tower of Hospental castle. 8km/5 miles from Realp is Hospental (1484m/4869ft; bypass), an old village (from hospitum, "hospice") situated at the point where the Furka-Reuss and Gotthard-Reuss join to form the Reuss, a popular health and winter sports resort. It is dominated by a church (1705–11) and 13th c. castle tower. From here follow road 2 to Andermatt.

Hospental

Appenzell

Cantons: Appenzell-Ausserhoden (AR, main town: Herisau)
Appenzell-Innerrhoden (AI, main town: Appenzell)

This attractive Pre-Alpine region in eastern Switzerland, just south of Lake Constance, reaching its highest point in the Säntis (2504m/8216ft) in the Alpstein range, is the only Swiss canton which is completely surrounded by another canton (St Gallen). It is subdivided into two independent half-cantons, established in 1597 following democratic votes in the two religious communities, Appenzell-Ausserrhoden being Protestant and Appenzell-Innerrhoden Roman Catholic. The division also reflects a geographical difference; Innerrhoden consists mainly of the Alpstein and Säntis massifs, while Ausserrhoden takes in the upland region to the north of the Säntis range. Both the half-cantons reach their most important political decisions

Situation and general

The town of Appenzell

at the Landsgemeinde, the annual meeting, held in the open air. It was 1990 before female suffrage was introduced in Innerrhoden.

History

In the Middle Ages Appenzell belonged to the Prince-Abbot of St Gallen, but at the beginning of the 15th c. it broke away after a valiant and determined struggle for independence, and in 1513 became the last canton in the 13-member confederation, which received no further accessions until the French Revolution. The canton owed its prosperity in earlier centuries to its flourishing textile industry, and many villages still have handsome houses with curved gables dating from this period.

Folk art and customs

According to legend the devil once flew over the region with his sack full of towns and villages. A sharp rock from Mt Säntis tore a hole in his bundle, through which thousands of houses fell and were scattered over the countryside, this being the reason for the typically wide dispersal of settlements. Folk art is deeply rooted in Appenzell traditions; in Innerrhoden in particular an ancient culture characteristic of these upland pastoral regions is still very much alive. Naïve peasant painting is to be seen everywhere in the canton, and other old crafts still practised are the making of bell harness and coopering. Folk music played by string bands (violins, cellos, double basses, dulcimers) and the elegant local costumes also play an important part in the ancient traditions of the sociably disposed people of Appenzell.

Landsgemeinde

The annual general meeting of the Landsgemeinde is an impressive experience for any visitor who is fortunate enough to be present. On the last Sunday in April all citizens entitled to vote – those over the age of 20 – make their way wearing swords, to the square where the meeting takes place. The men of Ausserrhoden meet alternately in Trogen, headquarters of the cantonal court and the cantonal police, and in Hundwil. The people of Innerrhoden, carrying their swords as evidence of their right to vote, meet in the cantonal capital, Appenzell. The landamman (chief magistrate) and other members of the cantonal government are elected by show of hands and solemnly sworn in on the spot. Every citizen has the right to speak, and can put forward a proposal for legislation or constitutional amendment.

Transport

Appenzell is served by good roads and by narrow-gauge railways. The Appenzellerbahn runs from Gossau, in the Unterland, via Herisau and Urnäsch to the town of Appenzell, and from there to Weissbad and Wasserauen; the Gaiserbahn links St Gallen and Altstätten with Appenzell, and there are other lines from Rorschach, St Gallen and Rheineck to Heiden, Trogen and Walzenhausen.

Around Mt Säntis

The highest peak in the Alpstein massif, which consists of three ranges lying between the Rhine valley, Toggenburg and the Vorderland of Appenzell, is the Säntis (2504m/8216ft), a mountain much favoured by hillwalkers, climbers and those who prefer to make the ascent by cableway. From the summit there are panoramic views of the Vorarlberg, Grisons, Glarus and Uri Alps and across Lake Constance and far into Southern Germany (Swabia). To the north-west of the peak the boundaries of the two half-cantons and of the canton of St Gallen meet.

★★Säntis

From the Schwägalp (1283m/4210ft; inn, 60b.) a cableway runs up, with only two intervening supports, to the Säntis (upper station 2476m/8124ft; length 2307m/7569ft, height difference 1193m/3914ft, time 10 minutes; restaurant and inn, 20b.). The ascent on foot takes 3½ hours from the Schwägalp and 4–5 hours from Wasserauen.

The railway line from St Gallen via Herisau (11km/7 miles; change trains) terminates at Urnäsch (23km/14 miles), from where there is a bus to the

Ascending the Säntis by cable-car ▶

Schwägalp (11km/7 miles; 30 minutes). The road from St Gallen to Urnäsch (32km/20 miles passes through the villages of Stein and Hundwil.

Urnäsch

Urnäsch (826m/2710ft; pop. 2300) is the largest in area and one of the oldest communes in Appenzell-Ausserrhoden. The village square with its trim wooden houses reflects the people's attachment to tradition, and Urnäsch is widely known for its rustic dances, New Year celebrations (in some places this is still celebrated on January 13th, in accordance with the Julian calendar) and other traditional observances. It has a museum of Appenzell traditions (open: Apr., Wed., Sat., Sun. 2–5pm; May–Oct. daily 2–5pm). Footpaths lead into the surrounding hills.

From Urnäsch it is 14km/9 miles to Appenzell. The road comes in 4km/2 miles to Jakobsbad (876m/2874ft; chalybeate spring), from which there is a cableway up the Kronberg (1663m/5465ft: length 3223m/10,575ft, height difference 772m/2533ft, time 8 minutes; restaurant). 2km/1 mile beyond this is Gonten (902m/2960ft).

Appenzell

Appenzell (780m/2560ft; pop. 5000) has been since 1597 capital of the Roman Catholic half-canton of Appenzell Innerrhoden. The town centre – especially the main street – is well preserved, with fine old traditional houses. Interspersed among the painted wooden houses are stone buildings dating from the 16th c., including the Town Hall, the Schloss and the parish church of St Mauritius (nave of 1823). Also of interest are the Landesgemeindeplatz, the square on which the annual meeting of the community takes place, the churches of the nunnery and the Capuchin friary, the Ziegelhütte cultural centre (open: June–Oct., Tues.–Thur. 2–5pm, Sat. 2–4pm, Sun. 4–6pm), the Appenzell Museum in its new premises and the "Im Blauen Haus" private museum (open: Mon.–Sat. 9am–noon, 1.30–6pm).

Gaiserbahn, Appenzeller-bahn

Appenzell is the terminus of the Gaiserbahn from St Gallen and a station on the Appenzellerbahn from Gossau, which runs via Weissbad (816m/2678ft; pop. 1500) to Wasserauen (872m/2861ft).

Ebenalp
★ Wildkirchli

There is a cableway to Ebenalp (1644m/5394ft; inn), from which it is a 10-minute walk down through a 75m/82 yard-long cavern to the Wildkirchli (1477m/4864ft; inn), a chapel in a cave which was inhabited by hermits from 1658 to 1853. In 1904 Palaeolithic implements and animal skeletons were found here. From Wasserauen there is a pleasant walk (1 hour) to the Seealpsee (1141m/3745ft) and from there to the Meglisalp (1520m/4987ft; inn) with its little church of "Maria zum Schnee".

Brülisau

Brülisau (922m/3025ft; pop. 700), the terminus of a postal bus service (Swiss postal buses convey both passengers and mail), has a cableway up the Hoher Kasten (1794m/5886ft), from which there is a geological trail to Staubern. A road leads from the Brühltobel gorge to the Sämtisersee and Fählensee (mountain inns). Other good climbs are up Fähnern (1506m/4941ft), with a little lake, the Forstseeli, and by way of the steep "Zahme Gocht" up the Alpsigel (1662m/5453ft).

In the Hinterland of Ausserrhoden

Herisau

Herisau (778m/2553ft; pop. 15,000), capital of the half-canton of Ausserrhoden, lies at the junction of the St Gallen – Wattwil (Bodensee – Toggenburg – St Gallen – Wattwil) and Gossach – Urnäsch – Appenzell (Appenzellerbahn) railway lines, and has a postal bus service to Hundwil–Teufen–Speicher–Trogen and Schwellbrun. The straggling little town has a beautiful square and is a local market and industrial focal point. Of interest is the church of St Laurence (Laurentiuskirche), dating from 1520, with its Rococo interior, and the Historical Museum in the old town hall (open: Apr.–Oct., Sun. 10.30am–noon).

A good impression of the character of the half-canton can be gained on the drive from Herisau to St Margrethen (49km/30 miles), via Waldstatt, Teufen (18km/11 miles), Trogen (25km/16 miles), Heiden (35km/22 miles) and Walzenhausen. The road crosses a number of deep gorges, including the Hundwiler Tobel near Waldstatt (concrete viaduct with a span of 105m/345ft).

Hundwil (793m/2602ft; pop. 1000; inn) has handsome old houses in the characteristic local style and a 13th c. church. The Hundwiler Höhi (1305m/4282ft), with a mountain inn, is a favourite local excursion.

Hundwil

1km/½ mile beyond Hundwil we turn off the road to Appenzell (8km/5 miles) to reach Stein (823m/2700ft; pop. 1050) where daffodils, a protected species, bloom in March. Tourists can visit a model cheese factory opened in 1978. The factory is open: Jan., Sun. 10am–5pm; Feb. and Mar., Tues.–Sat. 1.30–5pm, Sun. 10am–5pm; Apr.–Oct., Tues.–Sat. 10am–noon, 1.30–5pm, Sun. 10am–6pm; Nov. and Dec. see Feb./Mar.

Stein

About 4500 litres of fresh milk are delivered daily from the surrounding farms with the same amount again brought by tanker from more distant farms so that about 9000 litres of unpasteurised milk are processed daily.

★**Appenzeller model cheese factory**

The milk is first sieved, tested and weighed. If the milk needs to be stored before the next process it is cooled and stored in large vats at 10° C/50° F. The fat content of Appenzeller cheese is regulated to exactly 50% of the dry mass so some of the milk is skimmed in centrifuges.
   The skimmed and full cream milk then flow over a heat exchanger, where it is heated, into the so-called cheese kettle, which contains about 600 litres of milk. The milk is constantly stirred as it is heated to a temperature of 32° C/90° F, at which it coagulates, and the rennet and the lactic acid bacteria (natural coagulants and fermentation additives) are added. The cheese

Production of Appenzeller cheese

Appenzeller Cheese Factory Stein (AR)

Delivery of milk

Weighed

Storage

Cooler

tanks

Cheese Kettle

Moulds

Cream

Heat exchanger

Centrifuge

Cheese Cellar

Drying room

Salt dip

Whey

© *Baedeker*

then begins to ferment and after about 30–40 minutes it coagulates to form curds, which are broken up with the cheese sieve. The resulting crumbs – small lumps the size of maize kernels – separate from the whey. After the initial process has finished the curds are gently heated and stirred constantly until the necessary thickness has been reached.

During the next stage the lumpy mixture is siphoned up with the whey and poured into the pressing tub, where it is formed into blocks of cheese which are cut into pieces and shaped. The remaining whey is squeezed out of the fresh cheeses, which are turned several times.

The whey is completely skimmed of cream, after it has passed over the heat exchanger and through the centrifuge, before it enters the whey tank. It still contains protein and minerals and provides a valuable source of nutrition for pigs.

The temperature is regulated in the drying-room where the cheeses begin to form a crust. The salt dip promotes the formation of a perfect crust and determines the flavour and storage properties of the cheese.

The cheese is allowed to ferment and ripen naturally in cellars with a temperature of 14–15° C/57–59° F and a relative humidity of over 90%.

About five to seven weeks after manufacture the cheeses reach the retail trade, where they are stored and subjected to further quality controls relating to texture, hole formation, colour, appearance and smell.

The cheese-dealer regularly bastes the cheese with the so-called "Sulze" or "Schmiere", made from white wine, herbs and spices (a secret traditional recipe), which gives the "Appenzeller" its typical flavour and special aroma. After 3½–5 months the cheese is ripe and ready for sale.

Teufen
★ Fröhlichsegg

Teufen (837m/2746ft; pop. 5500) a favourite residential town a few kilometres from St Gallen, is situated on the southern slopes of the Fröhlichsegg (1003m/3291ft; 20 minutes to top; restaurant). In the handsome square stands an interesting church built in 1778 by the family of a local builder, Hans Ulrich Grubenmann. Domestic industry (embroidery, weaving).

Bühler

Beyond Teufen lies the pretty village of Bühler (828m/2717ft; pop. 1700), with trim houses in the local style.

Gais

Gais (933m/3061ft; pop. 2400) is a popular health resort with one of the prettiest squares in the region (typical houses with curved gables). This was the first resort to offer the whey cure – medical treatment involving the medicinal properties of milk. There is a school of folk art. From the top of the Gäbris (1247m/4091ft; 1 hour; inn) there are magnificent views in all directions (road closed on Saturdays and Sundays).

Stoss

4km/2 miles above Gais, on the Stoss pass (938m/3078ft; inn) are a chapel and a monument commemorating the victory of 400 Appenzellers over 3000 Austrians in 1405.

Speicher

5km/3 miles north-east of Teufen the health resort of Speicher (926m/3038ft; pop. 3350), is an idyllic village, to the north of which is the Vögelinsegg (959m/3146ft). Here stands a monument commemorating the Appenzellers' victory over the Abbot of St Gallen in 1403.

Trogen

Trogen (903m/2963ft; pop. 1950), the terminus of the St Gallen – Speicher – Trogen tramway, houses the cantonal court and the cantonal school. In the centre of the village is the Landsgemeindeplatz, the elegant square in which the cantonal assembly meets in even-numbered years (in Hundswil in odd-numbered years); the square is surrounded by fine 18th c. houses, a church built by Grubenmann in 1779 and the Town Hall.

Pestalozzi Children's Village

South-west of Trogen is the Pestalozzi Children's Village for orphans of many nationalities, founded by the Zurich philosopher Walter Robert Corti in 1946.

From Trogen a beautiful minor road leads via the Ruppen (1010m/3314ft; inn) into the Rhine valley.

Another winding road (14km/9 miles) runs via Wald and Scheidegg (side roads to Rehetobel and Oberegg) to Heiden (806m/2644ft; pop. 4000), a popular health resort in a park-like setting high above Lake Constance (rack-railway (cog-railway) from Rorschach, 7km/4 miles in 25 minutes). There is a museum in memory of Henri Dunant, founder of the Red Cross, who lived in Heiden from 1887 until his death in 1910. This village was rebuilt in the Biedermeier style following a fire in 1838.

Heiden

Dunant Museum

To the north, via Grub, lies the village of Wienacht (734m/2408ft) with the Tobel vineyards.

Wienacht

From Rheineck there is a rack-railway (1898m/6227ft long; 6 minutes to Walzenhausen (673m/2208ft; pop. 2000) above Lake Constance, and Oberegg (880m/2887ft; pop. 2500), an enclave of Innerrhoden, 3 km/2 miles south-west of which is the St Anton viewpoint (1121m/3678ft).

Rheineck, Walzenhausen, Oberegg

Between Herisau and Wattwil, on the Wasserfluh road, is Schönengrund (836m/2743ft), which has a chair-lift up Hochhamm (length 1345m/4413ft, height difference 328m/1076ft, time 15 minutes). On a ridge of hills is the highest holiday village in Ausserrhoden, Schwellbrunn (966m/3169ft; pop. 1200).

Schönengrund

Schwellbrunn

Arosa

R 8

Canton: Grisons (GR)
Altitude: 1740–1890m/5709–6201ft
Population: 2700

The popular summer and winter resort of Arosa seems in a world of its own, lying as it does in a sheltered hollow in the high valley of the Schanfigg, surrounded by mountains, well away from the main traffic routes of the Grisons. The road from Chur, almost 1200m/3937ft below, to Arosa is 30km/19 miles long and has many bends; there is also a narrow-gauge railway, opened in 1914, which takes just under an hour to reach the resort.

Situation

The first settlement in the Arosa valley, then accessible only by troublesome bridle-paths, was initiated about 1220 by the monasteries of Churwalden and Sankt Luzi in Chur, and soon afterwards the population was increased by some families brought in from the Valais by the Barons of Vaz. From 1320 to 1851 Arosa belonged to the parish and commune of Davos, but thereafter became an independent commune. In the 15th c. the village had a population of only 150. The little village church was built in 1490. In 1575 most of the mountain pastures were sold to the town of Chur, which still owns some land in the commune. By 1850 the population had fallen to no more than 50. In 1875, however, the post road from Chur to Langwies was constructed, and in 1890 it was extended to Arosa; in 1880 the Seehof hotel was built to provide accommodation for visitors. By the turn of the century Arosa had made a name for itself as a health resort, and in 1913 it ranked briefly as the leading resort in the Grisons. By 1930 the population had risen to 3724. The first ski school was opened in 1933, and the first three cableways were constructed in 1939.

History

With excellent facilities for walkers and climbers in summer and skiers in winter, provision for a great variety of sports and more than 150km/93 miles of footpaths, Arosa has developed into a leading resort. Other features of interest are the Late Gothic church (1493) in Inner-Arosa and the Schanfigg Local Museum (history of iron-mining and winter sports, open: Dec.–Mar., Tues., Fri. 2.30–4.30pm; mid June–mid Sept., Mon., Wed., Fri.

Townscape
★ Holiday resort

Arosa in winter

2.30–4.30pm). In summer a miniature railway operates at the Arosa Kulm Hotel. Driving is prohibited in the town after dark.

Arosa is an attractive town, with hotels dispersed about the beautiful sheltered valley and numerous small lakes. The tree-line passes through the resort, so that the skiing areas are almost completely open. The road from Chur runs from the Obersee (Upper Lake, 1740m/5709ft; rowing boats), beside the railway station, above the Untersee (Lower Lake 1694m/5558ft), in a charming wooded setting, past the Kursaal (gaming casino) and up above the tree-line to the Alpine meadows of Inner-Arosa, sloping gently uphill.

Maran

To the north is the mountain village of Maran, a favourite objective of walkers, reached on the "Eichhörnliweg" (Squirrel's Path). There are easy mountain walks over the Strela pass to Davos and by way of the Aroser Weisshorn to the Hörnligrat.

Cableways

Cableways from Arosa station to the Mittlere Hütte (2013m/6605ft) and the Weisshorn (2653m/8704ft; 30 minutes, restaurant) and from the lower station "Am Wasser" (1830m/6004ft) to the Hörnligrat (2493m/8180ft; 15 minutes; mountain hut, serviced).

Winter sports

Natural and artificial ice rinks (curling); toboggan run; cross-country ski-ing; ski-bob runs; ski-lifts on Tschuggen, Plattenhorn (2318m/7605ft), Hörnli, Carmenna (2177m/7143ft) and Alp Prätschli. The most popular ski runs are on the Weisshorn (2657m/8718ft), Brüggerhorn (2429m/7970ft; chair-lift) and Hörnli (2497m/8193ft); on all three are serviced ski huts.

Surroundings

Magnificent footpaths through the pine-forests and flower-spangled Alpine meadows: north over the Maran plateau to Alp Prätschli (2000m/6562ft; ski-lift), 1 hour from Inner-Arosa past the Schwellisee

(1919m/6296ft) to the romantic Aelplisee (2192m/7192ft), 1¾ hours; from the Untersee up the Welschtobel gorge to the waterfalls on the Alteinbach, 1 hour.

The best climbs are the Aroser Weisshorn (2653m/8704ft), 2½ hours by way of the Mittlere Hütte, easy, and the Aroser Rothorn (2984m/9791ft), 4 hours, rather more difficult, with superb views.

Ascona   N/O 11

Canton: Ticino (TI)
Altitude: 196m/643ft
Population: 5000

Thanks to its beautiful situation in a mist-free bay on Lake Maggiore, sheltered from the north winds, and to its sub-tropical vegetation, Ascona has developed from a little fishing village into one of Switzerland's most popular holiday resorts, excellently equipped for visitors. It has long hours of sunshine and a mild winter. The main areas of activity from spring into autumn are the picturesque town, a pedestrian precinct with numerous little shops, art galleries and antique dealers, and the piazza on the lake.

Situation and general

★Townscape

A prehistoric cemetery excavated in 1952 provided evidence of a Bronze Age settlement here (c. 800 B.C.). The town was "discovered" by a group of vegetarians and nature-worshippers who settled on Monte Verità before and during the First World War. The artists' colony of Ascona attracted such leading figures as Lenin, Leoncavallo, Isadora Duncan, J. C. Jung and Rudolf Steiner, and later residents included the writers Remarque and Herman Hesse and the painters Karl Hofer, W. Kandinsky, Paul Klee, M. von

History

Werefkin (to whom a museum is dedicated) and Jawlensky. In the 1930s many refugees from Nazism found a home on Lake Maggiore and, especially, in Ascona.

Sights

★Collegio
Pontificio Papio

The Collegio Pontificio Papio (c. 1584), by T. Pellegrini, has one of the finest Renaissance courtyards in Switzerland (two-storey loggias with Tuscan columns).

Santa Maria
della
Misericordia

The adjoining church of Santa Maria della Misericordia (1399–1442) has a cycle of frescoes by the Seregnesis and Antonio da Tradete, among others.

Parish church of
SS Pietro e
Paolo

The parish church of SS Pietro e Paolo (first referred to in 1264; rebuilt in the 16th c.), a pillared basilica with lateral aisles, has a high altar painting by Giovanni Serodine (1633), the "Coronation of the Virgin", and ceiling frescoes (1783) by Pietro Francesco Pancaldi-Mola.

Casa Serodine

Casa Serodine, or Casa Borrani, opposite the parish church, was built c. 1620 as a residence for the Serodine patrician family. It has a sumptuous three-storey façade of Baroque stucco (including a seated Madonna and balustrade friezes with mythical creatures and biblical scenes). They are by Giovanni Battista Serodine (1587–1626), brother of the artist Giovanni Serodine (1594–1630). The Libreria della Rondine which is housed here is the best bookshop in Switzerland on the subject of Ticino.

Museo
Comunale
d'Arte Moderna

In the former palazzo of Bartolomeo Papio in Via Borgo (No. 34; closed on Mon.) the Museo Comunale has an important art collection including works by Marianne von Werefkin (1860–1938), Richard Seewald (1896–1976), Franz Marc, Maurice Utrillo, Paul Klee, Hermann Hesse and Fritz Pauli. Special exhibitions are held during the summer months. Paintings are also exhibited in the Casa Beato P. Berno, a typical Ticinese Baroque house (craft centre; Via Collegio).

★Monte Verità

Monte Verità, 321m/1053ft, stands north-west of Ascona. In 1926 the Dutch Baron Eduard von der Heidt purchased a plot here to build the Monte Verità seminary hotel. Nearby stands the Casa Anatta, at one time the residence and social functions building of the founder of the local vegetarian co-operative. Today it houses a museum portraying the history of the socio-utopian reform movement in and around Ascona since 1870. In the neighbouring Casa Selma, built in 1900, there are more documents relating to the Monte Verità movement.

In the Chiaro Mondo dei Beati, rebuilt in 1986, hangs the circular painting, 25m/82ft in circumference, by the Baltic artist Elisar van Kupffer (1872–1942). All three exhibition buildings are open: Apr.–Oct. Tues.–Sun. 2.30–6pm.

Madonna della
Fontana

On the northern slope of Monte Verità stands the pilgrimage church of the Madonna della Fontana, built over a spring in 1617–77. It has no tower. The fresco decoration is also 17th c.

Other places of
interest

On a hill to the north of the town centre are the scant remains of the Castello San Materno, the town's oldest fortress which was probably razed to the ground in 1518. The Romanesque San Materno chapel has been preserved; in the apse is a *majestas Domini* (c. 1200).

Teatro
San Materno

Nearby stands the Teatro San Materno, built in 1927–28 to plans by Carl Weidemeyer in the Bauhaus style as a school of dancing for Charlotte Bara; today it is again being used for that purpose.

Epper Museum

The Epper Museum displays works by the Swiss Expressionist painters Ignaz and Mischa Epper (Via Albarelle 14; open: Apr.–Oct. Tues.–Sun. 3–6pm).

In the south-east, on the peninsula formed by the Maggia delta, lie the large lido, an 18-hole golf-course and the airport.

Surroundings

The road to Verbania (No. 13) follows the steep north-west shore of Lake Maggiore (see entry). To the right, high above the lake, is the picturesque village of Ronco; to the left are two small islands, the Isole di Brissago or dei Conigli ("Rabbit Islands"), on the larger of which is an interesting Botanic garden of Mediterranean flora. 3.5km/2 miles away is Port Ronco, where a minor road from Ronco joins on the right.

★★ Lake
Maggiore

3.5km/2 miles is Brissago (219m/719ft), a popular summer resort (bathing lido), also noted for the manufacture of cigars ("Brissago", a long thin Virginia cigar). The town is charmingly situated at the foot of Monte Limidario (2189 m/7182 ft), on the lower slopes of which are beautiful gardens with Mediterranean plants and vineyards. 2km/1 mile beyond Brissago, at the little Lombard-style Renaissance church of the Madonna del Ponte (1528), is the Italian frontier.

Brissago

Baden

L 3

Canton: Aargau
Altitude: 385m/1263ft
Population: 15,000

The health resort of Baden has long been an important market town. The picturesque old town, the core of the medieval settlement, lies in the Limmat defile under the Lägern hills; downstream is the spa, with its 19 sulphur springs (48° C/118° F), already used for medicinal purposes in Roman times. To the west of the spa, where the valley opens out, are the newer parts of the town, with large industrial plants, (Brown-Boveri).

Situation and
general

Known to the Romans as Aquae Helvetiae, Baden became in the Middle Ages the country's leading curative resort, the hot sulphurous water (1000 cu.m/35,310 cu.ft daily) being piped up from a great depth. The town's central situation and its political activity made it a place of importance in the old Confederation, and the Diet frequently met here. The first hydro-electric power station was brought into operation in Baden in 1892.

History

Sights

At the entrance to the fine old town, to the north, stands the 15th c. Bruggerturm (54m/177ft high). A little way south-east is the Roman Catholic parish church (built 1457–70, remodelled in Baroque style in 1612–98 and in Neo-Classical style in 1813–29), and facing it, to the north, the Stadthaus (Town Hall), with the Council Chamber (reconstructed in 1497) in which the Diet met between 1424 and 1712. The Swiss Children's Museum (29 Ölrainstrasse), situated about three minutes from the station, gives an insight into the history and manufacture of toys (open: Wed.,Sat. and Sun.). A covered wooden bridge (1810) leads across the Limmat to the Landvogteischloss (rebuilt 1487–89), the old governor's residence, which – together with adjoining extension built in 1992 by W. and K. Steib – now houses the Historical Museum (closed Mon.).

★ Old town

Children's
Museum

Historical
Museum

On a crag to the west of the old town (road and rail tunnel) is the ruined castle of Stein, formerly a Habsburg seat.

Castle Stein ruin

At Kappelerhof power station a small technical museum has impressive exhibits from the pioneering age of electricity production (open: Tues.– Sun. 2–5pm).

Kappelerhof

Baden, on the Limmat

★Brown Art Collection
The art collection of Sidney and Jenny Brown can be seen in the Langmatt Villa (Römerstrasse 30), built in the Art Nouveau style in 1900/1901 by R. Curjel and K. Moser. The collection includes works by Cézanne, Gauguin, Monet, Degas, Sisley, Bonnard, Van Gogh and Renoir. The furniture and fittings also provide an insight into the life-style of an industrial family in the first half of the 20th c. (open: Apr.–Oct., closed Mon.).

Spa
The spa is beautifully laid out with gardens, and has a Kursaal, with a gaming room, restaurant, inhalatorium (establishment where sulphur vapour can be inhaled) and an indoor thermal swimming pool. A high-level bridge crosses the Limmat to Ennetbaden (358m/1175ft; pop. 2900), on the right bank.

Surroundings

Baden is a good base for walks and climbs in the Lägern hills. 2¼ hours from Ennetbaden rises the Burghorn (863m/2832ft), the highest point in these eastern outliers of the Jura (views of the Alps and Black Forest); ½ hour east above the Limmat bridge, is Schartenfels (467m/1532ft; restaurant), and 2km/1 mile west Baldegg (572m/1877ft; restaurant), with a view of the Alps.

Wettingen
South of Baden the largest commune in the Aargau, Wettingen (395m/1296ft; pop. 19,500), was once a sleepy little wine-growing village, which has developed since the last war into a favourite residential town. In the bend of the Limmat is the best preserved Cistercian monastery in the country, now a teachers' training college. The abbey (founded 1227) has superb Late Renaissance and Rococo decoration, finely carved choir-stalls and in the cloister some of the best stained glass in Switzerland (182 roundels with coats of arms and figures, 13th–17th c.). The extensive renovations to the exterior and the redevelopment of the cloister and

★Cistercian monastery

Baden: Old Town, with Bruggerturm

Brugg: Vindonissa Museum

chapter-house were completed in 1988. Refurbishment of the interior commenced in 1990 and should last about four years.

10km/6 miles north-west of Baden lies Brugg (355m/1165ft), an old town of 7000 inhabitants and an important traffic junction near the confluence of the Aare, the Reuss and the Limmat. As the name indicates it grew up around its bridge, near which are the Black Tower (Schwarzer Turm, 11th c.) and the Town Hall. In the old-world main street (No. 39) stands the house in which the educationist Heinrich Pestalozzi (1746–1827) died; his grave is at Birr, 7km/4 miles south. The Vindonissa Museum contains a rich collection of material from the Roman fort of Vindonissa (first century A.D., now called Windisch).

Brugg

Vindonissa Museum

The Zurich road (No. 3) passes the former convent of Königsfelden (on left), founded in 1308 by Elisabeth , widow of the German King Albrecht I, on the spot where he was murdered by Duke Johann of Swabia. The convent was converted into a mental hospital in 1866–72. The choir of the Gothic church has magnificent 14th c. stained glass.

★Königsfelden convent

1km/½ mile beyond this is Windisch (568m/1864ft; to the left of road), on the left bank of the Reuss, the site of Roman Vindonissa (finds in Brugg – see above). On the road to Lucerne, which goes off on the left just before

Windisch

the village, are remains of a large amphitheatre which could seat 10,000 spectators.

Basle   H 3

Canton: Basel-Stadt (BS)
Altitude: 273–282m/895–925ft
Population: 200,000

★★Situation and Townscape

Basle (German Basel, French Bâle), Switzerland's second largest city, lying close to the French and German frontiers, has been an independent half-canton (Basel-Stadt) since 1833, the other half being Basel-Land. The city is built on both sides of the Rhine, which here takes a sharp turn northward between the Swiss Jura and the Black Forest to enter the Upper Rhine plain; upstream from Basle the river is known as the High Rhine (Hochrhein). Grossbasel (Great Basle), the city's commercial and cultural centre, lies on the higher left bank; Kleinbasel (Little Basel), where most of its industry is situated, on the flat right bank.

General

Situated on the Swiss frontier and at an important river crossing, Basle soon developed into an important commercial town. Its heavy commercial traffic is now served by two large railway stations and the Rhine harbour (Rheinhafen) at Kleinhüningen, 8km/5 miles north of the city on the right bank of the river (shipping exhibition, "Our Way to the Sea"; viewing terrace on the grain elevator, 55km/180ft high). At St Louis, 9.5km/6 miles north-west in French territory, is the Basle–Mulhouse–Freiburg International Airport, which is to be expanded into an International-European airport in the 1990s.

The city's main industries are the manufacture of chemicals and pharmaceuticals, machinery and electrical equipment, textiles and foodstuffs; it also has numerous banks including the head office of the Bank of International Settlements.

Basle: View across the Rhine to the Minster

In the second half of the 1st c. B.C. the hill on which the Minster now stands   History
was occupied by a Celtic settlement, remains of the ramparts of which have
been found in the Rittergasse. The proximity of the Roman town of Augusta
Raurica, founded in 44 B.C. (see p. 126), led to the establishment of a Roman
military station on the hill in 15 B.C. The name Basilia ("royal fortress") first
appears in the records in A.D. 374, and soon after that date there is a
reference to Basle as the see of a bishop. In the 10th c. the town belonged to
Burgundy, and in 1025 it became part of the German Empire. A long history
of conflict with the house of Habsburg ended in 1501 when the town joined
the Swiss Confederation. In 1529 it went over to the reformed faith. The
university, founded by Pope Pius II in 1460, became, thanks to the presence
of Erasmus from 1521 onwards, the principal centre of humanism, and its
fame was maintained by a series of distinguished scholars and teachers
in later periods: the physician Paracelsus lived in Basle in 1527–28, the
mathematicians Jakob and Johann Bernoulli taught in the university in the
17th and 18th c., the cultural and art historian Jakob Burckhardt from 1858
to 1893, the philosopher Friedrich Nietzsche from 1869–79. Among the
artists connected with Basle were Hans Holbein the Younger (b. 1497 in
Augsburg, d. 1543 in London), who spent many years in Basle between
1515 and 1538, and the 19th c. painter Arnold Böcklin (b. Basle 1827, d.
Fiesole 1901).

Museums, Galleries, etc.

Anatomical Museum (Anatomisches Museum)   **In the city**
Pestalozzistrasse 20
By arrangement; tel. (061) 2 67 35 35
Mon.–Fri. 8am–noon, 2–5.30pm

Antiquities, Museum of (Antikenmuseum) and Ludwig Collection
St-Alban-Graben 5
Tues.–Sun. 10am–5pm

Architectural Museum (Architekturmuseum)
Pfluggässlein 3
Tues.–Fri. 1–6pm, Sat. 10am–4pm, Sun. 10am–1pm

Basle Paper Museum and Museum of Script and Printing (Basler Papiermühle), St Alban-Tal 35–37
Tues.–Sun. 2–5pm

Botanical Garden of the University (Botanischer Garten der Universität)
Schönbeinstrasse 6, near the Spalentor (gate)
Jan.–Mar. and Oct.–Dec. Mon.–Sun. 8am–5pm; Apr.–Sept. 8am–8pm

Caricatures and Cartoons, Collection of (Sammlung Karikaturen und
Cartoons), St Alban-Vorstadt 9
Jan.–June, Aug.–Dec. Wed. 4–6pm, Sat. 3–5.30pm, Sun. 10am–4pm

City and Minster Museum (Stadt- und Münstermuseum; architectural
sculpture from Basle Minster from the 11th–15th c.)
Kleines Klingental, Unterer Rheinweg 26
Tues.–Sat. 2–5pm, Sun. 10am–5pm

Ethnographical Museum (Museum für Völkerkunde)
Augustinergasse 2
Jan.–Apr. and Nov.–Dec. Tues.–Sat. 10am–noon, 2–5pm, Sun. 10–5pm;
May–Oct. Tues.–Sun. 10am–5pm

Fire Brigade Museum
Kornhausgasse 18
Sun. 2–5pm

© Baedeker

Basel

200 m

Rheinhafen
Schweiz. Schiffahrtsmuseum   St.- Joseph- Kirche   Freiburg/Br.

Badischer Bahnhof (DB)

Frankreich

Elsässer
Rheinweg

Blasiring

Breisacher

Klybeckstrasse

Matthäus-
kirche

Bärenfelserstr.

Hammerstrasse

Maulbeer-
strasse

St.-Johannes-
Tor

St.-Johannes

St.-Johannes-Platz

Feldbergstrasse

Erasmus-
platz

Haltingerstrasse

Riehenring

Schweizer
Muster-
messe

Johanniterbrücke

Unterer

strasse

Sperrstrasse

Claragraben

Messe-
platz

Frankreich

Flughafen
Basel-Mulhouse

Frauen-
spital

Spitalstrasse

Schanzen

Rhein

Klingentalgr.

Klingentalstrasse

Clara-
matte

strasse

Drahtzug-

strasse

Kongress-
zentrum

Kantons-
spital

Prediger-
kirche

Johannis Vorstadt

Klingentalfähre

Weberg

Untere

Clara-

Riehenstrasse

Gewerbeschule

Skulpturenhalle

Hebelstrasse

Blumenrain

Petersgraben

Stadt- und
Münster-
museum

Rheinweg

Greifengasse

Clara-
kirche

Claragraben

Hammerstrasse

Universitäts-
bibliothek

Peters-
kirche

Petersgasse

Gerbergässlein

Utengasse

Rheingasse

Wettstein-
platz

Grenz-
acher
Str.

Bad Säckingen

Sportmuseum

Botan.
Garten

Peters-
platz

Stadt-
haus

Mitt. Rheinbrücke

Oberer

Rheingasse

St.-
Theodor-
Kirche

Alemannen-
gasse

Spalentor

Universität

Museum
für Gestaltung

Spalenvorstadt

Pharmaz.-
histor.
Museum

Martins-
kirche

Rathaus

Markt-
platz

Natur- und
Volkskunde-
Museum

Rheinsprung

Münsterberg

Pfalz

Rheinweg

Schaffhauser
Rheinweg

Jüd.
Museum

Feuerw.-
Mus.

Schützen-
graben

Leonhardsgraben

Korngasse

Heuberg

Freie

Gerbergasse

strasse

Münster-
platz

Münster

Rittergasse

St.-Alban-Rheinweg

Wettsteinbrücke

Rhein

Museum für
Gegenwartskunst,
St.-Alban-Kirche, Papiermühle

Holbein-
platz

Leonhards-
kirche

Kohlenberg

Barfüsser-
platz

Histor.
Museum

Antiken-
museum

St.-Alban-Gr.

Karikaturen-
Sammlung

St.-Alban-Vorstadt

Zürich, Bern
Augusta Raurica
St.-Alban-Tor

Eulerstrasse

Synagoge

Stei-

Musikinstr.-
Sammlung

nenberg

Casino

Steinenberg

Kunst-
museum

St.-Marien

Austrasse

Leimenstrasse

Theaterstrasse

Tinguely-
Brunnen

Stadt-
theater

Kunst-
halle

Elisabethen-
kirche

Dufourstrasse

Malzgasse

Gellertstrasse

Byfangweg

Holbeinstrasse

Komödie

Steinentorstrasse

Kirschgarten-
Museum

Aeschen-
platz

St.-Alban-Anlage

Engelgasse

Bahnhof
BTB

Heuwaageviadukt

Elisabethen-
schanze

Elisabethenstr.

Aeschengraben

strasse

Lange Gasse

St.-Jakobs-

Hallenbad

Birsig

Viaduktstrasse

Markthalle

Garten-

strasse

Nauenstrasse

Birsigstrasse

Schützenmattpark
Pauluskirche

Zoo-
logischer
Garten

Vivarium

Binningerstrasse

Erdbeergr.

Margarethenstr.

SNCF

Centralbahnstrasse

BIZ

Bahnhof
SBB

PTT

Rosenfeld-
park

Chr.-
Merian-
Park

Belfort   Delémont

Swiss Folk Museum (Schweizerisches Museum für Volkskunde; part of the Ethnographical Museum; Swiss folk culture in particular and that of Europe in general)
Münsterplatz 20
Jan.–Apr. and Dec., Tues.–Sun. 10am–noon, 2–5pm;
May–Oct. Tues.–Sun. 10am–5pm

Haus zum Kirschgarten (domestic culture and collections of arts and crafts 18th–20th c.)
Elisabethenstrasse 27
Nov.–Apr. Tues.–Sun. 10am–noon, 2–5pm;
May–Oct. Tues.–Sun. 10am–5pm

Historical Museum (Historisches Museum; Barfüsserkirche)
Barfüsserplatz
Mon., Wed.–Sun. 10am–5pm

Jewish Museum of Switzerland (Jüdisches Museum der Schweiz)
Kornhausgasse 8
Mon., Wed. 2–5pm, Sun. 10am–noon, 2–5pm

Museum of Form and Layout (Museum für Gestaltung)
Spalenvorstadt 2
Tues.–Fri. noon–7pm, Sat., Sun. noon–5pm

Musical Instrument Collection (Musikinstrumenten-Sammlung)
Leonhardstrasse 8
Tues., Fri. 2–5pm, Sun. 10am–noon, 2–5pm

Natural History Museum (Naturhistorisches Museum)
Augustinergasse 2. Tues.–Sat. 10am–noon, 2–5pm

Pharmacy, Swiss Museum of the History of (Schweizerisches Pharmazie-Historisches Museum)
Totengässlein 3. Mon.–Fri. 9am–noon, 2–5pm

Public Art Collection (Öffentliche Kunstsammlung)
Art museum, art gallery (mainly Renaissance artists, Flemish and Dutch masters of the 15th–17th c.; 19th c. Swiss artists and 20th c. Cubists)
St Alban Graben 16
Tues.–Sun. 10am–5pm
Collection of drawings, address as above (mainly views of the town by Matthäus Merians the Elder)
Tues.–Fri. 9am–noon, 2–6pm, Sat. 9am–noon, 2–5pm
Museum of Contemporary Art (Museum für Gegenwartskunst)
St Alban-Rheinweg 60
Tues.–Sun. 11am–5pm

Sculpture Hall (Skulpturhalle)
Mittlere Strasse. Tues.–Sun. 10am–noon, 2–5pm

Swiss Sports Museum
Missionstrasse 28 (near the Spalentor gate)
Mon.–Fri. 10am–5pm, Sat. 2–5pm, Sun. 10am–noon, 2–5pm

Jean Tinguely Museum
New building on the banks of the Rhine; planned to open in 1996

Zoological Garden (Zoologische Garten)
Binningerstrasse 40
Jan.–Feb. 8am–5.30pm, Mar., Apr. 8am–6pm, May–Aug. 8am–6.30pm, Sept., Oct. 8am–6pm, Nov., Dec. 8am–5.30pm

Basle

In the surrounding area	Augusta Raurica (Roman house, museum and domestic animal park)
Augst	Giebenacherstrasse 17
	Jan., Feb., Nov., Dec. Mon. 1.30–5pm, Tues.–Sun. 10am–noon, 1.30–5pm; Mar.–Oct. Mon. 1–5pm, Tues.–Sun. 10am–noon, 1.30–6pm. Domestic animal park: Jan., Feb., Nov., Dec. Mon.–Sun. 10am–4pm; Mar.–Oct. Mon.–Sun. 10am–5pm
Riehen	Cat Museum (Katzen-Museum)
	Baselstrasse 101
	Sun. 10am–noon, 2–5pm
	Toy Museum (Spielzeugmuseum)
	Baselstrasse 34
	(Wed. 2–7pm, Thur.–Sat. 2–5pm, Sun. 10am–noon, 2–5pm)
	Village and Viticulture Musuem (Dorf- und Rebbaumuseum)
	Baselstrasse 34 (opening times as for Toy Museum)
Rheinhafen	Switzerland's Transport Turntable and "Our Way to the Sea" (Verkehrsdrehscheibe Schweiz und unser Weg zum Meer)
	Westkaistr. 2, Kleinhüningen, Rheinhafen
Münchenstein	Brüglingen Mill Museum (Mühlenmuseum Brüglingen)
	Brüglingerstrasse 6 (entrance from car park near St Jakob Stadium in Basle)
	Visits by arrangement; tel. (061) 3 11 72 14
	Carriage and Toboggan Collection in the Historical Museum (Kutschen- und Schlittensammlung im Historischen Museum)
	Wed., Sat., Sun. 2–5pm
	Frog Museum (Froschmuseum)
	Grabenackenstrasse 8, Münchenstein
	First Sunday in the month 2–5pm and by arrangement; tel. (061) 4 11 77 03
Weil am Rhein	Vitra Design Museum
	D-79576 Weil am Rhein, Charles-Eames-Str. 1
	Wed.–Fri. 2–6pm, Sat., Sun. and public holidays 11am–5pm

Description of the Town

Gross-Basel (Great Basle) and Klein-Basel (Little Basle) are linked by six bridges over the Rhine. From the Mittlere Rheinbrücke (Middle Rhine Bridge, 1905), on the position of the first bridge in Basle, built in 1225, there is a fine view of the Minster. Upstream from this bridge are the busy Wettsteinbrücke (built 1879, widened 1937), the Schwarzwaldbrücke (Black Forest Bridge, 1973), which is designed for through traffic and the Eisenbahnbrücke (Railway Bridge), together with the dam of the Birsfelden hydro-electric power station. Downstream are the Johanniterbrücke (built 1882, rebuilt 1934). There are also three ferries, driven by the current, with no motors.

Gross-Basel, on the left bank of the Rhine, still preserves in the central area some features reminiscent of an old Imperial city, in spite of its many modern buildings and its busy commercial activity.

Around the Market Square

★**Rathaus**

The Mittlere Brücke leads into the Marktplatz (Market Square), which is dominated by the brightly painted Rathaus (Council House). The main building, with arcades, is in Late Burgundian Gothic style (1504–21); the front chancellery was added to the central section in 1606–08, while the

114

Basle: the Minster . . .   *. . . and façade of the Town Hall*

new wing to the left and the tall tower on the right are 19th c. additions. The clock is the work of the Master Wilhelms (1511/1512). The wall-paintings in the attractive courtyard are in part the work of Hans Bock (1608–11; restored). The statue (1574) on the outer staircase represents the legendary founder of the town, Munatius Plancus. When the council is not sitting visitors can see the two council chambers (the Regierungsratsaal with its impressive wood panelling and the Grossratsaal, which contains 15 coat-of-arms of the Swiss cantons).

A little way west, at the corner of the Marktplatz and Freie Strasse is the Renaissance Geltenzunfthaus (1578), the guild-house of the wine merchants. In the same street (No. 25) the guild-house of the locksmiths (Ruman Faesch 1488), charmingly decorated in Baroque style in 1733, now houses a restaurant. The guild-house of the Hausgenossen (No. 34), has attractive wall-paintings.

Freie Strasse

A little way west, at Stadthausgasse 13, we find the Rococo Stadthaus (Town House, 1771), and at Totengässlein 3 the Swiss Museum of the History of Pharmacy.

Stadthaus
History of
Pharmacy
Museum

North-west of the Marktplatz is the little Fischmarkt, with a Gothic fountain decorated with saints and angels playing harps, etc. (1851 reproduction: original in Historical Museum).

Fish market
fountain

★ Minster

South-east of the Marktplatz the long Münsterhügel (Minster Hill) rises above the Rhine (reached from St-Alban-Graben by way of Rittergasse). The spacious Münsterplatz, on the site of the Roman fort, is an elegant 18th c. square.

Minster Hill

Basle

The Minster stands on the highest point of the hill, dominating the city with its two slender spires, its masonry of red Vosges sandstone and its colourful patterned roof. The oldest parts of the building date from the 9th–13th c. It was rebuilt in Gothic style after an earthquake in 1356, and was a cathedral until the Reformation. The high altar and much of the furnishings were destroyed by militant Protestants in 1529. The church's greatest treasures were concealed in the vaulting of the sacristy and escaped destruction, but were sold when the canton was divided into two in 1833 and are now partly in the Historical Museum in Basle and partly dispersed among other museums throughout the world.

The West Front

The west front and towers are entirely Gothic, with the exception of the lower part of the north tower (St George's tower), which dates from the end of the 11th c. St George's tower, with its elegant upper part and spire, is 64.2m/211ft in height, the south tower (St Martin's), completed in 1500, is 62.7m/206ft high.

The sculptured friezes above the main doorway depict prophets in the outer frieze, roses in the middle one and dancing angels in the inner one. To the right of the doorway is a figure of the "Prince of this world" dallying with one of the Foolish Virgins: from the front he looks like a fine young man, but his back is crawling with adders and noxious vermin symbolising corruption. To the left of the doorway are depicted the founder of the church, the Emperor Henry II, with a model of the building, and the

Basle Minster

A Münch chapel
B Neuenburg chapel
C Aspelt chapel
D Schaler chapel
E Gallus chapel
F Stephen chapel
G Fröwler chapel
H Tegernau chapel
I   Bebelnheim chapel

1 Main doorway (c. 1300)
2 St George
3 St Martin
4 St George's tower (1421–28)
5 St Martin's tower (1488–1500)
6 Organ (1955)
7 Former choir screen (1381)
8 Fragments of stalls (c. 1375)
9 Hartung and Johannes Münch monuments (late 14th c.)

10 Monument of R. von Tierstein (d. 1318); tomb of Thüring von Ramstein (d. 1367)
11 Tombstones of Oregius de Conflens and Bartolomeo de la Capra
12 Monument of Erasmus (d. 1536)
13 St Vincent panel (c. 1190)
14 Tomb of Katharina von Baden-Tierstein (d. 1385)
15 Tomb of Georg von Andlau (d. 1466)
16 St Gallus doorway (12th c.)
17 Communion table (1580)
18 Choir-stalls (late 14th c.) used as rood-screen
19 Entrances to crypt (bishops' tombs, 10th–13th c.; ceiling frescoes, early 10th c.; lapidarium)

20 Tomb of Anna von Hohenberg (Habsburg)
21 Late Romanesque wall-paintings and dedicatory inscription of 1202
22 Font (1465)
23 Bishop's throne (1380)
24 Apostles panel (11th c.)
25 Pulpit (1486)
26 Fragment of pavement from an earlier church, with a drawing of a dragon (c. 1170)
27 Tomb recess of Walter von Klingen (d. 1380)
28 Gravestone of Heinrich von Flachslanden (d. 1353)
29 External crypt (9th c.)

Empress Kunigunde. Farther out, under the towers, two mounted saints represent St George (left) and St Martin (right) and above the latter are a clock and a sundial. On the central gable the figures of the founders appear again, and above them, enthroned and bearing the infant Jesus, is the Virgin (to whom the church is dedicated).

The St Gallus doorway (restored 1988/89) in the north transept (12th c.), with numerous Romanesque figures showing an archaic severity of style, is one of the oldest figured doorways in German-speaking territory. Between the slender columns on either side of the doorway are four figures, two on each side, identified by their symbols (the ox, the lion, the eagle and the angel) as Luke, Mark, John and Matthew. To right and left of the Evangelists are six tabernacles with representations of the Six Works of Mercy; above them are John the Baptist with the Lamb of God (left) and John the Evangelist; and above these figures again are two angels with the trumpets of the Last Judgment. The tympanum above the doorway depicts the Wise and Foolish Virgins, with Christ enthroned above them as the Judge of the world, flanked by Peter and Paul, who present to him the foundress and the sculptor. The large rose window above the St Gallus doorway symbolises the Wheel of Fortune. The choir, the lower part of which is Romanesque, has round arches borne on capitals with rich foliage decoration surmounted by figures of animals. In the paving east of the choir are lines showing the plan of a 9th c. external crypt which was discovered in 1947.

★ St Gallus Doorway

The church, which was carefully investigated and restored between 1963 and 1975, is 65m/213ft long by 32.5m/107ft across, with double lateral aisles; the outer aisles were originally a series of interconnected chapels. The raised choir is surrounded by an ambulatory, and under it is the crypt. The Gothic organ gallery was originally a rood-screen which until 1852 separated the chancel from the nave. In front of the pulpit, under glass, is a piece of the Late Romanesque pavement (12th c.). The Romanesque capitals in the nave and ambulatory are very fine. On the north side of the ambulatory is the sarcophagus of Anna von Hohenberg, wife of Rudolf of Habsburg, and her young son Karl (d. 1271).

Interior

Most of the interior furnishings were destroyed in 1529 by Protestants at the Reformation. The elaborately decorated High Gothic altar was the work of Hans von Nussdorf, builder of the Minster (1486). In the outer north aisle are a number of tombs and the monument of Erasmus, who died in Basle in 1536. The panel near here depicting eight scenes from the martyrdom and death of St Vincent of Saragossa and another panel depicting the Apostles in the outer south aisle date from the 11th c. and may be by the same sculptor. The choir-stalls, now at the entrance and the crossing as well as in the choir, are of the late 14th c. The Crypt, which can be entered from either side of the choir, contains the tombs of bishops of the 10th to the 13th c. and other monuments. The Romanesque frieze on the piers shows fabulous themes, hunting scenes and interlace ornament. The ceiling frescoes depict scenes from the life of the Virgin, the childhood of Christ and the lives of St Martin of Tours and St Margaret. On either side of the altar, formerly dedicated to the Virgin, are life-size Romanesque statues of bishops, dated by an inscription to 1202. On the right-hand side of the altar recess, also identified by an inscription, is Bishop Adalbero, builder of the earlier cathedral of 1019. Under the crossing are a collection of lapidary material and the recently excavated walls of a still earlier church of the early 9th c.

★Crypt

The very beautiful double cloister (entrance from Rittergasse), built in the 15th c. on Romanesque foundations, contains many monuments ranging over a period of five centuries, including that of the mathematician Bernoulli (d. 1705). The south tower can be climbed; access from inside the church.

★Cloister

Behind the Minster is the Pfalz ("Palace"), a terrace 20m/66ft above the Rhine with fine views of the river and the Black Forest hills.

Museum of Art

I. FIRST FLOOR

GROUND FLOOR (not shown)
Entrance courtyard: Sculptures by August Rodin ("The Burgers of Calais"), Alexander Calder, Hans Arp and Eduardo Chillida; temporary exhibitions, engravings (over 100,000 examples); study and reading room of the library lecture hall; museum café.

FIRST FLOOR

1–13 *German and Swiss painting of 15th and 16th c.*
 1 Romanesque wall-paintings
 2 Konrad Witz
 3 School of Witz (1450–80)
 4 Hans Fries, Hans Holbein the Elder ("Death of the Virgin")
 5 Holbein the Elder, Lucas Cranach the Elder
 6 Hans Baldung, Cranach, Niklaus Manuel-Deutsch ("Judgment of Paris")
 7 Mathias Grünewald, Albrecht Altdorfer, Baldung ("Death and the Maiden", "Death and the Woman"), Hans Leu
 8 Hans Holbein the Younger (selection of drawings)
 9 Ambrosius Holbein, Hans Holbein the Younger (double portrait of Jakob Meyer zum Hasen, burgomaster of Basle, and his wife; portrait of Bonifacius Amerbach; portraits of Erasmus)
 10 Holbein the Younger, religious paintings ("Dead Christ", "Last Supper", panel of the Passion)
 11 Holbein the Younger, late portraits ("Family Group")
 12 Hans Bock the Elder (also Dutch painting of the 15th–17th c.)
 13 Tobias Stimmer, Bock; El Greco

12, 14–21 *Dutch painting of the 15th–17th c.*
 12 Quentin Matsys, Katharina von Hemessen, Frans Floris
 14 Jan Breughel the Elder, Joos de Momper, Tobias Verhaecht, etc.
 15 Rembrandt ("David presenting Goliath's Head to King Saul"), Pieter Lastman, Govert Flinck,

Leonhard Bramer, etc.
16–17 Flemish and Dutch landscapes: David Teniers the Younger, Jan van Goyen, Salomon van Ruysdael, Jacob van Ruisdael, Frans Post
 18 Adriaen Brouwer, Teniers, Adriaen van Ostade, Paulus Potter, etc.
 19 Jan van der Heyden, Pieter de Hooch, etc.
 20 Nicolaes Maes, Casper Netscher
 21 Jan van de Velde III, Willem van Aelst, Jan Fyt, etc.

22–23 *18th c. painting*
 22 Hyacinthe Rigaud, Anton Graff, Hubert Robert, Johann Heinrich Füssli (Fuseli), etc.
 23 Swiss Alpine and landscape pictures: Caspar Wolf

24–25 *Romantic Neo-classicism*
 24 Peter Birman, Joseph Anton Koch ("Macbeth and the Witches"), Charles Gleyre
 25 Ferdinand von Olivier, Friedrich Overbeck, Moritz von Schwind, Carl Gustav Carus, Emilie Linder
 26 Early 19th c. Swiss landscapists

27–34 *19th c. French painting*
 27 Théodore Géricault, Eugène Delacroix, Camille Corot ("Italienne à la Fontaine")
28–34 Gustave Courbet, Edouard Manet, Auguste Renoir, Camille Pissarro, Claude Monet, Edgar Degas ("Le Jockey blessé"), Paul Cézanne ("Montagne Sainte-Victoire"), Paul Gauguin ("Ta Matete"), Vincent van Gogh
 29 *German painting of the 19th c. (second half)*
 Hans von Marées ("Self-Portrait in High Hat")

35–36 *19th c. Swiss painting*
 35 Ferdinand Hodler ("The Valiant Wife", Lake Geneva from Chexbres")
 36 Anselm Feuerbach ("Self Portrait", "Death of Pietro Aretino"), Arnold Böcklin ("Fight with Centaurs", "Island of the Dead", "Odysseus and Calypso", "The Plague")

118

Museum of Art

II. SECOND FLOOR

SECOND FLOOR

20th c. painting and sculpture

1 Pop art

2 Pablo Picasso ("Pains et compotier aux fruits sur une table", "L'aficionado", "Le poète", "Femme à la guitare")

3 "Les Fauves" art group around Henri Matisse ("La Berge", "La Danse" La Musique)

4 Henri Rousseau ("The Customs Officer", "La muse inspirant le poète", "Primeval landscape with setting sun"), Georges Roualt

5 Georges Braque ("Violon et cruche", "Le Portugais"), Juan Gris ("Le Violon")

6 The Blue Rider group, Orphism, Futurism

7 Marc Chagall ("Portrait de ma fiancée en gants noirs", "The Stockdealer")

8 Fernand Léger ("La femme en bleu", "Eléments mécaniques", "La femme et l'enfant")

9 Expressionism, New Functionalism: Paula Modersohn-Becker ("Self Portrait"), Lovis Corinth ("Ecce Homo"), Franz Marc ("Destiny of Animals"), Oscar Schlemmer ("Four Figures in space – Roman", "Frauentreppe"), Oskar Kokoschka ("Storm"), Max Beckmann ("Nice in Frankfurt"), Otto Dix ("The Artist's Parents")

10 Alberto Giacometti ("Self Portrait", "Palais à 4 heures du matin", "La Place")

11 Paul Klee ("Villa R", "Senecio", "Old Sound", "Ad marginem", "Rich Harbour"

12 De Stijl; Constructivism: Piet Mondrian ("Composition aux couleurs gris"); Theo van Doesburg ("Composition XII en blanc et noir"); El Lissitzky ("Proun 1 D"); Làszlò Moholy-Nagy ("Construction LIV"); Georges Vantongerloo ("Construction $Y = axy - bxx + cx$"); Antione Pevsner ("Construction surface développable") Hans Arp ("Cloud Arrow"; relief); Sophie Taeubner-Arp ("Moving picture circle")

13 Dadaism, Surrealism: Salvador Dali ("The Burning Giraffe"); Max Ernst ("La grande forêt")

14 Robert Rauschenberg, Cy Twombly, Jasper Johns

15 Ecole de Paris: Joseph Beuys ("Scene of the Fire", "Woman Throwing Discus")

16 *Modern American painting* Franz Kline, Barnett Newman, Clyfford Still, Mark Rothko, Frank Stella, Claes Olderburg, Andy Warhol, Carl Andre, Donald Judd, Sol Le Witt, Sam Francis ("Meaningless Gesture" on the staircase)

The Museum's largest collection of *20th c. Swiss painting and sculpture* (including Jean Tinguely, etc.) can be displayed only in selected groups, varying from time to time.

Around the Münsterplatz

Museum of
Natural History
and
Ethnography

In Augustinergasse, which runs north-west from the Münsterplatz, is a
Neo-Classical building (left) by Melchior Berri 1844–49 which houses the
Museum of Natural History and Ethnography (Natur- und Völkerkunde-
museum). The Natural History Museum, situated at the front of the build-
ing, contains a display cabinet from the 18th c. At the rear is the Museum of
Ethnography with exhibits from Melanesia and Oceania; the collections
are the result of the museum's own expeditions. Just a few yards away in
Rollerhof stands the Swiss Folk Museum (textiles, traditional paintings,
European masks).

Augustinerstrasse is continued by the Rheinsprung, which descends to the
Mittlere Brücke, passing the old University on the left. In Martinsgasse,
which runs parallel to the Rheinsprung on the side away from the river, are
two very elegant patrician houses, the Blaues Haus (Blue House) and
Weisses Haus (White House), built between 1763 and 1770 for wealthy
silk-merchants. At the west end of the Minster Hill, in a square with a
fountain, stands St Martin's church (consecrated 1398), the oldest parish
church in Basle.

St Martin's
church

★★Public Art Collection (Plans of floors see pp. 118–119)

Museum of Art

From the Minster, Rittergasse, lined by handsome Rococo houses, runs
south-east into St-Alban-Graben. At the corner of Dufourstrasse in a building designed by R. Christ and P. Bonatz (1932–36), is the Public Art Collection or Museum of Art (Kunstmuseum), which contains the finest collection
of pictures in Switzerland, including both old masters and modern art, and
also a Print Cabinet.
   On the first floor are the old masters, from Konrad Witz to Holbein the
Younger (both well presented), and a collection of French and Dutch pictures presented by Professor Bachofen. The second floor houses an out-

Museum of Art: "The Burghers of Calais"   *"Shrovetide Fountain", by J. Tinquely*

standing collection of 19th and 20th c. art, including Impressionists, Expressionists and Surrealists (Gauguin, Van Gogh, Corot, Corinth, Cézanne, Braque, Kokoschka, Picasso, Kandinsky, Léger, Chagall, Paul Klee, Juan Gris, Dali, Max Ernst), together with 20th c. works and special exhibitions.

Items of particular importance include the Heilspiegel (Mirror of Salvation) Altar by Konrad Witz (d. *c.* 1447), portraits by Holbein (16th c.), a "Crucifixion" by Mathias Grünewald (d. 1528), paintings by Niklaus Manuel-Deutsch (d. 1530) and Rembrandt ("David with Goliath's Head", 1627), Böcklin's "Island of the Dead" (earliest version, 1880) and works by Ferdinand Hodler (1853–1918).

The Italian Luciano Fabro was responsible for the "Giardino all'Italiana", a sculpture on Picasso Square (behind the art museum).

Between St-Alban-Graben and Theaterstrasse

At 5 St-Alban-Graben is the Museum of Antiquities (Antikenmuseum) and Ludwig collection with Greek works of art from 2500 to 100 B.C. and Roman and other Italian art from 1000 B.C. to A.D. 300 (including some items on loan) and an educational department. The growing collection made the creation of a "museum island" necessary between St-Alban-Graben and Luftgässlein. Four buildings and annexes different in style, function and date of origin surround a picturesque courtyard in the shade of a mighty lime tree.

Museum of Antiquities and Ludwig Collection

To the west of the Museum of Art, on the left-hand side of the street called Steinenberg, stands the Art Gallery (Kunsthalle), used for special exhibitions. At the far end of the street, on the right, is the Municipal Casino (Stadtcasino), with a wall-painting by A. H. Pelligrini (1940).

Art Gallery

The Municipal Theatre (Stadttheater, 1975) with its "state-of-the-art" technology dominates Theaterstrasse. The irregular-shaped building with its curved roof enjoys a high reputation among German-speaking theatres. There is an unusual "Carnival Fountain" (Fasnachtsbrunnen) 1977 by Jean Tinguely which produces ever-changing spray forms; its counterpart is the massive sculpture named "Intersection", made in steel by the American sculptor Richard Serra (1992).

Municipal Theatre

In Elisabethenstrasse, to the east of the Theatre, one of the finest of Basle's patrician houses, the Haus zum Kirschgarten (No. 27, 1777–80, built in early Classical style by J. U. Büchel) contains 25 rooms furnished in 18th c. style (including toys, porcelain, etc.).

Haus zum Kirschgarten

Around the Barfüsserplatz

In the busy Barfüsserplatz is the 14th c. Barfüsserkirche (church of the barefoot friars), which now houses the Historical Museum, with an important collection on the history of culture and art (renovated 1975–81; cellars constructed and reconstruction of the rood screen). Notable exhibits in the nave of the church are the Late Gothic tapestries, the religious art in the choir, the Minster treasure, the secular treasure-chamber, historical fittings, the modern portrayal of the history of Basle from the Celts to the present day, and the coin cabinet.

★Barfüsserkirche, Historical Museum

Above the west side of the church rises St Leonard's church (Leonhardskirche), rebuilt between 1480 and 1512 and restored in 1965. The crypt is Romanesque; the choir dates from the 13th–14th c. The former monastery adjoining the church, known as the Lohnhof, is now occupied by the police.

St Leonard's church

In the Teufelhof guest-house visitors can see an exhibition of the town medieval fortifications.

From the square in front of St Leonard's church is the beginning of the Heuberg which, together with the Lower Heuberg, the Gemsberg and Nadelberg, is one of Basle's most picturesque streets.

Spalenvorstadt

Jewish Museum of Switzerland

From the Steinenberg we go north-west along Kohlenberg and Leonhardsgraben. To the left in Kornhausgasse (No. 8), is the Jewish Museum of Switzerland. We then come into the Spalenvorstadt, which can also be reached from the Marktplatz up a picturesque flight of steps. At the near end of this on the right (No. 2), is the Industrial Museum (Gewerbemuseum: periodic special museums). Farther along on the left is the Spalenbrunnen, a fountain also known as the Holbein fountain (after Holbein and Dürer: original in Historical Museum).

Industrial Museum

St Peter's Church

In the centre of this part of the town is the tree-shaded Petersplatz, on the east side of which stands St Peter's church (Peterskirche), rebuilt at the time of the Council of Basle (15th c.), with a gallery running round the nave and reticulated vaulting in the choir from an earlier building (14th c.); interesting frescoes in the Eberler chapel and the nave. In front of the church is a bronze bust of the poet J. P. Hebel (b. Basle 1760). On the north side of the square is the handsome Wild'sches Haus (1763) and on the west side the Botanic Garden of the University. Beyond this a concrete building (1965) houses the rich University Library (Universitätsbibliothek), with numerous incunabula and manuscripts dating from the time of the Council of Basle (1431–87).

University

On the south side of Petersplatz stands the new university building (1938–46) by the Zurich architect Roland Rohn. At the entrance is a mosaic by Walter Eglin depicting scenes from daily life and in the corridors are pictures and busts of famous personalities and scientists, including one of Pope Pius II who founded the university in 1460. The great hall (Aula) contains ten stained glass windows and its beautiful courtyard has a water-lily pond.

★ Spalentor

To the west of the University is the Spalentor (1370), a fortified gate which marks the end of the old town. The town gate, once part of the old town walls, has stood alone since their destruction in the 19th c. On the left there is an old letter box by M. Berri (1801–54) with the emblem of the Basle pigeon.

Swiss Museum of Gymnastics and Sport

At 28 Missionsstrasse is the Swiss Museum of Gymnastics and Sport with exhibits relating to different sports, including the Olympic Games and the Swiss sports of "Hornussen" and "Schwingen".

Predigerkirche

At the foot of Petersgraben, which runs down to the Rhine from Petersplatz, is the Predigerkirche (Dominician church), a long building of the 14th–15th c. with a graceful roof turret. Opposite is the house in which the poet Johann Peter Hebel (1760–1826) was born (plaque).

St Antonius Kirche

In the north-west of the city St Anthony's church (St Antoniuskirche), built in an extremely plain style by Karl Moser in 1927, was in its day a pioneering example of concrete architecture (fine windows).

South of the old town

Railway station, Basle SBB

On the south side of the old town, behind the Elisabethenschanze with the Strasbourg monument of F. A. Bertholdi, is the main railway station

The Spalentor, at the end of the Old Town in Basle ▶

(Bahnhof SBB), built 1905–09 by Emil Faesch and Emanuel La Roche. The imposing Neo-Baroque façade with its high concourse is framed between domed towers. Adjoining it is the Centralbahnplatz (underground passage with shops, information bureau and café) surrounded by big hotels.

BIZ

Nearby stands the circular tower block (architect Burckhardt; 1977) of the Bank for International Settlements (Bank für Internationalen Zahlungsausgleich, BIZ), which was founded in 1930 at the Hague Conference and today is at the centre of the international gold and currency markets as well as the European money market.

★Zoo

To the west in the Birsig valley is the large and interesting zoo (Zoologischer Garten; restaurant), affectionately known as the Zolli by the people of Basle. Founded in 1874 with 510 European animals it contains mainly exotic species. It comprises a vivarium (fishes, penguins, reptiles), a bear enclosure with different species, an excellent monkey house (1970 orangutans, gorillas, proboscis monkeys, etc.), an aviary (1927) with indigenous and exotic birds, birds of prey, an antelope house and children's zoo. The zoo has been particularly successful in breeding rhinoceros. The elephants put on a performance in a special arena and give rides to children.

Basle Zoo

↕ Entrance/exit
← Exit only
00 Toilets
P Car Parks

1 Main entrance and director's office
2 Kiosk (books)
3 Fishes, penguins, reptiles
4 Aquatic birds
5 Somali wild asses, bongos
6 Brown bears, Malayan bears, spectacle bears, polar bears
7 Zebras, ostriches, flamingos
8 Orangutans, gorillas, chimpanzees, woolly monkeys, smaller monkeys
9 Birds from all continents
10 Waterfowl and waders
11 African and Indian elephants
12 Elephant arena
13 Otters, civets, ratels
14 Waders and waterfowl
15 Lions, tigers, panthers, fossas, servals
16 Okapi, giraffes, kudos, kangaroos
17 Rhinoceroses, pigmy hippopotamuses, tapirs
18 Parrots
19 Penguins
20 Barbary sheep, Himalayan thars
21 Reindeer
22 Birds of prey (golden eagle, bateleur eagle, vulture, raven)
23 Covered seating
24 Sea-lions
25 Owls (snowy owl, eagle-owl)
26 Marmots, porcupine, agouti
27 Sardinian wild sheep
28 Wolves
29 Camels, llamas, pigmy zebus
30 Wild pigs, musk-oxen, bison
31 Children's zoo (ponies, pigmy goats, domestic animals)

© Baedeker

Dorenbachviadukt

St-Alban-Vorstadt

To the east of the old town a stroll through the old town brings you to the square St-Alban-Tor, with its lower part finished in bulging stone blocks. An old town gate, it dates from the 13th c. when it was part of the fortifications. It was altered in 1871 with the addition of the watch house on the side facing the Rhine, being completely restored in 1976.

St-Alban-Tor

At No. 9 St-Alban-Vorstadt the constantly changing collection of caricatures and cartoons by famous artists is a source of amusement.

Collection of Caricatures and Cartoons

The Mühlenberg runs down to the old St Alban's monastery under the town walls. Part of its Romanesque cloister is preserved in a neighbouring house.

St Alban's monastery

To the east on the Gewerbebach an old Gallician paper mill has been turned into the Museum of Writing, Printing and Paper demonstrating the individual processes.

Basle Paper Mill

In St-Alban-Tal stands the Museum of Contemporary Art (Museum für Gegenwartskunst), an old paper mill with modern extensions (1980 Katharina and Wilfried Steib). Works on display range from c. 1960 and the contemporary part of the Emanuel Hoffmann collection. Especially noteworthy are works by Stella, Beuys, Chagall, de Chirico, Dali, Braque, Mondrian, Klee, Arp, Pevsner, Giacometti, Moore and Tinguely. There is an attractive trip across the Rhine to Klein-Basel by ferry.

★ Museum of Contemporary Art

Kleinbasel

In Kleinbasel a tree-lined promenade runs along the bank of the river, affording fine views of the old town. At 26 Unterer Rheinweg, a little way north-west of the Mittlere Brücke, is the City and Minster Museum (Stadt- und Münster Museum), notable particularly for its collection of sculpture from the Minster.

City and Minster Museum

In Claraplatz stands the Roman Catholic St Clara Kirche, a light-coloured roughcast building with a small turret. The Gothic nave has 19th c. additions by Amadeus Merian. The choir contains the Sunday Cross from Basle Minster.

St Clara Church

Near the Wettstein bridge is the St-Theodor-Kirchplatz, in which is the Late Gothic St Theodore's church (14th c.). Noteworthy are the sandstone font (c. 1500), the choir with a wall tabernacle (16th c.) and the old choir windows (c. 1375). Between the square and the river we find the old Carthusian monastery which has served as a monastery since 1669.

St Theodore's Church

One of the main traffic arteries of Klein-Basel is the Riehenring, along which extend the buildings of the Swiss Trade Fair (Schweizer Mustermesse) and the European World Trade and Congress Centre (EWTCC). Swiss trade fairs have a long history. Some of the most important international fairs include ART (20th c. art fair), the Swiss Trade Fair, Basle Autumn Fair, EUSM (European Clock and Watch Fair) and Nuclex, an international trade fair for the nuclear industry.

Swiss Trade Fair, European World Trade and Congress Centre (EWTCC)

A little way east, at the Vogelsangstrasse 15, is the Technical College (Gewerbeschule, 1961), which has a column by Hans Arp in the courtyard.

North-east is the Art Nouveau building (1906–13) of the Baden Railway Station (Badischer Bahnhof), the German Railways (DB) terminus. The allegorical statues above the entrance are by C. Burckhardt.
    Beyond the railway line, along the little River Wiese, is situated the popular Lange Erlen Zoo (Tierpark: cafés).

Baden Railway Station

Basle

In Riehen, a desirable residential area of Basle, are the Village and Toy Museum (400 teddy-bears) and probably the only Cat Museum. By 1996 the museum designed by the architect Renzo Piano for the Beyeler Collection of 20th c. art should be completed.

Surroundings

Boats leave from the Mittlere Brücke for trips on the Rhine or around the port installations; boats to Rotterdam from St Johann, Elsässerrheinweg.

From Basle to Kaiseraugst

Leave Basle on the east and join the motorway (N2/N3) which crosses the Rhine. After crossing the river Birs we arrive in 3.5km/2 miles at the exit for the Basle suburb of Birsfelden, on the north bank of the Rhine. Here there are port installations and a power station built in 1950–55 (visitors' gallery).

Augst

We continue along the south edge of the Hard forest and through a tunnel, beyond which the southern slopes of the Black Forest can be seen on the left. 6.5km/4 miles: Liestal-Augst exit. 5km/3 miles south is Liestal; 1km/½ mile north is Augst (275m/902ft), on the left bank of the Ergolz, which here flows into the Rhine and forms the boundary between the cantons of Basel-Land and Aargau. In Griebenbacherstrasse a Roman museum has exhibits from Augusta Raurica and the silver treasure from Castle Kaiseraugst. Also worth a visit is Roman domestic animal park (east of the Roman town wall).

★Augusta
Raurica

0.5km/½ mile uphill from the town (signposted) is the site of the Roman colony of Augusta Raurica, founded about 27 B.C., with a large theatre and

Augusta Raurica: a Roman theatre

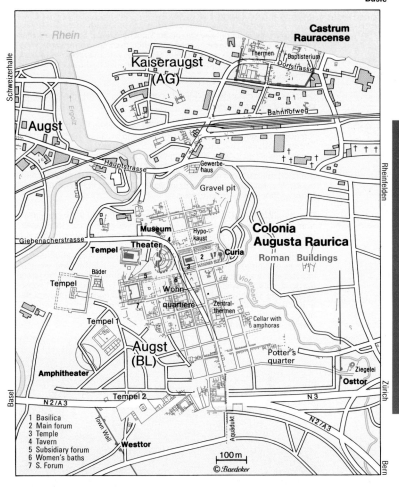

Schweizerhalle

Augst

Kaiseraugst
(AG)

Rhein

Ergolz

**Castrum
Rauracense**

Thermen   Baptisterium

Dorfstrasse

Bahnhofweg

Rheinfelden

Haupstrasse

Gewerbe-
haus

Gravel pit

Giebenacherstrasse

Museum   Hypo-
kaust

Theater

Tempel

**Colonia
Augusta Raurica**

Roman   Buildings

Curia

Bäder

Tempel

Wohn-

quartiere

Zentral-
thermen

Cellar with
amphoras

Violenbach

Tempel 1

Augst
(BL)

Potter's
quarter

Ziegelei

Osttor

Amphitheater

Tempel 2

Basel   N 2/A 3

Town Wall

Westtor

Aquädukt

N 3

N 2/A3

Zürich   Bern

1 Basilica
2 Main forum
3 Temple
4 Tavern
5 Subsidiary forum
6 Women's baths
7 S. Forum

100 m

© *Baedeker*

the remains of several temples. At the near end of the site, on the left, is a reconstruction of a Roman house (1953–57) containing a museum. To the right is the theatre (restored: performances in summer), and beyond this to the east the site of a temple, the main forum and a basilica. On a hill west of the theatre are the remains of a large temple, and to the south a residential district. South-west of the main complex is an amphitheatre discovered in 1959.

1km/½ mile north-east of Augst beyond the Ergolz, beautifully situated on the banks of the Rhine, the little town of Kaiseraugst has the remains of a Roman fortified post. On the Rhine is the Augst-Whylen power station (1907–12), which has a dam 212m/696ft long, and the Kaiseraugst nuclear power station which was finally halted in 1989 after years of strong opposition.

Kaiseraugst

From Basle via Dornach to Liestal

	Leave from the main railway station on Münchensteiner Strasse and after crossing the railway line take a road on the left; then, soon afterwards, keep straight ahead through the suburb of Neuewelt with the recreational park

Grün 80 — "Grün 80" (playground and lake), which is dominated by the stone statue of a dinosaur.

Münchenstein — Over the Birs 6km/4 miles lies Münchenstein (540m/1772ft) where there is a coach and sledge museum.

Arlesheim — After 2km/1 mile is Arlesheim (340m/1116ft), with a church built in 1681 and remodelled in Rococo style in 1760 (Silbermann organ of 1761) and many country houses. The Jazz Museum at Stollenrain 10 is open: Tues. 11am–3pm, Wed. 7–9pm, Fri. 11am–3pm. On the wooded hill above the town are Burg Reichenstein (480m/1575ft) and Schloss Birseck (private property), formerly the residence of the Prince-Bishops of Basle. Adjoining the latter is the romantic Hermitage Garden, laid out in 1789, with small lakes, grottoes and a country retreat.

Dornach, ★Goetheanum — Only 1km/½ mile farther lies Dornachbrugg (295m/968ft) with a Capuchin friary. It is another 1km/½ mile to the pretty village of Dornach (300m/984ft) towered over by the castle ruins of the same name. Opposite stands the massive concrete structure of the Goetheanum II, designed in 1925–28 by Rudolf Steiner. It is the World Centre of Anthroposophists and the Free College of Spiritual Science. The first Goetheanum, with twin wooden cupolas and designed by Steiner in 1913 for performances of his "mystery dramas", was burned down by arsonists in 1922/23. Constructed in Expressionist style, the present building conforms to the holistic thinking of the anthroposophists. Today concerts, theatrical and eurhythmic performances are held on the stage. Many adherents of anthroposophy have built their homes around the main building.

Goetheanum in Dornach

From Dornach the road winds uphill through wooded country for 7km/ 4 miles to Gempen (672m/2205ft) side road on left ascending the Gempenfluh (765m/2510ft), with magnificent views of the Jura and the Rhine, extending beyond Basle to Strasbourg.

★ Gempenfluh

From Gempen the road winds its way down for 10km/6 miles east to Liestal (330m/1083ft), chief town of the half-canton of Basel-Land. In the 18th c. Town Hall is the gold cup of Charles the Bold, Duke of Burgundy, which was captured at Nancy in 1477. The "Dichtermuseum" (Writers' Museum) has mementoes of the Nobel Prize winner Carl Spitteler (1845–1924), who was born in Liestal, Georg Herwegh and others. The museum is open on the first Sat. in the month and by prior arrangement (tel. (061) 9 22 08 95). The former Basle corn exchange and arsenal now houses the Cantonal Museum (Rathausstrasse 2; open: Tues.–Fri.). At the end of Rathausstrasse is the picturesque Oberes Tor (Upper Gate). North-west of the town, at Munzach, are the remains of a Roman villa (mosaics, etc.). In the Harmonium Museum some 100 instruments are on display (Widmannstrasse 9A; visits by arrangement; tel. (061) 9 21 64 10). 5km/3 miles north via the holiday resort of Bienenberg (431m/1414ft) is Bad Schauenberg (468m/ 1536ft); brine baths.

Liestal

From Basle to Laufen through the Birsig valley

Leave Basle by Oberwiler Strasse. Near the zoo take the Hohestrasse towards Allschwil (3km/2½ miles). Near the parish church of St Peter and Paul are several half-timbered buildings including a local museum.

Allschwil

Returning to the zoo take the main road heading south for 2km/1 mile to Binningen (285m/935ft) where there is a restaurant in Schloss Binningen, a former moated castle which is first mentioned in 1229 and also the smaller Schloss Holee with a stepped gable and tower (lookout terrace). The Mon-

Binningen, Monteverdi Car Collection

Allschwill: Local museum

Bottmingen: medieval moated castle

teverdi Car Collection in Oberwilerstrasse is interesting, a car museum of unique Swiss cars (100 cars and Europe's largest collection – 8000 – of model cars; open: Mon.–Sun. 1–5pm).

Bottmingen   Bottmingen (295m/968ft), 2km/1 mile to the north also has a medieval moated castle. The only castle with a lake in north-west Switzerland it dates back to the 14th c., but was renovated in the 18th and 20th c. (restaurant). There are interesting Baroque statues in the hall and a ceiling painted by Isaak Merian (18th c.).

Flüh   10.5km/6½ miles via Oberwil (515m/1690ft), Therwil (309m/1014ft) with a fine church and Ettingen we reach Flüh (381m/1250ft), just on the French frontier, with a chalybeate spring. On a hill beyond the frontier is the ruined castle of Landskron (546m/1791ft). Beyond Flüh the road climbs sharply. 2.5km/2 miles: Mariastein (515m/1690ft) has a Benedictine abbey on a steep-sided crag which was founded in 1645, dissolved in 1874, and re-occupied by Benedictines in 1941; there is also a pilgrimage church (1648–55) and the cave of Maria im Stein.

Laufen   Passing through Metzerlen (530m/1739ft) the road runs up on to the western slopes of Blauen and then descends steeply to (11km/7 miles) Laufen (358m/1175ft), a little town of 3500 inhabitants on the south side of the hill. Two town gates belonging to the old fortifications, the Baslertor and the Obertor; St Catherine's church (1698); palace of the Prince-Bishops, now the Prefecture. Large limestone quarry.

Bellinzona   P 11

Canton: Ticino (TI)
Altitude: 230m/755ft
Population: 18,200

Situation and general   Three important North–South routes – the roads over the Alpine passes of St Gotthard, San Bernardino and Lucomagno – meet in the valley of the

St. Gotthard, San Bernadino

Bellinzona

1 Castello Grande

2 Castello di Montebello

3 Castello di Sasso Corbaro

4 Church of SS Pietro and Stefano

5 Government Palace

200 m

© Baedeker

Castello Grande: the oldest fortress in Bellinzona

Ticino, and could in the past be closed by a barrier across the road at Bellinzona. The town thus occupied a key strategic situation for many centuries, and this led to its selection as the cantonal capital in 1878. It is now an educational focal point as well as the seat of cantonal administration. The town is still dominated by its three castles, an impressive example of a medieval defensive system which, together with a double circuit of walls, were built by the town's Milanese rulers in the second half of the 15th c.

The region was occupied by Rome for five centuries, from about 30 B.C. to A.D. 450. Bellinzona itself first appears in the records in A.D. 590. In 1242 it fell into the hands of Milan, ruled by the Visconti family and later by the Sforzas. In 1503 the Confederates established the governor's headquarters in the castles. In 1803 Bellinzona became part of the new canton of Ticino.

History

Sights

The main features of interest in Bellinzona are the three castles. The oldest Castello Grande, (known in the 14th c. as Castel Magnum, in the 17th c. as Burg Uri or Altdorf and in 1818 as San Michele), was constructed above a Roman castle. The Torre Bianca (27m/89ft) and the square Torre Negra (28m/91ft) form the most ancient part of the five defences. Situated 50m/164ft above the town the castle boasts wonderful views.

★ Castello Grande

The Castello di Montebello, (originally Castello Piccolo, later Burg Schwyz and in the 19th c. San Martino), stands on the east side of the town, where the old town walls divided. It is the most interesting of the three as an example of the art of fortification (originally centred on the keep, with a 13th c. palace and courtyard and further structures built between 1460 and 1480), which now contain a historical and archaeological museum.

★ Castello di Montebello

The square-shaped Castello di Sasso Corbaro (known as Burg Unterwalden and in the 18th c. S. Barbara), also called Castello di Cima by the

★ Castello di Sasso Corbaro

131

Bellinzona: Castello di Montebello . . .   *. . . and collegiate church*

Bellinzonese, was built in less than six months in 1479 following the Battle of Giornico to reinforce the defences of the Ticino valley (230m/755ft above the town). It houses the Ticino Museum (arts, crafts local costumes).

★ Collegiate church of SS Pietro and Stefano

The Roman Catholic Collegiate church SS Pietro and Stefano dates back to 1424. This fine Renaissance building was largely rebuilt in 1517 by Tomaso Rodari, master builder of Como Cathedral in Italy. The rich Baroque interior and façade were added in the 17th–18th c. The marble high altar is decorated with a representation of the Crucifixion (1658) by either Simone Peterzano or Tintoretto.

Historic Old Town

There is an interesting former Franciscan church S. Maria della Grazie with magnificent wall paintings by the Lombard artists working in Ticino (16th c.), the Palazzo del Governo (1738–43, altered 1848) and the old town which retains its Lombard character with its picturesque little streets, arcades, old doorways and wrought-iron balconies that inspired the English writer John Ruskin and the painter J. M. William Turner.

Villa dei Cedri

The art museum in the Villa dei Cedri has sculptures and paintings by early 20th c. Swiss artists and more recently by the 16th c. Italian Francesco da Basano.

Civica Galleria d'Arte

In the Civica Galleria d'Arte are exhibits by Augusto Sartoni (1880–1957), Giovanni Genucchi (1904–79) and Mario Marioni (1910–87).

Ravecchia

In the outlying district of Ravecchia (1.5km/1 mile south), off the road to the left, is the Romanesque church of San Biagio (St Blaise), with fine frescoes of the 14th–15th c.

Berne   H 7

Canton: Berne (BE)
Altitude: 540m/1772ft. Population: 142,000

The Swiss capital, Berne (German spelling Bern), is also capital of the country's second largest canton and a university town. The old town, dominated by the Minster (or basilica), is built on a sandstone ridge encircled on three sides by the Aare, flowing in a valley 35–40m/115–131ft deep. High-level bridges link it with the high ground on the right bank and with the newer parts of the city. The charming older part of Berne still preserves its original layout. The houses, with their arcades on street level (6km/4 miles of arcades altogether) and their projecting roofs, reflect the prosperity of the citizens of Berne in the 18th c. Most of the attractive fountains, painted in lively colours, were the work of Hans Gieng (1540–45).

The industries of Berne include textiles, machinery, chocolate, pharmaceuticals, foodstuffs, the graphic trades and electrical equipment, and it also has a considerable trade in agricultural produce. Over 12% of its working population are employed in administration, the highest proportion of all Swiss towns.

The town is believed to have been founded on its excellent defensive site by Berchtold V of Zähringen in 1191. The bear on the Bernese coat-of-arms, together with the bear-pit, commemorate the legend according to which a bear was the first animal to be killed by Berthold V in the year in which the city was founded. After the Zähringen dynasty died out the Emperor Frederick II granted Berne self-government and its own law court. In the Battle of Laupen (1339) the Bernese, led by Rudolf von Erlach, defeated the Burgundian nobility. In 1353 Berne became a member of the young Confederation, in which the military prowess of its citizens enabled it to play a leading role. In 1528 the Reformation came to the town and by 1536 Berne was the largest city state north of the Alps.

Since 1848 Berne has been the seat of the Federal Council and Federal Assembly; it is also the headquarters of important organisations including the Universal Postal Union (since 1874) and the international copyright and railway unions, and of an institute attached to the University for research into tourism.

Notable people born in Berne include the 18th c. scholar Albrecht von Haller, the writer Jeremias Gotthelf (1797–1854) and the painters Ferdinand Hodler (1853–1918) and Paul Klee (1879–1940). The famous physicist Albert Einstein (1879–1955) published his Theory of Relativity in Berne.

Berne was awarded the honour of being judged the best European City in Bloom by "Entente Florale" and accepted by UNESCO as a world cultural centre.

Museums, Galleries, etc.

Alpine Museum (Schweizerisches Alpines Museum),
Helvetiaplatz 4;
Mid-May to mid-Oct.: Mon. 2–5pm, Tues.–Sun. 10am–5pm.
Mid-Oct. to mid-May: Mon. 2–5pm, Tues.–Sun. 10am–noon and 2–5pm.

Art Gallery (Kunsthalle),
Hevetiaplatz 1;
Tues. 10am–9pm, Wed.–Sun. 10am–5pm.
(Temporary exhibitions of contemporary art).

Art, Museum of (Kunstmuseum),
Hodlerstrasse 12;
Tues.10am–9pm, Wed.–Sun. 10am–5pm.

Banknote Museum
Bundesplatz 1;
Mon.–Thur. 8am–5pm, Fri. 8am–4pm
(Appointments: tel. (031) 3 12 02 11).

Berne: The Old Town above the Aare valley

Bear-Pit (Bärengraben),
Nydeggbrücke;
Apr.–Sept. 8am–6pm, Oct.–Mar. 9am–4pm.

Botanic Gardens (Botanischer Garten),
Altenbergrain 21 at the north end of the Lorraine Bridge;
Outdoors: Mon.–Fri. 7am–6pm; Sat. and Sun. 8am–5pm.
Indoors: Mon.–Sun. 8–11.30am and 2–5pm.

Bundeshaus (Parliament), Bundesplatz;
conducted tours: weekdays at 9, 10, 11am, 2, 3 and 4pm;
Sun. 9, 10, 11am, 2 and 3pm.
(except during sittings of Parliament and on public holidays).

Cast Collection of Berne (Bernische Abguss-Sammlung),
Hallerstrasse 12 (2nd floor);
Sat. 10am–noon.

Clock Tower (Zeitglockenturm);
May 1st–Oct. 31st: daily at 4.30pm guided tours including astronomical
clock (about 1 hour). Meeting point: east side of tower. Numbers limited.
Nov. 1st–Mar. 30th: guided tours by arrangement; tel. (031) 3 20 32 11.

Einstein House (Einstein-Haus),
Kramgasse 49;
Mar.–Oct.: Tues.–Fri. 10am–5pm, Sat. 10am–4pm.

Historical Museum of Berne (Bernisches Historisches Museum),
Helvetiaplatz 5; Tues.–Sun. 10am–5pm.

Käfigturm
(Information Centre for the Canton of Berne),
Marktgasse 67;
Tues.–Thur. 10am–1pm and 2–8pm, Fri.–Sun. 10am–1pm and 2–5pm.

Kornhaus Collection of Applied Art,
Zeughausgasse 2;
Tues.–Sun. 10am–1pm and 2–5pm, Thur. 10am–1pm and 2–8pm.

Minster, Münsterplatz;
Easter Sun.–end Oct.: Tues.–Sun. 10am–5pm,
Nov.–Easter: Sat., Tues.–Fri. 10am–noon and 2–3pm, Sat. 10am–noon and
1–5pm, Sun. 11am–noon.
Tower ascents: until 30 minutes before the Minster closes.

Municipal Archives (Stadtarchiv),
Falkenplatz 4; tel. (031) 6 33 51 01.
Mon. 1.30–5pm, Tues.–Thur. 7.45am–noon and 1.30–5pm, Fri.
7.45am–5pm.

Municipal and University Library (Stadt- und Universitätsbibliothek),
Casinoplatz;
Issue of books on loan Mon.–Fri. 10am–noon and 2–6pm, Sat. 10am–noon;
Reading room Mon–Fri. 8am–9pm, Sat. 8am–noon.

Municipal Zoo, Dählhölzli (Dählhölzli Städtischer Tierpark),
Tierparkweg 1;
Summer: 8am–6.30pm; Winter: 9am–5pm.

National Library (Schweizerische Landesbibliothek),
Helvetiastrasse; Lending library and textbook collection.
Mon.–Fri. 9am–6pm (Wed. to 8pm), Sat. 9am–2pm.
Reading Room: Mon., Tues., Thur., Fri. 9am–6pm; Wed. 9am–8pm; Sat.
9am–4pm.

Natural History Museum (Naturhistorisches Museum),
Bernastrasse 15;
Mon. 2–5pm, Tues.–Sat. 9am–5pm, Sun. 10am–5pm.

Nature Reserve, Elfenau (Stadtgärtnerei Elfenau);
Indoor houses – winter: Mon., Tues., Thur. 11am–6pm, Wed. to 8pm, Sat.
and Sun. 10am–6pm.
Summer: normal working hours.

Postal Museum (Schweizerisches PTT Museum),
Helvetiastrasse 16;
Tues.–Sun. 10am–5pm.

Rathaus (Town Hall), Rathausplatz;
seen by prior arrangement, tel. (031) 6 33 75 50.

Schulwarte, Berner
Helvetiaplatz 2; Mon.–Fri. 10am–noon and 2–5.30pm.

Swiss Rifle Museum (Schweizerisches Schützenmuseum),
Bernastrasse 5;
Tues.–Sat. 2–4pm, Sun. 10am–noon, 2–4pm.

Theatrical Museum (Schweizerische Theatersammlung),
Schanzenstrasse 15;
Tues. 9am–noon, Fri. 1–4pm;
archives and library: Tues. 1–4pm, Wed., Thur. 9am–4pm, Fri. 9am–noon.

Psychiatric Museum (Psychiatrie-Museum)   Bern–Oster-
Ostermundingen, Psychiatrische Universitätsklinik Bern (Waldau), in the   mundingen
prebendary building.
Wed. 2–4pm.

Description of the town

Bubenbergplatz

Bürgerspital

The hub of the city's traffic is the long Bubenbergplatz. On its north side the handsome Bürgerspital (Municipal hospital, 1734–42; now an old people's home), built around two courtyards, is reminiscent of French models such

Heiliggeistkirche

as the Hôtel des Invalides in Paris. To the right is the Heiliggeistkirche (church of the Holy Spirit: Protestant), in French Baroque style, built 1726–29.

From here it is a short distance south along Christoffelgasse into the broad Bundesgasse, in which are the Bundeshaus and the Kleine Schanze.

Around the Bundesplatz

Bundeshaus

In the Bundesplatz (vegetable and flower market on Tuesday and Saturday mornings) is the Renaissance-style Bundeshaus (Parliament building), standing on the edge of the high ground above the river. The domed central block (by H. Auer, 1896–1902) contains the two chambers of the Swiss Parliament (open to visitors), the meeting-places of the National Council and the Council of States; in the east wing (also by Auer, 1888–92) and west wing (by F. Studer, 1851–57) are various Federal agencies and the Federal library.

From the Bundesterrasse, which rests on massive retaining walls, there are fine views of the river Aare 48m/157ft below (funicular into valley) and of the Alps beyond.

Noten Museum

In the Banknote Museum (Bundesplatz 1) can be seen Swiss and foreign banknotes and also forgeries.

★ Kleine
Schanze

Another popular viewpoint, with an orientation table, is the Kleine Schanze (Little Redoubt; restaurant) to the west, a relic of the old fortifications. In the gardens are a monument to Oskar Bider, who made the first flight over the Alps in 1913, and a monument (1909) commemorating the foundation of the Universal Postal Union.

Bundesplatz

Parliament
Building

Council of States
Chamber

Bundeshaus
West
(Bundes-
Rathaus)

Domed
Hall

Bundeshaus
Ost

National Council
Chamber

Wandelhalle

10 m

© Baedeker

Bundesterrasse

Bundeshaus Bern

Palais Fédéral Berne
Palazzo Federale Berna
Casa Federala Bern

CURIA
CONFOEDERATIONIS
HELVETICAE

Plan of first floor in the Federal
Parliament building (1894–1902)

1 Rütli group
2 Paper office
3 Newspaper room
4 Office of President of Council
  of States
5 Office of President of
  National Council
G Cloakrooms
V Antechambers

Berne: Church of the Holy Ghost . . .   *and the Parliament Building*

Between Theaterplatz and Münsterplatz

To the east of the Bundesplatz in the Theaterplatz are the Hauptwache (guard House), a small pillared hall of 1767, and the Hôtel de Musique (1771), once the fashionable assembly rooms of Berne. On the south-east corner of the square, at the end of the Kirchenfeld bridge, is the Casino (1906–09), an assembly and concert hall with a restaurant and large lookout terrace. To the north is the horseshoe-shaped site of the Municipal and University Library (Stadt- und Universitätsbibliothek), which was built in 1755 as the Corn Exchange but renovated in 1787–92 as the library by Sprüngli and Schmid.

From here Münstergasse (market for meat and dairy produce on Tuesday and Saturday mornings, every 1st Saturday in the month a craft market of hand-made goods) leads to the Münsterplatz, where stands the Moses Fountain (*c.* 1545, rebuilt 1790–91 in the original form). The so-called late Baroque Stiftsgebäude (Albrecht Stürler, 1748) is the seat of the Cantonal government.

Hôtel de Musique

Municipal and University Library

Münstergasse

Stiftsgebäude

★Minster

The Late Gothic Minster (dedicated to St Vincent), a three-aisled pillared basilica without transept, was begun in 1421 to the design of Matthäus Ensinger of Ulm, but the tower was not completed until 1893, with the addition of the octagonal upper section and the open-work spire.

The west doorway is richly decorated with sculpture (now copies); in the tympanum is a Last Judgment (originally 1495) containing a large number of figures, and on the side walls are paintings (1501, restored) of the Fall and the Annunciation.

    The nave and the choir have reticulated vaulting with fine 16th c. bosses (coats-of-arms).

★West Doorway

**Minster (St Vincent)
Berne**

1 Main doorway (1490–95), with 45 figures (copies:
   originals in Historical Museum)
2 Organ (1726–30)
3 Pulpit (1470)
4 Communion table from Lausanne Cathedral
5 Stone staircase, a relic of the rood-screen
6 North Doorway
7 Double rows of choir-stalls (1523–25)
8 Font (1524)
9 Sedilia (c. 1435)
10 Stained glass windows of choir (1441–50
   and 1868)

Interior

The finely carved choir stalls (1523) were the first Renaissance work of art in
Berne. In the apse are a Gothic font (1524), sedilla (15th c.: on right) and
beautiful stained glass (1441–50). At the end of the south aisle is a monument to Berchtold von Zähringen (1601), incorporating a coat-of-arms; at
the end of a marble memorial to the 702 men of Berne who died fighting the
French in 1798.

In the Matter chapel (seventh bay in the south aisle) can be seen the
Dance of Death window (1917), with 20 scenes from the "Dance of Death"
(1516–19) by Niklaus Manuel-Deutsch. There is a magnificent Baroque
organ (1726–30) with 5404 pipes and fine modern stained glass (1947) in
the south aisle.

From the tree-planted Minster terrace there is an attractive view down into
the Aare valley; and there are fine panoramic views from the gallery on the
Minster tower (254 steps).

Between Junkerngasse and Bärengraben

Erlacherhof

From here Junkerngasse, lined with arcaded houses once occupied by the
old patrician families of Berne, runs towards the east end of the old town. At
No. 47 is the handsome Erlacherhof (1749–52), now the seat of the State
President.

Nydeggbrücke

Junkerngasse joins the wide Nydegg-Gasse, at the far end of which is the
Nydegg bridge (1840–44) over the Aare gorge; the principal arch of stone
has a span of 55m/180ft and stands 26m/85ft above the river. On the left,
just before the bridge is the little Nydegg church, built in 1494 on the site of
an Imperial stronghold (restored 1956).

Bärengraben

On the far side of the bridge is one of Berne's great popular attractions, the
Bear-Pit (Bärengraben), a deep circular den in which bears, the heraldic
animal of Berne, have been kept since 1480.

From the road running up to the right (Muristalden) there is a fine view of
the Minster and the old town. Above the bridge to the left is the beautiful
Rose-Garden (Rosengarten), with views of the Aare and the old town. Just
downstream from the Nydegg bridge at the end of the old Untertorbrücke
(1461–87), in Läuferplatz are Berne's first town hall and the Läuferbrunnen
("Runner Fountain", 1543).

From the Nydegg bridge to the Bubenbergplatz

From the Nydegg bridge a series of picturesque streets (Nydeggsgasse, Gerechtigskeitsgasse, Kramgasse, Marktgasse and Spitalgasse), with many antique shops and art galleries, runs along the whole length of the old town for a distance of 1700m/1860yd to end in the Bubenbergplatz.

The Gerechtigkeitsgasse is lined on both sides by arcades and elegant shops. In the middle of the street is the Justice Fountain (Gerechtigkeits-brunnen, 1543) probably by Hans Gieng of Freiburg, with Justitia (since 1988 a copy) as the image of justice. The original statue was destroyed in 1986 and has been carefully restored in the Historical Museum.

★ Gerechtig-keitsgasse

At the far end of Rathausgasse, on right, leads to the Rathaus (Council House, the seat of the Great Council of the canton and of the Town Council), in Late Burgundian Gothic style, built in 1406–16, much altered in 1866 and restored in the original style in 1939–42. In the square in front of the Rathaus stands the Banner-Carrier or Venner fountain (1542).

Rathaus

The continuation of the Gerechtigkeitsgasse, the Kramgasse, also lined with arcaded houses, has three fountains – the Kramgassbrunnen (1778), the Simsonbrunnen (Samson fountain, 1544) and the Zähringerbrunnen (1544) which shows the heraldic animal in jousting costume.

★ Kramgasse

The world-famous physicist, humanist and Nobel prize winner, Albert Einstein, lived at 49 Kramgasse from 1903–05 before emigrating to the United States. The house is now a museum open to the public (photo-graphs, documents). In 1905 alone he wrote six epoch-making treatises, discovered quantum light, for which he was awarded the Nobel prize sixteen years later, and produced his "General Theory of Relativity", thereby revolutionising contemporary concepts of space, time and mass.

Albert Einstein House

Berne: Late-Gothic façade of the Town Hall   *Clock tower and Zähringer Fountain*

Berne

★ Clock Tower   The Kramgasse ends at the Clock Tower (Zeitglockenturm or Zytglogge-
turm), a notable Berne landmark, frequently rebuilt (the present stone
tower with its pointed spire is 15th c.) which was the west gate of the town
until about 1250. On the east side of the tower is an astronomical clock
(1527–30), with mechanical figures which perform four minutes before
every hour.

★ Marktgasse   Beyond this is the busy Marktgasse (pedestrian precinct), with old guild-
houses, arcades, shops and two more fountains, the Schützenbrunnen
(Marksman fountain) and Anna-Seiler-Brunnen, both of about 1545. At the
Käfigturm   far end of the street is the Käfigturm ("Cage tower", 13th and 17th c.), which
was once one of the town gates from 1250 to 1350.
     Beyond it is the Bärenplatz, from which the Spitalgasse (pedestrian
precinct), with the Pfeifferbrunnen (Piper's fountain, 1545), continues to the
Bubenbergplatz.

Between Kornhausplatz and the railway station

This line of streets cuts across two of the town's principal squares. In front
of the Clock tower is the Kornhausplatz, in which stands the curious Kind-
lifresserbrunnen ("Child Eater Fountain" or Ogre Fountain, with the figure
of an ogre devouring a child) of about 1540.

Kornhaus   On the west side of the square we see the handsome Kornhaus (1711–16),
with high-vaulted wine cellars (restaurant); on the first floor are the Industrial Museum and the Swiss Gutenberg Museum. The Kornhaus was
recently made into an "open house" for cultural and social purposes.

French Church   Behind it the French church (Französische Kirche), originally a Dominican
foundation (13th c.), has frescoes by the Berne "Master of the Carnation".

Sampson Fountain in the Kramgasse   *Berne: Historical Museum*

In the north-west corner of the square, at the end of the iron bridge called the Kornhausbrücke, is the Municipal Theatre (Stadttheater, 1903).

To the south of the Käfigturm the charming little Bärenplatz (pedestrian precinct: flower and vegetable market Tuesday and Saturday mornings) was once a bear-pit; to the north is the large Waisenhausplatz (partly pedestrianised), at the far end of which stands the elegant old Orphanage (Waisenhaus) of 1782, now the police headquarters.

Bärenplatz

Waisenhaus-platz

To the west of this, in the Hodlerstrasse (No. 12), the Museum of Art (Kunstmuseum), built in 1876–79, with a plain windowless extension of 1935, contains a large collection of Swiss art, pictures by Italian masters of the 14th–16th c. and works by French artists of the 19th and 20th c. Among the older Swiss masters represented are the "Master of the Carnation" (Paul Löwensprung d. 1499) and Niklaus Manuel-Deutsch (1484–1530), one of the leading Swiss painters of the Early Renaissance: among modern artists Karl Staufer (1857–91) and Ferdinand Hodler (1853–1918). Notable also are the Paul Klee Collection with over 2500 of Klee's works making it the largest such collection in the world, and the Rupf Collection of Cubist art (Braque, Gris, Léger, Picasso, Kandinsky, Feininger, etc.), together with works by Adolf Wölfli. The Print Cabinet contains works by both Swiss and foreign artists.

★ **Museum of Art**

The main railway station, in Bahnhofplatz, below the Grosse Schanze, was completely rebuilt between 1957 and 1974, with the tracks running underground for a distance of 200m/656ft (tourist information office, shopping, restaurants, café, car park, bus station). In the Christoffel underpass are remains of the fourth medieval defensive system (foundation of walls, round towers, remains of a bridge).

Main Railway Station

Elevators and flights of steps lead up from the station to the Grosse Schanze, the principal bastion in the old fortifications (built 1634, demolished 1834), now a park commanding extensive views.

Grosse Schanze

On the north-west side are the University, founded in 1834 (present buildings 1899–1930, with a monument to the Berne doctor and poet Albrecht von Haller (1708–77) in front of it, and the headquarters of the Swiss federal Railways (SBB-Direktion). To the left, beyond Schanzenstrasse, is the Supreme Court (Obergericht, 1909).

University

From Kornhausplatz the Kornhausbrücke (1898, a graceful iron bridge 48m/157ft high with a span of 115m/377ft, leads over the Aare into the newer part of the town. On a little hill immediately beyond the bridge, on the left, is the Schänzli, once an outer work in the town's defences, now occupied by the Kursaal (café-restaurant, concert hall, casino), from the terrace of which there is a magnificent view of Berne and the Alps.

Kornhausbrücke

Schänzli

Below the hill to the west are the Botanic Garden and the Lorraine bridge, a concrete structure of 1928–29 which links the Lorraine district of the town with the area around the station.

Botanic Garden

South of the Old Town

From the south side of the old town the Kirchenfeld bridge, a two-arched iron bridge built 1882–83, crosses the Aare to the residential district of Kirchenfeld, the central feature of which is Helvetiaplatz, a large square around the Telegraph Union Monument (1922) and surrounded by museums. To the left is the Art Gallery (Kunsthalle, 1918), which puts on special exhibitions of contemporary art. To the right are the Berner Schulwarte (1933), with a rich collection of teaching material and a library on

Kirchenfeld Bridge

Berne

★ Swiss Alpine Museum

Swiss Postal Museum

education, and the Swiss Alpine Museum (1934), which presents a fascinating picture of the Swiss Alps, covering their scientific study, communications, mapping and climbers (large relief model of the Bernese Oberland). In the same building is the Swiss Postal Museum, illustrating the history of the Swiss postal service, with a large collection of stamps.

★ **Historical Museum of Berne**

On the south side of Helvetiaplatz the Historical Museum of Berne (1892–94) is built in the style of a 16th c. castle, with collections of prehistoric material, folk art and traditions, ethnography and various types of decorative and applied art. Of particular interest are the Burgundian room, with trophies won at the Battle of Grandson in 1476 (weapons, tapestries, embroidery), the Henri Moser Charlottenfels Collection (weapons and objets d'art from the Islamic East), the Lausanne cathedral treasury and late medieval tapestries.

Natural History Museum

Beyond the Historical Museum, in Bernastrasse, are (No. 5) the Swiss Riflemen's Museum and (No. 15) the Natural History Museum (Naturhistorisches Museum, 1933), with excellently displayed collections of geology, mineralogy, palaeontology and zoology (series of dioramas of African mammals in the B. von Wattenwyl Collection; dioramas of the animals of other regions; collection of rock-crystal; collection of antlers; zoological laboratory).

Swiss National Library

Dählhölzli

Still farther south rises the massive building occupied by the National Library (Landesbibliothek, 1929–32). Thormannstrasse continues south to the Dählhölzli, in a bend of the Aare, with the Tierpark (nature park and zoo: restaurant). Footpath along the river (15 minutes) to the Elfenau nature reserve.

Surroundings of Berne

Bremgartenwald

To the north-west, between the town and the Aare, is a large wooded area, the Bremgartenwald, now encroached on by the motorway.

Halen

On the north side of the Aare, near the Halenbrücke, the interesting modern residential district of Halen (1959–61), is surrounded by the forest.

Walensee

To the north-west of the Bremgartenwald lies the Walensee, an artificial lake 15km/9 miles long formed by the damming of the Aare (motor-boat trips, rowing boats).

Ascent of Gurten

Gurten

Leave on the road to Belp, which runs south-east to the suburb of Wabern (556m/1824ft), 3.5km/2 miles away. From here (car park) a funicular ascends in 5 minutes to the summit of the green hill of Gurten (861m/2825ft). At the upper station, Gurten-Kulm (843m/2766ft), are the Gurten-Kulm Hotel, a large garden restaurant (view of Berne) and a miniature railway. From the Ostsignal (857m/2812ft: 10 minutes' walk east) and Westsignal (856m/2809ft: 3 minutes west) there are superb views of the Bernese Alps.

Through the Gürbe valley

From Wabern it is 3.5km/2 miles to Kehrsatz (573m/1880ft; bypass), with a 16th c. Schloss, now a state girls' reformatory.

Gürbetal

Belp

From here the direct road runs through the beautiful Gürbe valley (to the left Schloss Oberried, now a boys' school), via the neat little town of Belp (526m/1726ft), at the foot of the Belpberg (894m/2933ft), which has a picturesque 16th c. castle and a series of Gothic frescoes (1455–60) in the church of St Peter and Paul.

Then on to Toffen where there is a museum of veteran cars and motor-cycles in the Gürbestrasse and a medieval Baroque castle (1671). The castle in neighbouring Rümligen is also of Baroque style (18th c.); the last owner was the well-known Bernese Madame de Meuron. Past Seftigen, continuing over the ridge between the Gürbe and Aare valleys, the road reaches Thun (see entry) on the lake of the same name.

Toffen

Alternatively take a road on the right to Kehrsatz, and after a short distance uphill turn left into a ridge road which runs above the Gürbe valley (extensive views), passing below Zimmerwald, where the formation of the Third International (the Communist International Organisation) was discussed at a conference in September 1915 attended by Lenin.

Zimmerwald

The road runs sharply downhill to (12km/7 miles) Riggisberg (768m/2520ft), a little town of 2000 inhabitants (Abegg Collection of textiles and decorative art). From here via Gurnigel (1153m/3783ft: winter sports) to Schwefelbergbad (see p.203). Beyond this turn left (road on right to Gurnigel) 4.5km/3 miles: Burgistein (775m/2543ft) under a prominent 16th c. castle (813m/2667ft).

Riggisberg

Burgistein

2.5km/2 miles: Wattenwil (604m/1982ft), below the Staffelalp (983m/3225ft: far-ranging views; inn; 3km/2 miles by road). Continue through the Gürbe valley for 4km/2 miles to Blumenstein (661m/2169ft), with a 14th c. church (beautiful stained glass in choir) and a chalybeate spring (impregnated with iron). Finally, 4.5km/3 miles, we reach Oberstocken (672m/2205ft), at the foot of the Stockhorn, from which there are extensive views.

Wattenwil

From Berne to Fribourg via Schwarzenburg

In Köniz (575m/1887ft; pop. 32,000) a visit to the Morillongut country seat (1832) and the former Augustinian Provost St Peter and Paul is a must. The notable Romanesque church (Gothic choir with 14th c. glass and wall-paintings) was taken over by the Teutonic knights in 1226 and enlarged in the 17th c.

Köniz

About 5km/3 miles farther on the road cuts across the deeply cut valley of the Scherlibach. Another 10km/6 miles to Schwarzenburg (795m/2608ft) where there is a castle of 1573, the 15th c. little church of Maria Magdalena with a shingle-covered 17th c. clock tower and the Swiss short-wave radio transmitter.

Scwarzenburg

From here road 74 leads west towards Fribourg through an upland region with far-reaching views, crossing the gorge of the Sense River on a covered wooden bridge (1.3km/1 mile north, above the right bank of the river the ruins of the Imperial castle of Grasburg). Via Heitenried, 13km/8 miles, (760m/2494ft) is Tafers (655m/2150ft) with its notable church (oldest part 8th–10th c.; altered in 16th, 18th and 20th c.). After only a few kilometres the church towers of Fribourg (see entry) are visible.

Tafers

Bernese Oberland   F–L 8–10

Cantons: Berne (BE) and Valais (VS)

The Bernese Oberland is that part of the Swiss Alps lying between Lake Geneva and the River Reuss; it rises above the 4000m/13,124ft mark in the Finsteraarhorn (4274m/14,023ft), the Aletschhorn (4195m/13,764ft), the Schreckhorn (4078m/13,380ft), the Mönch (4099m/13,449ft) and the Jung-frau (4158m/13,642ft).

Situation

Lakes and Rivers	The massif is drained on the north by the Saane, Simme, Kander and other rivers, on the south by the Rhône, which is fed by the Aletsch glacier and Rhône glacier and by its right-bank tributaries. The Rhône forms the southern boundary of the Bernese Oberland until it flows into Lake Geneva. Below the north side are Lake Thun and Lake Brienz. The principal gateway to the mountains of the Bernese Oberland is Interlaken.
History	The regions bordering the Bernese Oberland have a long history of human settlement, as is shown by the Stone Age and Bronze Age material and the Roman remains which have been found by excavation, as well as by churches dating from before the year 1000. For many centuries the villages in the Bernese Oberland were wholly dependent on their stock-farming and pastoral economy, but the time came when the beauties of mountain scenery began to be appreciated. In the latter part of the 18th c. Goethe visited the Lauterbrunnen valley, and during the Romantic period there was an enthusiastic interest in natural beauty. This period too saw the beginning of modern mountaineering; the Jungfrau was climbed in the early years of the 19th c., and other peaks represented a challenge to climbers. Perhaps the best known of these is the Eiger, the north face of which was long regarded as unclimbable. The first successful ascent was in 1938 (by Heckmair, Vörg, Harrer and Kasparek), and the first winter ascent in 1961 (by Hiebeler, Kinshofer, Almberger and Manhardt).
Communications	The main north–south route through the Bernese Oberland is the 14.6km/9 mile railway tunnel under the Lötschberg; the busiest road is the one which runs over the Grimsel pass from Brienz to Gletsch, at the foot of the Rhône glacier (see Andermatt, Grimsel road).

★★Culture and Landscape

The Bernese Oberland has a number of major tourist resorts which are among the oldest established in Switzerland. Alexander von Humboldt,

Panorama from Niesen (2362 m — 7750 ft)

Labels (top row): ...rothorn(?) (3639 m) · Morgenhorn (3629 m) · Weisse Frau (3260 m) · Blümisalphorn (3664 m) · Oschinenhorn (3490 m) · Fründenhorn (3369 m) · Doldenhorn (3643 m) · Zahlershorn (2745 m) · Fisistock (2949 m) · Monte Rosa (4550 m) · Balmhorn (3709 m) · Altels (3629 m) · Rinderhorn (3454 m) · Dent Blanche (4357 m) · Lohner (3049 m) · Wildstrubel (3244 m) · Rätzligletscher · Gletscherhorn (2943 m) · Weisshorn (4505 m)

Labels (bottom row): Blümlisalpstock (3219 m) · Dündenhorn (2862 m) · Armighorn (2742 m) · Gerihorn (2130 m) · Birre (2505 m) · Kandergrund · Elsighorn (2341 m) · Adelboden

© Baedeker

Goethe, Kleist and Brahms were regular visitors to Lake Thun, the site of three famous castles, which today house Historical Museums. The neighbouring Lake Brienz is equally attractive. Interlaken, as the name suggests, lies on an alluvial delta between the two lakes. Lenk, Adelboden and Grindelwald, among others, were already attracting many visitors in the 19th c., and up to the First World War the region became the haunt of the nobility and successful artists from all over Europe. Today the Bernese Oberland, with its magnificent scenery and its excellent and steadily expanding facilities for winter sports, is perhaps still the best-known holiday region in Switzerland and it is not without good reason that it is often described as "The playground of Europe".	Lake Thun Lake Brienz
Summer in the Bernese Oberland means walking, hiking and climbing in magical countryside on well marked paths. A number of routes of varying difficulty await the climber while the lakes are a sailor's paradise.	In Summer
In winter the region is a skier's paradise offering marvellous pistes for both beginners and experienced skiers. With almost 500km/310 miles of routes the Bernese Oberland is a paradise for long-distance skiers. For non-skiers there are excellent indoor and outdoor facilities for curling, ice-skating, tennis and swimming.	In Winter
The finest mountains, and those affording the best views, are well provided with cableways and elevators — e.g. the Jungfraujoch (3545m/11,635ft) with Europe's highest cableway station. On the route to the "Top of Europe" one can enjoy unique views of the Alpine glaciers of the Swiss Alps (see Jungfrau region), e.g. the Eismeer (3160m/10,371ft), the Eigerwand (2865m/9403ft), the First (2168m/7115ft), the Schilthorn (2971m/9751ft) and others.	★★ Jungfrau region
The most impressive panoramic view is to be had from the 2362m/7750ft high Niesen, which rises above the south-west side of Lake Thun and can be reached by funicular from Mülenen. From the summit there is a panorama taking in Lakes Thun and Brienz, the 4000m/13,124ft peaks of the Jungfrau massif and the Valais Alps to the south.	★ Niesen

147

Spiez Castle on Lake Thun

Typical 18th c. timber house in Bönigen

Bernina Pass   S/T 9/10

Canton: Grisons (GR)
Altitude: 2323m/7622ft

One of the most rewarding routes through the Alps is the one which runs from St Moritz over the Bernina pass and down the Poschiavo valley into Italy, and usually remains open throughout the year for both road and rail traffic. The pass is not only the watershed between the Engadine and the Valtellina but also the boundary between Rhaeto-Romanic (referring to the language and culture peculiar to south-eastern Switzerland and the Tyrol) and Italian culture. The road, already being used in the 13th c. and built in its modern form between 1842 and 1865, traverses magnificent mountain and glacier scenery.

Situation and general

The journey from St Moritz to Tirano in Italy goes over the 58km/36 miles long pass road, via Pontresina (8km/5 miles) to the Bernina pass (24km/15 miles), and then via Poschiavo (17km/11 miles) to Tirano (34km/21 miles).

Communications

By rail on the Rhätische Bahn, the journey takes 3½ hours (the highest railway over the Alps). A tourist attraction is the Bernina-Express from Chur via the pass to Tirano, which can also be combined with the Glacier-Express (see Practical Information, Railways).

The road crosses the plateau via Samedan (airport) and Celerina, and begins to climb at Punt Muragl (cableway up Muottas Muragl: see p.333). At Pontresina there are views up Val Roseg to the right and Val Languard to the left. 4.5km/3 miles farther on a road goes off on the right to the Hotel-Restaurant Morteratsch (45 minutes climb from here to the Morteratsch glacier, 35 minutes up Chünetta). From the sharp bends at Monte-

Morteratsch Glacier

◀ *View from the Eiger over Grindelwald and First*

Walking to the Boval hut above the Morteratsch glacier

bello there are superb views of the Morteratsch glacier, Piz Palü (3905m/12,812ft), Bellavista (3827m/12,556ft), Piz Bernina (4049m/13,285ft) and Piz Morteratsch (3751m/12,307ft).

Two of Switzerland's finest cableways start from special stations on the Bernina railway.

★★ Diavolezza

The Diavolezza (2973m/9754ft), one of the most popular skiing areas in the Alps, is reached by a cableway starting just beyond Bernina Suot (length 3625m/11,894ft), height difference 883m/2897ft, time 10 minutes). The Diavolezza-Haus (2978m/9774ft), situated opposite the giant peaks of the Bernina group, affords magnificent views. From here there are numerous paths leading into the mountains, including the "Diavolezza-Tour", one of the easiest glacier walks (3 hours, with guide), going from the Diavolezza-Haus by way of the Pers and Morteratsch glaciers to the Morteratsch Hotel. Summer skiing.

★ Piz Lagalb

Piz Lagalb (2959m/9708ft: lower station Curtinatsch 2090m/6857ft, upper station 2896m/9502ft: restaurant, with panoramic view): wildlife park, view into the Valtellina. The cableway, 2381m/7812ft long, runs up from Curtinatsch (Bernina-Lagalb) in 8 minutes.

Bernina Hospice

The Bernina Hospice (2309m/7576ft: 40b.) is a good walking and climbing base. Two lakes, Lej Nair (Black Lake, 2222m/7290ft) and Lej Pitschen (2220m/7284ft), fed by springs, drain northward into the Inn; they are separated by a masonry dam from the Lago Bianco (White Lake, 2230m/7317ft), an artificial lake supplying the Brusio hydro-electric station. From the Alp Grüm (2091m/6861ft: railway station) there is a fine view of the Palü glacier (Alpine garden). Nature-lovers can observe many species of birds, from the golden eagle to the rock swallow, from the pigmy owl to the snow finch.

The Bernina road now leaves the railway track, which runs over the Alp Grüm and down into the Val di Pila, and climbs past the Lago della Crocetta to the Bernina pass (Italian Passo del Bernina, 2323m/7622ft), with the desolate landscape of ice-worn rocks commonly found on the high passes and beautiful views on both sides. From here the road runs sharply downhill in short bends and then descends in four hairpins, with magnificent views down into the valley, into the Val Agoné, the highest part of the Poschiavo valley. At La Motta a road branches off on the left over the Forcola di Livigno pass (2315m/7596ft) into the Val di Livigno, in Italy (3.5km/2 miles to the frontier, then 15km/9 miles to Livigno: large skiing area, customs-free zone).

★ Bernina Pass

5.5km/3 miles from the pass is La Rösa (1878m/6162ft), a picturesque little mountain village at the foot of Piz Campasscio. Then downhill above a wooded gorge, with beautiful views, followed by two sharp bends down to Sfazù (1666m/5466ft: restaurant) and over the Wildbach at the mouth of the beautiful Val di Campo (on left), a valley gouged out by a glacier (narrow mountain road, 8km/5 miles, maximum gradient 13%). 4km/2 miles beyond La Rösa, on the left, is the Pozzolascio restaurant (1530m/5020ft), near a small lake.

Val di Campo

The road continues high up on the wooded mountainside, soon affording an excellent view of the Poschiavo valley. On the opposite slope (view restricted by trees) are the boldly engineered bends of the Bernina railway. 10km/6 miles from La Rösa, at San Carlo (1095m/3593ft), the road reaches the floor of the Poschiavo valley (Italian Valle di Poschiavo). Before the village is a hydro-electric station belonging to the Brusio complex.

Valle di Poschiavo

From the Poschiavo valley into the Valtellina

The 34km/21 miles long Poschiavo valley, which descends from the Bernina pass to Tirano in the Valtellina, is a region of southern vegetation and Italian life-style. It remained part of the canton of Grisons after the cession to Italy of the Valtellina, which belonged to the Grisons from 1512 to 1797. In 1987 the valley was subject to catastrophic floods, but repairs were completed within a year.

The road continues on the south side of the Bernina pass is now of a good standard. In 17km/11 miles it comes to Poschiavo (1014m/3327ft: pop. 3600), the central area of population in a commune made up of six separate villages. Sights include the 17th c. Town Hall with Romanesque tower, the Late Gothic church of San Vittore (15th–16th c.) and the Baroque church of Santa Maria Presentata (17th–18th c.) with a beautiful ceiling painting in the nave from 1770. Not far from the Piazza are the elegant patrician houses. Colourful façades characterise the Spaniola quarter, which was settled in the 19th c. by emigrants returning from Spain.

4km/2 miles beyond Poschiavo is the summer holiday resort of Le Prese (965m/3166ft) on the Lago di Poschiavo.

Le Prese

The commune of Brusio (740m/2428ft: pop. 1340), which takes in the seven villages between the Lago di Poschiavo and the frontier, is an area of lush southern vegetation. The principal village is dominated by the towers of its 17th c. church.

Brusio

The road continues through tobacco plantations and forests of chestnut trees to Campascio (630m/2067ft) and Campocologno (553m/1814ft), the last place in Switzerland (customs), with the Brusio power station (33,000kW).

From the frontier crossing at Piatta Mala the road leads into the Valtellina. The Village of Madonna di Tirano (438m/1437ft) has a famous pilgrimage church (1503–33). The road now forks: to the right it runs down the Valtellina and continues via Sondrio and around Lake Como to Lugano (120km/

Madonna di Tirano

| Tirano | 75 miles: see entry); the road to the left runs up the valley to the old town of Tirano (429m/1408ft: pop. 10,000), straddling the River Adda, with old patrician houses of the 15th–17th c. |

Biel/Bienne   G 5/6

Canton: Berne
Altitude: 440m/1444ft
Population: 58,000

| Situation and general | This bilingual town (Biel in German, Bienne in French), with two-thirds of its inhabitants speaking German and one-third French, is the capital of the Swiss watchmaking industry. Several hundred small and medium-sized firms are engaged in the manufacture of watches and watch parts in the town, which is also a place of considerable commercial activity. The residential districts are mainly on the lower slopes of the Jura hills, which here slope down to the lake. In recent years the town has also made a name for itself as a convention capital. |

| History | The town was founded about 1220 by the Prince-Abbot of Basle and remained under the rule of successive Prince-Abbots until 1792. From 1798 to 1815 it belonged to France; thereafter it was incorporated in the canton of Berne and is now the second largest town in the canton. |

Sights

| Rathaus | The upper town with its historic old buildings is well preserved. In the Burgplatz are the Late Gothic Rathaus (Town Hall: built 1530–34, renovated 1676) and the Theatre, originally the armoury (1589–91; in front of the Rathaus stands the Justice fountain (1714). A market is held on the Burgplatz during the week. |

Biel/Bienne

© Baedeker

Biel/Bienne: Guild house of Foresters . . .   . . . and the Devil's Fountain

From here the Burggässli leads to the Ring, a square surrounded by arcaded houses. The old Zunfthaus der Waldleute (Guild-House of the Foresters, 1559–61), a Late Gothic building with a stepped gable and some Renaissance features, is now occupied by the Kunstverein (Society of Arts) and the School of Music. The Late Gothic parish church of St Benedict (1451–92: Protestant) has 15th c. stained glass and wall-paintings. In the Obergasse are the 16th c. Angel fountain and the former inn Zur Krone (1578–82), with a tablet commemorating Goethe's stay there in 1779. In the Rosiusplatz are towers and part of a moat belonging to the old fortifications, the old Clock tower (rebuilt on this site in 1843) and the Technikum (Technical College).

★Zunfthaus der Waldleute

The Omega Museum (96, Rue Stämpfli) has a clock collection ranging from the first watches to NASA's latest time measuring equipment. Viewing by appointment only; tel. (032) 42 92 11 and 42 93 04.

Museum

In the Seevorstadt, a street running down to the lake, is the Schwab Museum (closed Mondays), with material of the prehistoric period (lake-dwellings), Iron Age and Roman period.

In the Centre PasqART art centre (Seevorstadt 71; closed Mondays) visitors can view contemporary Swiss art, while the Neuhaus Museum houses the Karl and Robert Walser collections (Schüsspromenade 26, re-opened from autumn 1995.

To the south are the railway station and the modern Congress Hall in the Zentralstrasse (1961–66: swimming pool).

Congress Hall

Surroundings

From the north-western Jura hills above the town there are panoramic views of the Bernese Alps and the Mittelland, with the lakes. 2.5km/2 miles from Biel on the Delémont road (No. 8) a narrow road branches off on the

Magglingen	left and in 4.5km/3 miles reaches Magglingen (French Macolin: 875m/2871ft; pop. 2700), with the Federal School of Gymnastics and Sport; easy hill-walking in the surrounding area. There are cableways from Biel to Magglingen (length 1694m/5558ft, time 9 minutes) and to Leubringen/Evilard (length 933m/3061ft, time 6 minutes).
Taubenloch-schlucht	In the Taubenlochschlucht, a gorge 2km/1 mile east of the outlying district of Bözingen, the folding of the strata caused by the geological upheavals of the past can be observed in the rock face.

The wine villages around the lake

Lake Biel	The Bieler See (Lake Biel) or Lac de Bienne (429m/1408ft: area 39sq.km/15sq.miles), forms the boundary between two geological regions, the limestone formations of the Jura and the molasse (soft greenish sandstone) of the area around the lakes. On the north side of the lake the slopes of the Jura fall steeply down, with the German-speaking villages of Tüscherz, Twann and Ligerz, once belonging to Burgundy, set amid vine-yards at the foot. The shore on the south side, less visited by tourists, is flatter, and in prehistoric times was occupied by numerous lake-dwellings built on piles. At the south end of the lake lies the popular resort of St Peterinsel (St Peter's Island), the south-east side of which is the haunt of large numbers of waterfowl.
Regulation of the River Aare	In 1878, as a result of the control of the River Aare, the level of the lake was lowered by some 2m/7ft. The Aare, which had previously flowed past the lake 7km/4 miles to the east, was then diverted into the lake by the con-struction of a canal at Hagneck and brought back to its original bed by another canal from Nidau to Büren. As a result soil and debris carried down by the river were deposited in the lake.
Vine-growing	A circuit of the lake provides an opportunity of seeing the beautiful scenery of its shores and a series of attractive little towns and villages, in the largest vine-growing area in the canton of Berne. Three-quarters of the area is planted with the white Chasselas grape, a fifth with the red Pinot Noir. The local method of wine-making, involving early racking (separation of the wine from the sediment or "lees"), produces fruity wines of high carbonic acid content, mainly sold as Twanner, Schafiser and Erlacher, which are much sought after. Vines are also grown at Ligerz, Tüscherz, Vingelz, Tscugg, La Neuveville and Alfermée and on St Peterinsel. There is a Museum of Viticulture in Ligerz and visits to wine-making establishments can be arranged through the Informations- und Propogandastelle für Bieler-See-Weine, CH-2514 Ligerz.
Twann	A walk along the "wine route" from Biel to Tüscherz and Twann (2 hours), returning from Twann by boat or continuing on foot to Ligerz (½ hour), is a memorable experience. The road around the lake runs south-west via Vingelz and the old Burgundian settlement of Alfermée to the wine village of Tüscherz (435m/1427ft; pop. 2800), which has a railway station and landing stage and continues to Twann (French Douanne: 434m/1424ft; pop. 900), a sleepy little village of narrow winding streets and old houses which has preserved its medieval character. Excavations here in 1974–76 revealed remains of the earliest farming settlements (between 3000 and 2000 B.C.).
Ligerz	The next village is Ligerz (French Gléresse: 433m/1421ft; pop. 450; Wine-Growing Museum), from which there is a cableway to Prêles (Prägelz), on the Tessenberg (length 1200m/3937ft, height difference 379m/1243ft, time 7 minutes); from the terrace below Mont Chasseral there are superb views. Good walking among the vineyards, through the Twannbach gorge and to Schernelz.

The Blanche-Eglise (white church) of La Neuveville

The last Bernese commune on the lake is La Neuveville (German Neuen-   La Neuveville
stadt: 438m/1437ft; pop. 3900), the "Montreux of the Jura", with narrow
streets, old gates and towers which belonged to the town's fortifications,
and a 14th/15th c. church, the Blanche Eglise, with a wooden ceiling and
Gothic frescoes (restored 1988/90). The road now enters the canton of
Neuchâtel.

The first place beyond the cantonal boundary is Le Landeron (433m/1421ft;   Le Landeron
pop. 3400), a medieval market town with house fronts of the 16th and
17th c. The largest flea-market in Switzerland, the Fête de la Brocante, is
held here annually in September.

Continuing along the south side of the lake, the next town is Erlach (433m/   Erlach
1421ft; pop. 1000) with an old castle which is now a cantonal school hostel.
Late Gothic arcaded houses line Junkerngasse from the town hall to the
castle. The administrative district of Erlach also includes the farming and
vine-growing villages of Vinelz and Lüscherz.

The most popular excursion on the lake is to St Peterinsel (435m/1427ft: ★ St Peterinsel
Hotel), a place of idyllic beauty. Once an island it can be reached from Biel
or La Neuveville by boat, or (since the 19th c. regulation of the River Aare)
on foot from Erlach on the "Heidenweg". The inn was originally a Cluniac
priory (founded 1120, dissolved 1530); the room in which Rousseau stayed
in 1765 is shown to visitors. The return route from Erlach crosses the Aare
canal and just before Biel reaches Nidau (430m/1411ft; pop. 8400), which is
separated from Biel only by the Zihl canal, and is the starting point of the
Nidau-Büren canal; thus in effect Nidau lies on an artificial island. The
castle was the seat of the Bernese provincial governor from 1388; it now
houses the district council offices.

Aarberg (455m/1493ft; pop. 3300) 11km/7 miles south of Biel, a unique little   Aarberg
medieval town, was founded about 1220, and was for centuries one of the
countries most important road junctions. Its main features of interest are

Erlach Castle

the Stadtplatz with its ring of well-to-do citizens' houses and the old wooden bridge over the Aare. The castle (end of 17th c.) contains a gallery of coats-of-arms from over 80 provincial governors.

Lyss
Lyss (444m/1493ft; pop. 8300: swimming pool and ice rink): walks along the Alte Aare, the old course of the river (rich flora and fauna).

Büren an der Aare
Büren an der Aare (443m/1453ft; pop. 2900), a little medieval town, bright with flowers, lying between the Aare and the forest, with many fine old buildings. The town hall (*c.* 1500) and the provincial governor's castle from 1620 with picturesque Gothic stepped windows are worth visiting.

Val Bregaglia   R 10

Canton: Grisons (GR)

Situation and general
The Val Bregaglia (in German Bergell) is a wild and romantic gorge, enclosed between towering granite mountains, which descends in a series of terrace-like steps from the Majola pass (1815m/5955ft) to the Italian town of Chiavenna (333m/1093ft), 32km/20 miles south-west. The high valley of the River Mera, which eventually flows into Lake Como, begins by falling steeply down from the pass (the watershed between the Val Bregaglia and the Engadine) and then descends to Chiavenna in six stages, the first four of which are within the canton of Grisons. The oddly shaped crags, buttresses and pinnacles of this mountain world are a climber's paradise, and the picturesque villages with their old patrician houses are a reminder of the long history of this region, which began in Roman times.

Beyond the pass the road leads down in a series of 13 hairpin bends, with gradients of up to 9%, into the green valley below.

Casáccia
The highest village in the valley is Casáccia (1458m/4784ft; pop. 60), from which the old bridle-path, one of the busiest routes through the Alps in

medieval times, crossed the Pass da Sett (Septimer pass) to Bivio in the Sursés (Oberhalbstein) valley. The ruined Turratsch watch-tower and the 16th c. hospice are relics of these earlier days. A cableway 2500m/8203ft long belonging to the hydro-electric station which supplies power to Zurich (available for the transport of visitors by prior arrangement) leads up to the Albigna reservoir (2163m/7097ft: dam 115m/377ft high).

Vicosoprano (1067m/3501ft; pop. 400) was originally the chief settlement in the valley. Sixteenth century patrician houses; Senwelenturm, a 13th c. tower 23m/75ft high; courthouse, with torture chamber; Town Hall (1584); church (1761).

Vicosoprano

Stampa (994m/3261ft; pop. 180), a village which straggles along the road, was the home of the Giacometti family of artists. In the Ciäsa Granda (the "large house", open: June 1st–Oct. 20th, daily 2–5pm) is a fascinating museum devoted to the Val Bregaglia (collection of minerals, a weaving room, elegant living rooms and domestic utensils, as well as some paintings by the Giacomettis).

Stampa, Ciäsa Granda

The following defile, La Porta, marks the boundary between the Alpine and the more southerly parts of the valley; it was fortified in Roman times.

The hamlet of Promontogno (821m/2694ft) has a church (Nossa Donna), which dates in part from the 12th c., and a ruined castle (Castelmur).

Promontogno

From here a rewarding excursion (3km/2 miles) can be made to Soglio (1090m/3576ft; pop. 210) on a road which branches on the right and runs through a chestnut wood. The village was the ancestral home of the Salis family and has three palaces (16th–18th c.) which belonged to them. From the village, huddled around the tall tower of its church on a natural terrace above the valley, there are magnificent views of the Sciora group and the Val Bregaglia.

★ Soglio

22km/14 miles from the Majola pass the road reaches the Italian frontier at Castasegna (697m/2287ft; pop. 220), a trim village of southern aspect

Castasegna

View of the upper valley of the Mera from the Majola Pass

surrounded by luxuriant vegetation and the beautiful chestnut wood of Brentan. Underground hydro-electric power station (50 by 25m/164 by 82ft).

Chiavenna

The Italian town of Chiavenna lies at the junction of the Spluga (Splügen) and Majola pass routes. The Roman Clavenna occupied a key strategic position, as its name (from clavis, "key") implies. From 1512 to 1797 it was in the Grisons. Its principal church, San Lorenzo, has an octagonal baptistery (font of 1156).

Brig   K 10

Canton: Valais
Altitude: 684m/2244ft
Population: 10,000

Situation and general

The historic little town of Brig, on the south bank of the Rhône, is the capital of the German-speaking upper Valais (Oberwallis) and an important junction on the Simplon, Lötschberg, Furka–Oberalp and Brig–Visp–Oberalp railways. It has a number of notable buildings and is also the starting-point of the great roads over the Simplon, the Furka and Nufenen passes.

History

Brig was already of importance in Roman times as a staging point on the north side of the Simplon pass. Its name comes from its situation between two bridges (over the Rhône and the Saltina). It later became the see of a bishop, and enjoyed a period of great prosperity in the time of Kaspar Jodok Stockalper (see below).

Sights

★ Stockalper-schloss

The most notable building in Brig is the Stockalperschloss, the finest Baroque palace in Switzerland, which the town bought from the Stockalper family in 1948. Since then it has been thoroughly renovated and restored by a trust, with financial assistance from the Federal government, the canton and the town. This imposing structure, dominated by three square gabled towers, was built by the great Valais merchant Prince Kaspar Jodok Stockalper von Thurm (1609–91), who had occupied all the leading positions in the land. The palace, built between 1658 and 1678, pointed the way towards a great flowering of the Baroque in Valais. Linked by an arcaded walk to the house of Peter Stockalper (16th/17th c.), the palace now houses, in addition to the family library of the "King of the Simplon" and 12,000 documents, the archives of the Upper Valais Historical Society, the Valais Institute (Walser-Institut) and the Museum of the Upper Valais (May–Oct., Tues.–Sun., guided tours each hour). Also here are the Matza and Jadok galleries which both have special exhibitions.

Near the palace are the collegiate church of Spiritus Sanctus (1675–85) and the Gothic St Antony's chapel. Also of interest are the Fernanda Stockalper house (18th c.) opposite the palace, the Wegener house (17th–19th c.) and the Theiler house in Simplonstrasse.

★ Pilgrimage church of Unsere liebe Frau

West of Brig, on the Glisacker, stands the pilgrimage church of Unsere liebe Frau (c. 1540), representing the final phase of medieval architecture (Gothic and Renaissance), which contains the finest works of art in this part of Switzerland.

Also of interest are the monument to Dr Ernest Guglielmetti (known as "Dr Goudron" – i.e. "Dr Tar"), inventor of the asphalt-surfaced road (in the Marktplatz to the north of the Stockalperschloss) and the fountain commemorating the Peruvian aviator Geo Chavez, who flew over the Simplon for the first time in 1910 (in Sebastianplatz).

Brig: Stockalperschloss

Visp, at the mouth of the Vispa valley

Surroundings

On the north bank of the Rhône is Brigerbad (655m/2149ft; pop. 185) with the first thermal swimming bath in a cave (air-conditioned, 38–42° C/ 100–108° F).

Brigerbad

9km/6 miles south-west is Visp (660m/2165ft), a little town of 4000 inhabitants beautifully situated at the mouth of the Vispa valley, up which runs the road to Zermatt and Saas Fee. Remains of town walls; old houses with coats-of-arms. On a crag above the Vispa is a large church of 1761 with a Romanesque tower, and higher up the hill St Martin's church (1651, altered 1956), with an arcaded porch.

Visp

A road winds its way up the east side of the Vispa valley, through the highest vineyards in Europe (700–1200m/2297–3937ft: "Heidenwein", "heathen's wine"), for 10.5km/7 miles to the village of Visperterminen (1340m/4397ft), surrounded by a network of irrigation channels. From the village a path, with Stations of the Cross, climbs to the pilgrimage chapel of the Visitation (17th c.: old organ). Chair-lift from Visperterminen to Giw (1925m/6316ft).

Visperterminen

About 14km/9 miles west is Raron (640m/2100ft) with a pretty 16th c. castle church where the poet Rainer Maria Rilke lies buried.

Raron

To the north of Brig extends a magnificent glacier region. Between the Riederhorn (2230m/7317ft) and the Eggishorn (2937m/9636ft), a natural terrace exposed to the sun, from which the land falls steeply away, forms a transition to the Rhône valley. From Brig there are various routes to the Aletsch glacier which offer attractive day or half-day outings, with the help of cableways and lifts.

At the foot of the Aletsch glacier

From Brig-Naters there is a good road up the Chelchbach valley to Blatten (1327m/4355ft; pop. 50), a typical little Valais mountain village, from which

Blatten

Brig

Belalp

there is a cableway (length 1780m/5840ft, height difference 766m/2513ft, time 8 minutes) to Belalp (2080m/6824ft). From here a footpath (½ hour) leads to the Belalp Hotel (D, 30b.), at the foot of the Sparrhorn and above the western tip of the Aletsch glacier (see below).

Mörel

7km/4 miles up the Rhône valley from Brig is Mörel (800m/2625ft; pop. 600), formerly a post station and now a base for walks and climbs on the Riederalp. There are two cableways, one running up in two stages via Ried (length 3055m/10,123ft, height difference 1155m/3790ft, time 25 minutes) to the Riederalp, the other to the Greicheralp (length 2798m/9180ft, height difference 1141m/3744ft, time 15 minutes) with a continuation to the Moosfluh (length 1817m/5962ft, height difference 451m/1480ft, time 12 minutes), directly above the Aletsch glacier. From the Riederalp there is a chair-lift (length 1053m/3455ft, height difference 299m/981ft, time 7 minutes) to the Hohfluh, from which there is a splendid walk down to the Riederfurka (2064m/6772ft).

A well constructed road leads from the mountain station of the cableway Rieder-Alp–Moosfluh, along the Bettmerhorn to Lake Märjelen, and offers spectacular views of the Aletsch glacier and the surrounding peaks over 4000m/13,000ft.

★ Breiten ob
Mörel

8km/5 miles up the valley from Brig lies the modern holiday resort and spa of Breiten ob Mörel (900m/2954ft). This centrally-managed resort on a sunny terrace above the infant Rhône valley is the only brine spa in the Alps (33° C/91° F), with a well-equipped treatment and fitness centre (indoor heated swimming pool, solarium) and its own Alpine farm (cheese dairy of 1713).

★★ Great
Aletsch glacier

The Great Aletsch glacier is a unique feature of great magnificence – the largest stretch of firn (ice formed from snow) in the Alps and in Europe (area 170sq.km/66sq.miles, length 22km/14 miles). Its catchment area

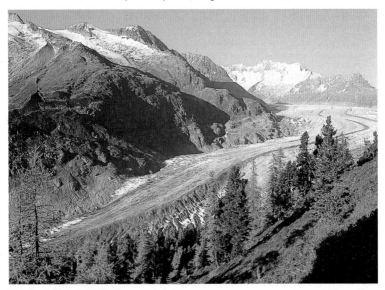

The Great Aletsch glacier

extends from the south side of the Bernese Alps, around the Jungfrau, to the almost level Konkordiaplatz (see below), where the ice is some 800m/2625ft deep, and from there southwards to the Aletschwald (nature reserve), one of the highest forests of stone pines in Europe.

The Aletsch area offers magnificent opportunities for walkers and climbers. The Villa Cassel, an elegant building erected by the British banker Sir Ernest Cassel at the end of the 19th c., on the Riederfurka was the first office for the protection of nature established by the Schweizer Bund für Naturschutz (Swiss Association for the Protection of Nature: exhibition, Alpine garden).

Villa Cassel, Riederfurka

The real gateway to the Aletsch glacier and the Aletschwald is the Riederalp (1950m/6398ft; pop. 300) which is accessible by three cableways from Mörel. The highest golf course in Switzerland (9 holes) is situated here. Popular attractions include guided glacier walks, excursions over the high mountain path from the mountain station Riederalp/Moosfluh to Lake Märjelen and the weekly cheese show at the Alpine museum. The well established pistes of the Riederalp are an ideal skiing area in winter with guaranteed snow (ski school offering courses in ski acrobatics). Particular features of interest are the Riederalp chapel (1679) and the nearby Blausee (Blue Lake; 2204m/7234ft).

★Riederalp

There is a pleasant, almost level, walk to the Bettmeralp (1950m/6398ft; pop. 150). The picturesque little mountain village, around the chapel of Maria zum Schnee (1679), is a popular resort both in summer and in winter, with excellent walking (walking, fishing and tennis weeks; glacier walks; climbing school). From the Rhône valley the Bettmeralp can be reached via Betten (10km/6 miles from Brig) on a cableway (length 2610km/8563ft, height difference 1120m/3675ft, time 10 minutes).

★Bettmeralp

The Aletsch area can also be reached from Fiesch, 18km/11 miles east of Brig (1050m/3445ft; pop. 700). Fiesch, which first appears in the records in 1203, has a chapel with an altar of 1704. There is a large health and holiday complex for young people, opened in 1966 (1050b., SB, gymnasium).

Fiesch

From the Eggishorn (2916m/9600ft) there are panoramic views in the Upper Valais. A cableway (length 4795m/15,732ft, height difference 1807m/5929ft, time 13 minutes) ascends to the Kühboden and from there to the summit (magnificent view of the Aletsch glacier). Under the north face of the Eggishorn is the Märjelensee (Lake Märjelen; 2345m/7694ft: nature reserve).

★Eggishorn

8km/5 miles north-east of the Eggishorn is Konkordiaplatz (2840m/9318ft: Swiss Alpine Club hut; guide required).

★Konkordia-platz

Passing through Lax and Ernen (see Rhône Valley), the road leads to Birn (1389m/4558ft; 28km/17½ miles north-east of Brig), a community made up of several hamlets. From here it is worth making an excursion into the Binntal, a valley 12km/7½ miles long and 1400–2400m/4600–7900ft above sea-level, in which six of the seven roads into Italy begin as mere footpaths. It is known for its unusual and varied flora and its mineral riches (150 of the 300 minerals found in Switzerland occur here).

★Binntal

At the end of the Binntal is the beginning of the Gomstal, the valley of the upper Rhône (see Rhône Valley).

Brunnen

Canton: Schwyz (SZ)
Altitude: 440m/1444ft
Population: 6300

Brunnen

<table>
<tr><td>Situation and general</td><td>The popular summer resort of Brunnen has a magnificent situation at the right-angled bend in Lake Lucerne formed by the Urner See (Lake Uri) and the Gersauer Becken (Gersau basin), at the beginning of the Axenstrasse (opened 1865), on the road over the St Gotthard. Since the construction of a bypass road it is a pleasantly quiet resort, with splendid views of the lake, the Seelisberg (with the Rütli Meadow) and the Bürgenstock. Above the wide Muota valley rise the two characteristically shaped horns of the Mythen; above the deep rocky trough of the Urner See towers the massive Urirotstock, almost 3000m/9843ft high; and to the rear of the Gersau basin is Pilatus, rising to over 2000m/6562ft.

The first reference to the town is in the Einsiedeln chronicles in 1217, but its traditions go much further back.

The Axenstrasse, with its fine views, was opened in 1865.</td></tr>
<tr><td>Sights</td><td>The historic Bundeskapelle (Federal Chapel), built 1632–35 by Landamman Heinrich von Reding, has an altarpiece by Justus van Egmont (1642), a pupil of Rubens. Late Baroque parish church of St Leonhard (1661, restored 1978) in Ingenbohl. Memorial to the composer Othmar Schoeck, a native of Brunnen (1959). Crypt dedicated to the foundress of the convent of the Sisters of Charity of the Holy Cross (1975).</td></tr>
</table>

Surroundings

<table>
<tr><td>Fronalpstock Morschach</td><td>From the Axenstrasse a steep road runs up to the natural terrace at the foot of the Fronalpstock (1922m/6396ft). 3km/2 miles: Morschach (645m/2116ft: pop. 550) has a superb view of the lake and the mountains, concerts, a forest park and a swimming pool.</td></tr>
<tr><td>★ Axenstein</td><td>From here it is 1km/½ mile to the Axenstein (708m/2323ft: nurses' home), an excellent viewpoint.</td></tr>
</table>

At the north end of Lake Uri . . .   *. . . lies Brunnen*

The 35km/22 mile-long "Weg der Schweiz" ("Swiss Way"), around Lake Uri, from Rütli to Brunnen, was completed in 1991 to mark the 700th anniversary of the Confederation. Each Canton was allocated a section of it – the length depending on its population – and was made responsible for making it environmentally friendly; for example Zurich, having the largest population, was allocated 6.9km/3¾ miles, while Appenzell had to be content with 71m/78yd.

Swiss Way

Bürgenstock   M 6

Canton: Nidwalden (NW) and Lucerne (LU)
Altitude: 878–1132m/2881–3714ft

The Bürgenstock is a limestone ridge 10km/6 miles long and between 1.5 and 3km/1 and 2 miles broad, covered with forests and Alpine meadows, which forms a peninsula in Lake Lucerne. Its north side rises steeply to a height of 500m/1641ft above the lake; the south side slopes more gently down to the Stans valley.

Situation

This select health resort and magnificent viewpoint can be reached by road from Stansstad (5km/3 miles) or from the landing-stage of Kehrsiten-Bürgenstock (30 minutes from Lucerne) by funicular (944m/3097ft, gradient 45%, 7 minutes). At the upper station of the Bürgenstock funicular, the oldest in Switzerland (opened in 1888), are the Bahnhofsrestaurant, the Park-Hotel and the Palace Hotel; 300m/328yd south-west is the Grand Hôtel, the furnishing of which include a notable collection of pictures.

General

Tour

(2 hours: strongly recommended). Starting from the hotels, walk along the Felsenweg on the Hammetschwand cliffs (30 minutes) to the Hammet-

★Felsenweg

View of Mt Pilatus from the Bürgenstock

schwand lift, which runs up the vertical rock face to the upper station (restaurant) at 1115m/3580ft.

Hammet-
schwand

Take the lift down again and continue on the Felsenweg, the finest stretch of which begins here: 20 minutes to the Honegg-Känzeli, and from there another 30 minutes, past the Kurhaus Honegg and the golf-course, back to the hotels.

The narrow road which runs from the hotels by way of the Honegg saddle to Ennetbürgen can be used by cars only from the Kurhaus Honegg.

La Chaux-de-Fonds   E 6

Canton: Neuchâtel (NE)
Altitude: 997m/3271ft
Population: 37,000

Situation and
general

Situated in a high valley in the Jura, the town of La Chaux-de-Fonds (rebuilt on a regular plan after a fire in 1794) is the capital of the Swiss watchmaking industry, which was first established here about 1705. The town is home of the Théâtre Populaire Romand, the only professional acting troupe of West Switzerland, and an important centre of Esperanto. La Chaux-de-Fonds was the birthplace of the Romantic painter Léopold Robert (1794–1835), of the famous pilot and automobile manufacturer Louis Chevrolet (1878–1941), the poet and writer Blaise Cendrars (Frédéric Sauser, 1887–1961) and the famous architect Charles-Edouard Jeanneret, better known as Le Corbusier (1887–1965).

Wintersports

Illuminated ski trails, lifts from town, cross-country skiing, ski-bob run, indoor and outdoor ice rinks, tobogganing, ski school.

La-Chaux-de-Fonds: Glockenspiel outside the International Clock Museum

International Watch and Clock Museum
La Chaux-de-Fonds

Plan

© Baedeker

Rue des Musées

Repair and Restoration

Reception

Multi-purpose hall

Documents and Library

Underground museum with an area of 2300 sq. m (2751 sq. yards) and 3100 exhibits

EARLY ERA

1 Tower clocks
2 Pre-history and antiquity
3 Renaissance
4 18th c. clockmakers
5 Marine clocks
6 Enamelled watches and engraved watch cases
7 Neuenburg clock making
8 French pendulum clocks
9 Foreign pendulum clocks
10 Automata, 19th c. fantasy clocks
11 Information area
12 Old and new professions

MODERN ERA

13 Scientific measurement of time
14 Glockenspiel
15 Basic movements
16 Motive power
17 Transmission of power
18 Oscillators
19 Assembly techniques
20 Clockwork mechanisms
21 Quality, precision and reliability
22 Finished product

A Reception
B Multi-purpose hall
C Exhibition areas
D Documentation office
E Administration

Section

© Baedeker

La Grande Fontaine . . .   *. . . and Musée des Beaux Arts*

Sights

★★ International Watch and Clock Museum

In Rue du Progrès is a Technical college, with a watchmaking school. At 29 rue des Musées the International Watch and Clock Museum (Internationales Uhrenmuseum/Musée International de l'horlogerie: partly underground; closed Mon.) takes as its theme "Man and Time", displaying the history of timekeeping from the Egyptians to the latest achievements of modern technology. It also has a workshop for the restoration of old watches and clocks which make its services available to collectors generally, a documentation office and library, audio-visual apparatus and a multi-purpose hall which is used for special exhibitions.

Museums

Other interesting museums in the Rue des Musées are the Museum of Fine Art (No. 33; Musée des Beaux-Arts; closed Mon.) and the Historical Museum (No. 31; Musée d'Histoire et Médailler; open: Sat., Sun. and by arrangement, tel. (039) 23 50 10), and the Natural History Museum at 63 Avenue Léopold-Robert; closed Mon. The Farmhouse Museum shows details of rural life and working conditions, as well as a lace collection (Musée Paysan et Artisanal; 5 Les Eplatures-Grise; open: May–Oct. daily except Fri., Nov.–Apr. Wed., Sat. and Sun.).

The Protestant church, built in 1794 after plans by M. Perret-Gentil, was rebuilt in 1921 after a fire.

There is a large sports centre in the east of the town.

Surroundings

Le Locle

8km/5 miles south-west is the modern industrial town of Le Locle (925m/3035ft), second only to La Chaux-de-Fonds as a hub of the watchmaking industry, which was founded in 1705 by Daniel Jean-Richard (monument at Post Office). In front of the Watchmaking school stands a monument to the first director of the school, J. Grossman (1829–1907), a native of the watchmaking town of Glashütte in Saxony. In the Rue Marie-Anne Calame

(No. 6) the Museum of Art has works by Swiss artists of the 19th and 20th centuries.

In the Château des Monts are a Watch and Clock Museum, with an interesting collection of watches and clocks and 35 automata, ranging in date from the 15th c. to the 18th c., and a small historical museum.

Near the town at Col-des-Roches the underground river Bied was harnessed as far back as the 16th c. The mills built into the mountains processed flour, hemp and flax for 200 years before the water became necessary for the new electricity works. The mills were forgotten and fell into disrepair until they were restored in 1973 by a preservation society, with the aim of establishing the Musée National de la Meunerie. (Open to visitors: May–Oct., Mon.–Sun. 10am–noon, 2–5.30pm; the temperature inside the mountain is 7° C/45° F all the year round!)

★Col-des-Roches, Mill Museum

Chur (Cuera/Cuoira)

R 7

Canton: Grisons (GR)
Altitude: 595m/1926ft
Population: 34,000

Chur, capital of the Grisons canton and oldest town in Switzerland, has developed into a considerable intellectual and cultural attraction thanks to its excellent strategic situation at the end of some of the most important passes through the Alps and also its mild climate. The town, known in

Situation and general

Chur (Cuera/Cuoira)

Chur: Episcopal court

Romansch as Cuera or Cuoira, grew up around the episcopal residence of the bishops of Chur (who are first mentioned in the records in 452), and became an important staging-point on the trade routes through the Alps. It is also the terminus of international railway lines and the starting-point of the Rhätische Bahn (narrow gauge) to St Moritz, the Chur–Arosa line and the "Glacier Express" to Zermatt, the Bernina-Express to Tirano (Italy) and the Furka–Oberalp line to Brig. There is a postal bus service from Chur via Lenzerheide to St Moritz (see Practical Information, Railways). The post stage-coach connection "Grand Cañon Express" from Chur through the Upper Rhine Valley to Laax is becoming increasingly popular.

History

Excavation has shown that the sight was occupied about 3000 B.C. In 15 B.C. after their conquest of Rhaetia (an ancient Alpine district), the Romans made this the chief town of Rhaetia Prima. The name is derived from the Celtic "kora" or "koria" (tribe, clan). In 284 Chur became the provincial capital, about 450 the see of a bishop. In the 12th c. the bishops of Chur were granted the status of princes of the Empire, but the Reformation deprived them of their secular authority. When the canton of Grisons was established in 1803 Chur became its administrative capital.

Sights

Bishop's Court

The town is situated on the River Plessur, which here flows into the Rhine. It is dominated by the picturesque Bishop's Court (Bischöflicher Hof), an extensive group of buildings surrounding the Hofplatz, on the site of a Roman fort.

★Cathedral

The cathedral, dedicated to the Assumption, is a Romanesque and Gothic building of the 12th and 13th c. (choir consecrated 1178, church 1272) with fine monumental sculpture and a richly decorated interior ranging in date from the Carolingian period to the Baroque.

Chur: High Altar in the Cathedral . . .   *. . . and St Martin's Well*

Inside the cathedral the carved altar, by Jakob Russ of Ravensburg (1486–92), is the finest Late Gothic altar in the country, and there are notable figured capitals in the nave and crypt (6th and 12th c.). In one of the aisles is the tomb (gravestone), discovered in 1960, of the Swiss patriot Jürg Jenatsch (b. 1596, murdered 1639), who fought for the return of the Valtellina region to the Grisons canton. In the choir is a fine triptych of 1492.

The Cathedral Museum displays the valuable Cathedral treasury, including the relics of St Lucius (2nd c.) and a 4th c. seal.

★Cathedral Museum

The Bishop's Palace (1732–33), an elegant Baroque building, has an imposing façade (stucco decoration). In the medieval Marsöl tower are the Bishop's chapel (17th c.) and a library.

Bishop's Palace

Above the cathedral to the east are the former monastic church of St Lucius, with a round Carolingian crypt (8th c.), a Romanesque crypt (12th c.), a seminary for the training of priests and a theological college.

★St Lucius church

Below the Bishop's Court is the Old Town, with interesting old buildings of the 15th–17th c. In the Regierungsplatz are the Vazerol monument, commemorating the union of the three Rhaetian leagues in 1471, and the Regierungsgebäude (Government Building), known as the "Graues Haus" (Grey House), with the cantonal chancery, the chamber in which the Little Council meets, the cantonal library and the state archives.

★Old Town
Regierungsplatz

In the Reichsgasse is the Rathaus (Town Hall), built in 1465, with the Citizens' Council Chamber (1538: 17th c. tiled stove), and the Town Council Chamber (1494: collection of precious stones). The trapezoid roof and the cross vaulting of the Town Hall are of 16th c. origin. In the Romantik Hotel are Swiss horse-drawn carriages, harnesses and bells from the 19th c.

Reichsgasse

At the end of the Reichsgasse St Martin's church (Protestant: originally 8th c., rebuilt in Late Gothic style 1476–91) has stained glass by A. Giaco-

St Martin's church

metti (1917). The fountain of the same name (1716), in front of the church, depicts a Roman soldier; it was erected in 1910 by A. Bianci as a copy of the original by F. Hundertpfund, which is lost.

Rhaetian
Museum

Above the church to the east, we find the Buolsches Haus (1674–80), now housing the Rhaetian Museum (Rätisches Museum: material of early historical period, cultural history, folk art; open: Tues.–Sun. 10am–noon, 2–5pm).

Postplatz, Art
Museum

In the middle of the town is the Postplatz, from which the Bahnhofstrasse and Grabenstrasse run respectively north-west and north-east to south-west. In the former Villa Planta (1874–76) in Bahnhofstrasse is the Art Museum (Kunstmuseum: pictures of the 17th–20th c., including works by Giovanni, Augusto and Alberto Giacometti, Giovanni Sergantini and Angelika Kaufmann; open: daily 10am–noon, 2–5pm, Thur. to 8.39pm).

Natural History
Museum

In Masaner Strasse (No. 31) is the Natural History Museum (Naturhistorisches Museum: also a national park museum; collections of rock and minerals and common species of animals; open: Tues.–Sun. 10am–noon, 2–5pm).

To the north-east is the Grossratsgebäude (Great Council Building), converted in 1958 from the old Armoury, which also houses the Municipal Theatre (Stadttheater).

Fontanaplatz

South-east of the Postplatz is the Fontanaplatz, with a monument to Benedikt Fontana, leader of the men of Grisons in the Battle of the Calven gorge in 1499.

Surroundings

Calanda

From the south side of the town a cableway ascends in two stages to Brambrüesch (1600m/5250ft), from which there is a chair-lift to the Dreibüdenstein (2180m/7153ft): walks and climbs on Pizokel and up Calanda (2806m/9206ft: wide views).

Bad Passugg

4.5km/3 miles from Chur on the Lenzerheide road is Bad Passugg (780m/2559ft: Hotel Kurhaus), which has chalybeate (iron-bearing) springs in the Rabiosa gorge (drinking-fountain). The road continues via Praden (1160m/3806ft) to the health resort of Tshiertschen (1343m/4406ft: pop. 200; two ski-lifts). From here it is a 2 hours' climb to the Churer Joch (2038m/6687ft) and a rewarding 3 hours' walk to Arosa (equally good in the reverse direction). Arosa: see entry.

Lake Constance   O–R 1–3

Within Germany, Switzerland and Austria
Cantons: Thurgau (TG) and St Gallen (SG)

Situation and
general

Lake Constance, (in German the Bodensee), lying below the northern edge of the Alps, with its shoreline shared between Switzerland, Germany and Austria, is by far the largest lake in Germany, the third largest lake in Central Europe (after Lake Balaton and Lake Geneva) and the second largest of the lakes bordering the Alps. From south-east to north-west it is divided into the Obersee, extending from Bregenz Bay to Eichhorn (Constance), and the much narrower, shorter and shallower Überlinger See, between the Bodanrück and Linzgau, and Untersee.

The Untersee is separated from the main lake by a strip of land which is traversed by the Rhine at Konstanz. At its northern end it splits into the Gnadensee, between the island of Reichenau and the Bodanrück, and the Zeller See, between the Höri and Mettnau peninsulas in Radolfzell Bay.

The whole of the southern shore of the lake is in Switzerland, much the greater part of it (running south-east to beyond Arbon) belonging to the canton of Thurgau and the rest (from the vicinity of Rorschach to the Old Rhine) to St Gallen.

Evidence of the ancient fauna of the region has been found in the form of animals' bones (mammoths, bison, reindeer, deer, wild horses, bears, etc.), and, in caves in the Thayngen area (canton of Schaffhausen), particularly in the Kesslerloch, works of art dating from the Late Palaeolithic period (c. 10,000 B.C.) – engravings on reindeer antlers, figures of wild horses, a carving of a musk-ox's head, etc. Many traces of human settlement in the Mesolithic period (c. 8000–5000 B.C.) have been identified around the lake; and occupation during the Late Neolithic and Early Bronze Age (c. 3000–2000 B.C.) attested by the pile-dwellings – huts occupied by hunters, fishermen and farmers – found, for example, at Ermatingen on the Untersee and between Botighofen and Seedorf on the Obersee. Remains of these houses, built on piles to provide protection from flooding, can be seen at low tide a short distance from the shore of the lake. Since the water level was 2–3m/7–10ft lower at the time the houses were built they would originally have been on dry land. There are also remains of whole villages of pile-dwellings dating from the Early Iron Age (c. 800 B.C.).

The land around Lake Constance was originally Celtic territory, into which the Romans penetrated in the 1st c. B.C. Among Roman foundations on the Swiss shore of the lake was "Arbor Felix" (Arbon). In the 3rd c. A.D. the Alemanni, a Germanic tribe from the north, thrust into the western Lake Constance area. The region was Christianised by Iro-Scottish monks including Columban and his disciple Gallus, who preached here about the year 610, and the 8th c. saw the foundation of the abbey of St Gallen, which developed into a major cultural hub whose influence extended far beyond the region. In the Appenzell war (1403–08) the confederation of towns on

Kreuzlingen: Night festival on the lake . . .   *. . . and the Seeburg*

171

Lake Constance supported the Abbot of St Gallen against the mountain peasants, who suffered a defeat at Bregenz in 1408.

Constance, a member of the Swabian League, lost all rights of sovereignity in the Thurgau under the Treaty of Basle at the end of the Swabian war (1498–99).

Facts and figures about Lake Constance

Geographical situation

Constance (lighthouse) lat. 47°39' north, long. 9°10' east; Bregenz (lighthouse) lat. 47°30' north, long. 9°44' east.

Mean water level: 395m/1296ft (with fluctuations, so far unexplained, unconnected with seasons or weather conditions). This change of water level, which occurs at regular intervals in calm weather, resembles the ebb and flow of the sea, yet occurs 26–38 times in 24 hours and varies only a few centimetres.

Sovereign territory

Although the borders between the countries neighbouring Lake Constance are not distinct, the respective areas are approximately as follows: Germany 55%, Switzerland 34% and Austria 11%.

Area

Total area: 545sq.km/210sq.miles (Obersee and Überlinger See together 476sq.km/184sq.miles, Untersee 63sq.km/24sq.miles).

Length

Greatest length: between Bregenz and Stein am Rhein 76km/47 miles (as the crow flies 69km/43 miles).

Between Bregenz and the mouth of the Stockacher Aach 63km/39 miles; longest direct line over water, from Hard to near the mouth of the Aach, 60km/37 miles. Between Bregenz and Constance 46km/28 miles.

Width

Greatest width: between Kressbronn and Rohrschach 14.8km/9 miles

Depth

Greatest depth: in the Obersee (between Fischbach and Uttwil) 252m/827ft, in the Überlinger See 147m/482ft, in the Untersee 46m/151ft (Zeller See 26m/85ft, Gnadensee 22m/72ft). New depth measuring works are in progress.

Circumference

Circumference at half-tide level: total 263km/163 miles, of which 168km/104 miles (64%) are in Germany, 69km/43 miles (26%) in Switzerland and 26km/16 miles (10%) in Austria.

Volume of water

Average volume of water: total 48,430 million cu.m/1,710,163 million cu.ft, Obersee and Überlinger See together 47,600 million cu.m/1,680,756 million cu.ft, Untersee 830 million cu.m/29,307 million cu.ft.

Tides (at Constance tide-gauge)

Mean high water (end June/beginning July) 440cm/173¼in. (highest recorded, beginning September 1817, 623cm/245¼in.).
Mean low water (end February) 280cm/110¼in. (lowest recorded this century, end March 1972, 237cm/93¼in.).

Visibility

Visibility from surface: annual average about 7.50m/25ft (in January down to 12m/39ft).

Water colour

In the Überlinger See and western Obersee the water is bluish-green in colour, whereas to the east – as a result of the cloudy Rhine water flowing in from the Alps – it becomes increasingly yellow. In summer the waters are covered with a shimmering layer of blue-green algae (known as the "Wasserblüte", or "water blossom"), while "Schwefelregen" ("sulphur rain") is the name given to the yellow pollen from coniferous trees which is blown into the quiet bays and harbour basins.

★ The Swiss side of Lake Constance

Kreuzlingen (404m/1326ft; pop. 17,000), sister city to the German town of Constance, is separated from that town only by the line of the frontier, which does not follow the Rhine but runs through the built-up area at some distance from the river. The town's name comes from a relic of the True Cross which is preserved in the conventual church.

Kreuzlingen

In the Hauptstrasse is the former Augustinian convent (since 1844 occupied by the Thurgau teachers' training college) built by Michael Beer in 1640–53 to replace an earlier monastic house destroyed during the Thirty Years' War and remodelled in Baroque style in 1765. St Ulrich's church, well restored, together with the rest of the conventual buildings, after a fire in 1963, has notable ceiling frescoes, a fine organ and a grille by Jakob Hoffner (1737). A representation of the Agony in the Garden (in the north lateral chapel) preserves 280 of its original 322 figures (1720–40), and a large Gothic cross bears a figure of Christ with natural hair.

Augustinian convent

St Ulrich

In the Tenants' house of Schloss Girsberg the Thurgau Doll Museum was opened in 1988, the oldest of its kind in the country containing over 400 dolls and old-fashioned children's toys (open: Oct.–mid May, Wed.–Sun. 2–5pm; mid May–end Sept., Mon.–Sun. 2–5pm).

Doll Museum

To the north of the town, by the lake, lies the ivy-clad Seeburg, built in 1598 as a country residence of the bishops of Constance, largely destroyed during the Thirty Years' War, and rebuilt in 1879–94. The "Kornschütt" on the eastern edge of the park, built by Augustinian monks in 1715, now houses the Lake Museum, with exhibits covering the history of the Lake Constance area, shipping and lakeside scenery (open: Nov.–Mar., first Sun. in the month 2–5pm; Apr.–June, Sept., Oct., Wed., Sat., Sun. 2–5pm; July, Aug., Tues.–Sun. 10am–noon, 2–5pm). The park contains a reserve for fallow deer and wildfowl.

Seeburg park

1km/½ mile east of the Seeburg, at the Fischerhaus camping site and restaurant, is a waterworks, and just offshore is a fountain, visible far and wide when it is working (illuminated at night).

Waterworks

South-west of the former convent stands the Rosenegg Heimatmuseum (Bärenstrasse 6; open: May–Oct., first Sun. in the month 2–4pm) with weapons, documents and furniture from Kreuzlingen and the surrounding area. Still farther south-west, in Bernrain, are an observatory and a Baroque pilgrimage chapel.

Rosenegg Heimatmuseum, Observatory

A good 12km/7 miles south-west on the main road to Frauenfeld, near Lipperswil is the recreational park of Conny Island with a dolphinarium, children's zoo and many amusements (open: daily 9am–6pm).

★ Conny Island

The road west from Kreuzlingen towards the Untersee arrives first at the village of Tägerwilen (406m/1332ft) with the church of SS Cosmas and Damian. 1.5km/1 mile south, above the village, Schloss Castell or Chastel, was built in 1661 near the palace of the bishops of Constance, which was destroyed in 1499; it was rebuilt between 1876 and 1894. Tägerwilen was the birthplace of Hermann Müller (1850–1927), who produced the Müller-Thurgau grape (a cross between Riesling and Sylvaner) which bears his name.

Untersee
Tägerwilen

To the north, on the Rhine, in the picturesque Gottlieben district of the town (398m/1306ft), stands a palace built in 1251 as a subsidiary residence of the bishops of Constance (enlarged 1480, rebuilt in Neo-Gothic style 1837–38), in which Jan Hus, his fellow Hussite Jerome of Prague and Anti-Pope John

Gottlieben

XXIII were imprisoned in 1415; the palace now belongs to the singer Lisa della Casa.

There are a number of handsome half-timbered houses, including the Drachenburg and the Waaghaus or Weigh-House (both 17th c.), as well as the so-called Burg (Castle) and Haus Rheineck.

A local speciality is the pastry called "Gottlieber Hüppen".

Ermatingen,
Lake Constance
Fishing Museum

Ermatingen (397m/1303ft: pop. 2000), 4km/2 miles farther west an old fishing village (attractive half-timbered houses and the Fishing Museum; open: May–Sept., Sun. 2–5pm), is also a holiday resort, situated on the Staad or Stad peninsula (on which remains of pile-dwellings have been found).

Mannenbach-
Salenstein

Farther west again, beautifully situated opposite the island of Reichenau (2km/1 mile: ferry), is Mannenbach (405m/1329ft), above which stands Burg Salenstein (505m/1657ft: originally 11th c., restored 1842).

★Schloss
Arenenberg

On a terrace to the east is Schloss Arenenberg (458m/1503ft: Napoleonic Museum, open: Oct.–Mar., Tues.–Sun. 9am–noon, 1.30–4pm; Apr.–Sept., Tues.–Sun. 10am–noon, 1.30–6pm), built 1540–46, with later alterations. From 1830 until her death in 1837 this was the residence of Napoleon's step-daughter Queen Hortense de Beauharnais, whose son Louis Napoléon, later Napoléon III, spent his childhood here. In 1906 the Empress Eugénie, Napoléon III's widow, presented the castle to the canton of Thurgau as a memorial to her husband.

Above Mannenbach to the west is the ruined castle of Sandegg (517m/1696ft: views), and 500m/1641ft farther south Schloss Eugensberg (544m/1785ft: private property), built in 1820 for Eugène de Beauharnais, Napoleon's stepson and brother of Queen Hortense.

Steckborn

Schloss
Turmhof

The road continues through the quiet resort of Berlingen (398m/1306ft), with a Town Hall of 1780, to Steckborn (404m/1326ft: pop. 3500), an ancient little town on a peninsula in the Untersee which is a popular holiday resort (picturesque half-timbered houses). The Turmhof, a castle on the lakeside, built about 1320 (17th c. domed tower and corner turrets) by Diethelm von Castell, Abbot of Reichenau, houses a local museum (contains Neolithic, Roman and Alemannian exhibits, Steckborn ceramics, examples of wrought-iron and turned wood from the 18th and 19th c.: open: mid May–mid Oct., Wed., Thur., Sat. 3–5pm). The Town Hall dates from 1667 and has a collection of weapons on the first floor (open weekdays). The Town church (1776), a plain Baroque building by F. A. Bagnato, has extensive wide views from the tower. The Roman Catholic Jakobuskirche (St James's church) was built in 1963.

At the south-west end of the town is the Bernina sewing-machine factory, with a sewing-machine museum.

Obersee

The road south-east from Kreuzlingen along the Obersee arrives in 2.5km/2 miles at the village of Bottighofen (398m/1306ft), which is attractively situated amid fruit orchards and has a well-equipped boating harbour.

Münsterlingen

1.5km/1 mile beyond this is Münsterlingen (398m/1306ft), a hotel resort situated on a peninsula. The church of the Benedictine convent (rebuilt 1709–16), now a cantonal hospital, has a fine Baroque interior, and since 1968, when the lake last froze, has housed the 16th c. bust of St John the Baptist, which traditionally transfers between Hagnau and Münsterlingen whenever the lake freezes.

Romanshorn

The road continues through Kesswil and Uttwil, both with fine half-timbered houses, to Romanshorn (403m/1323ft: pop. 8200), a lakeside resort which is also the largest port on Lake Constance and the base of the Swiss lake steamers (shipyard of Swiss Federal Railways).

Steckborn: Turmhof Castle

To the north of the Bundesbahnhafen (Federal Railways harbour) lies the Seepark, with the Old Church. The Schloss (now a hotel) dates in its present form from 1829. In the lake, to the north, is the "Inseli", a rocky islet. 1.5km/1 mile north-west can be found the Amriswil pumping-works.

The next town of any size is Arbon (398m/1306ft: pop. 12,300), a port and an industrial town situated on a peninsula, occupying the site of the Celtic settlement of Arbona and the Roman Arbor Felix. St Gallus died here *c.* 645. From 1285 to 1798 the town was held by the Bishops of Constance.
    North-west of the Alter Hafen (Old Harbour) and the Schlosshafen is the Roman Catholic parish church of St Martin (choir 1490, nave 1788; Madonna of 1525). Farther north-west is the 16th c. Schloss, built on the foundations of a Roman fort of A.D. 294, with a seven-storey tower originally dating from 400, which contains a local historical museum (closed in winter). Other features of interest are the Römerhof (*c.* 1500), the chapel of St Gallus (originally 10th c.; 14th c. frescoes) and the lakeside promenade 3km/2 miles long.

Arbon

From Arbon the road continues to Steinach (400m/1312ft), a fishing village with a Baroque parish church and a large granary (the "Gred") of 1473. Horn (398m/1306ft), an enclave belonging to the enclave of Thurgau, boasts a castle which belonged to the Landgrave of Hesse, and Rohrschach, the old port of St Gallen (see entries).

Steinach
Horn

Rohrschach

Farther east is Altenrhein, on the delta of the Old Rhine. Here is the hangar of the FFA aircraft and car factory (Flug-und Fahrzeugwerke Altenrhein: formerly the Dornier works) and the base from which the old Dornier flying-boats took off in the 1920s.

Altenrhein

South-east of the mouth of the Old Rhine is Rheineck (400m/1312ft: pop. 3000), the attractive little Swiss frontier town on the banks of the idyllic Old

Rheineck

175

Rhine. Rheineck has arcaded streets, and old town gate, a Town Hall of 1555, a Late Gothic and Baroque church (Protestant), two imposing 18th c. town houses, the Löwenhof and the Custerhof, and a ruined castle (views).

From here a narrow-gauge rack railway runs up (1.9km/1 mile, taking 6 minutes) to Walzenhausen (670–900m/2200–2950ft: pop. 2200), a hillside village in a commanding situation high above Lake Constance which is also a health and winter sports resort.

Walzenhausen

3.5km/2 miles south-east of Rheineck is St Margrethen (410m/1345ft: pop. 5000), a rail and road junction on the Swiss–Austrian frontier (customs) situated on the Old Rhine in a fertile fruit-growing region. It is also a spa (Kneipp treatment). St Margaret's chapel, a cemetery church dating from 1090, has frescoes and Late Baroque altars. Directly next to the motorway is the large "Rheinpark" shopping centre.

St Margrethen

To the south-west is Schloss Bergsteig, to the west Schloss Vorburg (open to visitors). The ruins of Burg Grimmenstein are also of interest.

Pleasant walks to the hill villages (good views) in the St Gallen and Appenzell areas.

Crans-Montana   H 10

Canton: Valais (VS)
Altitude: 1500–1680m/4922–5512ft. Population: 4500

The popular holiday and winter sports area of Crans-Montana lies north-west of the little town of Sierre in the Rhône valley. It is reached by any one of three roads from the Rhône valley or by a funicular from Sierre.

Situation

The attractive resort of Crans-sur-Sierre (1480–1500m/4856–4922ft), to the west, lies around a number of small lakes, the Etangs de Lens. For over 45 years the resort has been equally famous in summer for its "Open" on the two splendid golf courses (9 and 18 holes), hang-gliding, hot air balloon meetings and other sporting events as for its marvellous skiing in winter. The Alpine World Skiing Championships were held here in 1987.

Crans-sur-Sierre

From Crans a cableway 4480m/14,699ft long ascends in 25 minutes, via Merbé (1900m/6234ft) and Cry d'Err, to Bella Lui (2543m/8344ft: restaurant); on foot, the path to the top leads over the 2140m/7023ft high Mont Lachaux from which there are superb views. Another cableway, roughly parallel to the first, takes 13 minutes to reach Chetzeron (2100m/6890ft), from which there is a ski-lift to the Cry d'Err.

★ Bella Lui

A spectacular route, suitable only for experienced climbers, leads to the famous Bisse du Roh. Water from the mountains collected in these *bisses* (water channels) from where it flowed to the pastures and valleys.

Bisse du Roh

The popular mountain and winter sports resort of Montana (1500m/4922ft), 1.5km/1 mile to the east on Lac Moubra, lies on a natural terrace covered with forests and Alpine meadows 1000m/3281ft above the Rhône valley, sheltered by the mountains to the north, and has a mild, dry mountain climate. A cableway 540m/1772ft long climbs in 3 minutes to the Grand Signal (upper station 1712m/5617ft), from which there are ski-lifts to Verdet (1875m/6152ft) and the Cry d'Err. Another cableway, 2500m/8203ft long, runs up in 12 minutes to the Cry d'Err (2263m/7425ft: restaurant).

Montana

Above Montana, 1.5km/1 mile north, is Vermala (1670m/5479ft), with a ski-jump. From Vermala-Zaumiau a cableway 2545m/8350ft long goes up

Vermala

◀ *Scenic walks from Crans-Montana to Leukerbad*

via Les Marolires to the Swiss Alpine Club's Cabane des Violette (2208m/7244ft: restaurant), from which another cableway (3243m/10,640ft long) continues to the Plaine Morte (2927m/9603ft).

Aminona

10km/6 miles north-east of Montana is Aminona (1437m/4415ft), a popular winter sports resort with a group of tower-block hotels, from which there is a cabin cableway 2410m/7907ft long to the Petit-Mont-Bonvin (2411m/7910ft: numerous ski-lifts). Access to the pistes of Crans-Montana is via the Violettes, La Tza and La Barma.

Anzère

The mountain station of Anzère, separated from the deep valley of the Lienne, lies about 8km/5 miles west of Crans. This modern village, with its typical large chalets, is surrounded by excellent long-distance courses and pistes of varying levels of difficulty.

Winter sports

There are short training lifts in the valley. In the mountain area around Chetzeron, Mont Lachaux, Cry d'Err, Bella Lui, Signal, Violettes, etc., there are more than 40 cableways. chair-lifts and ski-lifts up the mountains, totalling more than 160km/100 miles in length. The longest ski descent is the 3.2km/2 mile-long Plaine Morte. Summer skiing in the Plaine Morte glacier area (3000m/9843ft: cableway from Violettes). Many ski-trails with lifts between Violettes (2208m/7244ft: cableway from Vermala-Zaumiau) and Petit-Mont-Bonvin (2383m/7821ft: cabin cableway from Aminona). There is splendid long-distance skiing between Crans, Montana and Vermala. National teams from all over Europe train on the high slopes of the Plaine Morte glacier. An artificial ice rink, curling, tobogganing and famous Swiss ski schools are also to be found here.

Davos   S 7

Canton: Grisons.
Altitude: 1560m/5118ft.
Population: 12,300

Situation and general

Davos, a high valley extending 16km/10 miles south-west from the Wolf-gang pass and traversed by the Landwasser, is the second largest com-mune in Switzerland (254sq.km/98sq.miles) – larger than the canton of Zug. The twin settlements of Davos Platz and Davos Dorf have increased their population five-fold over the last 100 years and have now united to form a built-up area 4km/2 miles long. Surrounded by forest-covered mountains and sheltered from rough north and east winds, Davos enjoys a

Davos – panorama

climate (bracing but not excessively so, with plenty of sunshine and dry air) which has made it one of Switzerland's leading summer and winter resorts. The foundations of Davos's fame as a health resort were laid by a Mannheim doctor, Alexander Spengler, who prescribed mountain air for his tuberculosis patients and brought the first summer visitors here in 1860 and the first winter visitors in 1865.

Since 1890 Davos has been linked with the Rhine valley (Chur) by the Rhätische Bahn (Rhaetian Railway), and since 1909 with the Albula valley and the Engadine. There are postal bus services from Davos over the Flüela pass to Susch/Süs (only in summer), to Clavadel and Sertig Dörfli (in winter only to Clavadel) and into the Dischma valley (in winter only as far as Teufi), and from Davos Glaris to Monstein. Local bus operators run services between Davos Platz, Davos Dorf, Davos Wolfgang and Dörfji (near which is the lower station of the Pischa mountain railway). There are numerous cableways and lifts and a wide range of facilities for sport and entertainment. *Communications*

The name of Davos (in the form Tavauns, which later became Dafaas) appears for the first time in 1160, in a document in the episcopal archives in Chur. In 1289 14 families from the Valais established households here. After the death of the last member of the Toggenburg family in 1436 the League of the Ten Jurisdictions was formed. In 1649 Davos purchased its freedom from Austrian sovereignty. A large ice-rink (24,000sq.m/28,704sq.yd) for the world figure-skating championships and the European speed skating championships was opened in 1899, and in the same year the Davos-Scatzalp toboggan run came into operation. *History*

Sights

The chief place of the valley is Davos Platz (1560m/5118ft), the only old buildings in which are the parish church of St John the Baptist (1481; nave **Davos Platz**

179

Davos

300m

Jakobshorn

1280–85, restored 1909), with a window in the choir by Augusto Giacometti (after 1928), and the adjoining Rathaus (Town Hall: restored 1930), with the panelled "Great Chamber" (Grosse Stube) of 1564.

★ Ernst-Ludwig-Kirchner Museum

In 1992 the Ernst-Ludwig-Kirchner Museum moved into a new building, designed by the Zurich architects A. Gigon and M. Guyer. The cubic building of dark glass is situated in Kirchner Platz and is open Tues.–Sun. 2–6pm. On display are oil paintings, sculptures, water-colours, drawings, woodcuts, etchings and lithographs by the artist Kirchner (1880–1938), who lived and worked in Davos-Frauenkirch from 1917 until he committed suicide in 1938.

Adjoining the indoor swimming pool (Hallenbad) stands the modern Congress House (Kongresshaus, 1969), in which a number of cultural events (theatre, concerts, exhibitions) are held.

Davos Dorf

In Davos Dorf (1563m/5128ft) is the 14th c. church of St Theodulus. At Museumstrasse 1 is the Old Prebend House (Altes Pfrundhaus), the only surviving example of an old burgher's house, which is now occupied by a local museum (Heimatmuseum; including an old corn-mill from Sculms; open: Wed. and Sun. 4–6pm). The Gemeindehaus (communal house) of Davos Dorf was built by Jürg Jenatsch in 1643 (altered 1886).

Recreation and sport

Bathing beach on the Davoser See; indoor and outdoor swimming pools (Hallenbad, Gartenbad) in the Kurpark. There is a 18-hole golf course on Davos Platz. Natural ice-rinks (22,000sq.m/26,312sq.yd: the largest in Europe), with areas for figure and speed skating, ice-hockey and curling; artificial ice-rink (1800sq.m/2153sq.yd), open in summer as well as winter: curling). Beautiful Kurpark (bandstand). 55 cableways and lifts with a total capacity of 55,000 persons, giving access to extensive mountain-walking and skiing areas. Toboggan run, Schatzalp-Davos. Davos is famous for the International Ice Hockey Tournament for the Spengler Cup, curling tournaments, skating events, ski races, "walking" weeks and its music festival.

Swiss Research Institute (Physical and Meteorological Observatory and World Radiation Centre, Institute of Medical Climatic and Tuberculosis Research, Laboratory of Experimental Surgery, Osteosynthesis Study Group); Federal Institute of Snow and Avalanche Research, Weissfluhjoch/Davos.

Scientific Institutes

Surroundings

A favourite walk from Davos is to the Davoser See, a natural lake (area 0.59sq.km/0.23sq.mile) which supplies a hydro-electric power station (walk around the lake 1½ hours).

Davoser See

Popular walks include the Hohe Promenade (level walk of 2.5km/2 miles from Davos Dorf to Davos Platz) and those to Wolfgang (1631m/5351ft) and Laret (1525m/5004ft), to the north-east, and to Frauenkirch (1532m/5026ft), Spinabad (1455m/4808ft), Glaris (1446m/4746ft), Schmelzboden (1590m/5217ft: Mining Museum) and Wiesen (1421m/4662ft) to the south-west.

Walks

To Parsenn and Weissfluhjoch

This is a renowned skiing area and also excellent walking and climbing country. The mountains on the west side of the Davos valley were made

Cableway from Weissfluhjoch to the summit of the Weissfluh

★ Davos–
Parsenn-Bahn

Weissfluhjoch

conveniently accessible by the opening in 1931 of the Davos–Parsenn-Bahn, a funicular 4106m/13,472ft, time 25 minutes). From the Höhenweg station (2km/1 mile: 2219m/7281ft) there are magnificent mountain walks without any real climbing. The funicular continues up to the Weissfluhjoch (2663m/8737ft: restaurant), with views of the Silvretta and Flüela groups, from Piz Buin to the Tinzenhorn. From the upper station there is a cableway to the summit of the Weissfluh (2844m/9331ft: restaurant), from which there are superb views in all directions. There is also a cableway from the Weissfluhjoch to the Parsenn hut (2200m/7218ft: restaurant), 2 hours' walk from Wolfgang.

Panoramaweg

One of the finest paths in the area is the Panoramaweg, which runs from the Parsenn hut through the Meierhofer Tälli valley to the Höhenweg funicular station and from there through the Dorf-Tälli and under the Schiahörner to the Strela pass. From the Parsenn hut it is a half-hour's walk to the Gotschnagrat (2285m/7497ft).

★ Schatzalp

From Davos Platz the Schatzalpbahn (funicular, length 716m/2349ft, height difference 301m/988ft, time 5 minutes) ascends to the Schatzalp (1861m/6106ft: hotel and restaurant); on foot 1–1½ hours. 350m/1148ft north of the Berghotel is the Schatzalp Alpine Garden (Alpinium), which contains 7500 plants and 550 species and sub-species (free admission with funicular ticket).

From the Schatzalp a rewarding walk via the Podestatenalp, Lochalp and Grüenalp leads to Davos (2¼ hours). The Schatzalp-Davos toboggan run is 2.5km/2 miles long with well-cambered bends.

Strela pass

The Strela pass (2350m/7710ft), reached by the Schatzalp-Strela cableway (length 1760m/5775ft, height difference 488m/1601ft, time 10 minutes; restaurant), passes larches over a thousand years old. From the Strela

Susch in the Inn valley ▶

pass a cabin cableway (opened 1981) ascends to the lower station of the Haupter-Tälli Ski-lift which goes up to the Weissfluhjoch.

The Jakobshorn and the eastern valleys

★Jakobshorn

There are also pleasant walks and climbs on the left side of the valley. A cableway constructed in 1954 runs up to the Ischalp (1931m/6336ft: restaurant), and from there to the Jakobshorn (2590m/8498ft: restaurant), from which there are splendid panoramic views. From here a waymarked path runs down through groves of rhododendrons to the Ischalp (1¼ hours). Ski-lifts from the Ischalp serve the Brämebüel skiing area (2477m/8127ft).

Clavadel

Another footpath from the Ischalp leads in 45 minutes to the Clavadeler Alp (1971m/6467ft) and from there in another 45 minutes to Clavadel (1664m/5460ft: postal bus), one of the sunniest spots in the valley. The walk from Davos Platz to Clavadel and back takes about 2 hours.

★Sertig Dörfli

In summer the postal bus runs up the Sertig valley to Sertig Dörfli (1861m/6106ft: restaurant), in a superb mountain setting (a popular trip with walkers, plant-lovers and animal lovers).

Rinerhorn

The magnificent walking and winter sports area on the Rinerhorn, a few kilometres south of Davos, can be reached by taking the chair-lift from Davos-Glaris to Jatzmeder (2054m/6741ft: restaurant), from which it is 1½ hours climb to the summit of the Rinerhorn (2528m/8294ft).

★Monstein

A short distance beyond Glaris a by-road branches off on the left to the little village of Monstein (1626m/5335ft), idyllically situated on a sunny terrace on the mountainside, where the old German dialect of the Upper Valais is still spoken. The Grisons Mining Museum is worth seeing.

Dischma valley

The Dischma valley is the longest (12km/7 miles) of the valleys on the left side of the Davos valley. On the right bank of the Dischmabach is a narrow road, on the left bank a pleasant footpath. The timber buildings to be seen here are typical of the older Davos. The last village in the valley is Dürrboden (2007m/6585ft: inn), which can be reached on foot in 3–4 hours from Davos Dorf. Postal bus in summer to Dürrboden, in winter to Teufi.

Dörfji
★Pischabahn

The Flüela valley is another good walking and skiing area (nature reserve). The road from Davos Dorf crosses the Flüelabach (waterfall, 5 minutes' walk) and comes in 4km/2 miles to Dörfji (1810m/5940ft: bus station, restaurant), from which the Pischabahn (length 2030m/6660ft, height difference 680m/2231ft, time 6 minutes) serves Pischa (2483m/8149ft: inn). From there it is a climb of 2 hours to the summit of the Pischahorn (2980m/9777ft).

Over the Flüela pass into the Engadine

Flüela pass road

The shortest route from the Rhine valley to the Lower Engadine goes from Landquart through the Prättigau to Davos Dorf and from there over the Flüela pass to Susch. The Flüela pass road between Davos and Susch (27km/17 miles), opened to traffic in 1867, is between 5.5 and 7m/18 and 23ft wide, with gradients of up to 10%. In winter the road is closed for 40 days, on average, due to the risk of avalanches. This problem should be solved in the future by the construction of a new tunnel (see "Vereina-Bahn").

Tschuggen

★Flüela pass

From Dörfji (1800m/5907ft: restaurant), from which there is a beautiful view to the rear of the Weissfluh, one can reach Tschuggen 7km/4 miles south-east (1938m/6360ft: holiday centre, 100 chalets; in summer postal bus service from Davos), amid magnificent expanses of rhododendrons and stone pines. 13km/8 miles beyond this is the Flüela pass

(2383m/7819ft: mountain inn), the highest mountain pass in the Grisons, 3¾ hours on foot from Davos Dorf. Beyond the pass, at the head of the lower Engadine, Susch (1426m/4680ft: pop. 222), straddles the Inn and the Susaca.

Susch

Construction began in 1988 of a tunnel which at the turn of this century will enable motorists to avoid using the Flüela pass between Davos and Unterengadin which is frequently impassable. A 19km/11 mile long tunnel is being excavated between Klosters and Susch/Lawin, through which the motor-rail "Vereina-Bahn" will travel.

Vereina-Bahn

Delémont   G/H 4

Canton: Jura (JU)
Altitude: 430m/1411ft. Population: 12,500

Delémont (in German Delsberg), the largest town in the Jura and capital of the newest Swiss canton, is an important railway junction on the Berne–Basle and Delle–Paris lines and the starting point of many postal bus services. It lies in the wide valley of the Sorne, which here flows into the Birs.

Situation

Delémont first appears in the records in 782 as a market village, and again in 1212 as a town founded by the Prince-Bishop of Basle. It was granted a municipal charter in 1289. After the Reformation it was a favourite residence of the bishops of Basle. From 1815 it was the chief town of a district in the canton of Berne, and in 1978 it became capital of the new canton of Jura.

History

Sights

As an important industrial, cultural and tourist area Delémont has developed into a modern town without losing its old-world character. The

Delémont: Town Hall

main features of interest are the church of St-Marcel (1762–66), a three-aisled basilica built over an earlier cruciform structure; the château of the Prince-Bishops (1716–21); the 13th c. Archive tower; the former Grand'rue, the wide main street, now Rue du 23 Juin; five large fountains; the Baroque Hôtel de Ville (1742–45); and the Musée Jûrassien (local history, prehistoric and Roman material).

Surroundings

Vorbourg Fortress	There are many places of interest in the immediate surroundings of the town, including the fortress of Vorbourg, an early medieval fortification, to the north-east of the town. The adjoining pilgrimage church of St-Maria, which was consecrated by Pope Leo IX in the 11th c., has an interesting 16th c. high altar.
Château de Domont	To the west of Delémont is the Château de Domont, dating from the middle of the 16th c.
Jura	Also to the west of Delémont a hilly region extends towards the French frontier. An interesting route into the Ajoie takes in the renowned medieval small town of St-Ursanne and Porrentruy. Heading south-west one comes to the scenic Franches Montagnes (see Jura) before reaching the town of Saignelégier, famous for its horse-breeding. There are other interesting excursions into the wildly romantic Jura, south-west towards Lake Geneva.

Disentis/Mustér   O 8

Canton: Grisons (GR)
Altitude: 1130m/3709ft. Population: 2500

Situation and general	The holiday resort Disentis (accent on first syllable: Romansch Mustér) lies in a wide green valley on the upper reaches of the Surselva at the junction of the Upper Rhine with the Medelser Rhein or Mittelrhein (Middle Rhine). The development of summer tourism in Disentis is due mainly to the building of the former Hotel Disenterhof (1870), which as a bathing and spa hotel utilises the waters of the St Placidus spring. This health and winter sports resort has over 150km/93 miles of walks of varying difficulty, and offers the visitor attractions such as river trips, tennis, mountain excursions on the Glacier-Express, well-prepared pistes and long-distance runs for the skier.

Sights

Benedictine Abbey, St Martin	Above the town is a Benedictine abbey founded by St Sigisbert about 720 and almost completely rebuilt at the end of the 17th c.; the abbey dominates the valley with its fine conventual buildings and St Martin's church (Vorarlberg Baroque, 1696–1712); it contains a collection of artistic and historical interest.

Surroundings

Cableway (2060m/6759ft, 5 minutes) from Funs (1228m/4029ft) north-west to Caischavedra (1842m/6044ft); from there ski-lifts to the slopes of Piz Ault (3027m/9932ft).

Over the Lucomagno (Lukmanier) pass to Biasca (65km/40 miles)

★ Höllen-schlucht	The road runs south from Disentis and climbs, with moderate gradients, through the Höllenschlucht (Hell's Gorge), a magnificent wooded defile. It

Spa resort of Disentis/Mustér

then continues uphill, with numerous bends, and passes through a number of tunnels, between which there are views to the rear of Disentis Abbey and later impressive views of the foaming waterfalls in the gorge below.

Curaglia (1332m/4370ft), with a church of 1672 (Late Gothic altar), is situated at the mouth of the Val Plattas, which runs down from Piz Medel (3210m/10,532ft: 7 hours with guide); to the east there is a rewarding climb (3½–4 hours) up Piz Mauraun (2897m/9505ft), from Monte Rosa to the Ortles (Ortler) group, and of the nearer Tödi group in the Glarus Alps.

Curaglia

★Piz Mauraun

Platta (1380m/4528ft), a straggling village (church with Romanesque tower) in an open part of the Val Medel. Further to the right there is a small waterfall.

Platta

Acla (1476m/4843ft: off the road to the right), with a chapel. The scenery now becomes wilder; Fumatschfalls, 30m/98ft high, on the Medelser Rhein. To the rear there is a view of the valley around Platta, with the Tödi massif rearing up beyond the Vorderrhein.

Acla

From Pardatsch (or Perdatsch), 1556m/5105ft, a hamlet with a small chapel, the road continues uphill under Piz Curvet (2248m/7376ft) to Sogn Gion (1615m/5299ft), a former hospice. It then climbs a lonely Alpine valley, with tumbles of rock, areas of sparse pasturage and rhododendrons. To the right are the pointed summit of Tgiern Sogn Gion (2677m/8783ft) and Piz Ganne-retsch (3040m/9974ft). In 8km/5 miles the Santa Maria lake (formed by a dam completed in 1967) can be seen below the road on the right. On the old road on the west side of the lake, at Santa Maria (1842m/6044ft), was the old hospice of "Sancta Maria in Luco Magno" which gave its name to the pass. Above the west side of the lake is Piz Rondadura (3016m/9895ft; 3½ hours), to the east the dark slaty peak of Scopi (3187m/10,457ft; 4–4½ hours).

Sogn Gion

Santa Maria Lake

The Lucomagno pass (Romansch Cuolm Lucmagn, German Lukmanier-pass: 1978m/6492ft), with an inn, a large stone figure of the Virgin and a

Lucomagno pass

chapel, is the lowest road crossing of the central ridge of the Swiss Alps, over which there was already considerable traffic in medieval times. It is flanked on the left by Scopi and on the right by Scai (2676m/8780ft). The pass marks the boundary between the cantons of Grisons and Ticino.

Pizzo Curvo

The road descends from the pass through a rocky valley, following the left bank of the Brenno, which is fed by numerous streams flowing down from Scai and Pizzo Lucomagno. To the left are the rock walls of Pizzo Curvo (2510m/8235ft). Then it continues through an area of high Alpine meadows with scattered summer chalets. Ahead can be seen the Rheinwaldhorn (3406m/11,175ft).

4.5km/3 miles beyond the pass, on the right, is the Aquacalda inn (1788m/5868ft; Albergo del Paso, 20b.), surrounded by a forest of stone pines, with a beautiful waterfall on the Brenno.

Valle Santa Maria

The road traverses the Alpine meadows of the Piano di Segno, passing above the huts of Campra, continues down the north side of the beautiful Valle Santa Maria, high above the Brenno, and then through a wooded gorge, passes close to the Albergo Grande Venezia and comes to the former hospice of Camperio. The road now leaves the Valle Santa Maria

★ Val Blenio

and runs down the Val Blenio, high up on the south side of the valley, with magnificent views of the valley itself, the precipitous buttresses of the Rheinwaldhorn, the Cima di Pinaderio and the Cima Giù (2369m/7773ft), and Olivone in its fertile valley, with the jagged granite peak of Sosto rearing above it.

5.5km/3 miles beyond Camperio there is a rewarding drive along a road which branches off on the left and after traversing a tunnel 1490m/4889ft long, which bypasses the narrow Gola di Sosto, reaches the mountain

Campo Blénio

village of Campo Blénio (1228m/4029ft), 4.5km/3 miles north, situated at the meeting of three valleys. Beyond this, 1.5km/1 mile up the Val Camadra, is Ghirone (1302m/4270ft), with a very picturesque old church; then 3km/2 miles east up the Val Luzzone to a large artificial lake (1590m/5217ft).

Olivone

The main road continues down to the village of Olivone (Romansch Uorscha, 893m/2930ft), a summer holiday resort beautifully situated at the junction of two arms of the Brenno under the massive pyramid of Sosto (2221m/7278ft), surrounded by fruit trees. It has a fine old house, still inhabited, the Casa Cesare Bolla (c. 1500), once the residence of the governor, and an interesting local museum. Beyond Olivone the road to Biasca winds its way down the fertile Val Blénio, on the left bank of the Brenno, to the valley floor.

Aquila

Aquila (788m/2585ft), with neat houses in the Ticinese style, lies at the foot of the Colma massif, which reaches its highest point in the Cima di Pinaderio (2490m/8170ft).

From here there are alternative routes to Dongio: either on a narrow by-road (5km/3 miles longer) which runs above the right bank of the Brenno through a series of pretty villages and chestnut groves (at Prugiasco, 7.5km/5 miles), detour on right, 30 minutes, up to the little Romanesque church of San Carlo Negrentino, with 13th–16th c. frescoes); or on the main road, which climbs up the left bank of the Brenno and beyond Dongio turns into the Val Soia, running down from the Rheinwaldhorn (3406m/11,175ft).

Torre

Torre (770m/2526ft) is prettily situated on a terrace, and here a southern vegetation of vines, mulberries and walnut-trees begins to feature more prominently in the landscape.

Lottigna

Farther down the valley, on the hillside to the left, is the village of Lottigna (695m/2280ft), the chief place in the Val Blenio, beautifully situated at the foot of Simano (2580m/8465ft), with a church of the 15th and 17th centuries.

Beyond this there is a superb view down the valley, with a view of the pyramidal peak of Sosto to the rear. Acquarossa (538m/1765ft), is a spa (mineral spring, 25.5° C/78° F).

Dongio (470m/1542ft) is a long straggling village surrounded by vineyards and orchards, where the by-road from Aquila comes in. To the south-west, on the other side of the Brenno, stands the chapel of San Reigio, with Romanesque wall-paintings.

Malvaglia (375m/1230ft), lies at the mouth of the deep Malvaglia valley, with the church of San Martino (originally Romanesque, altered in 1603: beautiful campanile). A narrow mountain road runs 10.5km/7 miles up the Val Malvaglia, passing an artificial lake, to Madra (1086m/3563ft).

Opposite Malvaglia, on the right bank of the Brenno, is the village of Semione (402m/1319ft), with the ruined castle of Seravalle (12th–14th c.). In the Casa San Carlo is the Museo di Minerali with fossils and minerals from Ticino and other areas of the country.

Below Malvaglia the valley becomes wider and more regular, with large areas of tumbled rocks on the valley bottom. Below the narrow mouth of the Val Pontirone the road skirts the Buzza di Biasca, a great mass of debris the result of a tremendous landslide in 1512. The place from which the rock broke away can be seen high above the road on Pizzo Magno (2298m/7540ft).

At Biasca (305m/1001ft) we join the road from the St Gotthard (see entry), which runs down the Ticino valley to Bellinzona (see entry).

Einsiedeln   N 5/6

Canton: Schwyz (SZ)
Altitude: 905m/2969ft
Population: 9600

The famous Swiss pilgrimage destination of Einsiedeln, situated in a high valley of the Pre-Alps between Lake Zurich and Lake Lucerne, has been a great focus of religion and culture for more than a thousand years, and its magnificent conventual buildings are one of the peak achievements of Baroque architecture. The Gnadenkapelle (chapel of Grace) with its Black Virgin, draws large numbers of pilgrims every year, and many visitors are also attracted by the quiet and beauty of the abbey's setting. For the winter sports enthusiast there are six ski-lifts and about 52km/32 miles of long-distance runs.

The famous "Grosse Welttheater" (Great Theatre of the World) by Calderón de la Barca has been performed here several times since 1924.

In 934 Eberhard, Dean of Strasbourg Cathedral, founded a community of hermits in the "Dark Forest" above the hermitage of a monk from Reichenau, Meinrad, who had been murdered in 861; and Duke Hermann of Swabia and his wife Reginlinde granted the monastic settlement enough land to provide for its maintenance. In 937 Einsiedeln was made a royal abbey, and its abbot became a prince of the Empire. The buildings were destroyed by fire on five occasions, in 1029, 1226, 1465, 1509 and 1577. The Reformer Ulrich Zwingli was for a time a secular priest at Einsiedeln. In 1639 the first peace negotiations between France and Bavaria during the Thirty Years' War were conducted here. The building history of the abbey covered the whole range from Romanesque through Gothic to Baroque. Einsiedeln later developed into an important area of intellectual activity, with a flourishing printing and publishing industry. It is the administrative heart of the district of the same name, which comprises the "quarters" of Bernau, Egg, Eutal, Gross, Trachslau and Willerzell.

Einsiedeln

A Gnadenkapelle
B Nave
C Dome
D Lower choir
E Sacristy and upper choir
F Confessional church
G Princes' Hall

1 "Black Virgin"
2 Patronal altar
3 Altar of St Joseph
4 Altar of St Meinrad
5 Altar of St Maurice
6 Entrance to confessional church and students' chapel
7 Choir screen
8 Doorway into conventual buildings (pilgrimage office)
9 Altar of St Sigismund
10 Altar of St Benedict
11 Altar of St Anne
12 Altar of the Rosary and grave of Brother Meinrad Eugster

Einsiedeln

Sights

★★ Benedictine Abbey of Maria Einsiedeln

The Benedictine Abbey of Maria Einsiedeln, built by the lay brother Kaspar Moosbrugger (1656–1723) of Au in the Bregenzerwald, is the finest example of Vorarlberg architecture in Switzerland. The conventual buildings, laid out in a regular square around four courtyards, cover an area of 34,000sq.m/40,664sq.yd. The twin-towered church (1719–35) is a sumptuous Baroque building, with ceiling frescoes by the Asam brothers of Bavaria (the largest fresco in the country), and a wrought-iron choir screen (1684), designed to give the effect of perspective. The Gnadenkapelle (Chapel of Grace), rebuilt in 1815–17 in Neo-Classical style after its destruction by the French in 1798, contains the carved wooden figure of the "Black Virgin", (15th c.). The library possesses 150,000 volumes, 1300 manuscripts produced in the great medieval scriptorium here and 1200 incunabula. The Princes' Hall (Fürstensaal: entrance from the south side of the conventual buildings), with stucco decoration by M. Roncati (1704–05), is used for special exhibitions.

Black Madonna

Bethlehem Diorama

Near the square outside the abbey is the Bethlehem Diorama, a representation of the manger in Bethlehem with 500 carved wooden figures. A little way beyond this a circular building houses a Panorama of the Crucifixion (originally 1893, reconstructed after a fire in 1960).

Surroundings

Sihlsee

An attractive feature of the surrounding area is the Sihlsee (892m/2927ft), an artificial lake 9km/6 miles long and just over 1km/½ mile wide on average (area when full 10.85sq.km/4sq.miles, depth 25m/82ft) completed in 1934, the first stage in the Etzelwerk hydro-electric complex. The road along the west side of the Sihlsee comes in 13km/8 miles to Unteriberg (931m/3055ft: pop. 1450). 2km/1 mile beyond this is Oberiberg (1123m/3685ft: pop. 550).

The Benedictine Abbey of Maria Einsiedeln

5km/3 miles farther south again is Weglosen (parking garage), from which there is a cableway up to the holiday and sports facility of Hochybrig (Weglosen-Seebil), at the foot of the Drusberg and the Forstberg, a recently developed walking and skiing area (1600–2200m/5250–7218ft: restaurant, chair-lifts, ski-lifts).

★Hochybrig

11.5km/7 miles south-west of Einsiedeln in the Alptal is the little hamlet of Brunni (996m/3268ft; pop. 330), from which there is a cableway up Holzegg: good walking country, starting-point for the climb of the Grosser Mythen (1902m/6240ft: mountain inn; wide views), Ibergeregg, Haggenegg and Hochstuckli. From the Ibergeregg pass (1406m/4613ft: inn) there is a pleasant walk to Rickenbach, from which a cableway 2446m/8025ft long runs up to the Rotenfluh (1565m/5135ft).

★Grosser Mythen

To the north is the Etzel pass, with St Meinrad's chapel (poor road to Pfäffikon), from which a footpath (20 minutes) climbs to the Etzel-Kulm (959m/3146ft: inn). Near the Teufelsbrücke (Devil's Bridge) in the Sihl valley is the house in which the scientist and doctor Theophrastus Paracelsus (1493–1541) was born (see plaque on nearby house).

Etzel Pass

Emmental

J/K 6/7

Canton: Bern (BE)

The Emmental (Emme valley), renowned for its cheese, is a fertile farming region extending east from Berne towards the Napf (1408m/4620ft), with a characteristic way of life which was described in the works of the 19th c. novelist Jeremias Gotthelf (Albert Bitzius), who was pastor at Lützelflüh. Until about 1800 it was thought that good cheese could be made only from the milk of the Alps; but the first cheese dairies in the valleys were then established in the Emmental, and the excellent cheese produced there is

Situation and general

now exported far and wide. A model Emmentaler cheese dairy has been opened in Affoltern.

<table>
<tr><td>Lakes and rivers</td><td>The Kleine Emme (Little Emme) rises on the Giswilerstock and flows down through the Mariental and Entlebuch valley to join the Reuss after a course of 58km/36 miles. The Grosse Emme (Great Emme) rises on the Hohgant (2197m/7208ft), north of Lake Brienz and flows through the Emmental to join the Aare east of Solthurn after a course of 80km/50 miles.</td></tr>
</table>

★ Culture and Landscape

The Emmental is a region of gently rolling country with a long tradition of good farming with many farms having belonged to the same families for centuries. Although traditional values are deeply rooted, the farmers of the Emmental have been among the pioneers of modern agriculture in Switzerland. The farmhouses have a distinctive character – substantial and well-built, with arcades, an abundance of flowers and often elaborate carved decoration – as have the barns and the little houses for the grandparents, and the inns with the old traditional names, the "Bear" and the "Lion", the "Star" and the "Crown". The region offers endless walking opportunities off the beaten track.

Communications

The Emmental is the shortest route from Berne to Lake Lucerne. Road 10 runs from Berne to Langnau (30km/19 miles) and from there via Wolhusen to Lucerne (92km/57 miles).

Burgdorf

Burgdorf (533m/1749ft: pop. 16,000), a fine town north-east of Berne, is the real gateway to the Emmental. 10th c. castle of the Zähringen family, with three towers (now a historical museum; closed Sat.); Late Gothic parish church (1490: organ gallery with sandstone tracery); fine old guild-houses; picturesque arcaded market and cantonal technical college.

Following its conversion in 1991 the 18th c. granary houses the Swiss Museum and Institute for Folk Music and Musical Instruments, a Swiss Costume Collection, and a large collection of musical equipment (closed

Burgdorf: Zähringer Castle

Mon.). Ethnological collections are also on show in Kirchbühl (open: Wed. and Sat.). Also of interest is the construction of the Wynigen Bridge (1764). There is an attractive marked walk from Binzberg to Wynigen.

Engadine

Canton: Grisons (GR)

The Engadine (in German Engadin, in Romansch Engiadina) is the valley of the Inn (in Romansch En), enclosed between mighty mountain chains and flanked by flower-spangled Alpine meadows and magnificent forests of larch and stone pine on the steep hillsides. The village houses are solid white-washed structures, often with sgraffito decoration, painting, handsome oriel windows or elaborate window grilles. The population is Rhaeto-Romanic and predominantly Protestant. Since 1938 the old Ladin place-names have been in official use.

Situation and general

★★ Culture and Landscape

From the Majola pass (1815m/5955ft), the boundary between the Engadine and the Val Bregaglia (see entry), the road runs north-east through the Upper Engadine, with its clear air and extensive views, to the international resort of St Moritz (see entry) and two smaller resorts, popular both in summer and in winter, Celerina (Schlarigna: Romanesque/Gothic church of St Jean), where the road to the Bernina pass branches off, and Samedan (Samaden: Gothic church of St Peter and many Engadine houses). It then continues to La Punt (road on left to Albula pass) and the old-world village of Zuoz, once the chief settlement in the Engadine with many fine old houses and a Gothic church. Beyond S-chanf it runs through a defile at Puntota to enter the Lower Engadine, where the valley becomes narrower and more densely forested.

★ Upper Engadine

Celerina
Samedan

Zuoz

★ Lower Engadine

After passing through Zernez, where the road through the Swiss National Park (see entry) to the Ofen pass and the Stelvio pass diverges to the right, the Engadine road turns north for 6km/4 miles to reach Susch, where the road to Davos over the Flüela pass branches off on the left.

From here we continue down the Lower Engadine, running under the south side of the magnificent Silvretta group, with a series of wild side valleys nestling on its sunny southern slopes. Throughout the centuries the old Imperial road (Reichsstrasse) avoided the impenetrable valley and ran through the upper villages.

★★ Swiss National Park

A narrow side road leads via steep hairpin bends to the linear village of Guarda (1653m/5425ft: pop. 179), which was awarded the Wakker Prize in 1975 for its harmonious architecture.

★ Guarda

The inns and guest houses of Guarda provide a prime example of the traditional Engadine house, which from the 14th c. has combined both house and stable under one roof. The "Suler" (passage) below the round arched doorway serves as the entrance to the "Tablà" (barn) and the lobby to the living-room, with the "Stüva" (parlour, lounge), the "Chadafö" (kitchen), and the "Chaminada" (pantry). Above these last two rooms are the bedrooms ("Chombra"), access to which is usually via stairs from the parlour. In addition there is a winch and more "Giodens" or "Gebens" (rooms) for the young men. Occasionally there is a finely panelled upper room. The external appearance is characterised by the mortar-coloured walls with inward-sloping window openings and a large door. The influence of neighbouring Tirol is clearly visible in the fascinating and varied wall decorations. Every style is reflected from Gothic to Rococo and Neo-Classical to Naïve, and typical decorative features include oriel windows, window grilles and heraldic animals.

Engadine House

Traditional Engadine house . . .　　*. . . with decorated façade*

. . . such as the Clalgüna-Haus in Ardez . . .　　*. . . or in Guarda*

The neighbouring village of Ardez (1470m/4825ft: pop. 463) also has many examples of typically decorated houses of the Lower Engadine region, with charming sgraffiti, oriel windows and gables. A notable example is the Clalgüna house.

★Ardez

The hamlets of Lavin (1430m/4693ft: pop. 200) and Ftan-Pitschen also have wonderful farmhouses in Engadine style.

Lavin, Ftan

The valley then opens up again, and the road reaches the Bad Scuol-Tarasp-Vulpera group of resorts (see entry), with Tarasp Castle on its precipitous crag dominating the scene.

Bad Scuol-Tarasp-Vulpera

Beyond Scuol the valley becomes wilder and more solitary, with the few villages (Sent, Ramosch, Tschlin) perched high above the road on the green meadows on the sunny side of the valley. The scenery becomes still more forbidding in the wooded Finstermünz defile beyond the last Swiss Village (Martina), in which, at the hamlet of Vinadi, the old frontier fortifications can still be seen. Here a boldly engineered road leads into the Samnaun valley, where secluded villages attract many visitors both in summer and in winter.

The road now crosses the Austrian frontier into Tirol and continues down the Inn valley, between the Samnaun group and the western ridge of the Ötztal Alps. After passing through Stuben-Pfunds and Prutz it comes to Landeck, where it meets the road from the Arlberg pass.

Landeck

Engelberg   M 7

Canton: Obwalden (OW)
Altitude: 1050m/3445ft
Population: 3400

The little town of Engelberg with its abbey, in a sunny basin under the north face of Titlis, is a popular winter and summer resort lying well away from the main traffic routes. Since 1815 it has been an enclave of the half-canton of Obwalden. It is a region of varied scenery; good walking country with hills and lakes, and with a number of cableways providing easy access to the mountains.

Situation and general

The Benedictine abbey was founded in 1120, and its abbot held independent sway over the territory. In 1798 the town was released from ecclesiastical authority and became part of the canton of Obwalden.

History

Sights

At the upper end of the town is the Benedictine abbey, founded about 1120, which ruled the whole valley until 1798. The handsome church, designed by Kaspar Moosburger, and the square complex of conventual buildings were rebuilt in 1730–37 after a fire. Rich library (men only admitted), with valuable manuscripts, incunabula and miniatures.

Benedictine Abbey

Also of interest are the adjoining charnel-house and below the village the chapels St Jakob in Espen (17th c.) and Maria im Horbis (17th c.) at the so-called "end of the world". To the south, on the left bank of the Aawasser, are beautiful gardens surrounded by forest.

Swimming (indoor and open-air pools), the new Erlen Sports Centre, riding, tennis, summer skiing (ski-lift at upper station of Titlisbahn, 3020m/9909ft). Skating rinks, curling rink, toboggan run from the Gershnialp (3.5km/2 miles), horse-drawn sleighs, hang-gliding and hobby courses.

Recreation and sport

Unique panoramic view of the Alps from Mt Titlis

Mountain railways and cableways	Terminus of narrow-gauge railway from Lucerne via Stans (1 hour); cableways; Engelberg–Trübsee (length 2755m/9042ft, height difference 800m/2625ft, time 10 minutes); Trübsee–Stand–Kleintitlis (length 3465m/11,369ft, height difference 1220m/4003ft, time 14 minutes); Trübsee–Joch pass (length 1459m/4787ft, height difference 439m/1440ft, time 13 minutes); Engstlensee–Joch pass (length 1631m/5351ft, height difference 273m/896ft, time 10 minutes); Rindertitlis-Laubersgrat (length 1183m/3883ft, height difference 385m/1264ft, time 8 minutes); Engelberg–Brunni (length 1193m/3914ft, height difference 582m/1910ft, time 6 minutes).
Climbs ★ Urirotstock	Titlis (3239m/10,627ft), usually starting either from the Trübsee Hotel or from Kleintitlis; Hutstock (2680m/8793ft: 6 hours; wild goats); Schlossberg (3135m/10,289ft: 8 hours); Engelberger Rotstock (2820m/9252ft: 6 hours, with guide); Urirotstock (2932m/9620ft: 8–9 hours, with guide).
Benedictine Way	The first stage of the Benedictine Way is from Engelberg village centre via Brunni/Ristis (1600m/5251ft), Alp Stafel (1694m/5560ft) and Walenalp to Wolfenschiessen (guest houses). It continues by cableway to Haldiwald (1400m/4595ft) or by cabin cableway to Schmidsboden (1215m/3988ft) climbing down the Underrist-Hütti to Dallenwil (inn).

Surroundings

★ Titlis	Titlis (3239m/10,627ft), covered by eternal snow and ice, is the highest viewpoint in central Switzerland, offering a unique panorama of the Alps (ice cave, glacier trail). Restaurants on Titlis and in Stand (2450m/8038ft). Since 1993 the Rotair shuttle service has operated between these two peaks; it revolves once on its own axis during the five-minute journey. Cableway Engelberg–Titlis (45 minutes).
Solar power station	The highest experimental solar power station at Stand came into operation in 1988 with energy being produced by a bank of solar panels. With a

nominal output at present of 2.3kW, an annual output of between 3000 and 3500kWh is expected.

From Engelberg there is a cableway by way of the steep Pfaffenwand to the Trübsee Hotel (1790m/5875ft); descent in 2 hours via the Trübseealp. From Trübsee by chair-lift (or on foot in 1¼ hours) to the Joch pass (2215m/7267ft: ski hut), and from there a bridle-path (1 hour) to the Engslensee (1852m/6076ft), in a magnificent mountain setting, and on to the Engstlenalp (1839m/6034ft), one of the finest areas of Alpine pasture in the country (rich flora, superb views) and the Melchsee.

Trübsee

★Engstlenalp

Other rewarding walks are to the Bergli (1341m/4400ft); to the Surenenalp and Tätschbach Falls (1090m/3576ft: restaurant); and by the Herrenrüti grazings to the Nieder-Surenenalp (1260m/4134ft: restaurant) and the Arnialp.

Entlebuch

K/L 6/7

Canton: Lucerne (LU)

The quickest route between Lucerne and Berne by either road or rail (92km/ 57 miles) is through the valleys of Entlebuch and Emmental. The region drained by the Great and Little Emme extends from the Brienzer Rothorn to the Napf: a land of many legends, it has preserved much of its traditional character, but what was once the home of woodcutters and charcoal-burners is now a favourite holiday area. From the borders of the cantons of Lucerne and Berne in the Emmental low passes lead through the hills to Lake Thun and Obwalden.

Situation and general

From Lucerne the road follows the Kleine Emme (Little Emme) by way of Emmenbrücke and the old market village of Malters to Wolhusen (20km/ 12 miles), the gateway to the Entlebuch valley. The picturesque village of Entlebuch (684m/2244ft; pop. 3500) lies above the Entlen, a torrential stream which flows into the Kleine Emme here. It has a parish church founded about 900 with an elegant Rococo interior and a tower of the 13th–14th c. Entlebuch is renowned as the culinary stronghold of the region, and every three years the traditional "Wyberschiessen" is held here.

Entlebuch

Schüpfheim (719m/2359ft; pop. 3800) is the chief town in the district of Entlebuch, with an eventful history as the place of execution of the Governor of Wolhusen. It is the starting-point of the panoramic road which runs via Flühli (883m/2897ft; pop. 1500), the principal commune in the Marien-tal, which also includes the holiday resort of Sörenberg, on the road to Giswil (1159m/3803ft; ski-lifts). From Sörenberg there is a cableway up the Brienzer Rothorn (length 2740m/8990ft, height difference 1040m/3412ft, time 8 minutes); and access to other walking and skiing areas is provided by a chair-lift from the Eisee to the Rothorn (length 1061m/3481ft, height difference 298m/978ft, time 11 minutes) and a cableway to the Rossweid (length 1457m/4780ft, height difference 305m/1001ft, time 8 minutes).

Schüpfheim

Flühli

Escholzmatt (553m/1815ft) marks the watershed between the Entlebuch valley and the Emmental.

A minor road goes off to Marbach (871m/2858ft; pop. 1300), from which there is a cableway to the Marbachegg (1470m/4823ft), with extensive views of the Bernese Alps.

Marbach, Mar-bachegg

Flims

Q 7

Canton: Grisons (GR)
Altitude: 1100m/3609ft
Population: 2400

Flims

<table>
<tr><td>Situation and general</td><td>The summer and winter resort of Flims lying on a south-facing terrace 500m/1641ft above the Vorderrhein, consists of the original mountain village of Flims Dorf and the hotel development of Flims Waldhaus to the south. The high plateau with its extensive forests and its beautiful lake, the Caumasee, is magnificent walking and climbing country.</td></tr>
</table>

This easily accessible resort – reached by leaving the motorway at Reichenau, 10km/6 miles west of Chur and taking a road which runs up to Flims in 12km/7 miles – lies on the great mass of debris resulting from the biggest landslide of the last Ice Age in Switzerland. The debris covers an area of 40sq.km/15sq.miles, reaching 14km/9 miles downstream and 6km/4 miles upstream, and blocks the Vorderrhein valley for a distance of 15km/9 miles between Kästris and Reichenau. The landslide brought down at least 12,000cu.m/423,720cu.ft of rock.

There is a wide choice of recreational activities including classical concerts and traditional plays, excursions and sporting events such as the Alpine triathlon, mountain bike racing, moonlight skiing and hot air balloon week.

Sights

<table>
<tr><td>Flims, Schlössli</td><td>The village of Flims (Romansch Flem), under the Flimserstein (Crap da Flem, 2696m/8846ft), has a Late Gothic church (1512). The "Schlössli" (1682) is now the headquarters of the commune (Gemeindehaus). 2km/1 mile east is the old German settlement of Fidaz (1178m/3865ft), with wooden houses (an unusual case of the adoption of a Rhaeto-Romanic practice).</td></tr>
<tr><td>Flims Waldhaus</td><td>2km/1 mile south of Flims Dorf is Flims Waldhaus (1103m/3619ft), a modern resort with hotels and holiday houses. In a pavilion in the park of the Waldhaus Hotel there is a hotel museum (open: Fri.–Sun.).</td></tr>
</table>

Flims, in the skiing area of the "White Arena"

198

Chair-lift (1400m/4595ft in 20 minutes) by way of Alp Foppa to Alp Naraus; Cableways
from there cableway (2200m/7218ft in 7 minutes) to Cassonsgrat. Cableway from Flims Dorf to Startgels (1590m/5217ft); from there Graubergbahn
at 2230m/7317ft, near the Berghaus Nagiens (2128m/6982ft).

Cableway (height difference 1100m/3609ft, time 10 minutes) to Crap
Sogn Gion (2228m/7310ft; restaurant).

(Experienced climbers only with guides.) Piz Segnes (3102m/10,178ft; 8 Climbs
hours) by way of the Segneshütte (2130m/6989ft; serviced). Vorab (3030m/
9941ft; 6 hours), with magnificent views of the Tödi group.

Several ice-rinks; curling rink; toboggan run (3km/2 miles) from Alp Foppa; Winter sports
skiing on Alp Foppa (1425m/4675ft) and Alp Naraus (1840m/6037ft;), and
on Cassonsgrat (2678m/8787ft; inn) and Alp Nagens; ski-lifts; cross-
country skiing. Flims-Laax–Fellers "Weisse Arena" ("White Arena"; see
below), with summer skiing on the Vorab.

Surroundings

From Waldhaus beautiful forest tracks run south-west (1 hour) to Salums Salums
(1015m/3330ft; restaurant) and south-east (1 hour) past the delightful Cau- Caumasee
masee, in the heart of the forest (1000m/3281ft; small funicular to shore), to
Conn (990m/3248ft; restaurant); from both places there are superb views
of the gorge of the Vorderrhein.

From Flims Dorf to the Cresta-See (850m/2789ft), on the Rhine valley
road in the direction of Trin.

Ascent of the Flimserstein (4½–5 hours): from Flims Dorf via Fidaz and Flimserstein
Bargis (1550m/5086ft; from here bear left uphill) to Alp Sura (3 hours;
2102m/6897ft); then over the Alpine meadows to the highest point (1¾
hours; 2696m/8832ft), with magnificent views to the north of Ringelspitz
(Piz Bargias, 3251m/10,667ft) and the Trinserhorn (Piz Dolf, 3028m/9935ft).

5km/3 miles west of Flims on the road to Ilanz (12km/7 miles; postal bus) is **Laax**
the village of Laax (1016m/3333ft; pop. 610), which in the time of King
Rudolf of Habsburg (13th c.) was the seat of a county, with the right to hold
a market and self-government. There is a Baroque church (1675) and the
local museum has an interesting local history collection.

Laax, Flims and Fellers (Romansch Falera, 1213m/3980ft) – where remains ★ Weisse Arena
of a Middle Bronze Age settlement and cult site were found – together form Falera
the famous "Weisse Arena" ("White Arena"). An extensive winter sports
region, it has recently been developed as a huge skiing complex, one of the
largest in the Alps, more than 140sq.km/54sq.miles in area. Since November 1978, with the provision of facilities for access to the Vorab glacier area
(3025m/9925ft), it has been possible to ski here all year round. There are
more than 52 trails, with a total length of some 220km/137 miles, reached
with the aid of four cableways, three cabin cableways, eleven chair-lifts and
fifteen ski-lifts.

From Mulania a cableway (length 4200m/13,780ft, height difference Crap Sogn Gion
1100m/3609ft, time 10 minutes) runs up to Crap Sogn Gion (2228m/7310ft),
the starting-point of the Laax skiing and climbing area, with a modern
mountain restaurant seating 600 and an indoor swimming pool.

Fribourg   G 8

Canton: Fribourg (FR)
Altitude: 550–630m/1805–2067ft
Population: 40,000

Musée d'Histoire Naturelle
La Roche, Bulle

Situation and general

Fribourg (in German Freiburg), capital of the canton of the same name, is the great stronghold of Catholicism in Switzerland, seat of the Bishop of Lausanne, Geneva and Fribourg and of a Catholic University. One of the finest old medieval towns in Switzerland, it lies on the River Sarine (German Saane), which flows in a deep valley through the Mittelland. The Auge and Bourg quarters leading to the upper town are picturesquely situated, like Berne, above the rocky banks of a bend in the river; in the lower town are the districts of Neuveville on the left bank and Planche on the right bank. Fribourg was founded by Duke Berchtold IV of Zähringen in 1157 and joined the Confederation in 1481.

Sights

★★Old Town

Town Hall

In the middle of the old town is the Place de l'Hôtel de Ville, where the Town Hall (Hôtel de Ville or Hôtel Cantonal), built 1501–22 by Gylian and Hans Felder the Younger, has an octagonal clock-tower (lantern added 1642) and two attractive arched friezes above the entrance (1881 Charles Iguel). The interior has Louis XVI style panelling and Gothic 16th c. windows by Martin Gramp decorate the "Hall of the Lost Steps".

Stadthaus

The adjoining Baroque-Classical Stadthaus (addition to Town Hall) was built 1730–31 by Hans Fasel.

View of the Old Town of Fribourg

To the east of the Town Hall stands the Cathedral of St Nicholas (Gothic, 14th and 15th c.) on the former site of a Romanesque building. Its front tower measures 76m/249ft and above the main doorway are fine 14th and 15th c. sculptures (Apostles, Angelic Salutation; Last Judgment in the tympanum). At the south door is a 14th c. representation of the Three Kings. Notable features of the interior are the pulpit, font (1498), choir screen (1474) and choir-stalls (15th c. Antoine Peneys), the burial chapel (1430–33), modern stained glass by Joseph de Mehoffer, a famous organ by Alois Mooser and the treasure in the sacristy.

★ **Cathedral**

In the adjoining Place Notre-Dame (Samson fountain by Hans Gieng, 1547, original in museum) is the 12th c. church of Notre-Dame, the oldest church in the town (altered 1787 and 1853) with a Baroque-Classical Façade.

Church of Notre-Dame

Immediately north is the Franciscan friary with a church (Eglise des Cordeliers; choir 1281, nave 1745–46) which contains some notable works of art, including an altarpiece by the "Master of the Carnation" (1481), a predella with a painting by Hans Fries, "The Death of the Usurer" (1506), and a carved and gilded wooden triptych (c. 1513).

Franciscan friary

Beyond this, to the north-west, the Musée d'Art et d'Histoire in the old Ratzehof houses sculpture and painting from the 10th to the 19th c. At the end of Rue de Morat, which continues north-west, is a well-preserved old town gate, the Porte de Morat (1414).

Musée d'Art et d'Histoire

Porte de Morat

Immediately opposite the museum, in a former tram depot, a small museum has been set up in memory of the sculptor Jean Tinguely (d. 1991), who was born in Fribourg in 1925. Also on display are works by Niki de Saint-Phalle, the artist's widow.

Espace Tinguely

From the Place de l'Hôtel-de-Ville we go up the busy Rue de Lausanne or the Route des Alpes (views) to Place Georges-Python (610m/2001ft), at the

Place Georges-Python

Fribourg Cathedral: font . . .   *. . . and organ*

top of a funicular from Neuveville (Place du Perthuis). On the east side of the square stands the Bishop's Palace (Palais Episcopal). Higher up, to the north, are the Albertinium, a seminary, the Cantonal and University Library (Bibliothèque Cantonale) and the Jesuit church of St Michel, with the tomb of St Peter Canisius (Hundlinger, 1521–97), the "first German Jesuit".

University

To the west, beyond the railway, is the Université Miséricorde (by Dumas and Honegger, 1941). The great hall is decorated with 17th c. tapestry.

Station quarter

To the south-west of the upper town is the newer district around the station, with the Grand' Places, from which there is a beautiful view of the old town and the Sarine valley. Since 1984 this has been the site of Tinguely's "Fontaine de Jo Siffert", a fountain erected in memory of the Formula 1 driver Seppi ("Jo") Siffert, who was killed at Brands Hatch in 1971. This is the artist's third "waterwork", following those he erected in Basle and Paris.

Beer museum

In the Passage Cardinal a beer museum was opened in July 1988 in the cellars of the Cardinal brewery by the Blanc-pain Foundation exhibiting photographs, documents and utensils connected with the history of brewing. Visits by arrangement; tel. (037) 82 11 51.

Quartier de Pérolles

From the nearby Place de la Gare the Avenue de Pérolles runs south through the Pérolles quarter, with the church of Christ the King (1954), to the Pont de Pérolles. Nearby is the natural history museum (Musée d'Histoire Naturelle, 6 Chemin du Musée; open: daily 2–6pm). To the west of Avenue de Pérolles the 16th c. chapel of St Bartholomé (restored 1970) has

St Bartholomé's chapel

fine stained glass in Renaissance style and a crucifix by Hans Geiler.

Neuveville

In Neuveville, in the lower town, are two attractive fountains – in Place du Perthuis (553m/1814ft; funicular to upper town) the Fontaine du Sauvage (1627), and at the end of Rue de la Neuveville the Fontaine de la Prudence (1550); Gothic house fronts. The Eglise de la Providence (church) was built in 1748–57.

In the old-world Auge-quarter, which also has fine 16th c. fountains, is a former Augustinian convent, on a peninsula in the bend of the Sarine. The church, dedicated to St Mauritius, dates from the 13th c. but was rebuilt in the 16th and 18th c. The conventual buildings now house the Cantonal Archives, with more than 30,000 parchment documents, the oldest dating from 928.

Auge
Augustinian
convent

From Auge a covered wooden bridge, the Pont de Berne (1580), leads to the Place des Forgerons, on the right bank of the Sarine, with the Fontaine de la Fidélité (by Hans Gieng, 1558). To the north are the Porte de Berne (13th–14th c., restored 1660), the Tour des Chats (1383) and the Tour Rouge (1250).

Place des
Forgerons

In the Planche area of the lower town, on the right bank of the Sarine, is the church of St-Jean (1259; later enlarged). Above Planche are the Couvent de Montorge and two chapels (see below).

    South-west of Planche, on the Banks of the Sarine, is the Couvent de la Maigrauge, a Cistercian nunnery with a church built before 1300.

Planche
St-Jean

Maigrauge

Surroundings

In the suburb of Villars-sur-Glane to the south-west, at 10 Route des Biches, are the headquarters of the Cartier Group, designed by the Parisian architect Jean Novel.

Villars-sur-Glane

Circuit on the right bank of the Sarine: 4.5km/3 miles from the cathedral cross the river on the Pont du Zähringen and turn right past the Tour Rouge; cross the Pont du Gotteron, with a fine view of the town, and continue past the Tour du Dürrenbühl to the west end of the village of Bourguillon (658m/ 2159ft; church of 15th–18th c.); then sharp right along the Beau Chemin to the Porte de Bourguillon, beyond which, to the right, is the chapel of Notre-Dame de Lorette (1648), with a view of the town; beyond this, to the right, the chapel of St-Jost (1684) and, to the left, the Capuchin friary of Montorge, founded in 1626; then down into the Planche quarter, returning to the upper town either by way of the Pont du Milieu and Auge or by the Pont St-Jean and Neuveville.

Round trips

★Pont du
Gotteron

Lorette chapel
Capuchin friary
Montorge

Leave Fribourg by Avenue du Midi. In 3km/2 miles the road crosses the Glâne, a short distance above its junction with the Sarine, on a bridge above the gorge of the river. 2km/1 mile beyond the bridge a road goes off on the left and runs 2km/1 mile south to the Cistercian Abbey of Hauterive (inn), in a bend of the Sarine. The church (1160), in the purest Cistercian style, has fine stained glass (1332) and richly carved choir-stalls (1480).

    From here it is worth making a detour to the Lac de la Gruyère (see Gruyère).

**From Fribourg to
Hauterive**

Cistercian
Abbey of
Hauterive

A beautiful run (22 and 33km/17 and 21 miles south-east) through the Fribourg Pre-Alps. The road runs via Bourgouillon and Giffers (767m/ 2517ft) to Plaffeien (18km/11 miles; 851m/2792ft), where it enters the valley of the Sense and the Fribourg Alps. 4km/2 miles: Zollhaus (902m/2959ft), at the junction of the Warme and the Kalte Sense. From here a road to the left leads to Schwefelbergbad (below); the road to the right ascends the valley of the Warme Sense to the Schwarzsee (1048m/3438ft; Hotel Gypsera, D, 28b.), a lake surrounded by beautiful wooded hills. From the north end of the lake a chair-lift 1436m/4712ft long runs up in 14 minutes to the Riggisalp (1500m/4922ft). From Kaiseregg (2189m/7182ft; 3½ hours from the lake) there are magnificent views; good skiing (ski-lifts).

**To the
Schwarzsee and
Schwefelbergbad**
Zollhaus

Schwarzsee

Schwefel-
bergbad

From Zollhaus the road to Schwefelbergbad leads east up the valley of the Kalte Sense by way of the Sangernboden (1005m/3297ft). 10km/6 miles: Schwefelbergbad (1398m/4587ft), with sulphurous springs, in a beautiful wooded setting at the foot of the Ochsen (2190m/7185ft; 2½ hours; view) and Gantrisch (2177m/7143ft). These mountains form a skiing area much favoured by the people of Berne (many ski huts; ski-lifts from Schwefelbergbad to 1700m/5578ft on the north face of the Ochsen).

Geneva   B 11

Canton: Geneva (GE)
Altitude: 377m/1237ft. Population: 160,000

Situation and
general

Geneva (in French Genève; in German Genf), the city of Calvin and the centre of the Reformation, lies in the extreme western tip of Switzerland at the south-west end of Lake Geneva (in French Lac Léman). The town is built on morainic hills of varying height on either side of the swiftly flowing Rhône, which here flows out of the lake and is joined on the south-west side of the town by its tributary the Arve, coming down from the Savoy Alps. Lying between the Jura to the north-west and the limestone ridges of Mont Salève and the Voirons to the south-east, Geneva enjoys a magnificent situation on the largest of the Alpine lakes, within sight of the majestic peak of Mont-Blanc. As a hub of European cultural life in which French savoir-vivre and Swiss solidity are happily combined, the venue of international meetings on the highest level, as well as conventions and exhibitions of all kinds, and not least as a major financial, commercial and industrial city, Geneva has a lively and cosmopolitan atmosphere which makes it perhaps the most attractive town in Switzerland and the one that attracts the greatest number of visitors. Evidence of its dynamic growth during the last few decades is provided by the large amount of new building in the city itself

The "Jet d'Eau", a landmark of Geneva

and in the surrounding area, where a number of residential suburbs and satellite towns of considerable importance have grown up.

The first human settlements in this area were established at the foot of Mont Salève at the end of the Ice Age: then about 2500 B.C. a large village of pile-dwellings grew up in the area of the modern port. The first fortified settlement on the hill now occupied by the old town is believed to have been an oppidum (town) belonging to a Celtic tribe, the Allobroges, who were first conquered by the Romans in 120 B.C. The first known reference to the town under the name of Geneva occurs in the "Commentaries" (I, 7) of Julius Caesar, who in 58 B.C. caused the strategically important bridge over the Rhine to be destroyed in order to hinder the advance of the Helveti into Gaul. In A.D. 443 the town became the Burgundian capital: in 534 it fell into the hands of the Franks. At the end of the 9th c. it passed to the second Burgundian kingdom, and together with Burgundy became part of the Holy Roman Empire in 1033.

History

The long continued conflicts between the Bishops (later Prince-Bishops) of Geneva, the Counts of Geneva and the Counts (later Dukes) of Savoy for control of the town were ended by the Reformation, to which Geneva firmly adhered. In 1536 Jean Calvin (1509–64) fled from Paris to Geneva and joined forces with the Reformer Guillaume Farel (1489–1565), who had been preaching the new faith in the town since 1532. Calvin acquired great influence in both ecclesiastical and state affairs, particularly after his return in 1541, when he established a theocratic régime based on strict and often intolerant church discipline. Through his foundation in 1559 of an Academy mainly designed to train Reformed theologians he turned the commercially minded town towards an interest in intellectual matters.

In 1602 Geneva beat off an attempt by the Duke of Savoy to capture the town (the "Escalade", December 11–12). The town was occupied by the French in 1798, and until 1813 was the administrative capital of the French department of Léman. In 1814 Geneva became the 22nd canton to join the Confederation. The International Committee of the Red Cross was established in Geneva in 1865, and from 1920 to 1946 it was the headquarters of the United Nations. Geneva was the birthplace of Jean-Jacques Rousseau (1712–78), the writer and philosopher whose ideas had so much influence on the French Revolution and on the Romantic movement.

The townscape of Geneva, though undramatic, is full of variety. On a steep-sided hill on the left bank of the Rhône rises the old town, dominated by the cathedral, with its picturesque old streets, flights of steps, fountains and historic buildings. On the west, south and east it is surrounded by a ring of imposing buildings and broad streets on the line of the old fortifications. The business life of the city is concentrated in the area below the old town to the north and in Saint-Gervais, formerly an outlying suburb. On both sides of the lake are elegant promenades and extensive parks and gardens. In the northern part of the town are the main railway station, industrial establishments, craft workshops and residential areas. Most of the international organisations have their headquarters still farther north, in spacious park-like grounds.

★★ Townscape

Geneva is the capital of the smallest Swiss canton, the République et Canton de Genève. It is almost entirely surrounded by French territory (free trade zones) and is connected to the rest of Switzerland only by the lake and a narrow corridor along the north-west shore of the lake. It has two small enclaves around Céligny in the canton of Vaud.

(Not all operating during the winter.) Regular steamer services to places on the lake, run by the Compagnie Générale de Navigation sur le Lac Léman (CGN; head office in Lausanne-Ouchy; branch office in Geneva, "Le Bateau", Jardin Anglais); round trips and cruises; shuttle services and short trips in the port area and round about by the Mouettes Genevoises (motor-launches) and by "Swiss Boat".

Boat services

See also Lake Geneva/Boat services.

Geneva

1 Palais de Justice
(Law Courts)
2 Collège de St-Antoine
(College)

3 Musée des Instruments
Anciens de Musique
(Museum of Historical
Musical Instruments)

4 Musée d'Art et d'Histoire
(Art Museum)
5 Ecole des Beaux-Arts
(Art School)

6 Athénèe (Atheneum; Library,
Special Exhibitions)
7 Monument de la Réformation
(Reformation Memorial)

Genève / Genf

300 m

© Baedeker

Lausanne

LES PÂQUIS

Palais Wilson

Lake Geneva

Grand Casino

Jetée des Pâquis

Phare

Église Américaine

Bains

Mouettes

Places des Alpes

Bus Station

Église Anglaise

Monument Brunswick

Phare

GERVAIS

Rade de Genève

Jet d'eau

Jetée des Eaux-Vives

Parc de la Grange

Roseraie

Thonon, Evian / Parc des Eaux-Vives

14

Île Rousseau

CGN

Pierres du Niton

Temple de la Fusterie

13

Promenade du Lac

Jardin Anglais

Quai Général Guisan

LES EAUX-VIVES

Tour du Molard

Place du Port

Ste-Marguerite

Maison Tavel

12

St-Joseph

Place des Eaux-Vives

Bahnhof (Gare des Eaux-Vives)

11

Cathédrale St-Pierre

Rond-Point de Rive

Carrefour de Rive

Mairie

Place de Jargonnant

Rathaus

Place du Bourg-de-Four

Immeuble Clarté

Museum d'Histoire Naturelle

Route de Chêne

Bastions

Palais Eynard

versité

Église Russe

Musée de l'Horlogerie

CONTAMINES

SAINT-LÉGER

Petit Palais

ce des ilosophes

Boulevard des Philosophes

MALOMBRE

FLORISSANT

Annemasse / Chamonix

8 Temple de l'Auditoire
(Protestant Church)

9 Conservatoire de Musique
(Music Conservatoire)

10 Musée Rath
(Special Exhibitions)

11 Ancien Arsenal
(former Corn Hall)

12 Temple de la Madeleine
(Germano-Swiss Reformed Church)

13 Monument National
("Helvetia" and "Geneva")

14 Sitzbild von Jean-Jaques
Rousseau (Statue of
Jean-Jaques Rousseau)

15 Tour de l'Ile
(Historical Island Tower)

Museums, Galleries, etc.

Bibliotheca Bodmeriana
21 Route de Guignard, Cologny;
Tues.–Sun. 2–6pm

Bibliothèque Publique et Universitaire
Salle Ami Lullin, Promenade des Bastions
Mon.–Fri. 9am–noon, 2–6pm, Sat. 9am–noon

Cabinet des Estampes
(Print Room; old and contemporary works, also special exhibitions)
5 Promenade du Pin
Tues.–Sun. 10am–noon, 2–6pm

Cathedral of St Peter
See Site Archéologique de la Cathédrale Saint-Pierre

CERN (European Organisation for Nuclear Research)
Route de Meyrin (bus from Cornavin station)
Guided tours by prior arrangement (minimum age 16)
Sat. 9.15am and 2.15pm (tel. 7 67 40 52 or 7 67 41 02)

Château de Penthes
See Musée des Suisses à l'Etranger

Château de Voltaire
Ferney-Voltaire (France)
Sat. afternoons in July and Aug. only

Collections Baur
8 Rue Munier-Romilly
Tues.–Sun. 2–6pm

Collection de la Fondation in Memoriam Comtesse Tatiana Zoubov
21 Rue des Granges
Guided tours only
Oct. 1st–June 14th, Thur. 6pm, Sat. 2.30 and 3.30pm; June 15th–Sept. 30th,
Mon.–Fri. 3.45 and 5pm
There is also a guided tour at 5pm on Fridays which forms part of the tour of
the Old Town (tour de la vieille ville); meet at the Town Hall (Hôtel de Ville).

Conservatoires et Jardins Botaniques
Route de Lausanne
Botanical collections:
Mon.–Fri. 7.45am–12.30pm, 1–5pm
Botanical gardens: Jan.–Mar., Oct.–Dec. daily 9.30am–5pm, Apr.–Sept.
daily 8am–7.30pm

Hôtel de Ville (Rathaus/Town Hall)
2–2b Rue de l'Hôtel de Ville
Conducted visits only as part of organised city tours
Cantonal archives
Mon.–Fri. 9am–noon, 2–5pm

Institut et Musée Voltaire
25 Rue des Délices
Mon.–Fri. 2–5pm

Maison Tavel
6 Rue du Puits-Saint-Pierre
Tues.–Sun. 10am–5pm

Musée Ariana
10 Avenue de la Paix
Mon., Wed.–Sun. 10am–5pm

Musée Barbier-Muller
Primitive and ancient art
10 Rue Jean Calvin
Mon.–Sun. 11am–5pm

Musée d'Art Moderne et Contemporain (MANCO)
Art since 1960
10 Rue des Vieux Grenadiers (near the Musée de l'Automobile)
Tues.–Sun. noon–6pm

Musée d'Art et d'Histoire
2 Rue Charles-Galland
Tues.–Sun. 10am–5pm

Musée de l'Automobile Jean Tua
28/30 Rue des Bains
Wed.–Sun. 2–6pm

Musée de Carouge
2 Place de la Sardaigne, Carouge
Tues.–Sun. 2–6pm

Musée d'Ethnographie
65/67 Boulevard Carl-Vogt
Tues.–Sun. 10am–noon, 2–5pm

Musée d'Histoire des Sciences, Villa Bartholoni
128 Rue de Lausanne
Tues.–Sun. 1–5pm

Musée d'Instruments Anciens de Musique
New premises are at present being sought, so the museum is closed until
further notice

Musée de l'Horlogerie
15 Route de Malagnou
Wed.–Mon. 10am–5pm

Musée de l'Ordre de Malte
Commanderie de Compesières;
By appointment (tel. 7 35 33 81)

Musée des Suisses a l'Etranger
Château de Penthes
18 Chemin de l'Impératrice
Tues.–Sun.10am–noon, 2–6pm

Musée de l'Institut Henry Dunant
Parc Mon-Repos
114 Rue de Lausanne
Mon.–Fri. 9am–noon, 2–5pm

Musée International de la Croix Rouge et du Croissant Rouge (MICR)
17 Avenue de la Paix
Mon., Wed.–Sun. 10am–5pm

Musée Philatélique des Nations Unies
Palais des Nations, Entrée Pregny, Porte 39
Mon.–Fri. 9am–noon, 2–4.30pm

Musée d'Histoire Naturelle
1 Route de Malagnou
Tues.–Sun. 9.30am–5pm

Petit Palais – Musée d'Art Moderne
2 Terrase St-Victor
Tues.–Sun. 10am–noon, 2–6.50pm

Musée Rath (special exhibitions)
Place Neuve
Tues.–Sun. 10am–5pm. Wed. noon–9pm

Observatoire
Sauverny (special exhibitions)
Library (tel. 55 26 11)

Palais des Nations (ONU/UNO)
Avenue de la Paix
Conducted tours only (Entrance 7) every hour, daily Apr.–Oct. 9.15am–
noon, 2–5.15pm; otherwise Mon.–Fri. 9.15am–noon and 2–4.15pm

Site Archéologique de la Cathédrale Saint-Pierre
Cour Saint-Pierre
Tues.–Sun. 10am–1pm, 2–6pm
Service on Sunday at 10am

Temple de l'Auditoire (John Knox Chapel)
Place de la Taconnerie
June 1st–Sept. 15th: Wed., Sat. 2–5pm

Description of the town

Pont du Mont-Blanc
One of Geneva's busiest traffic arteries is the Pont du Mont-Blanc (1862; rebuilt 1969), the first of its eight bridges over the Rhône, spanning the river at the point where it leaves Lake Geneva. At the southern end is the entrance to a car park under the riverbed.

Ile Rousseau
Between this bridge and the next one, the Pont des Bergues, lies the Ile Rousseau, with a statue of Jean-Jacques Rousseau (by Pradier, 1834). Then come the Pont de la Machine (pedestrian bridge; under it a dam) and the double Ponts de l'Ile (until the 19th c. the only bridge), crossing an island in the Rhône on which stands the Tour de l'Ile, a relic of the medieval fortifications.

Lower town

The Lower Town or "Rues Basses", lying between the south bank of the Rhône and the old town, is the city's main business and shopping quarter.

Rue du Rhône
the busiest streets are the Rue du Rhône and a succession of streets which run parallel to it – Rue de la Conféderation, Rue du Marché, Rue de la Croix-d'Or (these last two for pedestrians only) and Rue de Rive – with a series of squares (originally landing-stages), passages and cross streets linking the two. Opposite the island in the Rhône is Place Bel-Air, around which are a number of banks. Farther east is Place de la Fusterie, in the

Temple de la Fusterie
middle of which stands the Temple de la Fusterie, a Neo-Classical structure built by J. Vennes in 1713–15 as a Protestant church and restored in 1975–77 for use as an ecumenical facility.

Tour du Molard
Along Rue du Rhône, at the corner of Place Molard, is the Tour du Molard (built 1591, several times altered or restored), the remnant of an old arcaded building, with a bas-relief of 1920, "Genève Cité de Refuge".

★ Temple de Saint-Pierre

On the highest point of the old town (Vieille Ville: 404m/1326ft), occupying the site of a Roman temple and a number of earlier churches of the 4th–5th c. onwards, rises the Temple de Saint-Pierre, the post-Reformation name of the Cathedral of Saint-Pierre, a Romanesque church with Gothic elements which was built between about 1150 and 1232, with later alterations, particularly to the exterior. The two principal towers, never completed, date from the 13th c.; the metal spire over the crossing was built only in 1895, replacing a tower destroyed by fire in the 15th c. The original west front and doorway were replaced in 1749–56 by a portico of six Corinthian columns – a piece of stylistic nonconformity which does not, however, interfere with the unity of the interior. Extensive restoration of the church was carried out in 1888–98 and in 1974–79.

History

The interior of the cathedral (total length 64m/210ft) is of impressive effect with its harmonious proportions and the austere simplicity characteristic of Calvinist churches. The nave, with the aisles divided off by massive clustered piers, has a gallery, blind arcading and triforium; the transepts are short and narrow; the choir, with no ambulatory, ends in a semi-circular apse.

★ Interior

Against the walls of the aisles, in the second bay, are the gravestones of ecclesiastical and lay dignitaries of the 15th and 16th c., originally set into the ground. In the fifth bay are Late Gothic choir-stalls with delicate carving from the destroyed Chapelle des Florentins. In front of the last pillar on the

★ Choir-stalls

Cathedral of St Peter, Geneva
Temple de Saint-Pierre · Genève

1 Entrance
2 Organ
3 Gravestone of the Huguenot Théodore Agrippa d'Aubigné (1552–1630)
4 Tablet commemorating the first oecumenical service (20 February 1946)
5 Tablet commemorating the restoration of Genevese independence (31 December 1813)
6 Choir-stalls (from the Chapelle des Florentins, destroyed)
7 Tablet commemorating the Calvinist Reformation
8 Pulpit
9 Calvin's chair
10 Steps to N tower
11 15th c. door

NOTABLE CAPITALS
a Lions, dancers and acrobats
b Daniel in the lions' den
c Angels fighting with dragons
d Salome dancing in front of her father; demons, themes from the Apocalypse
e Melchizedek with bread and wine; Abraham's sacrifice
f Sirens; monks' heads with lions' bodies
g Ornamental motifs with human figures and animals; geometric arabesques
h Partridges billing and cooing, with grapes; acanthus ornament
j Orpheus charming birds
k Christ at Emmaus

wall of the north aisle is the "Chaise de Calvin", a triangular chair said to have been used by the Reformer.

In the transepts are chapels: in the north-east corner the plain Nassau chapel, north-west of the choir the Rohan chapel, with the tomb (1889) of Duc Henri de Rohan (1579–1638), leader of the French Protestants in the reign of Louis XIII.

Choir

The simple choir with blind arcading, dates from the 12th c.: the stained glass windows are copies of the 15th c. originals, now in the Musée d'Art et d'Histoire (which also has the surviving parts of the high altar, painted by Konrad Witz).

★ Capitals

The large gallery above the entrance houses a modern organ (1962–65) with 6000 pipes. The late Romanesque and Early Gothic capitals on the clustered piers of the nave and the pillars on the walls and windows of the aisles and in the choir and transepts are notable for their artistic quality and their variety of theme.

The recently opened archaeological excavations below the cathedral reveal an extensive underground labyrinth, evidence of early Christian settlement on the hill.

Chapelle des Macchabées

Adjoining the south-west corner of the cathedral is the Chapelle des Macchabées (1406, altered and restored in 1898), a superb example of High Gothic religious architecture, with beautiful window traceries.

Around the cathedral

Temple de l'Auditoire

On the south side of the cathedral the former church of Notre-Dame (originally early 13th c.) has been called since the Reformation the Temple de l'Auditoire, in which Calvin, Beza and John Knox preached. Partly rebuilt in the 19th c., it is now used by Scottish, Dutch, Italian and Spanish Protestants (John Knox Chapel; restored 1959; exhibition of historical documents).

Cour Saint-Pierre

To the west of the cathedral the peaceful tree-shaded Cour Saint-Pierre has a number of historic old houses, the most elegant of which is the Maison Mallet (Louis XV style, 1721).

★ Place du Bourg-de-Four

South-east of the cathedral in the picturesque Place du Bourg-de-Four, on the site of the Roman forum, stands the handsome Palais de Justice, built 1707–12, which has housed the law courts since 1860.

Hôtel de Ville

South-west of the cathedral is the Hôtel de Ville (15th–17th c.), seat of the cantonal government, which has a ramp without steps, leading to the upper floors. The Tour Baudet contains the cantonal archives. On the ground floor of the south-east wing is the Alabama room, in which the first Geneva Convention (on the Red Cross) was signed in 1864.

State Archives

Facing the Hôtel de Ville is the Old Arsenal, a former 16th c. granary which served as a weapons arsenal in the 18th c. Restored in 1971, it now houses the State archives.

Grand' Rue

Here is the beginning of the Grand' Rue (pedestrians only), the well-preserved main street of the old town, with house fronts of the 15th–18th c. (at No. 40 the birthplace of Jean-Jacques Rousseau).

Promenade de la Treille

South-west of the Hôtel de Ville, reached through a pillared gateway, is the Promenade de la Treille, lined with chestnut-trees (views of Mont Salève and the Jura). There are rows of bench-seats with a total length of 126m/138yd.

★ Maison Tavel

From the Arsenal the narrow Rue du Puits-Saint-Pierre leads north: at No. 6 is the Maison Tavel, the oldest private house in Geneva (first mentioned in

Grand Théâtre, opera-house of Geneva   *Arcaded courtyard of the Hôtel de Ville*

the records 1303, rebuilt 1334). Today it houses the Musée du Vieux Genève with a model of the town of Geneva in 1850 before the walls were destroyed (scale 1:250; 1880–96; A. Magnin) along with doors, carved inn and shop signs, bells, chairs and other exhibits from the town's history.

Below the old town, to the south-west, is the Place Neuve (equestrian statue of General Dufour).

Place Neuve

On the north side stands the Grand Théâtre (Opera House, 1874–79), with the Musée Rath (1824–25, in Classical style: exhibitions) on the right, and the Conservatoire de Musique (1858: annual music competition) on the west side. South-east of the square the Promenade des Bastions, is graced by old trees and busts of prominent citizens of Geneva.

Grand Théâtre
Musée Rath
Conservatoire
de Musique

Against the wall under the Promenade de la Treille can be seen the Reformation Monument (Monument de la Réformation, 1917). In the middle are figures of Calvin, Guillaume Farel, Théodore de Bèze or Beza and John Knox, and on either side are the statesmen who promoted the cause of the reformed faith and bas-reliefs with scenes from the history of the Calvinist Reformation, while at the ends are memorials to Luther and Zwingli.

★ Reformation
monument

On the south side of the Promenade des Bastions is the University, housed in its present buildings since 1873, which developed out of the Academy founded by Calvin in 1559 for the training of Reformed theologians. The Library in the east wing was founded in the 15th c., and contains some 1,200,000 volumes, a collection of portraits of leading theologians, scholars, writers and statesmen, 6000 valuable manuscripts, a Rousseau Museum (manuscripts, books, compositions, etc.) and a Reformation Museum.

University

At the east end of the Promenade des Bastions is the elegant Palais Eynard (1821: municipal reception rooms), and to the south-east of this the Neo-Classical Palais Athénée (art gallery; 1864).

Palais Eynard

Palais Athénée

213

Reformation Monument: Farel, Calvin, Bèze and Knox

Plaine de Plainpalais Museum of Ethnography

West of the University, beyond the spacious Plaine de Plainpalais, is the Museum of Ethnography (65–67 Boulevard Carl-Vogt), with a collection of more than 30,000 items from all over the world, only about a fifth of which can be displayed. In the front garden two Indian totem poles (19th c.) from Alaska have been erected.

Facing the museum rises a tower block with the headquarters of Radio Genève (radio and television).

Promenade de St-Antoine

At the south-east end of the hill on which the old town is built is the Promenade St-Antoine, a former bastion, below which is the Collège St-Antoine, founded by Calvin in 1559, now one of the eight cantonal secondary schools.

★ Musée D'Art et d'Histoire

Facing it to the south, between the Boulevard Jacques Dalcroze and Boulevard Helvétique, on a lower level, the Musée d'Art et d'Histoire has rich collections of applied art and archaeology, a collection of weapons and a fine picture gallery. On the lower ground floor Greek and Roman art treasures are displayed, together with Middle Eastern and Eastern Mediterranean antiquities, Greek, Roman and Etruscan pottery and Egyptian funerary art. On the main ground floor is the museum's collection of antiquities, with material from Geneva and the surrounding area ranging in date from the Paleolithic and the Iron Age through Roman and Gallo-Roman times to the Middle Ages. There are also objets d'art of the Gothic and Renaissance periods on display.

★Picture collection

On the first floor the museum's picture collection includes Italian, Flemish and Swabian old masters, works by Flemish, Dutch and French artists of the 16th–18th c. and pictures of the 18th and 19th c. Geneva school.

International Monument
of the Reformation
Geneva
© *Baedeker*
Schematic plan

On the upper part of the rear wall of the monument, on either side of the central figures, is an inscription in large Roman lettering, POST TENEBRAS LUX ("After darkness comes light"), the motto of the Genevese Reformation. On the plinth of the central group is the Christian emblem IHS. At the ends of the wall are inscribed the two most important dates in the history of Geneva – **1536** (adoption of the Reformed faith and introduction of compulsory schooling) and **1602** (the "Escalade").

STATUES
of the Genevese Reformers **Guillaume Farel** (1489–1565), **Jean Calvin** (1509–64) and **Théodore de Bèze** (1519–1605) and the Scottish Reformer **John Knox** (1505–72)
On either side of the main figures:
A Frederick William of Brandenburg (1620–88), the Great Elector
B William I, the Silent, of Nassau-Orange (1533–84)
C Admiral Gaspard de Coligny (1519–72), leader of the French Protestants
D Roger Williams (1603–83), the English settler in New England who fought for freedom of conscience in the North American colonies
E Oliver Cromwell (1599–1658)
F István (Stephen) Bocskay (1557–1606), Prince of Transylvania, the Hungarian statesman

BAS-RELIEFS of important events in the history of the Reformation:
1 The Great Elector issues the Potsdam Edict of 1685, offering asylum to Protestants driven from France by the Revocation of the Edict of Nantes
2 The States General in The Hague vote for the independence of the Netherlands (26 July 1581)
3 Henry IV of France signs the Edict of Nantes granting religious toleration (13 April 1598)
4 The Reformation is preached to the people of Geneva in the presence of envoys from Berne (22 February 1534)
5 John Knox preaches the Reformation in St Giles' Cathedral, Edinburgh (1565)
6 The Pilgrim Fathers sign a covenant on the "Mayflower" for the righteous colonisation of North Africa (11 November 1620)
7 The Lords and Commons present the Bill of Rights, providing for the establishment of constitutional monarchy, to William and Mary (13 February 1689)
8 Stephen Bocskay presents to the Hungarian Diet in Košice (Slovakia) the Vienna peace treaty which secures religious freedom for the kingdom of Hungary (13 December 1606)

East of the Old Town

The Ecole des Beaux-Arts (Art School) behind the Museum to the south-west, houses the collection of graphic art of the Cabinet des Estampes at 5 Promenade du Pin. A little way south is the Petit Palais (2 Terrasse St-Victor), a private museum of modern art. — Ecole des Beaux-Arts ★ Petit Palais

To the east of the Museum of Art and History, beyond the Boulevard Helvétique, stands the Russian Church (1866), with nine gilded domes. Nearby, at 23 rue Lefort, is the Musée des Instruments Anciens de Musique (Museum of Old Musical Instruments) and at 8 rue Munier-Romilly the private Collection Baur (Far Eastern art). — Russian church / Collection Baur

Farther east, at 11 Route de Malagnou, the important Musée d'Histoire Naturelle (Natural History Museum) contains informatively displayed collections and a specialised library. Of particular interest are the dioramas of regional fauna on the ground floor and the large fossils and palaeontological and mineralogical collections on the first floor. — Muséum d'Histoire Naturelle

Immediately east of the museum, at Route de Malagnou, is a mansion housing the Musée de Horlogerie et de l'Emaillerie (Museum of Watchmaking and Enamels). — Musée de l'Horlogerie et de l'Emaillerie

215

Museé d' Art et d' Histoire

LOWER GROUND FLOOR (Rez-de-Chaussée Inférieur)

111 Egypt: steles, reliefs, sarcophagi and mummies.

112 Near East; gravestones, vessels, bronzes, ceramic and gold articles (various regions).

113 Greek sculpture, vases and jewellery.

114 Etruscan art – pottery, ceramics and sculptures, urns, small bronzes (figure of Heracles).

115 Ancient Rome:
works of art and everyday objects, mainly from the Geneva area, fine marble head of Augustus.

UPPER GROUND FLOOR (Rez-de-Chaussée Supérieur)

Applied Art

212 Ecclesiastical Art of the Middle Ages: sculptures in wood, stone and ivory; enamel ware from Limoges, windows from the Cathedral of Saint-Pierre, Geneva (end of 15th c.) and from Saint-Fargeau, France (13th c.), capitals from Geneva Cathedral (11th c.), Madonna from Saas, Wallis (early 14th c.).

211 "Salle J.-J. Rigaud": sculptures. furniture, ceiling (15th c.), tapestries from Tournai (*c.* 1470), Swiss glass (16th c.).
Access to the rooms of the Château of Zizers in the mezzanine, rooms 306–300.

210 "Salle du Conseil d'Etat": carved wooden ceiling (early 18th c.) from the old council chamber of the Hôtel de Ville; furniture, tables (18th c.); Florentine marble table (16th c.).

209 "Salon de Cartigny": carved wooden ceiling (end of 18th c.) from the Château de Cartigny, near Geneva, by the Geneva sculptor Jean Jaquet (1754–1839); furniture, pastel drawing (end of 18th c.).

206/207 "Salle Renaissance": stucco work, articles of marble, bronze and ivory (Italy, France, 14th–16th c); French embroidery (*c.* 1580).

205 "Salle d'honneur" of the Château of Zizers (Grisons) (*c.* 1680): musicians' gallery, painted ceiling, doors, furniture, weapons (15th–17th c.).

204 European Weapons and Armour (15th–18th c.): guns, guillotine (1799), fine collection of pistols; windows from Sainte-Pierre (end of 15th c.).

202, 203 Silver from Geneva, the rest of Switzerland and France (18th c.).

201 Contemporary Art: special exhibitions sponsored by AMAN (Association of a Modern Art Museum).

Collection of Antiquities

218 Prehistoric articles: utensils, weapons, handmade articles, jewellery, principally from the Geneva region; especially a bronze helmet (950–750 B.C.) from Fillinges. Savoy.

213–217 Special exhibitions.

MEZZANINE (Entresol)

300, 301 Special exhibitions.

308 Numismatic collection, Byzantine art.

302 "Salle des étains": pewter from Geneva and other regions of Switzerland (16th–19th c.).

303 "Belle chambre": room from the Château of Zizers, tiled stove.

304 "Chambre peinte": room from the Château of Zizers (Regency style).

306 "Salle Anna Sarasin": coffered ceiling, stove from Winterthur.

FIRST FLOOR (Premier Étage)

Pictorial Art

Paintings and sculpture including panels by Ferdinand Hodler symbolising the Swiss cantons. A commission on the occasion of the National Exhibition of 1896.

- 400 Peristyle: special exhibitions.
- 401 Paintings of the German, Flemish, French and Italian schools. Notable paintings: winged altarpiece by Conrad Witz (b. Rottweil c. 1400–10, d. Basle or Geneva c. 1446), a triptych from Maria Stein Monastery, Upper Rhenish school, portraying the "Miraculous Draught of Fishes"; Juan de Flands (d. 1519): "Beheading of John the Baptist"; Fontainebleau school: "Sabina Poppaea" (c. 1570); Andrea Vaccaro (c. 1598–1670): "Triumph of David". Outstanding sculptures: "The Virgin in Majesty" (Auvergne), (c. 1150–80), "St John the Evangelist" (South Germany or Frankish, c. 1480), "Archbishop Giving Blessing" (Rhineland (?), c. 1460).
- 402 "Foundation Baszanger": Dutch and Flemish painting (15th–17th c.).
- 403 Dutch painting (16th–17th c.)
- 404 French and Italian paintings of the 17th–18th c.: Nicolas Régnier (c. 1590–1667), Mattia Preit (1613–99), Charles le Brun (1619–90) and Jean-Baptiste Oudry (1686–1755).
- 417, 418 Room with pictures of the Flemish type and Dutch portraits of the 17th c.
- 419 Dutch masters, painting in the Italian manner. Notable are two paintings by Nicolaes Berchem (1620–83): "The Miraculous Child" and "Abraham Receives Sarah from the hands of Abimelech".
- 420 French paintings of the 17th c.; noteworthy "The Visitation" by Philippe de Champaigne (1602–74).
- 421 Italian painting of the first half of the 18th c.
- 422 Pastels by Jean-Etienne Liotard (1702–89), wooden ceiling by the sculptor Jean-Jaquet, sculptures, furniture (18th c.).
- 405 First and foremost French portraits of the 18th c. (Nicolas de Largillière, 1656–1746; Maurice-Quentin de La Tour, 1704–88); among them a portrait of Didero by Levitzky, a likeness of Rousseau by La Tour and a bust of Voltaire by Jean-Baptiste Lemoyne (1704–78).

- 406 Paintings by Jean-Etienne Liotard; furniture of the 18th c.
- 407 Paintings from Geneva of the second half of the 18th c.: Jean-Pierre Saint-Ours, Pierre-Louis de la Rive.
- 408 Paintings and sculpture from Geneva from the end of the 18th and from the first half of the 19th c.: Jacques-Laurent Agasse (1767–1849), Adam-Wolfgang Töpffer (1766–1847), James Pradier (1790-1852).
- 409 Paintings from Geneva of the 19th c. François Diday (1802–77) and Alexandre Calame (1810–64).
- 423, 424 Temporary exhibitions of the Cabinet des Dessins.
- 410 Room entirely devoted to Camille Corot (1796–1875).
- 425–428 Room devoted to the pioneers of modern painting (Centre Bruno Lussato).
- 425 Works by Sonja Delaunay, Paul Klee (1879–1940), Fernard Léger (1881–1955) and Le Corbusier (1887–1965).
- 426 Works by Kurt Schwitters (1887–1948).
- 427 Works by Hans Richter (1902–69). Hans Arp (1887–1966) and Alexander Rodtschenko (1891–1956).
- 428 Works by Russian Constructionists.
- 413 Swiss paintings from the beginning of the 20th c.: Giovanni and Augusto Giacometti, Cuno Amiet (1868–1961), Edouard Vallet, Albert Traschsel and Hans Berger.
- 414 Paintings by Félix Vallotton (1865–1925).
- 415 Room devoted to sculpture from the end of the 19th c. and of the present day: Auguste Rodin (1840–1917), August Rodo, Antoine Bourdelle (1861–1929), Henri Laurens (1885–1954), Alexander Archipenko (1887–1964), Hans Arp, Alberto Giacometti, Max Bill (b. 1908), Henri Presset, Jean Tinguely (b. 1925), Robert Müller (b. 1920), César (b. 1921), Bernhard Luginbühl (b. 1929).

The *Cabinet des Dessins*, with about 10,000 drawings and sketches of various schools, can be visited by appointment.

Jardin Anglais: "Helvetia and Geneva"   *Brunswick Monument*

Immeuble Clarté	In a heavily built-up area below the Natural History Museum to the south-west rises the Immeuble Clarté, the only building of any size in the country designed by the Swiss architect Le Corbusier (along with his cousin P. Jeanneret). The outer walls, mainly of glass, of this block of apartments (1930–32) have no load-bearing function, being suspended from a steel skeleton.

On the south bank

Jardin Anglais	On the south side of the lake (the Rive Gauche) the Promenade du Lac runs east from the Pont du Mont-Blanc, flanked by the Jardin Anglais (large flower clock, café), with the Monument National (figures of "Helvetia" and "Geneva"), erected in 1869 to commemorate Geneva's entry into the Con-federation (1814). From here Quai Gustave-Ador leads north-east, follow-ing the shore of the lake (commercial and boating harbour). In the lake are
Pierres du Niton	two erratic boulders known as the Pierres du Niton ("Neptune's Stones"), on the larger of which is a Swiss Ordnance Survey reference point (373.6m/1226ft a.s.l.).
★Jet d'Eau	Beside the Jetée des Eaux-Vives, the breakwater enclosing the harbour (beacon), is the Jet d'Eau, a mighty jet of water which soars up to a height of 140m/460ft (1360 HP pump; does not operate in bad weather).
Parc de la Grange Parc des Eaux-Vives	Farther along the lakeside road, on the right, are the Parc de la Grange (rose-garden) and the Parc des Eaux-Vives (restaurant), both with beautiful mature trees and flower-beds. Beyond this are the yacht harbour and the Genève-Plage bathing area.

On the north bank

★Quai de Mont-Blanc	On the north side of the lake (the Rive Droite) the Quai de Mont-Blanc extends north-east from the bridge, with a view of the Mont-Blanc chain

| Aiguille du Midi 3842 m | Mont Blanc du Tacul 4248 m | Mont Maudit 4465 m | Mont Blanc 4807 m | Aiguille de Bionnassay 4052 m | Mont Saiève 1380 m |

Lac Léman (Lake Geneva) © *Baedeker*

(particularly fine in the late afternoon in clear weather). At the landing stage in front of the Hôtel Beau Rivage the Empress Elizabeth of Austria (b. 1837) was assassinated by an Italian anarchist in 1898.

Beyond this is the imposing Brunswick monument, a mausoleum modelled on the Scaliger tombs in Verona, which was built for Duke Karl II of Brunswick (1804–73), who left his money to Geneva.

Brunswick Monument

Beyond this again are the modern Grand Casino and the Jetée des Pâquis (breakwater; bathing area, beacon). From here Quai Wilson runs north past the large Palais Wilson in which the League of Nations met from 1925 to 1936, to the beautiful lakeside parks of Mon Repos and La Perle du Lac (Museum of the History of Science, summer only; restaurant).

Grand Casino

Palais Wilson
Mon Repos, La Perle du Lac

From the Pont du Mont-Blanc Rue du Mont-Blanc (pedestrian zone) goes north-west past the Hôtel des Postes (on right: the main Post Office, with a special philatelic department) to the main station, the Gare de Cornavin (Swiss and French Railways), with underground shopping passages and Geneva's tourist office.

Rue du Mont-Blanc

Beyond the railway line, to the west, is the Quartier Les Grottes, a model example of sympathetic restoration. Extensive and innovative renovation is planned with grants available in order to help preserve the character of the quarter and to allow the existing residents to remain.

Quartier Les Grottes

South of the station, extending towards the lake, is the old watchmaking quarter of Saint-Gervais, in the midst of which is the Temple of Saint-Gervais; the present church (Protestant) dates from the 15th c. (tower 1435).

Temple de Saint-Gervais

To the west of Saint-Gervais, in the district of Les Délices, we find the little property of the same name where Voltaire lived from 1755 to 1765, when he moved to Ferney, across the frontier in France. The mansion (1730–35, enlarged by Voltaire), set in a small park, is now occupied by the Institut et Musée Voltaire, with relics and mementoes of Voltaire. The adjoining library houses a large number of original manuscripts.

Institut et Musée Voltaire

International Organisations Quarter

International Organisations based in Geneva

A selection in alphabetical order: names and abbreviations in French and English

Accord Général sur les Tarifs Douaniers et le Commerce
General Agreement on Tariffs and Trade (GATT)

Alliance Internationale du Tourisme
International Touring Alliance (ITA)

Alliance Réformée Mondiale (ARM)
World Alliance of Reformed Churches

Alliance Universelle des Unions Chrétiennes de Jeunes Gens
World Alliance of Young Men's Christian Associations (YMCA)

Alliance Universelle des Unions Chrétiennes Féminines
World Alliance of Young Women's Christian Associations (YWCA)

Association Européenne de Libre-Echange (AELE)
European Free Trade Association (EFTA)

Bureau Internationale d'Education (BIE)
International Bureau of Education (IBE)

Bureaux Internationaux Réunis pour la Protection de la Propriété Intellec-
    tuelle (BIRPI)
United International Bureaux for the Protection of Intellectual Property

Centre Européen de la Culture (CEC)
European Cultural Centre (ECC)

Comité Intergouvernemental pour les Migrations Européenes (CIME)
International Committee for European Migration (ICEM)

Comité International de la Croix-Rouge (CICR)
International Committee of the Red Cross (ICRC)

Commission Economique pour l'Europe
Economic Commission for Europe

Conférence des Nations Unies sur le Commerce et le Développement
United Nations Conference on Trade and Development (UNCTAD)

Conseil Mondial de la Paix
World Council of Peace

Conseil Œcuménique des Eglises (COE)
World Council of Churches (WCC)

Fédération Luthérienne Mondiale (FLM)
Lutheran World Federation (LWF)

Haut Commissariat pour les Réfugiés
High Commissariate for Refugees

Ligue des Sociétés de la Croix-Rouge
League of Red Cross Societies

Organisations des Nations Unies (ONU)
United Nations (UN)
(European headquarters: main headquartes in New York)

Organisation Européenne pour la Recherche Nucléaire (CERN = Centre
    Européen pour la Recherche Nucléaire)
European Organisation for Nuclear Research

Organisation Internationale du Travail (OIT)
International Labour Organisation (ILO)
Executive agency:
Bureau International du Travail (BIT)
International Labour Office

Organisation Météorologique Mondiale (OMM)
World Meteorological Organisation (WMO)

Organisation Mondiale de la Santé (OMS)
World Health Organisation (WHO)

Union Européenne de Radiodiffusion (UER)
European Broadcasting Union (EBU)
Administrative headquarters of EUROVISION
(technical services in Brussels)

Union Internationale des Télécommunications (UIT)
International Telecommunications Union (ITU)

Union Internationale des Transports Routiers
International Road Transport Union

Union Interparlementaire (UIP)
Inter-Parliamentary Union (IPU)

Around the Place des Nations

The Place des Nations, 2km/1 mile north of the Pont du Mont-Blanc, is a
busy traffic intersection around which are the headquarters of many international organisations.

South of the square in the district of Varembé are a series of modern   Varembé,
buildings occupied by a variety of important institutions. Between the   International
Chemin des Colombettes and the Avenue Guiseppe-Motta are the United   Organisations

International Bureaux for the Protection of Intellectual Property (BIRPI: by P. Braillart, 1962) and the World Meteorological Organisation (WMO/OMM): by E. Martin, 1956). Between Avenue Guiseppe-Motta and Rue de Vermont is the International Telecommunications Union (ITU/UIT), a six-sided tower block by Bordigoni (1958). At the corner of Rue Varembé and Rue de Montbrillant is the Centre International, housing numerous international associations; and closely adjoining are the European Free Trade Association (EFTA: by Grand, Praplan and Fischer, 1969), with a beautiful inner courtyard, and the new International Conference Centre and Press House (CIGG: by A. and F. Gaillard and A. Camenzind, 1971).

Also in this area is a modern Roman Catholic church, Saint-Nicolas-de-Flüe (by Bouvier and V. and J. Malnati, 1967), which was visited by Pope Paul VI in 1969.

★Palais des Nations

North-east of the Place des Nations, in a large area of parkland sloping down towards the lake, stands the Palais des Nations, a monumental complex of buildings clad in light-coloured marble.

Parc de l'Ariana

This area, which now enjoys extraterritorial status with full judicial, fiscal and postal rights, was formerly part of the Parc de l'Ariana, which was bequeathed to Geneva by P. G. Revilliod in 1890. In 1929 the town handed over the area, 200,000sq.m/239,200sq.yd in extent, to the League of Nations, which had held an architectural competition in 1927–28 for the design of new headquarters.

History of the building

The most modern and progressive designs were those put forward by Le Corbusier and P. Jeanneret and by H. Meyer and K. Wittwer, but these were rejected and the choice fell instead on the rather ponderous designs submitted by an international group of architects – C. Broggi (Italy), F. Flegenheimer (Switzerland), C. Lefèvre and H. P. Nénot (France) and J. Vago (Hungary). The buildings were erected between 1929 and 1937, and the

Palais des Nations

1 S Gate (main entrance)
2 Porter's lodge (information)
3 First aid post
4 Garage
5 Bank
6 Post office
7 Gate 7: starting-point of conducted tours; Stamp Museum
8 Council Chamber (Salles des Conseils)
9 W Gate
10 Assembly Hall (Salle des Assemblées)
11 Lobby
12 Armillary sphere
13 Library
14 Space Memorial

100 m

© Baedeker

Palais des Nations: seat of the United Nations

League of Nations (hitherto housed in the Palais Wilson) was able in 1936 to transfer its headquarters to the new Palais des Nations, which was formally inaugurated in 1938 under the presidency of the Aga Khan. In 1940 the League of Nations ceased to operate, since after the exclusion of the Soviet Union it was no longer an effective international instrument, and it was dissolved in 1946 to give place to the United Nations Organisation (UNO/ONU), founded at San Francisco on October 24th 1945. The United Nations Organisation (at present with 159 members) has its main headquarters in New York but has established its European headquarters in the Palais des Nations. Conducted tours: library.

The extensive complex of buildings (25,000sq.m/29,900sq.yd), the second largest in Europe (after the Palace of Versailles), consists of three main sections. In the middle is the main range of buildings, with a wing at each end enclosing a terrace courtyard facing the lake; in this section are the Assembly Hall, Council Chamber, conference rooms and library. To the south is the Secretariat building, and to the north a higher block of offices completed in 1972, with a front wing (conference rooms) topped by two large polygonal domes.

The Palais des Nations has a total of some 30 conference rooms and 1100 office rooms, its own printing office with 36 polycopiers and 6 offset machines, a restaurant, a snack bar and a number of refreshment bars. The interior is comfortable and equipped with the most modern technical services. The large assembly halls have simultaneous interpretation facilities, enabling speeches to be translated into and out of the five official languages of the United Nations (English, French, Spanish, Russian and Chinese). The lavish decoration of the various halls and rooms was donated by different countries. The following are of particular interest:

Assembly Hall (Salle des Assemblées), a square chamber with seating for over 2000, the largest in the Palais, used for meetings of the United Nations and its associated organisations. The curtains, of raw silk, were a gift from

Salle des Assemblées

223

India. It is preceded by the Salle des Pas Perdus (Lobby), with a view of the Alps from the east side. The floor is of Finnish granite, and the walls are faced with Swedish marble. The two heavily gilded bronze doors at the ends, brought back from Italy by Napoleon, were presented to the League of Nations by Clemenceau.

Salle des
Conseils

Council Chamber (Salle des Conseils), with seating for 500. The wall and ceiling painting (by J. M. Sert, 1934–36) was a gift from Spain. Carried out in sepia on a gold ground, it depicts four related themes – technical, social and medical progress and, as a hope for the future, the abolition of war. In the middle (opposite the window side) is "Victors and Vanquished", and on the ceiling "Solidarity of the Five Continents". In this chamber was held the 1955 Four-Power Conference on the reunification of Germany (Eisenhower, Bulganin, Eden, Faure).

In the ante-chamber are three bas-reliefs by Eric Gill inspired by Michaelangelo.

Other rooms

Room III: birch and pearwood panelling; "Ship on a Calm Sea", a picture by the Genevese painter Barraud. Room V: decoration by an English artist, W. Allom; architectural motifs on the doors. Room VI: decoration presented by Switzerland (frescoes by K. Hügin; events from Swiss history on the insides of the doors). Room VII: decoration by Porteneuve. Room VIII: clad with wood inlay by a Dane, Petersen. Room IX: Panelled with beautifully grained stinkwood from South Africa. Room X: presented by Latvia (black intarsia oak floor). Room XI: by Mutters (Holland), with leather wall covering. Room XII: presented by Italy (used for showing films). Room XIV: by M. Simon.

Library

The library, donated by John D. Rockefeller Jr, was founded in 1920, and now possesses some 750,000 volumes and numerous manuscripts and letters from outstanding international figures. The stamp museum (door 39: video display) displays rare and interesting United Nations issues.

Cour d'Honneur

Between the wings of the main range of buildings is the Cour d'Honneur, a spacious terrace which merges into the park, with a magnificent view of the lake and the Alps. In the middle is a bronze armillary sphere with gilded signs of the Zodiac, by the American sculptor Paul Manship, presented by the Woodrow Wilson Foundation in 1939.

Space Memorial

On a marble terrace near the Library wing is a Space Memorial symbolising the conquest of space. The 26m/85ft high sculpture (architect Alexander N. Kolchin, sculptor Jurij Neroda) presented by the Soviet Union in 1971.

Around the Palais des Nations

Château de
Penthes

The Château de Penthes, north of the Palais des Nations (18 Chemin de l'Impératrice), houses the Musée des Régiments Suisses au Services Etranger (Museum of Swiss Regiments in Foreign Service) together with the Musée Militaire Genevois (Geneva Military Museum) and a restaurant.

★ Ariana

Above the Palais des Nations, to the west, stands the Ariana, a building in Italian Renaissance style erected in 1877–84 for the Geneva writer and philanthropist P. G. Revilliod (1817–90). With a sumptuously appointed interior, it now houses the International Academy of Ceramics and a rich collection of ceramics and porcelain begun by Revilliod.

Jardin
Botanique

To the south-east, lying between the Route de Lausanne and the Geneva–Lausanne railway line and between the Avenue de la Paix to the south and the Chemin de l'Impératrice to the north lies the Jardin Botanique, a botanic garden established in 1902, with glasshouses (exotic plants, etc.), a fine Alpine garden, a small animal enclosure (fallow deer, llamas, peacocks, cranes, parakeets) and a refreshment pavilion (summer only).

Double space-monument outside the Palais de Nations

On the east side of the Route de Lausanne is the Conservatoire Botanique, with an excellent specialised library and famous herbaria (in the garden pavilion), new greenhouses and an aviary.

Conservatoire Botanique

From the Place des Nations the broad Avenue de la Paix extends north in a wide curve, passing the Ariana on the right and the Soviet embassy on the left. Opposite the west entrance to the Palais des Nations is the attractive villa, Vieux-Bois, which houses the Geneva Hotel School (restaurant).

Villa Vieux-Bois

On higher ground to the north-west is the imposing headquarters of the International Committee of the Red Cross (Comité International de la Croix-Rouge). The International Red Cross, founded in 1864 on the initiative of Henri Dunant (1828–1910) and managed exclusively by Swiss citizens, is dedicated to pursuing humanitarian aims on the international level (e.g. by the register of prisoners of war and missing persons which it has maintained since 1916). The various national organisations (Red Cross, Red Crescent, Red Lion, Red Sun) belong to the League of Red Cross societies, which is also based in Geneva.

Comité International de la Croix-Rouge

The Musée de la Croix-Rouge et du Croissant Rouge, opened in November 1988, has information on the history of the organisation.

From the Place des Nations the Ferney road leads uphill in a north-westerly direction. After some 500m/550yd the Hôtel Intercontinental (1964), with its 15-storey tower, can be seen to the south. Beyond it is the high-class residential district of Parc de Bude.

Hôtel Continental

A little way along the old road to Ferney is the Centre Œcumenique (Ecumenical Centre), Headquarters of the World Council of Churches, the Lutheran World Federation, the Reformed World Federation and other non-Catholic associations.

Centre Œcumenique

The World Council of Churches, first discussed at the Edinburgh World Missionary Conference in 1910 and founded in its present form at Amsterdam in 1948, is composed of more than 220 Protestant, Orthodox, Old

Catholic and Anglican churches and maintains contacts with other Christian denominations, (in particular with the Roman Catholic Church; Papal visits 1969 by Pope Paul VI, 1984 by John-Paul II)

World Health
Organisation

North-west of the Ecumenical Centre (1km/½ mile from the Palais des Nations) is the headquarters of the World Health Organisation (Organisation Mondiale de la Santé; WHO/OMS:1962–66, by J. Tschumi, P. Bonnard, H. Curchid and P. Cotty), also known as the Palais de la Santé.

The World Health Organisation, founded in 1948, succeeded the International Office of Public Health, established in Paris in 1907. It is concerned with health care on an international basis, epidemic control, the training of doctors and other health care personnel, etc., and is active in the field of medical research. Its Geneva headquarters and its six regional offices on Copenhagen, Alexandria, Brazzaville, Manila, New Delhi and Washington have a total staff of almost 5000.

The main building, a rectangular eight-storey block 150m/492ft long built of prefabricated elements, rests on 22 concrete piles and contains 550 rooms. In front of it is a lower structure containing the main assembly hall, surrounded by gardens. The building contains many works of art and other features presented by member nations, notably a large wall decoration (7m/23ft square) presented by Brazil.

International
Labour Office

To the south of the World Health Organisation, on a previously undeveloped site at Le Grand Morillon rises the new headquarters of the International Labour Office (Bureau International du Travail ILO/BIT: 1969–73)

Designed by Beaudouin, Camenzind and Nervi, this has an 11-storey main building 190m/623ft long and 60m/197ft high on a biconcave ground plan borne on two supporting blocks (in the north one various services, in the south one conference rooms and the library). The outer walls (4000 windows) are of aluminium and glass, on a framework of steel and concrete. The building has some 2500 telephone extensions, facilities for simultaneous interpretation, 23 passenger and 7 goods lifts, a system for the transmission of documents within the office and a four-storey underground garage for 1450 cars.

Surroundings

★★ Lake
Geneva

See entry

Bois de la Bâtie

To the west of the town, at the "Jonction", the River Arve flows into the Rhône, its turbid yellowish water mingling with the clear greenish-blue water of the larger river. Beyond the Arve is the Bois de la Bâtie (woodland, meadows, animal enclosure; view of town).

Carouge

To the south-east of this is an artificial ice-rink, the Patinoire des Vernets (partly roofed over; seating for 10,000). The suburb of Carouge, still farther south-east was incorporated in the city in 1816, with the large goods station and bonded warehouses of La Praille. Carouge, originally founded by Savoy as a rival to Geneva, has some attractive squares and old houses.

3km/2 miles west of the city is the last of Geneva's eight bridges over the Rhône, the Pont Butin (built 1916–27, widened to eight lanes in 1970), spanning the valley at a point where it is 50m/164ft deep.

★ Cointrin
airport

5km/3 miles north-west of Geneva is Cointrin International Airport.

★ New
Exhibition and
Congress Centre
("Palexpo")

To the north-east, in the suburb of Grand-Saconneux, the New Exhibition and Congress Centre was opened in 1981. The Nouveau Palais des Expositions et des Congrès, abbreviated to "Palexpo", has 70,500sq.m/ 84,318sq.yd of floor space.

European atomic research centre CERN

About 2km/1 mile beyond this is the frontier town of Meyrin, a large residential suburb with an Alpine garden. Here, too, is the nuclear research facility CERN (Conseil Européen pour la Recherche Nucléaire: partly on French territory), with a 600 MeV synchro-cyclotron, a 28 GeV proton synchroton, storage rings and a super proton synchroton (7km/4 miles long ring tunnel). In 1989 the Large Electronic Position Storage Ring (LEP), 27km/17 miles long, was completed.

4km/2 miles west of the town, in a bend of the Rhône, is the residential development of Le Lignon, a striking example of modern architecture housing a population of 15,000.

7km/4 miles north-west, in French territory (bus services, on a road which passes under the runways of Cointrin airport in a tunnel), is Ferney-Voltaire (pop. 2000), once a potters' town. To the west of the little town is the château which Voltaire acquired in 1758 and later enlarged, where he held court until shortly before his death (mementoes). Above the former chapel is the inscription "Deo erexit Voltaire". In front of the Town Hall is a statue of Voltaire by Lambert.

9km/6 miles north (reached by rail or boat) is Versoix, an attractive little place on the west side of the Petit Lac, near the border between the cantons of Geneva and Vaud, with a beautiful lakeside promenade. The third Aga Khan, Head of the Ismaili sect, died here in his property of Le Barakat in 1957 (b. Karachi 1877; buried in Egypt). Near this house is the Château Rouge (the property of an Arab ruler).

In Genthod, just south of Versoix (fish restaurant on lake), are a number of fine old 18th c. houses, including the Maison Ami-Lullin, built in 1723–30 by F. Blondel, which was occupied by the scientist H. B. Saussure. In the Maison de la Rive (1730), above the railway line, Goethe stayed in 1779 with the philosopher and naturalist Charles Bonnet (1720–93).

Meyrin, CERN

Ferney-Voltaire

Versoix

Genthod

227

Coppet

14km/9 miles north (reached by rail or boat), in the canton of Vaud, is Coppet, a little town on the west shore of the lake, founded in the 14th c., with old arcaded houses and a 15th c. Gothic church. Above the town, in an extensive park, stands a large château on a horseshoe plan, built in 1767–71 by G. de Smethe on the site of an earlier 13th c. castle and purchased in 1784 by the Geneva banker Jacques Necker (1732–1804), later French Finance Minister. In the early 19th c. Necker's daughter Anne-Louise-Germaine, who became the Baronne de Staël-Holstein, better known as the free-thinking Mme de Staël (1766–1817), made the château a meeting-place of the leading social and political personalities of the day. Necker and Mme de Staël are buried in the park, in a walled area west of the château (visitors not admitted). The château is open to the public from March to October.

Céligny

4km/2 miles north, away from the lake, is the pretty village of Céligny, in a little enclave belonging to Geneva.

Cologny

Cologny (450m/1476ft) 1.4km/1 mile north-east (No. 9 bus or boat) on the hillside above the east shore of the Petit Lac, has a fine 17th c. country house and a number of modern villas. There is a magnificent view across the lake to the Palais des Nations and the Jura, particularly from the terrace between the Lion d'Or restaurant and the church and from the "Byron Stone" on the Chemin de Ruth. Byron stayed in the Villa Diodati in 1816 and met Shelley, then also living in Cologny.

1.8km/1 mile south at Chêne-Bougeries, is the modern residential development of La Gradelle, built since 1963.

Bellerive

6.5km/4 miles north-east, on the lake (No. 9 bus or boat), is Bellerive, with the 17th c. Manoir de Bonvent (near the landing-stage) and a 17th c. château.

Schloss Coppet: once meeting-place of artists and poets

14km/9 miles north-east, on the lake (No. 9 bus or boat), is Hermance, a
pretty little place founded in 1245 close to the French frontier. 12th c.
fortifications, château, 15th and 16th c. houses; Stone Age tombs.

★ Mont Salève

A good road and cableway ascend to Mont Salève, a long limestone ridge
south of Geneva, in French territory (good rock-climbing): 16 km/10 miles
to Monnetier, round trip 69km/43 miles, maximum gradient 6%.

Leave Geneva by the Route de Florissant and road 42, which runs south-
east via the suburb of Villette. 6km/4 miles: Veyrier (422m/1385ft) on the
French frontier (passport and customs control).
   Straight ahead is the lower station of a cableway 1180m/3872ft long
which runs up in 6 minutes to a height of 1143m/3750ft on Mont Salève.
Alternatively turn left beyond Veyrier into road 206 and in 3.5km/2 miles
right into 206A. 7km/4 miles: Mornex (572m/1877ft, a summer holiday
resort on the southern slopes of the Petit Salève. Almost opposite the
Protestant church is a house in which Richard Wagner lived in 1856.

The road continues up the beautiful valley of the Viaison. 3km/2 miles:
Monnetier (696m/2284ft), a health resort on a cleft between the Petit and
Grand Salève, from which it is a half-hour climb to the summit of the
Petit-Salève (900m/2953ft: beautiful views).

4.5km/3 miles above Monnetier, to the right, is the upper station of the
cableway (1143m/3750ft; restaurant), with a magnificent panorama of
Geneva, the lake and the Jura.
   1.5km/1 mile farther on a road branches off on the right to the Treize-
Arbres inn (1184m/3885ft). Above the inn (1212m/3977ft; orientation table)
there is a magnificent view of the Mont Blanc chain, Lake Geneva and the
Jura. A footpath leads up (30 minutes) to the Crêt de Grange-Tournier
(1308m/4292ft), the highest point on the Grand Salève.

The road continues along the slopes of the Grand Salève. 5km/3 miles: Col
de la Croisette (1176m/3858ft; restaurant), with roads running down to
Collonges on the right and La Muraz on the left. Then past the Grand Piton
(1380m/4528ft), the highest point in the Salève range, and then downhill,
with many bends. 16km/10 miles: Cruseilles (781m/2562ft), on the road
from Annecy to Geneva (N 201); then north on this road over the little pass
of Mont Sion (785m/2576ft) and through Le Châble and Saint-Julien to the
Swiss frontier, 26km/16 miles to Geneva.

★The Voirons

There are two alternative routes (each 37km/23 miles) to this long ridge in
French territory east of Geneva making an attractive round trip of 74km/
46 miles.
   Leave Geneva on the Chamonix road. 7km/4 miles: Annemasse (436m/
1431ft). From here on N 507 to Bonne-sur-Menoge and Pont-de-Fillinges
(10.5km/7 miles), from which a road to the left climbs (fine views) via Boëge
to the Col de Saxel (12.5km/8 miles: 945m/3101ft); then a road on the left
which winds its way uphill, passing through wooded country. 7km/
4 miles: Grand Chalet (1400m/4593ft), sanatorium. From here it is a 30
minutes' climb to the Calvaire or Grand Signal, on the summit of the
Voirons (1486m/4876ft), with magnificent views (Savoy Alps, Jura, etc.).
   8km/5 miles: Bons (548m/1798ft), on the road from Thonon (N 203); then
left along this road via Langin and Saint-Cergues to Annemasse (15km/
9 miles). 7km/4 miles to Geneva.

Lake Geneva B–F 9–11

Within Switzerland and France
Cantons: Vaud (VD), Geneva (GE) and Valais (VS)

★ Situation and general

Lake Geneva (in French Lac Léman or Lac de Genève), the largest of the lakes in the Alps, lies between the Savoy Alps, the Swiss Jura and the Vaud Alps at a mean height of 371m/1217ft above sea level. Of its total area of 581sq.km/224sq.miles 60% falls within Switzerland and 40% within France. Its maximum depth is about 310m/1017ft. The lake, which the River Rhône enters at one end and leaves at the other, extends in a flat arc 72km/45 miles long from east to west, with a maximum width of 14km/9 miles. While the French southern shore of the lake (department of Haute-Savoie) is only thinly populated, with Evian and Thonon as its largest towns, the sunny northern shore in the canton of Vaud, with the vine-growing areas of Lavaux and La Côte, is the Swiss equivalent of the Riviera, a popular holiday and tourist region.

Boat services

Regular steamer services between places on the lake, run by the Compagnie Genérale de Navigation sur le Lac Léman (CGN: head office Lausanne-Ouchy, branch office in Geneva at Le Bateau, Jardin Anglais); many round trips and cruises (evening trips with dancing on board); shuttle services and round trips in port and on the Petit Lac by the "Mouettes Genevoises"; short round trips on the motor-launches "Elma" and "Star of Geneva". A particular attraction is "Neptune", the last cargo-carrying sailing vessel on the lake, which can be chartered. Built in 1904 (length 24m/78ft, width 8.5m/28ft, weight 20 tonnes) it was used to transport stone blocks from Meillerie and gravel from Bouveret/Vieux Rhône to Geneva until 1968. Since 1976 it has been used for excursions.

Rolle Castle on Lake Geneva

The north bank of the lake

For centuries the beauty of the northern shores of Lake Geneva has been lauded (e.g. by Byron, Voltaire and Rousseau), the luxuriantly fertile slopes rising gently above the lake, the picturesque towns and old castles, the magnificent backdrop of the Savoy and Valais Alps to the south and east. The climate has a southern mildness in which the vine flourishes.

The road along the shore of the lake from Geneva runs through Genthod (restaurant on lake) and the little town of Versoix, enters the canton of Vaud (8km/5 miles) and comes to Coppet (see Geneva).

See entry.

Nyon

It then continues via the interesting little town of Nyon and Prangins (château of 1748) to reach the stretch of land along the lake known as La Côte, the fertile slopes descending from the Vaudois plateau, with flourishing vineyards, fruit orchards and farming land: a gentle prosperous landscape with many old castles and country houses.

La Côte

Rolle (376m/1234ft: pop. 3600) is a long straggling little town, an important wine-trading area, with a 13th c. castle (four towers) and old burghers' and vintners' houses lining the main street. On a small island in the harbour is an obelisk commemorating General de la Harpe (1754–1838), who played a part in securing the separation of Vaud from the canton of Berne in 1798. The local speciality is "petits pains au sucre" (sugar rolls).

Rolle

The road continues to Allaman (425m/1394ft: 16th c. castle with two towers) and St-Prex (373m/1224ft: pop. 2000), an old market town with a church which first appears in the records in 885. Cobbled streets; old street signs; Tour de l'Horloge (Clock Tower), the only gate-tower with loopholes in the canton of Vaud. Glassworks; beautiful lakeside gardens and villas.

St-Prex

Morges (381m/1250ft: pop. 12,700), on a site once occupied by a large village of pile-dwellings, is a town of fishermen, with the headquarters of

Morges

The "Neptune", a sailing-freighter

Morges Castle

the World Wildlife Fund. Founded by the Savoyards in 1286 and now known for its annual tulip and wine festivals, it was once the home of Paderevski and Stravinsky. There are handsome 18th c. burghers' houses, a church (1776) and 16th–17th c. Town Hall. In Blanchenay, an old patrician house which once belonged to the engraver Alexis Forel, is the Musée du Vieux Morges (furniture, sculpture, and pictures of the Renaissance and Gothic periods). The castle with its four round corner towers, typical of the "carré savoyard" style, (13th c.; alterations in 16th and 17th c.; restored 1948), today it houses the Vaudois arsenal containing a historical weapons collection and 10,000 lead soldiers.

L'Isle

From Morges an excursion can be made (10km/6 miles) to L'Isle (666m/2185ft), with the little late 17th c. château of Chandieu, set in parkland. A visit to the Tine gorge on the southern slopes of La Sarraz is worthwhile.

★ Vufflens-le-Château

Near here are the châteaux of Chardonney (18th c.) and Vufflens-le-Château (14th–15th c.). The latter, of North Italian design, was built by Heinrich von Colombier (1395–1430) with a large cemetery and four towers which are characteristic of Savoy. It is privately owned and not open to the public.

St-Sulpice

The road continues through the select residential suburb of St-Sulpice (Romanesque conventual church, 12th c.) to enter Lausanne, capital of the canton of Vaud.

Lausanne

See entry.

★ Corniche de Lavaux

To the east of Lausanne is one of the most beautiful parts of Switzerland, with many features of interest. Between Lutry (380m/1247ft) and Vevey the road runs past the Monts de Lavaux, the slopes of which are entirely covered with vineyards. There is a magnificent stretch of road on the Corniche de Lavaux (Corniche Vaudoise), running high above the lake through the vineyards and affording views of the mighty peaks around the upper end of the lake. The road runs via Grandvaux (565m/1845ft) and the wine-growing villages of Riex (450m/1476ft) and Epesses to a superb

★ Signal de Chexbres Chardonne, Corsier

viewpoint, the Signal de Chexbres (655m/2149ft), and the health resort of Chexbres (559m/1834ft; pop. 1700) to the vine-growing village of Corsier (445m/1460ft; pop. 3030), which has a fine 12th c. church with a Romanesque tower, the device of the House of Savoy and old bells (1427, 1523). Charlie Chaplin (Sir Charles Spencer Chaplin, 1889–1977) is buried here.

Cully

From Lutry the lakeside road continues via Villette to Cully (380m/1247ft), a vine-growing village with picturesque old streets. Near the landing-stage is a monument to Major Davel, a native of the village, who made an unsuccessful attempt (1723) to free Vaud from Bernese rule.

Rivaz

The main road continues past the famous Dézaley vineyards to Rivaz, the castle of Glérolles (12th c., rebuilt in the Gothic period).

St-Saphorin

It continues past the vine-growing village of St-Saphorin (376m/1234ft: pop. 300), with beautiful old houses and a 16th c. church. This was originally a country seat of the bishops of Lausanne. In a house of 1705 opposite the church is the restaurant A l'Onde (old inn sign, 1750). The "traffic regulations for coaches" written on a "Pierre à sabot" (1812) in the Place du Peuplier make interesting reading.

Vevey

See entry.

Montreux

See entry.

Villeneuve

The road then traverses the celebrated resorts of Vevey and Montreux and comes to Villeneuve (378m/1240ft; pop. 4500), a little harbour town at the end of the lake which was founded in the 13th c. on the site of earlier Celtic and Roman settlements. The triple-naved Romanesque parish church (St-Paul) is of 12th c. origin.

The south bank of the lake

Leave Geneva on road 37, which skirts the Parc des Eaux-Vives and passes below the hill of Cologny to Vésenaz, from which the main road to Thonon continues in long straight stretches through attractive rolling country, with the Yvoire peninsula to the left.

Beyond Corsier (a former Roman settlement), to the left of the road, the Swiss–French frontier is crossed (Swiss passport control). Then on N 5 through a customs-free zone to Douvaine (429m/1408ft: French frontier control).

Swiss-French frontier

The road continues below the vine-clad Mont de Boisy (735m/2412ft; on right) and in 5km/3 miles reaches Sciez (408m/1339ft), where the lakeside road via Yvoire comes in on the left. Beyond Jussy, on a hill to the right of the road, is the village of Les Allinges, with two ruined castles and a pilgrimage chapel (beautiful view).

Les Allinges

10km/6 miles beyond Sciez is Thonon-les-Bains (427m/1401ft; pop. 22,000), beautifully situated on the slopes above the lake (carbonated springs).

Thonon-les-Bains

Beyond Thonon N 5 cuts across the delta of the Dranse. Interesting detour (2.5km/2 miles) to the 15th c. castle of Ripaille, on the lake, where Duke Amadeus VIII of Savoy lived as a hermit before his election as Pope (Felix V, 1439–49).

Ripaille castle

2.5km/2 miles beyond Thonon on N 5 is Vongy, where the road from Ripaille joins the main road which then crosses the Dranse and continues to Amphion, on the shores of the lake.

6.5km/4 miles from Vongy is Evian-les-Bains (374m/1227ft; pop. 7000), a fashionable resort in a beautiful situation on the shores of the lake (alkaline thermal springs and numerous parks, including the Jardin Anglais by the lake). On the broad Quai Baron-de-Blonay are the spa establishment and the Casino (gaming). The church (14th–19th c.) has a 15th c. relief showing the Virgin Mary.

Evian-les-Bains

From Evian to St-Gingolph the road keeps close to the lake. It traverses Grande-Rive and Petite-Rive, on the outskirts of Evian, and at the Château de Blonay (16th c.) passes under the defensive walls. The hills alongside the lake now become steeper and higher; to the right is the Dent d'Oche (2225m/7300ft: from Evian by road to Bernex, 14km/9miles, then 4½ hours' climb with guide).

Château de Blonay
Dent d'Oche

The road then comes to Meillerie (385m/1263ft), a picturesque fishing village in a magnificent situation, with large limestone quarries.

Meillerie

Beyond this, on the right, are the steep slopes of Mont Chalon (1058m/3471ft); to the left is a superb view across the Lake to Vevey and Montreux, with the villages and villas on the slopes above, and of the peaks of the Vaudois Alps (Pléiades, Dent de Jaman, Rochers de Naye); to the right, on the shores of the lake, is Chillon castle (see Montreux).

At Le Locum is the French frontier control. The road now crosses a customs-free zone at the foot of the Pic de Blanchard (1472m/4830ft) and comes to St-Gingolph (391m/1283ft), a picturesque little town straddling the River Morge, here flowing through a deep gorge, which marks the French–Swiss frontier (Swiss passport and customs control).

St-Gingolph

Then on road 37 beneath the steep slopes of Le Grammont (2178m/7146ft; wide views; 5–5½ hours from St-Gingolph, with guide). 4km/2 miles from St-Gingolph is Bouveret (394m/1293ft), an attractively situated village near

★Grammont

Bouveret

233

the inflow of the Rhône, which creates a wave effect (the "bataillère") reaching far out into the lake.

The road (SP Martigny) now leaves the lake and runs up the broad Rhône valley, keeping close to the foot of the hills. To the left of the road is Port-Valais, with the Hôtel de la Tour, a former 16th c. castle.

After passing through Les Evouettes the road comes to Porte-du Secx, a narrow passage (formerly fortified) between the rock face and the river where a road branches off on the left to Villeneuve (8km/5 miles) and Montreux (see entry). The main road then continues to the large village of Vouvry (384m/1260ft, with a power station, and Martigny (see entry).

Glarus   O/P 5–7

Canton: Glarus (GL)

Situation

To the south of the picturesque Walensee the little canton of Glarus, occupies the basin of the River Linth, one of the most beautiful transverse valleys in the Alps, with the ridge of Glärnisch (2332m/7651ft) rearing above it on the west and the massive bulk of Tödi (3614m/11,858ft) closing its southern end. Surrounded on three sides by mountains, the canton is linked with the neighbouring canton of Uri by a road which runs south-west from Linthal over the Klausen pass.

General

The 37,000 inhabitants of the canton (area 685sq.km/264sq.miles), the land of St Fridolin, who appears on Glarus's coat of arms, are an independent-minded race, formed by this rugged mountain world. Industry (in particularly the cotton industry; spinning, weaving, coloured prints) established itself here at an early stage, using the water-power provided by the Linth. The main valley is served by a branch railway line from Rapperswil to Glarus and Linthal, connecting with the main line from Zurich to Chur at Ziegelbrücke. From Linthal there is a cableway to the traffic-free resort of Braunwald, and there is a bus service from Schwanden to Elm in the Sernf valley.

Specialities

Local culinary specialities are Schabzieger, a herb cheese, and Glarner Pasteten (fruit tarts).

History

From 1288 Glarus was under Habsburg jurisdiction, and after repeated threats to its independence became the sixth canton to join the Confederation. Since 1387 the cantonal meeting (Landesgemeinde) has been held every year in the Zaunplatz in Glarus on the first Sunday in May. In 1388 the men of Glarus finally shook off the Habsburg yoke by their victory in the Battle of Näfels. During the Reformation the canton was divided into two cantons, one Protestant and the other Catholic, but the two halves were reunited under the 1836 constitution.

Up the Linth valley

From the broad mouth of the valley at Ziegelbrücke (428m/1404ft) the road runs south to Linthal (651m/2136ft; 28km/17 miles) and from there over the Klausen pass to Altdorf in the canton of Uri.

Niederurnen, Schlössli

From Niederurnen (432m/1417ft; pop. 3500) there is a footpath up the Rebburg to the Schlössli (Burg Oberwindegg), with fine views of the Linth plain and the Walensee. The path then continues to Oberurnen (432m/1417ft) with a view of the Glarus Alps.

Näfels
★Freulerpalast

In Näfels (440m/1444ft; pop. 3700) is the finest building in the canton, the Freulerpalast with a magnificent Renaissance doorway and Early Baroque interior. Built by Colonel Kaspar Freuler, commander of the Swiss guard in

In the Linth valley   *Renaissance doorway of the Freuler Palace*

France (who was ennobled by Louis XIII), it has been occupied by the Cantonal Museum since 1942 and contains interesting collections (documents from Glarus's textile printing industry) and special exhibitions.

The Roman Catholic parish church St Fridolin and Hilarius (1778–81) is modelled on the parish church at Schwyz. The adjoining chapel commemorates the soldiers who died in the Battle of Näfels in 1388 against the Austrians. There is an interesting 17th c. Capuchin monastery Maria-Burg.

From here a steep road climbs to a charming little lake, the Obersee (989m/ 3245ft).

Obersee

Näfels shares a railway station with its twin town of Mollis (444m/1457ft; see Walensee). In the Steinacker is the birthplace of the Glarus humanist Heinrich Loriti (1488–1563), who was crowned as poet laureate by the Emperor Maximilian. On the road up the Kerenzerberg are Obstalden and Filzbach (sports facility, with a public indoor swimming pool).

Mollis, Obstalden, Filzbach, Kerenzerberg

Netstal (453m/1486ft; pop. 2800) is a long straggling village surrounded by hillocks formed by landslides of the past, with some industry and a hydro-electric power station (50,000 kW) built in 1909. The Late Baroque village church (1813) is a statutorily protected ancient monument.

Netstal

From Netstal a road (postal bus in summer) and footpath cross the Schwammhöhe (superb views of the Glarus mountains) into the Klöntal (850m/2789ft), one of the most beautiful and romantic of Alpine valleys, with the Klöntalersee and a series of tumultuous mountain streams. The lake was almost doubled in size by the construction of a dam. The road passes through Rhodannenberg (853m/2799ft; 5km/3 miles; inn) and follows the lake, above the south side of which rear the rock walls of Glärnisch (with the peaks of Vorderglärnisch, 2331m/7648ft, Vrenelisgärtli, 2904m/ 9528ft, Ruchen, 2905m/9531ft) and Bächistock (2920m/9583ft), to Vorauen (853m/2799ft; inn) and the Richisau (1095m/3593ft), an expanse of Alpine pasture at the beginning of the bridle-path over the Pragel pass (1554m/

★Klöntal

★Glärnisch

Glarus

Freuler Palace, cantonal museum of Glarus

5099ft) to Muothal (5 hours' walk). The Klöntal is a popular resort with climbers and hill-walkers (e.g. over the passes into the Sihl and Wägi valleys).

★ Glarus   Glarus (481m/1578ft; pop. 5700) lying at the foot of Glärnisch (Vorderglärnisch, 2331m/7648ft), is capital of the canton, rebuilt in 1861 on a regular grid plan after a devastating fire. The twin-towered Neo-Romanesque church (Protestant) was built in 1866; fine treasury. In the Town Hall (1865) is a relief model of the canton on a scale of 1:25,000. The Landesgemeinde (communal assembly) meets every year on the first Sunday in May in the Zaunplatz. In the courthouse are the cantonal archives and cantonal library, with a famous early map of Switzerland by Ägidus Tschudi (1570).

Kunsthaus   The Kunsthaus in the Volksgarten contains a natural history collection and mounts exhibitions of Swiss 19th and 20th c. artists (paintings and sculptures by F. Hodler, Ernst Ludwig Kirchner, Fritz Pauli), international graphics and the iconography collection of Hans Jenny-Kapers.

Out of the town are some houses which survived the fire, examples of the architecture such as Leuzinger-Paravicini house (16th c.) and the "Haus in der Wies" ("house in the meadow"), built for Johann Heinrich Streiff (1746–48), the founder of the Glarus textile industry

Schwanden   Schwanden (528m/1732ft; pop. 2600) lies at the junction of the Sernf and the Linth, which provide water for the Sernf-Niederenbach hydro-electric scheme. It is a good starting-point for a walk into the Niederental, and from there by cableway to the Mettmenalp (mountain inn) and the artificial lake on the Garichte. Good climbing in the Karrenstock and Kärpf area (the oldest wildlife reserve in Switzerland, with numerous chamois, marmots and ibex).

Sernftal   From Schwanden an attractive detour can be made into the Sernf valley (also known as the Kleintal); the road runs via Engi and Matt (oldest church

236

in Glarus, 1261) and comes in 15km/9 miles to Elm (977m/3206ft; pop. 800), in a quiet and secluded area which offers excellent walking.

The last settlement in the main valley is Linthal (653m/2142ft; pop. 1400), with mighty mountains rearing above the little town. Selbsanft (3029m/9938ft) lies above the artificial lakes supplying the Linth-Limmern hydro-electric scheme, with the Gries glacier; the Bifertenstock (3426m/10,722ft) and Tödi (3614m/11,858ft). Tierfehd, 5km/3 miles south is a good base for walks and climbs in the Tödi group.

Linthal

From Linthal (parking garage) the Braunwaldbahn (length 1314m/4311ft, time 10 minutes) ascends to the only traffic-free mountain and holiday resort in eastern Switzerland, Braunwald (1256m/4121ft; pop. 500), an ideal jumping-off point for walking and climbing. Experimental rhododendron nursery. Musical festival in July. Chair-lift to Gumen mountain inn (1900m/6234ft).

Braunwald

Over the Klausen pass to Altdorf

There is a magnificent drive over the Klausen pass from Linthal to Altdorf (see entry) in the canton of Uri (48km/30 miles). The road built in 1893–99 on the line of an old bridle-path, has a maximum gradient of 8.5% (1 in 12) and is usually open from June to November.

★ Klausen pass road

10km/6 miles from Linthal the road crosses the Scheidbächli, a stream which has marked the boundary between the cantons of Glarus and Uri since 1196, and comes to the Urnerboden (1313–1400m/4308–4593ft), a meadow-covered high valley some 7km/4 miles long through which flows the Fätschbach, following an almost level course for 4km/2 miles. A series of well-engineered bends leads up to the Vorfrutt (1812m/5945ft), from which four further bends take the road to the Klausen pass (1948m/6391ft; chapel, kiosk), 23km/14 miles from Linthal. The road then runs down 1.5km/1 mile to the Klausenpasshöhe Hotel (1838m/6030ft) and continues down the Schächen valley, with the 93m/305ft high Staubi falls. After passing through Urigen (1280m/4200ft) it reaches Unterschächen (994m/3261ft), at the mouth of the steep Brunni valley, with a view of the Grosse Windgälle (3192m/10,473ft) and the Grosser Ruchen (3136m/10,289ft). Between Spiringen and St Loreto is the Kinzigpass inn (640m/2100ft), with the 16th c. Loreto chapel. From Brügg a cableway (3.2km/2 miles in two stages) runs up in 15 minutes to the Biel mountain inn (1634m/5361ft), below the Kinzig pass (2076m/6811ft) over which the Russian General Suvorov was compelled to retreat into the Muota valley in 1799 with 18,000 men suffering heavy losses.

Urnerboden

★ Klausen pass

Schächen valley

After passing through the village of Bürglen we arrive in Altdorf.

Bürglen

See entry.

Altdorf

Grindelwald

K 9

Canton: Berne (BE)
Altitude: 1034m/3394ft
Population: 3600

The "glacier village" of Grindelwald, one of the most popular health and winter sports resorts in the Bernese Oberland and a favourite base for climbers, straggles over a considerable expanse of Alpine meadows on the slopes of the Schwarze Lütschine valley. Three towering mountains enclose the valley on the south: the Eiger (3970m/13,026ft), with its sheer north face, the most dangerous mountain wall in the Alps (first climbed in

Situation and general

1938 by Heckmair, Vörg, Kasparek and Harrer, taking four days), on which the lights in the windows of the Eigerwand station of the Jungfraubahn can be seen twinkling after dark; to the left of the Eiger the Mettenberg (3104m/10,184ft), one of the subsidiary peaks of the Schreckhorn; and the Wetterhorn (3701m/12,143ft), the most characteristic landmark of the Grindelwald valley. Between the three mountains are the two Grindelwald glaciers.

Townscape

★ Terrassenweg

The Talhaus, near the Protestant church, contains a local museum. The best general view is to be had from the Terrassenweg, which branches off the road 20 minutes' walk above the church, just before the Mühlbach bridge, and runs along the mountainside above Alpine meadows and through patches of forest to the hamlet of Duftbach (30 minutes), from which it is a 20 minutes' walk down to Grindelwald.

Mountain railways, cableways and lifts

Wengernalpbahn and Jungfraubahn to Jungfraujoch (18km/11 miles; see Jungfrau) via the Kleine Scheidegg. Cableway (1046m/3432ft long to Pfingstegg (upper station 1387m/4551ft; restaurant). Chair-lift (4354m/14,285ft in four stages) via Oberhaus, Bort and Egg in 30 minutes to First (2168m/7113ft; inn), with magnificent views and excellent skiing country (ski-lifts) on the Grindelalp, on the slopes of the Widderfeldgrätli, the ridge between the Faulhorn and the Schwarzhorn. The longest cableway in Europe is to the Männlichen (2343m/7690ft), a height difference of 1284m/4214ft in 30 minutes.

Winter sports

Skiing at Grindelwald and on the First, Kleine Scheidegg and Lauberhorn; tobogganing; ice-rinks (indoor and outdoor); curling.

Walking, climbing

Favourite walks include the Panorama Way to the First (round trip), Grosse Scheidegg–Schwarzwaldalp–Rosenlaui and the walk Pfingstegg–Marmor-

Travelling on the Wengernalpbahn, with Grindelwald and the Wetterhorn in the background

bruch–Gletscherschlucht and Pfingstegg–Oberergletscher (geological information; see below).

The Grindelwald Mountain Guides Association organises guided climbs of the surrounding mountains over 4000m/13,128ft from the climbing centre, opened in 1985.

Surroundings

To the Upper Glacier (1½ hours): from the church take road (closed to cars) to the turn-off of the road to the Grosse Scheidegg, and continue to the end of the glacier, which has recently been advancing again, with an artificial cave hewn from the ice. There are eight walks providing geological information about the area: Pfingstegg–Milchbach, Pfingstegg–Stieregg, Milchbach–Sulz, Rubiweid–Sulz, Pfingstegg–Sulz, Pfingstegg–Uf der Halten, Pfingstegg–Fielewald–Uf der Halten, Pfingstegg–Marmorbruch.

★Upper Glacier

To the Lower Glacier (1½–2 hours); from the church go down to the bridge over the Lütschine (990m/3248ft), and from there either turn right and continue through the hamlet of Mettenberg to the entrance to the impressive Lütschine gorge (accessible through a gulley cut through the rock) and so to the end of the glacier; or turn left into a steep path leading up to the Lower Glacier or Unteres Eismeer (1650m/5413ft), a large expanse of ice covered with rock debris.

★Lower Glacier, Lütschine gorge

Up the Faulhorn (2681m/8796ft), one of the most renowned viewpoints in Switzerland, from which the giant peaks of the Bernese Oberland can be seen in all their magnificence: either by the chair-lift (30 minutes) to the First station and from there an hour's walk north to the Bachsee or Bachalpsee (2264m/7428ft), or a 3½ hours' walk from Grindelwald to the Bachalpsee; then 1½ hours' climb to the summit (Berghotel, summer only).

★Faulhorn

A climb of 2½-3 hours up the slopes above the Checklibach leads to the Grosse Scheidegg (1961m/6434ft).

Grosse Scheidegg

See Jungfrau

★★Jungfrau region

Grisons

Q–T 8/9

Canton: Grisons (GR)

The canton usually known in English by its French name of Grisons (German Graubünden, Romansch Grischun, Italian Grigioni), is a typical mountain region, with its valleys lying at heights of between 900 and 2000m/2953 and 6562ft and its highest peak, Bernina, rising to 4049m/13,285ft. Two-thirds of its boundaries lie along the frontiers of Italy and Austria. Within the canton are the sources of the Rhine (which receives the water of three-fifths of the rivers in the canton) and the Inn (Romansch En); the rivers in the south-facing valleys on the Italian side drain into the Po.

★Situation and landscape

The climate of the Grisons reflects a variety of influences. In the catchment area of the Rhine a continental climate of northern type predominates, while the transverse valleys with a southern exposure show Mediterranean characteristics. Magnolias, chestnuts and vines flourish only a short distance away from the perpetual snow and ice.

Climate and vegetation

Grisons, the largest canton in Switzerland, owes its name to the Upper or Grey League (Ligue Grise, Grauer Bund) formed by the peasants of the region in 1395, like the League of the House of God and the League of the Ten Jurisdictions, to defend their interests against the Habsburgs.

Grey League

In 15 B.C. the Romans subjugated the Rhaetians and began to colonise the region, building roads over the Alpine passes which have not greatly altered their course since then. In 536 the Grisons fell under Frankish rule and, as Chur-Rhaetia, became part of the Duchy of Swabia. Later the people of the Grisons formed the three leagues mentioned above, which at the end of the 15th c. made common cause with Swiss Confederation. The Reformation was adopted by the region. During the Thirty Years' War it was plunged into bitter internal strife by the conflict between the supporters of France, led by the Salis family, and of the Habsburgs, led by the Planta family. In the 17th c. Jürg Jenatsch freed the Grisons from foreign influence, but the region was not brought together in a single canton until the 19th c. Of the present population of the Grisons 54% speak German, 31% Romansch and 15% Italian.

From very early times the Alpine passes played a vital role in the life of the Grisons. The road over the Septimer pass (Pass da Sett), built in the 14th c., is believed to have been one of the first Alpine roads usable by vehicles. During the 19th c. ten pass roads were built, of which the Julier (Passo dello Guglia), Flüela, Splügen (Passo dello Spluga) and Maloja passes, among others, are still of major importance. The opening of the San Bernardino tunnel in 1967 made available a north–south route open all year round.

The Rhätische Bahn (RhB), run by the canton of Grisons, is a narrow-gauge railway-system with a total length of 400km/249 miles and 500 bridges. The 6km/4 miles long Albula tunnel is the highest tunnel in the Alps (1883m/6178ft).
The famous "Glacier-Express" (see Practical Information, Railways) came into operation in 1930, a communal project by the Rhätische Bahn, Furka–Oberalp Bahn and the Brig–Visp–Zermatt Bahn.

Gruyère   F 8–10

Canton: Fribourg (FR)

The district of Gruyère (German Greyerzer Land), in the southern half of the canton of Fribourg, is a gently rolling Pre-Alpine region mainly devoted to intensive stock-farming and renowned as the home of Gruyère cheese. Its beautiful scenery, numerous remains of the past and vigorous folk traditions make it an attractive tourist region.

27km/17 miles south of Fribourg, on the left bank of the Trême, is Bulle (769m/2523ft; pop.7700), chief town and commercial and cultural heart of the Gruyère district and one of the most important traffic junctions in the canton of Fribourg. From 1196 to 1537 this small market town belonged to the bishops of Lausanne, who built a massive castle here in the 13th c. The town was rebuilt after fires in 1447 and 1805. It has preserved a number of fine old buildings – the parish church (Protestant), rebuilt in 1751, the Capuchin friary and the Town Hall. The 13th c. Schloss Bulle, altered in the 16th c., is a typical example of the "carré-savoyard" design.

Below the castle, in the Place du Cabalet, is the Musée Gruérien (closed Mon.), which houses the Tissot Collection of local history and customs. Also on display are paintings by Swiss, Italian and French artists, including A. Grimou, J.-E. Liotard, G. Courbet, F. Valloton and J. Crotti.
In the public park is a monument to Abbé Bovet (1879–1952), a composer of lieder.

From Bulle there are roads over the Jaun pass into the Simmental (see entry) and through the Sarine valley to Château-d'Oex in the Pays d'Enhaut. The local museum (Musée du Vieux d'Enhaut: closed Mon.) contains exhibits of the region's arts and crafts as well as local history.

★ *The Inn valley, near Zernez*

Gruyère

Bulle Castle

Gruyères, famous for its cheese

★Gruyères
6km/4 miles south-east of Bulle, on a green ridge of hills, is Gruyères (801m/2628ft; pop. 1200), famous for the cheese of the same name. Finely situated and still surrounded by its ancient walls, the town has largely preserved its old-world aspect. From 923 it was the capital of a county which was ruled by a succession of 19 counts; then in 1555 Fribourg and Berne divided the territory between them, and the castle (1493) became the residence of the governors until its acquisition by the Bovy family of Geneva in 1848. Since 1938 the castle has belonged to the canton of Fribourg, and now houses a museum (exhibits of particular interest being three mourning robes belonging to knights of the Golden Fleece, dating from the Burgundian wars). The town lies just off the main road from Bulle to Château-d'Oex but is closed to motor vehicles (car parks outside the town walls). The 15th–17th c. houses in the main street are statutorily protected as ancient monuments. At the entrance to the town is a Wax Museum (Musée de Cire; figures from Swiss history).

The commune of Gruyères also includes the villages of Epagny (712m/2336ft) and Pringy (746m/2448ft).

★Model cheese-dairy
Adjoining the railway station is a famous model cheese-dairy making Gruyère cheese (open: daily 8am–noon, 1–6pm)

★Le Moléson
4km/2 miles south-west of Pringy is Le Moléson, a rounded hill in the midst of the Gruyère district which has become a popular walking and skiing area. From the holiday complex of Moléson-Village (1110m/3642ft) a cable-way runs up in two stages to the summit of Le Moléson (2002m/6569ft), another to La Vudulla (1520m/4987ft).

Observatory
Le Moléson has an observatory (open: mid December to mid April and mid June to mid October) and a restaurant, from which there are far-ranging views, extending from Mont Blanc to Titlis; good walking and climbing.

Broc
Between Bulle and Gruyères is the little industrial town of Broc (719m/2359ft; pop. 1870) with a chocolate factory established by F. L. Cailler in

1898 (conducted tours). Broc lies at the south end of the beautiful Lac de la Gruyère (677m/2222ft; area 9.6sq.m/4sq.miles, greatest depth 75m/246ft, capacity 180 million cu.m/6356 million cu.ft), formed by a dam on the Sarine (Saane) and lying at the foot of the Dent-de-Broc (1833m/6016ft).

Lac de la Gruyère

Gstaad

G 10

Canton: Berne (BE)
Altitude: 1100m/3610ft. Population: 2500

The summer and winter resort of Gstaad in the high valley of the Saane, in the western part of the Bernese Oberland, has for many years enjoyed an international reputation, while still preserving its character as a village of holiday chalets. It is known for the Swiss International Tennis Championships, its Alpine golf-courses, the annual Menuhin Festival along with plays and concerts during the Alpine gala in September. The resort is a paradise for walkers and climbers, with cableways providing easy access to the mountains.

★ Situation and general

River-rafting (white-water trips) on the river Saane and the Simme, to the south, is becoming increasingly popular.

The Montreux-Oberland railway (built 1905) and the adjacent pass roads make Gstaad easily accessible from both German-speaking and French-speaking Switzerland.

To Wasserngrat (2000m/6562ft; length 2585m/8481ft, height difference 826m/2710ft, time 20 minutes), Eggli (1580m/5184ft; length 1451m/4761ft, height difference 514m/1686ft, time 10 minutes) and Höhi Wispile (1940m/6365ft; length 3039m/9971ft, height difference 865m/2838ft, time 20 minutes).

Cableways

Gstaad in winter

Ilanz

Winter sports   Together with Schönried, Saanenmöser and Château-d'Oex Gstaad has one of the most scenic skiing areas in the Bernese Oberland, the "Weisse Hochland" with 250 prepared runs and 69 cableways and ski-lifts. There are skiing areas in three directions: the Eggli with its southern slopes, the Wispile with its eastern slopes and the Wasserngrat to the north-east. A 25km/15 miles long-distance course runs from Gsteig via Gstaad, Saanen, Rougemont to Château-d'Oex. On the Eggli and in Turbach there is toboganning, curling and ice-skating (ice stadium).

Surroundings

Lauenen   7km/4 miles south-east is Lauenen (1250m/4101ft; pop. 760), a beautifully situated health resort with a Late Gothic church (1520). An hour's walk south is the Lauenensee (1379m/4524ft).

Gsteig   The road to the Col du Pillon leads to the resort of Gsteig (1192m/3912ft) of the Saane valley, which has preserved the character of an Alpine farming village; note particularly the Gasthof Bären (inn: 1756). The road continues over the Col du Pillon (1546m/5072ft) to Aigle in the Rhône valley.

Saanen   8km/5 miles north-west of Gstaad is Saanen (1020m/3348ft; pop. 1600), chief town in the Upper Saane valley, a climatic and winter sports resort (ski-lifts) surrounded by many isolated farms. Church (rebuilt in 15th c.) with a fine tower and 15th c. wall-paintings in the choir. A prosperous stock-farming and dairy-farming area, notable for its cheese (Saanen, a grating cheese).

     To the north of the town rises the Hugelirat (1902m/6240ft; 3 hours), from which there are superb views.

     From Saanen it is possible to continue to Lausanne, by either the Col des Mosses or the Col du Pillon.

Ilanz   P 8

Canton: Grisons
Altitude: 702m/2303ft
Population: 2200

Situation and general   Ilanz (Romansch Glion), the "first town on the Rhine", situated in the valley of the Vorderrhein, is the market town of the surrounding district of Surselva.

History   The town first appears in the records in 765, when the first church of St Martin was built. In 1395 it became the nucleus of the "Grey League" formed by the Abbot of Disentis together with the local feudal lords and peasants. The people of the Grisons were granted freedom of religious belief following a conference held in St Margaret's church in 1526.

Sights

Ilanz is a picturesque little town of winding streets with one or two buildings recalling its past greatness. Parts of the town fortifications, rebuilt following a fire in 1717, have been preserved. The Late Gothic parish church of St Margaret (Protestant) has fine ceiling paintings, Gothic scrollwork and a Rococo organ-loft. There are a number of Baroque mansions, including the Casa Gronda (1677), in which the Russian General Suvorov once stayed. The Casa Carniec houses the regional museum of Surselva (reopened 1988; open: Wed. 8–10pm, Sat., Sun. 2–4pm) with a comprehensive collection of folklore (including an Alpine dairy).

Surselva Regional Museum

Surroundings

A road runs west, climbing steeply up the northern slopes of Piz Mundaun (2067m/6782ft), to Flond (1075m/3527ft; toboggan run to Ilanz) and Meierhof (1302m/4272ft), the principal village in the extensive commune of Obersaxen, a German-speaking enclave (skiing). There is an interesting Catholic parish church (1904–05) in Meierhof and a dozen chapels, such as the Chapel of St Georg (17th c.) with a Late Gothic winged altar.

Obersaxen

Through the Lugnez valley to Vrin (22km/14 miles)

Leave Ilanz on a narrow road which goes through the Obertor and ascends the western slopes of the beautiful Lugnez valley (Romansch Lumnezia), through which flows the River Glenner. The road with a moderate gradient passes St Martin's church and below, to the left, can be seen the ruined castle of Castelberg; then beyond the Frauentor defile (formerly fortified), the St Moritzkapelle (St Maurice's chapel, 1068m/3504ft).

6km/4 miles above Ilanz a road goes off on the left to Peidenbad and the Vals valley. Beyond this point the main road climbs steeply for 1.5km/1 mile to Cumbels (1145m/3757ft), a large village below the south side of Piz Mundaun. The church has 17th c. sgraffito painting.

2.5km/2 miles: Villa (1244m/4082ft), with elegant 17th–18th c. houses and a Gothic church (16th c.; frescoes). Pleif, below the road on the left, has a church founded in the Carolingian period but much altered in later centuries. Opposite is the mouth of the Vals valley. The road continues along the side of the Lugnez valley. Below, to the left, is the village of Igels, with two Late Gothic churches. 6km/4 miles: Lumbrein (1410m/4626ft. After a bend at the mouth of the Val Miedra (on right) the road enters the Vrin valley, the highest section of the Lugnez valley.

Villa

6km/4 miles: Vrin (1454m/4771ft), a village with a Baroque parish church of 1675, a quiet summer holiday place and a good base from which to climb the numerous neighbouring peaks.

Vrin

From Ilanz to Bad Vals (21km/13 miles)

The road follows the left bank of the Glenner below the road to Vrin. At the ruined 13th c. castle of Castelberg it crosses through two gorges, the Rieiner Tobel (road tunnel) and the Pitascher Tobel.

8km/5 miles: Peidenbad (820m/2690ft), in a wooded setting (chalybeate spring). Above, to the right, is the village of Peiden.

Peidenbad

2km/1 mile: Uors-Lumnezia (German Furth), where the road enters the beautiful Vals valley. To the right, on the mountain spur between the two valleys, is the picturesquely situated little village of Surcasti (German Oberkastels). 4km/2 miles: St Martin (1000m/3281ft). the road now traverses a magnificent rocky gorge, with the river surging and foaming over waterfalls far below; then through the villages of Lunschania (1200m/3937ft) and Bucarischuna (1170m/3839ft), along a defile and over the Valser Rhein on the Hohen Brücke (High Bridge).

Vals valley

7km/4 miles: Bad·Vals (1248m/4095ft; pop. 1000; Therme Bad Vals and Häuser Zerveila/Tomül, 300b.) is a little spa frequented by holidaymakers, climbers and winter sports enthusiasts (cross-country skiing), with a church of 1669 and the "Stella Maris" spa establishment (spring containing calcium sulphate, 28° C/82° F; treatment facility, open-air thermal pool with artificial waves, indoor swimming pool).

Bad Vals

The surrounding area has much of geological, botanical and entomological (butterflies) interest to offer. Piz Tomül (Weissensteinhorn, 2950m/9679ft) can be climbed in 4½ hours: panoramic views.

Piz Tomül

Zevreila

From Bad Vals the road ascends up the right bank of the valley for another 7.5km/5 miles, passing through a number of tunnels, to the artificial lake of Zevreila (1862m/6109ft), beneath the towering bulk of the Zevreiler Horn (2900m/9515ft).

Interlaken   J/K 8

Canton: Berne (BE)
Altitude: 570m/1871ft
Population: 13,500

Situation and general

Interlaken, reached by way of the Berne motorway or the Brünig, Susten or Grimsel/Furka passes, lies between Lakes Thun and Brienz below the north side of the Jungfrau massif and offers an endless variety of walks, climbs and other excursions, particularly in the mountains of the Bernese Oberland, brought within reach by numerous mountain railways, cableways, etc. It is one of the oldest, best known and most popular summer holiday resorts in Switzerland, outstandingly well equipped to cater for the needs of visitors. Between the two lakes is an expanse of some 35sq.km/14sq.miles of alluvial soil, deposited over many millennia by mountain streams from the Bernese Oberland such as the Lütschine and the Lombach. On this green and level area, known as the Bödeli, live the 20,000 inhabitants of the separate communes of Interlaken, Böningen, Matten, Unterseen and Wilderswil.

History

The fertile alluvial soil of the Bödeli was probably settled at an early stage by Celtic tribes. Later the main settlers were Alemanni, driven from their homeland by Burgundian incomers. A major influence on the economic and cultural development of the area was the Augustinian house founded here (inter lacus) in 1133, joined in 1257 by a nunnery. The monks were pioneers of urban development and soon became the largest landowners in the Bernese Oberland. After Berne's adoption of the reformed faith in 1528 the monastery was dissolved (and is now occupied by district administrative offices). The first visitors began to come here in the 17th c., and as transport facilities improved – with the coming of the railway, boat services on the lakes and most recently the motorway – Interlaken became the

Interlaken

1 Alpine Wildlife Park

2 Protestant church

3 Catholic church

4 Augustinian convent

400m

© Baedeker

Interlaken

Traditional carved façade in Bönigen

major tourist attraction of the Bernese Oberland. Among the great attractions of the area were its local folk traditions and art. In 1805 and 1808 the peasant stock-farmers of the Alpine pasturelands celebrated their first great pastoral festivals at Unspunnen, near Interlaken; and at this time, too, the painter Franz Niklaus König was living in Schloss Unterseen and painting the pictures of mountains which became so widely popular.

Sights

The Höhematte in the midst of the town is a remarkable example of farseeing town planning. The area of 14 hectares/35 acres which had belonged to the Augustinian convent was acquired in 1860 by a group of 37 hotel-owners and private persons and left as an open space, with the Höheweg, a splendid avenue running between the east and west stations and affording a magnificent view of the Jungfrau, surrounded by hotels and flower-beds. Here, too, is the Kursaal, with a theatre, a café, a gaming room and beautiful gardens (flower clock). At the east end is the former Augustinian convent (1133–1528; inner courtyard with cloister, restored), with a Late Gothic church (stained glass of 1950) and the adjoining Schloss added in 1750 (now housing cantonal offices).

★ Höhematte

Höheweg

On the south-east side of Interlaken is Matten with its old timber houses.

Matten

The Marktgasse runs north-west from the post office over the Spielmatten islands to the little town of Unterseen (569m/1867ft; pop. 4700), at the foot of Mt Harder, tourist museum (open: May 1st–Oct. 11th). In the old part of the town stands the parish church, with Late Gothic tower (1471).

Unterseen

Tourist museum

On the right bank of the Aare opposite the Kursaal is the fresh water swimming-pool. There is an indoor pool, a golf course in Unterseen and trips on Lake Thun and Lake Brienz. For sporting enthusiasts there is sailing, windsurfing, riding and tennis.

Surroundings

Interlaken is an ideal base for day or half-day excursions in the surrounding area. A beginning can be made with the town's own hills, Harder and Heimwehfluh.

★Harder
Beyond the bridge over the Aare on the road to Brienz, at the Harder Alpine Wildlife Park (Alpenwildpark; marmots, ibexes), is a funicular (length 1447m/4748ft, height difference 725m/2379ft, maximum gradient 64% (1 in 1½), time 8 minutes) up Harder (upper station 1322m/4337ft), with the Harderkulm restaurant magnificent views of the Jungfrau area and the lakes). The return can be made by forest paths, via the Hardermannli lookout pavilion (1116m/3662ft) and the Hohbühl pavilion (memorial to the composers Mendelsohn, Wagner and Weber).

★Heimwehfluh
From the south end of Rugenparkstrasse another funicular (length 167m/548ft, height difference 120m/394ft, time 3 minutes) runs up to the Heimwehfluh (676m/2218ft; café-restaurant, lookout tower), which forms the north-west buttress of the Grosser Rugen (800m/2625ft).

Model-railway enthusiasts should see the layout of the Gotthard and Lötschberg lines, presented by the Heimwehfluh-Bahn-AG.

★Schynige Platte
Another popular trip from Interlaken is to the Schynige Platte (2000m/6564ft; Hotel Kulm 40b.), reached from Wilderswil, 3km/2 miles south of the town, on a rack-railway (cog-railway) opened in 1893 (7km/4 miles, 50 minutes). From the top there is one of the finest panoramic views of the Alps. Alpine garden with 500 species of flowers.

Wilderswil
3km/2 miles south of Interlaken is the little holiday town of Wilderswil (600m/1969ft; pop. 1900). North-west of the town is the ruined castle of Unspunnen, with the Unspunnenwiese, a meadow on which herdsmen's festivals were held at the beginning of the 19th c.

Saxeten
From Wilderswil a road runs 6km/4 miles up the Saxeten valley to Saxeten (1103m/3620ft; pop. 100), a picturesquely situated mountain village from which Sulegg (2412m/7914ft) can be climbed (about 4½ hours).

Bönigen
From the Höheweg a road goes east to reach the south shore of Lake Brienz at Bönigen (569m/1867ft; pop. 1900). The old part of the town has richly carved timber houses of the 15th to 18th c. The modern resort is well equipped with facilities for the entertainment of visitors.

Iseltwald
High above the south side of the lake is the village of Iseltwald (565m/1854ft; pop. 420), on a quiet little peninsula with no through road.

From Interlaken to Beatenberg (11km/7 miles)

From Interlaken station take the Thun road, which crosses the Aare into Unterseen, where the road to Thun bears left: continue straight ahead up the Scheidgasse. 2km/1 mile from Interlaken is a road junction, with a road on the right which runs up the Lombach valley to the prettily situated

Habkern
village of Habkern (6.3km/4 miles, 1067m/3501ft). The road to Beatenberg, to the left, begins to climb through wooded country (attractive view of Interlaken to left) and then takes two sharp bends up the hillside. 3.5km/2 miles Lueglibrückli restaurant (938m/3078ft; car park), with superb views. The road continues uphill on a moderate gradient (views of Lake Thun and the mountains to the left) and then takes another two sharp bends. Farther on it passes a number of children's homes under Amisbühl (1336m/4383ft; views) and then descends into the Sundgraben. 5.5km/3 miles: Beatenberg

Beatenberg
(1150m/3773ft), a popular health and winter sports resort which spreads out along a sunny sheltered terrace high above the north side of Lake Thun,

with magnificent views of the Bernese Alps, from the Schreckhorn to the Niesen.

From the Oberland Hotel (parking garage) a chair-lift runs up in 18 minutes to the Niederhorn (1957m/6421ft), on the Güggisgrat ridge, with still more extensive views. At the west end of the town is a funicular (1706m/5597ft, gradient 35–40%, 10 minutes) to Beatenbucht.

See Lake Brienz   Godswil

See Lake Brienz   Ringgenberg

Jungfrau   K 9

Cantons: Berne (BE) and Valais (VS)

The Jungfrau massif, with its group of three famous peaks, the Jungfrau (4158m/13,642ft), the Mönch (4099m/13,449ft) and the Eiger (3970m/13,026ft), has long had a powerful grip on men's imaginations. Originally difficult of access, this mighty range of mountains in the heart of the Bernese Oberland has now been brought within easy reach and attracts large numbers of visitors every year.

Situation and general

The Meyer brothers of Aarau first set foot on the summit of the Jungfrau in 1811; and a hundred years later, in 1912, the rack-railway to the Jungfraujoch was opened. The upper station (3454m/11,333ft) is the highest railway station in Europe.

The skiing area of the Jungfrau region around Grindelwald (see entry), Wengen, Lauterbrunnen (see Lauterbrunnen valley) and Mürren (see entry) offers 175km/109 miles of pistes with 43 stations. The 10km/6 miles long intermediate descent Lauberhorn–Grindelwald–Grund covers a height difference of 1450m/4759ft. The height difference between Männlichen and Grindelwald (6km/4 miles; intermediate) is 1200m/3938ft. Schilthorn–Lauterbrunnen (12km/7 miles; difficult) the height difference is 2170m/7121ft. The First, Eigergletscher and Lauberhorn all have deep snow.

Winter sports

Long-distance runs: Grindelwald–Bussalp (1800m/5907ft; length 4km/2 miles), Aspi–Grund (length 4km/2 miles), Lauterbrunnen valley (12km/7 miles), a circular course near Mürren and Lauterbrunnen–Stechelberg (12km/7 miles).

Climbs from the Jungfraujoch (only to be undertaken with a guide): the Jungfrau (4158m/13,642ft; 4 hours, difficult), so named (the "Maiden") in honour of the Augustinian nuns of Interlaken; the Mönch (4099m/13,449ft; 4 hours, easier), the "Monk"; the Finsteraarhorn (4274m/14,023ft; 6½–8 hours), the highest peak in the Bernese Alps. There is also a popular glacier walk to Konkordiaplatz (2840m/9318ft), on the Aletsch glacier and a two-day climb from the Jungfrau–Aletsch–Märjalensee–Kühboden.

Climbs

Mountain railways and cableways

The area of most interest to visitors extends north from the 4000m/13,124ft peaks of the Bernese Oberland towards Lake Thun and Brienz (see entries).

A railway line connecting the two lakes was opened between Därlingen and Bönigen in 1874 (the first steamer on Lake Thun having gone into service nearly 40 years earlier, in 1836). This was followed in 1888 by the Brünigbahn between Lucerne and Interlaken, in 1893 by the Thuner-See-Bahn (Lake Thun railway) and in 1913 by the Lötschberg railway, which provided a link with Italy. The first mountain railways in the Jungfrau area had been built some years previously.

History

Jungfraujoch
(3454 m ü.d.M.)

Section schematic

© *Baedeker*

Mönch (4099 m)

Aufstieg zum Mönch

1 Jungfraujoch station	6 Road to plateau	11 Sphinx tunnel
2 Berghaus Hotel	7 Ice Palace	12 Sphinx elevator
3 Restaurant	8 Entrance to Sphinx tunnel	13 Sphinx lookout terrace (3573 m – 11,723 feet)
4 Restaurant	9 Tourist House	14 Exit from Sphinx tunnel
5 Cinema	10 Research station	15 Ski school and huskies

The Jungfrau mountain railways, all under the same management, now have a total length of more than 70km/43 miles (all electric), with gauges of either 100 or 80cm/39 or 31in.

Opened 1890; from Interlaken Ost (East station) to Lauterbrunnen (796m/ 2612ft) and from Interlaken Ost to Grindelwald (1034m/3393ft). Total length 23.5km/15 miles; gauge 100cm/39in.; gradients up to 12% (1 in 8) (partly normal railway line, partly rack-railway).

Berner-Oberland-Bahnen (BOB)

Opened 1893 (associated with the Berner-Oberland-Bahnen since 1895); from Wilderswil (584m/1916ft) to the Schynige Platte (1967m/6454ft). Length 7.3km/5 miles; gauge 80cm/31in.; gradients up to 25% (1 in 4) (rack-railway).

Schynige Platte Bahn

Opened 1891; from Lauterbrunnen (796m/2612ft) to the Grütschalp (1487m/4879ft), cableway; Grütschalp–Mürren (1650m/5414ft), railway. Total length 5.7km/4 miles; gauge 100cm/39in.; gradients up to 61% (1 in 1.6) (cableway).

Bergbahn Lauter-brunnen–Mürren (BLM)

Cable railway opened 1912; from Mürren (1650m/5414ft) to the Allmend-hubel (1912m/6273ft). Length 536m/1759ft; gauge 100cm/39in.; gradients up to 61% (1 in 1.6).

Seilbahn Mürren–Allmendhubel (SMA)

Opened 1893: from Lauterbrunnen (796m/2612ft) to Wengen (1274m/ 4180ft), the Wengernalp (1873m/6145ft) and the Kleine Scheidegg (2061m/6762ft), and from Grindelwald (1034m/3393ft) to the Kleine Scheidegg (2061m/6762ft). Total length 10km/6 miles (the longest single stretch track of rack-railway line in Switzerland); gauge 80cm/31in.; gradients up to 25% (1 in 4).

Wengernalp-bahn (WAB)

First section, from the Kleine Scheidegg (2061m/6762ft) to the Eiger glacier (2320m/7612ft), opened in 1898; from the Eiger glacier (2320m/7612ft) to the Eigerwand (2865m/9400ft) in 1903; from the Eigerwand (2865m/9400ft)

Jungfraubahn (JB)

★ *The Jungfrau, queen of mountains*

251

to the Eismeer (3160m/10,368ft) in 1905; and from the Eismeer (3160m/10,368ft) to the Jungfraujoch (3454m/11,333ft) in 1912. Total length 9.3km/6 miles; gauge 100cm/39in.; gradients up to 25%. Tunnel 7.1km/4 miles long from the Eiger glacier to the Jungfraujoch. Rack-railway (cog-railway).

Drahtseilbahn
Interlaken–
Harder (HB)

Cable railway, opened 1908; from Interlaken (567m/1860ft) to the Harderkulm (1322m/4337ft). Length 1.4km/1 mile; gauge 100cm/39in.; gradients up to 84% (1 in 1½).

Useful tip

The best starting-point for a trip into the Jungfrau area is the East station in Interlaken (Interlaken-Ost). It is possible to go by car to Grindelwald and Lauterbrunnen. The round trip from Interlaken to the Jungfraujoch and back (either via Lauterbrunnen and Wengen or via Grindelwald) takes between 4½ and 5 hours. It is important to choose a day with favourable weather conditions, to be stoutly shod and to take sun-glasses.

Information

Information from Bahnen der Jungfrau-Region (Jungfrau Railways), CH-3800 Interlaken, tel. (036) 22 52 52.

★★ To the Jungfraujoch

There are two routes from Interlaken to the Kleine Scheidegg, either via Lauterbrunnen or via Grindelwald: the best plan is to go one way and come back the other. The line to both places is the same as far as Zweilütschinen, at the junction of two streams, the Schwarze Lütischine (Black Lütischine) coming from Grindelwald and the Weisse Lütischine (White Lütischine) from the Lauterbrunnen valley.

Grindelwald

See entry

Lauterbrunnen

See Lauterbrunnen valley

The rail journey from Interlaken Ost to Grindelwald takes 40 minutes, from Grindelwald to the Kleine Scheidegg 35 minutes. The line runs below the dreaded north face of the Eiger, the most dangerous rock wall in the Alps, which claimed many deaths before it was finally climbed in 1938 by an Austro-German team of four men (Vörg, Heckmayr, Harrer and Kasparek), who took four days for the ascent. The summit had already been reached by an Englishman, Christopher Berrington, in 1858, following a different route. The north face of the Eiger has since been climbed by over 700 men and women. A commemorative stone was unveiled in 1988 in memory of the first ascent.

The journey from Interlaken Ost to Lauterbrunnen takes 25 minutes, from Lauterbrunnen to the Kleine Scheidegg 42 minutes. There are parking facilities in Lauterbrunnen. The Wengernalpbahn runs up in 14 minutes to Wengen, on a sunny terrace, sheltered from the wind, high above the Lauterbrunnen valley (4km/2 miles).

Wengen

Wengen (1300m/4267ft; pop. 1150), the second largest winter sports resort in the Bernese Oberland and beautifully situated at the foot of the Eiger, Mönch and Jungfrau, is an ideal base for walks and climbs in the mountain world of the Bernese Oberland. There is a cableway up Männlichen (2343m/7687ft), and numerous attractive footpaths. Particularly rewarding is the climb to the Wengernalp, either direct (1¾ hours) or by way of the Mettlealp (1700m/5578ft; immediately opposite the Jungfrau; 3 hours).

Wengernalp

From Wengen the railway continues up for another 4km/2 miles to the Wengernalp (1873m/6145ft; Hotel Jungfrau, November–April, C, 45b.), from which there are splendid views of the Trümleten valley and the Jungfrau. There is a chair-lift from Wengernalp Wixi to the Lauberhornschulter (2310m/7579ft).

11km/7 miles farther on is the Kleine Scheidegg (2061m/6764ft; Scheidegg Hotels, open: December–September), the terminus of the rack (cog)-railways from Lauterbrunnen and Grindelwald and the starting-point of the Jungfraubahn, with tremendous views of the nearby 4000m/13,124ft peaks of the Eiger, Mönch and Jungfrau. Magnificent walks; splendid skiing country (Arven, Honegg and Lauberhorn ski-lifts). Sight-seeing flights over the glaciers from Männlichen.

Kleine Scheidegg

★★Jungfraubahn

The Jungfraubahn, built 1896–1912, runs up through Alpine meadows and an 87km/285ft long tunnel and after 2km/1 mile arrives at the Eigergletscher (Eiger Glacier) station (2320m/7612ft; inn), in magnificently wild scenery and then enters the long tunnel (7.1km/4 miles) which leads up towards the Jungfraujoch.

Eigergletscher

4.4km/3 miles: Eigerwand station (2865m/9400ft), with a magnificent view of Grindelwald, 1800m/5906ft below. From here the line runs under the Eiger. 5.7km/4 miles: Eismeer (Sea of Ice, 3160m/10,368ft) on the south face of the Eiger, 40m/131ft above the Upper Grindelwald-Fiescher Firn (névé, or frozen snow), with views over the much-crevassed surface of the glacier towards the Wetterhorn, the Schreckhorn, the Fiescherhörner and the great crevasse under the Mönchsjoch.

Eigerwand

Eismeer

After a journey of 50 minutes and 9.3km/6 miles the rack-railway reaches the Jungfraujoch (3454m/11,333ft), the highest railway station in Europe, which together with the accommodation for visitors, the research stations, the underground passages and the elevators forms a little subterranean town of its own. An outer lobby (post office, shops, restaurants, lookout gallery) leads into the Ice Palace (Eispalast), a cavern hewn out of the glacier, with ice sculpture. Next to a self-service restaurant the first-class

★★Jungfrau-joch

The "Top of Europe" restaurant on the Jungfrau

★ "Top of
Europe"

Top of Europe restaurant opened in 1987, offers magnificent views of the mountains and in fine weather the Aletsch glacier. From the Sphinx Tunnel an elevator (112m/367ft) ascends to the summit of the Sphinx (3573m/11,273ft), with an lookout terrace, a research institute and a weather station. There is also an exit from the tunnel giving access to a summer ski school; here, too, visitors can have a sleigh ride, pulled by husky dogs.

The views from the Jungfraujoch itself, the saddle of firn (névé) between the Mönch and the Jungfrau, are breathtaking. To the south can be seen the Aletsch glacier, 22km/14 miles long, to the north the mountain world of the Alps, the Mittelland and beyond this, on clear days, the Vosges and the Black Forest.

Jura Mountains   B–H 3–11

Cantons: Jura (JU), Neuchâtel (NE) and Vaud (VD).

Situation and
★ landscape

The Jura is the range of folded mountains lying north-west of the Swiss Alps and extending from Geneva to Schaffhausen. This is the central area of the Swiss watchmaking industry; but, lying as it does on the periphery of the country, has so far played a relatively minor part in the Swiss tourist trade. For this reason is popular with nature lovers.

Canton Jura

The new canton of Jura, the 23rd to become a member of the Confederation, was established on January 1st 1979, following a popular referendum in September 1977. It has an area of 837sq.km/323sq.miles and a population of 65,000, 87.6% of whom are Roman Catholics. The capital is Delémont, and the canton is divided into three districts of Delémont, Porrentruy and Franches-Montagnes, with a total of 82 communes.

From Basle through the Jura to Lake Geneva

Delémont

The road runs through the beautiful Birs valley and after 41km/25 miles arrives at Delémont (see entry). From here the road to Biel continues south through the picturesque narrow Val Moutier, which the River Birs has carved through the limestone rock.

Moutier

From Choindez the road continues to Moutier (532m/1745ft; pop. 8900), a former centre of medieval monastic culture with watchmaking and manufacture of machine tools. South-west of the town is the interesting Romanesque chapel of Chalières with ornate frescoes (c. 1020).

Tavannes

The road then runs through a picturesque defile, the Gorges de Court, and continues through the villages of Court, Malleray-Bévilard and Reconvilier (731m/2398ft; pop. 2600; important horse fair), birthplace of the famous clown known as Grock (Adrian Wettach, 1880–1959), to Tavannes (757m/2484ft; pop. 4000), near the source of the Birs.

Pierre Pertuis

From here the road ascends to the Pierre Pertuis, with a passage through the rock 12m/39ft high and 8m/26ft wide (Roman inscription), and then down to Sonceboz (656m/2152ft; pop. 1370), where the railway line from Biel to La Chaux-de-Fonds branches off.

St-Imier

The route then continues through the Vallon de St-Imier, the valley of the River Suze, to St-Imier (814m/2671ft; pop. 6300), an important watchmaking capital, with a 12th c. Romanesque church and the Tour de la Reine Berthe, a remnant of the Romanesque church of St Martin. In the Longines Museum the visitor can learn something of the history of these famous watch and clock makers (by appointment; tel. (039) 42 54 25): the Paris architect Jean Nouvel designed a factory for the Cartier group in 1993. Cableway up the Mont Soleil (1290m/4332ft).

Jura landscape

From here there is a direct road to Neuchâtel (30km/19 miles), past Le Chasseral (1610m/5282ft; hotel), from which there are beautiful panoramic views. The main road continues to La Chaux-de-Fonds (see entry).

★ Le Chasseral

La Chaux-de-Fonds

From La Chaux-de-Fonds an attractive excursion can be made via Le Locle (9km/6 miles) and the Col des Roches (917m/3009ft), 5km/3 miles beyond which is the watchmaking village of Les Brenets (849m/2786ft; pop. 1200), situated above the Lac des Brenets (753m/2471ft). The lake (length 4km/ 2 miles, breadth 100–200m/328–656ft, area 0.69sq.km/0.27sq.miles), enclosed by sandstone crags, is a natural formation on the River Doubs, which here forms the frontier between Switzerland and France. It is a 15 minutes' trip by motor-boat or a 45 minutes' walk to the Hôtel du Doubs, from which a 5 minutes' climb leads to a viewpoint opposite the Saut du Doubs, a waterfall 27m/89ft high. Immediately downstream from the Lac de Brenets is the Lac de Moron (4.5km/3 miles long).

Lac des Brenets

Saut du Doubs

14km/9 miles south-west of the Col des Roches we come to La Brévine (1046m/3432ft; pop. 700), and a further 14km/9 miles south, in the Val de Travers, Fleurier (743m/2438ft; pop. 4100). To the east of Travers it is a 30 minutes' round trip to former asphalt mines, (in operation until 1986), where natural asphalt, a mixture of bitumen and mineral (chiefly chalk), was mined.

La Brévine
Val de Travers, asphalt mines

14km/9 miles south-west of Fleurier the town of Ste-Croix (1092m/3583ft; pop. 5300), famous for its musical boxes, lies in a valley on the slopes of Le Chasseron (1611m/5286ft). There is an interesting Musical Box Museum in L'Auberson. Below the road from Ste-Croix to Vuiteboef wheel tracks can be seen in the rock of the old Roman road.

Ste-Croix

The road from La Chaux-de-Fonds to Neuchâtel (22km/14 miles) runs past the Vue des Alpes (9km/6 miles; 1283m/4210ft; inn), from which there is a beautiful panorama of the Alps (Mont Blanc).

Jura Mountains

Neuchâtel	See entry.
Yverdon	See entry.
La Sarraz	South-west of the Lac de Neuchâtel, via Orbe (see Yverdon), is La Sarraz (488m/1601ft; pop. 1000), with a massive 11th c. castle which was given its present form in the 16th c. The Musée Cheval has an exhibition of working, draught and riding horses as well as horses of the army and in art. As part of the project "Renovation 2000" the castle is undergoing extensive restoration. In the former parish church of St-Antoine (now the Town Hall) can be seen the tomb of Count François de la Sarraz (d. 1363).
Romainmôtier, ★ Abbey of St-Pierre et St-Paul	North-west of La Sarraz, on a by-road to the left of road 9, is the old-world little town of Romainmôtier (658m/2159ft) which has a monastery founded in the 5th c. and dissolved in 1537. The Abbey Church of St-Pierre et St-Paul, built under the direction of St Odilo of Cluny in the 10th–11th c. and reconstructed in the 12th–14th c., is one of the oldest and most important ecclesiastical buildings in the country. The Romanesque monastery church has valuable 14th/15th c. frescoes.
★ Dent de Vaulion Lac de Joux	The by-road continues along the foot of the Dent de Vaulion (1486m/4877ft; magnificent view) to the north-east end of the Lac de Joux. An attractive road follows the south side of the lake, passing through the little village of L'Abbaye, dominated by the massive tower of its church.
Le Brassus	Just beyond the south-west side of the lake is Le Brassus (1024m/3360ft), a winter sports resort with excellent skiing terrain (ski-lifts up Molard, 1570m/5151ft). From here it is possible to continue to Nyon (see entry), on Lake Geneva (see entry), either by way of the Col du Marchairuz (1447m/4748ft) or (passing through French territory) via La Cure, the Col de la Givrine (1228m/
St-Cergue	4029ft) and the winter sports resort of St-Cergue (1043m/3422ft); possible detour to the fine viewpoint of La Dôle, 1677m/5502ft.

From Delémont into the Ajoie

The so-called Pruntruter Zipfel (Porrentruy summit) is the name given to the hilly borderland with France, a chalk upland area which slopes down towards Burgundy. The road between Delémont and Porrentruy (German Pruntrut; 28km/17 miles) is part of the main route Berne–Belfort–Paris.

Develier, Corniche du Jura	Via Develier (church window by Bissière) along the beautiful "Corniche du Jura" (14km/8 miles) the road reaches the Les Rangiers pass (858m/2816ft) with magnificent views of the mountain ridge Mont Terri. 1km/about ½ mile farther on the right is a war memorial, erected in 1924, in memory of the battles of the First World War.
★ St-Ursanne	The "Corniche du Jura" continues via Les Malettes (inn) down through the Combe Maran and under a high railway viaduct (5km/3 miles) to St-Ursanne (German St Ursitz; 440m/1444ft; pop. 1100), a romantic little medieval town on the River Doubs, which bends sharply through Swiss territory. St-Ursanne was founded in the 7th c. on the site of the chapter-house, which dates back to the Irish monk Ursicinus (companion of Colomban). The church, a triple-naved basilica with buttresses and no transept (Romanesque choir, 12th c.; Gothic nave, 13th–14th c.; front tower, 1441), is one of the most attractive buildings in the west of Switzerland and contains a cloister, Merovingian sarcophagi and a Romanesque crypt. Of particular note are the Romanesque south doorway, the towers, the old bridge and the castle ruins. Motor enthusiasts will be interested in the International Rally St-Ursanne–Les Rangiers, the only Swiss motor race in the European Championships.

Hermitage of . . .   *. . . St Ursanne*

The road to Porrentruy runs down from Les Malettes with views of the village and ruins of Asuel, through the village of Cornol (503m/1651ft), lying in a narrow valley into the hilly countryside of the Ajoie (German Eisgau). After 8.5km/5 miles it comes to Courgenay (493m/1618ft), home of the legendary soldiers' mother "Gilberte de Courgenay".

Courgenay

5km/3miles to Porrentruy (426m/1398ft; pop. 7800), the commercial, industrial and cultural centre of the Ajoie. In 1988 it received the Wakker prize for its outstanding preservation of its medieval town centre.

Porrentruy

The old town is dominated by the castle, which became the seat of the prince-bishops following Berne's conversion to the new faith (1529). The 13th c. round tower Tour Réfouse (refuge) is the oldest building with the Porte de France (1563) in the Faubourg as evidence of the former fortifications. Notable sights include the Catholic parish church of St-Pierre (1349), with Late Baroque side altars, the former Jesuit church which is now used as the hall of the cantonal school and several Baroque buildings such as the Hôtel de Ville (1761–63; interesting bell towers), the Hôpital (now a local museum) with the Samaritan fountain by L. Perraud (1564), the Late Baroque Hôtel des Halles and the Hôtel de Gléresse (*c.* 1750), houses the library. The Botanical Garden of the cantonal school, founded by Lémane in 1795, is open daily.

From here it is 12km/7 miles to the Swiss border town of Boncourt (375m/1231ft; pop. 1700), with a 12th/13th c. church, a traditional tobacco factory (1814) and caves with stalactites.

Boncourt

From Delémont into the Franches-Montagnes

The road runs from Delémont via Saignelégier (33km/20 miles) through the Jura to Neuchâtel and Geneva. First along the Sorne valley through the villages of Courtételle and Courfaivre (bicycle factory; stained glass in

Sorne valley

Préfecture in Saignelégier

Combe Tabeillon	the church by F. Léger) for 10km/6 miles to the watchmaking village of Bassecourt (478m/1569ft), then the road climbs the slopes of the wild Combe Tabeillon into the Franches-Montagnes, an upland chalk area from 1000m/3282ft to 1100m/3610ft, with a network of maintained walks (some suitable for mountain bikes). It is ideal for exploring on horseback or even in a hired Romany caravan. There are many long-distance tracks.
Montfaucon	Montfaucon (1006m/3301ft; pop. 450) has a Classical parish church (late 19th c.) and there are the "Grand Ceux" caves.
Saignelégier	5km/3 miles farther lies Saignelégier (982m/3222ft), chief town of the Franches-Montagnes and horse-breeding centre with the National Horse Market ("Marché Concours") being held here the second weekend in August. The massive préfecture in the main street and its adjoining prison tower were built in the 16th c.
Noirmont, Les Bois	The village of Noirmont (970m/3183ft; pop. 1550) lies on the French border. In Les Bois (1087m/3567ft) there is a cheese dairy which is open to visitors ("Tête de Moine" = monk's head). Over the Col-de-Bellevue (1073m/3521ft) the road finally comes to La Chaux-de-Fonds.

Kandersteg J 9

Canton: Berne (BE)
Altitude: 1170–1200m/3839/3937ft
Population: 800

Situation and general	Kandersteg is a popular summer and winter resort in the Upper Kander valley, in the Bernese Oberland. The village, with some attractive old peasants' houses and a small 16th c. church, spreads out along the meadows of the valley floor for almost 4km/2 miles, enclosed by towering mountains.

To the north-east is the jagged Birrenhorn (2505m/8219ft), to the east the snow-capped Blümlisalp and the Doldenhorn, to the south-east the bare slopes of the Fisistöcke (2947m/9669ft) and to the south, closing the valley, the rugged Gellihorn (2289m/7510ft). At Eggenschwand, at the south end of the village, the Lötschbergbahn enters the Lötschberg tunnel, the third longest in the Alps (14.6km/9 miles; cars carried).

Cabin railway from Eggenschwand to Beim Stock (1837m/6027ft) on the Gemmiweg (6 minutes); from there a chair-lift (12 minutes) to 1947m/ 6388ft on Sunnbühl.

Chair-lift from the mouth of the Oeschinental (5 minutes from the church) to Oeschinen (1700m/5578ft; 9 minutes).

The Allmenalp cableway runs from Bütschels (10 minutes from the church) to Allmenalp station (1730m/5678ft) in 5 minutes.

Cableways and lifts

There are some 13km/8 miles of marked-out slopes suitable for beginners and average skiers, as well as 75km/47 miles of cross-country ski runs of varying degrees of difficulty. In addition there are facilities for curling, ice-skating and tobogganing as well as ski schools.

Winter sports

Surroundings

Some 5km/3 miles before reaching Kandersteg lie the crystal-clear waters of the Blausee (trout farming, breeding of St Bernard dogs; restaurant), surrounded by 20ha/50 acres of natural parkland.

Blausee

The Oeschinensee (1582m/5191ft; Hotel Oeschinsee, E) can be reached by a 1¼ hours' walk from the Victoria Hotel up the valley of the Oeschinen-bach, or by taking the chair-lift to the Oeschinen station and walking down from there over the Im Lager meadows (extensive views: 30 minutes). The lake lies below the Blümlisalp, mirroring the mountain's rugged shape in its clear water, in a setting of majestic beauty.

★Oeschinensee

From here it is a 3¾ hours' climb to the Blümlisalp hut (2837m/9308ft) and a 5 hours' climb (with guide) to the summit of the Blümlisalphorn (3664m/12,022ft), the highest peak of the mighty Blümlisalp.

Blümlisalp

Into the Gastern valley

¾ hour to Klus, 2¼ hours to Selden; also possible to drive to Selden on payment of a toll.

The narrow road runs through a tunnel in the rock into the Klus, a gorge through which the River Gander rushes and tumbles, and then continues uphill through a second tunnel on the left bank and another on the right bank. In 15 minutes it arrives at a magnificent stretch of the valley at Gasternholz (1365m/4479ft; on the left bank the Waldhaus inn), with the mighty rock walls of the Tatlishorn and Altels towering up on the right.

★Kander-Klus

From here it is a 1¼ hours' walk along the right bank to the huts of Selden (1590m/5217ft), under a grand mountain screen formed by the Hockenhorn (3297m/10,817ft; 8 hours with guide), the Doldenhorn (3643m/11,953ft; 8 hours with guide, from Kandersteg) and the Balmhorn.

Selden
★Hockenhorn

★Balmhorn

To the Gemmi pass

To Schwarenbach Hotel 3 or 1½ hours, to Leukerbad 6½, 5 or 3½ hours depending on route taken.

First a 30 minutes' walk to Eggenschwand (road passable for cars for 2.5km/2 miles to car park at lower station of Stock cableway); then either by cableway (6 minutes) or on foot (1¾ hours) to Beim Stock (1837m/6027ft; chair-lift to Sunnbühl).

Then a 1¼ hours' walk through wooded country high above the Gastern valley, and up the valley of the Schwarzbach and over the Spitalmatte (1900m/6234ft), an Alpine meadow littered with rock debris, to the Schwarenbach Hotel (2067m/6782ft), a good climbing base (climbing school), e.g.

★ Balmhorn   for the ascent of the Balmhorn (3709m/12,169ft; 6–7 hours with guide).

★ Gemmi pass   Then another 1¼ hours through a bleak and rugged region, past the Daubensee (2205m/7235ft; frozen for 8–10 months of the year) to the Gemmi pass (2316m/7599ft; Berghotel Wildstrubel, E), with astonishing views of the Rhône valley and the Valais Alps.

From the pass a cableway descends to Leukerbad (see entry). The walk down to Leukerbad on the old bridle-path (made in 1740) along a rock face which plunges precipitously down for almost 600m/1969ft, is to be recommended only to those with a good head for heights (2 hours).

Klosters   S 7

Canton: Grisons (GR)
Altitude: 1127–1209m/3698–3967ft
Population: 3500

Situation and general   The popular health and winter sports resort of Klosters, made up of a number of separate groups of houses and hotels, lies in the wide Prättigau valley, through which flows the River Landquart, within a framework of high mountains. The first official reference to it was in 1222, the "Klösterli im Walt". The construction of roads and the Rhätische Bahn railway in the 19th c. linked it with the Rhine valley.

Sights

In the main part of the resort, known as Zentrum (formerly Klosters Platz, 1209m/3967ft) are the large hotels and the parish church (restored 1921), which originally belonged to the Premonstratensian (an order founded at Premonstré, France in 1119) monastery of St Jakob, dissolved in 1528: hence the name of the village (Kloster=monastery). Nearby a shopping centre has several small shops selling local crafts.

Local museum Nutli-Hüschi   A renovated 16th c. farmhouse houses a local museum "Nutli-Hüschi" with local historical exhibits (open: beginning of July–mid Oct. Wed.–Fri. 4–6pm, in July and Aug. also Sat. 4–6pm; mid Jan.–mid Apr. 4–6pm).

1.5km/1 mile down the valley, at the mouth of the Schappin valley, is Klosters Dorf (1127m/3698ft).

Winter sports   Excellent ski-trails in the Parsenn area (53 in all, including Davos), in the Madrisa area and on the Saaseralp. The longest descent (14km/9 miles) Weissfluhgipfel-Küblis (medium) covers a height difference of 2030m/6662ft. Chuecalanda has the deepest snow with bob-sleighing in the areas of Gotschna/Parsenn and Madrisa. There are over 40km/25 miles of long-distance runs; ice-rink, curling, tobogganing.

Surroundings

Gotschnagrat   A cableway ascends from Kloster railway station by way of an intermediate station on the Gotschnaboden (1780m/5840ft) to the Gotschnagrat (2283m/7491ft; restaurant), with views of the Upper Prättigau and the Silvretta group. From here a footpath leads in 30 minutes to the Parsenn hut (2205m/7235ft; inn) from which it is another 2 hours' walk to the Höhenweg station

Klosters: Nutli-Hüschi

on the Davos–Weissfluhjoch funicular (2215m/7235ft). There is also a cableway from the Parsenn hut (2400m/7874ft, 8 minutes) to the Weissfluhjoch (2663m/8737ft).

Another cableway (2280m/7481ft, 11 minutes) runs up from Klosters Dorf to the Albeina station (1884m/6181ft; restaurant) on the Saaseralp (several ski-lifts) below the Madrisahorn (2826m/9272ft; another 3–4 hours with guide).

The Prättigau (Romansch Val Partens or Portenz), extending north-west **Prättigau** from Klosters is the narrow valley of the River Landquart. Although the neat little villages, situated among fruit orchards in the wider parts of the valley or on narrow terraces on the steeply sloping meadowland on the hillsides, have Romansch names dating from an earlier settlement they are inhabited by a German-speaking and mainly Protestant population. On the north side of the valley is the Rätikon chain (Scesaplana, 2967m/9735ft), **Rätikon** along which runs the frontier with Austria (Vorarlberg). The numerous summer holiday resorts in the Prättigau are mostly some distance off the road on the hillside (Seewis on the north side. Fideris and Bad Serneus on the south side) or in the side valleys (Valzeina to the south, St Antönien to the north). Küblis, with a late Gothic church, and Schiers, at the mouth **Küblis, Schiers** of the Schraubach, are both worth a visit.

A 5 hour walk through varied countryside with wonderful flora is marked **Prättigau Walk** from Madrisa station (1884m/6183ft) over the Jägglischhorn-Fürggli (2255m/7401ft), where there are marvellous views of Sulzfluh, Drusenfluh, Scweizertor and Scheseplana, to St Antönien (1420m/4660ft).

From Klosters a narrow road climbs the right bank of the Landquart into the highest part of the Prättigau, with beautiful views of the Silvretta group. 3km/2 miles: Monbiel (1313m/4308ft; restaurant). From here it is another 4km/2 miles (road closed to cars) to the beautifully situated Alp Noval **Alp Noval** (1368m/4488ft), at the point where the Sardascabach and the Vereinabach

In the Prättigau near Schiers

Berghaus
Vereina
Silvrettahaus

join to form the Landquart. A bridle-path ascends the Vereina valley (to the right) to the Berghaus Vereina (1944m/6378ft; inn, with beds), in a magnificent mountain setting (2¼ hours), a good base for climbers. 3½ hours' walk up the Sardasca valley, to the left, is the Silvrettahaus (2340m/7677ft; inn), in a magnificent situation under the Silvretta glacier (1 hour's climb). These are both good bases for climbs in the Silvretta group – the Silvrettahorn (3248m/10,657ft; 3½ hours, with guide), Piz Buin (3316m/10,880ft; 4½ hours, with guide).

Küssnacht am Rigi   M 6

Canton: Schwyz (SZ)
Altitude: 440m/1444ft
Population: 6500

Situation and
general

Küssnacht, chief town of the district of that name between Lake Lucerne and Lake Zug, famous for its associations with William Tell, lies at the farthest tip of the Küssnachter See, the most northerly arm of Lake Lucerne. It first appears in the records in 870, in connection with a gift to the monastery in Lucerne.

Sights

Hotel Engel

The Gasthaus Engel (Angel Inn) is a half-timbered building of 1552 with an old assembly hall and a Goethe Room. Parish church of St Peter and Paul (rebuilt in Baroque style 1708–10, enlarged 1968); Town Hall (1728).

William Tell

William Tell, the hero of Swiss legend who, the story goes, refused to recognise the authority of the Habsburg governor Gessler, won his freedom by shooting the apple on his son's head and later killed Gessler in the

Kussnacht: "Hohle Gasse", Tell Chapel . . .   . . . and Hotel Engel

Hohle Gasse, is a symbolic figure who has been a powerful inspiration throughout Swiss history.

The desire for freedom lay at the root of the striving by this people of herdsmen and forest-dwellers in the heart of Switzerland to achieve independence, and continued in subsequent centuries to inspire the Confederates in their struggle. Switzerland's development into the well-ordered European state of today passed through many troubles and vicissitudes; but the "Perpetual Pact" between the three forest states in 1291 was strong enough to endure and form the basis of the present Confederation of 26 cantons.

Surroundings

2km/1 mile north-east of Küssnacht on the road to Immensee is the Hohle Gasse ("Hollow Lane"), where tradition has it that William Tell shot the Austrian governor Gessler with his crossbow.

★ Hohle Gasse

The spot is marked by the Tell chapel (built 1638, restored 1895, with paintings by H. Bachmann of "Gessler's Death" and "Tell's Death"). The Hohle Gasse was purchased by the young people of Switzerland and presented to the Confederation.

Tell chapel

Above Küssnacht stands the ruined Gesslerburg ("Gessler's Castle"), the remains of a medieval stronghold which has no connection with Gessler. After visiting Küssnacht Goethe suggested the subject of William Tell to Schiller, and Schiller's play in turn inspired Rossini's opera.

Gesslerburg

5km/3 miles above Küssnacht on a narrow and winding mountain road (or 7 minutes by cableway), on the slopes of the Rigi, is the Seebodenalp (1030m/3379ft), from which a footpath leads in 1½ hours to Rigi Staffel and Rigi Känzeli.

Rigi

Rooterberg

4km/2 miles west of Küssnacht is Udligenswil, from which there is a footpath up the Rooterberg (798m/2618ft St Michaelkreuz chapel).

Just outside Küssnacht on the Lucerne road a Flemish-style memorial chapel is dedicated to Queen Astrid of Belgium, who was killed in a car accident here in 1935.

Lausanne   D 9

Canton: Vaud (VD)
Altitude: 380–530m/1247–1739ft
Population: 127,000

Situation and general

Lausanne, the lively capital of the canton of Vaud, is picturesquely situated on the north shore of Lake Geneva, on terraces rising above the lake which are broken by gorges. It ranks with Geneva as a focus of intellectual life in French-speaking Switzerland (Federal Court, University, College of Technology, Hotel School and many other technical colleges), and is also a popular convention and conference centre and the venue of important trade fairs (Comptoir Suisse in Autumn, International Tourism Fair in March). Major elements in the town's economy are the foodstuffs industries, vine-growing and the wine trade.

★ Townscape

In the attractive townscape of Lausanne the modern office blocks and the high-level bridges spanning the gorges (now built over) of the Rivers Flon and Louve form a striking contrast to the narrow lanes and steep flights of steps which run up to the old town (Cité), dominated by the cathedral (530m/1739ft) and the Château, while to the south pleasant residential districts extend down to the port of Ouchy (380m/1247ft).

History

There was a Celtic settlement at the mouth of the River Flon which later became the Roman Lousonium or Lousonna. After the destruction of this

Lausanne, capital of the canton of Vaud, with Notre-Dame cathedral

town by the Alemanni about 379 a fortified settlement was built on the hill now occupied by the Cité, and after that the transfer of the episcopal see from Avanches to Lausanne (c. 590) this became a town of some size which, like Geneva, belonged successively to the Burgundians, the Franks and the second Burgundian Kingdom before becoming part of the Holy Roman Empire in 1033. In the 15th c. the Vaud region was conquered by the Bernese, who soon introduced the Reformed faith. In 1798, however, Vaud recovered its independence as the République Lémanique, and in 1803 it became the 19th canton to join the Swiss Confederation.

On Lake Geneva (departures from Place de la Navigation, Ouchy) there are motor launches several times daily to lakeside towns in Switzerland and France; round trips and cruises.

Boat services

Tour of the town

In the centre

The hub of the town's traffic is the Place St-François, surrounded by large office blocks and the Head Post Office. In the middle of the square stands the former Franciscan church of St-François (13th–14th c.; beautiful stained glass of 1907 in choir), with a tower of 1523. A little way east is the Derrière Bourg park (fine views).

St-François church

From Place St-François take Rue de Bourg (pedestrians only) and Rue Caroline and then turn left over the Pont Bessières (1910) to reach the cathedral (below).

The Grand-Pont (1839–44), an arched viaduct 180m/591ft long from which there is an attractive view of the old town and the cathedral, runs north-west from Place St-François into the busy imposing Bel-Air Métropole office block (1932; restaurant and café), crowned by a tower block 67m/220ft high (20 storeys).

Bel-Air Métropole

From Place Bel-Air, Rue Haldimand runs north-east, passing on the right the Protestant church of St-Laurent (1719; Baroque façade).

St-Laurent church

To the north-east is the spacious Place de la Riponne. On its east side stands the Palais de Rumine (1898–1906), which houses the University, originally founded as as Academy in 1537. (A new university complex has been built at Dorigny, 5km/3 miles west of the town.) Also in the Palais de Rumine are the Cantonal and University Library (700,000 volumes, valuable manuscripts), the Cantonal Museum of Art (Musée Cantonal des Beaux-Arts; mainly pictures by 18th–20th c. artists of western Switzerland), the Natural History Museum and the Archaeological Museum (bust of Marcus Aurelius). There is also a display of medals (visits by arrangement) with some rare coins, seals and weights.

Palais de Rumine

Museum of Art
Natural History
and Archaeo-
logical Museum

Also of interest is a small museum on the theme of "man's hand in art" (21 Rue du Buynon; open: Tues.–Fr.).

Musée de la main de l'homme

From the church of St-Laurent Rue de l'Ale runs north-west to the Tour De l'Ale, a round tower 21m/69ft high which is the only remnant of the town's 14th c. fortifications.

Tour de l'Ale

A little way south of Place de la Riponne (pedestrian precinct) is Place de la Palud, in which is situated the Hôtel de Ville (Town Hall, 15th and 17th c.; 16th c. stained glass). From here the Escaliers du Marché, a covered flight of steps, lead up to the cathedral, in the Cité (which can also be reached-from Place de la Riponne by a flight of steps to the right of the University and Rue Pierre-Viret).

Hôtel de Ville

Yverdon, Neuchâtel

Collection de l'Art Brut,
Palais de Beaulieu

Lausanne

300 m

Tour de l'Ale

Place
Chauderon

Bel-Air
Métropole

Thé

St. Laurent

Pont Chauderon-
Montbenon Rue

de

Genève

Avenue de Tivoli

Avenue

Rath

Casino

Avenue M. Dufour

Avenue Louis Ruchonnet

Jules

Gonin

St-Fran

MONTBENON

R. du Petit-Chêne

Chemin des Fleurettes

Avenue du Mont d'Or

Boulevard

Place
de la Gare

Gare
Centrale

Ave

Milan

de

Avenue

de

Grancy

Avenue de Cour

Avenue

MONTRIOND

Ed Dapples

d'Ouchy

Jardin
Botanique

Avenue F. C.

Musée

Bibliothèque

Avenue

Théâtre
du Triangle

Ecole
Polytechnique
Fédérale (EPFL)

Avenue de

Cour

Avenue de

Chemin de Bellerive

de

la

Harpe

Avenue

d'Ouchy

Avenue de

Ecole
d'Art

Chemin des Mouettes

Chemin de Beau-Rivage

Mu
de l'Ely

Avenue

de

Rhodanie

OUCHY

Bassin
marchand

Avenue

Bassin de
Plaisance

Château
d'Ouchy

Place
du Port

Quai

d

Port
d'Ouchy

© Baedeker

Dorigny

Dorigny

Signal de Sauvabelin, Moudon, Bern

Centre
Hospitalier

Château
St- Maire
Policlinique

Hôpital
Cantonal

Av. Montagibert

Av. de Beaumont

lais de
mine

Théâtre

Cathédrale

usée
storique
Centrale

François

Rue St-Martin

Rue Caroline

Rue de Bugnon

Avenue de Béthusy

Avenue Secrétan

Piscine

Tribunal
Fédéral

Parc

Mon-Repos

Parc

Av. du Théâtre

Rue Beau- Séjour

Musée
des Arts
Décoratifs

Théâtre
Municipal

MON REPOS

Av. Juste Olivier

Synagogue

Av. Eglantine

Avenue du Léman

Avenue de Mousquines

St-
Rédempteur

de

Rumine

Ch. du Trabandan

Avenue

a Gare

Avenue des Alpes

Av. de Jungoz

de Mont-Choisi

Servan

Av. Fantaisie

ysée

Avenue

Chemin

de

Chandieu

Ch. de
Fantaisie

La Vuachère

Avenue C. F. Ramuz

Avenue C. F. Ramuz

Chemin du Pont du Diable

du

Denantou

Chemin de Champittet

Chemin de Chamblandes

Igique

Quai d'Ouchy

Parc du
Denantou

Avenue Général Guisan

man

Tour
Haldimand

Montreux, Bern, Fribourg

Vevey, Montreux

———○——— Métro

In the old town (Cité)

★Cathedral

The Cathedral of Notre-Dame (Protestant), consecrated by Pope Gregory X in the presence of King Rudolf of Habsburg in 1275, is an Early Gothic building with five towers (central tower, 75m/246ft high, 1876; a watchman calls out the hours from the bell-cage during the night). The main doorway (16th c.) and the "Apostles' doorway" (13th c.) have very fine sculptured decoration (copies: originals under the rose-window). The restoration work, which has been taking place for years, should be completed by the end of the century.

★Rose-window

The interior is notable for its noble proportions. In the south transept is a large rose-window with beautiful 13th c. stained glass (the Universe); the south aisle has carved choir stalls of 1509; in the choir are remains of early (13th c.) Gothic stalls and (on left) the tomb of the Minnesinger Otto of Grandson (d. 1328); in the crypt are to be found remains of an 8th c. basilica, with old tombs.

Musée Historique de l'Ancien Evêché

On the terrace to the south of the cathedral (beautiful view) is the tower (1373–83) of the old episcopal castle, which now houses the Musée Historique de l'Ancien Evêché (historical and iconographic collection, etc.; closed Mon.) and the Musée Permanent de la Cathédrale.

Ancien Academy

From the cathedral we go north, past the former Academy (1587), the forerunner of the University, where famous professors such as Sainte-Beuve and Adam Mickiewicz gave their lectures. In the Rue de l'Academie (No. 7) the Musée de la Pipe contains over 2500 examples documenting the history of the pipe (closed Sun.). Farther to the north is the Château St-Maire (1397–1431), originally the bishop's palace, residence of the Bernese government from 1536 to 1798, and now occupied by the cantonal government. This cubic building of sandstone and brick has 15th and 16th c. allegorical frescoes.

Musée de la pipe Château St-Maire

Grand-Conseil

To the left, on the west terrace, is the Grand Conseil (the cantonal parliament; 1803–06 by A. Perregaux), with its Classical façade.

East of the Old Town

Mon Repos

On the east side of the town is the beautiful old park of Mon Repos with an 18th c. palace of the same name rebuilt in the 19th c. by L. Damesme.

Cathedral Notre Dame Lausanne

©Baedeker

Porch — Aisle — Choir — Ambulatory

Place de la Cathédrale

1 W doorway (1515–36; statues restored 1892–1909)
2 Chapel of Maccabees, with late Gothic choir-stalls (1509)
3 S tower

4 Pulpit (16th c.)
5 Apostles' doorway (13th c.), with coloured statues (restored 1975–76; some are copies)
6 Central tower
7 Rose-window (c. 1240)

In Lausanne Cathedral . . .

. . . is beautiful stained glass

Cathedral of Notre-Dame

Château St-Maire

Old Presbytery

Palais de Beaulieu

QUARTIER DE LA VIOLETTE

Stables

Av. du Mont - Blanc

Avenue des Bergières

Palais de Beaulieu Lausanne

Convention and Exhibition Centre

The Comptoir Suisse or National Fair is held here annually in September

Pavillon des sports de Beaulieu

Avenue Jomini

© *Baedeker*

Nowadays, the building where Voltaire staged his play "Zaïre", is used for official visits.

Federal court   On higher ground to the north of the park the Federal Court (Tribunal Fédéral; conducted tours) is housed in a building erected in 1922–27.

North of the Old Town

★Signal de Sauvabelin
Fondation de l'Hermitage

Bois de Sauvabelin

Vivarium
Zoo de Servion

Above the town to the north (20 minutes' walk) is the Signal de Sauvabelin (647m/2123ft; restaurant), with a famous view of Lausanne. On the Route de Signal (No. 2) the impressive Fondation de l'Hermitage, situated in beautiful parkland, has art exhibitions. Beyond this is a large wooded park, the Bois de Sauvabelin, with a small lake (restaurant) and a deer park. To the north of the park, on the far side of the motorway along the banks of the Flon, is the Vivarium, with reptiles, insects, birds of prey and small animals (combined admission ticket which covers also the Zoo at Servion, 15km/9 miles north-west).

Palais de Beaulieu

On the north-west side of the town (1km/½ mile) from Place de la Riponne) stands the Palais de Beaulieu (1920; convention facility, restaurant, theatre), with the show and exhibition halls of the Comptoir Suisse, a sports complex and since 1987 the theatre of the "Béjart Ballett Lausanne".

Château de Beaulieu,
★Collection de l'Art Brut

To the south, beyond the Avenue Bergières, the Château de Beaulieu (1756) houses a collection of marginal art ("Art Brut") donated by Jean Dubuffet (closed Mon.).

Ouchy

On the lakeside 1.5km/1 mile south of the town's central district (6 minutes by underground train) lies the busy little port of Ouchy (380m/1250ft).

Ouchy: Yacht harbour

Between the old and the new harbours is a 12th c. castle, the Château d'Ouchy, now a hotel and restaurant, in which the peace treaty between Turkey, Greece and the Allies was signed in 1923.

Château d'Ouchy

There is a statue in the square by Dönninger of General Guisan, the commander of the Swiss army during the Second World War.

Near the Hôtel de l'Angleterre a plaque commemorates Lord Byron, who wrote "The prisoner of Chillon" here (Montreux see entry). Several historical treaties were signed in the famous grand hotels, such as in the Beau-Rivage Palace, where the "Accord de Lausanne" was signed in 1932.

From Port d'Ouchy, the old harbour, a beautiful lakeside promenade affording attractive views runs 1km/½ mile east to the Tour Haldimand and the pretty Parc Denantou. The Elysée Museum in the Avenue de l'Elysée presents the history of photography, from its beginnings to the present day (closed Mon.).

Port d'Ouchy

Musée de l'Elysée

The new Olympic Museum at 1 Quai d'Ouchy (closed Mon.) was opened in 1993. It provides details of the international Olympic movement from the time Pierre de Coubertin originally conceived the idea.

Musée Olympique

Above Ouchy to the north-west is the Parc Montriond (fine views), with the Botanic Garden; of particular interest are the alpinum, the Pharmaceutical garden and the arboretum.

Botanic Garden

Vidy

To the west of the suburb is Vidy, in Gallo-Roman times the port of Losonna. On the shores of the lake are a yacht harbour, a rowing facility, extensive sports grounds and a camping site. A "Promenade Archéologique" is to be found at the beginning of the motorway.

Musée Romain   To the north of the motorway, in the Chemin du Bois-de-Vaux, is the Vidy
                Roman Museum (Gallo-Roman material; closed Mon.).

Pully

Roman villa   To the east of Ouchy the suburb of Pully has modern bathing facilities and
                the remains of a Roman villa (destroyed in the 2nd c. A.D.) can be seen in
                the Place du Prieure (Fri. market). A monastery was later built on its site
                and excavations have uncovered a 20 sq.m/215 sq.ft wall-painting from the
                1st c. A.D.

Musée d'Art   A former dye-works on the lakeside (85 Avenue du Géneral Guisan;
Contemporain   closed Mon.) now houses a display of some 600 works by contemporary
                American, Italian and German artists.

Surroundings

Moudon   25km/16 miles north-east, off the west side of E4 the little industrial town of
                Moudon (513m/1683ft; pop. 3000) occupies the site of the Roman Minno-
                dunum. In the lower town is the beautiful Gothic church of St-Etienne, with
                richly carved choir-stalls of 1502, while in the upper town are attractive old
                houses, the 12th c. Tour de Broye, the little château of Rochefort (1595;
                local museum) and the château of Billens (1677).

Château Oron   20km/12 miles east of Lausanne on the road to Romont, in Oron-le-Châtel
                (above Oron-la-Ville), is the well-preserved Château Oron (13th c.;
                museum).

Lauterbrunnen Valley   K 9

                Canton: Berne (BE)

Situation and   The Lauterbrunnen valley to the south of Interlaken extends from Zweilüt-
general   schinen to the foot of the Breithorn, in the Jungfrau massif. The Trogtal, a
                typical high Alpine valley through which the Weisse Lütschine flows down
                to join the Schwarze Lütschine at Zweilütschinen, is enclosed between
                sheer rock walls over which plunge a number of magnificent waterfalls.
                  From Zweilütschinen the road climbs up the valley with a moderate
                gradient between limestone walls from 300 to 500m/984 to 1641ft high. On
                the right are the Sausbach Falls, and just beyond this, on the left, the
                Hunnenfluh (1334m/4377ft), rearing up like a semicircular tower.

Lauterbrunnen   Beyond this is Lauterbrunnen (800m/2625ft; pop. 1000), a popular summer
                resort and the starting-point of the funicular to the Jungfraujoch (see
                Jungfrau). Above the village are the Staubbach falls, which plunge down
                from an overhanging crag in a sheer drop of 300m/984ft. It was here, over
                200 years ago, that the privy councillor Johann Wolfgang von Goethe
                found the inspiration for "Gesang der Geister über den Wassern" ("Song of
                the Spirits over the Water"), which was later set to music by Schubert.
                  The Lauterbrunnen valley is renowned as a walkers' paradise offering
                beautiful climbs, while helicopter flights to the glaciers provide a bird's eye
                view of the mountains. There are also long-distance ski-runs (17.5km/
                11 miles), tennis courts and two swimming pools. A collection of agricultu-
                ral tools and equipment is on show in the museum.

Isenfluh   A rewarding excursion can be made on a mountain road which runs 3.5km/
                2 miles north to the village of Isenfluh (1084m/3557ft), situated on a steep
                natural terrace affording a superb view of the mountain giants from the
                Grosshorn to the Eiger.

Lauterbrunnen – between the Jungfrau region and the Schilthorn

The road to Stechelberg branches off on the left at the Staubbach Hotel in Lauterbrunnen, bends to the left and runs down to cross the Lütschine; it then continues up the valley of the Breithorn, passing two camping sites and the Staubbach falls (on right).

In 4km/2 miles it comes to the Trümmelbach Falls, which plunge down in five mighty cascades through the gorge carved out by the Trümmelbach (open: mid Apr.–end of Oct.; entrance fee; electric elevator, stepped paths, floodlighting). There are breath-taking views of the falls, ten of which are accessible, thundering down through the mountain at 20,000 litres per second. ★Trümmelbach falls

They are fed by the giant ice walls of the Eiger, Mönch and Jungfrau. Almost hidden inside the Schwarze Mönch they are the only waterfalls in Europe inside a mountain which are accessible.

From the hotel the road continues up the Lauterbrunnen valley. In 2km/ 1 mile a side road goes off on the right to the lower station (867m/2845ft; car park) of the Schilthornbahn, a cableway 6967m/22,859ft long which ascends in 34 minutes, via the intermediate stations of Gimmelwand (1367m/4485ft), Mürren (1638m/5374ft; see entry) and Birg (2677m/8783ft; restaurant with observation terrace), to the Schilthorn (2970m/9745ft; re-volving restaurant, sun terrace; summer skiing), from which there are magnificent views (telescope). ★Schilthorn-bahn

★Schilthorn

The road ends, 1km/about ½ mile beyond the turn-off for the cableway station, at the little village of Stechelberg (922m/3025ft). From here it is a 45–60 minutes' walk to the group of huts at Trachsellauenen (1263m/ 4144ft), and from there another 1¼ hours' walk to the Schmadribach falls or a 1½ hours' walk to the Alp Obersteinberg (1770m/5807ft), which affords a superb panorama of the mountains and glaciers around the upper part of the Lauterbrunnen valley. Stechelberg

★Schmadribach falls

273

Lenzerheide-Valbella   R 8

Canton: Grisons: (GR)
Altitude: 1470 and 1540m/4823 and 5053ft. Population: 2400

Situation

In the park-like and wooded high valley of Lenzerheide (Romansch Pla-nüra), the beauty of which has long attracted visitors, are the two resorts of Lenzerheide and Valbella, on either side of the Heidsee (the "Lei"; 1493m/4899ft; bathing beach), on the road from Chur to the Julier Pass and into the Engadine.

Townscape

To the east of the two resorts, which are popular both in summer and in winter, rear up the Aroser Rothorn (2984m/9791ft), the Lenzerhorn (2911m/9551ft) and the ridges of the Parpaner Rothorn (2824m/9266ft) and Schwarzhorn (2683m/8801ft); on the west, Alpine meadows extend up the slopes of Piz Scalottas (2324m/7625ft) and the Stätzerhorn (2574m/8445ft).

These two resorts have expanded to form one town which is characterised by its Swiss chalet architecture. For the active holidaymaker there is golf, horse riding, tennis, water sports, walking and climbing to choose from as well as winter sports.

Cableways and lifts

Chair-lift from Lenzerheide via Tgantieni (1730m/5676ft) to Piz Scalottas (2324m/7625ft); cableway from Valbella (Canois) via Alp Scharmoin (1900m/6234ft) to Parpaner Rothorn (2865m/9400ft; 15 minutes).

Winter sports

The Val Sporz region saw the advent of "mechanised" skiing with the first sledge-railway as the forerunner of the ski-lift in 1936. Nowadays this extensive area has over 50 prepared ski-lifts as well as numerous elevators below the Parpaner Weisshorn and Schwarzhorn (reached by cableway to Alp Scharmoin) and on the slopes of Piz Scalottas and the Stätzerhorn. The longest slope (8km/5 miles, 1385m/4546ft height difference) is from the Rothorn peak to Lenzerheide-Dorf. Cross-country skiing, tobogganing, skating, curling, horse-drawn sleigh rides. Three ski schools.

Surroundings

★Schin gorge

A by-road runs south-west from Lenzerheide to Zorten and down into the wild Schin gorge on the River Albula.

Lenz

The main road runs south, past the golf course, a camping-site and the Bual nature park, to Lantsch or Lenz (1320m/4331ft), with a church dedicated to the Virgin (1505). 2km/1 mile beyond Lantsch, below the road on the right, we see the farm of Vazerol (1130m/3708ft), where the three Rhaetian leagues agreed to unite in 1471.

Tiefencastel

8km/5 miles farther on is Tiefencastel (see Oberhalbstein/Sursés), a picturesquely situated village (parish church of 1660 with rich interior), at the confluence of the Julia and the Albula and at an important road junction. From here one road leads south over the Julier (Guglia) pass to Silvaplana and another goes east over the Albula pass to La Punt-Chamuesch.

From Valbella the road runs north over the Acl' Alva pass (1549m/5082ft), also known as the Valbella saddle or the Lenzerheide pass, which marks the linguistic boundary between German and Romansch (fine view of the Oberhalbstein Mountains).

The road then reaches Parpan (1511m/4958ft), another health and winter Parpan
sports resort, with a number of fine old houses, including the "Schlössli"
(16th–17th c.) of the Buol family, and a 16th c. church with a separate tower.

4km/2 miles beyond this is Churwalden (1230m/4036ft), a rambling village Churwalden
with a former Premonstratensian abbey (15th c. church, tower-like abbot's
lodging). Chair-lifts to the Alp Stätz (1824m/5985ft) and the Pradaschier
Alp (1817m/5962ft).

Leukerbad/Loèche-les-Bains   J 10

Canton: Valais (VS)
Altitude: 1411m/4629ft. Population: 1500

The well-known spa of Leukerbad (in French Loèche-les-Bains) lies amid Situation
the green Alpine meadows of a south-facing basin situated in a valley on
the north side of the Upper Rhône on the route to the Gemmi pass.
   Leukerbad can be reached by the ordinary motor road from Leuk or by a
romantic little by-road which winds its way up from Sierre via Salgesch.
From the motor road a daringly engineered path with eight rough wooden
ladders up a 100m/328ft rock face leads to the mountain village of Albinen.

Townscape

This high-altitude resort was known to the Romans; in modern times the
earliest reference to the village – then known as Baden – dates from 1315.
The scattered settlement has grown up around its 20 or so thermal springs;
the old wooden houses of the village are on the right bank of the River Dala,
the hotels and spa establishments on the left.
   The water (containing lime and sulphur, 51° C/124° F; temperature of
baths 28–41° C/82–106° F) is efficacious in the treatment of rheumatism,
gout and paralysis; there is an open-air pool with thermal water as well as
several indoor pools; polio clinic. With its cableways and a magnificent
sports centre. Leukerbad is now popular both as a summer and a winter
sports resort.

Surroundings

The Torrentbahn runs from Leukerbad and the Albinen ladders to the
Rinderhütte (2315m/7596ft). From the Hotel Torrenthorn (2462m/8078ft) it
is a 1½ hours' climb to the summit of the Torrenthorn (2998m/9836ft), from ★Torrenthorn
which there is a superb panoramic view taking in twenty 4000m/13,124ft
peaks.

The Gemmiweg, a path hewn from the rock in 1737–40, runs along a rock Gemmiweg
face with a sheer drop of 600m/1969ft, and is to be recommended only to
those with a good head for heights. A cableway (length 1984m/6510ft,
height difference 935m/3068ft, time 5 minutes) runs up to the Gemmi pass
(2316m/7599ft), from which a bridle-path runs along the shores of the
Daubensee and then down to Kandersteg (see entry) in the Bernese
Oberland.

At the mouth of the Dala gorge, above the Rhône, is Leuk Stadt (725m/ **Leuk Stadt**
2379ft; pop. 2800), a little market town and district administrative capital
which was once the summer residence of the Bishop of Sion. Features of
interest include a Late Gothic tower (1541–43) once occupied by a local
government official, the viztum; the bishop's castle (first mentioned in
1254); the late 15th c. parish church of St Stephan (R.C.); and the former
residence of the de Werra family (16th–17th c.).

Leukerbad: thermal baths

The Ringacker Chapel, on a natural terrace south of the town, is one of the finest Baroque buildings in the Valais (1690–94). The interior of this single-naved church is richly decorated in stucco and its monumental altar was completed at the beginning of the 18th c.

★Ringacker Chapel

At the Leuk satellite tracking station there is an exhibition on space communication with slide shows, demonstrations and models.

Satellite station

Principality of Liechtenstein   Q/R 5/6

Prince's arms

National Flag

Car Nationality plate

Arms on car number plates

◀ *The magnificently situated spa town of Leukerbad in the canton of Valais*

Principality of Liechtenstein

Country: Principality of Liechtenstein
Seat of government: Vaduz
Area: 157sq.km/61sq.miles
Altitude: 460–2124m/1509–6970ft
Population: 28,000

Situation

The Principality of Liechtenstein is an independent state in the Alpine region between Switzerland and Austria. It extends from the western slopes of the Rätikon ridge to the Rhine.

General

The most densely populated part of the country and the main agricultural area is the Rhine plain; the hillsides are mainly covered with forest, and in the high valleys Alpine meadows predominate. Its favourable tax laws have made it the headquarters of numerous holding companies. In proportion to its size Liechtenstein is the most highly industrialised nation in the world (metal-processing, chemical and pharmaceutical, textile and food industries), and its per-capita income is also one of the highest in the world. The language of the country is an Alemannic dialect of German.

History

Pre- and early history

The region of present-day Liechtenstein was already settled during the Early Stone Age. In the Roman period a road traversed the region from north to south.

Foundations

The county of Vaduz, established in 1342, was acquired in 1712 by Prince Hans Adam of Liechtenstein and combined with the lordship of Liechtenstein. On January 23rd 1719 Emperor Karl VI finally granted both counties the status of the Imperial Principality of Liechtenstein. In 1806 Liechtenstein was joined to the Rheinbund by Napoleon and subsequently the German Bund. With the dissolution of the German Bund Liechtenstein became an autonomous state. Prince Franz Josef II died in 1989, a week after his wife Gina, in his 51st year of office. He was succeeded by the Crown Prince Hans Adam II, who had already taken over the leadership of the government in 1984.

Associations

From 1852 until after the First World War Liechtenstein was joined with Austria in a currency union, but in 1924 it formed an economic union with Switzerland (using Swiss currency and under Swiss customs and postal administration but with its own stamps). The Principality of Liechtenstein is a member of the European Parliament and (EFTA). In 1993 a popular referendum decided in favour of joining the EU (even though Switzerland decided otherwise).

Constitution

The Principality of Liechtenstein is a constitutional monarchy, inherited through the male line. The Parliament consists of 15 delegates elected for four years by secret ballot. Legislation may be changed by referenda.

Vaduz

General and situation

Vaduz (460m/1510ft; pop. 5000), capital of the Principality of Liechtenstein, seat of its government and parliament and its main tourist attraction, lies near the right bank of the Rhine under the towering summit of Rätikon.

Schloss Vaduz

To the east, above the town, rises Schloss Vaduz (no admittance), which dates back to the 12th c. The cemetery and buildings on the east side form the oldest part; the chapel is probably High Middle Ages. The round bastions to the north-east and south-west were built in the 16th c. after it was burnt down in 1499 by the Confederates. The west side was rebuilt in the 17th c. and between 1901 and 1910 the castle was rebuilt in 16th c. style.

Vaduz

100m

Schloss-Strasse
Im Gässle
Schaan
Rotes Haus
Hinterdorf
Mitteldorf
Altenbach
Herrengasse
Bangarten
Städtle
Rathausplatz
Town Hall
Schloss Vaduz
Gemäldegalerie
Centrum für Kunst
Briefmarkenmuseum
Vaduzer Saal
Landesmuseum
Liechtensteinische Landesbank
Regierungsgebäude
Rheinberger-Haus
Landesbibliothek
Pfarrkirche
Kirchstrasse
Rhein
© Baedeker
Triesen, Malbun
Balzers

SCHWEIZ

Altenrhein
Staad **13**
Bodensee
Margrethen
Fussach
Buriet **202**
Gaissau
Höchst
Rheineck
Thal **463**
Walzenhsn.
St. Margrethen
Lachen
Au
Rheindorf
Schachen
Berneck
Lustenau
Dornbirn
Oberegg **445**
Reute
Heerbrugg
Wiesenrhein
Bäumen
Balgach
St. Anton
Marbach
Rebstein
Widnau
Lüchingen
Diepoldsau
N13
Altstätten
484
Kriessern **445**
Bauern
Allach **1**
Eichberg
Au
Mäder
Götzis
Hard
Montlingen
Koblach
Steinegg *1506*
Kobelwald
Oberriet
Au
Klaus
Fährnsspitz
Moos
Weiler
Hirschensprung
Meiningen
Sulz
Brülisau
Rüthi
Hoher Kasten *1795*
Plonen
Lienz *458* **13**
Bangs
Brederis
Rankweil
29
Sennwald
Glesingen
Notels
Altenstadt
Eugstisriet
FELDKIRCH
Ruggell
Tosters
Rungels
Frümsen
460
Gristen
Schellenbg.
Feldkirch
Sax
Salez
Mauren
Tisis **1B**
Gasenzen
Eschen
Frastanz **1**
Haag
Bendern
Schaanwald **11**
Ammerlügen
Nendeln
452
Gams **13**
Gurtis
16
Gröis
Planken
Gafadura-Alp
Gurtispp. *1781*
Werdenberg
2055
14
BUCHS
Schaan **16**
Drei Schwestern
447
452 **7**
211 *2124*
Gallinakopf *2202*
Gamserrugg
2009 Oberstoffel
Burgerau
Gaflei
Rafis
460
Masescha
Höchst *2038*
1112
Rans
VADUZ
Stachlerkopf *2085*
2025 Buchserberg
Faulfirst *2382*
St. Ulrich **13**
Ochsenkopf *2288*
Sevelen **17**
N13
Steg
1600
Plattis
Triesenberg *884*
Malbun *2005*
Oberschan
Wartau
1867
Sareiserjoch
Malans
Welte
2072
Valinaalp
Azmoos
Rappenstein
Trübbach
Balzers *474*
Lavena
Naafkopf *2574*
Mäls
22
2566
Sargans *482*
Falknis

SCHWEIZ

Alpenrheintal

Principality of Liechtenstein

ÖSTERREICH

© Hallwag

Principality of Liechtenstein

Liechtenstein: Alpine Rhine Triesen . . .   *. . . and Vaduz Castle*

Rathausplatz, Städtle, parish church.	In the middle of the town is the Rathausplatz, with the Rathaus (Town Hall). From here the town's main street, Städtle (one-way traffic in the opposite direction), runs south for some 500m/1641ft to the Neo-Gothic parish church (Pfarrkirche, 1869–73).
Post Museum ★ Liechtenstein Art Collection	On the left-hand side of the street, at No. 37, is the Engländerbau ("English-men's Building"), in which is housed the Postal Museum (open: daily 10am–noon, 1.30–5pm). The first floor is reserved for special exhibitions, while the second floor houses the Prince's Gallery, with "five hundred years of Italian art from the collections of the Princes of Liechtenstein".
Post Office	On the opposite side of the street is the Post Office.
Liechtenstein Landesmuseum	Then follows (No. 43) the Landesmuseum (relief model of the Principality on a scale of 1:10,000; prehistory and the early historical period; weapons; religious art). This museum will probably be closed until the end of the century for renovations.
Government offices	At the south end of the street, on the left, stands the Regierungsgebäude (government offices, 1903–05).
Rotes Haus, Rheinberger-Geburtshaus	Other places of interest are the Rotes Haus (Schloss-Strasse), the Wine Cellar (17th c.) and the Rheinberger-Geburtshaus with the Liechtenstein music school.
Wildschloss ruins	The ruins of the Wildschloss (840m/2756ft) tower over Vaduz and are a popular place to visit.

Other places in Liechtenstein

Triesenberg	The little towns and villages on the hills and in the Upper Samina valley are popular both with summer visitors and winter sports enthusiasts. From Vaduz a hill road winds its way, with steep bends and extensive views, into

the Samina valley (14km/9 miles to Malbun), going either via the beautifully situated village of Triesenberg (884m/2900ft; Walser Museum), 6km/4 miles from Vaduz, or via Rotenboden (1000m/3281ft), also 6km/4 miles from Vaduz, to a road junction at Gnalp (8.5km/5 miles from Vaduz); left to Gaflei, right to Malbun.

1km/½ mile past the above-mentioned junction, on the road to Gaflei, is the old Walser settlement of Masescha (1235m/4053ft; oldest Walser church, 14th c.; inn).

★Masescha

About 2½km/1½ miles beyond Masescha (12km/7 miles from Vaduz) the road comes to the car park of the Gaflei Alpine hotel (1483m/4866ft), situated amid Alpine meadows, with extensive views. From here a footpath (the Fürstensteig or "Prince's Path") leads up in 2¼–2½ hours to the Kuhgrat (2124m/6969ft; magnificent views), the highest peak in the Drei Schwestern (Three Sisters) massif.

Gaflei Alpine Hotel, Kuhgrat, Drei Schwestern

The road to Malbun, to the right, runs under the Kulm pass (1459m/4787ft) in a tunnel 850m/2789ft long to Steg (1312m/4305ft) in the Upper Samina valley, and continues along a side valley to Malbun, 14km/9 miles from Vaduz (1650m/5414ft) Liechenstein's winter sports centre.

Kulm, Steg, Malbun

From here a chair lift 850m/2789ft long ascends to the Sareiser Joch (2014m/6608ft), and Schönberg (2104m/6903ft) can be climbed in 2½ hours.

Sareiser Joch, Schönberg

4km/2 miles south of Vaduz is Triesen (463m/1519ft; pop. 3000), with old houses in the upper part of the village and chapels dedicated to St Mamertus and the Virgin. Walks and climbs on the Lavena, Rappenstein and Falknis hills.

Triesen

5km/3 miles beyond Triesen we reach Balzers (476m/1562ft; pop. 3500), with Gutenberg Castle, the chapels of Mariahilf and St Peter, and an old presbytery. Numerous prehistoric and historic finds have been made around Balzers.

Balzers

3km/2 miles north of Vaduz, at the foot of the Drei Schwestern massif, is Schaan (450–500m/1477–1641ft; pop. 4700), a busy little industrial town with the church of St Peter built on the foundations of a Roman fort. Idyllically situated above the town is the pilgrimage church Maria zum Trost ("Dux"; 18th c.). Various Roman remains have been excavated in the surrounding area of Schaan.

Schaan

From here a good minor road runs north-east to the village of Planken (800m/2625ft; pop. 300), situated on a beautiful natural terrace, with good views of the Rhine valley and the Swiss Alps beyond. The St Joseph chapel dates from 1768. Planken is an excellent base for walks and climbs in the Drei Schwestern area.

Planken

5km/3 miles north-east of Schaan on road 16 is Nendeln. This little town and Eschen, a few kilometres west, are the principal places in the lowland part of Liechtenstein. In both towns remains of the past have been found (in Nendeln the foundations of a Roman villa). The main features of interest are the Pfrundhaus (prebend house), the Holy Cross chapel on the Rotenberg (formerly a place of execution and of assembly) and the chapels of St Sebastian and St Roch in Nendeln. There is also an interesting model pottery here.

Nendeln, Eschen

To the west, on the western slopes of the Eschnerberg, lies the village of Gamprin-Bendern, from which the interesting "Eschnerberg History Trail" (Historischer Höhenweg Eschnerberg) runs to Schellenberg, with the ruined castle of Neu Schellenberg.

Gamprin-Bendern
Schellenberg

At Ruggell (pop. 1300), west of Schellenberg in the Rhine valley, is the Ruggeller Riet nature reserve, with interesting flora and fauna.

Ruggell

Locarno

O 11

Canton: Ticino
Altitude: 205m/673ft. Population: 15,000

Situation and general

The old Ticenese town of Locarno is magnificently situated at the north end of Lake Maggiore, with country villas, gardens and vineyards rising up the hillsides; the newer parts of the town are laid out in a regular pattern on the flat ground of the swiftly flowing River Maggia. With its mild climate, in which figs, olives and pomegranates flourish and in August myrtles blossom, Locarno is particularly popular in spring and autumn.

Boat services

Boat services on Lake Maggiore. Motor ships (in summer also hydrofoils) to the islands and places on the lake (departure from Lungolago G. Motta).

Sights

Piazza Grande

The town's main square is the broad Piazza Grande, which extends westwards from the landing-stage for some 400m/1312ft, with arcades containing shops on its north side. Along the south side are the Giardini Pubblici (Public Gardens) and the Kursaal (gaming rooms, restaurant). In Via della Pace, which runs south through the gardens to a fountain, is the Pretorio (Law Court) or Palazzo della Conferenza, in which the Locarno Pact was signed in 1925.

Public Gardens, Kursaal

The Piazza Grande runs into curving Via Francesco Rusca, from which four narrow streets lead up to the Old Town. Since 1987 the Pinacoteca in the Casa Rusca (17th c.) has housed the Hans Arp Collection and the Giacometi Foundation (closed Mon.). On the west side of Via Rusca is the Castello Visconti, the old castle of the Visconti Dukes of Milan, which was

Castello

Parco della Pace

Locarno   *Mediterranean flora in public gardens*

largely destroyed in 1518; it now houses the Museo Civico (closed Mon.), with Roman material recovered by excavations and a local history collection. To the north-east stands the Casorella (16th c.) with a Baroque portal and impressive stucco reliefs.

To the south-west, on higher ground, is the conventual church of San Francesco, a basilica (1528–72) with massive granite columns and 18th c. wall-paintings, now serving the German-speaking Catholics of the town.

San Francesco

To the north the 17th c. church of Sant'Antonio contains painting with perspective effect by G. A. F. Orelli. West of this are the cemetery and the former church of S. Maria in Selva (only the choir remains; note the important 15th c. wall-paintings showing scenes from the life of Christ) and the tomb of Hans Arp (1887–1966), with sculpture.

Sant'Antonio

Santa Maria In Selva

To the east of Sant'Antonio is the small but fine Baroque church of Santa Maria dell'Assunta, also known as Chiesa Nuova (17th c.). Its façade is dominated by a large statue of St Christopher; the interior contains beautiful stucco work.

Santa Maria dell'Assunta

A beautiful lakeside promenade, the Lungolago Giuseppe Motta, skirts the bay. To the south this leads to the Lido (swimming pool, camping site), the Parco della Pace and the Trade Fair grounds on the Maggia delta. To the east is Rivapiana in the district of Minusio.

★ Lakeside promenade

In the Muralto district to the east of the station stands the parish church of San Vittore, originally Romanesque (12th c.) but much altered in later centuries (campanile, completed only in 1932; fine Romanesque crypt).

Muralto, San Vittore
★ Crypt

Farther north-east is the outer district of Minusio, with the interesting old church of San Quírico. The bell tower (13th/14th c.) is a former watch tower.

Minusio, San Quírico

283

Pilgrimage church of the Madonna del Sasso

Cà di Ferro	On the lakeside is the imposing 16th c. Cà di Ferro, once a barracks occupied by mercenaries in the employ of the Governor Pietro à Pro. In the cemetery (north-east entrance in the wall on the right) is the grave of the German poet Stefan George (1868–1933).
★Madonna del Sasso	The pilgrimage church of the Madonna del Sasso, with a Capuchin friary on a wooded crag above Locarno (355m/1165ft) can be reached by funicular from Via Ramogna, between the station and the Piazza Grande, 825m/2707ft in 6 minutes; on foot, by a path with Stations of the Cross, in 30–45 minutes; or by road from Sant'Antonio via Monti or from Muralto via Orselina, 3.5km/2 miles. The church, founded in 1480, was rebuilt in 1616 and overloaded with decoration in the 19th c. (restored in 20th c.). To the right of the entrance is a major work by Bramantino, the "Flight into Egypt" (1536), and in the second side chapel an "Entombment" by A. Ciseri (*c.* 1865). The notable collection of ecclesiastical art in the monastery museum includes valuable manuscripts. From the terrace there are superb views over Locarno and Lake Maggiore.

On the hillside to the west and east of the Madonna del Sasso, commanding extensive views, are the residential suburbs of Monti (Monti della Trinità, 404m/1326ft and Orselina (456m/1496ft). |

Surroundings

Alpe Cardada	From the Madonna del Sasso a cableway 2km/1 mile long ascends in 10 minutes to the Alpe Cardada (1350m/4429ft; hotel), with magnificent views. Chair-lift (869m/2851ft, 6 minutes) to Cimetta (1676m/5499ft; good skiing with several ski-lifts).
Monte Bré, San Bernardo	From Monti a road (6km/4 miles) runs steeply uphill through the forest, with many bends, to the little mountain village of Mont Bré (1004m/3294ft).

1km/½ mile beyond this along the mountainside is San Bernardo (1096m/
3596ft), with a 16th c. chapel. From both villages there are splendid views.

To Mergoscia

(13km/8 miles: narrow and winding road, but well worth it.)
　　The road runs north-east from the Madonna del Sasso along the hillside,
with far-ranging views, via Orselina and Brione sopra Minusio (433m/
1421ft). 8km/5 miles: Contra (486m/1595ft), high above the mouth of the Val
Verzasca. The road continues, through galleries and over bridges, along
the west side of the valley.

Brione sopra
Minusio
Contra

5km/3 miles: Mergoscia (735m/2412ft), a beautifully situated village with a
view of the Verzasca dam and Pizzo di Vogorno (2446m/8025ft). The church
has 15th c. wall-paintings.

Mergoscia

★From Locarno into the Val Verzasca

The Val Verzasca (30km/19 miles) to Sonogno: reasonably good road, but
many bends; its attraction lies in the beauty of this remote and secluded
Ticinese valley with its Italian-style houses and churches, many of them
with campaniles; good footpaths.

General

Leave on the Bellinzona road. 4km/2 miles: Tenero on the west bank of the
Verzasca. 1km/½ mile: Gordola (208m/683ft, a neat village at the entry of
the Verzasca into the Ticino plain (Piano di Magadino). The road now winds
its way uphill to the left and continues along the left bank of the river high
up on the slopes of the deeply slashed Val Verzasca, an inhospitable valley
which has been considerably changed by the construction of a dam. It has

Gordola

★Val Verzasca

Lavertezzo in the Val Verzasca

Verzasca dam	few inhabitants except in summer. 3km/2 miles farther on is the mighty Verzasca dam, 220m/722ft high, built 1960–65, which has formed the Lago di Vogorno, an artificial lake with a capacity of 105 million cu.m/3708 million cu.ft. Beneath the dam is the hydro-electric power station (235 million kWh annually).
	The road continues up the east side of the lake (6km/4 miles long), passing through several tunnels, some of them on sharp bends. Mergoscia can be seen high up on the other side.
Vogorno	6km/4 miles: Vogorno (490m/16908ft), a picturesque village with 13th c. frescoes of saints in the upper church. 2km/1 mile: road on left (1km/½ mile) to the little village of Corippo (565m/1854ft).
★Lavertezzo	2km/1 mile: Lavertezzo (548m/1798ft), at the mouth of the wide Val Lavertezzo, a charming village with a two-arched bridge and a quarry of excellent granite.
	The road then climbs through the villages of Aquino (574m/1883ft), Motta (623m/2044ft) and Chiosetto (645m/2116ft) and crosses to the other bank of the river.
Brione-Verzasca	8km/5 miles: Brione-Verzasca (760m/2494ft), another picturesque village at the mouth of the Val d'Osola. The church is the finest in the valley, with a 14th c. figure of St Christopher on the outside and beautiful 14th–15th c. wall-paintings in the interior. The little castle with four towers belonged to the noble Marcacci family of Locarno.
Sonogno	The road continues through the straggling village of Gerra (826m/2710ft) and the closely huddled settlement of Frasco (885m/2904ft). 7km/4 miles: Sonogno (920m/3019ft), a beautifully situated mountain village at the end of the post road. The valley forks into the Val Vigornesso (to the right), with a number of other villages, and the Val Redorta (to the left).

★From Locarno into the Maggia Valley

	(45km/28 miles to Fusio: a good road, almost level as far as Bignasco.) Leave on the Centovalli road and in 4km/2 miles, at Ponte Brolla (260m/953ft, turn off to the right into a road which ascends the left bank of the Maggia, in a wide valley enclosed between steep wooded crags. 7.5km/5 miles: church of Santa Maria della Grazie di Campagna, with a wooden ceiling and 16th c. frescoes (key in Ristorante Poncini, Maggia).
★Maggia	0.5km/¼ mile: Maggia (347m/1139ft), among extensive vineyards. In the village are charming old houses with arcades, picturesque courtyards and wooden balconies. Above the village the Baroque Parish church of San Maurizio, the oldest in the valley, has fine stucco work and 17th c. statues inside. It is a short walk to a beautiful waterfall.
Sasso Trolcia	5km/3 miles: Giumaglio. Beyond the village, on the left, is the Sasso Trolcia, a rock wall over which the River Soladino plunges in a waterfall
Cevio	100m/328ft high. 8km/5 miles: Cevio (418m/1371ft), the chief place in the Maggia valley, with a 17th c. governor's house (pretorio), situated at the mouth of the beautiful Valle di Campo. A road runs up this valley to
Bosco-Gurin	Cimalmotto (14km/9 miles) and (in a side valley) Bosco-Gurin (15km/9 miles), the only German-speaking village in Ticino.
Bignasco Val Bavona	3km/2 miles: Bignasco (441m/1447ft), delightfully situated at the mouth of the Val Bavona (characteristic local style of building, beautiful little churches; hydro-electric installations). 11km/7 miles up the valley is San Carlo, with several cableways. Beyond this point the Maggia valley is
Val Broglio Val di Prato	known as the Val Broglio. 8km/5 miles: Prato (750m/2461ft), at the mouth of the Val di Prato, which runs down from Pizzo Campo Tencia. 2km/1 mile: Peccia (839m/2753ft), with a hydro-electric station. From here the road

climbs in sharp bends to the upper part of the Maggia valley, the Val Lavizzara which has interesting flora. 7km/4 miles: Fúsio (1281m/4203ft), picturesquely situated on the mountainside (parish church). Above the village lies an artificial lake Lago Sambuco.

Val Lavizzara, Fúsio

★From Locarno to the Val Centovalli

(19km/12 miles to Ponte Ribellasca.)

Leave Locarno on the Vai Vallemaggia, going north-west through Sol-duno. In 4km/2 miles the road crosses a bridge (33m/108ft high) over a gorge on the tumultuous River Maggia. At Ponte Brolla (260m/853ft), at the mouth of the Valle Maggia (on right), the Centovalli road turns left into the fertile Pedemonte, a level area in a wider part of the Val Centovalli. After passing through the picturesque villages of Tegna (255m/837ft) and Verscio (274m/899ft) it comes in 2.5km/2 miles to Cavigliano (296m/971ft), where a road branches off on the right into the beautiful Val Onsernone with a view to the rear of Lake Maggiore.

Ponte Brolla

Tegna
Vescio
Cavigliano

The road now passes under a railway bridge, over a road bridge (fine view), through a curving tunnel and over the Isorno to enter Intragna (342m/1122ft), a neat village situated among vineyards on a hill between the Isorno and the Melezza. Church of San Gottardo (1738), with a fine tower (1775) 70m/230ft high, the tallest in Ticino. The interior of the church is notable for the decorative galleries of stucco and a fine Rococo reredos. 2km/1 mile beyond the village is a parking place (view).

Intragna

Now begins the increasingly winding stretch of road through the beautiful Val Centovalli ("Valley of a Hundred Valleys"), between steep hillsides covered with chestnut trees and slashed by numerous gullies, with a series of picturesquely situated little villages. 2km/1 mile along the road is another parking place (view). A road goes off on the left, crosses a dam over the river and continues for 1.5km/1 mile to the village of Palagnedra (662m/2173ft) which has vivid 15th c. frescoes in the church of San Michele.

★Centovalli
Valley

Palagnedra

Beyond this there are magnificent views down into the valley, with the river swollen into the form of a lake by the dam and Monte Limidario rearing above it. 9km/6 miles from Intragna is Camedo (552m/1811ft), the last Swiss village (customs). The road then crosses a bridge (with parallel railway bridge) into the village of Ponte Ribellasca (562m/1844ft), on the Italian frontier (Italian customs).

Camedo

Ponte Ribellasca

An interesting alternative is to take the Centovallibahn, which crosses the frontier to Domodóssola.

★Cento-
vallibahn

Lötschental   J/K 10

Canton: Valais (VS)

The Lötschental, surrounded by seventeen 3000m/9843ft peaks in the Bernese and Valais Alps, has preserved much of its traditional character and customs. It now lies just off one of the great traffic routes through the Alps, the Berne–Lötschberg–Simplon railway. The people of the valley have kept their old local costume and their distinctive dialect, which even their compatriots from other parts of Switzerland find difficult to understand. The subject of study by folklorists, historians and naturalists, the Lötschental now mainly appeals to visitors in quest of peace and seclusion.

Situation and
general

From the north the valley is reached by way of Thun and the Kander valley (cars carried by train from Kandersteg to Goppenstein), from the south by way of the Rhône valley and Gampel (641m/2103ft), which lies at the mouth of the Lötschental.

Communica-
tions

From Gampel the road winds its way up through the wild gorge of the Lonza to Goppenstein (1220m/4003ft). The 2.4km/1½ miles Mittal-Tunnel to the car-loading station at Lötschberg is open all year round.

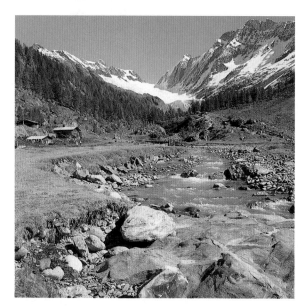

Fafler Alp – base for touring in the high mountains

Winter sports   The Lötschental was made accessible with lifts and cableways at the end of the Seventies. Today there are about 30km/19 miles of prepared descents of varying difficulty and long-distance courses along the Lonza.

Through the Lötschental

The Lötschental proper is 10km/6 miles long, with magnificent scenery.

Ferden   Beyond Ferden (1389m/4557ft) the valley opens out into a wide basin dotted with picturesque villages and hamlets and enclosed by a splendid ring of mountains (to the right the Bietschhorn, 3934m/12,907ft, to the left the Petersgrat, 3205m/10,516ft.

Kippel   Kippel (1376m/4515ft; pop. 430) is the chief place in the valley. In addition to the traditional single-storey houses characteristic of the Lötschental, it has 17th and 18th c. houses of two or more storeys with inscriptions and richly carved decoration. Several of the typical wooden granaries and barns can still be seen. The single-naved parish church of St Martin dates from 1779 with extension work at the beginning of the 20th c. It contains an interesting 18th c. high altar and a Renaissance tabernacle. The adjoining ossuary is of 16th c. origin. Kippel is the scene of colourful traditional processions. Its history is documented in the local museum.

There are attractive walks on the Kummenalp, which can also be reached by cableway.

Wiler   Wiler (1421m/4662ft; pop. 410) is the only place in the valley with a modern aspect, the old church having been burned down. The little church has beautiful stained glass by Richard Seewald.

Cableway to the Lauchernalp (1970m/6464ft), with good skiing and walking.

The last place in the valley is Blatten (1542m/5059ft), lying a little off the road which continues up the valley and past the Baroque Kühmad chapel, to the Fafleralp (1788m/5866ft), a good base for mountain walks and climbs.

Blatten

Fafleralp

Lucerne

L 6

Canton: Lucerne (LU)
Altitude: 436m/1431ft. Population: 65,000

Lucerne (in German Luzern), capital of the canton of the same name, lies at the north end of Lake Lucerne (Vierwaldstätter See – Lake of the Four Forest Cantons) at the point where the River Reuss flows out of the lake. For more than a century the town, with its well-preserved medieval core and elegant historic old buildings, has been one of the great tourist attractions of Switzerland. Famous conductors, soloists and orchestras appear at the annual International Music Festivals.

Situation and general

Lucerne first appears in the records in 840 as Luciaria. The name comes from the Benedictine monastery of St Leodegar, founded about 730. After the opening of the St Gotthard pass in the 13th c. it became an important trading town. In 1291 it fell into the hands of the Habsburgs, but in 1332 joined the Confederation. After the occupation of the whole of Switzerland by Napoleon in 1798 Lucerne was for a brief period capital of the Helvetian Republic.

History

Sights

The town symbol of Lucerne – and after the Matterhorn probably the most photographed feature in Switzerland – is the Kapellbrücke (Chapel Bridge),

★Kapellbrücke

Old Town Hall by the River Reuss

a covered bridge 204m/670ft long across the Reuss (1333). Much of it was destroyed in a serious fire in 1993, since when it has been faithfully restored. The fire also destroyed many of the 111 famous paintings hanging from the roof rafters. Painted in the early 17th c., they depicted local saints and scenes from the town's history. Photographic facsimiles have been hung in their place until the restoration work is complete and copies painted. Near the bridge is the octagonal Water Tower (Wasserturm, 13th c.), once part of the town's fortifications. Research has shown that the tower was used to store plunder during the Burgundian War (1476), as well as being a prison and torture chamber.

Reussbrücke	The nearby Reussbrücke (Reuss Bridge) was built in 1877 on the site of the oldest "Pons Lucernensis" (first mentioned in 1246 and 1253).
Spreuerbrücke	Farther downstream is another covered wooden bridge, the Spreuerbrücke (1406), decorated with scenes from the "Dance of Death" (17th c.).
Historical Museum	The Armoury (1568) now houses the Historical Museum (weapons, flags and uniforms since the late Middle Ages; closed Mon.).
Nature Museum	Nearby, at 6 Kasernenplatz, is the interesting Nature Museum (including ecological exhibit with living animals).
★ Old Town	The Old Town on the right bank of the Reuss, still preserves many old burghers' houses and little squares with fountains. In the Kapellplatz is the
St Peter's Chapel	oldest church in Lucerne, St Peter's Chapel (1178), which received its present form in the 18th c.
Old Town Hall	In the Kornmarkt is the Old Town Hall (Altes Rathaus, 1602–06), in Italian Renaissance style but with a very typical Swiss hipped roof. Unfortunately, the magnificent wood-panelled council chambers are not open to the public. The adjoining tower dates from the 14th c. and is by P. A. Isenmann.

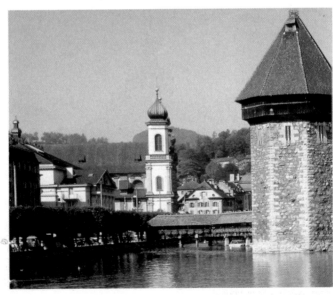

Lucerne:

Immediately east of the Old Town Hall (entrance in Furrengasse) stands the Am Rhyn-Haus (17th–18th c.) which houses a collection of important works by Picasso (Rosengart Donation: closed Mondays).

Am Rhyn-Haus
Picasso
Museum

To the west of the Kornmarkt is the picturesque Weinmarkt; the Late Gothic fountain (1481) by K. Lux is a copy (original in the courtyard of the Regierungsgebäude).

Weinmarkt

Along the north side of the old town runs the Museggmauer, a wall built between 1350 and 1408, with nine towers built in differing styles.

Museggmauer

Along the north shore of the lake, to the east of Schwanenplatz, extends a series of broad tree-lined quays lined with shops and hotels – Schweizerhofquai, Nationalquai and Spittelerquai – from where there is a magnificent panorama of the Alps. To the left is the Rigi group, in the middle the Bürgenstock, to the right the Stanserhorn and Pilatus, and beyond, in the distance, the Glarus and Engelberg Alps. In Nationalquai are the Kurplatz and the Kursaal (restaurant, gaming rooms).

North shore of
the lake

Kursaal

Above the Nationalquai, on the site of the old monastery of St Leodegar, is the twin-towered Hofkirche (R.C.), which was rebuilt in 1634–39 but preserved the towers (1525) of the previous church. On the north tower a Late Gothic sculpture depicts the Agony in the Garden. The church has a carved pulpit and choir-stalls of 1639 and a famous organ (recitals in summer). The treasury (visits by arrangement) contains a valuable Romanesque book-cover, a goblet and other treasures. In the picturesque arcades which surround the church are the tombs of members of old Lucerne families.

Hofkirche

From the Kurplatz Löwenstrasse leads north to the Löwenplatz, to the right of which is the Panorama, a large circular painting (11,000sq.m/ 118,360sq.ft) by the Geneva battle painter Castres, with the collaboration of

Löwenplatz

Kapellbrücke (chapel bridge)

Hodler and other Swiss painters (1877–79). The painting depicts in highly realistic fashion the retreat of the French Eastern Army into Switzerland in 1871.

★ Lion
monument

A little way north, to the rear of the pool is the famous Lion Monument (Löwendenkmal), a huge figure of a dying lion hewn from the face of the living rock. The monument (1820–21), designed by Thorwaldsen, commemorates the heroic death of the Swiss Guards (26 officers and over 700 troops) who were killed during the attack on the Tuileries during the French Revolution (1792).

★ Glacier
Garden

Above the Lion Monument is the Glacier Garden (Gletschergarten), a remarkable relic of the Ice Age which was exposed between 1872 and 1875 (open March–October): glacier-polished rock, erratic boulders and 32 potholes, some of them of huge size, with a working model showing the process of formation of a pot-hole. Higher up are an early climbers' hut and a lookout tower. In the museum are relief maps of Switzerland, groups of Alpine animals, specimens of rock and old domestic interiors.

Rotsee

On the outskirts of the town, 1km/½ mile farther north, is an elongated lake, the Rotsee, on which a well-known regatta is held every year.

Seebrücke

Railway station

On the south bank of the Reuss, extending east to the lake and linked with the Schwanenplatz by the busy Seebrücke (Lake Bridge; 1935–36), is the Bahnhofplatz; here are the new railway station (1991) and the docks used by the various boat services. In the gardens stands the Wagenbach fountain (1934).

The Baroque Jesuit church   *Spreuerbrücke*

At the east end of the square, adjoining the station, is the Kunst- und Kongresshaus (1932–33), which contains conference and concert halls and the Museum of Art (Kunstmuseum; closed Mon. in winter), with a fine collection of Swiss painters of the 16th–20th c., 20th c. European painters and the Rieder Collection (also special exhibitions). By the year 2000 a new congress centre and concert hall, designed by the Parisian architect Jean Nouvel, will be built here in four stages. The whole building will comprise four sections – a west wing with a Museum of Art, congress centre and restaurant, etc., a middle section (Municipal Hall and Museum of Art), an east wing with a concert hall and, finally, the south or service wing with a light, wing-shaped high roof.

Kunst- und Kongresshaus

In the part of the old town that extends west from the station along the left bank of the Reuss are the Municipal Theatre and the Jesuit church, a Baroque building (1666–77) with an elegant Rococo interior (1750).

Jesuit church

The Regierungsgebäude (Government Building) adjoining the church was formerly a Jesuit college, the core of which is the Ritter palace, a Renaissance mansion (1557–64 built by Lukas Ritter, a local dignitary who had grown rich in foreign service. In the handsome arcaded courtyard can be seen the original of the Weinmarkt fountain (1481). To the rear of the building is the Neo-Classical Chamber of the Great Council (1841–43). Close by are the Cantonal Archives.

Regierungsge-bäude
Ritter Palace

South-west of the Regierungsgebäude stands the Franciscan church (13th–17th c.; completely restored 1988–1989), the nave walls of which have paintings of flags and banners (carved pulpit 1628, choir stalls 1647–51). In front of the church (also known as the Barfüsserkirche or Church of the Barefoot Friars) is the Spitalbrunnen, a copy of the original of 1651.

Franciscan church

South-west of the station, at 10 Sempacherstrasse, the Central Library (Zentralbibliothek) contains over 400,000 volumes and pamphlets, 2500 manuscripts and over 800 incunabula.

Central Library

293

Thorwaldsen's Lion Monument

Swiss Transport Museum

★ Dietschiberg

On the north side of the lake, just off Haldenstrasse, is situated the lower station of the (now unused) funicular to the Dietschiberg (632m/2014ft). There is a fine view of the town and the lake from the top. Near the upper station there are a golf-course and a miniature railway (scale 1:10). Below, to the south-west, is a park with the interesting Utenberg Costume and Folk Museum/Harmonica Museum (Schweizer Trachten- und Heimat-museum Utenberg).

Utenberg Costume and Folk Museum

★★ Swiss Transport Museum
Open:
Daily 10am–4pm

Beyond the funicular station Haldenstrasse continues to the fascinating Verkehrshaus der Schweiz (Swiss Transport Museum, Schweizerisches Verkehrsmuseum; entrance in Lidostrasse). The museum is a large complex of exhibition halls and outdoor exhibits covering all forms of transport, including air and space travel (cosmorama), communications and tourism, with railway locomotives and rolling-stock, ships, aircraft rockets and automobiles (originals or models), together with a Planetarium. By means of 150 projectors the sky can be seen through a 18m/59ft-wide dome.

The tourism department, opened in 1984, contains the largest pin-ball machine in the world and is an entry in the Guinness Book of Records.

At the east end of the complex is the Hans-Erni-Haus which contains paintings and graphic art by the well-known Lucerne artist of that name, and also a lecture hall with an impressive mural.

Gütsch

To the west of the town, on the edge of the extensive Gütschwald, is the Gütsch, another hill which affords extensive views. It is reached by funicular from Baselstrasse or on foot by way of the Gütschweg (1.5km/1 mile).

Surroundings

Emmen

A 16th c. gallows was excavated in the suburb of Emmen in 1988–89. This was the first to be found in Switzerland and had been in use until the 18th c.

Swiss Transport Museum

Convair CV 990 'Coronado'

Picknick-Platz

Douglas DC 3

DS 'Rigi' (Restaurant)

© Baedeker

Lidostrasse   Lidostrasse   Lidostrasse

Swiss Transport Museum Lucerne
Schweizerisches Verkehrmuseum Luzern
Musée Suisse des Transports Lucerne
Museo Svizzero dei Trasporti Lucerne
Museum Svizzer da Traffic Luzern

1 Entrance, kiosk, transport archives
2 Model of St Gotthard Railway
3 Locomotive cab simulation
4 RAIL TRAFFIC HALL
  Normal and narrow gauge original rolling stock of
  Swiss railway companies of various dates on more
  than 1 km of track;
  Steam locomotives and historically interesting
  electrically driven vehicles;
  Wagons, railway equipment
5 SBB dining car of 1914 (restaurant)
6 Workshops
7 ROAD TRANSPORT HALL

Ground Floor:	Swiss cars, milestones of motoring history
First Floor:	Chassis and engines, fuel, accident prevention
Second Floor:	Coaches, history of land transport, bicycles, motorisation in the post-war period

8 Connecting halls
9 Lecture hall
10 POSTAL SERVICES HALL

Ground Floor:	Postal sorting centre, airmail, travel post, film show, original postal coach
First Floor;	postage stamps

11 TELECOMMUNICATIONS HALL

Ground Floor:	International telephone network, Marconi radio transmitter, transmission of sound and pictures, TV studio
First Floor:	Amateur radio station, telephone service

12 Administration
13 Restaurant

14 "Longines" PLANETARIUM (Commentary through
   headphones in English, French, German and
   Italian)
15 Cosmorama (see No. 16, second floor)
16 HALL OF AIR AND SPACE TRAVEL

Ground	History of aviation
Floor:	"Lighter than air" flying, Swissair, airports
	Aircraft: Fokker VIIa, P 51 "Mustang"
	Heliswiss and rescue service
	Military aviation, Swiss aircraft industry
First	Flight safety, control tower
Floor:	Swiss Aero-Club, flight meteorology, Basis of flying
	Aircraft: Bücker "Jungmeister", Lockheed "Orion", Fieseler "Storch", Blériot, Dufaux
Second	Gliders WF 7 and S 21, Piper seaplane,
Floor:	helicopters Bell 47G, Alouette III, Messerschmitt aircraft Me 108B
	COSMORAMA Mercury and Gemini space capsules, moonsuit, lunar rocks; multi-media show (on 18 canvas screens) on the history of space travel

17 SHIPPING Shipping on the Swiss lakes and rivers,
   models of historic and modern craft, dioramas
18 CABLE RAILWAYS Original cabins, including one
   from the Wetterhorn lift (first aerial cableway in
   Switzerland), scenes and models of various
   systems
19 TOURISM Swiss National Tourist Office
   Working models and equipment illustrating Swiss
   tourism
20 SWISSORAMA Multivision show about Switzerland
   (360° circular projection; 20 minutes)
21 HANS-ERNI MUSEUM About 300 works of the
   Lucerne artist Hans-Erni (b. 1909; in the auditorium
   can be seen his wall painting "panta rhei"
   (= "everything flows"; 18×2 m), with personalities
   who have left their mark on western philosophy.
   "Hans Erni" video show (45 minutes).

Lucerne

Tribschen

On a hill south-east of the town, on the west side of the lake (also accessible by motor-boat), stands Tribschen, a country house in which Wagner lived from 1866 to 1872 and composed the "Mastersingers" and other works. The house is now a museum, with original scores, pictures, prints and a collection of old musical instruments (closed Mon.).

Kriens

Sonnenberg

South-west of Lucerne is the industrial suburb of Kriens (482m/1582ft), with the little castle of Schauensee (1595, with a 13th c. round tower). From here there is a funicular up the Sonnenberg (780m/2559ft), which affords superb views. Here too is the lower station of a cableway up Mt Pilatus.

★Maria Loreto
pilgrimage
chapel

5km/3 miles south-west of Kriens at Hergiswald there is the beautiful 17th c. pilgrimage chapel of Maria Loreto (flight of 1000 steps; timber ceiling with more than 300 symbolic images of the Virgin by K. Meglinger, 1654).

The road continues to the mountain resort of Schwarzenberg (831m/2727ft).

★Ascent of Mt Pilatus

A popular round trip going up by the cableway and down by the cog-railway.

Alpnachstad

Cableway from Kriens (4968m/16,300ft; 30 minutes) to the Fräkmüntegg (1415m/4643ft; skiing), and from there another cableway (1400m/4593ft; 7 minutes) to the Pilatus-Kulm (2070m/6792ft). Visitors can also travel by rail, boat or road (16km/10 miles on the road to the Brünig pass) to Alpnachstad (440m/1444ft). From there travel on the cog-railway (4.6km/3 miles; 30 minutes, gradients up to 48% (1 in 2)), which runs up through Alpine meadows (orchards) and forests to the passing station at Ämsigen (1350m/4429ft) and then continues over the rock-strewn Mattalp and up the steep rock face, through four tunnels, to the upper station on Pilatus-Kulm (2070m/6792ft).

★Pilatus

From here it is a 6–10 minutes' climb to the summit (surrounded by a wall) of the Esel (2122m/6964ft), the central but not the highest peak of Pilatus, from which there are magnificent views of the Alps, from Säntis to the Blümlisalp, Lakes Lucerne and Zug, and the Swiss uplands. The name of the mountain probably comes from the Latin pileatus, "covered (with clouds)", although legend ascribes it to Pontius Pilate, said to have been buried in a former lake on the Upper Bründlenalp. Until the 17th c. Pilatus was known as Frakmunt (from fractus mons).

Tomlishorn

From the Pilatus-Kulm it is a 30 minutes' walk to the Tomlishorn (2132m/6995ft), the highest point in this rugged limestone massif.

Wolhusen,
Werthenstein
convent

To the west of Lucerne, in the valley of the Kleine Emme, is the industrial town of Wolhusen (568m/1864ft; pop. 3500). On a hill near the town is situated the convent of Werthenstein, which boasts a beautiful pilgrimage church (1608–16) and a fine cloister.

Willisau

From here road 2 runs north-west to the old-world little town of Willisau (557m/1828ft; pop. 2900) with well-preserved town walls and an upper tower dating from 1551. Nearby the 17th c. pilgrimage chapel of Heiligblut has a fine wooden ceiling with biblical decoration. The tower of the former governor's castle (17th c.) is part of the walls, built about 1400.

To the Sempach, Baldegg and Hallwil lakes

Sempacher See

Sempach

North-west of Lucerne lie three beautiful lakes. Road 2 leads to the south end of the attractive Sempacher See (507m/1663ft), on the east side of which is the pretty little town of Sempach (520m/1706ft; pop. 1500), with a fine half-timbered town hall (1737; old coat-of-arms in council chamber).

Sursee: St Martin's Church . . .   *. . . and Late-Gothic Town Hall*

On the Kirchbühl north of the town stands St Martin's church (first recorded in 1349). By this lake, to the south of the town, the Swiss Bird-Watching Station (Schweizerische Vogelwarte), houses an ornithological museum.

2km/1 mile north, above the town on the road to Hildisrieden, is the Schlachtkapelle (Battle Chapel), built in 1473 to commemorate the Confederates' victory over Duke Leopold III of Austria on July 9th 1386, a victory traditionally attributed to the self-sacrifice of Arnold von Winkelried.

Schlachtkapelle

At the north end of the lake, from which the river Suhre flows north, is the tranquil little country town of Sursee (507m/1663ft; pop. 5000) which has a Baroque parish church (1641), a late Gothic town hall (1546) and 18th c. burghers' houses. Neat rows of houses and two towers surround the moated Mühlplatz (mill square). There is an interesting Museum of the Swiss Capuchin Province in the Capuchin monastery; visits by arrangement; tel. (045) 21 31 30. The old Roman road along the lake heading south is of interest to walkers.

Sursee

From here road 25 runs north-east to Bermünster (642m/2106ft; pop. 1700), with St Michael's church, which belonged to a monastic house founded by Count Bero of Lenzburg about 980. The church, originally Romanesque, was rebuilt in 1606 and remodelled in Baroque style in 1775; fine choir-stalls of 1609, rich treasury. Castle (local museum), in which the first book printed in Switzerland was produced in 1470.

Bermünster

To the east of Beromünster is the Seetal (Lake Valley) in which lie the Baldegger See and Hallwiler See. Hochdorf, at the south end of the Baldegger See, has a fine church of 1768. On a hill 3km/2 miles east stands a former commandery of the Knights of St John, Hohenrain (614m/2015ft), now a special school. Continue up the east side of the lake on road 26. On the Lindenberg, to the right of the road, is Schloss Horben (1701), from which there is a beautiful view of the Alps.

Baldegger See, Hochdorf

Schloss Horben

Lugano

Gelfingen, Schloss Heidegg	At Gelfingen is Schloss Heidegg which has a massive 12th c. tower house, with a hall decorated by Ticinese artists.
Hitzkirch	From Gelfingen a road goes off on the right to Hitzkirch (473m/1552ft), with a former commandery of the Teutonic Order (main building 1749, church 1680), which now houses a teachers' training college and a lake-dwelling museum.
Hallwiler See, Beinwil	Road 26 continues to the south end of the Hallwiler See. Beinwil (522m/1713ft), on the west side of the Hallwiler See, lies at the foot of the Homberg (792m/2599ft; inn), which commands extensive views.
Schloss Hallwil	1km/½ mile north-east of Boniswil on the north bank of the lake stands Schloss Hallwil (9th–16th c. Museum; local collection). Countess Wilhelmine von Hallwyl had the moated castle restored at the beginning of the 20th c. with important items going to the Landesmuseum in Zürich, where they are now on display.
Schloss Brestenberg	The road back to Lucerne along the east side of the lake passes Schloss Brestenberg (462m/1516ft), a country house with a park built in 1625, which is undergoing redevelopment as a hotel, restaurant and museum.
	From Gelfingen road 26 returns to Lucerne.

Lugano   O 12

Canton: Ticino (TI)
Altitude: 272m/892ft
Population: 29,000 (Greater Lugano 50,000)

★★ Situation and townscape	Lugano, the "pearl of Lake Lugano", lies in a bay half-way down the lake, flanked by Monte San Salvatore (912m/2993ft) and Monte Brè (925m/3036ft). It is the largest and most important town in Ticino, and the beauty of the town and its setting makes it one of Switzerland's most popular holiday resorts during the warmer months of the year. The architecture and way of life of Lugano show distinctly southern characteristics, as does the plant life. After Zurich and Geneva, Lugano has become Switzerland's third largest financial centre.
Climate	Lugano has a notably temperate climate. The summers are pleasantly warm with occasional welcome showers of rain, while the winters are mild and dry.
Transport	Cars are best parked in the multi-storey parks in the middle of town (signs). Trolley service between Paradiso and Castagnola, from Pregassona to Breganzona, from the centre to Vezia, from the station to Viganello and Cornaredo. Local boat services to several destinations. Funicular (1½ minutes) from the station to the old town (Piazza Cioccaro). Bus from Lugano to Brè-Dorf. The town and surrounding area lie directly on the important north–south traffic route, both road and rail, over the St Gotthard. Alternatively, it can be reached by way of the St Bernardino road on the south side of the Alps. Flights from Lugano–Agno airport to Zürich, Geneva, Basle, Berne, Paris, Nice, Venice and Florence.
History	Along the shores of Lake Lugano traces of the Etruscans and the Gauls have been found, together with remains of the Roman, Lombard and Frankish periods. During the Middle Ages the town was under the jurisdiction of the Bishop of Como and thus became involved in the conflicts between Milan and Como. After the conquest of Ticino by the Confederates Lugano was from 1512 to 1798 the seat of the district governor. The opening of the St

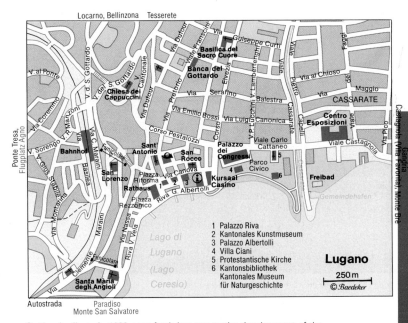

Locarno, Bellinzona   Tesserete

1 Palazzo Riva
2 Kantonales Kunstmuseum
3 Palazzo Albertolli
4 Villa Ciani
5 Protestantische Kirche
6 Kantonsbibliothek
  Kantonales Museum
  für Naturgeschichte

Lugano
250 m
© Baedeker

Autostrada   Paradiso
Monte San Salvatore

Gotthard railway in 1882 gave fresh impetus to the development of the
town, particularly as a tourist and holiday resort.

Sights

The pulsating activity of Lugano revolves around three squares surrounding the Town Hall (Municipio, Palazzo Civico, Town Hall, 1844–45 by G.
Moraglia from Milan). To the north is the Piazza della Riforma, with the
former Pretorio (Law Court; 15th–18th c.), now occupied by the Cantonal
Bank, and a number of cafés. By the lake is the Piazza Riziero Rezzonico and
the Piazza Manzioni (gardens), and in front of the 18th c. Palazzo Riva is the
Debarcadero (dock). The long lakeside promenade from Cassarate to Paradiso has sub-tropical gardens with modern sculptures by G. Genucchi, O.
Zadkine and P. Selmoni.

Municipio

The Old Town of Lugano contains a number of historic buildings.

★Old Town

Outstanding among the churches is the Cathedral of St Lawrence (San
Lorenzo). Originally Romanesque, it was enlarged in the 13th–14th c. and
underwent extensive alteration in the 17th and 18th c. It has an imposing
Renaissance façade, rich fresco decoration and a Baroque interior.

St Lawrence
Cathedral

North-east of the Piazza della Riforma in the Via Canova the Museo cantonale d'arte in the Palazzo Reali has modern art exhibitions. The adjoining
handsome Palazzo Albertolli was built in the 19th c.; in the Piazza Maghetti
is the 16th c. church of St Roch (San Rocco) with its 20th c. façade and the
new Centro Maghetti. Still further east we come to the Piazza Indipen-
denza, on the south side of which is the Kursaal.

Museo
cantonale d'arte

Centro Maghetti

299

Villa Ciani: Ticino art from the Baroque to the present

★ Parco Civico
Congress centre
Villa Ciani

The extensive and beautiful Parco Civico (Municipal Park) with old trees and sub-tropical plants is the site of the Palazzo dei Congressi (convention facility; 1965–75 by Rolf Otto) and the Villa Ciani. The Palazzo houses the Museo delle Belle Arti (Ticinese art from Baroque to present day, European masters, special exhibitions; closed Mon.).

From the Piazza della Riforma the Via Pretoria runs north into Viale Stefano Franscini. On the left-hand side stands the Villa Saroli and new building (Banca del Gottardo) by Mario Botta.

Santa Maria
degli Angioli

The conventual church of Santa Maria degli Angioli (1499–1515) on south side of town contains a fine fresco of the Passion by Luini (1529).

Madonna di
Loreto

The nearby pilgrimage church of the Madonna di Loreto (1524) has 17th c. frescoes.

Castagnola
Villa Favorita

Following the renovation of the gallery extension, the Villa Favorita, situated in the east of the town in a beautiful park, has been re-opened. Until 1992 the former Palazzo di Beroldingen (17th c.) housed the world-famous private collection of Baron Thyssen-Bornemisza. After the most valuable and important part of the collection had been ceded to Madrid and Barcelona some 130 pictures now remain exhibited in 13 rooms, under the title "Europe and America". In addition to examples of American painting between 1835 and 1900, 20th c. work is also shown (open: Fri.–Sun. 10am–5pm); the villa has no public car park, so visitors are asked to use other forms of transport, e.g., bus No. 1.

Surroundings

The town's two hills, Monte San Salvatore and Monte Brè, offer attractive day and half-day trips.

View of San Salvatore from Municipal Park

Monte San Salvatore (912m/2992ft). From Paradiso, on the lake, a cable-way 1658m/5440ft long, with gradients of 38–60% (1 in 2½–1 in 1½), as-cends in 10 minutes to the upper station at 884m/2900ft (restaurant and viewing terrace). From the summit there are magnificent panoramic views of the town and the lake, the Bernese and Valais Alps (Monte Rosa) and the north Italian plain. Footpaths to Carona, Melide, Morcote and Figino; return by rail, postal bus or boat.

★★ Monte San Salvatore

Monte Brè (933m/3061ft). From Cassarate, to the east of the little stream of the same name, a cableway 1621m/5319ft long, with gradients of 47–60% (1 in 2–1 in 1½) arrives in 15–25 minutes at the upper station (restaurant), from where there are fine views extending to the Valais Alps. This favourite viewpoint can also be reached by car on a narrow and winding road (11km/7 miles) from Lugano, via Castagnola, Ruvigliana and Aldesago).

★★ Monte Brè

There are also a variety of possible excursions further afield. From March 1st to October 31st a reasonably priced holiday ticket covering travel on all train, boat and postal bus services for a period of 7 days can be obtained from travel agencies and tourist information offices.
  For trips on the lake, see under Lake Lugano, below.

Holiday saver ticket

From Lugano into the Malcantone

An attractive drive through this area between Lugano and the Italian fron-tier, of about 50km/31 miles, with Agno (8km/5 miles west of Lugano) as its starting-point, might take in the health resort of Cademario (795m/2608ft), Breno (802m/2631ft; base for the ascent of Poncione di Breno, 1658m/5440ft, 3 hours) and Miglieglia (751m/2464ft), from which a chair-lift (2673m/8770ft, 18 minutes) goes up Monte Lema (1624m/5328ft; upper station 1550m/5086ft; inn, superb views). Also worth seeing are the vil-lages of Novaggio (644m/2113ft), Banco (585m/1919ft) and Astano (633m/

Agno
Cademario
Breno

★ Monte Lema

2077ft; surrounded by chestnut forests) as well as Caslano on Lake Lugano, from which the return road runs north-east to Agno.

South-west of Agno on the Swiss-Italian border lies Ponte Tresa.

From Lugano to Tesserete

Tesserete

An excursion (20km/12 miles) into the densely populated valley of the Cassarate, running through romantic villages including Vezia, Cureglia and Tesserete (532m/1745ft), chief place in the hilly Capriasca district; then into the Val Colla, returning from Bogno (963m/3160ft via Sonvico, Dino and Cadro.

From Lugano to Gandria

★Gandria

(5km/3 miles) via Cassarate and Castagnola to the Gandriastrasse (Gandria road), which runs south to Porlezza and Lake Como (Italy). The last part of the trip must be done on foot, to the picturesque village of Gandria (300m/984ft; pop. 196), a typical Ticinese settlement clinging picturesquely to a steep slope rising from the lake (narrow lanes, arcades, Baroque church) and surrounded by terraced vineyards.

Customs
museum

On the other side of the lake (boat service), to the south is the Cantine di Gandria dock, with an interesting Customs museum, situated near the Italian frontier (containers for smuggled goods, weapons). To the south-east is the Italian village of Santa Margherita, from which there is a funicular to the Belvedere di Lanzo (887m/2910ft; good views).

Lake Lugano   O/P 12/13

Within Switzerland and Italy
Canton: Ticino (TI)

Situation and
general

Lake Lugano (in Italian Lago di Lugano or Ceresio), on the southern edge of the Alps, lies mainly within the Swiss canton of Ticino, the remainder being in the Italian province of Varese and Como. Lying at an altitude of 270m/886ft, it has an area of 48.7sq.km/19sq.miles, with a maximum depth of 288m/945ft. From the west end of the lake the River Tresa flows into Lake Maggiore. The climate already shows distinct Mediterranean characteristics.

Boat services

Very pleasant round trips on the lake are run by the motor-ships of the Lake Lugano Shipping Company (SNL; head office in Lugano, information in harbour).

Towns on ★★ Lake Lugano

★★Lugano

The principal town on Lake Lugano is Lugano (see entry), on the north shore of the lake.

Melide

From there a road runs south alongside the lake to Melide (277m/909ft), situated on a peninsula from which a causeway crosses the lake.

★ Switzerland in
miniature

A feature of interest here is "Switzerland in Miniature", which reproduces many of Switzerland's principal tourist attractions (towns, castles, monuments, transport) on a 1:25 scale.

View of Lugano from Monte Brè

Melide: "Switzerland in miniature"

Lake Lugano

Lake Lugano

Campione d'Italia	Across the causeway, to the north, is the Italian enclave of Campione d'Italia, with the 14th c. church of the Madonna dei Ghirli and a gaming casino.
★ Morcote	South of Melide, on the southern slopes of Monte Arbostora (839m/2753ft), a promontory projecting into the lake, is the old-world little town of Morcote (277m/909ft; pop. 650), one of the most picturesque places in Switzerland and a great tourist attraction, with its beautiful setting and its well-preserved old houses and streets. In a commanding situation above the village stands the pilgrimage church of the Madonna del Sasso (originally 13th c., rebuilt 1462, remodelled in Baroque style 1758), with a separate campanile; it contains fine 16th c. frescoes and a valuable organ. From the church a flight of 408 steps goes down to the village on the shores of the lake. The chapel of San Antonio di Padova (1676) is also of interest. In the cemetery are the graves of Moissi, Eugen d'Albert and the dramatist Georg Kaiser. There is a beautifully laid out park, the Parco Scherrer, designed in the 1930s by Arthur Scherrer.
	Facing Morcote across the lake is Brusino-Arsizio, which can be reached from Melide by way of Melano and Capolago.
Bissone	From Melide we cross the causeway and go south along the far side of the lake to Bissone (274m/899ft; pop. 720), which dates back to Roman times. It has well-kept patricians' houses with impressive arcades and façades. The Tencalla museum contains ancient exhibits with an exhibition of painting and sculpture by local artists.
Melano	Melano (296m/971ft; pop. 875) at the foot of Monte Generoso, has patricians' houses including the Haus Fogliardi with fine Baroque decoration.

At the south end of the lake is Capolago (277m/909ft), from which a rack-railway (cog-railway) serves Monte Generoso (1704m/5591ft; hotel-restaurant), with superb views of the Alps and the Lombard plain, including Milan.

Capolago
★★ Monte Generoso

1km/½ mile west of Capolago in the village of Rlva San Vitale there is an octagonal baptistery (5th c.) and the church of Santa Croce (16th c.), one of the finest Renaissance churches in Switzerland.

Riva San Vitale
★ Baptistery,
★ Santa Croce

Beyond this is Brusino-Arsizio (277m/909ft; pop. 380), which lies within the administrative district of Lugano, but from the tourist point of view belongs to the fertile and densely populated Mendrisiotto area. This picturesque village lies at the foot of Monte San Giorgio.

Brusino-Arsizio

A cableway runs to Serpiano (645m/2116ft; extensive views), reached by cableway or by road from Mendrisio.

Serpiano

Through the Mendrisiotto to Chiasso

The administrative district of Mendrisiotto (pop. 47,590), with a total area of 133.61sq.km/51½sq.miles, lies at the southernmost tip of Switzerland (most southerly point in Chiasso-Pedrinate). The most easterly finger of Lake Lugano drives a wedge through this area which is in contrast to the more mountainous surroundings.

★ Mendrisiotto

To the south of Brusino-Arsizio, surrounded by fertile fields and vineyards, lies the village of Meride (583m/1913ft; pop. 270), now a protected area. There are interesting 18th c. houses, such as the Haus der Oldelli with magnificent arcades and colonnades, and a local museum.

Meride

The chief town of the region Mendrisio (354m/1162ft; pop. 6900) has been an important political centre since the Middle Ages. Neolithic and Roman remains provide evidence of an earlier settlement. Its picturesque territory extends as far as Bellavista on Monte Generoso. Interesting sights include the church of SS Cosma and Damiano (1875), Palast der Edelleute Rusca (mansion; former 15th c. courthouse), the Torrianische Palast (15th–16th c.) and the recently renovated Palast Pollini (1715). A former monastery houses an art museum where exhibitions, concerts and other cultural events are held.

Mendrisio

Not far to the west at Rancate (359m/1178ft; pop. 1200) are the Grosse Palast (Great Palace) and the Cantonal art collection, housed in a former church hall, which consists of around 200 paintings by Ticinese artists.

Rancate

Just before the Italian border we come to Bezasio (501m/1644ft; pop. 410), known for its "brocatello" red marble.

Bezasio

Ligornetto (364m/1194ft; pop. 1300) lies at the junction of the roads to Stabio and Genestrerio. The Vela artists such as the sculptors Vincenzo and Apollonio Pessina are supposed to come from here. Exhibits relating to the family are on display in the Vela Museum.

Ligornetto,
Vela Museum

Stabio (375m/1230ft; pop. 2800) dates back to Pre-Roman times with evidence of Etruscan, Roman and Langobard settlements having been found. It was the chief town in the region under the Romans and contains interesting burghers' houses and a local museum.

Stabio

The road from Mendrisio to the Italian border passes Balerna (310m/1017ft; pop. 3500), which joins up with the commercial centre of Chiasso. It was once an important religious centre. There is a ruined castle, Schloss Ponte-gana, which was built before the Langobard period.

Balerna

Chiasso

Chiasso (239m/784ft; pop. 8850) developed into an important centre for trade and transport due to its strategic location. First mentioned in 1127 Chiasso gained independence in 1416. Surrounded by hills it has long been a transit town, its status as a customs-point contributing to its economic growth. The Palast Züst (1906 by C. Brambilla) and the 18th c. Neo-Classical Camponovo Palast (formerly Matti) are worth visiting.

Lake Maggiore   M–O 11–14

Within Switzerland and Italy
Canton: Ticino (TI)
Altitude: 194m/637ft

Situation and
general

Lake Maggiore, known to the Romans as Lacus Verbanus, is the second largest of the north Italian lakes (area 212sq.km/82sq.miles, length 60km/ 37 miles, breadth 3–5km/2–3 miles, greatest depth 372m/1221ft). Less intricately patterned than Lake Como and without the sheer rock faces of the northern part of Lake Garda, it nevertheless offers scenery of southern splendour.

The northern part of the lake, with the town of Locarno, is in Switzerland, but the greater part of it is in Italy, the east side belonging to Lombardy and the west side to Piedmont. The lake's principal tributaries are the Ticino and the Maggia to the north and the Toce on the west side. The river which flows out of the south end, having carved a passage through massive morainic walls, preserves the name of Ticino.
The northern part of the lake is enclosed by mountains, for the most part wooded, while towards the south the shores slope down to the plain of Lombardy. In clear weather the water in the northern part of the lake is green, in the southern part deep blue.

Climate and
vegetation

The climate is mild. From midnight until morning the tramontana blows, usually coming from the north; from midday until the evening the inverna

Locarno: Panorama with the pilgrimage church of Madonna del Sasso

blows from the south. The plant life of Lake Maggiore, like that of Lakes Garda and Como, includes many sub-tropical species: figs, olives and pomegranates flourish in the mild climate, and in August the myrtle blossoms. On the Borromean Islands lemons, oranges, cork-oaks, sago-palms and carob-trees grow.

The most popular tourist areas are around Ascona and Locarno (see entries), and on the western arm of the lake between Pallanza and Stresa, where the Borromean Islands with their sub-tropical gardens are the main attraction.

★ Ascona,
★ Locarno
★★ Borromean Islands

One very attractive excursion is a boat trip from Locarno to Arona (service through the year, twice daily in summer; also hydrofoil services), calling alternatively at places on the east and west sides of the lake.

Boat services

Martigny   F 12

Canton: Valais (VS)
Altitude: 477m/1565ft. Population: 13,000

The ancient little town of Martigny, the Roman Octodurum, situated on the great bend in the Rhône at the inflow of the River Drance, lies on the important through route from Lake Geneva to the Simplon pass and on the roads to the Great St Bernard pass and the Col de la Forclaz (Chamonix – Mont Blanc Tunnel).

Situation and general

Sights

In the newer part of the town, Martigny Ville, is the attractive Place Centrale, with the 19th c. Hôtel de Ville (Town Hall). Close by is the former inn La Grande Maison, where famous personalities such as J. W. Von Goethe and A. Dumas stayed. Haus Supersaxo (16th c.), at Rue des Alpes 1, is the oldest house in the town.

2km/1 mile south is the old-world Martigny Bourg, with the Old Town Hall (17th c.) and the old residence (17th–19th c.) of the bishop's representatives.

The cantonal education department opened the Valais Film Centre in 1988, which specialises in films and photographs connected with Valais.

Valais Film Centre

On the vine-clad hillside above the town (30 minutes from Martigny Ville) can be seen the ruins of the 13th c. castle of La Bâtiaz (destroyed in 1518), which belonged to the Bishops of Sion; the tower was restored in 1898.

Burg La Bâtiaz

To the south-east, close to the remains of a Roman amphitheatre, around the foundations of a Gallo-Roman temple, stands the cultural centre of the Fondation Pierre Gianadda, the idea of Léonard Gianadda (in memory of his brother) and Umberto Guglielmetti. There is a Gallo-Roman museum, exhibition galleries and a veteran car collection of over 40 vehicles from 1897 to 1939. On display are Benz, Alfa 1750c, Rolls-Royce, Mercedes SSK, Bugatti, Pic-Pac and the famous Delaunay-Belleville owned by Tsar Nicholas II of Russia.

★★ Fondation Pierre Gianadda

The upper gallery is reserved for Gallo-Roman exhibits. The main finds of the excavations at Martigny are on display here (bronze statues from Octodurum, discovered in 1883, the Roman forum Claudii Vallensium) and enjoy international acclaim.

The garden contains famous sculptures by famous artists such as A. Rodin ("La Méditation avec Bras", 1885), J. Miró ("Tête", 1979–85), H. Moore ("Large Reclining Figure",1982) and C. Brancusi ("Grand Coq IV", 1949).

La Bâtiaz Castle

Pierre Gianaddas' vintage-car collection

Every September as part of the Montreux-Vevey Festival concerts take place with international ensembles and soloists.

Surroundings

From the end of Martigny Bourg a narrow winding road runs east through the forest on the slopes of Mont Chemin. 3km/2 miles: Chemin-Dessous (774m/2539ft). 3.5km/2 miles: Col des Planches (1409m/4623ft), with fine views which is the starting point for the ascent of the Pierre à Voir (2476m/8124ft: 4 hours), the highest peak between the Rhône and the Drance and a commanding view-point. From here there is also a beautiful footpath along the mountainside, level for most of the way, to Isérables (4 hours).

Sembrancher

From the Col des Planches the road descends steeply, with many sharp bends, to Sembrancher (9km/6 miles), in the Drance valley, which has a parish church of 1676 with a fine Late Gothic tower.

★ Verbier

From Sembrancher (which can also be reached from Martigny on the excellent main road, No. 21) it is 15km/9 miles to the well-known winter sports resort of Verbier, situated on a natural terrace facing south, with views of the Grand Combin and the Mont Blanc group (1420m/4659ft).

Access to the skiing area is provided by numerous cableways. It is a popular area with skiers (over 85 lifts and 320km/199 miles of pistes) as it is still possible to ski up to 3300m/10,830ft in summer. There are well laid out runs for long-distance skiing.

Into the Val de Trient

This is a short valley west of Martigny, gorge-like in places, through which the Trient flows to join the Rhône.

Henry Moore: "Large reclining figure"   *Finds from the Roman Octodurum*

The steep and narrow mountain road runs north-west through La Bâtiaz, crosses the Trient on the Gueroz viaduct and turns south-east.

7km/4 miles: Salvan (927m/3041ft), a health resort, from which a daringly engineered road climbs by way of Les Granges (1044m/3425ft) to the Lac de Salanfe (8km/5 miles), an artificial lake 2km/1 mile long formed between 1947 and 1952 (1914m/6280ft; hotels; skiing). From Les Granges there is a footpath to the impressive Gorges du Dailly.

Salvan

Gorges du Dailly

1.5km/1 mile south-west of Salvan is the summer and winter resort of Les Marécottes (1100m/3604ft; "Reno Ranch" Alpine Zoo, natural swimming pool), from which a chair-lift 1470m/4823ft long (lower station 1140m/3740ft) goes up to Creusaz (1780m/5840ft).

Les Marécottes

The Val de Trient road continues beyond Salvan to Le Trétien (4km/2 miles), from which it is possible to reach Finhaut, higher up the valley, but only by rail.

Over the Col de la Forclaz to Chamonix (France)

Just south of Martigny on the road to the Great St Bernard (see entry) turn right into a road which winds its way up, with a number of sharp bends, through the villages of La Fontaine and Le Fays to the Col de la Forclaz (1527m/5010ft), between the Croix de Prélayes and the Mont de l'Arpille (2089m/6854ft; chair-lift; extensive views).

Col de la Forclaz
Mont de l'Arpille

It then runs down with attractive views of the Trient valley and the Trient glacier, to Trient (1305m/4282ft), a summer and winter sports resort in a more open stretch of the valley.

Trient

After passing through Le Châtelard (1120m/3675ft) it comes to the French frontier, from which it continues over the Col des Montets to Chamonix.

Le Châtelard

Meiringen   L 8

Canton: Berne (BE)
Altitude: 600m/1969ft
Population: 8000

Situation and general

Meiringen the chief town in the Hasli valley, lies on the Aare, which flows into Lake Brienz a few kilometres west of the town. It is a popular summer holiday resort and a good base for excursions into the Bernese Oberland, and has a long tradition of wood-carving and hand-weaving.

Sights

The parish church, on higher ground, was built in 1684 on the remains of an earlier church (13th c.), and has an 11th c. crypt. The tower, with round-arched windows, dates from the 14th and 17th c. and contains the oldest bell in the canton (1351). There is also an interesting local museum, the Haslimuseum.

Sherlock Holmes Museum

The Neo-Gothic English church (1893) became a museum for the famous English fictional detective Sherlock Holmes in 1989 with a reconstruction of his drawing-room at 221B Baker Street, London. Memorabilia relating to the immortal character is on show and a life-size statue by John Doubleday, complete with deerstalker and pipe, stands in the tree-lined church square.

Surroundings

★ Aare gorge

2km/1 mile south-east is the Aare gorge, 1400m/4593ft long, through which there is a footpath (½ hour, through tunnels and galleries; open: May to Oct. 8am–6pm) to the Lammi inn, on the road to Innertkirchen.

Meiringen: Aare gorge   *Sherlock Holmes Museum*

From the left bank of the Aare (car park) a funicular takes 5 minutes to reach the Upper Reichenbach Falls. From the upper station there is a good view of the falls, which plunge down in two stages. This is the spot where Arthur Conan Doyle had Sherlock Holmes killed in a fight with his arch enemy Professor Moriarty.

★Upper
Reichenbach
Falls

The Meirengen Tourist Bureau organises trips to the Gerstenegg crystal ravine near the Grimsel pass (see Andermatt; circuit of three passes; tel. (036) 71 43 22).

Kristallkluft
Gerstenegg
(crystal ravine)

To the Schwarzwaldalp

(13km/8 miles to the Scwarzwaldalp). A narrow road branches off the Grimsel road in the hamlet of Willigen and winds its way up through the forest. 3km/2 miles Schwendi (779m/2556ft). 2km/1 mile Zwirgi inn (976m/3202ft), with a fine view to the rear of Hasli valley and Hasliberg.
  The road then continues high above the Reichenbach on the slopes of the Hohbalm (1371m/4498ft). Straight ahead is the Wellhorn, with the Wetterhorn and Eiger to the right.

Willigen

4.5km/3 miles Gschwandemaad (1298m/4259ft), from which there is a celebrated view of the Engelhörner (2781m/9124ft), the Rosenlaui (1330m/4364ft), in a magnificent setting. A footpath, largely hewn from the rock, winds uphill (½ hour) through the Rosenlaui gorge (open: June–Sept. 8am–4.30pm), carved out by the Weissenbach.
  The road climbs in a sharp bend and comes in 2.5km/2 miles to the Schwarzwaldalp (1467m/4813ft).

Gschwande-
maad
Rosenlaui,
★Rosenlaui
gorge

Schwarzwaldalp

From here a bridle-path leads in 2–2½ hours to the Grosse Scheidegg or Hasli-Scheidegg (1961m/6434ft), from which there is a view of the Grindel-wald basin (descent, 2 hours).

Grosse
Scheidegg

See Sarnen

Hasliberg

Montreux   F 10

Canton: Vaud (VD)
Altitude: 375m/1230ft
Population: 20,000

With a magnificent situation and an unusually mild climate which make it the most popular resort on Lake Geneva, Montreux extends for some 8km/5 miles along the shores of the lake, incorporating a number of smaller places which were formerly independent communes.
  The charm of the town's setting depends on its variety of geography and vegetation, ranging from the gardens on the lakeside, through the Alpine meadows and forests around Caux and Les Avants, to the lofty peaks of the Rochers de Naye and the Pléiades (skiing).

Situation and
general

Sights

The main part of the resort, Montreux Ville, lies on the steep slopes above the Baye de Montreux, a swiftly flowing mountain stream. On the shores of the lake is the Casino. From the terrace in front of the parish church (1507), higher up, there is a beautiful view of the lake.
  To the west, in Vernex, opposite the famous Montreux Palace Hotel (1904), stands the modern Maison des Congrès, and beyond this lies the attractive residential suburb of Clarens.

Montreux Ville

Maison des
Congrès

To the east the district of Territet is situated on a narrow coastal strip below the steep slopes of Glion. The Grand Hôtel (1887) by Maillard ranks among

Territet

311

Montreux Palace

the great hotels built at the end of the 19th c. A museum for audio and video technology was opened here, documenting the history and development of information technology. At the station a marble monument (1902) commemorates the Empress Elisabeth of Austria, murdered in Geneva in 1898.

★★ Château de Chillon

General	1.5km/1 mile beyond Territet, in the outlying district of Veytaux, is the popular tourist attraction of Chillon Castle, a stronghold of the Counts and Dukes of Savoy. Situated on a rocky islet close to the shore, it commanded the road from Burgundy over the Great St Bernard into Italy.

The castle, which now belongs to the canton of Vaud (conducted tours), was built in the 9th or 10th c., enlarged in the 11th–12th c. and given its present form in the 13th c. In the basement are large dungeons hewn from the native rock. Many Genevese were confined here for expressing their views too freely, among them François de Bonivard, Prior of St Victor's in Geneva. He was incarcerated here by the Duke of Savoy in 1530, fettered to an iron ring which is still shown to visitors, but was released in 1536 when Bernese conquered Vaux and, with the help of ships from Geneva, took the castle. He is the hero of Byron's poem "The Prisoner of Chillon" (1816). Other illustrious poets and writers such as Victor Hugo, Rodolphe Töpffer and Juste Olivier have written about the castle.

Nowadays it is hard to distinguish the 25 buildings that make up Chillon castle, closely grouped around three courtyards; the oldest being the keep and the Duke's Tower, which are linked by an internal wall, the square tower, which dominates the entrance and the living quarters.

St Pantaleon Chapel	Of special interest is the 10th c. Chapel of St Pantaleon of which only the St Tryphon crypt remains. Although it was filled-in in the 13th c. it has recently been rendered accessible again. The chapel contains the first Christian altar of the region – after the one at St Maurice. A reliquary dating from Carolingian times is displayed in the armoury.
Basement	The imposing underground vaults, which are actually at water level and replaced the old timbers of the ground floor, are double-naved halls with mighty pillars and Gothic vaulting. The largest vault was Bonivard's prison.

Château de Chillon

Chillon Castle

© Baedeker

Level I   Level II   Level III   Level IV

1 Entrance
2 Guard-room
3 First courtyard
4 Magazine
5 Arsenal
6 Dungeon
7 Gallows
8 Prison
9 Bonivard Column
10 Castellan's Hall
11 Second courtyard

12 Museum (formerly Banqueting Hall)
13 Bedroom
14 Guest-room
15 Heraldic Hall
16, 17 Duke's apartments
18 Latrine (13th c.)
19 Living-room (14th c.)
20 Old living quarters (13th c.)
21 Chapel
22 Third courtyard

23 Count's Great Hall
24 Torture chamber
25 Bedroom
26 Latrine (13th c.)
27 Clerks' room
28 Museum (models, sculpture)
29 Fourth courtyard
30 Keep
31 Defensive towers
32 Exit

On the ground floor are the large kitchen ("Grosse Bernerküche") with massive chestnut pillars and the courtroom.

Castle kitchen

On the upper floor are the former Banqueting Hall, the adjoining Bernese Room decorated with pretty bird and floral motifs and the splendid Heraldic Hall, formerly known as "aula paramenti" or the Knights' Hall with an interesting gallery of shields bearing the coats-of-arms of the Bernese governors. In the old tower, in the Duke's apartments, traces of the rich 13th and 14th c. decoration with birds and flowers are still visible. There are more living quarters and the little St Georg's Chapel where the ribbed vaulting on six low pillars is completely decorated with figures and tendrils.

Banqueting Hall
Heraldic Hall

St Georg's Chapel

Crossing the upper courtyard we come to the Count's Great Hall (Grosser Grafensaal; "magna aula", "aula vetus") with a 15th c. coffered ceiling. Notable are the four windows with charming quatrefoils above two lanceolate 13th c. Gothic arches.

Count's Great Hall

Through the treasury, the former prison and Vaud arsenal with its magnificent arches and Gothic ribbed vaulting we come to the medieval main tower ("magna turris"), 26m/85ft high, and completed in three stages (12th–14th c.). From the top are marvellous views of the castle and the outline of the Alps. During the restoration work begun at the end of the 19th c. the original moat was restored.

Surroundings

To Les Avants

Les Avants (8km/5 miles). From the station take Rue de la Gare; then left along Avenue de Belmont and into a road which climbs up in sharp bends (daffodils in flower in May).

On the left is the massive Château Châtelard, built by Jean de Gingins as a refuge for the people of Montreux in 1476. Partly destroyed by the Confederates it was later rebuilt; the large dungeon is of north Italian style.

Château Châtelard

Château de Chillon

Chamby

Cross N 9 and continue uphill in long bends, via the villages of Fontanivent (559m/1834ft), Chernex (603m/1978ft), Sonzier (664m/2179ft) and Chamby (752m/2467ft; Railway Museum (Chemin de Fer Musée Blonay-Chamby); open: mid May–end Oct., Sat. afternoons and Sun., also by appointment; tel. (021) 9 43 21 21 and 9 46 26 36; light railway to Blonay, (mid May–end Oct.).

Les Avants

The road continues to climb, along the east side of Mont Cubly, towering above the Gorge de Chauderon. 9km/6 miles: Les Avants (974m/3196ft), a summer and winter resort high above the valley of the Baye de Montreux.

Col de Sonloup

3km/2 miles farther on is the Col de Sonloup (1158m/3799ft; hotel), which can also be reached from Les Avants by funicular.

From Montreux to the Col de Jaman

Glion

To the Col de Jaman (14km/9 miles). Leave by Rue de la Gare and the district of Les Planches; then a road which runs uphill in a wide curve. 3km/2 miles: Glion (692m/2270ft), with beautiful views of the lake and the Alps; funicular down to Territet.

Caux

The road now climbs steeply, with numerous sharp bends. 3.5km/2 miles: Caux (1054m/3458ft), a health resort in a magnificent situation, with extensive views; meeting-place of the "Moral Rearmament" movement. From here there is a cog-railway to the popular skiing area (ski-lift) on the

★Rochers de Naye

Rochers de Naye, and from the upper station (1973m/6473ft; hotel) it is a 10 minutes' climb to the summit (2045m/6710ft), which has superb views of the Alps and Lake Geneva; Alpine garden.

★Col de Jaman

From Caux a mountain road runs up 7.5km/5 miles to the Col de Jaman (1516m/4974ft; restaurant), with far-ranging views.

Montreux on Lake Geneva, with Dent de Jaman and Rochers-de-Naye in the background

From Montreux to the Pléiades

To the Pléiades (15km/9 miles to Lally; mountain road). Leave on the Lausanne road, and in Clarens turn right into a road which crosses the N 9 and winds its way uphill via Chailly (485m/1591ft) and comes in 6 km/ 4 miles to Blonay (623m/2044ft), where Paul Hindemith (1895–1963) spent his last years. The castle dates back from the 12th c. The town (which for administrative purposes is part of Vevey; see entry) is noted for its almost champagne-like wine. From here there is a cog-railway to the Pléiades (4.7km/3 miles), 25 minutes.

Blonay

The road from Blonay to the Pléiades climbs in sharp bends, passing a side road on the right to the spa (sulphurous water) of L'Alliaz (1044m/3425ft). 9km/6 miles Lally (1237m/4059ft), at the end of the road. From here it is 4 minutes on the cog-railway from Blonay or 20 minutes on foot to the Pléiades (1364m/4475ft; pension and restaurant), from which there is a beautiful view.

L'Alliaz
Lally

★Pléiades

Mürren

K 9

Canton: Berne
Altitude: 1650m/ 5414ft. Population: 320

The holiday and winter sports resort of Mürren lies on a sunny terrace 700m/2297ft above the Lauterbrunnen valley, with magnificent views of the Jungfrau massif.

Situation

First mentioned in the records in 1257, Mürren developed during the 19th c. into a popular resort, particularly favoured by the British. The Mürrenbahn (narrow-gauge railway) was opened in 1891, the Allmendhubelbahn (funicular) in 1912.

History

Mürren

Townscape

Mürren is traffic-free. Only vehicles from the hotels and shops are allowed on the narrow streets of this rustic chalet village. Access is from Lauterbrunnen by funicular (6.5km/4 miles) to Grütschalp (1490m/4889ft) and from there by the narrow-gauge railway (5.5km/3 miles), or from Stechelberg by cableway (the Schilthornbahn) to Gimmelwald (1367m/4485ft) and Mürren.

Wengen, situated on the rocky plateau opposite is also accessible by cableway (see Grindelwald).

The British made this resort, lying at the foot of the Schilthorn, famous for sport. The revolving restaurant "Piz Gloria" was inspired by a James Bond film. The biggest amateur race in the world, the "Inferno Race", started by the British, still takes place here annually.

A new Alpine sports centre close to the skiing area offers a wide choice of activities (indoor swimming pool, tennis and squash courts, sauna, library and games room, etc.). Guided glacier walks and helicopter skiing are popular.

Winter sports   Difficult slopes on the Schilthorn; medium to easy on the Gimmeln, Schiltgrat and Winteregg slopes. The Jungfrau region also has 175 kilometres of downhill slopes and a 2km/1 mile circular course near Mürren.

Surroundings

★Allmendhubel   To the north-west is a mountain commanding panoramic views, Allmendhubel (1938m/6359ft; restaurant), which can be reached either by the funicular or by walking (30 minutes).

The Eiger and Mönch, seen from Mürren

Piz-Gloria revolving restaurant on the Schilthorn

From Gimmelwald (1367m/4485ft; pop. 140), which is accessible either by the Schilthorn or on foot (30 minutes), there is a footpath (1½ hours) along a mountain terrace into the Sefinental and to the Gspaltenhorn glacier.

Gimmelwald

Gspaltenhorn glacier

The upper sections of the Schilthornbahn lead by way of Birg (2676m/8780ft) to the Schilthorn (Piz Gloria, 2970m/9745ft; revolving restaurant), from which there are ski trails (moderate and difficult) to Mürren. The longest descent (12km/7 miles) runs to Lauterbrunnen (height difference 2170m/7122ft).

★Schilthorn

Murten/Morat   F 7

Canton: Fribourg (FR)
Altitude: 450m/1476ft. Population: 4600

Murten (the German form: French Morat) lies on a ridge of hills marking the linguistic boundary between French and German, on the south-east side of the idyllic Murtensee (Lac de Morat). This beautiful little medieval town has preserved, more completely perhaps than anywhere else in Switzerland, the old-world character derived from its many surviving buildings of the 15th–18th c. The old town is still surrounded by its circuit of walls (with a wall-walk).

Situation and general

★★Townscape

In 515 King Sigismund of Burgundy presented a property at Murten, on the road to Valais, to the monastery of St Maurice. In 1013 Murten was a stronghold held by King Rudolf III of Upper Burgundy. The real foundation of the town was the work of the Zähringen dynasty between 1157 and 1177.

History

Murten's main claim to fame is the battle fought here in 1476 in which the Confederates defeated the troops of Charles the Bold of Burgundy. The field of battle ranged from Cressier (572m/1877ft) to Greng (442m/1450ft), where a memorial now stands.

317

Sights

★ Town walls	The town walls (12th–15th c.) are a remarkable example of a medieval defensive wall; access to the wall-walk is by flights of steps at the German church and the Käfigturm (Cage tower). From the walls there are fine views over the roofs of Murten.
Schloss	At the western tip of the old town stands the castle, built by Peter of Savoy in the 13th c. Nowadays it serves as the prefecture with open-air concerts in the courtyard in summer. At the north-east end of the picturesque Haupt-
★ Hauptgasse	gasse, is the Berne gate (Berntor, 1777–78), a late Baroque reconstruction, with one of the oldest clocks in Switzerland (1712).
Town Hall French church German church	The Town Hall was rebuilt after 1416, and was given a Neo-Classical façade in 1832. Also of interest are the Late Gothic French church (1478–80) and the German church (1710–13). Opposite the latter is the birthplace of the writer Jeremias Gotthelf (whose real name was Albert Bitzius, a pastor, 1797–1854).
Haus Rübenloch Historical Museum	One of the town's most picturesque old buildings is the Late Gothic Rüben-loch, with a frontal gable. The old town mill now houses a Historical Museum, opened in 1978 (weapons, banners and uniforms from the Bur-gundian wars, and an old oil-mill). In Schulhausplatz a "world sundial" shows the time in different parts of the world.
Boat trips	There is a 1 hour round trip on the Murtensee (Lac de Morat) and trips encompassing three lakes: Murtensee, Neunburger See (Lac de Neuchâtel) and Bieler See. It is popular with water sports enthusiasts.

Murten/Morat: the main street . . .   *. . . and the medieval town fortress*

Surroundings

From the Bodenmünsi hill south of Murten there are magnificent panoramic views of the lake and the Jura mountains.

Archaeologists have discovered what is thought to be the oldest village in Europe in the countryside around Murten-Muntelier. The settlement has been dated at 3867 B.C.

Murten-Muntelier

From Murten to Avenches

Leave on the Lausanne road, which runs through the suburb of Meyriez and begins to climb. 2km/1 mile from the middle of the town, at the junction with the bypass road (on right), is the monument to the Battle of Murten, an obelisk erected in 1823 on the site of an ossuary destroyed by the French in 1798. It commemorates the decisive victory of the Confederates over Duke Charles the Bold of Burgundy on June 22nd 1476.

Monument to the Battle of Murten

The road runs close to the south-east shore of the Murtensee or Lac de Morat (433m/1421ft; area 27sq.km/10sq.miles, length 9km/6 miles, greatest depth 46m/151ft), which is linked with the Lac de Neuchâtel by the River Broye (motor-boat traffic). To the right is the flat-topped Mont Vully or Wistenlacher Berg (657m/2156ft) which lies between the Murtensee and the Lac de Neuchâtel.

Murtensee or Lac de Morat

2km/1 mile beyond the monument is Faoug (pronounced Foo; German Pfauen), from which a road descends on the right to a beach station and camp site (inn), 2.5km/2 miles west on the wooded shores of the lake, and follows a fairly straight and level course to Avenches, passing the remains of the Roman town just before reaching the modern town.

Lac de Morat

Avenches
Castle, Aviation
Museum

★Aventicum

Avenches (474m/1555ft; pop. 2000; bypass), a little town situated on a hill, with a medieval castle (remodelled in Renaissance style) and attractive old houses. The castle houses the Musée de l'AMVANAS, a museum of the history of flight in Switzerland, with documents, models and navigational instruments. It occupies the site of the old capital of the Helveti and the Roman town of Aventicum, which had its heyday in the 1st and 2nd c. A.D., when it had a population of some 20,000; it was destroyed by the Alemanni about 260. The excavated remains of the Roman town can be seen to the east of modern Avenches: a theatre (semicircular in form, with a diameter of 106m/348ft) which could seat 10,000 spectators; the "Tornallaz", the only surviving remnant of the town's 6km/4 miles circuit of walls; the remains of the Forum baths; and a 12m/40ft high Corinthian column, probably from the Forum, known as the Cigognier from the stork's nest which formerly crowned it. The numerous finds from the site are displayed in a museum adjoining the amphitheatre.

Neuchâtel   F 6

Canton: Neuchâtel
Altitude: 430m/1411ft
Population: 33,000

Situation and
general

Neuchâtel (German Neuenburg), capital of the canton of the same name, lies on the north shore of the Lac de Neuchâtel (Neuenburger See), below the Jura mountains. It is the seat of a University and has a Commercial College and the Swiss Watchmaking Research Laboratory. The public buildings are mainly on the shores of the lake around the harbour; the residential districts, with their houses of yellow Jurassic limestone, rise above the lake on the foothills of the Chaumont, surrounded by parks and vineyards.

1 Museum of Ethnography
2 Market Hall
3 Temple du Bas/Music Salon
4 College Latin/Municipal Library
5 Natural History Museum
6 Archaeological Museum
7 Hôtel du Peyrou
8 Museum of Art and History
9 University
10 Commercial College
11 Catholic Church

The town first appears in the records in 1011 under the name of Novum Castellum, and in the course of the 11th c. it became part of the Holy Roman Empire. Thereafter it changed hands several times. The Counts of Neuchâtel gave place to the Counts of Freiburg im Breisgau, who in turn were succeeded by the Counts of Hochberg. From 1504 to 1707 the town belonged to the the Dukes of Orléans-Longueville, and then passed to the Crown of Prussia. In 1848 a federal and republican constitution came into force, and in 1875 King William IV of Prussia renounced his claim to Neuchâtel. During the 18th c. the town developed into a commercial and industrial centre (watch-making, fabric printing) and in 1815 it became the cantonal capital.

History

Motor boats ply between the other towns on the lakeside. The trip around the three lakes (Lac de Neuchâtel, Bieler See and Murtensee) is highly recommended.

Boat services

Sights

On the long quays which extend on either side of the harbour are a series of fine late 19th c. buildings. In Place du Port is the Post Office and in Place Nume Droz (to the south) the Collège Latin (1835), with the Municipal Library.

Collège Latin

At the near end of Quai Léopold-Robert, north-east of the harbour, stands the Museum of Art and History (closed Mondays), which houses a comprehensive collection of Swiss 19th c, paintings, antiques, automata (mechanical figures) and clocks and watches.

Musée d'Art et d'Histoire

Parallel to Quai Léopold-Robert is the broad Avenue du Premier-Mars, which runs past the Jardin Anglais to the University (1909), successor to an Academy founded by King Frederick William III of Prussia in 1838. Behind the University, on the shores of the lake, stands the Commercial College (Ecole Supérieure de Commerce).

University

321

Neuchâtel

Neuchâtel: near the harbour . . .   *. . . stands the Musée d'Art et d'Histoire*

Faubourg de l'Hôpital Hôtel du Peyrou Musée d'Histoire Naturelle Musée d'Archéologie	To the north of the Jardin Anglais lies a select part of the town, the Faubourg de l'Hôpital, with handsome 18th c. patrician houses, including the Hôtel du Peyrou (1764–70; beautiful garden), which is now used for receptions and banquets, and the Grande Rochette (1730; private property). The adjoining Musée d'Histoire Naturelle (Natural History Museum) has important departments of zoology, mineralogy and geology. Behind the Hôtel du Peyrou the Archaeological Museum (Musée d'Archéologie) contains an interesting collection of excavated material from La Tène.
Old Town, Town Hall Maison des Halles	The Old Town lies north-west of the harbour, rising up the hillside towards the Château. On its east side are the Town Hall (Hôtel de Ville; 1784–90), with a pillared portico, and the Theatre (1775). The main street, Rue de Seyon, occupies the bed of a stream which was diverted in 1844. Side streets on the left lead to the elegant Renaissance Market Hall (Maison des Halles, 1570–75).
Fountains	There are a number of fine 16th and 17th c. fountains: the Banner Carrier fountain (1584), the Griffin fountain (1664), the Justice Fountain (1547) and the Lion fountain (1655; the lion itself 1664).
Château	From Rue de Château a stepped lane and a street lead up to the château, which belonged to the Counts and Princes of Neuchâtel and is now occupied by cantonal government offices. The west wing dates from the 12th c., the remainder from the 15th to the 17th c.; the interior has undergone much alteration.
Collegiate Church ★Monument of the Counts of Neuchâtel	The Collegiate church was built in the 12th–13th c. (west towers 1867–75). Until 1530, when it was taken over by the Reformed faith, it was the Catholic Collégiale Notre-Dame. In the very dark Romanesque choir the monument of the Counts of Neuchâtel (1372) has 15 painted effigies and is the finest Gothic memorial in the whole of Switzerland.

Collegiate Church Neuchâtel

1 St Guillaumes Chapel
2 St Michel's Chapel (Upper Storey)
3 14th century fresco
4 Remains of Romanesque Cloister

5 Seal of Farel
6 St Pierre's Doorway
7 Tomb of Counts of Neuchâtel
8 Reformation Inscription

On the north side of the church is a Romanesque cloister (restored). Outside the west front of the church stands a statue of the Reformer Guillaume Farel (1489–1565); from the terrace there are extensive views.

South-west of the park in Rue St Nicolas, is the Museum of Ethnography, with an excellent permanent collection and occasional special exhibitions from Asia, Africa and Oceania.

Museum of
Ethnography

From Rue de l'Ecluse, on the edge of the old town, a funicular ascends to the Cret du Plan (598m/1962ft), from which there are extensive views of the lake and the Alps.

★Cret du Plan

Surroundings

5km/3 miles north-east, in La Coudre, is a funicular to the summit of Chaumont (1177m/3862ft), which can also be reached on a steep road from Neuchâtel. From the top there are far-ranging views of the Mittelland with its lakes, and a panorama of the Alps from Sântis to Mont Blanc.

★Chaumont

Near St-Blaise, at the end of the lake, in the hamlet of La Tène, is a famous Late Iron Age site first excavated in 1858.

La Tène

In neighbouring Marin there is a butterfly garden where over 1000 species of butterflies, as well as fish and birds, are on show among the tropical plants of the Papillorama. An artificially created atmosphere maintains the ideal conditions necessary for the butterflies and moths.

Marin,
★Papillorama

★From Neuchâtel to Yverdon

The road (39km/24 miles) skirts the north-west side of the Lac de Neuchâtel, the largest of the three Swiss lakes on the fringes of the Jura (39km/24 miles long, up to 8km/5 miles wide). The hillsides are mostly covered with vineyards.

Leave Neuchâtel by way of Quai L. Perrier and road 5. In the suburb of Serrières are the Suchard chocolate factory (1826) and a tobacco factory (visitors admitted).

Auvernier (460m/1509ft) is a vine-growing village with a school of viticulture. It has a number of elegant patrician houses (16th c.) with Renaissance doorways.

Auvernier

Colombier (460m/1509ft; pop. 4000) has a massive castle, built in the 12th c. on Roman foundations and rebuilt and enlarged in the 14th and

Colombier

Hôtel du Peyrou, in Louis XIV style

Collegiate church . . .   *. . . with pointed vaulting*

16th c. From 1754 it was occasionally used as a residence by the Prussian governor of Neuchâtel. It now contains a military museum and a collection of pictures. The surrounding vineyards produce an excellent wine.

Boudry (470m/1542ft; pop. 3000) is a picturesque little town at the mouth of the Gorges de l'Areuse with a 16th c. castle which houses a museum of viticulture. Boudry was the birthplace of the French politician Jean-Paul Marat (1743–93) and of Philippe Suchard. Boudry

The road continues, with beautiful views, to Bevaix (476m/1562ft), which has a Gothic church and a 1722 mansion-house. Gorgier (518m/1700ft) has a castle of the 14th and 16th c., restored in Romantic style in the 19th c. (view). Bevaix Gorgier

St-Aubin (474m/1555ft) is the most important town in the district of La Béroche which lies on the slopes of the Montagne de Boudry with many picturesque villages and country houses. Beyond this, to the right, stands the castle of Vaumarcus, and on the left the former Carthusian house of La Lance, with a beautiful Late Gothic cloister. St-Aubin

La Lance monastery

The road continues via Grandson (see Yverdon) to Yverdon (see entry), at the south-west end of the lake.

Nyon

C 10

Canton: Vaud (VD)
Altitude: 404m/1326ft
Population: 14,000

The little old-world town of Nyon is beautifully situated on the north-west shore of Lake Geneva, at the end of a mountain road over the Col de la Givrine to La Cure. Situation

Roman columns . . .   *. . . in Nyon*

History | There was a settlement of the Helvetii here (Noviodunum) and Julius Caesar established the Roman station of Civitas Iulia Equestris. The town enjoyed a period of prosperity under Bernese rule in the 16th c. when many fine burghers' houses were built. From 1781 to 1813 there was a porcelain factory in Nyon. It was the birthplace of the writer Edouard Rod (1857–1910) and the pianist Alfred Cortot.

Sights

The town, with its old houses and its church (12th c.; Roman walling in substructure), is picturesquely situated on the slopes of a hill which is crowned by the five-towered castle (12th and 16th c.). The castle now houses the Historical and Porcelain Museum, including an exhibition of Nyon porcelain (1781–1813). Other museums include the Musée Romain (Roman finds) and the Musée Léman (flora and fauna of Lake Geneva, marine and natural history subjects). From the castle terrace there is a magnificent view of the lake with the Alps and Mont-Blanc. In the Bourg-de-Rive are Roman columns.

Castle
Museums

★Roman
columns

Surroundings

★Gingins | In Gingins, 8km/5 miles north-west of Nyon, an extension to the 15th c. castle houses the Neumann Collection of Art Nouveau and Art Deco vases (open: Thur.–Sun.).

Bonmont Abbey | 9km/6 miles north-west is the former Cistercian abbey of Bonmont (concerts in summer).

Coppet, Crans-près-Céligny | 8km/5 miles south-west of Nyon are two châteaux: Château Coppet and Château Crans-près-Céligny, an elegant 18th c. residence.

Oberhalbstein/Sursés   R 8/9

Canton: Grisons (GR)

Situation and general | Oberhalbstein (Romansch Sursés) is the name given to the valley of the river Julia, which flows down from the Julier (Guglia) pass to join the Albula at Tiefencastel. There was already a road here in Roman times, runing from the Engadine over the pass and down the successive levels of the valley. The language of the valley is Romansch.

Over the Julier pass into the Engadine

The road from Chur and Lenzerheide (see entries) was built between 1820 and 1840 and later improved. At the north end of the Oberhalbstein valley is Tiefencastel (Romansch Casti; 851m/2792ft; pop. 350), situated at a road junction on the site of the Roman station of Imacastra. On a rocky hill between the rivers Julia and Albula stands the parish church of St Stephen (1660), with a richly decorated interior. To the south-west lies the village of Mon (1227m/4026ft); in the church are 15th c. frescoes.

Tiefencastel

Mon

St Peter | A few kilometres before Tiefencastel, high above the Albula gorge, is St Peter in Mistail. Recently excavated remains of frescoes indicate it was built in the time of Charles the Great, around 800.

Bergün, Albula pass | The road continues to climb for 30km/19 miles via the old village of Bergün (1376m/4516ft) to the Albula pass (2312m/7588ft).

The Rhätische Bahn railway line winds its way across the romantic countryside between Bergün and Preda through tunnels and viaducts. In early 1985 a "railway history walk" was opened with information boards at regular intervals.

Railway history walk

Savognin, below the Piz Mitgel

Roman column on the Julier Pass

The road to the Julier pass runs up from here to the limestone wall of Crap Sès, above which the next stage of the valley opens up – Oberhalbstein ("above the rock").

Julier road

Cunter (1182m/3878ft) is a beautifully situated village frequented both by summer visitors and by winter sports enthusiasts. From here a narrow road (8.5km/5 miles) runs south-west via Riom up to Radons (1864m/6116ft; also reached by cableway from Savognin), from which Piz Caquiel (2970m/9745ft) can be climbed (4 hours).

Cunter

Savognin (1210m/3970ft; pop. 1000) is the primary town in the Oberhalb-stein, situated at the mouth of the Val Nandro, which runs down from the south-west to join the Oberhalbstein. The village has three 17th c. churches, a Valley Museum (open: July, Aug., Christmas–Easter, Tues., Sun. 7.30–9pm, Thur. 2–4pm; Sept.–Oct. 15th Tues. 7.30–9pm), and num-bers of attractive houses. At the upper end of the village, on the left, is a tablet commemorating the residence of the painter Giovanni Segantini (1886–94). Savognin is also a popular winter sports resort (many ski-lifts). The "Lei Barnagn" leisure centre may be used as a car-park in winter.

To the west of the village is Piz Curver (2972m/9751ft; 6 hours, with guide). Chair-lifts via Tigignas to Somtgant (2143m/7031ft) and via Malmi-giucr to Radons (see above).

Savognin

Farther up the valley is Tinizong (1232m/4042ft; pop. 360), on the site of the Roman station of Tinnetio. In the parish church (1647) is a carved altar (Late Gothic, 1512) by Jörg Kändel of Biberach in Swabia. At Rona (1420m/4659ft) the road reaches the next "step" in the valley.

Tinizong

The road continues via Mulegns to the step above this, on which is Lai da Marmorera (1680m/5512ft; car park), an artificial lake with a capacity of

Lai da Marmorera

327

60 million cu.m/2118 million cu.ft. Further along the road, on the left, the new village of Marmorera replaces the old village which was submerged by the lake.

Bivio

In the highest part of the valley is Bivio (1776m/5827ft; pop. 250), so called (Latin bivium, "roadfork") because a busy medieval road, now represented only by a bridle-path, branched off here and ran over the Septimer pass (Pass da Sett, 2311m/7582ft). In Bivio four different languages are spoken: German, an Italian dialect from the Val Bregaglia, Ladin and the Surmeirian dialect.

★ Julier pass

Beyond the village the road climbs to the Julier pass (Passo dal Guglia, 2284m/7494ft), with the stumps of two columns which probably belonged to a Roman shrine on the pass. To the right, is a small lake.

The road now descends the rocky valley of the Ova, past Piz Julier (3385m/11,106ft), on the left, to a lookout with a magnificent view of the Bernina massif (4049m/13,285ft). It then continues down to Silvaplana, where it enters the Engadine (see entry).

Olten   K 4

Canton: Solothurn
Altitude: 396m/1299ft
Population: 19,000

Situation and general

Olten, an important railway junction, with the main workshops of the Swiss Federal Railways, and a considerable industrial town (engineering), lies astride the river Aare at the foot of the Hauenstein (824m/2704ft), which commands extensive views.

History

The place was founded by the Froburg family on the site of a Roman castrum and first appears in the records as a town in 1201.

Olten: Old Town on the Aare

Sights

The handsome twin-towered parish church dates from 1806, the modern Stadthaus from 1966. An old covered wooden bridge leads into the Old Town, the most notable landmark of which is the Late Gothic tower of St Martin's church (demolished in 1844). The Old Town Hall (1701) now houses the municipal library. At Kirchgasse 10 is the Museum of Art (Kunstmuseum), with works by the Olten-born painter Martin Disteli (1802–44), and to the north, in Konradstrasse, the Historical Museum.

Surroundings

North of the town is the ruined castle of Froburg (excavations). Road 2 runs south up the Aare valley, enclosed between wooded hills.

Froburg ruins

It comes in 4km/2 miles to Aarburg (415m/1362ft), a picturesque little town of 6000 inhabitants situated above the junction of the Aare and the Wigger, with an 11th c. castle much altered in later centuries, now a penal establishment for young offenders.

Aarburg

On the Engelberg (667m/2188ft) is the "Säli-Schlössli", the ruined castle of Wartburg-Säli. A fire-watching post was established here in 1547, and remained the responsibility of the Säli family for 300 years.

Säli-Schlössli

South-west of Aarburg via Rothrist and Roggwil-Wynau stands the former Cistercian abbey of St Urban (founded 1184), in the north-west corner of the canton of Lucerne. The Baroque church (completed 1716) has a fine organ and richly carved choir-stalls, which were acquired by a foreign purchaser in 1854 but were later bought and returned to St Urban by the Gottfried Keller Foundation.

Cistercian Abbey of St Urban

Payerne   F 7

Canton: Vaud (VD)
Altitude: 452m/1483ft
Population: 7000

The name of this charming little old town, on the River Broye, has its origins with the Roman family Paterni. From the 10th c. the town has been the home of the Burgundian kings. The Benedictine monastery founded by Empress Adelheid, wife of Otto I, in 962 is an outstanding example of Cluny architecture.

Situation and general

Sights

Founded in the 11th c. on the ruins of a Roman villa the Abbey church is one of the chief examples of Romanesque architecture in the country. Constructed in the shape of a Latin cross this triple-naved pillared basilica has a large, semi-circular apse with apsides, a central nave with cross-vaulting in the lateral naves. The transept has notable 11th c. block capitals and chapels surround the choir, the capitals of which are of Burgundian influence. The yellow and grey stone blocks of the light interior are impressive, and 12th c. frescoes (Deesis) can be seen in the vestibule. Extensive renovations and excavations were carried out (including the grave of Queen Bertha, who died 1000 years ago) in the second half of this century.

★ Abbey Church

Jean de Grailly, verger and later vicar of Payerne, had his own chapel built in Gothic style, to the right of the choir, in the middle of the 15th c. It suffered severe damage during the Reformation. Restoration work on the chapel's frescoes along with those of Romainmôtier, Moudon, Lausanne Cathedral and Château Chillon was completed in 1982. On the north wall are St Moritz, the Compassionate Virgin and Mary Magdalena, while on the

Grailly Chapel

Abbey Church of Payerne

├─ 10 m ─┤

Development of Building

© Baedeker

Graillÿ Chapel

N ↗

Previous building and	☐ 10th c. Church	☐ 11th c. (4th Phase)
Periods of Building	■ 11th c. (1st & 2nd Ph.)	■ 11th c. (5th Phase)
☐ Roman Villa	■ 11th c. (3rd Phase)	☐ Late Middle Ages

12th c. frescoes in the abbey church

south wall are St Martin and La Pietà. The outer wall is decorated with a representation of the Triple Throne with Jean de Graillÿ, dressed in the dark attire of the Cluny monks, kneeling before it.

Only the chapter-house (rebuilt in the 16th c.) remains of the convent building. There is a local history collection, an interesting exhibition of Romanesque churches in Switzerland and a museum to General Jomini who was born in Payerne.

Next to the Abbey church is the triple-naved Protestant parish church of Notre-Dame (14/16th c.). A wall-painting in the southern lateral aisle depicts The Shroud of Christ (16th c.).

Notre-Dame
parish church

Four 13–14th c. towers remain of the medieval town. Fine Renaissance painting by H. Maraschet (1576) can be seen in the Late Gothic Law Court building (1571–72) next to the parish church. Close by are the Banner Carrier's fountain and the fountain of Serruriers (16th c.).

Law courts

◀ *Payerne: Nave of the abbey church*

Pontresina S 9

Canton: Grisons (GR)
Altitude: 1800m/5906ft
Population: 1820

Situation

Pontresina (Romansch Puntraschigna), once a mere village on the road to the Bernina pass and now a popular health resort, climbers' base and winter sports capital, lies in a sheltered spot in the highest side valley of the Upper Engadine, on a natural terrace facing south-west. It is surrounded by forests of stone pines and larches and enclosed by the majestic peaks of the Alps.

General

The two famous skiing areas of Diavolezza and Piz Lagalp (see Bernina) make Pontresina a popular winter sports centre.
  There are about 500km/310 miles of walks in the region. Guided tours of the glaciers are popular with climbers as are the nature walks. Golf, fishing, tennis, ice-skating, long-distance skiing, curling and tobogganing as well as winter sports and summer skiing are some of the activities on offer.

History

Pontresina first appears in the records in 1129, but evidence has been found of human settlement here dating back to the Bronze Age. The name has been thought to derive from one Saracenus who built a bridge here. (Pons Sarasinae).

Sights

Pontresina has some elegant hotels from the Belle Epoque period, typical stone houses with sgraffiti and window grilles.

The Punt Ota bridge is of 12th c. origin. In the Laret district the village church (Protestant) was built in 1640. The Museum Alpin (open: Mon.–Sat. 4–6pm) has interesting stone and mineral collections, etc. Between Piz

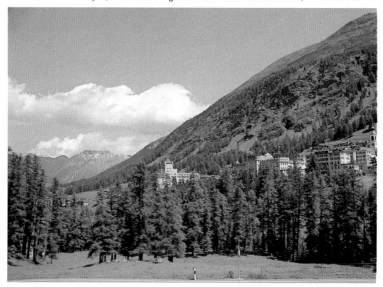

Pontresina, among stone-pines and larch woods

Rosatsch and Piz Chalchagn a beautiful glimpse of the Roseg valley and Roseg glacier can be enjoyed. Near here is a plant reserve with an Alpine garden.

On the hillside above Ober-Pontresina are the ruins of the pentagonal Spaniola tower and the little Romanesque Chapel of Santa Maria, with a ceiling of stone pine (1497) and frescoes of the 13th–15th c. The west wall was part of the previous building and retains wall-paintings from the 13th c. (God's appearance, The Baptism of Christ and the Last Supper). The life of Christ is depicted from the south wall to the north. The life of the Virgin Mary is shown on the north wall (moved from the west wall during restoration work in 1962–76).

Chapel of Santa Maria

Surroundings

Ascent of Muottas Muragl: 3km/2 miles from Pontresina on the St Moritz road a funicular (length 2200m/7218ft, gradient 13–54%) takes 15 minutes to reach Muottas Muragl (2456m/8061ft; restaurant), which commands the finest view of the Bernina group and the lakes of the Upper Engadine. A good return route is by a path which skirts the Schafberg to the Unterer Schafberg restaurant (1 hour; see below) and on to the Alp Languard (2250m/7382ft; 45 minutes); then by chair-lift (ski-lift) or on foot (45 minutes) to Pontresina.

★★Muottas Muragl

Alp Languard

The Schafberg (Munt della Bes-cha, 2731m/8960ft) is reached from Pontresina in 2¾ hours by way of the Unterer Schafberg restaurant (2230m/7317ft), from which there are magnificent views. On the summit, which has a prospect embracing the whole of the Bernina group, is the Segantini hut, with a tablet commemorating the painter Giovanni Segantini, who died here in 1899.

★Schafberg

Roseg glacier (Vadret da Roseg). A narrow road (6km/4 miles; closed to traffic; horse-drawn carts) leads up the Roseg valley to the Roseg-Gletscher restaurant (2000m/6562ft) from which it is a 30–45 minutes' walk under a fine row of stone pines to the end of the glacier, now much reduced in size.

★Roseg Glacier

There are more extensive views from the Alp Ota (2257m/7405ft; 1¼ hours from the restaurant) and the Tschierva hut (2573m/8442ft; 2 hours). From the Roseg glacier it is a 2¼ hours' walk to the Fuorcla Surlej and the Murtel station on the Corvatschbahn (see St Moritz).

★★Alp Ota

Morteratsch glacier (Vadret da Morteratsch). Leave Pontresina on the Bernina road and in 4.5km/3 miles take a little road on the right to the Morteratsch Hotel (1908m/6260ft).

Morteratsch Glacier

From here it is an hour's walk to the end of the glacier. A finer view of the glacier can be had by climbing Chünetta (2096m/6877ft; 35 minutes). 2 hours beyond this is the Boval hut of the Swiss Alpine Club (2495m/8186ft; inn with beds), from which there is a superb view of the Bernina group.

★Chünetta

Boval hut

Possible climbs from the Boval hut (to be undertaken only with a guide) include Piz Morteratsch (3751m/12,307ft; 4½–5 hours; easy, for those with a good head for heights), with superb panoramic views; Piz Palü (3905m/12,812ft; 6–7 hours), a beautifully shaped peak; and Piz Bernina (4049m/13,285ft; 7–8 hours, very strenuous).

Climbs

Ascent of the Diavolezza (on foot from the Morteratsch Hotel or by cableway from Bernina-Suot; see Bernina.

Another rewarding climb from Pontresina is the ascent of Piz Languard, to the east (3268m/10,722ft; 4 hours), with fine views. There is a restaurant 15 minutes below the summit.

From the cableways to the Diavolezza (summer skiing) and Piz Lagalb (see Bernina).

Cableways

Bad Ragaz
Q 6

Canton: St Gallen (SG)
Altitude: 517m/1696ft
Population: 4000

Bad Ragaz, attractively situated in the Rhine valley at the mouth of the Tamina gorge, is one of Switzerland's leading spas. The warm radioactive springs (37° C–99° F), with a flow of 3000 to 10,000 litres/660 to 2200 gallons a minute, are used in the treatment of rheumatism, paralysis, metabolic disorders and injuries of all kinds. The springs rise in the Tamina gorge and the water has been piped down to Ragaz since 1840.
Situation and general

Sights

On the left bank of the Tamina stands the parish church (1703) of St Pancras with 18th c. ceiling paintings. In the churchyard is the grave of the German philosopher Friedrich Wilhelm von Schelling.
Catholic Church

On the right bank we find the Kurgarten with the Kursaal, baths, a restaurant and a golf course.
Spa
   North-west of the town are the Freudenberg ruins which were destroyed in the 15th c. by the Confederates. Close by stands the St Leonhard chapel with an Italian style choir. To the north is the Giessen Park, with a lake.

Surroundings

8km/5 miles to the north-west is the little town of Sargans (482m/1581ft), its old town was completely destroyed by fire in 1811. The 19th c. Town Hall (Gallatihaus) is built in Classical style. The parish church of St Oswald and Cassian is of 18th c. origin, restored and extended in the 19th and 20th c. There are two interesting chapels in the hamlet of Vild – St Sebastian and St Maria. In Züricherstrasse (No. 5) there is an interesting private collection of cars, motorcycles and accessories (visits by prior arrangement). Sargans is dominated by the castle, former seat of the Counts of Werdenberg-Sargans. First mentioned in 1282 and partly rebuilt in the 15th c. it was the official seat of the provincial governors until the end of the 18th c.; today the keep houses a local historical museum.
Sargans

A road (4km/2 miles; closed to motor vehicles) climbs the left bank of the Tamina between schist walls almost 250m/820ft high to Bad Pfäfers (685m/2247ft; public baths), the buildings have the appearance of a monastery and date from 1704.
Bad Pfäfers

In the spa (Badehaus) tickets are issued for admission to the Tamina gorge. Long passages run down to the gorge (500m/1641ft long), at the end of which is a narrow steam-filled gallery where the principal spring emerges from a deep chamber in the rock. In 1242 a gangway was constructed on the rock face, supported on projecting beams, and in about 1465 a chamber was excavated above the spring, from which patients were let down on ropes.
★Tamina gorge

Another road parallel to the Bad Pfäfers road runs west up the valley to the developing spa of Bad Valens (915m/3002ft).
Bad Valens

◀ *The Tamina Gorge, near Bad Ragaz*

Bad Ragaz: Kursaal . . .   *. . . and evangelical church*

Wartenstein	3km/2 miles south-east of Ragaz we come to the Wartenstein (see below), with the Hotel Wartenstein (751m/2464ft), from which there is a beautiful view of the Churfirsten. Below the hotel are the ruins of Wartenstein Castle (13th c.) and St George's Chapel.
Guschakopf	West of Ragaz, above the right bank of the Tamina, is the Guschakopf (751m/2464ft; ¾ hour), from which there is a fine view.
★Pizol	South-west of Ragaz Pizol (2848m/9344ft), can be reached by way of a cableway (3.5km/2 miles, 22 minutes) to Pardiel (1630m/5348ft; mountain inn), from which a chair-lift leads up to the Laufböden (2222m/7290ft), near the Pizol hut (2229m/7313ft; cableway from Wangs; first-rate ski trails).

From Ragaz to Vättis (15km/9 miles)

Pfäfers	The road winds its way up to the Wartenstein. 4km/2 miles: Pfäfers (822m/2697ft; several inns), with the former Benedictine monastery of St Pirminsberg (founded *c.* 740, rebuilt 1672–93), now a cantonal home.
Vättis	The road continues along the east side of the deep Tamina valley, via Ragol and Vadura. 11 km/7 miles: Vättis (951m/3120ft), a quiet and beautifully situated summer resort under the west side of the towering Calanda (2806m/9206ft).
Piz Sardona	From here a very narrow road (excursions by minibus from Ragaz to St Martin, 1350m/4429ft, beyond this jeeps only: information from Verkehrsverein, Vättis) runs west up the beautiful Calfeisental to the Alp Sardona (1742m/5716ft; 12km/7 miles), from which Piz Sardona (3059m/10,137ft) can be climbed (4¼ hours, with guide) by way of the Sardona hut (2161m/7090ft).

Rapperswil

Canton: St Gallen (SG)
Altitude: 409m/1342ft
Population: 7700

The old-world little town of Rapperswil is picturesquely situated on a peninsula on the north side of Lake Zurich, which is crossed at this point by a causeway 1000m/3281ft long.

Situation

The town appears to have been founded about 1200, and first appears in the records in 1229. The line of the Counts of Rapperswil died out at an early stage. In 1358 Duke Rudolf built a wooden bridge over the lake, which stood until 1878, when it was replaced by a masonry-walled causeway carrying the road and railway. From 1415 to 1464 Rapperswil was a free Imperial city and in 1803 it was incorporated in the canton of St Gallen.

History

Sights

In the main square stands the tall Town Hall (1471), with a richly carved door at the entrance to the council chamber. The town library and a cultural forum are housed in the adjoining Haus Zum Pfauen.

Main square

From the square a broad flight of steps leads up to the Schlossberg (Castle Hill) or Endingerhügel (436m/1431ft), with the 15th c. parish church (restored 1887; two massive east towers) on the right and the imposing 13th c. castle on the left. The castle, on a triangular plan, with a keep and two other towers (restored 1988–89) was built by the Counts of Rapperswil and from the middle of the 15th c. was the seat of the Confederate governors. It houses the Polish Museum (Polenmuseum; the Renaissance, the Turkish

Castle

Polish Museum

Rapperswil: Yacht harbour and landing stage

Rapperswil: rose garden of Capuchin friary   *Historic fresco on the Curti-Haus*

wars, Copernicus, Zeromski, Chopin, the struggle for freedom against Russia in 1868) and a small library.

Hintergasse

Three rows of houses run down to the lakeside, among them are Marktgasse and Hintergasse with attractive old arcades and neat little shops.

Lindenhof, Deer Park

From the tree-lined west bastion, the Lindenhof, there are charming views of the town and the lake. On the north side of the hill is the Hirschgarten (Deer Park), on the south side a vineyard.

Brenyhaus, Local Museum

On the Herrenberg, east of the parish church, is the Heimatmuseum (local museum), in the 15th c. Brenyhaus (formerly Haus Landenberg; restored).

Harbour

There is a pretty little harbour with a dock for the lake boat services. Two wall-paintings on "Curti-Haus" (private) in the Engadinergasse commemorate the destruction of the town by the Zurich mayor Rudolf Brun and later the town's entry into the Confederation. Close by the lakeside is the "Heilig Hüsli" (c. 1600) which was part of the wooden bridge built in 1358, replaced by a stone dam in the 19th c. On the western promontory

Capuchin Friary

is a Capuchin friary (founded 1650), with a rose-garden, and nearby is a small vineyard first referred to in 972.

Knie National Circus Children's Zoo

On the Strandweg (lakeside road) south of the station, is a Children's Zoo belonging to the Knie National Circus, which is based in the town (dolphin show).

Surroundings

Hurden

A road runs over the causeway (Seedamm) along the Hurden peninsula, via the fishing village of Hurden (chapel of 1497), to Pfäffikon, on the south side of the lake (see Lake Zurich).

It is a 10 minutes' trip by motor-boat or motor-launch to the island of Ufenau (nature reserve; restaurant in old farm), which belonged to Einsiedeln abbey from 965 onwards (church and chapel of 1141). On Zwingli's advice the humanist Ulrich von Hütten sought refuge here in 1523, but died two weeks later; he is buried in the churchyard of the old parish church.

Ufenau

A lakeside road (10km/6 miles) runs south-east from Rapperswil through the commune of Jona to Busskirch, with an old church, and continues to Wurmsbach, which has a former convent of Cistercian nuns (16th–17th c.), now housing a girls' boarding school. The road then continues via Bollingen to Schmerikon, at the end of the lake.

Lakeside road

From Rapperswil road 8 runs east over the Ricken pass (805m/2641ft; beautiful view) into the Toggenburg district (see entry).

Toggenburg

The Rhine

Cantons: Grisons (GR), St Gallen (SG), Thurgau (TG), Schaffhausen (SH), Zurich (ZH), Aargau (AG), Basel-Land (BL) and Basel-Stadt (BS).

The Rhine (a name probably of Celtic origin: Latin Rhenus, German Rhein, French Rhin, Romansch Reno, Dutch Rijn) is Europe's most beautiful river and most important waterway. The first 375km/233 miles of its total length of 1320km/820 miles are in Switzerland. Its source is in the eastern part of the St Gotthard massif, from which the two principal arms of the river flow separately westward for the first 60km/37 miles.

Situation

Source

The Vorderrhein flows out of the Tomasee (2345m/7694ft), at the foot of Mt Badus (2928m/9607ft). The Hinterrhein originates in the névé of the Rheinwaldhorn (3402m/11,116ft). 10km/6 miles west of Chur, at Reichenau, the two streams join to form the Alpenrhein (Alpine Rhine), which flows north into Lake Constance.

Vorderrhein and Hinterrhein Alpenrhein

Emerging from the west end of the lake, the river plunges over the Rhine Falls at Schaffhausen and, as the Hochrhein (High Rhine) continues west to Basle. In its passage through Switzerland to this point the Rhine drains two-thirds of the country's total area, including 548sq.km/212sq.miles of glaciers.

Hochrhein, ★★Rhine Falls

Levels of the Rhine between Lake Constance and the North Sea

Height Difference (rounded)
400 m between Constance and Rotterdam
270 m between Basle and Rotterdam
80 m between Mainz and Rotterdam
40 m between Cologne and Rotterdam
10 m between Nijmegen and Rotterdam

© Baedeker

Eglisau on the bank of the Rhine

Upper Rhine, Middle Rhine and Lower Rhine

At Basle the river leaves Switzerland, with an average flow of 1027cu.m/36,263cu.ft of water per second, and turns north, flowing through the Rhenish Uplands as the Middle Rhine. Below Bonn it is known as the Lower Rhine. In Holland it splits up into a number of arms which flow into the North Sea.

Sights along the Rhine

N.B.

In this section, for the convenience of visitors coming from the West, the routes along the Rhine valley are described from west to east, going upstream.

The High Rhine (Basle to Lake Constance)

★Basle

From Basle (see entry) the road runs along the north bank of the swiftly flowing High Rhine (navigable to above Basle), which supplies power to many hydro-electric stations. The pleasant valley is bounded on the north side by the Black Forest and on the south by the Swiss Jura.

Rheinfelden

The first place of any size is Rheinfelden (277m/909ft), a little town of 7000 inhabitants beautifully situated on the left bank of the river facing the southern slopes of the Black Forest. It is a popular salt-water spa, with two indoor salt-water baths. The water has one of the highest salt contents in Europe. The waters of the springs are drunk for medicinal purposes.

The attraction of Rheinfelden lies in its picturesque old town, with ancient walls and towers rising above the rapidly flowing river. Notable features are the Town Hall (16th–18th c.) and St Martin's church (15th c., with Baroque interior). In the Haus zur Sonne (12 Marktgasse) is the Fricktaler Museum (local history). The Model Castle Museum (Rindergasse 6) and the Veteran Car Museum are also of interest.

At Rheinfelden we cross the Rhine and take a secondary road which runs north of the motorway to Möhlin and the village of Stein, where it joins road 7. Bad Säckingen, opposite on the north bank of the river, can be reached by the longest covered wooden bridge in Europe. This road continues east to Laufenburg (318m/1043ft; pop. 2000), opposite the German town, also called Laufenburg, on the north bank (bridge, with border control), at one of the most beautiful spots in the Rhine valley between Basle and Lake Constance, framed by wooded hills. The town has a tall Late Gothic parish church (1489) with a beautiful interior.

Stein,
★ Wooden
Bridge

Laufenburg

After an attractive bend in the valley the road continues via Leibstadt (to the north of which a nuclear power station is under construction) to a bridge over the Aare (5.5km/3 miles), just above its junction with the Rhine. Opposite, on the north bank, is the German town of Waldshut. Beyond the bridge a road goes off on the right to Brugg (Berne, Lucerne).

The Schaffhausen road continues to Koblenz (321m/1053ft), an important road junction near the confluence (hence its name – Latin Confluentia) of the Aare and the Rhine. From here road 7 runs via Winterthur and St Gallen to Rorschach. The Schaffhausen road turns left over the Rhine bridge (border control) into Germany.

Koblenz

In 6km/4 miles road 7 reaches Zurzach (342m/1122ft; pop. 3500), on the site of the Roman fort of Tenedo, a little town which was formerly a considerable river port, noted for its fairs, and is now a well-known spa. The hot springs (40° C/104° F), the spa facilities (including three outdoor swimming pools) the Turm Hotel and the Rheumatic clinic lie west of the town.

Zurzach

Zurzach has a number of fine old burghers' houses and a church of the 10th and 14th centuries (sarcophagus of St Verena, 1603, in crypt; tombstone of a Roman legionary of 1st c. A.D. built into wall). Opposite Zurzach (bridge) is the German village of Rheinheim.

The road, signposted to Winterthur, continues along the left bank of the Rhine and in 12km/7 miles reaches the old-world town of Kaiserstuhl (350m/1148ft), with a massive 13th c. tower and a Gothic church, picturesquely situated above the Rhine opposite the German village of Hohentengen (bridge).

Kaiserstuhl

Road 7 then leaves the Rhine and comes to Glattfelden (359m/1178ft), on the River Glatt just above its junction with the Rhine. This was the home town of the Swiss writer Gottfried Keller and is frequently referred to in his novel "Der grüne Heinrich".

Glattfelden

At a crossroads 2km/1 mile farther on, where the right-hand road runs south to Zurich, turn left to cross the Rhine on a stone bridge into the picturesque old town of Eglisau (360m/1181ft), which has 18th c. church situated on a higher road.

Eglisau

The road then cuts across the Ratzer Feld, an area surrounded on three sides by Germany, and a projecting finger of German territory linked with the district of Waldshut only by a narrow corridor. To the east of the German village of Jestetten is the small Swiss town of Rheinau, almost completely enclosed within a loop in the river, where there is a dam on the Rhine (motor-boats to the Rhine-Falls). The sumptuously appointed Baroque church (1705) belonged to a Benedictine abbey founded in the 9th c. and dissolved in 1862.

Rheinau

From Jestetten the road runs north-east into Switzerland again to the industrial town of Neuhausen, at the Rhine Falls (see entry).

★★ Rhine Falls

3km/2 miles farther on is Schaffhausen (see entry). From Schaffhausen take road 13, which runs 10km/6 miles east to Diessenhofen (416m/1365ft), a medieval town of 3000 inhabitants, once a free Imperial city, with handsome old burghers' houses, old town walls, the Siegelturm, a church of

Schaffhausen
Diessenhofen

Kaiserstuhl: Oberer Turm

Rheinau, on an island in the Rhine

1602 and conventual buildings of 1571. On the opposite side of the river is the German village of Gailingen.

Then along the river to Stein am Rhein (see entry). ★Stein am Rhein

2km/1 mile beyond this, at Eschenz, the Rhine opens out into the Untersee, the most westerly arm of Lake Constance (see entry).
Lake Constance

Along the Alpine Rhine

From the south-east end of Lake Constance road 13 leads up the wide valley of the Rhine to the village of Heerbrugg, with an old castle, and Altstätten (457m/1499ft; pop. 10,000), an ancient town with attractive arcaded houses (Marktgasse), a parish church of 1794 and a Heimatmuseum (local museum) in Prestegg, an old burgher's house (restaurant).
Altstätten

   Here a road goes off on the right and over the Stoss pass to Gais (Appenzell, St Gallen), and another road crosses the Ruppen pass, through beautiful scenery, to Trogen (see Appenzell) and St Gallen (see entry).

The road continues through Oberriet and comes in 29km/18 miles to Buchs (450m/1476ft; pop. 6000), chief town of a district and a road and rail junction. Buchs is a busy town (many haulage firms) on the route into Austria (Feldkirch–Innsbruck–Vienna).
Buchs

From Buchs the route continues either through the Principality of Liechtenstein (see entry) or on road 13, which runs along the west side of the valley to Balzers. Then either on the motorway via Bad Ragaz (see entry), or via Maienfeld (525m/1723ft; pop. 1500), an ancient Grisons town, with handsome patrician houses, the medieval Schloss Brandis ("Roman Tower"; inn) and Schloss Salenegg (17th–18th c.). In the cemetery is the grave of the writer John Knittel (1891–1970).
Principality of Liechtenstein

Bad Ragaz
Maienfeld

   From Maienfeld there are two possible routes to Landquart. The direct road (expressway) traverses the Rhine plain in a straight line (5km/3 miles) to the bridge which crosses the river Landquart into town. The alternative route, 2km/1 mile longer, is on an attractive minor road which follows the hillside through the orchards and vineyards of the old "Bündner Herrschaft" (Grisons Lordship) to the old-world village of Jenins, famous for its wine, and then continues below the ruined castles of Aspermont, Wyneck and Klingenhorn and past the lower station (1km/½ mile before Malans, on left) of a cableway which runs north-east to Aelpli (1802m/5912ft) under the summit of Vilan (2376m/7796ft; 1½ hours), to the vine-growing village of Malans (568m/1864ft), with handsome old patrician houses, under Burg Bothmar (16th and 18th c.).
Malans

Landquart (527m/1729ft) is a busy road and rail junction (paper-making). The motorway to Chur continues south between the railway and the right bank of the river (with strong side winds when the föhn is blowing).
Landquart

On the hillside to the east (not visible from the road) is Schloss Marschlins, with its four towers (538m/1765ft; 13th and 17th c.), commanding the entrance to the Prättigau. It can be reached by a side road (1 km/½ mile) off the old road via Zizers. Beyond this, to the east of the road, lies the village of Igis, with a college of agriculture in the Plantahof. In another 5km/3 miles the road passes Zizers station, serving the old market town of Zizers, Romansch Zizras (540m/1772ft), which lies off the road to the left and has two churches and two 17th c. mansions which belonged to the Salis family (the Unteres Schloss and the smaller Oberes Schloss, in the upper part of the town).
Schloss Marschlins

Zizers

The road then comes to Chur (see entry) and continues, bearing west, to the village of Domat Ems (583m/1916ft), with a church of the Assumption in Italian Baroque style (1730–38). On a rocky hill are the Late Gothic St John's church (1515; carved high altar of 1504) and the Romanesque St Peter's chapel.
Chur

The Rhine

Reichenau

3km/2 miles further on we leave the motorway at the Reichenau exit, just before it comes to an end. To the left is Reichenau (603m/1978ft), picturesquely situated on a rocky hill at the confluence of the Vorderrhein and the tumultuous Hinterrhein, with an old castle (altered in 1775 and 1820) belonging to the von Planta family; from the beautiful castle gardens there is a view of the junction of the two branches of the Rhine.

Along the Vorderrhein

Tamins

From Reichenau road 19 (signposted to Flims and Disentis), after crossing the Rhine, goes up to the village of Tamins (Romansch Tumein, "hill", 668m/2192ft; bypass), dominated by the prominent spire of its 16th c. parish church. The road then curves round to cross the Lavoi-Tobel (gorge) and winds its way up the hillside, with views to the left of the Domleschg (valley of the Hinterrhein) and Schloss Rhäzuns, one of the many old castles in the valley, and of the gorge carved by the Vorderrhein through the great Flims landslide.

Shortly before Trin the highest point on this section of road (895m/2936ft) is reached. On a crag to the left is the old tower of Hohentrins castle.

Trin

4km/2 miles from Tamins is Trin, German Trins (890m/2920ft), attractively situated on a terrace above the gorge of the Vorderrhein.

The road then continues downhill, with a view to the rear of the tower of Hohentrins. In 1km/½ mile it bends to the right, and one can see on the left the hamlet of Digg, picturesquely situated on the hillside. Then follows a fairly level stretch of road under the sheer cliffs of the Porclas defile, with meadowland and forest on the valley floor below. At the Trinsermühle (Romansch Trin-Mulin, 833m/2733ft; restaurant), an old mill, there are beautiful waterfalls. The road then climbs again, with many bends, along the edge of the gigantic masses of rock debris which tumbled down from the Upper Segnes valley during the Ice Age, covering some 52sq.km/20sq.

Valley of the Vorderrhein

miles of the Rhine valley. Off the road to the left is the little Cresta-See (850m/2789ft). Beautiful view of the valley below.

6.5km/4 miles beyond Trin is Flims (see entry). The road then passes a parking place (on right) for two cableways and bends to cross the Neue Stennabrücke (new Stenna bridge) over the Flembach (Segnesbach). After passing through the park-like landscape of the hotel settlement of Flims Waldhaus (see Flims) the road winds its way through a beautiful stretch of woodland and meadowland. 1km/½ mile further on a side road goes off on the left to a camp site; then in another 1km/½ mile, at Mulania (on right), is the lower station of a cableway 4045m/13,272ft long to Crap Sogn Gion (upper station 2220m/7284ft; large restaurant ski-lifts) and Crap Masegn (2477m/8127ft). The road then runs downhill and uphill again on a moderate gradient, crosses the Laaxer Bach and descends again above the deeply slashed Laaxer Tobel (gorge). Flims

The road continues via Laax (see Flims) to Ilanz (see entry) and from here it follows a fairly straight and level course to Disentis along the left bank of the Vorderrhein, close to the Rhätische Bahn, through a stretch of the valley known as the Pardella. Ilanz

2km/1 mile beyond Ilanz is Strada (720m/2362ft; bypass), with the charmingly situated little village of Schnaus higher up on the right. 2.5km/1 mile farther on is Ruis station (736m/2415ft; the village is above the road on the right). The road crosses the Panixer Bach, with the ruins of Jörgenberg Castle (495m/1624ft) on a wooded crag on the right.

4km/2 miles beyond Strada a road goes off on the right and winds its way up (3km/2 miles) to Waltensburg (Romansch Vuorz, 1010m/3314ft), where there is a church containing fine 14th and 15th c. frescoes. From Waltensburg a by-road, with extensive views, runs along a natural terrace to Brigels (5km/3 miles; see below). Waltensburg

Flims: "Schlössli"

The Rhine

The main road continues along the left bank of the Vorderrhein, then crosses to the other bank and curves under the railway.

Tavanasa

It reaches Tavanasa (800m/2625ft), at the narrow mouth of the Tscharbach valley, above which are two ruined castles, Schwarzenstein to the left and Heidenberg to the right. Here a side road on the right crosses the river to

Brigels

Danis and winds its way up (6km/4 miles north) to the village of Brigels, Romansch Breil (1283m/4210ft), a popular summer and winter sports resort in a sunny expanse of Alpine meadows, with the Late Gothic churches of St Maria (restored 1963–66) and St Martin. In the surrounding area (good walks with far-ranging views) are a number of pretty chapels, including the chapel of St Eusebius, with 14th c. frescoes on the exterior. Route over the Kisten pass (2638m/8655ft) to Tiefehd (9–10 hours).

Zignau

From Tavanasa the road to Disentis continues along the wooded slopes above the right bank of the Vorderrhein. Off the road to the left is Zignau, at the mouth of the wild Val Zavragia, and the ruins of Ringgenberg Castle.

St Anne's Chapel

Then on a stretch of concrete road to a bridge over the Vorderrhein and past St Anne's Chapel (1716, on right), on the spot where the "Upper" or "Grey" League of the people of the Grisons against the oppressions of the nobility was renewed in 1424.

Trun

6km/4 miles from Tavanasa is Trun, German Truns (855m/2805ft), a village of 1600 inhabitants at the mouth of the Val Punteglias, which runs down from the Brigelser Hörner (3250m/10,663ft; 10 hours, with guide). In the village are the parish church of St Martin (1660–62) with a Romanesque tower, and the former residence of the Abbots of Disentis (1675), now housing the district court and a museum, with handsome rooms (interesting coat-of-arms of the communes belonging to the Grey League and of all district judges since 1424). Above the village stands the 17th c. church of St Maria della Glisch.

Rabius

The road now climbs gradually to the village of Rabius (955m/3133ft), where a road on the left crosses the Rhine to Surrhein (892m/2927ft) and

Val Sumvitg

climbs the wooded Val Sumvitg (Somvixer Tal to 6.5km/4 miles south) Tenigerbad, Romansch Bagn Sumvitg (1273m/4177ft) (indoor pool). From Tenigerbad the road continues 1.7km/1 mile to Runcahez (1300m/4265ft), on a small artificial lake.

Somvix

The main road continues from Rabius to Somvix, Romansch Sumvitg (summus vicus, "highest village"; 1050m/3445ft), with the Gothic chapel of St Benedict. Below, on the Rhine, lies the village of Compadials (965m/3166ft). Beyond this is a beautiful stretch of road high up on the hillside, running through a defile and then over a new bridge (to the right the old covered wooden bridge) spanning the deep gorge of the Val Russein, which runs down from Mt Tödi. The road then ascends the rocky hillside

Disentis

and comes to Disentis (see entry), 7.5km/5 miles from Somvix.

Val Tavetsch

From Disentis road 19 leads up the Val Tavetsch on a moderate gradient, high above the river, with picturesque views of Disentis and its white abbey to the rear and the villages on the slopes of the valley downstream. Ahead can be seen, on the hillside to the right, the villages of Acletta (chapel), Segnes (1336m/4383ft) and Mompé Tujetsch (1397m/4584ft).

The road then continues, with expanses of coniferous forest, passes close to a high viaduct on the Furka–Oberalp railway and curves round to cross a mountain stream, the Bugnei.

Sedrun

9km/6 miles from Disentis is Sedrun (1401m/4597ft), chief place in the Val Tavetsch (Val Tujetsch), beautifully situated on gently sloping Alpine meadows and popular both with summer visitors and winter sports enthusiasts (ski-lift); enclosed swimming pool. The church of St Vigilius (1693), has a Romanesque tower and a carved altar (1491). Chair-lift to the spring pastures of Cungieri (1900m/6234ft; restaurant).

To the south is Piz Pazzola (2582m/8472ft; 4 hours), from which there are magnificent views. Further up the valley there is a fine view of Mt Badus (Six Madun). At Camischolas the road crosses a stream flowing down from the Val Strim. From here a narrow road (closed to traffic) runs up 8km/5 miles to the Lai da Nalps, an artificial lake (1909m/6263ft).

★Piz Pazzola

Rueras (1450m/4757ft) is a little village in the Val Milar, with a small church and fine wooden houses. The road then winds its way up again from the valley floor to the hillside and crosses streams flowing down the Val Milar and Val Giuf. To the left can be seen a tower of the ruined castle of Pontaningen (Pultmenga) and beyond this the chapel of St Brida. 1.5km/1 mile before Tschamut a road branches off on the left via the village of Selva to the hamlet of Sut Crestas (1540m/5053ft) lying in the valley, and which has a charming little church.

Rueras

The road then comes to the beautifully situated hamlet of Tschamut (1648m/5407ft), opposite the mouth of the Val Curnera (on left), crosses the Gämmerrhein, which flows down from the Val de Val (on right), and bears right at the foot of Mt Calmot into the Val Surpalix. To the left the Vorderrhein flows out of the Tomasee, at the foot of Mt Badus.

Tschamut

Along the Hinterrhein

The road south from Reichenau, where the Vorderrhein and the Hinterrhein join, crosses the Hinterrhein and runs along a terrace above the left bank of the river to Bonaduz.

From Bonaduz (660m/2165ft; pop. 1000) a road goes off on the right via Versam to Ilanz and Disentis. Here a road goes off on the right via Versam to Ilanz and Disentis. The main road (signposted to Thusis) continues south on the terrace above the river. High up on the left can be seen the Late

Bonaduz

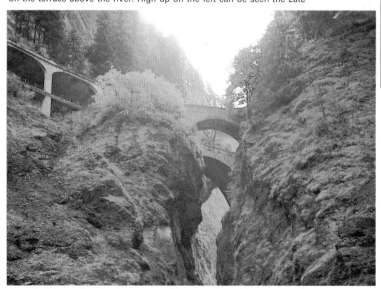

The Via Mala on the Hinterrhein

Romanesque chapel of St George, with fine wall-paintings of the 14th–15th c. and a Late Gothic carved altar (key at Rhäzuns station).

Rhäzuns

The road then comes to Rhäzuns (648m/2126ft). To the right is the village, with the Romanesque church of SS Peter and Paul and another church of 1702. To the left, on a steep crag above the Hinterrhein, stands the imposing Rhäzuns Castle, the oldest parts of which date from the 13th c., and which commands the entrance to the Domleschg (below). At the end of the village, on left, is the lower station of a cableway, 2100m/6890ft long, to Feldis.

The road follows the railway on the wooded hillside above the Hinterrhein, whose broad stony bed is enclosed between massive levees. On the opposite bank is a tower of the ruined castle of Nieder-Juvalta.

2km/1 mile beyond this, on the right, is the Rhäzuns mineral spring ("Rhätisana" table water; visitors can tour bottling plant). In another 2km/1 mile, just before the Rothenbrunnen railway station (625m/2051ft; to left), the valley opens out and the road forks. The valley floor and the gentle lower slopes on the east side are known as the Domleschg, the steeper west slopes as the Heinzenberg. On both sides are vineyards, and cornfields reaching high up on the hillsides. The main road to Thusis skirts the left bank of the river under the Heinzenberg; the very attractive side road to the left passes through the numerous villages in the Domleschg and rejoins the main road at Thusis. The castles built on projecting spurs of rock were almost completely destroyed at the end of the 15th c.

Through the Domleschg to Thusis

(11km/7 miles; well worth the extra 1.5km/1 mile).

The road to the left crosses the Hinterrhein and comes to the village of Rothenbrunnen, under high rock walls, with the ruined castle of Ober-Juvalta. It has a chalybeate (iron-bearing) spring containing iodine (bottling plant).

Farther on, beyond the bridge over the Scheidbach (on right), is the large Ortenstein castle (754m/2474ft), with an early medieval keep and 15th c. domestic quarters. 350m/1148ft south is the ruined pilgrimage church of St Lawrence.

Tomils

3km/2 miles from the road junction a mountain road (not dust-free, with some steep gradients; in winter open only as far as Scheid) runs up on the left via the village of Tomils or Tumegl (800m/2625ft; Late Gothic church with an altarpiece of 1490 and 16th c. wall-paintings) and continues with many bends, through Unterscheid and Oberscheid to (8km/5 miles north-

Feldis

east) Feldis or Veulden (1472m/4830ft), a health resort in a sunny spot commanding extensive views (cableway from Rhäzuns).

Paspels

The Thusis road continues to Paspels, with St Lawrence's chapel (Romanesque wall-paintings) and Alt-Sins Castle (restored). Beyond this, higher up on left, is the ruined castle of Neu-Sins or Canova.

Rodels

Rodels (700m/2297ft) has attractive 17th and 18th c. houses. Above the village, to the east, can be seen the 12th c. castle of Rietberg or Rätusberg, which features in Conrad Ferdinand Meyer's "Jurg Jenatsch".

Beyond this is Pratval, with the ruins of Hasensprung castle.

Fürstenau

At Fürstenau are two castles which belonged to the Planta family; the Haus Stoffel has 15th and 16th c. wall-paintings. Higher up, on the left, is the beautiful village of Scharans (780m/2559ft), where Jürg (Georg) Jenatsch was pastor in 1617–18. The road then crosses the Zollbrücke over the Albula, which emerges from the Schin gorge a little higher up the hill and flows down to join the Hinterrhein. To the left are Baldenstein castle and St Cassian's chapel (13th c.).

Sils, Thusis

At Sils (Seglias, 683m/2241ft) we join the road from Tiefencastel through the Schin gorge and turn right along this to reach Thusis (722m/2369ft).

The main road to Thusis (No. 13) continues from Rothenbrunnen station along the left bank of the Hinterrhein under the Heinzenberg, with views of the villages and castles of the Domleschg. To the left are Alt-Sins castle and the ruins of Neu-Sins.

Heinzenberg, Rothenbrunnen

In 5.5km/3 miles the road reaches Cazis (600m/1969ft) where we find an old Dominican nunnery (1504) (church with wall-paintings in choir) and the Romanesque chapel of St Wendelin.

Cazis

Beyond this is an attractive view, to the left, of the mouth of the Schin gorge, with the village of Scharans (on left) and Baldenstein castle (on right), the Tinzenhorn (3179m/10,430ft) rearing up above the gorge and in front of it the snow-capped Piz Curvèr (2972m/9751ft). 1km/½ mile beyond Cazis a road goes off on the right to Präz. Farther on, above the road on the right, are the little villages of Masein and Tagstein castle. Ahead, barely discernible, is the entrance to the Via Mala, with the ruined castles of Hohen-Rhätien and Ehrenfels.

4km/2 miles from Cazis we come to Thusis, Romansch Tusaun (722m/ 2369ft), a handsome market village at the junction with the road through the Schin gorge to Tiefencastel. The village was almost completely destroyed by fire in 1845. The Protestant parish church dates from 1506, the new Catholic church from 1965. All round Thusis are the ruins of medieval castles. On a steep crag at the entrance to the Via Mala, 246m/807ft above the river, perches the 12th c. castle of Hohen-Rhätien or Realta (950m/ 3117ft; 45 minutes' climb from the village); at Sils are Ehrenfels and Baldenstein; to the left, above the entrance to the Nolla valley, is Ober-Tagstein (1130m/3708ft; 1¼ hours on a forest track) from the slopes of the Heinzenberg stands the castle of Tagstein or Nieder-Tagstein (848m/2782ft; ½ hour).

Thusis

From Thusis the road to Splügen and the San Bernardino pass continues past the end of the Tiefencastel road, crosses the river Nolla, which flows into the Hinterrhein here.

The road then enters the Via Mala, a magnificent gorge on the Hinterrhein, enclosed between limestone walls 500m/1641ft high; the lowest section of the gorge, the Verlorene Loch ("Lost Hole"), is particularly wild and has been passable only since the construction of a road in 1822. The medieval bridle-path bypassed the gorge, running up from the Nolla valley to the right of the wooded crag of Grapteig; the road follows the windings of the gorge. The present road runs through a short tunnel and soon afterwards, high up on the hillside, enters a gallery leading into the 500m/1641ft long Rongellen Tunnel. 2.5km/2 miles from Thusis at the little hamlet of Rongellen (863m/2832ft), the gorge opens out into a small basin. It then closes in again, and in this narrower section, the real Via Mala of medieval times, the old road branches off the new road (No. 18).

★Via Mala

Rongellen

In 1988 a signposted educational walk through the narrow Via Mala gorge between Thusis and Zillis was opened. Information boards and maps explain the geological history and hydrology of the area and highlight man's great feats of engineering.

Via Mala Walk

The new road (distances about the same as on the old road described below) runs through a gallery, beyond which the old road, going in the opposite direction, comes in on the left. It then traverses a winding tunnel, crosses the Hinterrhein on a pre-stressed concrete bridge 170m/558ft long and runs through another curving tunnel 400m/1313ft long, beyond which the old road, with the bridge at Rania, can be seen lower down on the right. Then through a gallery and a short tunnel to an access road to the expressway, 5.3km/3 miles from Rongellen and 1km/½ mile north of Zillis.

N 13 expressway

The old road through the Via Mala (closed to large cars) branches off 1km/½ mile beyond Rongellen, immediately before a gallery. 800m/2625ft

Old Via Mala road

farther on, beyond the second gallery, is the Erste Brücke (First Bridge), built in 1941 on the site of an earlier bridge of 1738. Immediately beyond the bridge, on the right, are a parking place and a kiosk, from which a flight of 257 steps leads down to a gallery 120m/394ft long running above the tumultuous river (admission charge). 300m/984ft beyond this, after the third gallery, is the Zweite Brücke (Second Bridge: 800m/2887ft, built 1941), alongside the old bridge of 1739, 50m/164ft above the river. Above, to the right, can be seen the new road. In 1.3km/1 mile is the Dritte Brücke (Third Bridge: 885m/2904ft, at the end of the Via Mala, beside the little restaurant at Rania (on right). The road now enters the pleasant open valley of Schams (Romansch Sassám), with the pointed summit of Hüreli or Hirli (2855m/9367ft) in the background. 1km/½ mile before Zillis is an access road to the N 13 expressway.

Zillis
St Martin's
Church

★★Wooden
Ceiling

1km/½ mile south is the village of Zillis, Romansch Ciraun or Ziran (933m/3060ft), with the very interesting church of St Martin. The nave and tower are Early Romanesque, the choir Late Gothic; the whole structure was carefully restored in 1938–40. Its most notable feature is the 12th c. painted wooden ceiling, made up of 153 square panels depicting Biblical scenes – one of the oldest completely painted wooden ceilings in the West. Under the ceiling is a Romanesque frieze revealed in 1940.

Near the church in the Schams museum (Tgea da Schons) is a collection of tools, furniture and manuscripts from Schams, Avers and the Rheinwald.

Donath

From Zillis a narrow and winding road runs 2km/1 mile south-west up the Schamserberg, on the left bank of the Hinterrhein, to the village of Donath (1033m/3389ft). Above the village are the ruins of Fardün castle (1214m/3983ft), famous for the story of a 15th c. castellan who, during a peasant rising, spat into the dinner of a peasant named Johannes Calcar, who thereupon thrust his head into the bowl and suffocated him, with the words "Maglia sez il pult cha ti has condüt" ("You've salted the dish; now eat it!").

Zillis: Panels Nos. 136/137 and 143/144

E (Chancel)

1	2	3	4	5	6	7	8	9
48	49	50	51	52	53	54	55	10
47	56	57	58	59	60	61	62	11
46	63	64	65	66	67	68	69	12
45	70	71	72	73	74	75	76	13
44	77	78	79	80	81	82	83	14
43	84	85	86	87	88	89	90	15
42	91	92	93	94	95	96	97	16
41	98	99	100	101	102	103	104	17
40	105	106	107	108	109	110	111	18
39	112	113	114	115	116	117	118	19
38	119	120	121	122	123	124	125	20
37	126	127	128	129	130	131	132	21
36	133	134	135	136	137	138	139	22
35	140	141	142	143	144	145	146	23
34	147	148	149	150	151	152	153	24
33	32	31	30	29	28	27	26	25

S — N

W (Entrance)

☐ 140 original panels   ▨ 13 panels restored 1939–40

Romanesque painted ceiling in St Martin's Church (12th c.)

Zillis (GR)

38 Dragon swallowing a winged fish
39 Dragon
40 Fish-tailed animal with small nereid
41 Two dragons biting one another
42 Fish-tailed unicorn
43 Fish-tailed elephant
44 Fish-tailed lion
45 Fish-tailed wolf
46 Fish-tailed boar
47 Fish-tailed ram
48 Sea-horse biting the tail of a fish-tailed roebuck

INNER PANELS

49–51 Kings David, Solomon and Rehoboam
52, 53 The Synagogue and the Church
54, 55 Annunciation
56, 57 Joseph's Doubts
58 Visitation
59 Annunciation to the Shepherds
60–62 Nativity
63–66 The Three Kings on their way to see Herod
67–69 The Three Kings before Herod; three horses in waiting
70–73 Adoration of the Infant Jesus by the Three Kings
74–76 The Three Kings returning home
77 The Three Kings
78 Purification of the Virgin
79 Presentation in the Temple
80 Joseph's Dream
81–83 Flight into Egypt
84 Holy Family
85–90 Slaughter of the innocents
91 The Child Jesus gives life to clay birds
92, 93 The 12-year-old Jesus in the Temple
94–97 John the Baptist preaching in the wilderness
98 Baptism of Christ
99–101 Christ tempted by the Devil
102 Christ with two angels
103, 104 Marriage in Cana
105 Christ and the centurion of Capernaum
106, 107 Christ healing the sick
108 Christ casts out a devil
109 Christ heals the Canaanite woman
110, 111 Christ heals the impotent man at the pool of Bethesda
112 Christ heals a paralytic
113–115 Raising of Lazarus
116 Christ and the woman of Samaria
117, 118 Christ teaching in the school of Nazareth
119 Christ and the children
120–122 Mission of the Apostles
123–125 Transfiguration
126–130 Entry into Jerusalem
131, 132 Cleansing of the Temple
133–134 Judas's betrayal
135 Washing of the feet
136, 137 Last Supper
138, 139 Agony in the Garden
140–143 Christ taken prisoner; Judas's kiss
144 Christ before Pilate
145 Mocking of Christ
146 Christ is crowned with thorns
147, 148 St Martin with the beggar
149 St Martin consecrated as an acolyte by St Hilary
150 St Martin raises a man from the dead
151–153 The Devil appears to St Martin in the guise of a king

MARGINAL PANELS (including some copies)

1 Auster, the S wind
2 Dragon
3 Fish-tailed cock
4 Nereid with horn
5 Nereid with harp
6 Nereid with fiddle
7 Eagle
8 Dragon
9 Aquilo (written in mirror script), the N wind
10 Fisherman
11 The prophet Jonah
12 Part of a ship
13 Naked woman riding on a fish-tailed bird
14 Fish-tailed goose
15 Fish-tailed fox swallowing a fish-tailed cock
16 Monkey riding on a fish
17 Siren and fish-tailed stag
18 Naked man with axe riding on a fish
19 Fish-tailed wolf
20 Fish-tailed bear
21 Fish-tailed camel
22 Fish-tailed wolf
23 Fish-tailed lion
24 Fish-tailed ram
25 Angel
26 Dragon-tailed bird with snake
27 Dragon
28 Nereid with horn
29 Nereid with harp
30 Nereid with fiddle
31 Fish-tailed goose
32 Dragon-tailed bird with snake
33 Angel
34 Fish-tailed cock
35 Dragon
36 Fish-tailed boar
37 Fish-tailed he-goat

From Donath the road climbs another 6km/4 miles west to the quiet little mountain village of Mathon (1521m/4990ft), from which Piz Beverin (2997m/9833ft) can be climbed in 5 hours.

The N 13 expressway continues south up the Hinterrhein valley, coming in 3km/2 miles to the village of Clugin, on the left bank of the river (to right of road), with a picturesque little Romanesque church. 500m/1641ft south-west of the village are the ruins of Cagliatscha castle.

Beyond this, also on the right of the road, in the hamlet of Bad (Romansch Bogn), there is an alkaline chalybeate (iron-bearing) spring, the water of which is piped to Andeer. On the bridge over the Pignieuer Bach, which flows down from Piz Curvèr (2976m/9764ft), is a 15th c. Latin inscription.

5km/3 miles from Zillis is the exit for Andeer (979m/3212ft; pop. 1000), chief town in the Schams area, in medieval times an important trading station and now a health resort (mineral swimming pool) and winter sports facility, with a large parish church (1673: Protestant) and a number of fine 16th c. houses with sgraffito decoration, notably the Haus Padrun.

The old road continues through the Rofla gorge to join the new road (the distance is much the same). From Andeer there are rewarding and fairly easy climbs: to the west Piz Vizan (2472m/8111ft; 4½ hours); to the south-east Piz la Tschera (2632m/8636ft; 5 hours).

The new road (N 13) continues above Andeer in a wide curve, twice crossing the old road on bridges and passing below the village of Bärenburg (1042m/3419ft). Through the trees can be seen the ruined castle of the same name; to the right is an artificial lake.

The road then traverses a tunnel of some length and crosses the Averser Rhein to reach the junction, at Avers, with the old road coming up from Andeer on the right, which gives access to the Rolfa gorge and the Avers valley.

For the Rofla gorge, bear right into the old road to Avers soon branches off on the left. 1km/½ mile farther downhill is the Roflaschlucht inn (1097m/3599ft), at the entrance to the Rofla gorge (or Rofna: access to gallery hewn from rock, admission fee payable at the inn).

Beyond this is a reservoir (maximum capacity 1 million cu.m/35 million cu.ft, a compensation basin for the reservoir at Sufers, from which water is carried down under pressure through a tunnel 13km/8 miles long to a power station at Sils in the Domleschg. The old road then crosses under the new one twice and comes in 2km/1 mile to Andeer.

A rewarding excursion can be made into the beautiful high valley of the tumultuous Averser Rhein, which is divided into two parts by a narrow defile – the Romansch-speaking Val Ferrera and the German-speaking Averser Tal (Avers valley). It is reached on a good minor road (18km/11 miles to Cresta) which branches off the old road to the Rofla gorge, passes under the expressway and then continues up the wild Val Ferrera, first on the left bank and then on the right bank.

3.5km/2 miles up this road is Ausserferrera (1321m/4334ft), in a wider part of the valley. The road then runs through the Ragn da Ferrera defile. To the right are the Ferrera turbine house (185,000kW), hewn from the rock, and a compensation basin (230,000 cu.m/8 million cu.ft) for the reservoir in the Valle di Lei. Then, opposite the mouth of the Val d'Emet or Val Niemet, the village of Innerferrera (Romansch Canicül or Canlantgil, 1480m/4856ft) is reached. The road next crosses the Averser Rhein, runs through a tunnel

◀ *The Rofla gorge of the Rhine, near Andeer*

(200m/656ft) and then another grandiose defile (natural rock arch), with a waterfall at the mouth of the Val Starlera on the left. After another tunnel (500m/1641ft) it comes to the new bridge (lower down, the old bridge) over the Reno di Lei. This river issues from the Italian Valle di Lei, in which a dam was built in 1957–61 as a joint Swiss-Italian enterprise (Valle di Lei-Hinterrhein hydro-electric scheme).

100m/328ft beyond the bridge the road goes through another tunnel (250m/820ft), and 1.3km/1 mile farther on a road branches off on the right to the dam. This runs uphill, with two sharp bends, and in 2.5km/2 miles reaches a tunnel 1km/½ mile long (traffic lights; closed in winter), at the far end of which are the Swiss–Italian frontier, the Swiss customs (on right) and beyond this the dam (car park). The dam rises to a height of 138m/453ft above the foundations and is 635m/2083ft long at the top. The artificial lake

Lago di Lei   formed by the dam, the Lago di Lei (1931m/6336ft, capacity 197 million cu.m/6956 million cu.ft), lies in Italian territory. The water is carried down under pressure in a tunnel 6.9km/4 miles long to the Ferrera turbine house (above).

Avers valley   The main road continues past the turning for the dam along the Avers valley, whose German-speaking population originally came from the Valais (Wallis) and adopted the Reformed faith as early as 1530. After passing through the hamlet of Campsut (1670m/5479ft) the road comes to Cröt (1720m/5643ft: inn), at the mouth of the Madriser Tal, with the Cima di Lago (3082m/10,112ft) and Piz Gallgione (3135m/10,286ft) rearing up in the background. It then climbs the wooded hillside in sharp bends, crosses the Rhine once again and after a number of other sharp bends reaches the highest part of the valley.

Cresta   Cresta (Avers, 1960m/6431ft), beautifully situated amid flower-spangled Alpine meadows, attracts many visitors as a mountain resort and a climbing base, and offers good skiing. Outside the closely huddled village of brown wooden houses is the picturesque little 17th c. church. On the east side of the valley are the three peaks of the Weissberg (3057m/10,030ft; 3 hours) and the bold pyramidal silhouette of Piz Platta (3398m/11,149ft; 4–5 hours).

Juf   From Cresta the road continues for another 6km/4 miles, past the Podestatshaus (2042m/6700ft; built 1664), to Juf (2133m/6998ft), the highest permanently inhabited settlement in the Alps. From here it is possible to walk to Casaccia over the Septimer pass (Pass da Sett) or to Bovio.

Beyond the junction with the road to Andeer, the N 18 expressway to Splügen and San Bernardino continues through a long gallery above the Rofla gorge, and then through two tunnels, one fairly long, the other shorter. Below, to the right, is the Hinterrhein.

Sufner-See   Farther up the valley, on the left, is the Sufner-See (1401m/4597ft; capacity 18.3 million cu.m/646 million cu.ft), formed by a dam 58m/190ft high (viewing platform), which is linked with the reservoir in the Valle di Lei. Beyond this, on the right (exit road from expressway), is the little village of Sufers (1387m/4551ft).

Rheinwald Valley   The road continues through a beautiful expanse of forest. Soon afterwards the magnificent prospect of the Rheinwald valley opens up, with its backdrop of mountains: on the left the pyramid of Pizzo Tambo, to the right of this the blunt summit of Guggernüll (2886m/9469ft), beyond this the sharp peak of the Einshorn (2944m/9659ft) and in the background the Hohberghorn (3005m/9859ft).

Splügen   Farther on the exit for the Splügen pass and the village of Splügen (1450m/4757ft), in a wide valley at the foot of the Kalkberg, above which rears the Teurihorn (2973m/9754ft). The village, with handsome stone-built houses and a parish church of 1690, is a popular summer and winter resort (ski-lifts to the Danatzhöhe, 2160m/7087ft), and also attracts considerable through traffic as a result of its location on the route to the Splügen and San Bernardino passes. From the "Burg" (1527m/5010ft: 15 minutes north-east), a remnant of the old fortifications of the village, there is a fine view of the valley and the Tambohorn.

There is an attractive walk (2½ hours south-east) to the three Surette lakes (2270m/7448ft), in a grandiose mountain setting at the foot of the Surettahorn (3031m/9945ft); and Guggernüll (2886m/9469ft) offers a rewarding climb (4½ hours, with guide). For the continuation of the road over the Splügen pass to Chiavenna (see San Bernardino Pass).

The road to the San Bernardino pass (see entry) continues past the village of Splügen and runs up through the meadows of the Hinterrhein valley, following a fairly straight and almost level course, with beautiful views.

In 2.5km/2 miles it comes to the little village of Medels in Rheinwald (1533m/5030ft), consisting of three groups of houses (to right; exit from expressway). 4km/2 miles beyond this, also on the right (expressway exit), is the trim village of Nufenen (1568m/5145ft), opposite the mouth of the Areuetal, which runs down from the Tambohorn, with Guggernüll (2886m/9469ft) to the left and the Einshorn (2944m/9659ft) to the right.

3.5km/2 miles farther on, to the right, is Hinterrhein (1624m/5328ft), the last village in the Rheinwald valley, which comes to an end beneath the snow-capped peaks and glaciers of the Rheinwald or Adula Massif. There is a rewarding walk up the valley to the Zapport hut (2276m/7468ft; 4 hours), at the lower end of the Rheinwald glacier, the source of the Hinterrhein. From here there are many possible climbs (experienced climbers only) – e.g. the Rheinwaldhorn (3406m/11,175ft; 4 hr), the Güferhorn (3396m/11,175ft; 3½–4 hours, with guide), the Zapporthorn (3149m/10,332ft; 4 hr).

Hinterrhein

Rhine Falls N 2

Cantons: Schaffhausen (SH) and Zurich (ZH)

The Rhine Falls (Rheinfall) at Schaffhausen, the mightiest falls in Central Europe, surge over a ledge of Jurassic limestone 150m/492ft across and between 15 and 21m/49 and 69ft high, with two higher rocks standing in the

Situation and general

The Rhine Falls

middle of the river. The flow of water is at its greatest in June and July, after the melting of mountain snow.

Schaffhausen

The falls can be reached from Schaffhausen (see entry) on either side of the river.

Neuhausen

To reach the north side, leave Schaffhausen by way of Mühlenstrasse and road 4, which runs south-west to Neuhausen. There is a fishing museum (37 Rosenbergstrasse) with a collection of equipment, models and photographs documenting amateur and professional angling.

★★Rheinfall

Schloss Laufen

A footpath leads from the car park to the Rheinfallbrücke (192m/630ft long), which carries the Schaffhausen–Winterthur railway line. From here it is a 15 minutes' walk to Schloss Laufen (16th c., restored; restaurant), on the south bank from where there is a good general view of the falls.

A short walk through the park leads down to a number of viewpoints – the "Pavillon", "Känzli" and the "Fischez", an iron structure which brings the spectator almost within touching distance of the surging river.

Schloss Wörth

From the lower gate of the park a ferry can be taken across the river to the little Schloss Wörth (restaurant), with the best general view of the falls. From here it is a 10 minutes' walk up the right bank of the Rhine, past the Park Restaurant and then up a flight of steps to the left, to the car park.

Rhône Valley

B–N 9–11

Cantons: Valais (VS), Vaud (VD) and Geneva (GE)

Situation

The Rhône rises in the Bernese Oberland, flows through Swiss territory for 260km/162 miles and then enters France, eventually reaching the Mediterranean after a total course of 810km/503 miles.

★Rhône Glacier

★★Lake
Geneva

The source of the Rhône is the Rhône glacier, which comes down from the Dammastock, near Andermatt (see entry). The river, also known as the Rotten in its passage through German-speaking territory, flows south-west along the southern margin of the Bernese Oberland, with the Valais Alps on its south side, draining both these massifs through tributaries on either bank. At Martigny (see entry) it turns sharply north-west and flows into Lake Geneva (see entry). After passing along the whole length of the lake it emerges again at Geneva (see entry), leaves Switzerland and in a few kilometres makes its way into the French Jura.

Through the Rhône valley

The best way of seeing the Rhône valley is to travel upstream. In this direction the route passes through a great variety of scenery, rising to a culmination in the majestic landscapes of the High Alps.

Rhône Valley/
Vallée du Rhône

The Rhône valley, which with its lateral valleys occupies the whole of the canton of Valais (German Wallis), is a longitudinal trough up to 3km/2 miles wide between the steeply scarped southern slopes of the Bernese Alps, from which tumble a succession of short and swift mountain streams, and the main ridge of the Valais Alps, some 30–40km/19–25 miles away, the deep side valleys of which originate for the most part on terraces above the Rhône valley. The valley floor, originally littered with rock debris, has mostly been brought into cultivation through the regulation of the river and is now covered with fields of maize and vegetables and fruit orchards. At the bottom and on the lower slopes of the hills are vineyards, on the higher

Rhône glacier: Birth of the Rhône near Gletsch

slopes and terraces, fields, forests and Alpine meadows. Irrigation is necessary due to the shortage of rain and is provided by a network of channels (bisses), mostly fed by glacier water.

The Rhône valley road runs north-east from the old town of Martigny (see entry), from which roads run south to the Great St Bernard and the Col de la Forclaz, and then up the left bank of the river, traversing a region of fruit orchards on the valley floor, flanked by rocky hillsides, and often passing between long rows of poplars. It then crosses to the right bank and continues through a famous wine-growing region to the old episcopal and cantonal capital of Sion (see entry), dominated by its two old castles, and the little town of Sierre (see entry), situated amid a jumble of hills created by a huge prehistoric landslide, in an area offering numerous attractive excursions. ★Rhône Valley Road

Beyond Sierre the road returns to the left bank and enters the German-speaking Upper Valais (Oberwallis), passing within sight of the interesting little towns of Leuk (see Leukerbad) and Gampel on the sunny right bank.

After passing through the picturesque little market town of Visp (see Brig), where the road to Zermatt branches off, we soon come to the old town and road junction of Brig (see entry), where the towers of the Stockalperschloss form a distinctive landmark at the beginning of the road over the Simplon pass. The road continues via Lax (where it branches off to the Binntal) to Fiesch (see Brig).

Goms/Val de Conches

The character of the landscape now gradually changes. Although there are still walnut-trees and chestnuts to give something of a southern air, the rock faces now come closer, wooded gorges and steeper gradients make it clear that we have entered the region of high mountains.

Picturesque wooden houses and . . .　　*. . . wood-carving in Ernen*

A series of steep steps divides the lower Rhône Valley from Goms, whose name is derived from "Conches" (hollow, basin), the uppermost section of the Rhône Valley between Fiesch and Gletsch (as an illustration, Brig lies at 684m/2245ft, whereas Fiesch is at 1049m/3443ft). The Goms is a trough-shaped mountain valley running from south-west to north-east, along the bottom of which flows the Rhône, here known as the Rotten.

Here can be found numerous pretty villages, eight of which – Ernen, Mühlebach, Niederwald, Blitzingen, Selkingen, Ritzingen, Reckingen and Geshinen – are listed as places of prime cultural interest. The Goms Upper Way, along the north face, is particulary popular with walkers (for information contact the Walliser Vereinigung für Wanderwege, Postfach CH-1951, Sion).

Settlement

Evidence of temporary settlements date back to the Stone and Bronze Age. The first permanent settlement is thought to have been in the early Iron Age (from the 5th c.) with large clearings being left by the Alemannic tribes in the 8th c. During the Middle Ages settlement spread from the valley floor to individual farms and hamlets on the upper slopes. The region flourished economically and culturally during the 16th c. with the cattle trade, traffic using the pass and high political office bringing prosperity. Many elaborately decorated churches and artistic craftwork are the result of the religious Baroque revival in the 17th–18th c.

Ernen

Ernen, at one time the major town in the Goms, lies on a northern terrace of the valley, 1200m/3938ft above sea-level. Its picturesque wooden houses, 16th–18th c., their walls decorated with frescoes, coats-of-arms and mottoes, include the "Tellenhaus" (1578), with scenes from the Tell legend. The interior of the church is richly furnished.

Niederwald

Niederwald is the birthplace of the painter Raphael Ritz (1829–94) and the famous hotelier César Ritz (1850–1918).

At the mouth of the Blindental, dominated by the 3378m/11,087ft high Blindenhorn, lies Reckingen (1337m/4388ft), with one of the finest Baroque churches in Valais (1745).

Reckingen

Münster (pop. 450) is the chief town of the Goms. Note the church, rebuilt in 1678; the choir from the old church remains, and it has a fine altar (1509).

Münster

By way of Oberwald there is a final climb to Gletsch, at the foot of the famous Rhône glacier (see Andermatt). From here magnificent pass roads lead over the Grimsel into the Bernese Oberland and via the Furka road to the St Gotthard road (see Andermatt).

The traditional building, as elsewhere in the Inner Alps, is the Streuhof (barn). In contrast to the Mittelland, where living quarters, barn, threshing room and food store are all incorporated under one roof, the buildings here are single-purpose. The house is a high-walled block with a flat ridge roof. The oldest date from the Late Middle Ages and are colloquially referred to as "Heidenhäuser" ("Heathens' houses"). They are characterised by a ridge which holds together the grooved wall beams of the gable ends. In the 16th c. the wide "Renaissance houses" were built; in the 17th and 18th c. the multi-storey "Baroque house". The traditional functional building is the grain store, a towering block supported by typical stone "Mäuserplatten" ("mouse dishes") built on top of a lower construction, which served different purposes and in the Upper Goms even consisted of two floors. There is also a smaller store, of similar design, which was used as a food store and meat drying room. Due to the importance of cattle-rearing the most commonly found functional building is the cow stall or "Gade", as it is known in the Goms. Above the lower floor is the hay loft.

Buildings

Rigi

M 6

Cantons: Schwyz (SZ) and Lucerne (LU)

The Rigi, the most famous mountain viewpoint in Switzerland, 1800m/5906ft high, rises in isolation above Lake Lucerne, Lake Zug and the Lauerzer See, and is brought within easy reach by two cog-railways and a cableway. The roads from Küssnacht, Weggis and Gersau terminate halfway up the mountain.

Situation and general

The Rigi massif is an extensive range with a summit ridge some 50km/31 miles long.

The most popular viewpoints are the Kulm (1800m/5906ft), the Rotstock (1662m/5453ft) and the Scheidegg (1665m/5463ft). The many attractive footpaths and the mountain air, however, make it well worth while spending more time on the Rigi than a brief period for the sake of the view. The best places for winter sports are the sheltered hotel settlements of Kaltbad, with the excellent facilities provided by the Hostellerie Rigi, and Klösteri (several ski-lifts).

The view from the Rigi-Kulm is impressive both for the nearer view of the three surrounding lakes and the more distant panorama of the Alps; this prospect extends for some 200km/124 miles from end to end, with Säntis and Glärnisch, preceded by the Mythen, standing out with particular prominence in the east, Tödi in the south-east and the giants of the Bernese Oberland in the south-west; Pilatus closes the range of mountains in the west, and farther right one sees the Mittelland with its lakes, and beyond this the Jura and the Black Forest. On Rigi-Kulm, too, are the high tower antenna (the "Rigi-Nadel" or "Needle of the Rigi") and other installations of the Swiss Post Office.

★★ Landscape

Rigi

Mountain Rail- and Cableways

Vitznau-Rigi Line
Vitznau

Vitznau to Rigi-Kulm, the first cog-railway in Europe, built 1871 and electrified 1937 (length 7km/4 miles), maximum gradient 25% (1 in 4), time 35 minutes). During periods of heavy snow in winter it runs only as far as Staffelhöhe.

Rigi-Kaltbad

★Känzeli

★Rotstock
Rigi-Kulm

The line climbs up through Alpine meadows, the views becoming more and more extensive. 4.5km/3 miles: Rigi-Kaltbad (1440m/4725ft) lies in a sheltered hollow. Footpath to the First, and in 20 minutes to the Känzeli (1470m/4823ft), with fine views of the mountains and a prospect of Weggis, 1000m/3281ft below. 5km/3 miles: Staffelhöhe (1552m/5092ft). Beyond this the view of Lake Zug appears. 6km/4 miles: Staffel (1606m/5269ft), the station for the Rotstock (1662m/5453ft; 15 minutes), with a view similar to that from the Kulm. 7km/4 miles: Rigi-Kulm (1750m/5742ft). In summer there are also some steam trains.

Weggis–Rigi-Kaltbad

There is a cableway from Weggis to Rigi-Kaltbad (7 minutes). It is a beautiful walk by moonlight.

Arth–Rigi Line
Arth-Goldau

Arth-Goldau to Rigi-Kulm: cog-railway, opened 1875, electrified 1906 (length 9km/6 miles, maximum gradient 21% (1 in 5), time 35 minutes). The best views are on the right-hand side. The line runs uphill in a wide curve to the passing station at Kräbel (766m/2513ft: cableway to Scheidegg, 6 minutes) and then continues up the Kräbalwand, with views of the Rossberg and Lake Zug.

Klösterli

Rigi-Kulm

6km/4 miles: Klösterli (1315m/4315ft), in a sheltered hollow, with the pilgrimage church of Maria zum Schnee (Our Lady of the Snow: founded 1689, rebuilt 1721; pilgrimages on July 2nd and September 8th).

1.8km/1 mile: Staffel, where the view to the north and west opens up. The line then runs close to the Vitznau line, from where it is 9km/6 miles to Rigi-Kulm.

Regina Montium towers over the Lauerzer See

Special trips by boat and Rigi cableway are organised to see the famous sunrises and sunsets over the Rigi.

There are rewarding walks from either Kaltbad or Klösterli to Rigi-Schei- **Walks**
degg (2 hours).

The initial stage is to the Rigi-First (1454m/4771ft; 20 minutes); then by the "Felsenweg", with superb views, to Unterstetten (1440m/4725ft; 25 minutes); and from there either by way of the Nollen and Dossen (1688m/5538ft) in 1¼ hours or on the "Seeweg" (fine view down to the lake) to the ridge between the Dossen and Scheidegg (45 minutes) and from Scheidegg there another 30 minutes to the Scheidegg (1665m/5463ft; inn, with terrace café), from which there are good views to the south.

Rorschach   Q 3

Canton: St Gallen (SG)
Altitude: 398m/1306ft. Population: 10,800

The old port of Rorschach, lying at the foot of the Rorschacher Berg in a Situation and
wide bay, the most southerly in Lake Constance (Obersee), was once an general
important trading post for the town of St Gallen. Its principal industries are textiles, metalworking and piano manufacture ("Sabel").

The pumping station for the supply of Lake Constance water to St Gallen is here.

The development of Rorschach was closely bound up with economic pros- History
perity of the abbey of St Gallen. As early as A.D. 947 it was granted the right to hold markets, coin money and levy tolls by the Abbot of St Gallen. The old dock was enlarged in 1484, enabling the town to carry on a considerable trade, particularly in corn. In the 18th c. the linen trade also flourished. In 1803, on the dissolution of the abbey, Rorschach passed to the canton of St Gallen.

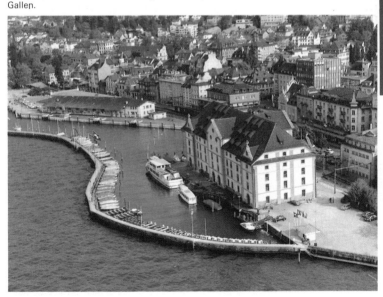

Rorschach on Lake Constance

Sights

Harbour, ★Kornhaus	At the federal harbour there is a harbour station and the Kornhaus (Granary: built 1746, restored 1956–58), now houses a local museum (closed in winter; well-displayed collection of prehistoric material).
Seepark	To the east of the park stretches the beautiful Seepark (fountains) with a lakeside promenade. Not far south of the park and the harbour the main road runs parallel to the lake with a number of prettily decorated 18th c.
St Columban	houses. Further south stands the Roman Catholic parish church of St Columban (Baroque, 1645–67; nave altered 1783).
Mariaberg monastery	On the hillside above the town is the former monastery of Mariaberg (440m/1444ft), a teachers' training college since 1805, with a beautiful cloister (1519) and a Gothic chapter-house (music room).
Staad	The cliffs "Grosser Schrönteler" and "Kleiner Schrönteler" can be seen from the easterly suburb of Staad.

Surroundings

St Anna Schloss, ★Rossbüehel ★View	Past the Mariaberg monastery turn left to reach, 2km/1 mile from Rorschach, St Anna Schloss (568m/1864ft; private property), with extensive views; then to the top of Rossbüehel (964m/3163ft; 1 hour), with views of five countries.
Wilen, Schloss Wartegg	From Mariaberg monastery take the Goldach road which runs 3km/2 miles east to Wilen, with Schloss Wartegg (1557: beautiful park) where the Austrian royal family took refuge after the First World War.
Goldach, Schloss Sulzberg	4km/2 miles south-west of Rorschach by way of Goldach is Schloss Sulzberg or the Möttelischloss (550m/1805ft; private property), with a 13th c. tower.
Rorschach– Heiden Line	7km/4 miles south of Rorschach in the canton of Appenzell are the holiday resorts of Heiden and Wienacht, which can be reached by cog-railway in 25 minutes.
Altenrhein	In the fishing village of Altenrhein (397m/1302ft), situated on the delta of the Alter Rhein (Old Rhine), is a nature reserve. The Altenrhein aircraft and vehicle manufacturing works (FFA, owned by Dornier since 1985) and Altenrhein airport, from where the legendary Dornier Flying Boats (including DO–X) took off in the Twenties, are to found here.
Altenrhein Marina	To the north-east of Altenrhein, on the left-hand finger of the Alter Rhein (Unterer Rheinspitz), is the Altenrhein marina or yachting harbour. A beautiful recreational park is in Buriet, to the south of Altenrhein.

Saas Valley   K 11/12

Canton: Valais (VS)

Situation and general	The narrow Saas valley, through which the Saaser Vispa flows down to join the Rhône, extends for some 28km/17 miles to the south of the little town of Visp, on the Rhône, at heights of between 1000 and 2000m/3281 and 6562ft, with the popular resorts of Saas Grund, Saas Fee and Saas Almagell. The starting-point of the valley is the village of Stalden, where the Zermatt and Saas valley roads separate.
History	The name of Saas Fee first appears in the records in 1217, in a document in which the Bishop of Sion disclaims responsibility for the protection of the Antrona pass road. About 1400 the commune of Saas became an independent parish, and in 1893 Fee was also made a separate parish. The local

priest, Johann Josef Imseng (1806–69), began to experiment with skis in 1849, and is honoured as the pioneer of winter sports in Switzerland.

In the Saas valley

Saas Grund

The lowest part of the commune of Saas is Saas Balen (1487m/4879ft; pop. 470), which has a round church (Baroque). 24km/15 miles higher up is the chief place in the valley, Saas Grund (1562m/5125ft), situated in meadowland on the valley floor, with a large parish church (1939). Lying between the Mischabel group (the main peak of which is concealed behind lower mountains) to the west and the Fletschhorn (3996m/13,111ft; not visible from valley floor) and Weissmies (4023m/13,199ft) to the east, it is a popular base for climbers. Indoor swimming pool in Touring Hotel.

Mischabel Group, Fletschhorn Weissmies

Saas Fee

From Saas Grund a minor road (4km/2 miles long, gradient 8% (1 in 12) with two hairpin bends) runs up to the "road terminus", just below Saas Fee (car park, parking garage, service garages; no cars beyond this point). The village of Saas Fee (1798m/5899ft), in a magnificent location facing the great Fee glacier, with the peaks of the Mischabel group towering above it in a wide arc, is a popular health resort, with winter sports (indoor swimming pool, ski-lifts, ice-rinks, curling, toboggan run) and climbing. The modern church (1963), with a separate tower, is well adapted to its setting. In the churchyard is the grave of the writer Carl Zuckmayer (1896–1977), an honorary citizen of Saas Fee. The nearby Saas Museum contains furniture,

★Situation

Saas Museum

Saas valley – chair-lift to the Felskopf

fittings and the original study belonging to him, along with the history of the glacier.

Spielboden ★ Längfluh	A cableway 3400m/11,155ft long runs south-west (23 minutes), via an intermediate station at Spielboden (2450m/8038ft; marmots), to the Längfluh (2865m/9400ft; restaurant, climbers' hostel), which can be reached on foot from Saas Fee via the Gletscheralp (2135m/7005ft) in 2½–3 hours (from Gletscheralp chair-lift 560m/1837ft long, winter only).
★ Allalinhorn	The Längfluh is the starting-point for the ascent of the Allalinhorn (4027m/13,213ft; 4 hours, with guide), the least difficult peak in the Mischabel group, the highest point of which is the Dom (4545m/14,912ft), the highest mountain entirely in Swiss territory.
Plattjen	A cableway runs south-east from Saas Fee (12 minutes) to the Plattjen (2567m/8422ft; restaurant, chair-lift; Berghaus Plattjen 30 minutes lower down), from which it is a 2½ hours' climb to the Britannia hut (3029m/9938ft). Cableway from Saas Fee to Hannig-Alp (2400m/7874ft), to the west.
Felskinn, Metro Alpin

Mittelallalin | From Saas Fee to Kalbermatten a cableway 3652m/11,982ft long runs south (9 minutes) to the Felskinn (2990m/9810ft; restaurant, ice cave, geological trail; skiing area, with summer skiing). The Metro Alpin, opened in 1985 (the highest underground funicular in the Alps), runs from Felskinn to Mittelallalin (3500m/11,487ft), where the highest revolving restaurant in Central Europe has marvellous views. |

Saas Almagell

From Saas Grund the road continues south-east up the valley, with moderate gradients, passing through Zenlauenen and Moos, and in 4km/2 miles reaches Saas Almagell (1679m/5509ft), the highest village in the valley, a health resort, winter sports (ski-lifts, ice-rink) and climbing base. Chair-lift to 1950m/6398ft on the Furggstalden (good skiing; ski-lift). Walk to the Almageller Alp (2225m/7300ft; 1¼ hours).

Almageller Alp	(see text above)
Mattmarksee

Monte Moro Pass

Macugnaga | The road continues for another 7.5km/5 miles, past the hamlet of Zermeiggern (1716m/5630ft) and the huge moraine of the Allalin glacier, to the dam (115m/377ft high, 780m/2559ft long at the top), completed in 1967, which has formed the Mattmarksee. A massive fall of ice from the Allalin glacier crashed down on the construction site in August 1965, killing 88 workmen. From the dam it is a 45 minutes' climb to the Monte Moro pass (2862m/9390ft), which until the construction of the Simplon road was the principal route from the Valais into Italy (Swiss–Italian frontier). From the pass a cableway (large cabins) descends to Macugnaga (1307m/4288ft), in the Val d'Anzasca. |

Great St Bernard   G 13

In Switzerland and in Italy
Canton: Valais (VS). Height of pass: 2469m/8101ft

Situation and general	The road over the Great St Bernard pass, between the Mont Blanc group and the Valais Alps, the highest pass road in the Swiss Alps after the Umbrail road, is for the most part excellently engineered (maximum gradient 11%), but is usually open only from the middle or end of June until October. The drive through the defiles of the Drance valley on the north side and above all the descent from the rugged world of the mountains into the southern beauty of the Aosta valley is a great scenic experience.

The construction of the St Bernard tunnel (5828m/19,122ft long, carriageway 7.5m/25ft; toll) in 1959–63 made the road passable throughout the year and shortened the distance between western Switzerland and Italy in winter by several hundred kilometres.

This ancient and historic traffic route was used by the Celts, from 105 B.C. onwards by the Romans, in A.D. 547 by the Lombards and later by many German emperors travelling to Italy (Charlemagne in 773, Henry IV on his journey to Canossa in 1077, Frederick Barbarossa in 1175). In May 1800 Napoleon led an army of 30,000 men over the pass to Aosta and Milan in order to expel the Austrians from Italy (Battle of Marengo).

History

From Martigny the road climbs the wild narrow valley of the Drance, passing through the village of Sembrancher at the mouth of the Val de Bagnes, to Orsières, and then up the featureless Vallée d'Entremont to Bourg-St-Pierre (1634m/5631ft; by-pass), a little market town in a wider part of the valley at the mouth of the Valsorey. The parish church (1739) has an 11th c. tower. Beside the church is a Roman milestone (4th c. A.D.). From here a number of difficult climbs can be undertaken including Mont Vélan (3765m/12,353ft; 7–8 hours, with guide) and the Grand Combin (4317m/14,164ft; 11 hours, with guide).

Martigny

Bourg-St-Pierre

★ Grand Combin

From Bourg-St-Pierre a covered concrete road (8m/26ft wide, maximum gradient 6% (1 in 16) runs up the east side of the valley above the Défilé de Saraire and past the Lac des Toules (1800m/5906ft), an artificial lake (capacity 20 million cu.m/706 million cu.ft) formed by a dam 80m/262ft high (short tunnel).

The road then reaches Bourg-St-Bernard, at the entrance (station, 1915m/ 6283ft; passport and customs control; toll charge) to the Great St Bernard tunnel. To the left are the Petit Vélan (3233m/10,607ft) and the snow-capped summit of Mont Vélan. Cableway (2530m/8301ft, 14 minutes) to the Col de Menouve (2753m/9033ft; Super-St-Bernard winter sports centre; magnificent ski trails of varying degrees of difficulty).

★ Great St Bernard Tunnel

On the Great St Bernard Pass

From here the route continues either through the tunnel (maximum speed in tunnel 60 km p.h./37 m.p.h.; toll charge) and on a covered road (9.5km/6 miles long, 9m/30ft wide) to beyond St-Rhémy, or on the old road over the Great St Bernard.

Over the Great St Bernard

The road over the Great St Bernard runs south-west over the Alpine meadows, strewn with rock debris, of the Plan de Proz to the Cantine d'en Haut (1905m/6250ft), and from there through a wild gorge, the Pas de Marengo, to the huts of Hospitalet (2100m/6899ft). After crossing the Drance on the Pont Nudry (2190m/7185ft) it winds its way up to the pass through the desolate Combe des Morts, which is filled with snow right into the height of summer.

★Great St Bernard Pass

The Great St Bernard pass (2469m/8101ft; Hôtel de l'Hospice), used since ancient times, crosses the main ridge of the Alps, between the Mont Mort (2867m/9407ft) on the left and the Pic de Drona (2950m/9679ft) on the right. In summer the Swiss customs control takes place here.

Hospice

The famous Hospice founded about 1049 by St Bernard of Menthon (d. 1081) to succour distressed travellers is now occupied by Augustinian Canons. Most of the monastery buildings date from the 18th c. The new building (1898) has been occupied by a hotel since 1925. In the church (1676–78) is the tomb of the French General Desaix, who was killed in the Battle of Marengo. The Museum contains Celtic and Roman antiquities from the Plan de Jupiter, documents relating to the history of the pass, as well as a collection of minerals and insects. The Hospice is famous also for the St Bernard dogs bred by the monks and used to scent out travellers lost in the snow. Chair-lift (10 minutes) to La Chenalette (2800m/9187ft) from which there are superb views.

Plan de Jupiter

The road to Aosta skirts a small lake, rarely ice-free even in summer, through which runs the Swiss–Italian frontier (Italian customs control in summer). To the right is the Plan de Jupiter, with a stone cross (1616) and a bronze statue of St Bernard (1905). The name Plan de Jupiter, like the earlier name of the pass, Mont Joux (Mons Jovis), recalls a Roman temple to Jupiter Poeninus which stood here.

The road now descends in a wide curve past the hamlet of La Baux and a large crag, the Gour des Fous, to the Cantine d'Aoste (2217m/7274ft; Italian customs), in a green hollow.

Vallée du Grand-St-Bernard

From here it winds its way down to Aosta. To the left is the exit from the tunnel (1875m/6152ft; Italian and Swiss passport and customs control for entry to Switzerland). The road then crosses the expressway coming from the tunnel and descends, with two sharp turns, to the left bank of the Torrente Artanavaz and the village of St Rhémy (1632m/5355ft) which is situated in a wooded defile. The expressway bypasses the village to the west. The road then bears right through the deeply eroded Combes des Bosses, and in another 2.5km/2 miles is joined by the expressway from the tunnel exit (9.5km/6 miles).

St Gallen   Q 4

Canton: St Gallen (SG)
Altitude: 670m/2177ft. Population: 75,000

Situation and general

St Gallen lies about 15km/9 miles south-west of Lake Constance, in a narrow high valley of the Pre-Alps, here dissected by numerous streams (the Goldach, the Steinach, the Sitter) flowing through constricted gorges. The motorway and express trains connect the town with Zurich-Kloten airport and other important towns in Switzerland. St Gallen is the capital of the canton of the same name and the commercial hub (embroidery, textile and metal industries; largest shopping centre in Eastern Switzerland; trade fairs) and cultural centre of Eastern Switzerland as well as a popular congress resort.

The town takes its name from the Irish missionary monk Gall or Gallus who established a hermitage here about 612. This developed into the Benedictine abbey which became a flourishing seat of religion and scholarship in the 9th c.; its school and library made it one of the focal points of European culture north of the Alps. In the 10th c. St Gallen, until then no more than a settlement of craftsmen and tradesmen which had grown up around the abbey, achieved the status of a town which in the 15th c. shook off the authority of the abbey and, in 1524, under a burgomaster named Vadian, adopted the Reformed faith. In the 16th–18th c. the town became exceedingly prosperous through its linen industry and grew considerably in size. The craft of embroidery, introduced in the 18th c., developed about 1830 with the advent of the hand-operated embroidery machine and later the shuttle embroidery machine into a considerable export industry (Textile Museum). Other industries, in particular metal-working, were established later.

History

Sights

In the northern part of the old town, which has handsome 17th and 18th c. burghers' houses with oriel windows, is the Marktplatz. At the corner of

Marktplatz

| 1 Kirchoferhaus | 2 Weigh-House | 3 Vadian Monument | 4 Schibener Tor | 5 Textile Museum | 6 Müllertor |

Marktgasse and Neugasse stands a statue of the 16th c. burgomaster Joachim von Watt (Vadian).

Musical Box Cabinet

Heading south from the Marktplatz No. 23 Marktgasse houses the Labhart musical box cabinet.

Bohl, Waaghaus

To the east of the Marktplatz is the broad street known as the Bohl, at the end of which is the 16th c. Weigh-House (Waaghaus); this houses the Council Chamber. Also here is the Hotel Hecht, the oldest inn in the town.

St Katharinenhof, St Mangan's church

To the north of the Bohl is the St Katharinenhof, a relic of the former cloister of 1504. Still farther north is St Mangan's church (founded c. 900 but much altered in later centuries), with a 16th c. tower.

Multergasse, St Lawrence's church

From the Marktplatz the Marktgasse runs south – on the right Multergasse, a well known shopping street in the pedestrianised zone – to St Lawrence's church (St Lorenz; restored 1851–54).

★ ★ Benedictine Abbey

To the south is the spacious Klosterhof (Abbey Yard), around which is the former Benedictine Abbey. The extensive range of buildings, dating from

Plan of St Gallen Monastery

Carolingian idealised plan (circa 820)

1 Saint's tomb (beneath High Altar)
2 Scriptorium (below) Library (above)
3 Sacristy (below) Robing Room (above)
4 Chapter House
5 Clerical guests
6 School Master
7 Gatekeeper
8 Visitors' room
9 Old People's Warden
10 Heating room (below) Dormitorium (above)
11 Provision store (cellar below)
12 Refectorium (below) Wardrobe (above)

W Business rooms
00 Lavatories

Generalised plan

© Baedeker

the 17th and 18th c., now accommodates the bishop's palace, the residences of the cathedral clergy and cantonal government offices.

The Late-Baroque three-aisled former collegiate church, now the cathedral, was reconstructed on the site of the earlier abbey church which had been pulled down. The most notable features are the colourful ceiling-paintings by Christian Wenzinger, the stucco work in the choir by the Gigi brothers, the ceiling-paintings by J. Wannenmacher (1722–80), the wrought-iron choir-stalls by Josef Feichtmayr, with carved scenes from the life of St Benedict. The interior of the cathedral was thoroughly restored and renovated in 1962–67 making the old ceiling paintings in the choir visible again.

★Cathedral

In the crypt, part of which dates from the 10th c. can be seen the tombs of all the bishops of St Gallen. The monastic treasury is also worth seeing.

The Abbey Library (May–Oct. Mon.–Fri. 9am–noon, 2–5pm; Sun. 10.30am–noon, June and Aug. also 2–4pm; some 130,000 volumes, 1650 incunabula, 2000 manuscripts), housed in a charming Rococo Library Hall by Peter Thumb (1758–67), with stucco work by the Gigi brothers and ceiling-paintings by Josef Wannenmacher, possesses works which belonged to the old abbey school, one of the leading European capitals of learning in the 9th–11th c., notable particularly in the fields of book illumination, poetry and the translation of Latin works into Alemannic. The finest items in the library are displayed in rotation and include the 9th c. "Psalterium Aureum", the "Casus Monasterii Sancti Galli" by Ekkehard IV (11th c.) and Manuscript of the Nibelungenlied (13th c.). The famous plan of St Gallen abbey in 820, displayed under glass, presents the model of a large monastic establishment, a plan which was followed until the end of the Middle Ages. A double sarcophagus of sycamore wood contains a mummy from Upper Egypt (700 B.C.).

★Abbey Library

In Gallusplatz and Gallusstrasse, to the west of the cathedral, are elegant old burghers' houses of the 17th and 18th c., such as the Haus zum Greif (House of the Griffin, Gallusstrasse 22), with a carved oriel window. There are other interesting old houses at Schmiedgass 15 and Kugelgasse 8 and 10.

Gallusplatz, Gallusstrasse, Haus zum Greif

In Moosbruggstrasse, immediately south of the abbey, are two remnants of the old town walls, the Karlstor (reliefs of 1570) and a round tower.

Karlstor

Next to the Spisertor stands the historic Schlössli. South-east of Gallusplatz, at the falls on the Steinach, is a terrace with a memorial to St Gall.

Spisertor, Schlössli, St Gall Memorial

North-west of Gallusplatz the Textile Museum (Vadianstrasse 2) has an important collection of embroidery and lace from the 14th to the 20th c., finds from Egyptian tombs (Coptic period, 4th–12th c.) and antique books.

Textile Museum

In the Oberen Graben is the Broderbrunnen (Broder fountain; 1896) commemorating the opening of Lake Constance waterworks in 1894. Along the Vadianstrasse is the modern shopping centre "Neumarkt" with an iron sculpture of St Gall by Max Oertli.

Broderbrunnen

Neumarkt

North-east of the Bohl is Museumstrasse, in which are the Tonhalle (1907; concert hall) and, on the right, the Municipal Theatre (Stadttheater, 1966–68) in modern style.

Tonhalle, ★Municipal Theatre

Farther to the left, at Museumstrasse 27, is the Kirchhoferhaus Museum (prehistoric material from caves; Züst collection of silver, 16th–19th c.).

Kirchhoferhaus Museum

Beyond this, on the right-hand side of the Stadtpark (Museumstrasse 23), stands the recently reopened (1987) Museum of Art and Natural History, which was built in Classical style in 1877. The Natural History section contains collections of minerals and precious stones and geology and

Museum of Art and Natural History

Treasures of the famous . . .   *. . . Abbey library*

holography exhibitions. The art collection includes works by Romanticists and Impressionists, paintings by Segantini, folk art and modern art.

Beyond this again (No. 50) is the Historical Museum or Neues Museum (New Museum), with prehistoric, historical and ethnographic collections, domestic interiors and utensils, porcelain, etc.)

Historical Museum

North-west of the Historical Museum, at Notkerstrasse 22, the Municipal Library (Stadtbibliothek Vadiana), founded in 1551, houses the Municipal Archives. To the north-east are the exhibition grounds where the annual Agricultural and Dairy Show (OLMA) is held.

Municipal Library Vadiana

OLMA

To the north of the town, on higher ground, is situated the School of Economic and Social Sciences (Hochschule für Wirtschafts- und Sozial-wissenschaften; conducted tours by appointment, tel. 23 31 35), a fine example of modern architecture (1960–63), with the Institute for Tourism and Transport, student residences and a sports hall. Within the buildings and grounds are numerous works by leading artists, including Jean Miró, Alexander Calder, Alberto Giacometti, Antoni Tàpies, Georges Braque, Otto Müller, Hans Arp and Carl Burckhardt.

School of Economic and Social Sciences Institute for Tourism and Transport

The Botanic Garden lies north-east of the town.

Botanic Garden

Surroundings

3km/2 miles south of the town is the Freudenberg (887m/2910ft; restaurant), from which there is a magnificent view of the town, Lake Constance and Säntis.

Freudenberg

◄ *St Gallen: the Late-Baroque cathedral*

St. Gallen HSG

General-Guisan-Strasse

Vonbüelstrasse

Theodor-Curti-Strasse

Dufourstrasse

School of Economic and Social Sciences

A Main Building
B Refectory
C Great Hall and Chapel
D Economic Research Institute

ART WORKS

1 Zoltan Kemeny: Brass relief
2 Umberto Mastroianni: Aluminium sculpture
3 Alicia Penalba: Reinforced concrete sculptures
4 Jean Arp: "Schalenbaum" (Bronze)
5 George Braques: "Oiseau" (Mosaic)
6 Soniatta: Wood Relief on ceiling
7 Etienne Hajdu: Beaten lead reliefs
8 Joan Miró: Ceramic frieze
9 Pierre Soulages: Tapestries
10 Alexander Calder: Mobile (Aluminium)
11 Alberto Giacometti: "Stehende" (Bronze)
12 Antoni Tàpies: Wall decoration
13 Ferdinand Gehr: Flower paintings
14 Max Gubler: "Nachtlandschaft" (Oil painting)
15 Coghuf (Ernst Stocker): three four-part reliefs (iron and glass)
16 Coghuf+Silvia Valentin: Tapestry
17 Coghuf: Ceiling relief
18 Otto Müller: interior of chapel with brass cross, bronze relief, lead relief, gilded glass sculpture
19 Walter Bodmer: iron and glass sculpture
20 Jean Baier: Coloured reliefs (enamelled aluminium)
21 Francois Stahly: Bronze sculpture
22 Carl Burckhardt: "Amazone" (Bronze)
23 Max Oertli: Bronze sculpture

★ Wildpark Peter und Paul	3.5km/2 miles north is the Rotmonten, Wildpark Peter und Paul (Wildlife Park; 800m/2625ft) with Alpine animals (chamois, ibex, marmots, etc.)
★ Säntis Leisure Park	In Abtwil, near the N 1 (St Gallen-Winkel exit), the Säntispark leisure and shopping centre was opened in 1987.
Teufen	7km/4 miles south-east of St Gallen the village of Teufen (837m/2747ft), a desirable suburb of St Gallen, has an interesting museum.
Gossau	Gossau lies about 11km/7 miles west of St Gallen between the rivers Glatt and Sitter in Fürstenland. It is the centre of agricultural production in the canton of St Gallen (butter and cheese dairies, mills) and has a variety of industries. There is a motorcycle museum and a small zoo.
Schloss Oberberg	4km/2 miles to the west is Schloss Oberberg (restaurant; museum) with a 13th c. tower.
Oberbüren	About 8km/5 miles west of Gossau lies the district of Oberbüren. Its former castle, the Glattburg, which was later converted into the Benedictine monastery of St Gallusberg, is mentioned in a historical document from 788, making it the oldest castle site in the country.
Wil	27km/17 miles (motorway) is Wil (574m/1883ft), an industrial town which at one time was a favourite summer residence of the Prince-Abbots of St Gallen. The beautiful old town lies around the Hofplatz (also known as the "Goldener Boden" or "Golden Ground"), with the former Abbot's palace (the Hof), now housing a local museum, and the Baronenhaus (1795). Nearby is the parish church of St Nicholas (1429–78) and to the south-west (originally Gothic) church of St Peter.

St Gotthard N 9

Cantons: Uri (UR) and Ticino (TI)
Height of pass: 2108m/6916ft

The St Gotthard massif in central Switzerland is one of Europe's most important watersheds, with the sources of the Rhine, the Rhône, the Reuss and the Ticino (Tessin). This rugged mass of crystalline schists and granite was for many centuries an obstacle to transit through the Alps, and it was only the bold road-building operations of the 18th and 19th c. and the construction of the St Gotthard railway that opened up this shortest route from north to south for modern traffic. In 1980 after 11 years' work the St Gotthard road tunnel was completed.

Situation and general

There was already a bridle-path over the St Gotthard pass in the 13th c. The first section of the modern road, between Andermatt and Airolo, was constructed in 1819–30, and this was later extended farther south. The construction of the St Gotthard railway (Gotthardbahn) in 1874–82 was an outstanding technical achievement for its day, costing the lives of 177 men, including the engineer in charge, Louis Favre.

History

The railway tunnel (15km/9 miles long) runs under the summit of the St Gotthard massif at a height of 1154m/3786ft. The Gotthardbahn from Basle or Zurich to Lugano takes 4 or 3 hours respectively through the Gotthard Tunnel.

★ Gotthardbahn

The William Tell Express (first stage by steamer from Lucerne to Flüelen) runs to Lugano from the end of May to the end of October (see Practical Information, Railways).

★ William Tell Express

The Gotthard Post has a nostalgic route from Lucerne to Lugano using old post vans and horse-drawn carriages (five-day trip; information from Historische Reisepost, CH-6002 Lucerne; tel. (041) 50 22 33).

★ Historic post route

The new St Gotthard Road Tunnel (toll) is the longest road tunnel in the world (16.91km/10 miles), passing through the mountains at a height of 1175m/3855ft. Its completion means that the St Gotthard route is now open all year round. The opening of the N 2 in 1986 means that it is possible to drive direct from Basle to Chiasso, leading to an increase in through-traffic along the valleys of the Reuss and Ticino. In view of the growth in the volume of traffic as a result of the single market in the European Union (EU) plans for a 50km/31 mile long tunnel, from Amsteg in the Reuss valley to Bodio in Ticino, are under discussion.

★★ St Gotthard Road Tunnel

From Andermatt to Bellinzona over the St Gotthard Pass (85km/53 miles)

From Andermatt (1444m/4138ft; see entry) the road to the St Gotthard at first follows an almost level course through the wide Urseren valley, with views of the Furka.

Andermatt

Hospental (1484m/4869ft), an old village (Lat. hospitium, "hospice") situated at the point where the Furka-Reuss and Gotthard-Reuss join to form the Reuss, is now a health and winter sports resort (ski-lift to 2000m/6562ft on the Winterhorn) with heavy through traffic. Church (1705–11); tower of 13th c. castle.

Hospental

The road to the Furka pass (see Andermatt) goes off on the right. The St Gotthard road, bearing left, now climbs up into the desolate valley of the Gotthard-Reuss with five hairpin bends. The view to the rear of the Urseren valley and the chain of mountains to the north, from the Spitzigrat (2560m/8399ft) to the Galenstock (3597m/11,802ft), like the later views towards the pass, reveals the landscape of the St Gotthard massif in all its austerity – bare gneiss and granite crags, sometimes containing rare minerals, which have been little affected by glacier action but have been worn smooth by earlier ice, with many small lakes gleaming between the hills.

St Gotthard Road

St Gotthard

Gamsboden

Guspis Valley

The road continues up the long stretch of valley known as the Gamsboden (1640m/5381ft), subject to dangerous avalanches in winter, climbing at a moderate gradient. To the left is the Guspis valley, below the Pizzo Centrale and the Guspis glacier.

Mätteli

4km/2 miles farther on we reach the Mätteli (1791m/5876ft; inn), at the foot of the Winterhorn of Piz Orsino (2661m/8731ft; 3½ hours' climb from Hospental), to the right. The road then climbs more sharply in a double hairpin bend. At the Brüggloch (1908m/6260ft) the cantonal boundary between Uri and the mainly Italian-speaking Ticino is crossed. Ahead can be seen La Fibbia (2742m/8997ft).

The road continues, following a fairly straight course, past the Capanna di Rodont (1966m/6450ft) to the Lucendro bridge (2015m/6611ft) over the Reuss, which flows out of the Lago di Lucendro (2077m/6815ft; 30 minutes up on the right; detour recommended), an artificial lake supplying a power station at Airolo. From the lake it is a 3½ hours' climb (with guide) to the summit of the Piz Lucendro (2964m/9725ft), from which there are superb views.

Lago di
Lucendro

★ St Gotthard
Pass

The road then climbs in a series of sharp bends to the St Gotthard pass (2108m/6916ft), a bare flat depression with a number of small lakes. To the left is Monte Prosa (2471m/8107ft; 2½ hours), to the right La Fibbia (2742m/8997ft; 2½ hours, with guide), sloping down sharply into Val Tremola. The St Gotthard group of mountains, forming a link between the Valais and the Grisons Alps, lies in the centre of Switzerland – the core around which the Confederation grew up. Here the valleys carved out by the Reuss and the Ticino have prepared the way for this magnificent route over the central ridge of the Alps.

100m/328ft beyond the pass is a fork at which the old road continues straight ahead and the new road bears right.

St Gotthard
Hospice,
Gotthard
Museum

500m/1641ft beyond the pass, on the old road, is the St Gotthard Hospice (2095m/6874ft; founded in the 14th c. but frequently rebuilt and now a protected national monument) with a hotel of the same name, a weather station and the National Gotthard Museum (Museo Nazionale del San Gottardo). The collection records the development of the pass (relief models, minerals, weapons, uniforms, documents, etc.).

From here it is a 45 minutes' walk to the Sellasee (2231m/7320ft) and a 3½ hours'climb (with guide) to the summit of the Pizzo Centrale (3003m/9853ft).

★ Val Tremola

Beyond the hotel the road descends the slopes of the wild Val Tremola ("Valley of Trembling") in 38 well-engineered bends, some of them supported on retaining walls. In 5.5km/3 miles it comes to the Cantoniera Val Tremola (1695m/5561ft), from which the view down into the Val Bedretto and the Valle Leventina opens up.

The new road, 7.8km/5 miles long, bypasses the Val Tremola on the west, with some remarkable examples of road engineering (three tunnels). It then crosses the old road and later joins it.

Airolo

Continuing down in 13 sharp bends, the road comes to Airolo (1154m/3786ft; pop. 2000), a summer and winter sports resort in a magnificent mountain setting in the upper valley of the Ticino, known above the town as Val Bedretto and below it as Valle Leventina. To the west is the Rotondo group (Pizzo Rotondo, 3192m/10,473ft). After a great landslide from the Sasso Rosso in 1898 the place was rebuilt and provided with a protective wall. In the Gotthardbahn station, just outside the tunnel, is a bronze relief commemorating the men killed during the construction of the tunnel. Above the bridge over the Ticino stands the Lucendro power station (completed 1945). South-west of Airolo is the lower station of a cableway up the Sasso della Boggia (2065m/6775ft; skiing area).

St Gotthard Hospice by the lake

From Airolo a road, narrow in places, goes west up the Val Bedretto, passing through a number of small villages which offer quiet summer holiday accommodation. The road through Fontana is particularly constricted. Villa (1358m/4456ft) has a five-sided church tower designed to resist avalanches. 1km/½ mile farther on we come to the picturesque mountain village of Bedretto (1405m/4610ft).

From All'Acqua (1605m/5266ft) it is a 3 hours' walk to the San Giacomo pass, which leads into the Toce valley (Domodóssola).

The road continues over the Nufenen (Novena) pass (2478m/8133ft; view) into the Rhône valley.

From Airolo to Biasca the Bellinzona road descends the valley of the Ticino, here known as the Valle Leventina: a superb Alpine valley which drops down in a series of stages, its slopes at first clad with green meadows and mountain forests, which soon give way to chestnuts and walnut-trees (many waterfalls).

At the mouth of the wild Val Canaria the road traverses the Stretto di Stalvedro, passing under four natural rock arches.

Beyond Piotta (1012m/3320ft), in a wider part of the valley, to the left on the other side of the Ticino is the Ritom power station (50,000kW), which supplies the St Gotthard railway. From here a funicular 1360m/4462ft long (average gradient 72% (1 in 1.3) serves the cantonal Gotthard Sanatorium (1177m/3862ft) the picturesque mountain village of Altanca (1346m/4416ft; also reached by road from Piotta; beautiful church of 1603) and Piora (1795m/5889ft; 24 minutes). From the funicular station it is a 15 minutes' walk to the Ritomsee (1830m/6004ft), an artificial lake which supplies the Ritom power station; from here it is a 3 hours' climb to the summit of Taneda (2670m/8760ft; magnificent views).

Val Bedretto

All'Acqua

Nufenen Pass

Valle Leventina

Piotta

Altanca
★Val Piora

Ritomsee

★Taneda

375

View of Airolo

From Ambri (980m/3215ft) a narrow mountain road winds up to a number of villages high in the mountains (1.5km/1 mile to Quinto, 6km to Ronco, 7km/4 miles to Altanca).

Rodi-Fiesso

Rodi-Fiesso (945m/3101ft) is a double village beautifully situated between steep hillsides clad with larches and firs (summer holiday accommodation). From here there is a pleasant walk up to the Lago Tremorgio (1828m/8998ft; 2 hours), to the south-west, nestling picturesquely in a deep rocky hollow. There is also a narrow mountain road from Rodi to the little village of Prato Leventina (1030m/3379ft; 2km/1 mile south-east), on a natural terrace high above the Ticino valley, with a beautiful, Romanesque campanile. 4km/2 miles beyond this is the village of Dalpe (1140–1200m/3740–3937ft), above the Piumogna gorge, from which it is a 2¾ hours' climb to the Campo Tencia (3072m/10,079ft), the highest peak in Ticino.

Prato Leventina

Dalpe

★ Campo Tencia

★ Piottino Gorge

Just beyond Rodi-Fiesso, at the old customs post of Dazio Grande (949m/3114ft), the road enters the wild Piottino gorge, with a number of tunnels through the rock, between which (on right) the waterfalls on the river Ticino can be seen.

Faido

Faido (725m/379ft; pop. 1500), in a beautiful location, is the primary town in the Valle Leventina, and attracts many summer visitors. The stone-built houses of Ticinese type which now appear alongside the 16th c. timber houses with carved decoration, together with the first chestnuts and mulberry-trees, are the first imitations of a more southern landscape. On the western side of the valley the Piumogna plunges down in three beautiful waterfalls to join the Ticino.

Chiggiogna

In Chiggiona (668m/2192ft), beyond the railway line, stands the parish church of the Madonna di Ascente (13th c., rebuilt in the 16th c.).

The road continues through wooded country, with waterfalls on both sides. Just before Lavorgo, on the right, are the Cribiasca falls, pouring down in a cloud of spray.

Lavorgo (622m/2041ft) lies in a magnificent setting, with the long crest of the Monte di Sobrio on the left and a series of ridges running down from Campo Tencia and the Cima Bianca (2630m/8629ft) on the right.
Below Lavorgo a narrow road goes off on the right, crosses the Ticino and runs up (4km/2 miles) to Chironico (800m/2625ft), a beautiful mountain village with a fine Romanesque church (12th c.) and the 14th c. Torre dei Pedrini.

Beyond this, in the Biaschina gorge, the Ticino bursts through into the lowest part of the Valle Leventina (beautiful waterfall).

The village of Giornico (378m/1240ft) straddles the Ticino, with handsome old stone houses and two fine Romanesque churches on the right bank. To the right of the road the church of San Nicolao (12th c.), has a beautiful three-aisled crypt; higher up, amid vineyards, is Santa Maria di Castello. At the end of the village stands a monument commemorating a victory by 600 men of the Valle Leventina and the canton of Uri over a force of 10,000 Milanese on December 28th 1478. The local museum and the Hans Josephson museum are of interest.

Beyond this, after crossing the railway, a beautiful waterfall on the Cramosina is seen on the right. After the next crossing of the railway, also on the right, is the Biaschina power station (30,000kW). The vegetation now takes on an increasing southern character (figs, mulberries); the vines are grown on pergolas, in the manner characteristic of the south.

Biasca (305m/1001ft; pop. 3500) lies in a fertile basin in the Ticino valley, at the mouth of the Val Blenio (the valley of the Brenno), through which a road

Giornico: San Nicolao Church

descends from the Passo del Lucomagno (Lukmanier pass); granite quarries, timber trade, railway workshops. On the hillside is the beautiful Romanesque church of Santi Pietro e Paolo (11th–13th c.; interior remodelled in 1685), from which a path with Stations of the Cross runs up to the Petronilla Chapel (384m/1260ft) and a waterfall on the Frodalunga. To the east is the Pizzo Magno (2298m/7540ft).

Riviera

Osogna

The road to Bellinzona now continues down through the wide and almost straight valley of the Ticino, which from here to Bellinzona is known as the Riviera, with purely southern vegetation (vines, chestnuts, walnuts, mulberries, figs). At Osogna (280m/919ft; bypass), above the village, is the chapel of Santa Maria del Castello (altar of 1494, 17th c. frescoes).

Claro

At Claro (253m/830ft), on the slopes of the Pizzo di Molinera (2293m/7525ft), to the left, stands the Benedictine monastery (founded in 1490), of Santa Maria (650m/2133ft).

4km/2 miles beyond Claro the road from Chur over the San Bernardino pass (see entry) comes in on the left.

Arbedo

Arbedo (283m/929ft; bypass), which has a fine 15th c. parish church (the "Chiesa Rossa" or Red church), lies at the mouth of the Valle d'Arbedo (on left): there was a landslide here in 1929 from the Motto d'Arbino, which had been in gradual motion since 1888. In a battle at Arbedo in 1422, during the war with the Duchy of Milan, a force of 3000 Confederates was defeated by an army six times their number, 2000 of them being killed in the battle.

Bellinzona

At Bellinzona (230m/755ft) the road divides: straight ahead for Lugano, to the right for Locarno (see entries).

St Maurice   F 11

Canton: Valais (VS)
Altitude: 420m/1378ft. Population: 3500

Situation and general

The little town of St Maurice is picturesquely situated in a narrow pass in the Rhône valley, some 25km/16 miles south of the end of Lake Geneva, at the end of a road which runs via Monthey to Champéry. This was the site of the Celtic settlement of Agaunum, where the legend has it that St Maurice and his companions of the Theban Legion were martyred by Roman soldiers about the year 300.

Sights

Augustinian Abbey

At the north end of the town is an Augustinian abbey founded about 515 in honour of the martyrs, the oldest monastic house in Switzerland. The present church dates from 1611 to 1627; the beautiful Romanesque tower (11th c.) survives from an earlier building. The conventual buildings (now occupied by a secondary school and commercial college) were largely rebuilt in 1707–13. In the courtyard, between the cliffs, foundations and catacombs belonging to the earliest church on the site, including a 4th c. chapel, have been brought to light. The famous Treasury contains some outstanding works of art, largely of the Merovingian period, including several reliquaries, a gold-enamelled jug of Oriental origin and a Roman vessel of sardonyx.

★ Treasury

The triple-aisled parish church of St Sigismond (18th c.) has beautiful Baroque side altars. The two-storeyed Town Hall, the Haus de la Pierre with an arcade of three storeys and the Haus de Bons date from the same period.

Also of interest are the pilgrimage church of Notre-Dame-du-Scex and the 13th c. castle above the Rhône, built by the Savoyards and restored in the 16th c.; now houses a military museum.

St Maurice: Rathausplatz   *Augustinian abbey*

To the north, above the town (footpath from the bridge over the Rhône), is a stalactitic cave, the Grotte aux Fées, with a restaurant and a view of the town.

Grotte aux Fées

Surroundings

At Bex, 8km/5 miles north of the town is the only working salt mine in Switzerland (open to visitors: Apr.–mid Nov., about 17° C/63° F). The labyrinth of tunnels and shafts, only part of which is accessible to visitors, stretches for up to 50km/31 miles as far as the villages of Villars, Chesières and Arveyes. A film show of the development of the tunnels from 1684 to the present-day is held in a former salt water reservoir (1826). A "Bähnli" (small train) takes visitors to the mining area.

Bex, Saltmine

6km/4 miles north-west is Monthey (428m/1404ft), a busy little town of 11,000 inhabitants with a medieval castle (rebuilt in the 16th and 18th c.; museum). From here a road runs south-west into the Val d'Illiez, first climbing up the steep hillside in sharp bends and then continuing up the slopes of the valley high above the left bank of the Vièze. Amid the vineyards and woods of chestnut-trees are many large boulders brought here by glacial action, including the Pierre à Dzo, resting on a base no bigger than a man's hand, and the Pierre des Marmettes, with a small house on the top.

Monthey

Val D'Illiez

In 6km/4 miles the road comes to Troistorrents (760m/2494ft), a prettily situated village at the mouth of the Val de Morgins, through which a road runs up to Morgins.

Val de Morgins

The road continues beyond Troistorrents ascending the beautiful valley (many waterfalls) alongside the cog-railway, with views of the Dents du Midi and the Dents Blanches. 3.5km/2 miles farther on is Val d'Illiez (952m/3124ft), a village which attracts summer visitors.

Champéry

The road continues up the valley, dotted with huts, and in another 3.5km/ 2 miles reaches Champéry, a village of 1000 inhabitants at the upper end of the Val d'Illiez, surrounded by forests and flanked by imposing peaks, popular as a health resort and especially for winter sports (heated swimming pool, tennis, golf, climbing school; curling with an indoor rink; cross-country skiing). Two cableways, one (1.7km/1 mile long, 7 minutes) leaving from the south end of the village, the other (2.2km/1 mile, 10 minutes)

Planachaux

1.5km/1 mile north of the Monthey road, go up to the skiing area of Planachaux (1800m/5906ft; several restaurants, mountain inn; many ski-lifts; beautiful views).

There are many attractive walks and climbs from here. Walks: 1¼ hours

★ Croix de Culet

south-west to the Chalets d'Ayerne (1473m/4833ft; good general view of the valley), 1¾ hours south to the Chalets de Bonaveau (1556m/5105ft; inn).

★ Dents du Midi

Climbs: Croix de Culet (1966m/6450ft; superb views), 2½–3 hours west (30 minutes from Planachaux); Dents Blanches (2645–2764m/8678–9069ft), 7 hours south (with guide); Dents du Midi (Haute Cime, 3260m/10,696ft), 7–8 hours east (with guide).

From St Maurice to Les Diablerets

Leave St Maurice on road 9 (E 2), which runs north down the Rhône valley, and in 13km/8 miles turns right into a steep and winding but very beautiful

Ollon

mountain road which comes in 3km/2 miles to Ollon (15th c. church). From here the road continues uphill, with beautiful views into the Rhône valley, curves round to enter the Gryonne valley and climbs in several sharp bends to the village of Huémoz.

Chesières

It then runs along the hillside, with a view of Villars, and climbs again in a double hairpin bend to the health resort of Chesières (1220m/4003ft). 10km/

Villars-sur-Ollon

6 miles from Ollon is Villars-sur-Ollon (1256m/4121ft), a popular health

Les Diablerets in winter

resort (salt-water swimming pool, golf-course, climbing school) and winter sports resort (several ski-lifts; cross-country skiing trail 25km/16 miles long; ski-bobbing run; artificial ice-rink; curling; ski-flying school), magnificently set on a sunny terrace high above the Rhône valley, with views extending to the Mont Blanc group. It is the terminus of an electric railway from Bex (1¼ hours), connecting with the line over the Col de Soud (1523m/4997ft) to the Col de Bretaye (1850m/6070ft), which is reached in 20 minutes: beautiful views and good skiing (lift to the Petit Chamossaire, 2030m/6660ft). From the Col de Bretaye a chair-lift (12 minutes; on foot ¾ hour) ascends Grand Chamossaire (2120m/6956ft), from where there is a famous panoramic view embracing the Bernese, Valais and Savoy Alps and Lake Geneva, and (summer only) a chair-lift to the Lac Noir and the Chaux Ronde (2027m/6651ft).

The narrow road continues east over the Col de la Croix (1780m/5840ft) and comes in 16.5km/10 miles to Les Diablerets (1163m/3816ft; pop. 1200), a magnificently situated health and winter sports resort (climbing school, ski-lifts, toboggan run) in the Vallée des Ormonts, a high valley surrounded by wooded hills and dotted with huts. The valley is bounded on the south by the Creux de Champ, a semicircle of rock under the peaks of the Diablerets (Teufelshörner, 3246m/10,650ft; 7–8 hours, with guide; cableway from the Col du Pillon), with numerous waterfalls which join to form the Grande-Eau (pleasant walk, 1½ hours, up the valley). Cableway (2.4km/1 mile, 15 minutes) to Isenau (1770m/5807ft; ski-lift).

★Les Diablerets

★Creux de Champ

From Les Diablerets it is possible to continue over the Col du Pillon (1546m/5072ft) to Gsteig, Gstaad and Saanen (see Gstaad).

Col du Pillon

St Moritz

S 9

Canton: Grisons (GR)
Altitude: 1768m/5803ft. Population: 6000

The world-famed winter sports resort (Winter Olympics 1928 and 1948) of St Moritz (Romansch San Murezzan), in the midst of the Upper Engadine, is in two parts. St Moritz Dorf – a "village" which has all the appearance of a town, with its large and palatial hotels – is situated on a sunny terrace, sheltered from the north wind, above the St Moritzer See (Lake of St Moritz, 1768m/5801ft), through which the river Inn flows from south to north. St Moritz Bad, on the valley floor at the south-west end of the lake, has iron-bearing springs of high carbonic acid content which were already being used in Bronze Age times.

Situation and general

The beautiful scenery with 25 crystal clear mountain lakes, forests and glaciers, the legendary "Champagne climate" and intense sunshine provide an unforgettable setting for an action-packed holiday. Along with winter sports (see below) in the colder months, in summer there are watersports (sailing, windsurfing and rafting on the river Inn), summer skiing, tennis, horse-riding and golf.

The magnificent view from St Moritz embraces the mountains from Piz Languard in the east to Piz Julier in the west, the most prominent peaks being Piz Rosatsch with its glacier, above the lake, to the right of this Piz Surlej and Piz Corvatsch, and in the distance the beautiful Piz della Margna.

Access is from Chur, over the Julier pass or from Landeck. The airline companies Air Engadinia and Crossair fly regularly to Zurich. There are four memorable Alpine rail journeys to St Moritz with the Rhätische Bahn (see Practical Information, Railways): Glacier-Express (St-Moritz–Zermatt), Bernina-Express (St Moritz–Tirano/Italy), Engadin-Express (St-Moritz–Bad Scuol–Landeck) and the Palm-Express (St Moritz–Ascona–Zermatt).

Transport

St. Moritz

200 m

St. Moritz Dorf

St. Moritzer See
(1768 m above sea-level)

St. Moritz Bad

Silvaplana
(Julier pass, Maloja pass)

© Baedeker

Cableways ★Corviglia

From St Moritz Dorf a funicular (2.1km/1 mile) ascends in 20 minutes via an intermediate station at Chantarella (2005m/6578ft) to Corviglia (2486m/8157ft; restaurant), with fine views and excellent skiing; from there a cabin cableway (2450m/8038ft, 10 minutes) up Piz Nair (3057m/10,030ft; magnificent view).

From St Moritz Bad the Signalbahn (cabins; 1460m/4790ft, 5 minutes serves the Signalkuppe (2150m/7054ft; several ski-lifts).

Winter sports

The origins of winter tourism in St Moritz go back to the end of the last century. From those early days with the first ski-runs it has developed into a world famous modern skiing metropolis with 25 snow cannons. It features artificial and natural ice-rinks; curling, toboggan run, the famous Cresta Run or Skeletonbahn (1400m/4593ft); bobsleigh run to Celerina-Cresta (1600m/5250ft); Olympic ski-jump. Every year there are three international horse races on the frozen lake, as well as winter golf, polo and greyhound racing.

This excellent skiing country with descents of varying difficulty is easily accessible by the funicular, cableways and numerous lifts. The new slopes opened in 1988 and the glacier on Corvatsch and Diavolezza make skiing possible from November to May. There are cross-country trails to Majola and Zuoz.

Sights

★St Moritz Dorf

The heart of St Moritz Dorf is the Schulplatz (Pl. da Scoula), in which stands the Town Hall. To the south-east, lower down, is the Tourist Information Office, to the north, on higher ground, the Protestant church (1786), and beyond this, in the idyllic Old Cemetery, the Schiefer Turm (Leaning Tower), all that remains of the old Romanesque church of St Maurice.

Segantini Museum

In the Via Somplatz (towards Suvretta) is the Segantini Museum (closed Mon.), a domed granite building (1911) containing pictures by Giovanni Segantini, including a large triptych with an Alpine setting, "Coming into Being, Being and Passing Away" (1897–99).

Opposite the museum stands a monument commemorating the victors in the Winter Olympics of 1928 and 1948.

St Moritz village

The Engadine Museum in the Via del Bagn 39 (closed Sat.) contains domestic interiors, embroidery, costumes, implements and utensils. Exhibits excavated in the Engadine from Neolithic and Bronze Age periods and Roman finds from the Septimer and Julier passes are on display.

Engadine Museum

In St Moritz Bad (1.5km/1 mile south of St Moritz Dorf), with its high-rise buildings, is the Roman Catholic church (1867), with a separate tower.

St Moritz Bad

On the eastern fringe of the forest are the Spa Establishment (1973–76), an open-air swimming-pool and the Kurhaus.

Spa Establishment

Attractive paths run along the wooded slopes.

Surroundings

There are fine views from Oberalpina (1990m/6529ft; 30 minutes south-west of St Moritz Dorf), Alp Nova (2185m/7169ft; 1 hour west) and Alp Laret (2101m/6893ft; 1 hour north). From Oberalpina there is a ridge path by way of the Chantarella funicular station to the Alp Laret (1 hour).

Oberalpina

2km/1 mile from St Moritz Dorf on the east side of the lake are the Meierei hotel-restaurant and café. From there it is another kilometre to the Staz Hotel and restaurant on the eastern shore of the Lej Staz (Stazer See, 1808m/5932ft; swimming pool), from which it is an hour's walk on forest paths to Celerina or Pontresina.

St Moritz Lake

From St Moritz Bad it is an hour and a half's walk on beautiful forest paths by way of the Quellenberg (1920m/6300ft) or the Johannisberg (2002m/6569ft) to the Hahnensee (2159m/7084ft; restaurant) and a further 2 hours along the slopes of Piz Surlej (3192m/10,473ft) to the Furocla Surlej (2755m/9039ft), from which there is a breathtaking view of the Bernina

Hahnensee

★Furocla Surlej

Panorama of St Moritz in the Upper Engadine

★Piz Corvatsch

group and the Engadine lakes. From here a 2½ hours' climb brings the walker to the summit of Piz Corvatsch (3451m/11,323ft; cabin railway from Silvaplana; superb views; summer skiing on the glacier (3303m/10,837ft with two ski-lifts).

★Piz Julier

To the west of St Moritz there is a rewarding climb (not difficult for experienced climbers) by way of the Alp Suvretta (2211m/7254ft) to the summit of Piz Julier (3385m/11,106ft; 5 hours), which offer magnificent distant views.

Silvaplana

Surlej

7km/4 miles south-west, at the junction with the road over the Julier pass, is Silvaplana (1815m/5955ft; bypass), a health and winter sports resort situated on the green alluvial fan of the Ova dal Vallun, with a Late Gothic parish church (1491). A bridge crosses the narrow neck of the lake on which it lies to a 19th c. baronial mansion, the Crap da Sass (private property), and the houses and chalets of Surlej ("above the lake"). 15 minutes' walk farther up is the lower station (1870m/6135ft; car park, restaurant) of the Corvatsch cableway.

Silvaplaner See
Silser See

Sils

5km/3 miles farther south-west on the road to the Majola pass, lying to the left of the road between the Silvaplana lake (Silvaplana See, 1794m/5886ft; area 2.6sq.km/1sq.mile, depth 77m/253ft) and the Silser See (Romansch Lej da Segl, 1797m/5896ft; area 4.2sq.km/2sq.miles), is the popular summer and winter sports resort of Sils (Romansch Segl). This is in two parts: Sils Maria (1795m–5891ft; the "Maria" is actually a corruption of a word meaning "farm"), the main tourist attraction at the mouth of the Val Fex, and Sils Baselgia at the outflow of the River Inn from the Silser See. In both parts of Sils there are elegant houses in the style of the Engadine. Sils Maria has a Baroque church (1764), and beside the Edelweiss Hotel is a modest museum devoted to Nietzsche, who spent the summer months here from 1881 to 1889 (commemorative tablet). Sils Baselgia has a church dating from 1448. From both parts of Sils there are pleasant footpaths (15 minutes) to the wooded peninsula of Chasté (1838m/6030ft; nature

Piz Bernina

reserve), with scanty remains of an old castle and a Nietzsche quotation carved in the rock.

On the south-east shore of the Silser See (45 minutes' walk) lies the hamlet of Isola (inn), which is abandoned in winter: behind it, in the gorge of the Fedozbach, is a beautiful waterfall. From here it is another 45 minutes' walk to the Majola pass.

From Sils Maria a narrow road (closed to cars) runs south up the Val Fex to Crasta (3km/2 miles, 1948m/6391ft) and Curtins (6km/4 miles, 1976m/6483ft), from which there is a beautiful view of the mountains framing the Fex glacier. ★Val Fex

East of Sils Maria (1¼ hours) is the Marmorè (2203m/7288ft; ski-lift), with a magnificent view into the Upper Engadine. Marmorè
    A good footpath (3½ hours) leads east to the Fuorcla Surlej (2756m/9042ft).

To the south of Isola (4–4½ hours, with guide) is the Piz della Margna (3159m/10,365ft; superb views). ★Piz della Margna
    A cableway ascends to the Alp Präsura (2311m/7582ft), giving access to the Furtschellas (2800m/9187ft; ski-lifts).

San Bernardino Pass   P 9/10

Canton: Grisons (GR)
Height of pass: 2065m/6775ft

The San Bernardino pass is the highest point on the San Bernardino road, a very convenient link between Lake Constance and Ticino. From Thusis onwards it is now mostly of expressway standard, and since the construction of the San Bernardino tunnel (1961–67) it has been the fastest Situation and general all-year-round route from Lake Constance through eastern Switzerland to northern Italy.

Access

From Chur the road follows the Rhine and Hinterrhein valleys to Thusis, and from there takes a new line by way of the famous Via Mala (see The Rhine) to Splügen (bypass).

Splügen

From Splügen over the San Bernardino to Mesocco

San Bernardino
Road
Splügen pass

The San Bernardino road to Bellinzona (69 or 76km/43 or 47 miles) continues past Splügen, where the road branches off south over the Splügen pass (2113m/6933ft), on the Italian frontier, and continues to Chiavenna, from where one can drive east into the scenic Val Bregaglia (see entry).

San Bernardino
Tunnel

The road to San Bernardino continues up the Hinterrhein valley. Beyond the valley of Hinterrhein the old road branches off to cross the pass, while the expressway (N 13) passes a parking place (on right: kiosk-restaurant) and over the Hinterrhein, here still quite small, to the northern entrance (1613m/5292ft) of the San Bernardino tunnel (length 6.6km/4 miles, width of carriageway 7.5m/25ft, highest point 1644m/5394ft; emergency telephones; maximum speed 80 km p.h./50 m.p.h., overtaking prohibited; toll-free). The tunnel runs in an almost straight line under the pass, emerging just to the west of the village of San Bernardino. The route through the tunnel is 7km/4 miles shorter than the road over the pass.

San Bernardino
Pass Road

The road over the pass climbs in 18 hairpin bends (maximum gradient 9% (1 in 11.1) up the steep slope below the Mittaghorn (2609m/8560ft; on left), with beautiful and constantly changing views to the rear of the Rheinwald valley and the peaks rising to over 3000m/9843ft on its north side. In 4km/ 2 miles it reaches the bare valley of the Thälialp (1920m/6300ft) and then ascends in nine hairpins to the pass.

San Bernardino Pass

The San Bernardino pass (2065m/6775ft; simple hospice), which may have been used as early as the Bronze Age as a route through the Alps, was originally known as the Vogelberg ("Bird Mountain"). It takes its present name from San Bernardino of Siena, who is said to have preached here in the early 15th c. On the pass, with its rocks worn smooth by the ice, is the Lago Moèsola, in which is a small rocky islet. To the east is the pointed summit of Pizzo Uccello (Bird Mountain, 2716m/8911ft), to the west the blunt top of the Marschalhorn (2902m/9521ft), beside which the Zapporthorn, with the Muccial glacier, comes into view as the road continues south.

San Bernardino Pass

The road skirts the lake and then continues down in 21 hairpin bends, following the course of the River Moèsa, through a rugged landscape, with magnificent views of the surrounding peaks, particularly of the precipitous Pan de Zucchero (2600m/8531ft) and (to the rear, on the left) Pizzo Uccello, which towers up ever more imposingly as the road descends. To the east are Piz Lumbreda (2977m/9768ft) and Piz Curciusa (2875m/9433ft). After the last hairpin the southern exit from the tunnel (1631m/5351ft) is seen on the right.

Just beyond this point is the village of San Bernardino (1607m/5273ft), the highest place in the Val Mesocco and now a developing holiday and winter sports resort. There are many attractive footpaths through the meadows and woodland of this high valley below Pizzo Uccello (3½–4 hours). Cableway from the Alpe Fracch (1630m/5348ft) to Confin (1953m/6405ft; restaurant), ski-lifts to 2500m/8203ft, ice-rink, cross-country skiing. 2km/1 mile south, on the old road, is the Lago d'Osso (1646m/5401ft), surrounded by forest.

San Bernardino

From the tunnel exit N 13 continues south over the moorland plateau, passing on the right an artificial lake (1604m/5263ft), curves round to cross the old road and then continues downhill, passing through two tunnels and two galleries. In 11km/7 miles it passes (on right) the scattered houses of Pian San Giacomo (1172m/3845ft), from which the old road runs down on the right to Mesocco.

Pian San Giacomo

N 13 then goes down in wide curves and several hairpins (beautiful views) into the Val Mesocco, which descends in a series of steep steps, with several hydro-electric stations. To the south-east are the twin peaks of Cima di Pian Guarnei (3015m/9892ft) and Piz Corbet (3026m/9928ft).

Just before Mesocco N 13 crosses the old road, which traverses the village, while N 13 passes above it (short tunnel) and then descends to the valley floor in a hairpin turn.

Mesocco or Misox (769m/2525ft; pop. 1500), formerly known as Cremeo, is a village of fine stone houses, the chief place in the Val Mesocco or Mesolcina (Misoxer Tal), and, like the Val Calanca which runs parallel to it on the west, belongs to the canton of Grisons but is inhabited by an Italian-speaking and Roman Catholic population. The two valleys together are known as the Moèsano (from the River Moèsa which flows down the Val Mesocco).

Mesocco

★ Misoxer Tal

Below Mesocco the road passes under a crag crowned by the ruined Castello di Misox (748m/2453ft), the ancestral castle of the Counts Sax von Misox, which was purchased by the Trivulzi family of Milan in 1483, destroyed by the people of Grisons in 1526 and restored by Swiss students in 1922–26 (magnificent view of the deep trough of the Val Mesocco).

★ Castello di Misox

At the foot of the hill on which the castle stands is the 12th c. church of Santa Maria del Castello, with 15th c. wall-paintings.

Further down the valley is Soazza (bypass), where the expressway comes to an end.

Santa Maria del Castello

Sarnen   L 7

Canton: Unterwalden. Half-canton: Obwalden (OW)
Altitude: 476m/1562ft. Population: 7300

Sarnen, capital of the half-canton of Obwalden, lies at the north end of the   Situation and
Sarner See, on the road from Lucerne to Interlaken over the Brünig pass.   general
The Landsgemeinde, the communal assembly, meets on the Landenberg
here on the last Sunday in April.

Sights

In the Town Hall (Rathaus, 1729–32) is kept the "White Book" (Weisses   Town Hall
Buch), containing the earliest account (c. 1470) of the history of the Confederation. The neighbouring church of St Andreas dates from the
17th–18th c.

At the north end of the town at 12 Brünigstrasse is the Heimatmuseum   Local Museum
(local museum) which surveys the cultural history of the canton of Ober-
walden. The collection includes prehistoric and early material, some from
the Roman settlement of Alpnach, weapons, religious art of the 14th–
18th c. (wooden statues, altars, liturgical items), pictures and sculpture by
local artists from the 17th–20th c., furniture, coins, agricultural implements
and a reconstructed alpine hut.

On a hill to the south-east stands the twin-towered Baroque parish church   St Peter's
of St Peter (by the Singer brothers, 1739–42). It occupies the site of a earlier   Church
Romanesque building first mentioned in 1036. The interior contains rich
stucco work
     The painted carving (1507) in the neighbouring charnel house (c. 1500) is
the work of Peter Tischmacher from Uri.
     To the west, on the Landenberg, is the Baroque Schützenhaus (Rifle-
men's Clubhouse, 1752) and nearby an armoury.

2.5km/2 miles south-west, on the sunny western shore of the lake, lies the   Wilen
attractive outlying district of Wilen, from which a road follows the lake via
Oberwilen to Giswil.

Surroundings

To Schwendi-Kaltbad

A beautiful road 11km/7 miles long leads up the hillside (known as   Stalden
Schwendi) above the lake, reaching Stalden (797m/2615ft), a small health
resort, after 3km/2 miles. The road continues through the hamlet of Gassen
and over the Alpine meadows on the Schwendiberg; then road on right to
(8km/5 miles) Schwendi-Kaltbad (1445m/4741ft), with an iron-bearing   Schwendi-
spring. Beyond the turning for Schwendi the road goes on into the Entle-   Kaltbad
buch valley (see entry).

From Sarnen into the Melchtal

(22km/14 miles to Melchtal-Frutt). Leave Sarnen on the road to Stans,
which runs east, crossing N 8. 2km/1 mile: Kerns (569m/1867ft), a village   Kerns
frequented by summer visitors. Turn right into a road which climbs the east
side of the valley of the Grosse Melch-Aa. 3km/2 miles: Zuben.

◀ *Sarnen: the parish church*

Sarnen

Flüeli-Ranft

Here a road branches off on the right, crosses the Melch on a bridge 97m/318ft high and reaches Flüeli (2km/1 mile: road recommended as return route from the Melchtal), a hamlet commanding extensive views, and which boasts a pilgrimage chapel of 1618 and a house said to have belonged to the 15th c. hermit Nikolaus von der Flüe. His hermitage is lower down on the slopes of Mt Ranft (close by, a chapel of 1700).

St Niklausen

3km/2 miles: St Niklausen (839m/2753ft), with a 14th c. chapel and the old Heidenturm ("Heathens' Tower").

Melchtal

4km/2 miles: Melchtal (894m/2933ft), a beautifully situated mountain village and health resort. Cableway (1200m/3937ft) to the Rütialp (1350m/4429ft; restaurant; view). The road continues uphill over the Balmatt, at the foot of the precipitous Rämisfluh (1866m/6122ft). 4km/2 miles: Stöckalp (1070m/3511ft), from which there is a cableway (3333m/10,936ft) to Melchsee-Frutt.

Melchsee-Frutt

The road (alternate one-way traffic) continues, with many bends, up the valley of the Keselnbach, below the rock walls of the Brünighaupt (2315m/7396ft). 6km/4 miles: Melchsee-Frutt (1920m/6300ft), a popular mountain resort and winter sports resort magnificently situated in a green valley on the shores of an Alpine lake, the Melchsee (1838m/6030ft), from where an unobstructed view of the whole Titlis chain may be enjoyed. A good base for climbs, e.g. to the Erzegg (2176m/7139ft; 1¼ hours; ski-lift) and the Hochstollen (2484m/8150ft; 2–2½ hours); easy and pleasant footpath to the Engstlenalp (3 hours). Chair-lift from the southern end of the Melchsee (1900m/6234ft; 20 minutes) to the Balmeregghorn (2230m/7317ft).

Over the Brünig Pass to Brienz

Sachseln

Leave Sarnen on Road 4, which runs south along the east side of the Sarner See to Sachseln (475m/1558ft), a prettily situated lakeside village which is

Sachseln: Pilgrimage church of St Theodul

popular with summer visitors. In the choir of the church (rebuilt 1672–84; lower part of tower Romanesque) is a glass sarcophagus containing the remains of St Nikolaus von der Flüe (1417–87), popularly known as "Bruder Klaus", whose conciliatory approach brought about the admission of Fribourg and Solothurn to the Confederation in 1481.

A museum (Dorfstrasse 4), the former house of the Landamman P. Ignaz von Flüe, contains literature and paintings commemorating the mystic and politician Klaus von Flüe. It also has a collection of manuscripts and works by the writer Heinrich Federer (1866–1928).

In celebration of the 150th anniversary of the Federal Department of Topography the geographical centre of Switzerland was officially marked. It is situated in the Kleiner Melchtal on Alp Äggli (district of Sachsen), where a resting-place has been built, surrounded by a stone wall in the shape of Switzerland. A pyramid stands in the centre as a symbol of land surveying.	Alp Älggi, Geographical Centre of Switzerland
Giswil (488m/1601ft), in a green hollow in the valley surrounded by fine mountains, has a church (above the village) and ruins of an old castle. A winding mountain road runs west, affording fine views, over the Moerli-Alp (1100m/3609ft; restaurant), a popular skiing area.	Giswil
Kaiserstuhl (701m/2300ft): view on right of the picturesque Lungernsee (692m/2270ft). The road runs along the lake (viewpoints, on right), to which water is conveyed from the valleys of the Grosse and the Kleine Melch in a tunnel 10km/6 miles long, producing some 50,000kW of electricity (power station between Giswil and Kaiserstuhl). To the south can be seen the Schwarzhorn chain, to the left the three peaks of the Wetterhorn (3701m/12,143ft).	Kaiserstuhl, Lungernsee
Lungern (715m/2346ft), a popular summer holiday place beautifully situated at the southern end of the lake in a setting of steep wooded hills, with a Neo-Gothic church above the village. In 1323 the town of Berne and the three original cantons of Uri, Schwyz and Unterwalden formed an alliance against the Habsburgs here (commemorative tablet at the near end of the village, on left). From Lungern-Obsee a cableway runs up west via the intermediate station of Turren (1531m/5023ft) to Schönbüel (2010m/6595ft; skiing), from which there is a path (4km/2 miles) to the Brienzer Rothorn and a ski-lift to the Hohe Gumme (2209m/7248ft).	Lungern
The road now comes to the Brünig pass (1008m/3304ft), on the wooded ridge between the Wilerhorn (2006m/6582ft; 3–3½ hours), to the west, and the Giebel (2039m/6690ft). To the left is the Brünig-Hasliberg station (restaurant). The view embraces the Engelhörner (2783m/9131ft) and the Faulhorn chain; below, to the left, is the Aare valley, extending west from Meiringen to Lake Brienz (see entries), with its beautiful waterfalls.	Brünig Pass
From the Brünig pass it is worth while taking a well-engineered panoramic road branching off on the left along the Hasliberg, a sunny mountain terrace high above the Aare valley which is a popular holiday area, with good skiing in winter.	Hasliberg
The road comes first to the health resort of Hohfluh (1049m/3442ft), with far-ranging views, and then continues past the lower station (1160m/3803ft) of a cableway to Käserstatt (1840m/6050ft; restaurant; chair-lift to Hochsträss, 2120m/6956ft; ski-lift to Hochbühl, 2037m/6683ft) to Goldern (1053m/3455ft). It then passes through Alpine meadows and crosses the	Hohfluh
gorge of the Alpbach in a wide bend to reach the health resort of Reuti (1045m/3429ft; extensive views). From here there are cableways via Bidmi (1423m/4670ft; restaurant in winter) to the Mägisalp (1706m/5600ft; restaurant), from where a chair-lift continues up to Planplatten (2245m/7368ft)	Reuti

and down to Meiringen (see entry). In winter there is also a chair-lift operating between Bidmi and Käserstatt.

From the Brünig pass the road to Brienz leads down through wooded country, with attractive glimpses to the left of the Hasli valley (the valley of the River Aare) and the Faulhorn chain. 1.5km/1 mile below the pass is a road junction, where an excellent road goes off on the left and winds its way down the slopes of the Hasliberg to Meiringen (8km/5 miles; see entry), in the valley of the canalised Aare.

Brienzwiler

The Brienz road bears right and descends, with a very fine view of the Aare valley, to the village of Brienzwiler (709m/2326ft), on a terrace above the Aare.

Ballenberg,
★★ Open-Air
Museum

Brienz

It then continues along the Aare valley below the Ballenberg (727m/2385ft; Swiss Open-Air Museum; see Lake Brienz) to the hamlet of Kienholz (570m/1870ft), where Lake Brienz comes into sight. Then beneath the Brienzer Rothorn to Brienz (see Lake Brienz), on the lake of the same name.

Schaffhausen   N 2

Canton: Schaffhausen (SH)
Altitude: 404m/1326ft. Population: 34,000

Schaffhausen

Schaffhausen, capital of the canton of that name, situated close to the Untersee and north of the Rhine, is enclosed on three sides by Germany.

Its well preseved medieval town centre and the picturesquely situated Kastell Munot make it one of the most interesting towns in Switzerland. Schaffhausen is also an important hub of communications and industrial town (iron and steel works, chemical plants, engineering works, clocks, textiles and playing cards).

Schaffhausen grew up as a transhipment point for traffic on the Rhine, here interrupted by the Rhine Falls. In 1045 the Emperor Henry III granted Count Eberhard von Nellenburg the right to mint coins here, and about 1050 the Benedictine abbey of All Saints was founded. From 1330 to 1415 the town was mortgaged to the Habsburgs, and thereafter, until 1501, was a free Imperial city. In 1454 Schaffhausen concluded an alliance with the Confederation, of which it became a member in 1501. From 1798 to 1803 the town and canton were part of the Helvetian Republic.

Sights

In the heart of the old town is the Fronwagplatz, with the Fronwag tower and two fountains, the Moor's fountain (Mohrenbrunnes, originally 1520) and the Metzgerbrunnen, 1524), which has a striking figure of a landsknecht (mercenary).

To the north of the Fronwagplatz is the Vorstadt, with a whole series of houses with oriel windows and coats-of-arms on the façade, which ends at the Schwabentor (Swabian gate, 14th–16th c.); to the west the short Oberstadt, at the far end of which is the Obertor (upper Gate, originally 13th c.).

To the east of Fronwagplatz the long Vordergasse opens out into a square. On the right of the Vordergasse the 15th c. Rathaus (Council House), with the fine Chamber of the Great Council (Grossratssaal, 1632) and the Council Arcade (Ratslaube, 1586). In the nearby Sporrengasse (No. 7) the private Stemmler museum has stuffed birds and mammals from all over Europe.

Beyond this, at the corner of Münstergasse, is the colourful Haus zum Ritter (1485), with paintings on the façade by Tobias Stimmer (originals, 1570, removed in 1935, now in All Saints Museum; reproductions of 1938–39, restored 1943). Diagonally across the street the Late Gothic St John's church (Protestant) has an imposing tower.

In a spacious square south of Fronwagplatz, Herrenacker, are the old Kornhaus (Granary, 1679) and the Municipal Theatre (rebuilt 1956). In a small square immediately east, the Beckenstube, is situated the Cantonal Government Building (Regierungsgebäude), a skilful conversion of the old Arsenal (17th c.), with a magnificent doorway.

The Minster (Münster), a pillared basilica with a single tower (1087–1150), was originally the church of the Benedictine abbey of All Saints and is now the Protestant parish church. The spacious nave, flat-roofed (restored 1950–58), is a fine example of Romanesque religious architecture. The choir contains remains of old wall-paintings. Outside the Minster, on the north side, is a bronze figure of David with Goliath's head (by K. Geiser, 1959). On the south side the cloister (freely accessible) has delicate 12th c. arcades.

In the forecourt of St Anne's chapel, adjoining it on the east, is the famous Hosanna Bell (Osannaglocke), cast in 1486, with a Latin inscription ("Vivos voco, mortuos plango, fulgura frango" – "I call the living, I mourn the dead, I quell the lightning") which inspired a well-known poem by Schiller, the "Song of the Bell" ("Das Lied von der Glocke").

Schaffhausen

★All Saints
Museum

The handsome conventual buildings of the abbey now house All Saints Museum (Museum zu Allerheiligen), one of the richest local museums in Switzerland (closed Mon.), with collections of prehistoric material (mainly from the Kesslerloch at Thayngen), works of religious art, a series of rooms furnished in period style, weapons, relics of the old guilds, traditional costumes, etc., and a large picture gallery, notable in particular for the works by modern Swiss artists.

Of the old conventual buildings St Erhard's chapel (1104), St John's chapel (1064), a Romanesque loggia (1200) and the Kreuzsaal (c. 1620) are noteworthy.

★Hallen für
Neue Kunst

South of All Saints Museum, at Baumgartenstrasse 23, the Hallen für Neue Kunst, a museum for international contemporary art (1960s and 70s), has been built in a former textile factory (closed Mon.).

★Kastell Munot

To the east, dominating the town on a vine-clad hill is Kastell Munot (1564–89), a circular structure designed in accordance with Dürer's principles of fortification, with walls more than 5m/16ft thick and vaulted gun-ports below. The principal tower has a ramp in place of a staircase to allow supplies to be carried up to the artillery. From the battlements there is a fine view of the town.

★★Rhine Falls   See entry

Rhine   See entry

Surroundings

Diessenhofen

About 10km/6 miles to the east of Schaffhausen lies the old-world former Imperial town of Diessenhofen (416m/1365ft; pop. 3000), with its fine Gothic burghers' houses, old fortifications (Siegelturm, 1545), parish

Schaffhausen: Kastell Munot

church of St Dionysis (1200; rebuilt 15th c.) and the Dominican convent of St Katharinental (1571; Baroque conventual church).

An old wooden covered bridge crosses to the opposite bank of the Rhine to the health resort of Gailingen (pop. 2500; neurological rehabilitation centre), with a St Nikolaus chapel (1100) and an interesting Jewish cemetery (1676); in the 19th c. there were as many Jews as Christians in Gailingen.

Gailingen

Schwyz   N 6

Canton: Schwyz (SZ)
Altitude: 517m/1696ft
Population: 12,000

The old town of Schwyz, which gave its name to the whole country, is capital of the canton of the same name. It is charmingly situated on the edge of the orchard-covered plain between Lake Lucerne and the Lauerzer See, under the towering twin horns of the Mythen (1815 and 1902m/5955 and 6259ft).

Situation and general

Sights

Schwyz has many beautiful 17th and 18th c. patrician houses. In the main square is the richly decorated Baroque parish church of St Martin (1774), and opposite it the Rathaus (1642–43), its façade decorated with frescoes (1891) of scenes from Swiss history. The Great Council Chamber contains a series of portraits of Landamänner (cantonal presidents) from 1544 to 1850; the Little Council Chamber has beautiful panelling and a carved ceiling of 1655 (restored 1989/90).

St Martin
Rathaus

Schwyz: Rathausplatz ...   *... guarded by the statue of Justina*

Federal archives of Switzerland in Schwyz

Turmmuseum

In the tower south of the Rathaus is the Cantonal Historical Museum and a small geology collection.

Bundesbrief-
archiv

In the Bahnhofstrasse (the road to Seewen) can be seen the Bundes-briefarchiv, in which the original deed of confederation (Bundesbrief) between Schwyz, Uri and Unterwalden, signed on August 1st 1291, is displayed as well as other historic documents and mementoes.

Ital-Reding Haus

The Ital-Reding Haus in Reckenbachstrasse offers an insight into 17th c. social history.

Haus Bethlehem

On the same site is the Haus Bethlehem, the oldest wooden house in Switzerland (1287; restored 1988/89).

Above the town is the Kollegium Mariahilf, a large Roman Catholic seminary, rebuilt after a fire in 1910.

Surroundings

★ Stoos

Take the road which runs south-east up the Muota valley and arrives in 4km/2 miles at Schlatti. From there a funicular (1.5km/1 mile long, gradient up to 77%, time 8 minutes) climbs the steep wooded hillside to Stoos (1280m/4200ft, barred to vehicles since 1988), situated on a terrace commanding extensive views, with a large area of excellent skiing terrain. 8 minutes' walk south-west of the Kurhaus a chair-lift (in winter a ski-lift) takes 15 minutes to reach the Karrenstöckli (1740m/5709ft). From here it is a 10 minutes' walk to the Luegi viewpoint. Another chair-lift goes to the summit of the Fronalpstock (1922m/6325ft; inn), from where superb views of Lake Lucerne and the mountains can be enjoyed.

Fronalpstock

★ Grosser
Mythen

From Schwyz it is a 4 hours' walk by way of the Holzegg inn (1407m/4617ft; cableway from Brunni) to the summit of the Grosser Mythen (1902m/6240ft), with a splendid view of central Switzerland.

1.8km/1 mile south-east of Schwyz is Rickenbach, from which a cableway 2466m/8025ft long ascends in two stages by way of Husernberg to the upper station (1565m/5135ft) on the Rotenfluh.

Rickenbach

(20km/12 miles to Bisisthal.) The road (in good condition as far as Bisisthal) climbs through flourishing fruit orchards to the foot of the Giebel (918m/3012ft), where it enters the wooded gorge of the Muota. 4km/2 miles: Schlattli (573m/1880ft), with the lower station of the Stoos funicular. The road continues past a number of beautiful waterfalls, running through the hamlets of Ried (chair-lift via Illgau to the Oberberg, 1150m/3785ft) and Föllnis. 8km/5 miles Muotathal (612m/2008ft) has a beautiful parish church (1792) and the picturesque nunnery of St Joseph (1684–93). 2km/1 mile: Hinterthal, where a road goes off on the left into the Starzlenbach valley. 6km/4 miles: Bisisthal (870m/2854ft), in a beautiful setting.

From Schwyz in the Muota valley

Schlatti

Muotathal, St Joseph nunnery

The road up the Starzlenbach valley comes in 1km/½ mile to the entrance to the Höllochgrotten, a cave system with extensive branches (total length of passages about 160km/100 miles; 1km/½ mile open to visitors; tel. (062) 71 27 71), and ends in 5km/3 miles at the Gutentalboden (1281m/4203ft), from which it is a 2¾ hours' walk on a bridle-path over the Pragel pass (1554m/5097ft) to Richisau in the Klöntal (see Glarus).

★Höllochgrotten

Gutentalboden

See entry

Brunnen

See entry

★★Rigi

See entry

★★Vierwaldstätter See

Bad Scuol/Schuls-Tarasp-Vulpera   U 7

Canton: Grisons (GR)
Altitude: 1203–1268m/3947–4160ft
Population: 1900

The village of Scuol, situated on the left bank of the Inn along the main road from St Moritz to Landeck bypass, combines with Bad Tarasp, only a short distance upstream, the summer holiday village of Vulpera, a little way south above the right bank of the river, and the village of Tarasp-Fontana below Schloss Tarasp to form the leading resort in the Lower Engadine. Scuol is a spa (recommended for liver and bile ducts, stomach disorders, etc.), a health resort and offers a wide choice of sporting facilities.

Situation and general

Sights

The heart of the resort is the lively little town of Bad Scuol or Schuls (1250m/4102ft; pop. 1900), in a beautiful sunny setting on a gently sloping area of Alpine meadows. In the spa quarter, Oberschuls (Scuolsura), is the old Badehaus (Pump room), to which water of Vi, Sotsass and Clozza springs (high carbonic acid content) is piped. Extensions and additions to the spa centre, including a new pump room, were to have been opened in 1993. The Museum d'Engiadina Bassa (Plaz 66; open: May 15th–end June, Tues., Thur. 3–5pm; July–Sept., Tues.–Fri. 10–11am, 3–5pm) displays rural implements, Romanesque culture, weapons, a mill, etc.

Bad Scuol
Oberschuls,
Spa Quarter

In the old village of Unterschuls (Scuol-sot) are richly decorated old Engadine houses and the Protestant parish church of St George (1516).
On the south-west side of Scuol the Inn gorge is spanned by the Gurlaina viaduct (40m/131ft high). From here it is a half-hour walk to Vulpera.

Unterschuls

Bad Tarasp (1470m/4822ft; pop. 280), 2km/1 mile south-west of Scuol, has sodium sulphate and chalybeate (iron-bearing) springs which are similar in

Bad Tarasp

397

Engadine house in Bad Scuol

Schloss Tarasp

their action to those of Karlsbad. On the left bank of the Inn stand the large Kurhaus and the Kurhotel, on the right bank the Trinkhalle (Pump room).

Vulpera

From here a road climbs 1km/½ mile, with sharp turns, to Vulpera (1270m/4167ft), a quiet little place beautifully situated on a narrow terrace above the river, amid attractive parks and woodland.

Tarasp-Fontana

From Vulpera a road winds up for 3km/2 miles to the little village of Tarasp-Fontana (1444m/4738ft), delightfully set on a small lake.

★ Schloss
Tarasp

Perched on a high schist crag is an imposing medieval castle, Schloss Tarasp (1505m/4938ft), which became the residence of Austrian governors and was much altered during the 16th–18th c. (restored 1907–16 by a Dresden industrialist and made habitable; private property).

★ Kreuzberg

To the east is the Kreuzberg (Munt la Crusch, 1477m/4846ft), from which the best view of the castle is to be had.

Surroundings

From Bad Scuol a cableway 2.3km/1 mile long leads up the Motta Naluns (2136m/7030ft; restaurant; winter sports area), to the north-west.

Val Sinestra

Sent

Val Sinestra (11km/7 miles to Bad Val Sinestra).
From the east end of Bad Scuol a road on the left climbs to 4km/2 miles Sent (1440m/4725ft; pop. 800), a village with fine Engadine houses and the picturesque ruins of St Peter's chapel (12th c.), originally belonging to the castle. It is also a winter sports resort (ski-lift, toboggan run). The road continues (turn left beyond the village) into the deep and narrow Val Sinestra, running high above the River Brancla. 7km/4 miles: Bad Val Sinestra (1471m/4826ft), in a sheltered setting among beautiful forests, with arsenical chalybeate (iron-bearing) springs.

Ftan (6km/4 miles west). From Oberschuls a road runs up the valley past the open-air swimming-pool and the lower station of the cableway, and then climbs steeply, with many turns, to the village of Ftan or Fetan (1650m/5415ft; with the villages of Pitschen and Grond), a summer holiday place and winter resort (chair-lift, ski-lift) on a high terrace of meadowland on the north side of the valley, opposite Tarasp.

Ftan

Val da S-charl (12km/7 miles south). After crossing the Gurlaina viaduct a narrow road, straight ahead, winds its way up through the forest. 2km/1 mile from Scuol a road branches off on the left (1km/½ mile) to the farm of San Jon (1469m/4834ft), with fine views of the Inn valley and the Lischanna group. The road to S-charl continues through the beautiful Val da S-charl, the eastern boundary of the Swiss National Park (see entry). 10km/6 miles: S-charl or Scarl (1810 m/5940 ft), a tiny village in a remote and beautiful setting; 11th c. Romanesque church, with later restoration.

Val da S-charl

Sierre   H 11

Canton: Valais (VS)
Altitude: 538m/1765ft
Population: 11,000

The little town of Sierre (German name Siders) in the Rhône valley, lies near the linguistic boundary between French and German. It is set amid vine-clad hills formed by a gigantic rock-fall in prehistoric times, facing the gorge-like mouth of the Val d'Anniviers. On the left bank of the Rhône, at Chippis, is a large aluminium plant.

Situation and general

Sights

In the main street is the 16th c. Château des Vidomnes, with four corner turrets, residence of the episcopal bailiffs (vice domini). Close by stands the church of Notre-Dame-des-Marais, which dates in its present form from the 15th to the 16th c; the Baroque parish church is 17th c. (restored 1947). The Château de Villa (16th c.), in the north-west of the town, contains one half of the Valais Wine Museum (the other half is in Salgessch; open: Nov.–Feb. Fri.–Sun., Mar.–Oct. daily except Mon.).

Château des Vidomnes

Close to the railway station, in the north-west of the town, is the Hôtel Château-Bellevue (Rue de Bourg; open: Mar.–Oct. daily except Mon.; otherwise Fri.–Sun.; restaurant). Built in the 17th–18th c. and restored in the 20th c. it houses a collection of pewter and the Rilke room with mementoes of the poet Rainer Maria Rilke (1875–1926).

Hôtel Château-Bellevue

On a commanding crag (590m/1936ft) above the town to the east is the massive Tour de Goubing (13th c.).

Tour de Goubing

To the south, on a rocky hill above the two Lacs de Géronde (bathing lido), stands the former Carthusian monastery of Géronde.

Carthusian monastery

Surroundings

To the ★ Val d'Anniviers

(German Eifischtal: 26km/16 miles to Zinai, on a good road.) Leave Sierre on the road up the Rhône valley to Visp and in 2km/1 mile, at Pfynwald, turn right onto a road which climbs steeply uphill, with numerous hairpin turns. Below, to the right, is the Chippis aluminium plant.

Sierre: Château des Vidomnes

Entrance to St Catherine's Church

Niouc	(900m/2953ft), situated high above the River Navigenze or Navisence, which flows down through the Val d'Anniviers. The road then skirts the mouth of the Pontis gorge (short tunnel), beyond which is the Sentier de Sussillon viewpoint (1029m/3376ft). From here a steep and narrow road on the left climbs up (3km/2 miles) to Susillon (1386m/4547ft), from which it is a 2 hours' walk to Chandolin (1936m/6352ft), one of the highest mountain villages in Switzerland, with a superb view (road from St-Luc). The road up the Val d'Anniviers continues to the hamlet of Fang (1095m/3593ft), above the road on the right. Beyond this Chandolin can be seen high up on the left.

Susillon
Chandolin

Vissoie

Vissoie (1221m/4006ft) is the chief place in the valley (pop. 400); it has a square stone tower dating from the 14th c. From here it is worth making an excursion on a road to the left which runs steeply up in seven hairpin bends (gradients of up to 12%, 1 in 8) to the village of St-Luc, 6km/4 miles east (1643m/5391ft), situated on a steeply sloping expanse of Alpine meadows. This is a popular health and winter sports resort (several ski-lifts) with magnificent views of the Val d'Anniviers and its ring of mountains and over the Rhône valley to the Bernese Alps. Above the village is the Pierre des Sauvages (1714m/5624ft), with prehistoric engravings.

St-Luc

★Bella Tola

Chair-lift to the Alm Tignousa (2050m/6726ft; restaurant). Rewarding climb (4 hours) to summit of Bella Tola (3028m/9935ft), with a superb view over the Bernese and Valais Alps to Mont Blanc. From St-Luc a road runs 5.5km/3 miles north to Chandolin.

Grimentz

From Vissoie a side road on the right (8km/5 miles) descends to a bridge over the Navigenze and continues along the left bank to the little village of Grimentz (1570m/5151ft; bypass), picturesquely situated on a little mountain stream, the Marais, above the mouth of the Val de Moiry. The village is a popular summer vacation spot, and also attracts winter sports enthusiasts (ski-lift).

Lac de Moiry

The road continues south and in 5km/3 miles reaches the artificial Lac de Moiry (capacity about 75 million cu.m/2648 million cu.ft; parking place by

Grimentz in the Val d'Anniviers

the lake, beyond a short tunnel; restaurant near the dam). It then follows the east side of the lake to the Moiry glacier (2350m/7710ft), 4km/2 miles from the dam. From here it is a 1½ hours' climb south-east to the Moiry hut (2850m/9351ft).

The road up the Val d'Anniviers continues from Vissoie along the right bank of the Navigenze to the hamlets of Quimet and Mission (1307m/4288ft), opposite the mouth of the Val de Moiry.

Quimet, Mission

It then climbs with a double hairpin to Ayer (1484m/4869ft), a large village of Valais-style houses preserved intact, which is surrounded by forest and Alpine meadows.

Ayer

From here it is 5km/3 miles up the highest section of the valley, the Val de Zinal, to Zinal (1678m/5506ft), a popular climbers' base, health resort, winter sports centre (ice-rink, toboggan run) in a magnificent mountain setting. At the head of the valley is the Zinal or Durand glacier (1¾ hours), and above it tower the Zinal-Rothorn (4221m/13,849ft; 12 hours, with guide), the jagged twin peaks of Besso (3668m/12,035ft; 9 hours, with guide), the Pointe de Zinal (3806m/12,487ft; 9 hours, with guide) and the Dent Blanche (4357m/14,295ft; 15 hours, with guide, very difficult).

Zinal

To the west of the Zinal-Rothorn is a Swiss Alpine Club hut, the Cabine du Mountet (2886m/9469ft; 5 hours from Zinal). Easier climbs are to the Alpe de la Lex (2188m/7179ft; 2 hours) and the Roc de la Vache (2587m/8488ft; 3 hours), which both afford splendid views; 1½–2 hours north-east of the Roc de la Vache is another SAC hut, the Cabane de Tracuit (3256m/10,683ft). From the near end of Zinal a cabin cableway (2000m/6562ft) ascends to the Alpe de Sorebois (2470m/8104ft; restaurant), a good skiing area (two ski-tows up to 2900m/9515ft).

Climbs

From Sierre via Montana-Vermala to Crans

A funicular goes up via St-Maurice-de-Laques (change cars) to Montana (4.2km/2 miles, gradient 39%, (1 in 2), 30 minutes).

There is also a well-engineered road to Crans (15km/9 miles) which winds its way up the steep hillside through vineyards and forest. From the first bend there is a view of the little Château de Muzot (not open to the public), in which the German poet Rainer Maria Rilke lived at one time.

Venthône,
Randogne

4km/2 miles: Venthône (800m/2626ft), a picturesque village with a Gothic church and a 15th c. castle. 5km/3 miles: Randogne (1250m/4101ft), with the Montana sanatoria (pulmonary tuberculosis, tuberculosis of the bones and joints).

Montana
Vermala

4.5km/3 miles: Montana (1500m/4922ft; see Crans-Montana). 1.5km/1 mile north, higher up, is Vermala (1680m/5512ft; see Crans-Montana).

Crans sur Sierre

1.5km/1 mile west of Montana is the separate resort of Crans sur Sierre (1480–1500m/4856–5922ft; see Crans-Montana).

Lens

From here an excellent road, with extensive views, runs south-west to Lens (5km/3 miles), a small health resort in a commanding situation, and from there to Sion (see entry).

Sion

From Sierre to Vercorin (18km/11 miles)

Chippis

The road runs south from Sierre and over the Rhône to Chippis (2km/1 mile; 534m/1752ft), at the entrance to the Val d'Anniviers, where there is a large aluminium plant (Alusuisse).

Chalais

From here a road runs 3.5km/2 miles down the Rhône valley to Chalais (521m/1709ft), at the near end of which, on left, is a cableway up to Vercorin (1820m/5971ft, 7 minutes).

★ Vercorin

From Chalais a winding mountain road, with sharp bends and two tunnels, continues up 10.5km/7 miles to Vercorin (1342m/4403ft), a beautiful old village 800m/2625ft above the Rhône valley. A cableway runs south to Sigeroula (1865m/6119ft). Still farther south is Mont Tracuit (2332m/7651ft).

Simmental   H/J 8–9

Canton: Berne (BE)

Situation and
general

The Upper Simmental extends down from Lenk in the Bernese Oberland by way of Zweisimmen to Weissenbach, going almost due north; the Lower Simmental then turns east, bounded on the north-west by the steep limestone crags of the Fribourg Alps. At Spiez the valley opens out and the River Simme flows into Lake Thun. With its handsome timber houses, its typically "Oberland" church towers, its herds of cattle (the famous Simmentaler breed) and its Alpine meadows dotted with huts, the Simmental is a very characteristic stretch of Bernese farming country.

Spiez
★ Niesen

At the west end of Spiez (see Lake Thun) turn off the lakeside road to Thun into road 11 (on left), which climbs, with a fine view of the Niesen (2367m/7766ft), to Spiezwiler (652m/2139ft), where the Kandertal road goes off on the left via Mülenen (7km/4 miles; funicular up the Niesen) to Kandersteg and Adelboden.

Road 11 continues straight ahead and then curves down to enter the valley of the Kander, which it crosses (to the left a view of the Blümisalp, 3671m/12,045ft).

View of the Niesen

It then continues through wooded country to Wimmis (631m/2070ft), below the north side of the Niesen, with attractive old wooden houses and a 10th c. church. Above the village on the Burgfluh stands the imposing Weissenburg Castle (14th c.), which now houses the Nieder-Simmental communal offices (on the ground floor a room furnished in Simmental style).

Wimmis

Weissenburg Castle

Beyond Wimmis the road passes the end of a section of motorway and crosses the Simme to join a road coming in from Thun on the right. It then continues alongside an artificial lake, the Simmensee, and through the Port, a narrow passage between the high rock walls of the Burgfluh (990m/3248ft) and the Simmenfluh (1456m/4777ft). Now in the Lower Simmental, it ascends on a moderate gradient, with a view of the Jungfrau area to the left, to Latterbach (703m/2307ft), in the commune of Erlenbach.

Lower Simmental

From here an attractive detour can be made on a narrow road to the left which runs through Oey and then 14km/9 miles south-west up the Diemtigtal to the Grimmi-Alp (1222m/4009ft), with far-ranging views, from which the Seehorn (2283m/7491ft; 3 hours) and the Männifluh (2654m/8708ft; 4½ hours) can be climbed (fine views from both peaks).

Grimmi-Alp

Erlenbach (707m/2320ft; pop. 1580) is a typical Simmental village, with 18th c. timber houses. Situated on high ground is its old church (11th–13th c.), with an octagonal steeple (fine wall-paintings, mainly 15th c., with some late 13th c. work at the south-east corner of the nave). Important cattle markets. A cableway 4040m/13,255ft long runs north, via an intermediate station at Chrindi (1640m/5381ft; restaurant), to the Stockhorn (2190m/7185ft; upper station 2160m/7087ft: restaurant; mountain hut, magnificent view) in 15 minutes (on foot 4½ hours).

Erlenbach

★ Stockhorn

5km/3 miles beyond Erlenbach lies the village of Därstätten, also with fine 18th c. timber houses on the south bank of the Simme (in particular Haus Knutti, 1756). 2.5km/2 miles north-west in Nidfluh (920m/3019ft) is the oldest farmhouse in the Simmental (1642).

Därstätten

Nidfluh

Simmental

Weissenburg

Weissenburg (776m/2546ft). 1.5km/1 mile north-west is Weissenburgbad (844m/2769ft), a former spa (sulphurous spring, 31° C/88° F) which no longer operates. From Weissenburg the main road continues steadily uphill through a wooded valley, with villages situated on a terrace higher up on the right. It then comes to Boltigen (850m/2790ft; pop. 1420), in a wider part of the valley, with the precipitous limestone peak of the Mittag-fluh (1890m/6201ft) rearing above it.

Boltigen

Reidenbach

Beyond this, at Reidenbach (840m/2756ft), a road goes off on the right over the Jaun pass to Bulle and Lausanne.

Weissenbach

The main road continues up through the green Alpine meadows of the Simmental to Weissenbach (846m/2776ft), and 2km/1 mile beyond this through a narrow passage which separates the Lower from the Upper Simmental. Beyond the crag of Laubeggstalden (ruined castle; waterfall on the Simme) the valley opens out again. The road passes the ruined castle of Mannenberg (1016m/3333ft), on the left.

Zweisimmen

It then comes in to Zweisimmen (954m/3130ft; pop. 3000), the chief place in the Upper Simmental, situated in a wide expanse of meadows at the junction of the Grosse and Kleine Simme. The little town attracts many summer visitors, but is particularly favoured by winter sports enthusiasts (30km/19 miles of cross-country skiing; toboggan run; indoor tennis courts). It has a fine church with a typical Simmental tower (15th c.; 15th–16th c. stained glass). Cableway (5.1km/3 miles, 30 minutes) up the Rinderberg. To the west is the Hundsrügg (2049m/6723ft; 4`hours), with extensive views.

Upper Simmental

From Zweisimmen the main road continues to Saanen (see Gstaad), while the road to Lenk through the Upper Simmental branches off on the left, running alongside the Grosse Simme to Betelried (960m/3150ft), with the 18th c. Schloss Blankenburg (local government offices).

Zweisimmen: chief town in the Upper Simmental

It then continues to St Stephan (993m/3259ft; 15th c. church), with the Wildstrubel (3253m/10,673ft) in the background, and to Matten (1026m/3366ft), at the mouth of the Fermelbach valley.

5km/3 miles farther on (views of Wildstrubel) is Lenk (1068m/3504ft; pop. 2280), in a beautiful setting of woodland and meadows at the head of the Upper Simmental, with the grandiose bulk of the Wildstrubel closing the valley to the south. Lenk is a health and winter sports resort (ice-rink, curling, cross-country skiing) and also a spa (sulphurous springs). The spa establishment lies to the south-west of the village.

Lenk

Cableway (3698m/12,133ft, 26 minutes) via intermediate stations at Stoss and Betelberg (1650m/5414ft; restaurant) to the Leiterli station on the Mülkerblatten (2000m/6562ft), with beautiful views and good skiing. From the Wallbach a chair-lift (3241m/10,634ft, 28 minutes) also provides access to the Mülkerblatten via an intermediate station at Wallegg (1580m/5184ft).

Mülkerblatten

A narrow road (8km/5 miles; alternate one-way traffic) runs south from Lenk up the Pöschenried valley, past the Iffigen Falls (130m/427ft high) to the Iffigenalp (1618m/5309ft). From here there are rewarding climbs (not difficult for experienced climbers, with guide) by way of the Wildhorn hut (2315m/7596ft) up the Wildhorn (3248m/10,657ft; 6 hours) and by way of the Wildstrubel hut (2793m/9164ft) up the Wildstrubel (west peak 3251m/10,667ft, east peak 3253m/10,673ft; 7 hours), from both of which there are magnificent views of the Valais Alps and the Mont Blanc group.

★Iffigen Falls, Iffigenalp
★Wildhorn

★Wildstrubel

A new road (N 6) is planned to run through a tunnel 4km/2 miles long into the Valais. Another road leads south-east from Lenk up the Simme valley, past a cableway to Metsch (1480m/4856ft), to Höhenhaus (5km/3 miles; 1103m/3619ft), at the head of the valley. From here a footpath (1 hour) ascends past the Simme Falls to the huts on the Räzliberg (1404m/4607ft; restaurant), near which the Siebenbrunnen (1446m/4744ft), the main source of the Simme, gushes out of seven clefts in the rock walls of the Fluhhorn (2139m/7018ft).

Simme Falls
Siebenbrunnen

Finally a road running east from Lenk climbs with steep bends to the Bühlberg restaurant (6km/4 miles; 1660m/5446ft), from which it is an hour's climb to the Hahnenmoos pass (1957m/6421ft).

Bühlberg, Hahnenmoos

Simplon Pass

K/L 10–12

Canton: Valais (VS)
Height of pass: 2005m/6578ft

The road to the Simplon pass (Italian Passo del Sempione), constructed on Napoleon's orders between 1801 and 1805, is the shortest route between Valais and southern Ticino or northern Italy. The road is usually open throughout the year; but it is always possible for motorists to avoid the pass by loading their cars on to the train which runs through the 19.8km/12 mile long Simplon tunnel between Brig and Iselle (Italy).

Situation and general

Over the Simplon pass to Domodóssola (Italy)

The road, which offers a tremendous scenic experience, ascends from the old town of Brig, at an important road junction in the Upper Rhône valley, with numerous turns and constantly changing views of the deep tributary valleys of the Saltina and the magnificent peaks of the southern Bernese Alps, and continues over the pass and down to Domodóssola (Italy) and Locarno.

The Simplon road (64km/40 miles to Domodóssola) branches off the Rhône valley road at Brig and winds its way up towards the towering Glishorn

★ Simplon road

Simplon Pass road

Brig

(2528m/8294ft), with beautiful views of Brig (see entry) to the rear. It then climbs the Briger Berg in the direction of the Klenenhorn (2695m/8842ft), affording an attractive view, to the left, of Brig and the Rhône valley. Ahead is the Belalp, with the Sparrhorn (3026m/9928ft) rearing above it; to the left the Nesthorn (3820m/12,533ft), and to the right, higher up, the conical peak of the Eggishorn (2934m/9626ft).

Schallberg
Refuge Hut

Beyond Ried-Brig (938m/3078ft) the road continues uphill through wooded country, passing under a cableway to Rosswald (2000m/6562ft) to the south-east. At the Schallberg Refuge hut (Schutzhaus II, 1320m/4331ft) the view of the pass, with the Bellevue Hotel opens up. To the rear are the Bernese Alps, from the Bietschhorn to the Aletschhorn.

Ganter valley

The road now curves round into the wooded Ganter valley, beyond which (from left to right) are the Bortelhorn (3194m/10,480ft), Furggenbaumhorn (2991m/9813ft) and Wasenhorn (3246m/10,650ft).

Berisal

Berisal (1526m/5007ft), a little hamlet with accommodation for summer visitors. The road continues to wind its way up the mountainside through forests of larch, with beautiful views of the Bernese Alps. At Rothwald (1750m/5742ft; inn) the magnificent summit of the Fletschhorn (3996m/13,111ft) comes into view above the pass (to right).

Rothwald
★Fletschhorn

100m/328ft further on a side road on the left runs up through the forest (0.5km/¼ mile) to the commandingly situated Taferna Hotel.

★Simplon Pass

The main road now makes straight for the pass, running high above the Taverbach, with beautiful views down into the valley on the right. Schallberg Refuge Hut (Schutzhaus V, 1934m/6345ft). The Simplon pass (2005m/6578ft; Hotel Bellevue and Simplon-Blick) is a ridge covered with Alpine meadows at the foot of the glaciated Monte Leone (3553m/11,657ft; 7 hours, with guide) and the black rock walls of the Hübschhorn (3192m/10,473ft), lying closer to the pass.

The road now crosses a fairly level stretch of ground, passing a large stone eagle on a mound to the right which commemorates the manning of the frontier by Swiss troops during the Second World War. Beyond this, on the left, is the Simplon Hospice (2001m/6565ft), established by Napoleon, which has been occupied since 1625 by monks from the Great St Bernard Hospice (see Great St Bernard).

Simplon Hospice

The road then descends the wide valley of the Krummbach, enclosed by snow-covered mountains, with fine views of the magnificent Fletschhorn. Below the road on the right can be seen the tall building of the Altes Spital (Old Hospice; 1872m/6142ft), established about 1660 by Kaspar Stockalper, the great merchant prince of Brig (see entry).

At the Engeloch (1795m/5889ft) the road leads down to the valley floor, crosses the Krummbach (1617m/5305ft) to Eggen (1660m/5250ft), at the mouth of the Rossboden or Sengbach valley, from which there was a devastating rock fall and avalanche from the Rossboden glacier in 1901.

Eggen, Rossboden valley

Simplon Dorf (Italian Sempione, 1479m/4853ft) is beautifully situated in an expanse of green Alpine meadows in a wider part of the valley. To the east is Monte Leone, to the south the Fletschhorn (3996m/13,111ft) and Weiss-mies (4023m/13,199ft).

Simplon Dorf

Gabi or Gstein (1232m/4042ft) is situated at the confluence of the Krumm-bach and Laggienbach, forming the Diviera or Doviera River, which the road now follows downstream. Beyond the Gabi gallery is the rugged Gondo gorge, one of the wildest and deepest ravine roads in the Alps. The road continues through the Gondo gallery and crosses the Alpienbach, which flows down from the Alpien glacier on Monte Leone, forming beauti-ful waterfalls.

Gabi or Gstein

★Gondo Gorge

Gondo (858m/2815ft), picturesquely situated below the rock walls of the ravine opposite the mouth of the Zwischenbergen valley (waterfall), is the last village in Switzerland (customs; Swiss passport control). The church dates only from 1968, but has an older choir; the high square tower was built by the Stockalper family of Brig about 1660 for the protection of travellers.

Gondo

1km/½ mile beyond this is the Swiss–Italian frontier (800m/2625ft; Italian passport and customs control). From here the road runs down the valley, now known as the Val Divedro, to Iselle (657m/2156ft). At Iselle station, 1km/½ mile beyond the village, the railway emerges from the southern end of the Simplon tunnel; cars loaded here for Brig.

Val Divedro

Iselle

After passing through Crévola d'Ossola the road runs in a long straight stretch through the wide and fertile valley of the Toce, here known as the Valle d'Ossola, in which the vegetation already has a southern character (chestnut, fig and mulberry trees, fields of maize, vineyards), and comes to Domodóssola (278m/912ft), a town of 20,000 inhabitants, with an attractive market square, the Piazza del Mercato. From here a road runs east through the Val Centovalli to Locarno (see entry).

Valle d'Ossola

Domodóssola

Sion

G 11

Canton: Valais (VS)
Altitude: 520m/1706ft. Population: 25,000

Sion (German Sitten), capital of Valais, occupies the site of the Roman town of Sedunum and has been the see of a bishop since the 6th c. It is now an important market town for the wine (Provins Valais depot; conducted tours), fruit and vegetables of the fertile Rhône valley, with many features of interest. The old town is built on the detrital fan of the river Sionne, dominated by two picturesque castle-crowned crags. Here the river

Situation and general

Borgne, coming from the Val d'Hérens to the south, flows into the Rhône, carrying down boulders and scree which the Rhône has thrust against its northern bank.

Sights

Place de la Planta

In the spacious Place de la Planta are the Palais du Gouvernement (cantonal offices) and a monument commemorating the centenary of Valais' admission into the Confederation (1815).

Maison Supersaxo

At 7 rue de Conthey stands the Maison Supersaxo, built by Georg Supersaxo, the provincial governor, in 1505; it has a fine hall with an elaborately carved and painted ceiling.

Rue de Grand-Pont, Town Hall

In the main street, Rue du Grand-Pont, which is built over the conduited river Sionne, is the Hôtel de Ville (Town Hall, 1660), with an astronomical clock. Built into the hall on the ground floor are a number of Roman inscribed stones, including one of A.D. 377 which is the earliest evidence of Christianity in Switzerland.

Cathedral Notre-Dame-du-Glarier

To the north-east the Cathedral of Notre-Dame-du-Glarier, was rebuilt in the 15th c. and has a 12th c. Romanesque tower. It contains 15th c. bishops' tombs and 17th c. choir-stalls; among the many valuable items in the

Sion: Rue du Grand-Port   *Château de Tourbillon*

treasury are a number of reliquaries of the 8th–10th c. In 1988 the great organ, a more than 100-year-old masterpiece by the famous organ builder Carlen of Reckingen, was brought back into service after being restored.

Facing the cathedral, to the south-west, is the church of St Théodule, a sober building of 1516. The Bishop's Palace (Evêché) on the west side of the square was rebuilt in 1840.

St Théodule's Church, Bishop's Palace

From here the narrow Rue de la Tour runs north to the Tour des Sorciers (Wizard's Tower, 12th c.), a relic of the medieval fortifications. Close by, at the junction of Rue de Gravelone and Avenue St-François, stands the Muli (Mule) monument (by M.-E. Sandoz, 1966).

Tour des Sorciers

In 1988 a cultural centre was opened in the Grenette building (1860) with capacity for concerts, exhibitions and other performances.

Grenette Cultural Centre

At 40 Avenue de la Gare there is an interesting Museum of Natural History with geology, mineralogy, botany and zoological departments (dinosaur finds, 1979).

Natural History Museum

From the Town Hall another narrow street, Rue des Châteaux (No. 19 Cantonal Museum of Art), leads up to the castles. (It is possible to drive as far as the All Saints chapel and park there.) On the left are the remains of the Château de la Majorie, which now houses the Valais Museum of Art. In front of the castle is a monument to St Theodulus (Bishop of Valais).

Valais Museum of Art

The Museum of Antiquities is at No. 12 Place de la Majorie with prehistoric finds and Gallo-Romanic exhibitions.

Museum of Antiquities

Beyond this is All Saints chapel (Tous-les-Saints), still in Romanesque style though it was built as late as 1325 (with some 17th c. rebuilding). From here it is a few minutes' walk to the Château de Tourbillon). The Château de

Château de Valère

409

Sion

★Notre-Dame-de-Valère

Valère (621m/2038ft) and the former collegiate church of Notre-Dame-de-Valère (12th–13th c.), built on Roman foundations, combine to form an impressive architectural group (floodlit on summer evenings). The church is a three-aisled pillared basilica, with fantastically decorated capitals in the choir; the carved wooden altar is 16th c., the beautifully carved choir-stalls 17th c., the stone rood-screen 13th c., and the organ, in a painted loft, 15th c. (one of the oldest that can still be played). Beside the church is the cantonal Musée de Valère with Roman antiquities and medieval sculpture.

Musée de la Valère

Château de Tourbillon

On the higher of the two hills above the town (655m/2149ft) are the imposing ruins of the Château de Tourbillon (built 1294, destroyed by fire 1788), from which there is a view embracing the Rhône valley from Leuk in the east to Martigny in the west.

Surroundings

★St-Pierre-de-Clages

Road 8 runs down the Rhône valley via the wine-producing village of Vétroz to St-Pierre-de-Clages (526m/1726ft), which has a church of the 11th-12th c. with an octagonal tower, one of the finest Romanesque churches in the country (stained glass of 1948).

To the Val de Nendaz

(16km/10 miles to Haute-Nendaz, 27km/17 miles to the Lac de Cleuson.) Leave Sion on the Val d'Herens road and after crossing the Rhône take a road on the right which gradually leads uphill and comes in 5km/3 miles to Arvilard (684m/2244ft), where a road branches off on the left to Mayens de Sion. 1km/½ mile: Baar (738m/2421ft), beyond which the road turns south into the narrow Val de Nendaz. 2km/1 mile: Brignon (895m/2936ft). 2km/1 mile: Basse-Nendaz (992m/3255ft).

Arvilard
Baar

Early-Romanesque architecture . . .   *. . . of St-Pierre de Clages priory church*

**Saint-Pierre
-de-Clages**

**Plan of
Romanesque Church**
(Founded *c.* 407; first
mentioned in 1152)

Nave — Crossing Tower — Choir

10 m   © *Baedeker*

Haute-Nendaz (1370m/4495ft), a holiday and skiing resort high above the Rhône valley. Cableway (2270m/7448ft, 12 minutes) to Tracouet (2200m/7218ft; skiing), at the foot of the Dent de Nendaz (2463m/8081ft; 2–3 hours).

Haute-Nendaz

The road continues south up the valley above an irrigation channel (bisse). 2km/1 mile: Le Bleusy (1412m/4633ft), with a chapel. 3km/2 miles: L'Antie (1565m/5135ft). 3km/2 miles Siviez (1758m/5770ft; several ski-lifts). From here a road (2km/1 mile) runs to the Alpe de Tortin (2039m/6690ft), from which there is a cableway (2280m/7481ft, 12 minutes) to the Col de Chassoure (2734m/8970ft); from there a chair-lift to the Lac des Vaux. Cableway from Tortin-Col des Gentianes to Mont Fort.

Le Bleusy
Siviez

Lac de Cleuson (2115m/6939ft), an artificial lake 1200m/3937ft long created in 1958.

Lac de Cleuson

From Beuson a steep and narrow mountain road climbs 3.5km/2 miles to Veysonnaz (1233m/4045ft), from which a cableway ascends to the holiday and winter sports resort of Thyon 2000 (2068m/6785ft; blocks of flats; indoor swimming pool, ski-lifts), which can also be reached by road (13km/8 miles) from Vex via Les Collons (1800m/5906ft).

Thyon 2000

To Mayens de Sion

(15km/9 miles.) At Arvilard (5km/3 miles) on the Val de Nendaz road turn left into a road which climbs in large bends via Salins (847m/2779ft) to (13km/8 miles) Les Agettes (1030m/3379ft). 2km/1 mile Mayens de Sion (1300–1400m/4265–4593ft), a summer village of chalets widely dispersed over the Alpine meadows, which are supplied with water by irrigation channels (bisses). Magnificent views of the Bernese Alps, in particular the Wildhorn (3248m/10,657ft), due north above Sion.

Mayens de Sion

To the Lac de Tseuzier

(23km/14miles: the Rawil road.) The road runs up the Sionne valley and then climbs in sharp turns up the east side of the valley. 3.5km/2 miles: Champlan (714m/2343ft), a village surrounded by vineyards. 2.5km/2 miles Grimisuat (881m/2891ft), on a rocky spur. From here a narrow mountain road ascends steeply to Arbaz (1146m/3760ft), immediately above Grimisuat to the north.

Grimisuat

3.5km/2 miles: Ayent (978m/3209ft), a widely scattered settlement made up of a number of separate villages. Road to Crans via Lens. In neighbouring La Giète (1154m/3786ft) the road goes off on the left to Anzère (see below). The main road now climbs up through the forest in two large bends. 7km/4 miles: Praz Combeira (1620m/5315ft), beyond which the road passes through three tunnels. 4km/2 miles: Lac de Tseuzier (1777m/5830ft), an artificial lake (1956–58) 1km/½ mile long and 600m/1969ft across, in wild and lonely country. A footpath follows the west side of the lake.

Ayent

Lac de Tseuzier

From La Giète a road (5km/3 miles) goes up to Anzère or Antsère (1500m/4922ft), a developing winter sports resort beautifully set on a mountain

Anzère

411

terrace (ski-lifts). Cableway (2180m/7153ft) to the Pas de Maimbré (2362m/7750ft; view; ski-runs). To the north is the Wildhorn (3248m/10,657ft), the highest peak in the western Bernese Oberland (5½ hours, with guide). Several chair-lifts.

To the Col du Sanetsch

(27km/17 miles; to the Sanetschsee 32km/20 miles.) Road 2–6m/7–20ft wide, maximum gradient 18% (1 in 5½); closed in winter. The winding road runs north-west from Sion through vineyards. 5km/3 miles: St Germain (820m/2690ft). The road then passes through the commandingly situated villages of Granois (857m/2812ft) and Chandolin (818m/2684ft) and turns north above the wild valley of the Morge. 6km/4 miles: Pont du Diable (919m/3015ft), where it crosses to the right bank. It then continues winding its way uphill, crosses the Morge again and later the Nétage, and climbs, with many turns to (16km/10 miles) the Col du Sanetsch or Col de Senin (2243m/7359ft), on a ridge between the Arpelistock (3035m/9958ft) to the east and the Sanetschhorn (Mont Brun, 2942m/9653ft) to the west. From both of these peaks (respectively 3½ and 2½ hours' climb from the pass) there are magnificent views. The road continues for another 5km/3 miles to the dam (42m/138ft high) at the north end of the Sanetschsee, a reservoir (2.7 million cu.m/95 million cu.ft) on the upper course of the River Saane (Sarine).

Col du Sanetsch

Sanetschsee

The Val d'Hérens

(52km/32 miles to Les Haudères.) The road runs south-east from Sion, turns right over the Rhône bridge towards Val d'Hérens.

Vex

Vex (957m/3140ft; pronounced Veh) is commandingly situated high above the gorge of the Borgne, which flows down through the Val d'Hérens. A narrow road goes off on the right and ascends the Val d'Hérémence, running from above the Val d'Hérens road to the picturesque village of Hérémence (1236m/4055ft), with the church of St Nicolas (by W. M. Förderer, 1963–71).

Hérémence

Val
d'Hérémence
Motôt
Grand-Dixence
Dam

The road continues up the Val d'Hérémence via Pralong (1608m/5276ft) to Motôt (1925m/6316ft), with a parking place (1970m/6464ft). From here it is a 2 hours' walk (5.5km/3 miles) to the Grande-Dixence dam (2365m/7760ft; completed 1961; 284m/932ft high; top 748m/2454ft long, 15m/49ft wide, in the Val des Dix). Its water is carried in underground tunnels to the Fionnay power station and beyond this, under pressure, to the main power station at Nendaz in the Rhône valley. At the end of the road, beneath the dam, is a hotel and restaurant with a large car park. From here a cableway runs up to the lake (motor-boat). Prominent among the peaks forming the magnificent mountain setting of the lake are the Rosablanche (3336m/10,945ft), Mont Blanc de Cheilon (3871m/12,701ft) and the Aiguilles Rouges d'Arolla (3650m/11,976ft).

Walks: along the lake (2½ hours); to the Cabane des Dix (4 hours; by boat 2 hours); to the Col de Riematten (4 hours); to Arolla (6 hours).

★ Val d'Hérens
★ Earth Pillars

The road to Les Haudères continues along the hillside, following an almost level but winding course. On the opposite side of the valley is the pretty village of Vernamiège. After crossing the River Dixence, coming from the Val d'Hérémence, the road turns into the Val d'Hérens (German Eringertal) and passes through a tunnel under a series of earth pillars, columns of morainic debris which have been protected from erosion by a large boulder or capstone.

Euseigne

Euseigne or Useigne (970m/3183ft): road on right into Val d'Hérémence. On the opposite side of the valley is the village of St-Martin.

Val d'Hérens: earth pillars near Euseigne

La Luette (1020m/3347ft), beyond which the road crosses the grey waters of the Borgne on a high bridge, the Pont Noir de Lugnerez (1001m/3284ft). 1km/½ mile farther up the valley, at Praz-Jean (1100m/3609ft), a narrow road goes off on the left and passes through a number of hamlets and the villages of St-Martin and Mase, standing high above the right bank of the Borgne and offering fine views. The road then runs down in steep bends to Bramois and across the Rhône to Sion (5km/3 miles).

La Luette

Praz-Jean

The Val d'Hérens road continues to Evolène (1378m/4521ft), the chief town in the valley (pop. 1500) and a popular holiday resort, lying in the wide green stretch of valley between Sasseneire (3259m/10,693ft; 5½ hours with guide) to the east and the Pic d'Arzinol (3001m/9846ft; 5–5½ hours) and the Mont de l'Etoile (3372m/11,064ft; 6 hours, with guide) to the west. Higher up the valley the view is dominated by the bold outline of the Dents de Veisivi and the massive Dent Blanche (to left).

Evolène

★Sasseneire

The road continues along the right bank of the Borgne and in 4km/2 miles reaches Les Haudères (1433m/4702ft), a health resort. It is the highest village in the Val d'Hérens, which divides at this point into the Val d'Arolla and the Combe de Ferpècle.

Les Haudères

A good road ascends the Val d'Arolla to Arolla, properly Mayens d'Arolla (1962m/6437ft), winter sports and mountain resort (ski-lifts, cross-country skiing, toboggan run, curling) magnificently set facing the Pigne d'Arolla (3801m/12,471ft; 5–6 hours) and Mont Collon (3644m/11,956ft; 7 hours, with guide).

Arolla

A narrow and sometimes steep road runs up the Combe de Ferpècle from Les Haudères to the huts of Ferpècle or Salay (6.5km/4 miles, 1800m/5906ft), near the end of twin glaciers, the Glacier du Mont Miné and the Glacier de Ferpècle.

Ferpècle

From here it is a 2 hours' climb to the Alpe de Bricolla (2462m/7960ft), with the Dent Blanche (4364m/14,318ft; 9–10 hours, with guide) rearing above it

★Alp Bricolla

on the left, and the Glacier du Mont Miné, with the Dents de Bertol, the Aiguille de la Za (3673m/12,051ft) and the Dents de Veisivi (3425m/11,237ft; 5½–6 hours).

Solothurn/Soleure   H 5

Canton: Solothurn (SO)
Altitude: 442m/1450ft
Population: 16,000

Situation and general

Solothurn (French Soleure), capital of the canton of the same name, lies astride the river Aare at the foot of the Jura hills. Numerous Renaissance and Baroque buildings bear witness to the one-time splendour of the town, which in the 16th, 17th and 18th centuries was the residence of the French ambassadors to the Confederation.

The number 11 is significant for Solothurn. It was the 11th canton to join the Confederation in 1481, there are 11 churches and chapels, 11 historic fountains and 11 towers. St Ursen Cathedral has 11 altars and 11 bells and its staircase is divided into sections each with 11 steps.

History

The town of Salodurum ranked with Trier in Germany as one of the oldest Roman settlements north of the Alps. In A.D. 303 two members of the Theban Legion, Ursus and Victor, were martyred here. Solothurn joined the Swiss Confederation in 1481.

Sights

★St-Ursen Cathedral

Just inside the Baseltor (Basle Gate, 1508), where the Baselstrasse enters the old town, stands the Cathedral of St Ursen (St Ursus: 1763–73), in Italian Baroque style, which has been the cathedral of the diocese of Basle since 1830.

★Treasury

On the ground floor of the 60m/197ft high tower is the rich Treasury containing goldsmiths' work, textiles of 15th–19th c. and papal coins. On

Solothurn

1 Landhaus
2 Palais Besenval
3 St Peter
4 St Ursens' Cathedral
5 Old Arsenal
6 Franciscan Church
7 Buristurm
8 Clock Tower
9 Jesuit Church
10 Theatre
11 Nature Museum

200 m

© Baedeker

Solothurn: St Peter's Chapel and cathedral

Statue of St Ursen on a fountain

Old Arsenal: collection of weapons from the Middle Ages to the present

Solothurn: Rathaus . . .

. . . and Mauritius Fountain

the steps leading up to the cathedral are two fountains with figures of Moses and Gideon.

★Old Arsenal The Old Arsenal (Altes Zeughaus, 1610–14), north-west of the cathedral, houses the largest collection of arms and armour of Europe (closed Mon.). The extensive arsenal has weapons and uniforms from the 16th and 17th c. to the present-day.

Town Hall Almost opposite is the Rathaus (Town Hall), of the 15th and 17th c., with a fine Renaissance doorway; in the north tower a cantilevered winding staircase dates from 1632.

Market In the nearby Marktplatz is the 12th c. clock tower (Zeitglockenturm), with mechanical figures (1545) of a king flanked by Death and a soldier. Close by is the Mauritius fountain decorated with a figure by the famous master Hans Gieng of Fribourg.

Jesuit Church In Hauptgasse stands the Jesuit church (1680–89) with an interior decorated with stucco work by Ticenese artists. In the cloister is an interesting lapidarium with Roman inscriptions.

St Peter's Chapel This much-restored chapel contains the tombs of the Theban martyrs Ursus and Victor.

Nature Museum At No. 2 Klosterplatz is the Nature Museum (closed Mon.). From the Marktplatz the Gurzelngasse leads west to the Bieltor (Biel gate, originally 12th c.) and a 16th c. tower, the Buristurm.

Museum of Art At No. 30 Werkhofstrasse, in the old town, is the Museum of Art (closed Mon.), housing works by old masters (including a Madonna by Hans Holbein the Younger) and by 19th and 20th c. artists.

Farther north, at Blumensteinweg 12, is the Schloss Blumenstein Historical Museum, and next door is the Pre-History Department (closed Mon.).

Blumenstein Historical Museum

On the western outskirts of the town St Mary's church (1953), has the largest stained-glass windows in the country (some 100sq.m/1076sq.ft) by H. Stocker.

St Mary's Church

Surroundings

Grenchen 11km/7 miles west, has a Museum of Modern Art in the Girard-haus (open: Tues.–Sun.) and a memorial to the Italian freedom fighter Guiseppe Mazzini (1805–72; open: Mon.–Fri.).

Grenchen

For Weissenstein (10km/6 miles) leave Solothurn by the Bieltor and Biel-strasse and bear right along Weissensteinstrasse into a road which runs through the watchmaking town of Langendorf (artificial ice-rink in winter) to Oberdorf. 4.5km/3 miles: Oberdorf station (658m/2159ft), from which a chair-lift (2369m/7773ft, 16 minutes) ascends to the Weissenstein (1284m/4214ft).

To the Weissenstein

Oberdorf
★Weissenstein

The road then climbs in steep bends up the Nesselboden (1051m/3448ft), with a celebrated view of the Alps extending as far as Mont Blanc. Marked footpaths lead to various viewpoints in the hills, which offer excellent skiing in winter.

There are numerous walks along marked paths, of which the Planetenweg (Planet Way) is recommended. It represents on a scale 1 to 1 billion the distance between the sun and the planet Pluto. Other walks encompass the flora (Botanical Garden) and geology of the Jura.

Planet Way

For safety reasons visitors to the "Nidenloch" caves must report to the Gasthaus Hinterweissenstein before and after visiting the caves. In the entrance are wire cable ladders; stout footwear is essential.

Nidenloch

Not far to the west at Altreu is the oldest and most well known stork colony in Switzerland.

Stork Colony, Altreu

Schloss Waldegg, lying 4km/2 miles from Feldbrunnen (north-east), was built in 1682–90. It is surrounded by a Baroque garden and is one of the most beautiful country houses in the Solothurn region. Visitors can view its 17th–19th c. furniture and pictures. It is also the headquarters of the organisation of the same name, which seeks to promote contact between the different linguistic areas of Switzerland (open: May 15th–Oct. 31st Tues.–Sat. 2–5pm, Sun. 10am–noon also).

★Schloss Waldegg

About 10km/6 miles north-east from Solothurn is the medieval little town of Wangen, with a very well-preserved medieval centre which is almost of a square design. The covered wooden bridge over the Aare was built in the 16th c. Worth seeing are the parish church of the Holy Cross and St Maria (1825; 14th and 15th c. frescoes) and the castle (restored 1680; Baroque ceiling paintings by J. Werners). The Gemeindehaus by the clock tower contains documents about the town's history and ceramics.

Wangen on the Aare

The little picturesque town of Wiedlisbach was, like Solothurn, founded by the Counts of Fribourg (c. 1280). A corner tower remains from the old fortifications in the "Hinterstädtli", and in St Catherine's chapel (Katharinenkapelle; 1338) there are Late Gothic frescoes. The Kornhaus contains a small local collection of ceramics, glass and tin from Bernese and Solothurn studios.

Wiedlisbach

Landshut castle (1624–30) in Utzensdorf (11km/7 miles south of Solothurn) houses an exhibition of 17th c. domestic culture and of hunting and shooting themes (closed Mon.).

Utzensdorf

Stein am Rhein   O 2

Canton: Schaffhausen (SH)
Altitude: 405m/810ft
Population: 3000

Location and   The little town of Stein am Rhein, situated at the western tip of the
★★ Townscape   Untersee, the arm of Lake Constance by which the Rhine leaves the lake, is,
                      with Morat, one of the best-preserved medieval towns in Switzerland.

Sights

★ Marketplace/   In the very picturesque Marktplatz (fountains) stands the Rathaus (Town
Town Hall   Hall, 1539), which contains the town's historical collections, including
                      weapons, heraldic crests and valuable stained glass (open: Mon.–Fri.).

Eschenz, Stammheimertal, Frauenfeld, Konstanz

Stein on the Hochrhein

From the Marktplatz the Hauptstrasse (with an old house, the Weisser Adler or White Eagle, at No. 14) runs north-west to the Untertor (Lower Gate). On the north side of the old town is the Obertor (Upper Gate).

At 17 Rathausplatz there is an exhibition of phonographs and gramophones from 1877 to 1940 (open: daily).

Phonograph Museum

In the house at 33 Unterstadt (closed Tues.), furnished in the Empire style, there is a small exhibition of the Late Impressionist work of the painter Hermann Knecht (1893–1978).

Lindwurm Museum

South-east of the Rathaus stands the former Benedictine Conventual Church of St George, a 12th c. Romanesque basilica which is now the Protestant parish church; it has old frescoes in the choir. The adjoining former Benedictine Monastery, founded by King Henry II and his consort Kunigunde c. 1005, was dissolved in 1524; the present buildings date from the 14th–15th c. and house the St George's Abbey Museum (Klostermuseum St Georgen) with original 15th and 16th c. furnishings. Associated with the museum is a local collection (closed Mon.) of prehistoric finds from the Island of Werd and from the surroundings of the town.

St George's Abbey

Benedictine Monastery

★Abbey Museum

The Great Hall of the abbey has fine wall paintings (1515–16) by Thomas Schmid and A. Holbein, and in the Late Gothic cloister are old tombstones.

West of the Town Hall at Schwarzhorngasse 136 is a doll museum (closed Mon.) containing more than 500 old dolls and automata from central Europe.

Doll museum

Near the landing stage for boats in the south-west of the Old Town is a miniature steam railway for children.

Landing stage Miniature steam railway

On the left bank of the Rhine is the district of Burg. On the hill (views) are remains of the Roman castrum of Tasgaetium (A.D. 294). Within the castrum

Tasgaetium

stands the parish church of St John (originally 5th c.), with frescoes of about 1400.

Benedictine abbey
1km/¾ mile west of Stein am Rhein is the outlying district of Wagenhausen, with the remains of a former Benedictine abbey built 1090–92 and dissolved in 1529. The Romanesque pillared basilica (1083–87) has been preserved.

Surroundings

Burg Hohen-klingen
On the Klingenberg (593m/1946ft), a wooded hill north of the town, is a well-preserved 12th c. castle, Burg Hohenklingen (armoury, 16th c. stained glass; restaurant), once the home of the minnesinger Walther von Klingen (c. 1215–86). From the tower (worn steps) there is a fine view over the town and the Rhine.

Eschenz
Not far south of Stein am Rhein, at the end of the Untersee, lies the village of Eschenz (406m/1332ft; pop. 1300). It occupies the site of the Roman town of Tasgaetium (see above) from which the name of the village is derived.

Werd Island
Near the district of Untereschenz lies the little island of Werd, where more than 5000 years ago people dwelt in houses built on piles (excavation finds in the local museum of the Benedictine monastery). The pilgrimage church of St Othmar dates from the 15th c.

Freudenfels castle
South-east of the village of Obereschenz (1.5km/1 mile; narrow road) stands Freudenfels castle (528m/1733ft).

Stamm-heimertal
On the far side of the Stammer Hill, south-west of Stein am Rhein, lies the charming Stammheimer or Stammer valley which was formed during the Ice Age. Idyllic lakes (Nussbaumersee, Hüttwilersee and Hasensee) nestle in wooded hills of glacial moraine, with neat little villages of typical half-timbered houses.

Ober-stammheim
The Gasthof zum Hirschen, an inn in Oberstammheim, built in 1684, with oriel windows dating from 1730, is one of the finest half-timbered houses in eastern Switzerland.

Swiss National Park   T 8

Canton Grisons (GR)

Location and general
The Swiss National Park (Schweizerischer Nationalpark, Parc National Suisse, Parco Nazionale Svizzero, Parc Naziunal Svizzer), founded in 1909, lies in the Lower Engadine to the north-west of the Ofen pass (Pass dal Fuorn), and covers an area of 168sq.km/65sq.miles. In the south it borders on Italy for a distance of 15km/9 miles. It is a mountainous region of eastern Alpine character, with some Dolomitic features. The highest peak in the National Park is Piz Pisoc (3174m/10,414ft), to the north, closely followed, in the south, by Piz Quatervals (3164m/10,384ft) from which radiate the four valleys referred to in its name. The permanent snow level lies between 2900m/9515ft and 3000m/9843ft.

The only area of habitation in the park is the Il Fuorn Hotel on the busy Ofen pass road (Ofenberg road), which runs from Zernez into Val Müstair. Along this road are nine parking places, from which radiate a network of footpaths (marked white–red–white) with a total length of 80km/50 miles. Visitors must not leave the marked paths: the National Park is subject to strict regulations designed to ensure that the natural conditions are not disturbed in any way.

Information can be obtained from the Nationalparkhaus in Zernez (see below).

About a third of the park's area is covered by forest. The characteristic tree is the mountain pine; larches and stone pines, forest pines and spruces feature less prominently, and deciduous trees (birch, aspen, willow) play a very minor role. Above the tree-line dwarf shrubs predominate (rhododendrons, dwarf willows, junipers, crowberries, etc.). On the dry limestone crags the commonest form of grass cover is the brownish type of turf known in Switzerland as "crooked sedge turf" (Krummseggenrasen, Caricetum curvulae). On the sunnier hillsides the predominant vegetation is blue grass (Sesleria semperviretum). The type known as "milk-grass pasture" (Milchgrasweide), which includes a wide variety of species, prefers wetter ground, while on poor soil the mat grasses form a thick felt-like carpet. Particularly attractive flowers are found in small hollows on shaded slopes which become impregnated with melt-water. The brilliantly yellow Rhaetian Alpine poppy manages to find a foothold even on steep scree slopes. — Flora

Reptiles and amphibians are represented by the grass frog, Alpine newt, viviparous lizard and adder. The commonest rodents are the marmot, the blue hare and the squirrel. Altogether thirty species of mammals are found – among the larger game are red deer, chamois, ibex and small numbers of roe-deer; among the predators the fox, the marten and the ermine. There are more than a hundred species of birds, the commonest being nutcrackers, ring ouzels, Alpine titmice and greater spotted woodpeckers; the game birds include capercaillie, black grouse, rock partridge, ptarmigan and hazel hen; and the crags provide nesting-places for ravens, Alpine choughs and, in many places, golden eagles. — Fauna

★★Walks in the Park

Marked footpaths run through some of the most beautiful parts of the National Park, with opportunities for observing the wildlife. The animals — Note

Nature reserve . . .   *. . . on the Ofen Pass*

are wary of man, so that they can usually be seen only at distances of 500 to 1000m/550 to 1100yd. Observers should therefore be properly equipped (field glasses, telephoto lens).

Route I: to Margunet

From parking place 7 on the Ofen pass road through the wooded Val dal Botsch to the first rest area (Rastplatz), from which chamois can be observed; then on to the large rest area at Margunet (2308m/7573ft), with a beautiful view (Munt la Schera, Piz Nair, Piz dal Fuorn; red deer); down from here to another rest area (red deer) and the Stabelchod hut (park-keeper's house; colony of marmots); then back to the Ofen pass road and along a path parallel to the road, past parking places 9 and 8, to parking place 7. The path continues to Il Fuorn. Time about 3 hours.

Route II: to the Grimmels Alp

From Il Fuorn north-west over Plan Posa and through Val Ftur; then climb to the Champlönch dry valley and the Alpine meadows of Grimmels (2050m/6726ft: marmots, sometimes in the early morning red deer hinds), with a beautiful view (Ofen pass, Munt la Schera, Piz dal Fuorn). Then either back to Il Fuorn or down (west) to parking place 1, 2 or 3 on the Ofen pass road. An easy walk of 2–2½ hours.

Route III: to Munt la Schera

The route starts from Buffalora, just outside the National Park boundary: from there south through a forest of stone pines to Marangun, then west over the flower-spangled meadows of Fop da Buffalora to enter the park beneath Munt Chavagi. After about 2 hours' walking bear right up Munt la Schera (2586m/8485ft), with magnificent views of the Ortler group (3900m/12,796ft) in the south-east, of the snow-covered Bernina group (4000m/13,124ft) in the south-west and the whole area of the National Park. Then down the south side of the hill to the Alp la Schera (rest area: marmots; red deer may be seen on the southern slopes of Munt la Schera). From there on the upper forest path to Il Fuorn; then either back on the postal bus to Stradin Buffalora or on the footpath to the right of the road (1¼ hours). The day's outing occupies about 5 hours.

The route starts from the parking place at the junction of the Mingèr with the Clemgia on the road from Scuol to S-charl. After crossing the Clemgia the path leads south-west through tall spruce forest to Mingèr Dadora, past a sandstone crag known as the Hexenkopf ("Witches Head") and on to the Alpine meadow of Mingèr Dadaint (2090m/6855ft): good opportunities for observing red deer and marmots. At the head of the valley are the precipitous peaks of Piz Plavna Dadaint (3166m/10,388ft). Return by the same route, or alternatively continue west to Il Foss and then via Alp Plavna to Tarasp. This half-day outing lasts about 3½ hours.

Route IV: to the Mingèr Dadaint Alp

Starting from Zernez, cross the covered bridge over the Spöl at the east end of the village and continue over the Selva meadows to a clearing at Al Pra (beautiful view from the Bellavista viewpoint). Then down to the valley floor and a short climb on the other side to the Cluoza hut (Blockhaus Cluoza, 1882m/6175ft: food, dormitory accommodation – booking at the tourist office in Zernez). From the hut the tracks of Dinosaurs 200 million years old can be seen through a telescope. Then up the hillside to the left and by way of Alp Murtèr to the Murtèrgrat (2545m/8350ft), with fine views of Piz Quattervals and Piz del Diavel to the south and the Fuorn valley and Piz Terza to the north, with an opportunity to see chamois and marmots. Descend by way of Plan dal Poms to the Praspöl meadows, then over the Spöl and up to the Ofen pass road at Vallun Chafuol (postal bus stop). Time about 6 hours.

Route V: by way of the Cluoza hut to the Murtèrgrat

From the bridge over the Inn north-east of S-chanf make for Mulins Varusch; then continue along the stream in the direction of Val Casana and at the next junction take a path on the left through Val Trupchun. Along the park boundary and opposite the mouth of Val Müsschauns there are opportunities for observing wildlife (chamois, ibex, eagles' nests). Then climb to the hut on Alp Trupchun (2040m/6693ft), with numbers of animals (including ibexes) in almost every direction. Return along the right bank, past the mouth of Val Müschauns, to reach the National Park boundary at Chanels; then on to the Varusch hut (refreshments), and from there back to the parking place. The day's outing takes about 5 hours.

Route VI: to Alp Trupchun

Over the Ofen pass into Val Müstair

The village of Zernez (1474m/4836ft; pop. 1000), situated in a broad valley basin, is the best base from which to visit the National Park (of which a good general impression can be had in the Nationalparkhaus). Part of the village was burned down in 1872 and rebuilt in rather urban style. In the older part, standing on higher ground, is the parish church (1607), with rich stucco decoration. Another old building that has survived is the Schloss Planta-Wildenberg (17th–18th c.). – From here take the Ofen Pass road, which runs E from the main road through the Engadine to St Moritz, following the Spölbach upstream through the wooded gorge of La Serra; then a well-engineered stretch of road up the rocky wooded hillside, passing through three galleries designed to provide protection from avalanches. In 3·5km (2 miles) there is a fine view down to the right of the wild Val Cluozza, the oldest part of the National Park with the glacier descending the slopes of Piz Quattervals (3164m/10,381ft) in the background. The road then follows a fairly level course over the forest-covered Champ Sech, beyond which the Piz del Diavel (3072m/10,079ft) comes into sight, and then descends down in a wide curve to the Wegerhaus Ova d'Spin (on left: car park), at the W entrance to the National Park.

Zernez

Nationalparkhaus

Ofen Pass road

La Serra

Val Cluozza

Wegerhaus Ova d'Spin

The road runs downhill, crosses the Ova d'Spin (parking place) and continues along the wooded slopes above the river, then above the Spölbach (parking place) and the Ova del Fuorn, flowing down from the Ofen pass, and comes to the Punt la Drossa (1710m/5611ft): Swiss customs; parking place), in a narrow pass, where the road crosses to the left bank of the Ova

Punt la Drossa

The Nationalparkhaus . . .   *. . . in Zernez*

del Fuorn. On the right is the entrance to a road tunnel 3·3km/2 miles long, belonging to the Munt la Schera hydro-electric complex, which reaches the Italian frontier at the Punt dal Gall (1963m/6441ft) over the River Spöl, at the N end of an artificial lake 8km/5 miles long (dam, alt. 1805m/5922ft, 540m/1771ft long, 130m/427ft high, 10m/33ft thick; capacity 164 million cu.m/5791 million cu.ft). A road runs down the W side of the lake through a customs-free zone to Livigno (19·5km/12 miles, 816m/2677ft: large skiing area, four ski-lifts). Beyond the Punt la Drossa the road to the Ofen pass climbs gradually; then comes a fairly level stretch, in which the road emerges from the forest; and finally it returns to the right bank of the Ova del Fuorn and reaches the Park Naziunal Hotel, in the lonely high valley of Il Fuorn (German *Ofen*, 1804m/5919ft), named after an iron-smelting works which once stood here. From here a marked footpath ascends Munt la Schera (2590m/8498ft: 2½ hours), from the limestone summit plateau of which there is a fine general view of the National Park.

Punt dal Gall

Livigno

Il Fuorn

Munt la Schera

From the hotel the road continues uphill through the coniferous forests in the high valley of the Ova del Fuorn, past the mouths of the wild Val dal Botsch and Val da Stabelchod, at the foot of Piz Nair (3010m/9876ft); several parking places. In 4·5km (3 miles) it comes to the Alp Buffalora (1963m/6441ft), in a marshy valley bottom, with Val Nüglia running down from Piz Tavrü (3168m/10,394ft) on the left and Munt da Buffalora (2629m/8626ft) on the right. The road then climbs more steeply to the Ofen Pass (Romansch Süsom-Givè or Pass dal Fuorn, 2149m/7051ft: hotel), from which there is a view of the Ortler group. It then winds its way down, with three hairpin turns, first over Alpine meadows and then along the slopes of the valley, through stretches of forest, with fine views.

Alp Buffalora

Ofen Pass

Tschierv (1664m/5460ft): Hotel Sternen; camping site) is the highest village in Val Müstair, the valley of the Rom. Here the road crosses the river and runs down the S side of the valley, with patches of woodland, on a moderate gradient.

Val Müstair

Fuldera (1638m/5374ft; pop. 112: bypass) is a little hamlet at the foot of Piz Turettas (2958m/9705ft). Beyond this a road goes off on the left to Lü (3·5km/2 miles, 1918m/6293ft), the highest village in its valley. The main road now runs down more steeply to Valchava (1410m/4626ft; pop. 217: bypass), where the first fruit-trees appear. Beyond this, on the right, is the mouth of the beautiful Val Vau.

Santa Maria (1388m/4554ft), the chief town in Val Müstair (pop. 350; Prot.), lies at the mouth of Val Muraunza, which runs down from the Umbrail pass. It has pretty painted houses, a church of 1491 and a local museum. Down the valley the view embraces the castles of Taufers and the Ötztal Alps, with the snow-capped peak of the Weisskugel. From Santa Maria a road goes off on right to Umbrail and Stelvio (Stilfserjoch) passes. The main road continues down Val Müstair, through Müstair village, into Upper Adige valley. In Müstair the Benedictine monastery (founded *c.* 780) is of interest. The church of St John contains important frescoes and a 12th c. statue of Charlemagne.

Fuldera

Valchava

Santa Maria

Müstair

Thun

J 8

Canton: Berne (BE)
Altitude: 560m/1838ft
Population: 40,000

The old-world town of Thun (French Thoune), which has belonged to the canton of Berne since 1384, lies on the River Aare just below its outflow from Lake Thun. Charmingly situated on both banks of the swiftly flowing green river and on a 1km/½ mile-long island in the middle, with its castle on a hill 30m/98ft high dominating the town, it is the gateway to the Bernese Oberland. An unusual feature of the old town is the flower-bedecked pedestrian walkways running along above the arcades containing the shops on ground level in the main street (Hauptgasse).

★ Location and general

Sights

From the Rathausplatz, with the handsome Rathaus (Town Hall: 1589, rebuilt 1685), a covered flight of steps leads up to the castle, whose massive keep with its corner turrets is a prominent landmark of the town. It was built in 1191 by Duke Berchtold V of Zähringen; later it became the seat of the Counts of Kyburg, and in 1492 was enlarged by the addition of an official residence for the chief magistrate of Berne. Since 1888 it has housed the Historical Museum (open: Apr.–Oct.), with arms and armour and 14th and 15th c. tapestries in the large Knights' Hall, prehistoric and Roman materials, furniture and ceramics in the three lower rooms and a collection illustrating 19th c. Swiss military history in the upper hall. From the castle and from the Protestant parish church (rebuilt 1738, with an older tower) on the south-east slopes of the castle hill there is a superb view of Lake Thun and the Alps (the Stockhorn chain, the Niesen and, to the left, the snow-covered Blümlisalp).

Rathaus
Castle Historical Museum

In the Thunerhof (Hofstettengasse 14; closed Mon.) is the Municipal Art Gallery, containing painting and sculpture of the 19th and 20th c., particularly by Swiss artists. Pop-art and photorealism are also represented. The paintings include Swiss and foreign work, both old and modern.

Art Gallery

On the site of the former Schadau market garden (about 17,000sq.m/ 183,000sq.ft) a museum is being established (1991 "pre" Museum; 1994 actual museum), illustrating the history of the steam-engine. Exhibit No. 1 is the paddle-wheel steamer "Blümlisalp" which used to ply on Lake Thun.

Swiss Steam-engine Museum

Brahms Quay by Lake Thun

Other exhibits will include the steamship "Lötschberg" (from Lake Brienz) as well as steam-trains of the Schynige–Platte, the Brünig and the Brienz–Rothorn railways.

Brahms Quai   The Aare basin is lined by the Johannes Brahms Quai, where there is a bronze monument to the Late-Romantic musician who spent several summers in Thun and who dedicated a violin sonata to the lake.

A series of little wooded islands extend opposite the shoreline with a romantic path; to walk along this is called "Inseli-Kehr machen" (doing the round of the islands).

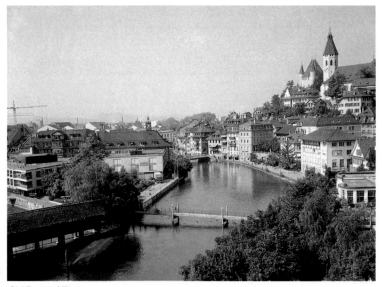

Old Town of Thun

Surroundings

1½km/1 mile south the village of Scherzlingen on the lake has a little 12th c. church (frescoes).

Scherzligen

Where the basin of the Aare broadens out into the lake and an unexpected wonderful panorama meets the eye, Schloss Shadau towers up on the shore. The castle, a smaller replica of the château of Azay-le-Rideau on the Loire, was built in 1852 for the de Rougemont family of Neuchâtel. Since 1988 it has housed the Swiss Museum of Gastronomy (open: Apr.–Oct. Tues.–Sun.), with exhibits of crockery, cutlery and kitchen utensils and mock-ups of interiors of some of the large hotels of the Bernese Oberland; temporary exhibitions are an additional feature. In the library the visitor can find rare cookery books from Japan, Russia, China and South America, the oldest of which dates from the time of the Thirty Years' War.

Schadau Castle
Gastronomic
museum

In the park of Schadau is the Wocher Panorama, a larger circular painting (38 × 7.5m/125 × 25ft) by Marquard Wocher (1760–1830) of the town of Thun as it was about 1810.

On the right, in Dürrenast can be seen the shipyard of the Lake Thun Shipping Company.

Shipyard of
Lake Thun

The pleasant promenade along the shore, which is part of the scenically beautiful Lake Thun circular route, leads to the outskirts of the village of Hilterfingen. Here stands Schloss Hünegg, another gem of the lovely lakeside landscape. The name recalls the early-Germanic tumuli ("giants' graves") which were discovered on a hill near the lake at the beginning of the 19th c. Hünegg Castle is also reminiscent of the French châteaux, particularly those of Blois and Chenonceaux. The industrialist G. Lemke-Schukkert of Wiesbaden gave the castle a new aspect at the turn of the century. Some rooms were carefully converted to reflect old styles, others in pure Art Nouveau. Since 1966 the building has been a museum of Historicism and Art Nouveau (open: May 12th–Oct. 13th). From the park there is a wonderful view of the lake and the Alps.

Hilter-
fingen/Schloss
Hünegg
Art Nouveau
Museum

Some 5km/3 miles north-east of Thun is the health resort of Goldiwil (1010m/3314ft; pop. 1000).

Goldiwil

About 6km/4 miles south-west is the village of Amsoldingen (644m/2113ft) on the shores of a small lake. It has a castle and a fine Romanesque church (St Mauritius) of the 10th or 11th c. which shows Lombardian influence.

Amsoldingen

8km/5 miles north-west on the Berne road is Kiesen, where a visit to the dairy museum is highly recommended. Here can be seen apparatus used in cheese-making, and a village cheese dairy has been reconstructed (sound-film and slide show).

Kiesen

Lake Thun and Lake Brienz

Canton: Berne (BE)

Lake Thun   J 8

Lake Thun (560m/1837ft) is 18km/11 miles long and between 2 and 2.8km/1 and 2 miles wide, with an area of 48sq.km (19sq.miles); its greatest depth is 217m/712ft. There are roads from Thun to Interlaken along both the north and south shores of the lake. Boat services operate during the season (Apr.–Sept.) from Interlaken-West via Spiez to Thun, and from Interlaken-Ost to Brienz (see Lake Brienz); there are also various round trips, cruises and excursions.

Location and
general

Sailing regatta on Lake Thun

Along the north shore of Lake Thun

★ **Shore Road**
Thun

The road along the north side of the lake (23km/14 miles), which affords a succession of beautiful views, leaves Thun by way of Hofstettenstrasse along the banks of the Aare, passing on the right the Municipal Art Gallery in the Thunerhof and on the left the Kursaal. It then follows the northern shore of Lake Thun (trolley-bus to Beatenbucht). Sheltered from north and east winds, the lake has an unusually mild climate. Many southern plants including laurels and fig-trees flourish in the gardens of the charming lakeside villages which attract many visitors in spring and autumn as well as in summer. Almost all the way along the lake there are magnificent views of the giants of the Bernese Alps. At the entrance to the Kandertal and Simmental the conical Stockhorn (2190m/7185ft) can be seen on the right and the pyramidal peak of the Niesen (2362m/7750ft) on the left, with the three peaks of the Blümlisalp (3664m/12,022ft) further to the left. To the right of the Blümlisalp a series of summits come gradually into view – from left to right the Fründenhorn (3369m/11,054ft), Doldenhorn (3709m/12,169ft), Balmhorn (3709m/12,173ft), Altels (3629m/11,907ft) and Rinderhorn (3453m/11,329ft). In the direction of Interlaken the most prominent peaks are (from right to left) the Ebnefluh (3960m/12,993ft), Jungfrau (4158m/13,642ft), Mönch (4099m/13,449ft) and Eiger (3970m/13,026ft), and beyond these the Schreckhorn (4078m/13,380ft) and Wetterhorn (3701m/12,143ft).

Hilterfingen
Schloss Hünegg

3.5km/2 miles: Hilterfingen (562m/1844ft) has a small church of 1470 and the 18th c. Schloss Hünegg. Thuner See sailing school.

Schloss
Oberhofen/
Historical
Museum

Adjoining Hilterfingen (575m/1887ft) the feudal castle of Oberhofen, picturesquely situated by the lake, can be seen from afar. The fortress was built in the 12th c. by the Lords of Oberhofen but had to be surrendered to the Austrians in 1306. After the Battle of Sempach in 1386 the castle was occupied by Berne; later it came into the possession of the Scharnachtal family. The western domestic wing, with its lipped roof, dates from the time

Schloss Oberhofen: Bernese domestic museum

of the Landvögte (governors; 1652–1798). In 1844 the Prussian Count Friedrich von Pourtales de Castellane Norante gave the castle a romantic aspect by adding numerous turrets, balconies and dormer windows. Regularly patterned flower-beds were laid out on the lakeside terrace and exotic trees were planted. An American, W. M. Measy, inherited the castle in 1926 and had a branch museum (open: May 14th–Oct. 15th) of the Bernese Historical Museum installed, which gives a graphic picture of the domestic life of the town and countryside including Bernese rural pottery of the 18th and 19th c., a Turkish smoker's saloon and a children's chalet.

To the right there is a fine view of the Niessen before reaching Gunten, (567m/ pop. 600) a pretty health resort at the mouth of the Gunter stream which breaks through a gorge above the village. By the lake are a bathing beach and a water-skiing and surfing school.

Gunten

The by-road to the left goes inland and here the gentle hills suddenly end at the steep slopes of the Alpine foothills. In 3km/2 miles we reach the well-known hill resort of Sigriswil (800m/2626ft; pop. 800) on a sunny plateau.

Sigriswil

From here a narrow but very beautiful road (toll charge; alternate one-way traffic) leads to Beatenberg (12km/7 miles: see Interlaken).

Beatenberg

Continuing along the shore of the lake we reach in 3½km/2 miles the resort of Merligen (568m/1864ft; pop. 710) in a very sheltered situation at the mouth of the Justis valley.

Merligen

The road goes on to Beatenbucht where the lake steamers call. This is the terminus of the trolley-bus line from Thun and from here a funicular takes passengers up to Beatenberg (1150m/3773ft; see Interlaken).
   The lakeside road now changes in character. The gently sloping shore with its villages and gardens gives way to a steep wooded scarp, along which the road climbs in a series of bends. 1.5km/1 mile farther on it passes

Beatenbucht

in two tunnels through a rocky promontory, the Nase. 1km/½ mile beyond this, there is a beautiful glimpse of the lake to the right.

Beatushöhlen

The road now comes to the parking place for the Beatushöhlen or St Beatus's caves (623m/2044ft: 8 minutes' walk from the road), an extensive complex of stalactitic caves of which 2km/1 mile are accessible to visitors. According to legend the caves were occupied by St Beatus (6th c.) and until the Reformation were a place of pilgrimage (conducted tour, 1 hour; Waldhaus restaurant). In the 8km/5 miles of caves which have so far been explored, are several impressive waterfalls, lakes and stalactitic formations.

The route continues through three tunnels and around a sheer rock face which, in places, actually overhangs the road, to Sundlauenen (609m/1999ft). It then runs along below the crag above the lake; in another 1.5km/1 mile it passes a camping site and at the Neuhaus bathing station (on right; camping site on left) comes to the end of Lake Thun.

2km/1 mile farther on the road passes the Hotel Beau-Site and crosses the "Bödeli", an area of alluvial soil deposited by the Lombach, to Unterseen (old church), an outlying district of Interlaken, where a road branches off on the left to Beatenberg (see Interlaken). The road then bears

Interlaken

right and crosses the Aare to enter Interlaken (see entry).

Along the south shore of Lake Thun

Shore road

The road along the south side of the lake offers two alternative routes between Thun and Interlaken. One way is to go south from the old town over the Aare and continue under the railway and then south-west for 3km/2 miles to join the motorway from Berne (N 6), which runs at some distance from the lake to Spiez (10km/6 miles). Alternatively, after passing under the railway, turn left along Frutigenstrasse and continue past the bathing beach at the end of the town (on left: beautiful gardens, camping site). This road, at some distance from the lake, comes in 4.5km/3 miles to Gwatt (564m/1850ft), beyond which a turn on the right leads to the Simmental. Then over the River Kander and up a winding stretch of road, with beautiful views of the bay of Spiez and the Niesen. Below the road, on the left, is the village of Einigen (590m/1936ft) with a Romanesque church (11th and 13th c.). 5.5km/3 miles from Gwatt is Spiez (630m/2067ft). At the near end of the town a road goes off on the right to the Simmental (see entry) and via Mülenen (8km/5 miles: funicular up the Niesen) to Frutigen (Kandersteg,

Spiez

Abelboden). The picturesquely situated town of Spiez (pop. 10,500) is a popular health and water sports resort (sailing school), and it is also an important junction for the roads and mountain railways into the Kandertal and Simmental.

Schloss Spiez

From an intersection in the upper part of the town near the parish church (1907) a street runs down to the medieval castle, delightfully situated in a cove. It has a massive 12th c. keep and fine buildings added in the 14th–18th c. This noble estate, which, in the time of the kings of Neuchâtel, bore the title of the "Golden Court on the Wendelsee", was for centuries owned by the Erlach family. Today the castle is the headquarters of the municipal council. It also houses a museum (drawing and reception rooms of the 13th–18th c., including Renaissance panelled rooms and an Early-Baroque hall; open. Good Friday–end of Oct.). Concerts are also held here.

The neighbouring little 11th c. church has three Romanesque apses and fine Gothic frescoes.

An attractive path leads along the lake from Spiez to Faulensee (30 minutes).

Aeschi

6km/4 miles south-east of Spiez is the village of Aeschi (860m/2822ft), a popular summer resort on the hill between Lake Thun and the Kander

Schloss Spiez

valley. The Protestant church, dating in part from the 12th to the 13th c., has frescoes in the choir (probably 14th c.) which were exposed in 1966.

From Spiez, take the Kandersteg road to Mülenen (8km/5 miles), from which a funicular 3.5km/2 miles), maximum gradient 68% (1 in 1·4), 30 minutes) serves the Niesenkulm Hotel (2362m/7750ft), a few minutes below the summit of Niesen (2362m/7750ft; see entry), with superb views of Lake Thun and Lake Brienz, the Jungfrau massif and the Blümlisalp. Descent to Wimmis on foot, 2 hours. **To the Niesen**

★★ Niesen

To the Griesalp (22km/14 miles): From Spiez take the Kandersteg road to Reichenbach (9km/6 miles); then turn left into a narrow road which winds its way up to the village of Scharnachtal and continues through the narrow wooded Kiental (6km/4 miles). Kiental (906m/2973ft), a village which attracts many summer visitors, with a beautiful view of the Blümlisalp. From here a chair-lift (1405m/4510ft: 18 minutes) ascends to a skiing area (1500m/4922ft) on the east side of the Gerihorn (2133m/6998ft). **Kiental**

Then on to the Tschingelalp (1151m–3776ft), and beyond this a series of narrow turns up the wooded hillside (gradients of up to 20% (1 in 5)) and past the Pochten Falls (curious rock forms resulting from erosion) to the Pochtenalp (1400m/4593ft). Pochtenalp

Finally, continue (3km/2 miles) to Griesalp (1407m/4616ft), which attracts summer visitors and skiers (interesting nature reserve). From here it is a 3 hours' climb to the Blümlisalp hut (2837m/9308ft) (see Blümlisalp) to the south. (See also Kandersberg). Griesalp

The Interlaken road continues straight ahead through the upper part of Spiez, with parking places 1km/½ mile and 1.5km/1 mile from the town which afford beautiful views of the bay of Spiez and its picturesque castle. ★ View

It then skirts a wooded promontory projecting into the lake and comes to Faulensee (587m/1926ft; pop. 900), attractively set in a bay (bathing beach). On the left, above the road, is the church of St Columban (1962). Faulensee

Lake Thun and Lake Brienz

There follows a beautiful but winding stretch of road closely following the lake (parking places). 2km/1 mile farther on an expressway from Spiez comes in on the right. Just before Leissigen an attractive road branches off on the right to Aeschi (6.5km/4 miles).

Leissigen

6.5km/4 miles from Spiez is Leissigen (573m/1880ft; pop. 800), among beautiful orchards, with an old church.

The road now runs along above the lake, with a view of Beatenberg (see Interlaken) high up on the opposite side. The next place is Därligen (564m/1850ft; pop. 350) with a bypass to the south of the village.

Interlaken
★ Heimwehfluh

The road then goes uphill and down again to the lake (railway on the left). Leaving the lake, it continues along the edge of the wide Aar valley to Interlaken (see entry). On the right at the entrance to the town is the lower station of the cable railway up to the Heimwehfluh (see Interlaken). The bypass continues straight on to Grindelwald and Lauterbrunnen, with the main road into the centre of Interlaken on the left.

Lake Brienz   K 8

Location and general

Lake Brienz (567m/1860ft) is 14km/9 miles long and between 2–2.5km/1–2 miles wide, with an area of 29sq.km/11sq.miles); its greatest depth is 259m/850ft. The lake, which is in effect an enlargement of the valley of the River Aare, lies between the limestone ridge of the Brienzer Grat and the Jurassic Faulhorn group.

Lake Brienz was originally connected with Lake Thun, but now lies 7m/23ft higher. The slopes of the surrounding hills are wooded and this gives the landscape an exceptionally charming aspect.

Along the north shore of Lake Brienz

From Interlaken the road along the north side of Lake Brienz crosses the Aare, on the banks of which to the right are a camping site and motel, and winds up the wooded slopes of the Harder (funicular: station on left), from which there are extensive views.

Goldswil

In 2km/1 mile it comes to Goldswil (612m/2008ft), a prettily situated little village with a ruined castle surrounded by a beautiful cemetery. Beyond this, on the right, is the Burgseeli bathing beach.

Ringgenberg

The road now keeps rather closer to the water and comes to the village of Ringgenberg (599m/1965ft) in a sheltered situation on a terrace above the lake. Here are weathered brown timber houses and a church (1671–74), with an Early Baroque interior, which stands above the village in the ruins of a castle.

Planet Path

An excursion (12km/7½ miles) to the "Planet Path" is recommended. The walk, of about five hours, takes the visitor through the whole of the solar system at a scale of one to one billion. Walking at a normal pace corresponds to the five-fold speed of light.

Then on, through a short rocky defile, to Niederried (580m/1903ft), situated amid orchards at the foot of the Augstmatthorn (2140m/7012ft) and Oberried (592m/1942ft), before passing through the little village of Eblingen to Brienz.

Brienz

Brienz (571m/1874ft; pop. 2800) attracts many summer visitors and has many more passing through on their way between Lucerne and Interlaken. It is beautifully situated on the lake, with steep wooded slopes rising above the town to the precipitous Brienzer Grat, which reaches its highest point in

Lake Brienz   *Brunnengasse in Brienz*

the Rothorn. The long, straggling little town is the centre of the Oberland craft of woodcarving, with a woodcarving school and the Swiss Violin-Making School (open to visitors). Beside the Protestant church, with an early 12th c. Romanesque tower, is the house in which the Swiss writer Heinrich Federer (1866–1928) was born. Other features of Brienz are the village museum in the Wiesplatz and the 19th c. wooden houses in the Brunnengasse, with beautifully carved friezes on the façades.

The Brienzer Rothorn (2350m/7710ft), with a magnificent prospect of the Appenzell, Uri, Engelberg, Berne and Valais Alps extending from Säntis to the Diablerets. There is a cableway from Sörenberg and a splendid four-hour mountain walk (stout footwear required) from the Brienzer Rothorn to the Brünig Pass, or to the mountain station of Schönbüel (1½ hours).

★Brienzer Rothorn

In 1988, the Brünig railway celebrated the centenary of the section between Alpmachstad and Brienz. Extensions to Lucerne and Interlaken were not built until 1916. This, the smallest rack-and-pinion railway of the Swiss federal network (length 74km/46 miles; electrified 1941/42), crosses 124 bridges and climbs gradients up to 1 in 8 on its scenically attractive trip over the 1002m/3289ft-high Brünig Pass.

Brünigbahn

★★Swiss Open-air Museum of Rural Life

The main entrance of the Swiss Open-air Museum of Rural Life, north-east of Brienz, is reached by road via Schwanden in Hofstetten (car park; bus service from Brienz; side-entrance in Brienzeiler.) The extensive grounds cover some 50ha/124 acres of Alpine countryside on the Ballenberg. A series of regional groups, some still in course of construction, display the traditional way of life in different parts of Switzerland in old houses and other buildings brought here from their original sites, with appropriate furniture, utensils and implements. Old crafts and traditional customs have

Swiss Open-Air Museum of Rural Life

REGIONAL GROUPS
(as planned, numbered items are complete)

1 Jura
No. 111 Farmhouse (1617) from La-Chaux-de-Fonds (Neuchâtel)

2 Central Mittelland
No. 211 House (1617) from Villnachern (Aargau)
No. 221 Farmhouse (1609) from Oberentfelden (Aargau)
No. 222 Pigsty (19th c.) from Brugg (Aargau)
No. 231 Farmhouse (1675) from Therwil (Basel-Land)

3 Bernese Mittelland
No. 301 Cereal fields
No. 302 Herb garden
No. 303 Instructional garden of useful plants
No. 311 "Alter Bären" inn from Rapperswil (Berne)
No. 312 House with stove (1796) from Oberwangen (Berne)
No. 321 Farmhouse from Madiswil (Berne)
No. 322 Granary (18th c.) from Kiesen (Berne)
No. 325 Textile worker's house from Herzogenbuchsee (Berne)
No. 326 "Stöckli" with herb room (19th c.) from Köniz (Berne)
No. 331 Farmhouse (1797) with collection of old clocks, and
No. 332 Barn (18th c.) from Ostermundigen (Berne)
No. 333 "Stöckli" from Detlingen (Berne)
No. 334 Journeyman's house (1760) from Detlingen (Berne)
No. 341 Barn (1702) from Faulensee (Berne)
No. 351 Farmhouse (17th c.) from Eggiswil (Berne)
No. 352 Granary (18th c.) from Wasen (Berne)

4 Rural Trades
No. 411 Sawmill (c. 1841) from Rafz (Zurich)
No. 421 Linseed press (18th c.) from Medel (Grisons)
No. 491 Charcoal kiln
No. 492 Lime burning oven
No. 495 Refuge hut

5 Western Mittelland
No. 501 Tobacco field
No. 511 Farmhouse (17th/18th c.) from Tentlingen (Fribourg)
No. 532 Farmhouse (1800) from Villars-Bramard (Vaud)
No. 532 Granary (17th c.) from Ecoteaux (Vaud)
No. 551 Farmhouse (1762, 1796, 1820) from Lancy (Geneva)

6 Eastern Mittelland
No. 611 Half-timbered house (c. 1780) from Richterswil (Zurich)

No. 612 Wash-house from Rüschlikon (Zurich)
No. 613 Storehouse from Männedorf (Zurich)
No. 615 Trotte (17th c.) from Schaffhausen
No. 621 Half-timbered house (17th c.) from Uesslingen (Thurgau); bread museum on 2nd floor
No. 622 Granary (1760) from Wellhausen (Thurgau)
No. 631 Wine cellar from Schaffhausen with beam-press from Flesch (Grisons)
No. 641 General purpose building (1680) from Wila (Zurich)
No. 642 Granary (15th/16th c.) from Lindau (Zurich)
No. 691 Sawmill (c. 1840) from Rafz (Zurich)
No. 692 Bone-grinder (19th c.) from Knonau (Zurich)

7 Central Switzerland
No. 711 House (17th, 19th c.) from Sachseln (Obwalden)
No. 714 Bee-hive
No. 721 House (17th c.) from Erstfeld (Uri)
No. 722 Cold store (18th c.) from Unterschächen (Uri)
No. 723 Hay barn (18th c.) from Spiringen (Uri)

8 Ticino

9 Eastern Switzerland
No. 911 Appenzell cross-ridged house (18th c.) from Brülisau (Appenzell-Innerrhoden)
No. 931 House (15th, 18th c.) from Wattwil (St Gallen)

10 Bernese Oberland
No. 1011 Miner's house (1698) from Adelboden (Berne)
No. 1012 Cheese store (1608) from Lütschental in the Grindelwald valley
No. 1021 House (17th c.) from Matten (Berne)
No. 1022 Granary (1656) from Niederried (Berne)
No. 1024 Hay barn (19th c.) from Brienzwiler (Berne)
No. 1031 House (18th c.) from Brienz (Berne)
No. 1032 Drying oven (18th c.) from Brienzwiler (Berne)
No. 1051 Pottery (19th c.) from Unterseen (Berne)
No. 1052 Smithy (19th c.) from Bümpliz (Berne)
No. 1061 Alpine cheese dairy (19th c.) from Kandersteg (Berne)
No. 1062 Cheese store (18th c.) from Guttannen (Berne)
No. 1063 Cheese store (1780) from Leissingen (Berne)

11 Valais
No. 1111 House (1568) from Blatten (Valais)
No. 1112 Hay barn (19th c.) from Blatten (Valais)
No. 1121 Post-mill (19th c.) from Törbel (Valais)
No. 1122 Mill (1872) from Naters (Valais)
No. 1141–1145 Alpine buildings (16th–19th c.) from Bellwald (Valais)

12 Grisons

13 Alps

Traditional interior . . .

. . . and exterior

In Ballenberg open-air museum . . .

. . . a farmhouse room from Ostermundigen

also been revived. A tour (guide available by prior arrangement) through the museum lasts 2½–3 hours; open daily 9am–5pm Apr. 15th–Oct 31st).

Along the south shore of Lake Brienz

Axalp

To reach the Axalp (9km/6 miles) you take a narrow road which branches off the Lucerne road on the right at the hamlet of Kienholz, 3km/1 mile from Brienz. The road skirts the east end of the lake at the inflow of the Aare and climbs up the slopes on the south side of the lake, past a turning to the Giessbach (see below). It then winds its way up to the Axalp (1460–1549m/ 4490–5053ft; good walking and skiing, with ski-lifts) from which there are far-ranging views. From here there is a beautiful footpath into the Upper Giessbach valley, and also a 1¼ hours' walk to the Hinterburgsee, a beautiful mountain lake in the Hinterburg nature reserve.

★Giessbach
Falls

The Giessbach (663m/2175ft) can be reached by the road referred to above or by boat to the Giessbach See landing-stage (15 minutes from Brienz) and from there either on foot (20 minutes) or by funicular (345m/1132ft). The best view of the Giessbach, which tumbles down from a height of 300m/ 984ft, to the lake in a series of falls over successive ridges of rock on the beautifully wooded hillside, is to be had from the terrace in front of the Park Hotel. There are footpaths up both banks to the highest of the three bridges, under which the stream emerges from a narrow gorge and plunges into a rock basin 60m/197ft deep.

Thurgau   O–Q 3

Canton: Thurgau (TG)

Location and
general

The canton of Thurgau in north-east Switzerland lies on the south side of Lake Constance, occupying most of the Swiss shoreline of the lake. It is bounded on the west by the canton of Zurich and on the east by St Gallen. It has an area of 1006sq.km/388sq.miles and a population of 185,000. The canton is a region of markedly pre-Alpine character, with its highest points rising to barely 1000m/3281ft. The main source of income is fruit-growing.

History

There were many settlements in the canton in Roman times, as is shown by the results of excavation at Arbon (Arbor Felix) and Pfyn (Ad Fines). Later, the area was occupied by Alemannic tribes. In medieval times, it was held by the Zähringen and Kyburg families and, from 1264, by the Counts of Habsburg. In 1460, Thurgau was taken over by the Confederates from the excommunicated Duke Sigismund and governed as a "common province". From 1798 to 1803 it was part of the Helvetian Republic; thereafter, it became an independent canton.

Frauenfeld

The cantonal capital is Frauenfeld (414m/1359ft; pop. 19,000, situated on the river Murg just south of its junction with the Thur. In the upper town,

Castle

rebuilt to a rectangular plan after a fire in the 18th c., stands the castle high above the Murg. It was once the seat of the Confererate landvögte (governors) and has a massive 12th c. tower, from which there is a fine view. The tower was built by the Kyburgs of Findlingen in about 1227. Additions to

Museum

the fortress were made at intervals. The castle now houses the Thurgau Cantonal Museum which has a rich collection of exhibits ranging from Neolithic times to the Early Middle Ages. Of particular interest are the furnished rooms of town and country dwellers (17th–19th c.), the exhibition illustrating the history of the town and a comprehensive collection of religious art, especially of the 14th c. (open: Tues.–Sun.). The church of St Lawrence in the suburb of Oberkirch has some valuable 14th c. stained glass.

Luzernerhaus
Nature Museum

The Lucerne House which, like the Berne and Zürich Houses, has an impressive Baroque façade, is now the Cantonal Nature Museum, present-

Camp site
Wil, St. Gallen

ing the history of the development of our planet and its biospheres in a
most vivid manner (open: Wed., Sat. and Sun.).

A few kilometres north-west of Frauenfeld, above the Thur, is the former ★ Ittingen
Carthusian monastery of Ittingen, founded as an Augustinian house in Monastery
1152 and taken over by the Carthusians in 1461. Much of the monastery
was destroyed by fire in 1524. The cloister dates from about 1540; the
church was built in 1549–53 and re-modelled in Baroque style in the 18th c.

Tour of Thurgau

From Frauenfeld road 14 runs east to Wellhausen, where, on a hill 500m/
547yd south, stands Wellenberg Castle (13th c.).

The road now crosses the Thur and comes to the busy little town of Weinfelden
Weinfelden (432m/1417ft; pop. 8500), seat of the cantonal parliament and
court. Above the vineyards on the slopes of the Ottenberg is a castle of 1180
(restored c. 1860).

The road continues through Bürglen (442m/1450ft), where a 16th–17th c. Bürglen
castle is a prominent landmark and comes to Amriswil (437m/1434ft; pop. Amriswil Coach
9200) a lively little industrial town. The private Sallmann Coach Museum Museum
has horse-drawn wagons and post coaches, including Napoleon III's battle
wagon.

Frauenfeld: Old Town . . .   *. . . and castle above the Murg*

Schloss Hagenwil	In Hagenwil, 3km/2 miles south-east, can be seen a well-preserved moated castle, with a chapel and Gothic knights' hall.
Bischofszell	South-west of Amriswil, above a loop in the Thur, lies the ancient town of Bischofszell (510m/1673ft). The Gothic parish church of St Pelagius (14th–15th c.) in the centre of the town has a notable treasury. The attractive Town Hall (1743) with its artistic iron balustrade, was designed by the architect Kaspar Bagnato. The former Bishop's Palace (13th–15th c.) is now the headquarters of the local public works department. At Marktgasse 4, the Bodenturm houses a museum of local history.
Sirnach Fischingen	From Bischofszell we go south-west to join road 7 and follow it westwards to Münchwilen, from which a detour can be made a short distance south to Sirnach (550m/1805ft; pop. 4200), with attractive old half-timbered houses, and Fischingen (620m/2034ft) which has a church belonging to the former Benedictine abbey (rebuilt 1795; richly decorated 18th c. interior).
Frauenfeld	From Münchwilen, road 7 returns to Frauenfeld.

Ticino   M–P 9–13

Canton: Ticino (TI)

Location and general	Ticino (German Tessin), the most southerly of the Swiss cantons, takes its name from the River Ticino, a left-bank tributary of the Po, which rises on the Nufenen pass (Passo della Novena), flows through Lake Maggiore and joins the Po after a course of 248km/154 miles.
	The canton has an area of 2811sq.km/1085sq.miles and a population of some 250,000. Its capital is Bellinzona (see entry), situated near the junction of the roads from the St Gotthard (see entry) and the San Bernardino pass (see entry). The canton's main sources of revenue are agriculture and tourism. In the past, many German-speaking Swiss and Germans from the Federal Republic have settled in the canton, particularly by the lakes, which

The "Paradise" of Lugano below Monte San Salvatore

has led to a considerable change in the population structure. The indigenous population is almost exclusively Italian-speaking, but with a local dialect.

The territory of Ticino, occupied in the early historical period by Rhaetians and Lepontii, was later incorporated in the Roman province of Gallia Cisalpina. Between the 5th and 8th c. it was successively occupied by the Goths, the Lombards and the Franks. In the 15th c. the Confederates gradually wrested it from the overlordship of the Dukes of Milan. It became an independent canton in 1803.

History

Along the northern boundaries of Ticino are high-Alpine regions with their characteristic plants and animals. Farther south, Mediterranean vegetation increasingly predominates, flourishing particularly in the south-facing valleys. By the lakes, palms and citrus fruits are found. The animal life, particularly insects and reptiles, also shows clear Mediterranean characteristics.

Flora and Fauna

The markedly southern orientation and the protection against influences from the region north of the Alps, which result from Ticino's geographical situation, are reflected also in the architecture of the houses and public buildings. In many places, the churches are built of natural stone without any external rendering, as in northern Italy, and the canton has a rich heritage of Renaissance and Baroque architecture.

Architecture

★Ascona; ★Bellinzona; ★Locano; ★★Lugano; ★★Lake Lugano; ★★Lake Maggiore; see entries.

Toggenburg

O–Q 3–5

Canton; St Gallen (SG)
Capital: Lichtensteig

Toggenburg

Location and general	The Toggenburg district, a region of varied scenery lying south of Thurgau, comprises the Upper Thur valley and its tributary valleys. Once an independent county, it is now part of the canton of St Gallen.

Tour of Toggenburg from Wil to Buchs

Untertoggenburg

General	South of Wil (see St Gallen) the road passes through the pleasant area of Untertoggenburg. On the slopes of the hills are elegant farmhouses of Alemannic type and, in the villages, are 18th c. "manufacturers' houses" (Fabrikantenhäuser) dating from the period when the region's flourishing textile industry was established.
Flawil	The chief town and trading centre of Untertoggenburg is Flawil (610m/ 2002ft; pop. 9000), a village situated above the river Glatt, with a flourishing spinning and weaving industry. Flawil still has a few richly painted houses (Hof "Gupfen", "Dorfschmiede" village smithy) and an interesting museum.
Oberglatt	A little way to the east lies Oberglatt which was, for centuries, the ecclesiastical centre of the district. Every year in summer the "Musikzychus" (music cycle) takes place.
Burgau, Magdenau Convent	About 1½km/1 mile south-east of Flawil lies the charming old village of Burgau, with fine old houses (law court of 1639), and another 1½km/1 mile west is the Cistercian Convent of Magdenau, founded in 1244, which has 17th and 18th c. buildings.
Burg Landegg (ruin)	Not far south-west of the convent stands the parish church of St Verena and, to the west, the ruins of Landegg Castle.
Retonio's Magic Casino	Further south-east, in Degersheim, is Retonio's Magic Casino, with mechanical organs, automata and magicians' equipment.

★ Obertoggenburg

	Beyond Neu-St Johann the road runs through the Starkenbach defile into Obertoggenburg, a beautiful mountain region between the limestone massifs of Säntis and the Churfirsten which is a popular health and winter sports area.
Wildhaus	It then crosses the Wildhaus pass (1098m/3602ft; climbing frames for children) and through the beautifully wooded Simmigorge into the Rhine valley.
Lichtensteig	By taking road 8 from St Gallen (see entry) or road 16 from Kreuzlingen via Wil, we reach Lichtensteig (618m/2028ft; pop. 2200), an old-world little town which is picturesquely situated on a rocky hill above the right bank of the Thur. It is the principal place in the Toggenburg region with some handsome old arcaded houses. In the Toggenburg Heimatmuseum can be seen a notable collection of rural crafts and popular art, including documentation of alpine husbandry as well as musical instruments and costumes. Also of interest is the church of St Gallus, a modern building (1966–72) by W. M. Förderer, and Freddy's Mechanical Music Museum in the Hans Zur Frohburg.
Wattwil	2km/1 mile south of Lichtensteig on road 16 is Wattwil (617m/2024ft; pop. 9000), a long straggling town which is the economic hub of Toggenburg, with a variety of industry (Textile College). The popular Swiss writer Ulrich Bräker (1735–98) worked here as a weaver.

Lichtensteig – chief town of Toggenburg

On the hillside to the right of the road can be seen the Franciscan nunnery of St Maria zu den Engeln (574m/1883ft: 17th c.) and, opposite it, to the south, Iberg Castle (13th c., restored). A road on the right leads via Ricken to Surih or Glarus.

St Maria zu den Engeln

The road to Buchs continues from Wattoril up the Thur valley, here wide and fertile, and in 5.5km/3 miles reaches Ebnat–Kappel (633–650m/2077–2133ft), actually two towns with a combined population of 5500 inhabitants and a variety of industry. The twin towns attract summer visitors and winter sports enthusiasts. The Ackerhus has a notable exhibition concerning traditional Toggenburg customs.

Ebnat–Kappel

Beyond this, the valley closes in. Ahead the Churfirsten (on right) and the Stockberg (on left) come into sight. At Krummenau (716m/2349ft) the valley briefly opens out again. At the far end of the village, on the right, is a large parking place near the chair-lift (2025m/6644ft) from Krümmenschwil (740m/2427ft) to Rietbach (1120m/3675ft), from which there is a ski-lift to the Wolzenalp (1456m/4777ft).

Krummenau

Beyond Krummenau, the Thur flows under the natural rock bridge known as the Sprung and through the Kesseltobel gorge, with the road running on the hillside high above it.

"Sprung"

2.5km/2 miles from Krummenau is Neu-St Johann (760m/2494ft), a village set amid meadows in a wider part of the valley (summer holiday accommodation, winter sports), with a fine 17th c. Baroque church belonging to a former Benedictine monastery.

Neu-St Johann

A reasonably good road (12km/7 miles to the lower station of the cableway) branches off the main road to Nesslau in Neu-St Johann and climbs the slopes above the Luternbach valley, with a fine view of the Säntis. Reaching the top of the hill in 1.5km/1 mile, it runs level past the Ennetbühl and then descends gradually to cross the Luternbach gorge.

From Neu-St Johann to the Säntis

Toggenburg

Rietbad Beyond this, a good road winds its way up to Rietbad (927m/3041ft), with a well-known spring of sulphurous water (drinking fountain 100m/328ft beyond the Kurhotel), at the foot of the Stockberg (1784m/5853ft; 1 hour; extensive views).

Seeben The road now follows a level course through the meadows of a high valley,
Kräzeren pass passing in 1km/½ mile the Kurhaus at Seeben. It then climbs over the meadows of the Alp Bernhalde (1283m/4210ft) and continues through forest to the Kräzeren Pass (1300m/4265ft). A short way downhill you arrive at the Schwägalp inn.

Schwägalp In Schwägalp you pass the road from Umäsch coming in on the left and then it is a drive of 1km/¾ mile up to the lower station (1350m/4462ft) of the Säntis cableway which was opened in 1935 and which has been renewed
★★ Säntis several times, most recently in 1974. It takes seven minutes to reach the summit of the Säntis (upper station 2433m/8116ft, see Appenzell) from where there is a breathtaking panorama over the Vorarlberg, Bündner, Glarus and Uri alps, as well as across Lake Constance into Swabia. In good weather, the view even takes in the Vosges and the Jura.

Nesslau From Neu-St Johann, road 16 continues through the adjoining village of Nesslau (762m/2400ft), frequented as a summer vacation and winter sports
★ Speer resort. Towering above it to the south-west is the Speer (1954m/6411ft), which offers a rewarding climb (5 hours).

Giessen Falls Higher up the valley is Germen, where the road runs through a narrow wooded pass, with the two Giessen Falls on the Thur (hydro-electric station). It then winds its way uphill to the little vacation spot of Stein (860m/
Starkenstein 2823ft) and continues up through the Starkenbach Pass (894m/2933ft; on
Castle (ruin) the right the ruins of Starkenstein castle) into the Alpine high valley of
★ Obertoggen- Obertoggenburg, with innumerable farms and huts dotting its green
burg meadow-covered slopes. To the right is the jagged ridge of the Churfirsten; to the left is a first glimpse of the Wildhauser Schafberg.

Alt-St Johann 5km/3 miles from Stein is Alt-St Johann (897m/2943ft), a popular health and winter sports resort, founded in the 12th c. as the monastery of St John.

Sellamatt Alp At the end of the village, on the right, is the lower station of a chair-lift (1.5km/1 mile, 15 minutes) to the Alp Sellamatt (1390m/4561ft; Schlamatt mountain inn): panoramic views, near which are the Churfirsten hut (1450m/4757ft) and the Iltiosalp (30 minutes' walk). Good walking and cross-country trekking.

Unterwasser Road 16 continues to Unterwasser (927m/3041ft), a popular health resort (swimming pool) and winter sports resort in a beautiful sheltered setting between the Säntis chain and the Churfirsten, at the junction where the two streams combine to form the River Thur. In the Haus Rotenbrunnen in the village street is an alpine dairy museum, with exhibits illustrating milk processing and showing a kitchen and living-room.

Kühboden From Unterwasser a narrow mountain road climbs steeply up (2km/1 mile north) to the Kühboden Alp (1050m/3445ft); from here it is an hour's walk to
Gräppelensee the charming little Gräppelensee (1302m/4272ft).

Schwendi Lakes Another little road runs 3.5km/2 miles south-east to the Schwendi (1165m/3822ft) from where there is a road 3.5km/2 miles to Wildhaus.

★ Iltiosalp A funicular 1.2km/1 mile long goes up from Unterwasser in 6 minutes to the much visited Iltiosalp (1350m/4429ft), from where a magnificent view of the Säntis massif can be enjoyed. There is excellent skiing (ski-lift to Alp Stöfeli, 1480m/4856ft).

Chäserrugg From the Iltiosalp a cabin cableway (3450m/11,319ft, 8 minutes) runs up to Chäserrugg (2250m/7382ft); Stöfeli mountain inn).

Unterwasser in Obertoggenburg

Footpaths (extensive views) lead east to the Schwendi-Seen (30 minutes) and west to the Alp Sellamatt (30 minutes). The ascent of the Hinterrugg (2309m/7575ft), the highest peak in the Churfirsten chain, takes 3½ hours.

★ Churfirsten

The main road continues up from Unterwasser in a double hairpin bend and comes in 2.5km/2 miles to the hamlet of Lisighaus (1056m/3456ft: commune of Wildhaus), with the modest house in which the reformer Ulrich Zwingli (1484–1531) was born.

Lisighaus

Zwinglihaus

Barely 5km/3 miles from Unterwasser is Wildhaus (1098m/3603ft), a widely scattered health and winter sports resort (indoor swimming pool; climbing school; holiday courses in hand-weaving; ice-ink, curling rink, cross-country skiing), magnificently situated on an open pass below the south side of the Wildhauser Schafberg (2384m/7822ft).

Wildhaus

From here an 800m/2625ft long chair-lift goes up to Oberdorf (1270m/4167ft) from which another chair-lift continues up to the Gamserrugg (1771m/5811ft) on the Gamsalp.

Oberdorf

There is yet another chair lift from Wildhaus north-westwards to the Gamplüt (1334m/4377ft).

Gamplüt

1½km/1 mile north of Wildhaus lies the little Schönen lake, with a bathing beach.

Schönen-bodensee

From Wildhaus the road goes downhill on a moderate gradient over Alpine meadows flanked by mountains, then enters the forest and runs more steeply down through the wooded Simmi gorge to the Zolhaus inn (706m/2316ft).

Simmitobel

From here it winds its way down the slopes of the Gamser Berg, with extensive views (parking place in 200m/656ft, on right) and magnificent vistas of the Rhine valley and the Liechtenstein Alps.

★ Gamser Berg

Gams	Gams (504m/1654ft) is a neat village with a church above it on higher ground. From here there is a road east to Hagg.
Rhine Valley	Road 16 now turns south along the edge of the wide Rhine valley and comes to Grabs.
Grabs	Grabs (482m/1581ft) is a large village surrounded by orchards. Here a steep and narrow mountain road (10km/6 miles) turns off on the right and winds its way up the Grabser Berg to the Kurhaus Voralp, below the beautiful
Voralpsee	Voralp Lake (1116m/3662ft).
Buchs Schloss Werdenberg	From Grabs the road continues along the densely populated valley to the straggling village of Buchs (450m/1476ft; see Rhine) to join the road from St Margrethen to Chur beneath Werdenberg castle. Chur is set picturesquely above a lake.

Valais Alps   F–K 11–13

Canton: Valais (VS)

Location	The Valais Alps (German Waliser Alpen; French Alpes Valaisiennes) lie between the Upper Rhône valley and the Italian river Dora Baltea. The Swiss–Italian frontier runs along the main ridge of the massif which forms part of the southern Swiss Alps.
★★Landscape	The principal valleys in the Valais Alps are accessible on side roads opening off the main road along the Rhône valley (see entry). Two important north-south routes run through the massif, over the Great St Bernard (see entry), in the west and the Simplon pass (see entry) in the east. Rising to well over 4000m/13,124ft, the range includes some of the mightiest peaks in Swit-
★★Matterhorn ★★Dufourspitze	zerland, including the Matterhorn (4478m/14,692ft) and the Monte Rosa group, with the Dufourspitze (4634m/15,204ft), the country's highest

Stalden in the Mattertal   *Monte Rosa massif*

mountain. One notable man-made feature is the artificial lake of Grand-Dixence (see Sion) in a grandiose mountain setting.

The beauties of the Valais Alps were discovered by tourists relatively early. The best-known resorts are Zermatt (see entry) and Saas Fee (see Saas Valley), but in recent years a number of other resorts such as Verbier (see Martigny), Grimentz (see Sierre) and Zinal (see Sierre) have developed into popular winter sports areas.

★★Zermatt
★Saas Fee

Vevey   E 10

Canton: Vaud (VD)
Altitude: 385m/1264ft. Population: 16,000

Vevey, the chief town of the Canton of Valais, lies on Lake Geneva at the mouth of the river Veveyse and is dominated on the north by Mont Pèlerin (1084m/3557ft) and the Plèiades (1364m/4475ft). On the slopes to the north are the famous Lavanx vineyards. Every twenty-five years the "Fête des Vignerons", a unique vintners' festival is held here (last in 1977), which includes many folkloristic events. Vevey lies on the Simplon railway line and is a motorway junction (N9/E2 and N12/E4).

Location and general

In Roman times, Vevey (Viviscus) was the most important port on Lake Geneva. The town received its municipal charter about 1200 and, during the Middle Ages it rose to prosperity as a trading station on the road from Burgundy to Piedmont. It began to develop into a major tourist attraction in the 19th c.

History

Sights

The finest feature of the town is the Grand' Place, an unusually large market square on the shores of the lake. At its north end is the colonnaded Grenette (Corn Exchange, 1808) and, beyond this, near the Theatre, is the Auberge de la Clef, in which Rousseau stayed in 1730 (commemorative plaque).

Grenette

In house No. 5 is the Swiss Camera Museum which has an interesting collection of old cameras and photographic equipment (closed Mon.). On the west side of the Grand' Place is the Jardin du Rivage (concerts during the season), with the beautiful Seahorse Fountain.

Camera museum

From the market square and the Quai Perdonnet to the east there are magnificent views over the lake to the Savoy Alps, with Le Grammont (2172m/7126ft) in the foreground. In the middle of the quai stands the "Charlot Memorial" (John Doubleday) to the great film artist Charlie Chaplin, who died here in 1977.

Quai Perdonnet

Nearby is the Alimentarium, a museum of the history of food, a Nestlé foundation opened in 1985. At the east end of the quay (800m/2625ft long) in front of a small park is an amusing bronze sculpture group, "Première chevauchée de Bacchus" (1930) and a bust of the poetess Anna de Noailles (1876–1933).

Alimentarium

No. 2 Avenue de la Gare, which leads east from the station square, houses the Musée Jenisch (established in 1897; closed Mon.). The collection includes pictures and sculpture by Swiss artists of the 19th and 20th c., including Hodler, Steinlen and Gimmi, and also etchings and natural history exhibits. Temporary art exhibitions are also held here.

Jenisch museum

As a memorial to the Austrian painter and writer Oskar Kokoschka, an exhibition of his works was opened in 1988 in the Jenisch Museum. On view are paintings, water-colours, drawings and etchings by the artist. His literary works were left to the Zurich central library.

Kokoschka Foundation

Vevey: La Grenette, the former corn-hall

Musée du Vieux-Vevey et Musée de la Confrérie des Vignerons

In the Rue d'Italie, north of Quai Perdonnet, are the Musée du Vieux-Vevey (Museum of Old Vevey) and Musée de la Confrérie des Vignerons (Museum of the Confraternity of Vintners; closed on Mondays), housing pre-historic material, fine old furniture, weapons, costumes, and documents on the history of wine.

St Martin's Church

On a terrace above the railway line (fine views: orienteering tablet) stands the church of St Martin (14th–15th c., with 20th c. stained glass).

Palais Nestlé

On the north-western outskirts of the town, near the Lausanne road, is the Y-shaped Palais Nestlé (1960), headquarters of the famous Swiss firm.

La Tour de Peilz Castle, Museum of Games

To the east, contiguous with Vevey, is the little town of La Tour de Peilz, dominated by a 13th c. castle, which, since 1987, has contained the Musée Suisse de Jeu. The interesting collection comprises games from all over the world and of various periods, and includes educational, strategic, simulated games, and games of chance. In the Place du Temple stands a "Freedom Monument" by Gustave Courbet, who died here in 1877. A walk along the shore of the lake by the fine yacht harbour is recommended.

Surroundings

★ Mont Pèlerin

From the hotel colony (806m/2644ft) on the slopes of Mont Pèlerin (1084m/3557ft) there are fine views of Lake Geneva, the Rhône valley and the Savoy Alps. It can be reached either by road (12km/7 miles, via Corsier) or by funicular (1.6km/1 mile, 10 minutes), via Corseaux (429m/1480ft: swimming pool), where there is a house built by Le Corbusier for his parents in 1924 (museum), and Chardonne. In summer a tourist railway runs between Vevey and Chamby. In 1988 the Dalai Lama, who was awarded the Nobel Peace Prize in 1989, opened a new cultural centre on Mont Pèlerin. This

Tibetan Centre

forms part of the Tibetan centre of 1977 in which live about a dozen monks.

La Tour de Peilz: the yacht harbour

The centre is intended as a meeting-place for Tibetans who are exiled in Europe, and also to give interested Europeans the opportunity to learn something of Tibetan culture and Buddhism.

The route (by road 5km/3 miles, by electric railway 6km/4 miles in 20 minutes, continuation to the Pléiades 12km/7 miles in 45 minutes) passes the English church and continues up the Route de Blonay, turning left up the hill in 1km/½ mile. After passing the 18th c. Château de Hauteville (off the road to the right: beautiful private gardens, with lookouts) it runs through the villages of St-Légier (champagne-style wine) and La Chiésaz, where the grave of the composer Paul Hindemith (1895–1963) can be seen in the cemetery and where there are a number of houses with humorous external paintings by A. Béguin. Finally, the road runs below the massive 12th c. Château de Blonay, which has remained in the possession of the Blonay family since it was built. 5km/3 miles: Blonay (623m/2044ft). For description of village and continuation of road to the Pléiades: see Montreux.

For details of the Corniche de Lavaux to Lausanne: see Geneva.

From Vevey to Blonay

Hauteville Castle

★ Blonay Castle

Vierwaldstätter See — L–N 6/7

Cantons: Uri (UR), Schwyz (SZ), Unterwalden (NW) and Lucerne (LU)

The Vierwaldstätter See or Lake of the Four Forest Cantons (the three original cantons of Uri, Schwyz and Unterwalden together with the canton of Lucerne) is commonly referred to in English as Lake Lucerne, but this is, in fact, only one of the lake's many arms. Lying at an altitude of 437m/1434ft, it is the fourth largest of the Swiss lakes (area 114sq.km/44sq.miles), length from Lucerne to Flüelen 38km/24 miles; greatest depth 214m/702ft), but is second to none in magnificence and scenic variety.

Location and
★★ Landscape

447

Vierwaldstätter See

General

The great mountains with their endless scope for walks and climbs are reflected in the spacious surface of the lake. The famous lookouts of the Rigi, Pilatus and the Stanserhorn are brought within easy reach by mountain railways and cableways. The beautiful shores of the lake with their southern vegetation offer numerous bathing places. The neat towns and villages provide luxurious or modest accommodation at the visitor's choice. These attractions, plus the lake's associations with the origins of the Swiss Confederation and the legend of William Tell all help make the Lake of the Four Forest Cantons one of the most popular tourist areas in Europe.

Lake Lucerne
Alpnacher See
Küssnachter See

The lake begins in the west as the beautiful Luzerner See (Lake Lucerne), with the Bucht von Stansstad (Stansstad Bay) and the Alpnacher See to the south and the Küssnachter See (Lake Küssnacht) to the north-east. Then come the Weggiser Becken (Weggis Basin) and, beyond the Rigi and Bürgenstock promontories, which reduce the width of the lake to only 825m/902yd, the Gersauer Becken (Gersau Basin) and the Buochser Bucht (Buochs Bay).

★Lake Uri

Running south from Brunnen is the Urner See (Lake Uri), a fjord-like strip of water enclosed between massive rock walls, scenically the most magnificent part of the lake.

Boat services

From Lucerne to Flüelen: 48km/30 miles, 3–3½ hours.

The full beauty of the lake and its mountain setting can best be appreciated by taking a boat trip, which will provide a pleasant alternative to the journey by car. Even a one-way trip is worth taking if you can arrange to have your car driven to meet you.

There are also boat services from Lucerne to Küssnacht (15km/9 miles, 1 hour) and from Lucerne via Kehrsiten–Bürgenstock and Stansstad to

Fronalpstock on Lake Uri

Alpnachstad (25km/16 miles, 1¼–1½ hours). In summer, services between Lucerne and Flüelen operate in conjunction with the William Tell Express excursion; there are connections with the railway to Locarno or Lugano (see Practical Information: Railways).

Water-taxis (maximum 10 passengers) of the St Niklausen Schiffsgesellschaft run throughout the day, stopping at any place by request.

★Around the Vierwaldstättersee by road

From Lucerne to Flüelen along the northern and eastern shores

Leave Lucerne (see entry: 438m/1437ft) on the Haldenstrasse, going past the Kursaal (on right) and the beautiful lakeside gardens and continuing close to the shore of Lake Lucerne. In 2km/1 mile a side road goes off on the right (0.5km/¼ mile) to the public beach (park, camp site, restaurant) and the Swiss Transport Museum (see entry). The main road passes the Liliput-bahn (a miniature steam railway). Beyond this a road comes in on the right from the beach.

Lucerne
Lake Lucerne

Then the hotels on the Bürgenstock and later the Rigi (see entries) come into view. The first place to be reached is Seeburg (440m/1444ft; beach), an outlying suburb of Lucerne. Beyond this, the road winds its way up to cross the Megger Berg (496m/1627ft), with fruit orchards and many houses, past the Meggenhorn, a little wooded peninsula on the right.

Seeburg

Meggen is a long straggling village (483m/1585ft). In Vorder-Meggen we find Schloss Neu-Habsburg (1869), with the tower of an older castle which Rudolf von Habsburg had built in 1240, but which was destroyed by the men of Lucerne in 1352. The mansion of Schloss Meggenhorn (1886–99) was built by Viktor von Segesser on the model of French Renaissance Châteaux; the Neo-Gothic chapel is worth seeing. The parish church of Hinter-Meggen dates from the 18th and 19th centuries.

Meggen

The road now enters the canton of Schwyz and continues along the northwest side of the Küssnachter See. 2km/1 mile beyond the village of Merlischachen (444m/1457ft), below the road on the right, is the Astrid Chapel (1936), moved here in 1960 from its previous position on the left of the road, commemorating Queen Astrid of the Belgians, who was killed in a car accident here (spot marked by a cross) on August 29th 1935.

Lake Küssnacht

The road now descends to Küssnacht (440m/1444ft; see entry), from which the main road (No. 2) continues via Arth to Brunnen (see entry). The more attractive road via Weggis and Gersau branches off on the right and follows closely to the east side of the Küssnachter See, passing through pleasant countryside below the west side of the Rigi. In 0.5km/¼ mile, it passes the lower station of the cableway to the Seebodenalp (on left). In 5km/3 miles, on right, is the village of Greppen (454m/1490ft). The road now climbs (beautiful view of the lake to the rear) over a hill, with the Hertenstein peninsula to the right, and runs down to a junction.

Küssnacht

Here a road on the right leads to the popular resort of Weggis (440m/1444ft), prettily situated on the lake. A pleasant detour can be made to the public beach and to the Hertenstein peninsula (8km/5 miles) and to the east a narrow road climbs 5.5km/3 miles up the slopes of the Rigi (see entry; no road to the summit). The main road, bypassing Weggis, runs uphill again. 2.5km/2 miles beyond the turning for Weggis, the old road comes in on the right. Nearby is the lower station of the Weggis–Rigi–Kaltbad cableway (see Rigi). Then follows a beautiful stretch of road, running close to the lake at the foot of the Rigi, with splendid views. To the right can be seen the Bürgenstock (see entry) and its well-known hotels. Further on, there is a charming view of the narrowest part of the lake between the two

Weggis

449

promontories, the Obere and the Untere Nase, and of the Bürgenstock, with the Buochsehorn and Stansehorn rearing up behind it.

Vitznau
★★ Rigi

Vitznau (440m/1444ft): a popular summer holiday resort affording extensive views, from which a rack-railway ascends the Rigi (35 minutes: see entry). (There is another rack-railway up the Rigi from Arth-Goldau, to the east.) At the far end of the village, on the left, are two cableways, one to Hinterbergen, the other to Weissenfluh (Wissifluh, 936m/3071ft: hotel), both giving access to fine walking country. The road continues past the beach and then winds its way around the Obere Nase, skirting the shore of the lake or running a little above it, with extensive views. 5km/3 miles from Vitznau is the terminal of a car ferry to Beckenried on the south side of the lake (service every hour, taking 15 minutes).

Gersau

Gersau (440m/1444ft) is the oldest health resort on the Vierwaldstätter See, occupying a charming sheltered site. From here, a mountain road leads north (5.5km/3 miles) to the lower station, at Gschwend (1012m/3320ft: inn), of a cableway which runs north-west to the Burggeist guest-house, 20 minutes below the Rigi-Sheidegg peak (1665m/5463ft).

Beyond Gersau, the road continues close to the shore or on the wooded slopes above the lake. It passes the old Kindlimord chapel (rebuilt 1708), at the foot of the Rigi-Hochfluh (1702m/5584ft), with a view of the two peaks of the Mythen. Soon after this, the Lake Uri comes into view beyond the Treib promontory. 4km/2 miles further on, to the left, is a cableway up the Urmiberg.

Brunnen

In Brunnen (440m/1444ft: see entry) we join the St Gotthard road, coming from Lucerne and Zurich via Arth. The lakeside route from Brunnen to Flüelen follows this road. At the Wolfsprung Hotel an attractive little mountain road (3km/2 miles) goes off on the left via the health resort of Morschach and the holiday centre of Axenfels (turn left), past the Rütliblick

★ Axenstein

Hotel to the Axenstein (708m/2323ft; see Brunnen), with a superb view of both arms of the Vierwaldstätter See.

★ Axenstrasse
★ Lake Uri

The road to Flüelen continues along the magnificent Axenstrasse, which runs above the steep east shore of the fjord-like Urner See (Lake Uri), passing through numerous tunnels and galleries blasted from the rock (it is possible to walk along some stretches of the old road, built in 1863–65). The St Gotthard railway running parallel to the road, sometimes below it, also passes through many tunnels. On the far side of the lake can be seen the crag known as the "Schillerstein" (named after the German dramatist whose works include "William Tell") and, higher up on the Seelisberg the Rütli meadow where the original Swiss Confederation was established. Just before Sisikon, the road enters the canton of Uri.

Sisikon

Sisikon (457m/1499ft), at the mouth of the Riemenstalden valley, has a modern church built in 1968. Beyond this, the road continues through more tunnels to the Tellsplatte Hotel (512m/1680ft), with a car park and beautiful gardens (view of the massive Urirotstock, 2932m/9620ft). From here, a

Tell's Chapel

footpath (7 minutes) leads down to the famous Tell's Chapel (known to have existed since at least 1500; restored 1881, with paintings by Stükelberg), on the spot where William Tell is traditionally supposed to have leapt out of Gessler's ship during a storm. From the hotel, a cableway runs up in 4 minutes to the Axen station (825m/2707ft). 1km/½ mile further on the Axenstrasse enters its last tunnel, with an old gallery (lookout) on the right.

Flüelen

Flüelen (440m/1444ft), a port and holiday resort at the south end of the Lake Uri, is built on the delta at the mouth of the canalised river Reuss (see below). Near the station, behind the old parish church of St George and St Niklaus (1665) stands the little Schloss Rudenz, which once belonged to the lords of Attinghausen, whose estate extended to the shore of the lake and who controlled the customs station. Here stands an iron sculpture

"Schwurhände" which Witschi created for the 1964 exhibition. There is a cableway up the Eggeberge (1440m/4775ft).

Flüelen is the landing-stage for boats from Lucerne. Passengers who have booked the "William Tell Express" excursion transfer here to the railway to continue their trip into southern Ticino (see Practical Information: Railways).

The Reuss plain is the only large level area in the canton of Uri which does not form part of the mountainous region. In 1966, work was begun to reform the Reuss delta, which had been partly canalised between 1850 and 1863 and from 1939 provided with flood protection. An opening in the dam on the left permits the water to flow into the plain and thus create a new shallow water zone; a new channel is to be created on the right. The mouth of the river which has hitherto extended far into the lake will be restricted and, eventually, previously inaccessible supplies of gravel for quarrying will be made available.

Reuss delta
project

For the continuation of the road via Altdorf to Isenthal (see Altdorf).

Altdorf

From Lucerne to Seelisberg along the western and southern shores (37km/23miles)

Leave Lucerne (438m/1437ft; see entry) by Pilatusstrasse and Obergrundstrasse (to left). Just after Paulusplatz a road goes off on the left to Horw (445m/1460ft) from which it is possible either to travel south-east to Winkel, attractively situated in a bay on the lake, or to continue along the shores of the lake to Hergiswil.

Lucerne

The main road continues straight on past the turning for Horw. In 0.5km/550yd, we bear left on to the N2 motorway which we follow, at first running below Pilatus (see Lucerne) at some distance from the lake, and then above the lake, a beautiful view of the Rigi, the Bürgenstock and the Stanserhorn.

★Pilatus

To the left (motorway exit) is the summer holiday resort of Hergiswil, on the lake (445m/1460ft; bathing beach. Glass Museum at Seestr. 12; closed Mon.). At Brunni (825m/2707ft) 1.5km/1 mile farther on, is a cableway which takes 6 minutes to reach the Gschwänd Alp (1216m/3990ft) on the north side of Pilatus.

Hergiswil

The motorway continues on a beautiful stretch of road above the lake, running along the slopes of the Lopperberg (965m/3166ft), an outlier of Pilatus, and comes to a junction where the road diverges on the right to the Brünig Pass (see Sarnen; which can also be reached by taking the Sarnen exit after Hergiswil).

★Lopperberg

The N2 continues over the channel, only 150m/492ft wide, between the Vierwaldstätter See and the Alpnacher See to the exit for Stansstad (438m/1437ft: bathing beach), the port for Stans, a summer holiday resort and the beginning of the road to the Bürgenstock and the road and railway to Engelberg. On the shores of the lake stands the Schnitzturm, a relic of old fortifications. 1km/½ mile north-east on the Harissenbucht (restaurant and night-club) is a funicular (382m/1253ft) which climbs in 4 minutes to the Kurhaus Fürigen (650m/2133ft).
From Stansstad a very attractive road runs east, climbing through the forest, then through the meadows of a high valley and finally through another stretch of forest to the parking place (fee) at the great complex of fine hotels on the Bürgenstock (878m/2881ft; fine views: see entry).

Alpnacher See
Stansstad

Bürgenstock

The motorway continues through the fertile valley (fruit orchards) between the Bürgenstock and the Stanserhorn to the exit for Stans (455m/1493ft), a little market town (population 6000), the capital of the half-canton of

Stans

The Schnitzturm of Stansstad

Nidwalden, the eastern half of the canton of Unterwalden. In the main square are the parish church (rebuilt in Baroque style 1641–47) and a monument to Arnold von Winkelried, hero of the Battle of Sempach (1386). To the right of the church is a double chapel of 1482 (charnel-house); to the left, above the church, stands the Town Hall (1715) where can be seen an interesting collection of paintings of Swiss cantonal officials. The Höfli is a restored medieval secular building. To the east of the centre the Kollegium St Fidelis has a small natural history collection. The former salt and corn store (1700) on the Stansstad road near the Stanserhorn funicular houses special exhibitions. The Historical Museum has been housed since 1993 in the Winkelfriedhaus, a late 16th c. half-timbered building.

★ Stanserhorn

A combined funicular and cableway ascends in 25 minutes to the pan- oramic restaurant on the Stanserhorn–Kulm (1849m/6067ft) 5 minutes below the summit of the Stanserhorn (1901m/6237ft), from which there are superb views of the Uri, Unterwalden and Bernese Alps, the Vierwald- stätter See and the Alpine foreland.

Engelberger Aa

From Stans, the road to Seelisberg (Treib) branches off on the left and rejoins the N2 motorway, which crosses the fertile open valley of the Engelberger Aa and then the river. To the left is the Bürgenstock, to the right the Buochsehorn, ahead the Rigi.

Buochs

The next motorway exit leads to Buochs (440m/1444ft), a village, beauti- fully situated on the bay of the same name, which attracts many summer visitors; it has a church prominently located on higher ground.

Ennetbürgen

From here, a good road runs north to Ennetbürgen, below the east side of the Bürgenstock. Beyond Buochs, the road to Seelisberg skirts the lake, with a beautiful view of the Rigi.

Beckenried

Haus Treib

At the near end of Beckenried, on the left, is the departure point of the car ferry to Gersau. Beckenried (440m/1444ft), a long straggling village at the end of the lakeside road, also popular as a quiet holiday resort.

Beckenried

A cableway runs up to the Klewenalp (1600m/5250ft) from which there is a beautiful view embracing the lake, the Rigi, the Mythen, the Glarus Alps and the Alpine foreland area with its lakes (good skiing; ski-lifts).

Klewenalp

Beyond Beckenried, the road to Seelisberg leaves the lake and crosses the motorway to Emmetten (762m/2500ft), another straggling village and summer holiday resort in a sheltered setting. The road continues uphill for a short distance before descending steeply near the church into a beautiful green Alpine valley and then climbing again on a moderate gradient to the Niederbauen (1927m/6322ft: on right, a cableway from Emmetten) and the Stutzberg.

Emmetten

Niederbauen

From Emmetten there is a cableway to the Stockhütte (1286m/4219ft).

Stockhütte

In another 3km/2 miles, the road winds its way up through forest and then runs down and passes through a tunnel, beyond which there is a picturesque view of the Seelisberger See far below (736m/2415ft; bathing beach).

Seelisberg Lake

Beyond the lake a road branches off on the right to the Rütli meadow in the middle of the forest, where tradition has it that the Swiss Confederation was established. Here, in 1291, the three "forest cantons" of Schwyz, Uri and Unterwalden joined in an alliance which became the foundation of the "Perpetual League" against the Habsburgs. The Tell legend, which received its classical form in Schiller's drama "William Tell" (1804), was a later addition to the traditional story.

Rütli

The road continues to the health resort of Seelisberg (804–845m/2638–2772ft), situated on a wooded terrace high above the Vierwaldstätter See.

Seelisberg

Rütli meadow, where the Swiss Federation was traditionally founded

The road passes the pilgrimage chapel of Maria-Sonnenberg (1667) and the funicular to Treib, and then descends through the forest, after which there is a superb view of the Vierwaldstätter See and the Rigi.

Treib

Treib (440m/1444ft), picturesquely set on the tongue of land between the Vierwaldstätter See and the Urner See, was formerly a little trading town and a haven for shipping on the lake. A funicular goes up to the Seelisberg (1149m/3770ft, 8 minutes) where there is a charming inn, built in 1903 in imitation of the previous inn (1658). Treib, where the road ends, has a landing-stage for the lake ships.

Seelisberg Tunnel

The motorway south-east of Beckenried, opened in 1980, passes through the 9.3km/5.8 miles long Seelisberg Tunnel to the south bank of Lake Uri and thence to the St Gotthard road.

Walensee   P/Q 5/6

Cantons: St Gallen (SG) and Glarus (GL)

Location

The Walensee (15km/9 miles long, up to 2km/1 mile wide and up to 151m/495ft deep) lies at an altitude of 423m/1388ft between the Glarus Alps to the south and the Churfirsten, which tower up on the north to a height of almost 1000m/3281ft above the light green waters of the lake (Hinterrugg 2309m/7576ft).

Weesen

At the west end of the lake is Weesen (431m/1414ft), a charming little town (population 1500) and holiday resort. From the shady lakeside promenade there are very beautiful views. 1km/½ mile east, beyond the wooded detrital fan of the Flibach, is the hamlet of Fli or Fly.

Walensee, on the south flank of the Churfirsten ▶

Walensee

Betlis

A little road which branches off the road to Amden at Fli (alternate one-way traffic) runs along the north side of the lake. The road is cut from the rock for most of the way, with two tunnels. After passing the Muslen falls and the ruins of Strahlegg castle it comes to the little village of Betlis, 5km/3 miles east of Weesen (520m/1707ft; boat service from Weesen), from which a footpath (15 minutes) leads up to the Seerenbach falls.

Amden

A road, north-east from Weesen via Fli (6km/4 miles: views), winds steeply up from the lake with two hairpin turns to the summer and winter sports resort (several ski-lifts) of Amden (911m/2989ft), lying high above the lake on sunny Alpine meadows between the Mattstock (1939m/6362ft: chair-lift, 1400m/4593ft in 15 minutes to the Alp Walau, 1285m/4216ft) and the Leistkamm (2105m/6907ft: 5 hours).

★Speer

There is a rewarding climb from Amden to the summit of the Speer (1951m/6401ft: 3 hours).

The N3 motorway follows the south side of the lake from the Glarus exit to Walenstadt, with viaducts (electrically heated in winter to prevent icing) and numerous tunnels and galleries.

Detour via Näfels and the Kerenzerberg
Näfels

There is also a slightly longer route via Näfels and the old road over the Kerenzerberg. 3.3km/2 miles south of Niederurnen (see Glarus) is Näfels (440m/1444ft), a busy little market town of 4000 inhabitants (mainly Roman Catholic) at the mouth of the Linth valley. The richly appointed Freulerpalast contains the Glarus Cantonal Museum (see Glarus).

Obersee

A steep road runs 6km/4 miles west from Näfels to a charming little lake, the Obersee (989m/3245ft).

Mollis

In Näfels, take a road which branches off the Glarus road on the left and crosses the Linth. The first place on the road to the Kerenzerberg is Mollis

Mollis: Hatli-Haus ...   *... and orangery of the Höfli-Haus*

(448m/1470ft), below the mighty Fronalpstock. It has a number of fine old burghers' houses, including the Zwickyhaus (1621), in the Kreuzgasse, which has a fine gable-roof and, on the Kerenzerberg road, the former mansion of Haltli (1772–84) which was designed by Konrad Schindler; it is now a special school. Hans Hof and the neighbouring Höfli, which were built in the second half of the 18th c., now form part of an old people's home. In the garden is an orangery, framed by beautiful beds of roses. The Fabrikhof on the Netstal road, built about 1760, has three fine curved gables.

Beyond Mollis, road 3, of excellent quality, climbs with many bends and sharp turns but with a moderate gradient. To the rear there are beautiful views of Näfels and over the Linth plain, bounded by the Hirzli, as far as Lake Zurich; to the left are the Weggis chain, the Glämisch and the Tödi. In 2km/1 mile the Talblick inn is passed on the right, after which the road turns through the forest, with the first glimpses of the Walensee.

5½km/3 miles from Mollis, on the left, is the Café Kerenser Berghaus (730m/ 2395ft), on the Kerenzerberg (1375m/4511ft), with a beautiful view of the Walensee and the Churfirsten; to the left, below the Mattstock, is Amden and, at the west end of the lake, the village of Weesen. Here, the road reaches its highest point and begins to descend.

Kerenzerberg

★ Churfirsten

Filzbach (720m/2362ft) is a village and health resort, magnificently located on a terrace of meadowland 270m/886ft above the Walensee, below the pyramidal summit of the Mürtschenstock (2442m/8012ft). 1¼ hours' walk south is the little Talalpsee (1100m/3609ft). A chair-lift (1650m/5414ft; 14 minutes) ascends from Filzbach to the Habergschwänd Alp (1280m/4200ft; restaurant).

Filzbach

From Filzbach, the road continues gently uphill and circles the Sallerntobel gorge, with beautiful views at the Café Seeblick (1.5km/1 mile) just before reaching Obstalden.

Obstalden (700m/2297ft), in a beautiful setting similar to that of Filzbach, has an old church. The road on the right leads into the Hüttenberge (5km/ 3 miles) and then winds its way down (views) into the Merenbach valley and passes through a short tunnel to join the road along the Walensee at Mühlehorn.

Obstalden

5km/3 miles beyond the Glarus exit the N3 motorway comes to a parking place and just beyond this, on the left, is the Walensee restaurant.

★ Along the
Walensee shore

1km/½ mile further on is an exit (cars only) to the village of Mühlehorn (426m/1398ft), at the inflow of the Merenbach into the Walensee. The road continues along above the lake, traversing two tunnels, and past the Müh-lehorn/Kerenzerberg junction where the road from the Kerenzerberg comes in.

Mühlehorn

The motorway now begins to climb a little. In another 1.5km/1 mile it comes to the village of Murg (430m/1411ft), situated below the road (exit only on left) on the alluvial cone of the river Murg, which forms a promontory projecting into the lake. There is a pleasant walk (4–5 hours) up the quiet Alpine valley of the Murg to the three beautiful Murg Lakes (1673–1825m/ 5489–5988ft). On the north side of the lake opposite Murg (motor-boat service), beneath the Leistkamm (2105m/6907ft) at the west end of the Churfirsten massif, is the very attractive little village of Quinten (Au inn), with beautiful southern vegetation. Like Terzen and Quarten, the village takes its name from the Latin numbering of ecclesiastical properties in the Middle Ages.

Murg

Quinten

The road continues past parking places on either side and then descends towards the shore of the lake. After 1km/½ mile, on left is the Rössli hotel and restaurant, and 1.5km/1 mile beyond this, on the right, the Mühle hotel.

Walensee

Unterterzen
Then comes Unterterzen (429m/1408ft), a little industrial town (cement works, match factory, etc.) of 8000 inhabitants. A road goes off on the right and runs up 3km/2 miles via Quarten (574m/1883ft) (convalescent home) to Oberterzen.

Oberterzen
Oberterzen (662m/2172ft) is a health resort and a cross country-skiing base. From here it is a 2½ hours' walk to the three Seeben lakes (1643m/5391ft). At the far end of Unterterzen, the Chur road passes the lower station of a cableway which ascends via Oberterzen to the Flumserberge.

Mols
About 2km/1 mile from Unterterzen is Mols (432m/1417ft), after which the road curves to the right under a wooded spur with the ruins of Bommerstein Castle. It then passes a camping site on the left and the Walenstadt bathing beach at the end of the lake.

Walenstadt
Crossing the Seez Canal you reach Walenstadt (430m/1411ft): population 3500; another popular summer holiday spot, it lies 1km/½ mile from the east end of the Walensee below the steep rock-faces of the Hinterrugg.

Walenstadtberg
From here, an attractive mountain road winds its way up to the health resort of Walenstadtberg (800–900m/2625–2953ft), 4km/2 miles north-west, on a terrace of meadowland above the north side of the lake, beneath the jagged peaks of the Churfirsten. 1.5km/1 mile farther on is the Knobli-shühl sanatorium (982m/3222ft) from where a narrow little road runs up another 2km/1 mile to the Schrina-Hochrugg restaurant (1313m/4308ft), near which is a temple-like monument to Peace by Karl Bickel.

Seez valley
From Walenstadt, the Chur road continues up the broad Seez valley below the Alvier massif (on left). To the right, on a projecting spur above Flums, stands the ruined castle of Gräpplang.

Berschis
Berschis (446m/1463ft: bypass). On a wooded crag above the village to the left (easy climb) the pilgrimage chapel of St George (592m/1942ft: 12th and 15 c.) has wall-paintings (key from priest's house in the village).

Flums, at the mouth of the Schils valley

Beyond Berschis, at the beginning of the motorway to Chur, a road branches off on the right, crossing the railway and the Seez canal, to the neat village of Flums (444m/1457ft) at the mouth of the Schils valley, with the Weissmeilen (2490m/8137ft) and the curiously shaped Spitzmeilen in the background. By the Seez canal is the church of St Justus, the nave of which was altered in the 17th c. (painted timber ceiling); under the Late Gothic choir (tabernacle of 1488) are the remains of an earlier Carolingian structure. Above the village are the ruins of the 13th c. Gräpplang castle (469m/1539ft) and 15 minutes south-west of this is St James's chapel (St Jakob), which is partly Romanesque.

Flums

From Flums two attractive little roads lead up to the Flumserberge, a region of Alpine meadows dotted with huts, visited both in summer and during the winter sports season (several ski-lifts, ice-rink, indoor swimming pool). To the south-east, above the east side of the Schilsbach valley, is the Kleinberg, with the Frohe Aussicht restaurant (900m/2953ft), 4.5km/3 miles from Flums; higher up are the Sässliwiese (1200m/3937ft) and Schönhalden hotels (1494m/4902ft): hotel cableway from Saxli.

Flumser Berge

To the south-west, above the west side of the valley, is the Grossberg. A good road (11km/7 miles) climbs up, passing a number of inns, to Tannenheim (1220m/4003ft; chair-lift via the Prodalp, 1576m/5171ft, to Prodchamm, about 2000m/6562ft), with restaurant and the Tannenboden Alp (1400m/4593ft; cableway from Unterterzen, with several hotels and many chalets). From here a cableway ascends via the Kreuz hotel (1610m/5282ft) to the Maschgenkamm (Maschgenlücke inn, 1960m/6931ft), on the Spitzmeilen (2501m/8208ft).

Tannenheim

Tannenboden Alp

Winterthur

N 3

Canton: Zurich (ZH)
Altitude: 449m/1473ft. Population: 87,000

Winterthur, the second largest town in the canton of Zurich, lies in a wide basin near the river Töss in the pre-Alpine region, half-way between the Rhine and Lake Zurich. It is widely renowned for its engineering industry (Gebrüder Sulzer, Schweizerische Lokomotiv and Maschinenfabrik, etc.) and its textile factories and institutions, such as the Cantonal Technical College.

Location and general

Winterthur

1 Theatre
2 Museum of Art
3 Galerie Oskar Reinhart
4 Summer Theatre
5 Casino
6 Industrial Museum
7 Technical School
8 Museum Lindengut
9 Weigh House

300 m

© Baedeker

Winterthur

<table>
<tr><td>History</td><td>Winterthur was founded by the Kyburgs about 1150 as a market village, and received its municipal charter from Rudolf of Habsburg in 1264. Pottery, watchmaking and weaving were early local industries, followed in the 19th c. by engineering.</td></tr>
</table>

Sights

Old Town

Art treasure and a cultural inheritance bearing witness to the thriving craftwork of former times are good reasons for paying a visit to Winterthur. The little triangular Old Town still preserves streets with rows of old burghers' houses. Of special interest are the Waaghaus (weigh house) in Moorish-Gothic style, the former Early Classical Stadthaus, also the Oberes Spital (upper hospital, 1790) and the old Unteres Spital (lower hospital, 1806–1814), now an old people's home. The semi-detached house "Zur Geduld" with an Early Baroque façade was built between 1690 and 1717; the "Hans zum Adler" at the Obertor (upper gate) is an elegant example of Rococo. The fascinating graffiti on the Hans zum Hinteren Waldhorn where the Winterthur painter Hans Haggenberg lived from 1440 to 1494, have also partly survived.

Stadtkirche

The town church, a three-aisled basilica, was built 1264–1615; its two 65m/213ft-high towers were added in 1659 and 1794.

Gewerbe-museum

At Kirchplatz 14 the industrial museum houses a stored collection of applied and decorative art and occasionally special exhibitions (closed Mon.).

Rathaus

In the Marktgasse stands the Early-Classical town hall (18th–19th c.); in its assembly hall can be seen a magnificent stucco ceiling by Lorenz Schmid. On the ground floor, Josef Bösch created a shopping arcade in Italianate style at the end of the 19th c. and this links the Marktgasse with the Stadthausstrasse.

Winterthur: parish church

Fortuna fountain

In a rear wing (No. 20) can be seen the Kellenberger Collection of Watches and Clocks (sundials, sand and oil timepieces and especially mechanical clocks of 16th–19th c.; closed Mon.). In the same building is the Jakob Briner Collection of paintings by minor Dutch masters of the 17th c., together with miniatures by English, French, German and Swiss artists of the 16th to the 19th c.

Kellenberger collection of watches and clocks; Briner bequest

The old town is bounded on the north by the Stadthausstrasse, which runs east from the station. At No. 6 is the Oskar Reinhart Bequest, with a fine collection of works by Swiss, German and Austrian artists of the 18th–20th c., including many Romantics (C. D. Friedrich, K. Blechen, A. Böcklin, L. Richter, R. G. Kerstling, P. O. Runge, R. F. Wasmann, etc.), and modern Swiss artists, including F. Hodler, C. Amiet, G. Segantini and G. Giacometti. At the east end of the Stadthausstrasse stands the Stadthaus, a prestigious building of 1865–69, built by Gottfried Semper and enlarged 1932–34; inside is the concert hall of the Collegium Musicum (1629); the hall extends over three storeys.

★Oskar Reinhart Bequest

Stadhaus

Not far from the town park can be seen the theatre (Theater am Stadt-garten), opened in 1965. The building, in echelon form, was designed by Frank Krayenbühl.

Theater am Stadtgarten

The Museum of Art at Museumstrasse 52, north-west of the Stadthaus, contains pictures by Swiss painters of the 17th–20th c. (including Meyer, Graff, Bierermann, Füssli, Hodler, Giacometti, Valloton, Klee, Bill, Lohse, Thomkins and Roth), international works from the Impressionists onwards (van Gogh, Redon, Bonnard, Vuillard, Kokoschka, Picasso, Braque, Gris, Delaunay, Léger, Klee, Arp, Miró, Ernst, Magritte, Calder, Le Corbuisier and others); 19th and 20th c. sculptures by Rodin, Maillol, Brancusi, Bill Rabino-witch, etc., and a large collection of drawings.

★Kunstmuseum

In the same building is the municipal Natural History Museum (palaeon-tology, zoology and reliefs of Swiss landscapes).

Natural History Museum

Museum of Art and scientific collection

Winterthur

Coin Collection

Nearby at Lindstrasse 8 the Villa Bühler houses the municipal coin collection, mainly Greek coins and examples of Graeco-Roman artwork (closed Mon.).

Lindengut Museum

In the mansion of Lindengut, at Römerstrasse 8, is the Lindengut Museum with exhibits illustrating the history of the town from Roman times to the 19th c.; there is also a special exhibition in the coach-house (closed Wed., Sun.). The aviary (1958, extended 1988) in the adjoining part is worth seeing.

★Oskar Reinhart Collection

To the north of the town at Haldenstrasse 95 in Römerholz (closed Mon.) is the celebrated private collection of the great art patron Oskar Reinhart. It includes works by a large number of old masters, including Cranach the Elder, Breugel the Elder, Grünewald, Rubens, Rembrandt, El-Greco and Goya, and paintings by 19th c. French artists, including Corot, Courbet, Daumier, Delacroix, Renoir and Cézanne.

Schloss Wülflingen

Decorative painting and carving can be seen in the rooms of Schloss Wülflingen (Wülflingerstrasse 214) which is now a restaurant. Ch. Kuhn painted the panels in the law court; the Salomon-Langholt Room has 17th c. decoration; the "Rose Room" is Rococo style. In almost all the rooms can be seen examples of stoves decorated in the Winterthur style.

Photo Museum

Post-1945 international photography is on display in a former factory at Grüzenstr. 44 (closed Mon.).

Oberwinterthur

The Frauenfeld road (N 1) leads to the suburb of Oberwinterthur (445m/1450ft), on the site of the Celto-Roman settlement of Vitodurum. The ancient finds are on display in the Lindengut Museum (see above). The 14th c. wall-painting in the Romanesque church (12th c.) is interesting.

★Technorama

In Technoramastrasse (closed Mon.), near the motorway exit, is the Technorama of Switzerland, opened in 1982. Science and technology are presented in a vivid manner to the visitor. Apparatus, materials and experiments which visitors can do for themselves form an intrinsic feature of the complex.

In the grounds of the museum there is also a laboratory for young people and other attractions.

Surroundings

Schloss Hegi

In the neighbouring village of Hegi stands a notable moated mansion dating from the 15th–18th c. Since 1947 the estate has been owned by the town of Winterthur; in addition to a collection illustrative of the history of rural and urban life of eastern Switzerland, there is also a youth hostel.

Eschenberg

To the south of the town rises the wooded Eschenberg (585m/1919ft) with a lookout tower and the "Bruederhus" game park. An instruction trail explains the origins of the district.

Kyburg

Road 15 (the Rapperswil road) leads south to Sennhof (485m/1591ft), from which a road runs west to the Kyburg, splendidly situated on a hill (634m/2080ft). The castle, first mentioned in the 11th c., was restored in 1925 and now houses a historical museum; there is a fine view from the keep.

Schloss Mörsburg

Road No. 1 runs beneath the motorway and passes the village of Sulz, from where a detour should be made to Mörsburg Castle. This contains a Romanesque chapel (1250) and a museum of the Historical and Antiquarian Society of Winterthur (weapons, ceramics and a knights' hall).

Yverdon-les-Bains

Canton: Vaud (VD)
Altitude: 435m/1477ft
Population: 22,000

The old-world town of Yverdon, capital of northern Vaud and a well-known health resort, lies at the south-west end of the Lac de Neuchâtel. From ancient times this has been an important traffic junction.

Location and general

Yverdon-les-Bains occupies the site of the Roman camp of Eburodunum. Traces of the earliest inhabitants were found when the inland waters of the Jura sank in the flood plain of the Orbe in the 19th c. According to the most recent excavations, the first settlements built on piles are dated to about 2800 B.C. At the beginning of the 5th c. Burgundians invaded the area. In the 13th c. the Dukes of Savoy built the massive castle in which the famous educationalist Pestalozzi ran his school from 1805 to 1826.

History

Sights

The town centre is dominated by the mighty château, with four towers, once surrounded by water. It was originally the property of the Dukes of Savoy and it was Peter II who built it in the characteristic "Savoy square" form. Later, the castle came into the hands of the Bernese governors (Landvögte) and, from 1805, it was the headquarters of the Pestalozzi Institute, where Johann Heinrich Pestalozzi ran his school for twenty years. The two rooms in which he lived (Salle Pestalozzi) contain the furniture and memorabilia of the pedagogue. Since 1912, the castle has housed a library and a historical museum, with interesting finds from the locality and an ethnographical collection.

Castle

Nearby in the Maison d'Ailleurs (5 rue du Four), the Science Fiction Museum, originating from the collection of Pierre Versin, encompasses the whole gamut of Utopian fantasy, ranging from books to magazines, comics, pictures, games, video-tapes and films (open: Tues.–Sun. 2–6pm).

Science Fiction Museum

Baroque parish church

Yverdon Castle

Hôtel de Ville Parish Church	In the "Place" (the main square) stands the Hôtel de Ville (town hall), built 1769–73 by A. D. Burnand, and on the west side of the square the parish church (1755–57), designed by the Geneva architect J. M. Billon. The curved gable end of the façade has as its decoration an allegory of faith. The choir-stalls (1499–1502) by C. Chapius and B. Bottolier are of considerable merit. Outside the church stands a monument to Pestalozzi by A. Lanz (1889).
Museum of Clothing	The Musée de l'Habillement, opened in 1982, exhibits in contemporary setting several thousand handmade articles of clothing and accessories from 1850 to the present day.
Centre Thermal	The Centre Thermal (reconstructed 1977) contains the sulphurous spring (34°C–93°F) which was used for curative purposes from Roman times.

Surroundings

Ste-Croix, Museum of Musical Automata	Some 19km/12 miles west in Ste-Croix an interesting collection of musical automata, musical boxes and mechanical musical instruments can be seen in the Centre International de la Méchanique d'Art CIMA, at 2 rue de l'Industrie.
Ursins	About 7km/4 miles south-east in the village of Ursins is the medieval church of St Nicolas, built on the foundations of a 2nd century Roman temple.
★Château de Champvent	South-east of Yverdon you pass the castle of Champvent, an imposing four-towered 13th c. castle (no admission).
Orbe	In 14km/9 miles you reach Orbe (479m/1572ft; population 4000) occupying the site of the Roman settlement of Urba. In the Ferme de Boscéaz (Route

d'Yverdon), to the north of the town, the visitor should not miss the
collection of Roman mosaics which were discovered in 1841. They came
from a Roman villa and display representations of divinities and animals.
From the 7th to the 15th c., Orbe was a fortified Burgundian residence. Of
interest is the medieval church of Notre-Dame, with a magnificent Gothic
doorway. Its richly decorated arch is adorned with wonderfully carved
keystones. In the 13th c. Amadeus III of Montfalcon built a fortress on a hill
overlooking the town, but only the round keep and a rectangular tower
remain. The two-storeyed town hall (1785–89) has a ballustrade decorated
with the arms of the town. Local history is featured in the Musée du Vieil
Orbe in the Rue Centrale.

Church of
Notre-Dame

On the west bank of the Lac du Neuchâtel, north of Yverdon, lies the old
little town of Grandson (439m/1440ft; pop. 2000). It has a mighty five-
towered castle on a hill on the bank of the lake. The 13th and 15th c. fortress,
the ground plan of which is an adaptation of the "carré savoyard" form, is
now in private ownership. Of special interest here are the Knights' Hall
(choir stalls of 1620), the collection of weapons and the museum of vintage
cars (open: Mar.–Oct. daily 9am–6pm; at other times only on Sun.).

Grandson
★Castle

The Romanesque church of St-Jean-Baptiste is all that remains of the
former Benedictine monastery which was founded here in 1049. From
1140, the priory was made subordinate to the Abbey of La Chaise-Dieu in
the Auvergne, and the influence of the abbey can be seen in the Romanesque architecture. There was also a close connection to the abbots of
Cluny. After the Burgundian wars, Grandson was ruled by Berne and
Fribourg and, as a consequence of the Reformation, the monastery was
finally dissolved in 1554. Relics of the first church are the remains of the
walls in the north chapel. The building of the cornered cupula and the
reconstruction of the former nave into a basilica with three arched aisles
can be attributed to the monks of La Chaise-Dieu. The beauty of the church
is mainly due to the lightness of its architecture. As in the church of

★Church of
St-Jean-Baptiste

Grandson Castle by Lake Neuchâtel

Church of Saint-Jean-Baptiste in Grandson

Capitals

1 Thorn Motif
2 St Michael and the Dragon
3 Hell
4 Virgin Mary
5 Lions
6 Lions with Common Head
7 Eagle

A Fresco "Christus-Eucharistie"
B Prior's Seat
C Fresco "Burial of Christ"

Capital motif

St-Aimable-de-Riom in the Auvergne, the side aisles have half-barrelled or double-barrelled roofs. The nave has a round-barrelled roof of tuft, supported by beautiful marbled pillars, with capitals full of fanciful decoration. The seat of the priors (who included St Hugo, a former monk of the "Grande Chartreuse") has a representation of his swan and is considered the finest carving of its kind in Switzerland. A special mention should be made of the frescoes of the 15th c. in a niche in the south chapel and the wall tabernacle (1470) by Pierre Chapuiset in the north chapel. The great Romanesque capitals of the main aisle form a unity of the highest artistic work. In spite of their varied inspirations, they form a unified synthesis of spiritual themes concerning the tragedy of human existence and the mystery of Christ.

In the Battle of Grandson the Confederates gained their first victory on March 2nd 1478 over Duke Karl the Bold of Burgundy, who lost all his artillery and a great deal of treasure which can now be seen in the Historical Museum of Berne.

From Yverdon to Payerne
(30km/19 miles)

Estavayer-le-Lac

Leave on a road going east along the south-east side of the Lac de Neuchâtel at some distance from the shore (marshy in places), from which there is an attractive view across the lake to Grandson. 19km/12 miles from Yverdon is the old-world little town of Estavayer-le-Lac (448m/1470ft: pop. 2500; bathing beach; youth hostel; camping site), with arcaded houses, gate towers and the Late Gothic church of St Laurent. The three-aisled collegiate church has beautifully carved choir-stalls of 1572 which were the work of the Geneva artist J. Mattelin. A visit is recommended to the Dominican monastery (14th and 18th c.) in the Grand Rue and a number of notable buildings, of which the Hôtel du Cerf (16th c.) and the Maison de la Dime (15th c.) in the Rue du Musée should be mentioned. The latter (open: Nov.–Jan. Sat., Sun; at other times daily except Mon.) houses the museum of local history (including prehistoric finds, medieval kitchen utensils and a collection of old railway lanterns) and also "The François Perrier Frogs". Perrier (1813–60) served in the Swiss Guard, and returned to his home town in 1849 and indulged in his hobby of catching and preserving frogs and arranging them to illustrate scenes depicting some of the less attractive characteristics of the human race. The house at No. 142 rue Châtel dates from the 15th c. and was the last residence of the lords of Estavayer.

Château
Chenaux

The great Château Chenaux was originally also a foundation by the Savoyards (13th c.). It was partly destroyed in the 15th c. and re-erected after the Burgundian wars, later being restored and rebuilt on several occasions.

Chenaux Castle

The road now turns south-east and comes to Payerne, where the Benedictine abbey is one of the major Romanesque buildings in the country.

Payerne
★Benedictine Abbey

Zermatt

J 12

Canton: Valais (VS)
Altitude: 1620m/5317ft
Population: 4200

The mountain village of Zermatt (from "zur Matte", "on the mountain pasture") is the leading climbing and winter sports capital in the Valais and one of Switzerland's great international resorts. Nestling in a green valley enclosed between steeply scarped mountains, it is dominated by the "mountain of mountains", the huge and gracefully curved pyramid of the Matterhorn. The Nikolai valley, at the head of which Zermatt lies, is open to cars only as far as Täsch; Zermatt itself is without motor cars (local transport is by electric vehicles and horse-drawn cabs). Among the old timber houses, weathered brown with age, are numerous hotels, all built in a style adapted to the setting. A rack-railway, several long cableways and numerous ski-lifts bring the various walking, climbing and winter sports areas within easy reach. There are magnificent long ski-runs of all grades of difficulty.

★★Location and general

Leisure activities include tennis, swimming, walking and mountain-climbing (mountaineering tuition). Visitors who would like to have a bird's eye view of the area can have a circular flight in a helicopter. The landing place ("heliport") is situated at the north end of the village. Since 1988, there has been a mountain trail for cyclists which runs from the Winkelmatten beyond Zermatt up to the Furi.

Until the end of the Middle Ages the glaciers were higher up and the tree-line was at about 2600m/8531ft so that the Theodul pass offered a

History

467

Zermatt

Zermatt: climbing and winter sports capital

fairly easy route through the mountains, and this was used from Roman times onwards. Zermatt itself is first recorded in 1218 under the Latin name of Pratoborgno. By the 17th c. its hundred or so families had purchased their freedom from the landowners of the Rhône valley and formed a citizen body, to which after 1618 only the 19th c. hotelier Alexandre Seiler was admitted. The mountains around Zermatt were first mastered from 1830 onwards almost exclusively by British climbers, who were the first to climb 31 out of the 39 principal peaks (Breithorn 1830, Monte Rosa 1855, Matterhorn 1865). The famous climbers' hotel, the Monte Rosa, was opened in 1854, the railway from St Niklaus in 1891, the Gornergrat rack-railway in 1898. 1898 also saw the appearance of the first skier, but Zermatt's rise into a great winter sports resort did not really begin until 1927.

Access to Zermatt

The road from Visp, in the Rhône valley, is open to cars only as far as Täsch (30km/19 miles), which has a large parking area (fee) at the station. In winter, depending on weather conditions, it may be advisable to take the railway from Visp or St Niklaus. The railway from Visp to Zermatt (the Brig–Visp–Zermatt or BVZ narrow-gauge electric line; 35km/22 miles, journey time 1¼/1½ hours) runs alongside the road into the Nikolai valley.

Stalden-Saas

In 7km/4 miles we come to Stalden-Saas (803m/2635ft), at the junction of the Saas valley (through which flows the Saaser Vispa) and the Nikolai valley (Matter Vispa). The old timber houses in Valais style cluster around the white parish church on high ground. A cableway ascends the east side of the valley to Staldenried and the Gspon plateau (1893m/6211ft); a road on the west side leads to the mountain village of Törbel (1491m/4892ft, 8km/5 miles north-west).

St Niklaus

The Zermatt road now climbs up the Nikolai valley through the Kipfen gorge and in another 8km/5 miles reaches St Niklaus (1130m/3708ft), the largest village in the Nikolai valley which is closely hemmed in by mountains. It has a fine parish church of 1964 with a medieval tower and three beautiful Baroque altars.

From St Niklaus, a narrow and winding road climbs 8km/5 miles north-east to Grächen (1617m/5305ft), which stands on a commanding mountain terrace traversed by irrigation channels (bisses). It is a village which attracts both summer visitors and winter sports enthusiasts and it has an indoor swimming pool. There is a cableway to the Hannigalp (2110m/6923ft; skiing). 26km/16 miles further on you pass through Randa (1410m/4626ft) at the foot of the Mischabel group, before reaching Täsch in 29km/18 miles, a picturesque little village. The peak of the Matterhorn now comes into view.

Grächen

Täsch

Sights

The life of the resort is primarily on the main street, which runs from the station to the market square, with a charming contrast between hotels and elegant shops and old village houses.

Bahnhofstrasse

In the gardens of the Mont Cervin Hotel is a stone pyramid (1902) with marble plaques of Alexandre Seilder and his wife, to whom the development of Zermatt as a resort was due.

Mont Cervin Hôtel

Here, too, is the very interesting Alpine Museum, with an extensive display of material concerning the climbing of the mountains around Zermatt (local guides and famous alpinists). The cartographic and folkloristic exhibits are also notable and include furniture, minerals, indigenous flora and fauna.

Alpine Museum

Above this are the guides' and ski school office and the English church (1871), built by the Alpine Club (founded 1857), which has the graves of climbers in the churchyard. Farther up the village is the Monte Rosa Hotel (1852), for 30 years the headquarters of all climbers in Zermatt, which has preserved much of its original character. A bronze plaque (1925) commemorates Edward Whymper, who made a series of attempts on the Matterhorn between 1860 and 1865. The neat little parish church to the left of the hotel dates from 1576.

English church

Around the market square are the Gemeindehaus (communal council house) and six characteristic old village houses, on one of which is a tablet commemorating Whymper's guides, the two Taugwalders (father and son). Here, too, is the charming Marmot Fountain (1902). The handsome church of St Maurice, rebuilt in 1914, has a tower modelled on that of the earlier church.

Market Square

At the bridge over the Vispa, on a strip of land between that river and its tributary the Triftbach, is the cemetery, with the graves of many climbers who met their death on the mountains, including Whymper's guide Michel Croz and his companion Hadow. Higher up in the village a few of the old larch-wood storehouses still survive, with large circular slabs of stone on the supporting posts to deter mice.

Cemetery

The Matterhorn (French Mont Cervin, Italian Monte Cervino: 4478m/14,692ft) was first climbed on July 14th 1865 by a British team consisting of Edward Whymper, Charles Hudson, Lord Francis Douglas and Douglas Hadow, with Michel Croz and the two Peter Taugwalders, father and son, as guides. On the way down, 400m/1312ft below the summit, Hadow slipped and fell on to the Matterhorn glacier, dragging Hudson, Douglas and Croz with him: Whymper and the Taugwalders were saved by the breaking of the rope. The ascent of the Matterhorn from Zermatt is no longer considered to be particularly difficult, as it is achieved by some 3000 people every summer, but it should be attempted only by experienced climbers (4½–6 hours from the Hörnli ridge; the Italian or south-west ridge was climbed a few days later by a guide named Carrell, the Zmutt ridge in 1879,

★★ Matterhorn

the difficult Furgg Ridge in 1911. The west face was climbed in 1927, the ice-covered north face and the south face in 1931 and the east face in 1932; the first winter climb of the north face was made in 1962.

Mountain Railways
★ Gornergratbahn

It takes 45 minutes to climb 10km/6 miles to the summit of the Gornergrat by the Gornergratbahn, the highest mountain-railway in Europe running over open country (see Surroundings of Zermatt). A cableway from the upper station (restaurant) crosses the Hohtälligrat (3286m/10,785ft; restaurant) to the Stockhorn (3532m/11,592ft; upper station 3407m/11,182ft). There are also cableways from Zermatt–Winkelmatten via Furri (or Furi; 1886m/6190ft; restaurant; to the south at 1955m/6416ft is a glacier garden) to the Schwarzsee (black lake; restaurant) and via Furri and Furgg (2431m/7979ft) to the Trochenen Steg (2939m/9646ft: large restaurant) at the upper Theodul Glacier. From the Trochenen Steg a ski-lift (open also in summer) goes up to the Furgg saddle (3365m/11,044ft) on the Italian border. Another ski-lift runs via Gandegg to the Theodul Pass (3317m/10,886ft) from where there is a further lift to the Testa Grigia (3480m/11,421ft).

★ Cableway to the Kleines Matterhorn

There is a spectacular trip on the highest cableway in Europe from the Trochenen Steg to the north face of the Kleines Matterhorn (3820m/12,537ft). From the upper station there is a lift to the summit of the Kleines Matterhorn (3884m/12,747ft).

A cableway from Furgg leads to the Schwarzsee (restaurant).

Gornergrat station at 3130m/10,270ft

The so-called "Alpine-Metro", a funicular in a tunnel runs from the centre of Zermatt to the Sunnegga sun-terrace (2289m/7512ft; with restaurant) from where a cableway goes via Blauherd (2580m/8468ft) to the Unterrothorn (3103m/10,184ft). From Blauherd, yet another cableway runs to Gant (2180m/6155ft); ski-lift to the skiing-ground (2814m/9236ft). You can also go down from Sunnegga by a winter chair-lift to Findeln (2164m/7102ft).

Other mountain railways

Zermatt provides facilities for skiing throughout the year, with skiing grounds all lying at an altitude between 2500m/8250ft and 3900m/12,800ft. They are accessible by numerous lifts: Schwarzsee–Trockener Steg–Theodul, Riffelberg–Gornergrat–Stockhorn, Sunnegga–Blauherd–Unterrothorn; in summer it is possible to ski on the Breithorn plateau (cableway to the Kleines Matterhorn) and on the Plateau Rosa (3500m/11,487ft) near the Theodul Pass. A special thrill can be had with heli-skiing or by taking part in a high-altitude ski-tour. There are delightful cross-country ski-runs (including a night-track of 3km/nearly 2 miles, from Winkelmatten to Tutra) and about 50km/30 miles of ski-tracks. In addition there are two natural-ice skating rinks and several curling rinks.

Winter sports

Surroundings

★ Ascent of the Gornergrat

The rack-railway climbs the east side of the valley, crosses the Findelnbach on a high bridge and then runs through the curving Unteralp tunnel. 4km/2 miles): Riffelalp (2213m/7261ft), with a superb view of the Gabelhorn group. The line continues up the slopes of the Riffelberg in a wide curve, with ever more impressive views of the Matterhorn. (6km/4 miles): Riffelberg (2582m/8472ft) with the hotel of the same name. 7.5km/5 miles from Zermatt lies Rotenboden station (2819m/9249ft). A few minutes' walk

★ Gornergrat-bahn

★★ Gornergrat

below the station is the Riffelsee, with the pyramidal peak of the Matterhorn mirrored in its water (particularly fine in the morning). The line then runs high above the Gorner glacier to the summit station (9km/6 miles, 3089m/10,135ft), from which it is only a five-minute climb to the famous Gornergrat (3130m/10,270ft: observatory), a rocky ridge rearing above the Gorner glacier. From here there is one of the most magnificent panoramas in the whole of the Alps: in the middle the Matterhorn, with the Breithorn, the Zwillinge ("Twins" – Castor and Pollux), the Lyskamm and Monte Rosa to the left; to the north the peaks of the Mischabel group, including the Dom (4545m/14,912ft), the highest purely Swiss mountain; and to the west the mountains between the Zermatt and Zinal valleys.

Walks

The return walk from the Gornergrat to Zermatt is highly recommended; the path at first drops steeply (1½ hours) to the Findel Glacier Restaurant.

**★ Findeln
Glacier**

From here, a detour can be made uphill in ¾ hour to the steeply inclined Findeln Glacier (2298m/7542ft). From the restaurant the walk continues via the summer village resort of Findeln (2164m/7102ft) where cereals are grown (in winter a chair-lift goes down to the Sunnegga cabin) and, in another hour, Zermatt is reached.

Gorner Gorges

About ½–¾ hour south of Zermatt lie the Gorner Gorges through which thunders the Matter Vispa, the outflow of the Gorner Glacier.

★ From Zermatt to the Schwarzsee

**Schwarzsee
hotel
★ Panorama**

This tour on foot, an alternative to the cableway trip, lasts about three hours. The route follows the left bank of the Vispa and then the Zmuttbach, in ¼ hour it crosses the stream (magnificent view of the Matterhorn), and continues by way of the Sum See (1763m/5784ft) and Hermettji huts to the Schwarzsee hotel (2583m/8475ft) from which there are superb panoramic views. A few minutes' walk below the hotel is the little Schwarzsee (2552m/8373ft), with the guides' chapel of Maria zum See (18th c.). 2½ hours higher up are the Belvédère mountain inn (3263m/10,706ft) and the Hörnli hut (3260m/10,696ft: 50 sleeping places), starting-point for the ascent of the Matterhorn. An hour's walk to the north-west is the Staffelalp.

To the Staffelalp

★ Staffelalp

20 minutes above the Zum See huts on the road to the Schwarzsee take a road on the right which ascends through beautiful mountain forests, high up on the right bank of the Zmuttbach, to the Staffelalp (2206m/7238ft: restaurant), with a magnificent view of the Matterhorn and the Zmutt glacier, littered with rock debris. The Smuttbach has been dammed and harnessed to produce electric power.

To the Theodul pass

**★ Theodul
Glacier**

This tour lasts 5–5½ hours with a guide, but you can also use the cableway. First, in 1¼ hours to Hermettji then, in a further 2¼ hours at the moraine of the Upper Theodul glacier (Oberer Theodulgletscher, 2713m/8901ft), either with a rope directly across the much-crevassed glacier to the pass (2 hours) or via the Gandegg hut (3029m/9938ft: 1 hour) and over the glacier to the pass.

Theodul pass

The Theodul pass (Matterjoch, 3317m/10,883ft), which was already in use before the 4th c. A.D. lies on the frontier with Italy (magnificent views). From nearby Testa Grigia, a cableway runs down to Breuil (Italians' Cervina).

★ Breithorn

Popular tours from the Theodul pass include the ascent of the Breithorn (4165m/13,665ft; magnificent views) with a guide; to the Kleines Matterhorn (3884m/12,743ft; cableway); from Rotenboden station on the Gorner-grat railway in two hours to the Monte Rosa hut (2795m/9170ft) and from there in 6–6½ hours with a guide to the Dufourspitze (4634m/15,204ft), the highest peak in the Monte Rosa massif and in Switzerland, with one of the most breathtaking panoramas in the Alps.

★Dufourspitze
★Monte Rosa

Zofingen   K 5

Canton: Aargau (AG)
Altitude: 437m/1434ft
Population: 10,000

The great road and rail cross-country routes of Switzerland, Basle–St Gotthard–Ticino, and Lake Constance–Lake of Geneva, intersect in the lower Wigger valley, the most westerly point of the canton of Aargau.

Location and general

Of the twelve historic towns of Aargau, the old town of Zofingen is the most extensive. It was founded by the Counts of Frohburg who, in the third quarter of the 12th c., began to secure their lands to the north and south of the upper Hauenstein with eight new towns and several castles. The first known mention of the place was in 1175 or 1179; in 1201 the "Canonici de Zovingen" were acknowledged. As early as the 1st c. A.D. a Roman estate existed outside the line of the walls which were built later. During the Bernese domination, which lasted almost 400 years, the town was granted a certain measure of self-government and, in 1803, it was raised to the status of a district capital. From 1830, increasing industrialisation (printing, processing of textiles, chemical works and engineering, etc.) took place. Important educational buildings followed from the 19th to the mid-20th c., including, in 1974–78, the modern educational centre, embracing six schools, in the Wigger plain between Zofingen and Stengelbach.

History

Zofingen: Niklaus-Thut-Platz

Zofingen

Aarburg, Olten

Sursee, Lucerne

© Baedeker

1 Lower Town Gate (Lion Fountain)
2 Farmers' Guildhall
3 Strecke Tower
4 Old Chancellery
5 St Urbanof
6 Upper Town Gate (Officials' houses)
7 Weibelhaus
8 Archive Tower
9 Butchers' Guildhall
10 Thut Fountain
11 Neuhaus
12 Latin School
13 Former Parish Custodian's house
14 Sexton's house, old Guardhouse
15 Klösterli (little convent)
16 Powder Tower
17 Old Guardhouse
18 Museum

Sights

★ Thut Square

The very well maintained Old Town contains many attractive features. The broad Niklaus Thut Square, originally called "Am Spitzberg", forms the town centre. A fountain of the same name (1894) commemorates Mayor N. Thut who carried the town banner in 1386 at the Battle of Sempach.

Also to be seen here are the Baroque Town Hall (1792–95) by N. E. Ringer, with a Classical assembly hall, and the impressive former Butchers' Guildhall (c. 1602), the restoration of which was completed in 1985. Of the former steward's house at the north-east corner of Thut Square, only a small part (dated 1595) now remains. In its top storey is a glockenspiel of sixteen bells which has been working since 1985. The Neuhaus, built by Ringer in 1770, is now the headquarters of the Swiss Banking Union. The hand of the architect Antoni Stal can be recognised in the former municipal Assistance Office (1598–99).

Town Hall
Butchers'
Guildhall

The Market Hall (once the headquarters of the butchers) and a cloth-hall, later to become the library, form links to the Vorderer Hauptgasse (outer main street). The last named is a narrow Baroque building with a hipped roof and open arcades. Since reconstruction in 1984, the weekly market is accommodated here, together with banqueting and conference rooms.

Market Hall

The old 18th c. town chancellery, which adjoins on the west, was restored in 1982; it has a huge hipped roof and now serves as a local administration building.

Old Chancellery

The oldest parts of the Reformed Church of St Mauritius (restored 1981–83) are Romanesque but the building was greatly altered in the 14th and 15th c. In 1979, the roof of the church collapsed and this necessitated the reconstruction of the nave with a wooden roof, as well as making the west gallery smaller.

Town church

Interesting features of the church are the 16th c. choir, the crypt and the west tower. The last named was built in 1649 to a design by Antoni Tierstein; it is a prominent landmark and its oldest bell is dated 1409. Inside the church are six gallery windows of 1518, Late-Gothic choir-stalls, a new organ (1983) and fine stained glass (the middle window of the choir depicts a passion cycle in 12 parts, dating from about 1400). Near the church stands the Hans Bögli which was completely restored in 1985.

The old Schützenhaus (1825), built in mid-18th c. style, in which the municipal art collection is housed, is worth a visit, as is the museum in General Guisan Strasse 18 which has a comprehensive historical and natural history collection. Also of interest are the funeral hall of the old cemetery in the Schützenmasse, which dates from 1873 and which was restored internally in 1983/1985, the 19th c. Gemeindeschulhaus (parish schoolroom), the Küstorei (sexton's house). "Loffelberg" (now a regional centre), the St Urbanhof (which once served the established monastery of St Urban as a sexton's house), and the Lateinschulhaus (Latin school house) by A. Stab (1600–02), in which the civic library (established in 1693) has been housed since 1974 are all noteworthy.

Schützenhaus
Museum

In the Hintere Hauptgasse (outer main street) where the nobility once lived, the silk manufacturer J. A. Senn set up an alpine dairy, completed in 1732. In the domestic wing on the south side can be seen fine linen tapestries showing panoramic scenes and genre landscapes.

Sennerhof

Remains of an encircling wall, mentioned in the 13th c., are the Schwarz or Pulvertum (black or powder tower) a well-known landmark in the southeast of the town, and the Strecke or Folterturm (rack or torture tower), now part of the Jelmoli department store. In the area of the Oberer Tor (upper gate) which was demolished in 1846 stand two original cottages in the Classical style.

Town fortifications

Lovers of nature can relax in the nearby zoo above the town or they can enjoy walks in the neighbourhood (there is an excellent nature trail). From the hill known as the "Bergli" there are good views over the upper Wigger valley and the Alps.

Zoo

Zug

Lindengeviert   From the Lindengeviert in the Heiternplatz the view embraces the whole of
                    the Old Town and extends to the Jura.

Roman finds   Where the Hotel Römerbad now stands, there was in the middle of the first
                    century a Roman villa rustica. During excavations in 1826–27, three Roman
                    mosaic pavements were discovered; these were dug up and provided with
                    protective covers in the style of Grecian temples. The pavements were
                    re-protected in 1974. Finds from excavations can be seen in the museum.

Zug   M 5

Canton: Zug (ZG)
Altitude: 426m/1398ft
Population: 24,000

Location and   Zug, capital of the canton of the same name, lies at the north-east end of the
general   Zuger See (Lake Zug), above which rises the flat-topped ridge of the Zuger-
                    berg. Tax advantages have attracted over 1300 multi-national companies to
                    the town.

History   Zug was founded in 1242 by the counts of Kyburg. In 1273, it was inherited
                    by the Habsburgs and became an important stronghold against the forest
                    cantons which, in 1352, founded the confederation. In 1415, Zug was given
                    a charter as a free imperial town and when the canton was formed in 1803
                    Zug was made the capital.

Sights

Lakeside   From the lakeside promenade, there is a fine view of the Rigi, Pilatus and
                    the Bernese Alps (Eiger, Mönch and Jungfrau). The Landsgermeindeplatz

Zug: Kolinplatz; statue of Wolfgang Kolin

(citizens' assembly area), near the Stadt landing-place, was laid out to a new plan at the beginning of the 1980s; there are cafés and restaurants where visitors can relax.

By way of the fish market we reach the old town with its attractive burghers' houses and fountains. Several buildings are noteworthy: the Baroque gabled building of the municipal planning office (18th c.), the 16th–17th c. mint and the nearby Rococo Glorietti Pavilion, and the 16th c. Brandenberg House which has a Rococo façade and houses the African Museum (Oswaldgasse 17; open: Mon.–Fri.).

★**Old Town**

The Late Gothic Rathaus (town hall) was completed in 1505; in a council room on the top floor fine carvings of 1507 have been preserved. Also of interest are the Renaissance doorway and the panelling in the Small Council Chamber.

Rathaus

From here a gateway under the picturesque Zytturm ("Time Tower" (about 1200), with an astronomical clock) into the Kolinplatz where there is a fountain bearing the figure of the standard-bearer Wolfgang Kolin, who fell at the Battle of Arbedo against the Milanese.

Kolinplatz

To the south, stands the Late-Gothic St Oswald's church (1478–1545) a three-aisled basilica; the main doorway ("King's Portal") is decorated with beautiful sculptures depicting St Oswald and St Michael on either side of the Virgin Mary.

St Oswald's Church

Nearby (Kirchgasse 11) the so-called "Burg" (13th c. castle), once the official headquarters of the Kyburg and Habsburg governors, houses the historical and cultural museum of the town and the canton. The collection includes items of pre- and early history, stained glass, clocks, weapons, uniforms and implements used in agriculture and crafts. North-east of the Kolinplatz on a hill stands the Capuchin friary (1595–97) with a church dating from 1676.

Museum in the Castle

At Aegeristrasse 56 (open: Mon.–Fri.) is the Cantonal Museum of Pre-history, containing finds from the canton of Zug, dating from the Mesolithic era to the early Middle Ages. Among the exhibits are objects excavated from a Neolithic lakeside settlement and from the Roman estate of Cham-Hagendorn.

Cantonal Museum of Pre-history

The Fishery Museum at Untergasse 16 houses a small collection of fish and birds which inhabit Lake Zug (open only by appointment).

Fischerei-museum

The former 15th c. Corn Exchange at Untergasse 14 has been converted into a museum of art which mounts temporary exhibitions, specialising in 19th and 20th c. art of Zug and the heartland of Switzerland. Four watch-towers and remains of the walls of the old town fortifications can still be seen.

Kunsthaus

Those interested in bee-keeping should pay a visit to the Hotel Rosenberg, where the collection of the German-Swiss Bee-keeping Association is on display. The collection covers bee-keeping, the life and anatomy of bees and the production of beeswax.

Bee collection

Surroundings of Zug

To the south-east of the town is the Zugerberg (988m/3242ft), with pleasant woodland walks and views of the Alps, particularly from the Hochwacht. It can be reached either by the direct road up the hill (9km/6 miles) or by driving via Guggithal to Schönegg (3km/2 miles) and taking the funicular (2km/1 mile, 8 minutes). On the top stands the Zugerberg Hotel.

Zugerberg

Cham 5km/3 miles west on the Lucerne road (No. 4) we come to Cham (421m/ 1381ft; pop. 6500), at the junction of several roads. The church, built in 1786, has a slender steeple added in 1853. By the lake is the Schloss St Andreas, with a chapel of 1488 built on Carolingian foundations. The smart Villa Villette has, since 1988, been a meeting place and cultural centre.

Baar 3km/2 miles north of Zug is the little industrial town (textiles) of Baar (447m/ 1467ft). In the main street are the fine parish church of St Martin (14th c.), rebuilt in 1771) with a massive Romanesque tower with a Baroque helm roof, and the Town Hall (1676). In the cemetery stands a Late Gothic chapel (1507). An attractive excursion (7km/4 miles south-east) can be made over a hill covered with fruit-trees and the deep Lorzentobel gorge to the Höllgrotten ("Caves of Hell"; restaurant) with magnificent stalactitic formations.

From Zug to the Ägerisee

The distance to Oberägen is 13km/8 miles, to Schwyz 29km/18 miles, 4km/ 2 miles more than by the main road via Arth.

Leave Zug on a secondary road which runs east to Thalacker and crosses the Lorze gorge on a high bridge. In 5km/3 miles we reach Nidfurren (654m/ 2146ft). The road continues along the east side of the Lorze valley. 5km/ 3 miles: Unterägeri (729m/2393ft), a busy little village and holiday spot at
Ägerisee the north end of the charming Ägerisee (725m/2379ft; 5.5km/3 miles long). The road runs along the north east side of the lake.

Oberägeri About 3km/2 miles further lies Oberägeri (737m/2418ft), a village of 3500 inhabitants which is also a holiday resort. The road then crosses a low ridge which forms the boundary between the cantons of Zug and Schwyz, where, on November 15th 1315, the Battle of Morgarten was fought, marking the Swiss Confederates' first victory over the Habsburgs. On the shores of the lake is the Morgarten monument (1908), and on the pass are the Schlachtkapelle (battle chapel) of 1603 and a defensive tower of 1320.

Sattel Then comes Sattel (827m/2713ft), on the road from Pfäffikon, which con
Schwyz tinues south to Schwyz (9km/6 miles; bypass; see entry). Alternatively, take a road which branches off on the right in Sattel and winds its way down the southern slopes of the Rossberg (fine views of Rigi and the Mythen), passing through the hamlet of Ecce Homo (735m/2412ft; chapel of 1667) and the village of Steinerberg (629m/2064ft; pilgrimage church of 1570),
Arth and then continues past the scene of a great landslide at Goldau to Arth (11km/7 miles).

★Zuger See

The beautiful Zuger See or Lake Zug (417m/1368ft, length 14km/9 miles, area 38sq.km/15sq.miles, greatest depth 198m/650ft), extends south from Zug, its northern end surrounded by gentle hills, its southern end enclosed between the steep scarps of the Rossberg and the Rigi (see entry).

East shore 2½km/1½ mile south of Zurich, on the east shore of the lake is Zug-Oberwil (420m/1378ft), attractively situated at the foot of the Zürichberg, along the foothills of which the road now runs. To the right, on the west shore, can be seen Schloss Buonas (15th and 17th c.) and the little village of Risch; then comes the Kiemen peninsula jutting out into the lake. After 4km/2½ miles you pass the Restaurant Lothenbach, where the stream of the same name flows into the lake (waterfall), then the road passes through two short
Walchwil galleries and finally reaches the summer resort of Walchwil, a popular lakeside resort in a picturesque situation amid chestnut groves and vineyards.

Beyond Walchwil the boundary between the cantons of Zug and Schwyz is crossed, and you continue along the foot of the Rossberg, with fine views across the lake to the Rigi; to the right is Immensee near the "Hohle Gasse" (hollow road), and straight ahead is Arth.

At the southern end of Lake Zug lies Arth (420m/1451ft; pop. 3000), a little town which has grown up around an important road junction. It has a Baroque church dating from the late 17th c. The station of Arth-Goldau is the starting point of a rack railway up the Rigi (see entry).

Arth

★★Rigi

For the south-west shore of Lake Zug and Immensee, see Küssnacht am Rigi.

Zurich

M 4

Canton: Zürich (ZH)
Altitude: 410m/1345ft
Population: 360,000

Zurich (German spelling Zürich), Switzerland's largest city and capital of the canton of Zurich, is also the country's economic and cultural hub; but with all its bustling activity it is still one of the finest Swiss towns, with carefully cherished traditions and much to attract and interest the visitor. The town lies at the lower north-western end of Lake Zurich astride the river Limmat which flows out of the lake at this point, between the Uetliberg on the west and the Zürichberg on the east. It has both a University and the Federal College of Technology. Three of the five major Swiss banks have their head offices in the famous Bahnhofstrasse, one of the finest shopping streets in Europe. Zurich is also a great financial and industrial capital (mainly textiles, engineering and electrical equipment). In addition it is the country's leading tourist attraction, with about a million visitors a year. A fifth of the country's total national income is earned in Zurich.

★★Townscape
and general

Zurich is also the most important focus of communications in Switzerland. It has the country's largest airport; its railway station is on the great international through routes from Vienna and Munich to southern France and Spain and from Stuttgart to Milan; and a number of motorways meet at the city. The motorways all end, however, at the city boundary, since the citizens of Zurich – who have a large say in the matter – have been unable to agree on the line of an urban motorway. As a result, all through traffic has to find its way through the city, which can be very time-consuming. The suburban railway in course of construction is scheduled to be completed in 1994.

Communica-
tions

The city of Zurich has a total area of 92sq.km/36sq.miles. The population in 1892, before the incorporation of suburban communes, was 87,400. In 1960 the population of the enlarged city had risen to 440,170 – its highest point – but by 1987 it had fallen to 353,000 (840,320 for the whole urban area). Less than half the resident population belong to the canton of Zurich. Until the end of the 18th c. the population of Zurich was almost entirely Protestant but by 1979 the proportion of Roman Catholics had reached almost 40%, giving Zurich the largest number of Catholics of any town in Switzerland.

Area and
Population

Since 1830 Zurich has been capital of the canton of Zurich, the seventh largest of the Swiss cantons in terms of area (1729sq.km/668sq.miles) and the largest of them all in terms of population (1,131,000 (1987)). Situated in the Swiss Mittelland, it has a green and gentle landscape, reaching its lowest point in the Rhine valley (330m/1083ft) and its highest in the Schnebelhorn (1292m/4239ft). It has much to offer the visitor, with its charming little towns and neat villages, its beautiful countryside and well-kept vineyards.

Canton of Zurich

The earliest traces of human occupation on the site of Zurich were a Neolithic settlement excavated on the Bauschänzli, the little island in the

History

479

Zurich

Zurich: city centre astride the Limmat

River Limmat. The Roman fortified settlement of Turicum was established on the Lindenhof, where there had been a Roman military station as early as 15 B.C. According to the legendary story the town's patron saints Felix and Regula fled to Zurich with the Theban Legion and were beheaded there; their remains were preserved in the Grossmünster (begun not later than the 9th c.). The works of Hartmann von er Aue and the poems by other medieval minnesingers preserved in the Manesse Manuscript (written in Zurich but now in the University Library of Heidelberg) are a reminder of the great days of chivalry. The development of Zurich into a city state was given a considerable stimulus when the guilds obtained equal rights with the nobility after an assault on the Town Hall in 1336 and, in 1351, it became a member of the Confederation. In 1523 Ulrich Zwingli (1484–1531) established the Reformation in Switzerland and made Zurich one of the great cities of the Reformed faith, ranking equally with Wittenberg and Geneva. The town rose to prosperity through its silk and cotton industries; but when a federal state was established in the 19th c. the status of capital passed from Zurich to Berne. In the 18th c. Zurich became influential in intellectual life, with such figures as the theologian Johann Caspar Lavater, the educationalist Heinrich Pestalozzi, the great scholar Johann Jakob Bodmer and the writer Salomon Gessner. During the 19th and 20th c. the town continued to be a pivotal point of liberal thought, and among the notable personalities who stayed here were Gottfried Keller, Conrad Ferdinand Meyer, Georg Büchner, August Bebel, Lenin, James Joyce, C. G. Jung, Ludwig Klages and Thomas Mann. In 1916 the Dadaist school was founded in Zurich. In 1980 and 1981 serious confrontations occurred between young people and police (including the occupation and clearance of a youth centre). In June 1982 the autonomous Youth Centre of Zurich was closed.

One of Europe's most important newspapers, the "Neue Zürcher Zeitung", is published in Zurich. Founded in 1780 by Salomon Gessner, it now has an editorial staff of 100 and a circulation of some 145,000.

Newspaper

Shopping

The Bahnhofstrasse in Zürich is one of the most attractive streets in Europe for shopping. Here there are fashion houses, boutiques, department stores and specialist shops (especially jewellery, watches and clocks, shoes, furs and fashion accessories). Small boutiques and antique dealers can be found mainly in the old town to the south of the Lindenhof (Rennweg, Strehlgasse, Augustinergasse, St Petershof, Münsterhof) and north of the Grossmünster. The Limmatquai (right bank), with its fine guild houses, is also a favourite shopping street. Unusual articles and curiosities can be found in the side streets of the old town, in Oberdorf and Niederdorf, where there are many bars, cafés and restaurants. The Löwenstrasse district and the adjoining "Shopville" in the station subcourse is another popular shopping area. The pedestrian zone around the Oerlikon market place is only a few steps from the exhibition centre.

Local souvenirs are sold by the Schweizer Heimatwerk at Rudolf-Brun Bridge, Bahnhofstrasse 2, Rennweg 14 and at the airport.

A large flea-market is held every Saturday between 6am and 4pm on the Bürkliplatz from May until October and many handmade and exotic articles are on sale at the Rosenmarkt curiosities market (Thur. 10am–9pm; Sat. 10am–4pm).

Leisure and Sport

Among the sports and recreational activities available in Zurich are sailing on Lake Zurich and boating on the Limmat. There are football stadia in Letzigrund and Hardturm, a covered stadium and a race-track in Oerlikon. The Allment indoor sports complex is in Zurich-Wiedikon. Other facilities include a swimming bath with wave-making equipment and an artificial ice-rink in Dolde. There are covered municipal swimming baths at the Silhporte and in Oerlikon.

Museums, Galleries, etc.

Architectural Forum
(contemporary architecture, special exhibitions)
Wed.–Fri. 2–7pm. Thur. to 8pm, Sat. 11am–5pm, Sun. 11am–3pm

Art Gallery (Kunsthaus Zürich)
Heimplatz 2
Tues.–Thur. 10am–9pm, Fri.–Sun. 10am–5pm

Bärengasse Museum of Domestic Life (Wohnmuseum)
(Zürich domestic interiors 1650–1840)
Sasha Morgenthaler Doll Museum
Bärengasse 22, c/o Talstrasse
Sept. 16th–Dec. and Jan.–June 14th: Tues.–Sun. 10am–noon, 2–5pm, Sat. to 4pm only; June 15th–Sept. 15th: Tues.–Sun. 10am–5pm, Sat. to 4pm only (closed Mon.)

Bellerive Museum
(international applied and decorative art of the past and present; also special exhibitions)
Höschgasse 3, Seefeld
Tues.–Sun. 10am–5pm, Wed. 10am–9pm

Beyer Museum of the Measurement of Time
Beyer Watch and Clock Shop, Bahnhofstr. 31
Mon.–Fri. 10am–noon, 2–4pm

E. G. Bührle Collection
(European art, especially French 19th and 20th c, including Impressionists)
Zollikerstrasse 172
Tues., Fri. 2–5pm, Wed. to 8pm

Criminal Museum
Near the former barracks; adults only (by prior arrangement)
Mon.–Fri. 8–9am, 2–3pm; tel. 2 47 22 11

Foundation of Constructive and Concrete Art
(special exhibitions – see daily press for details)
Tiefenbrunnen, Seefeldstr. 317
Tues.–Fri. 2–5pm, Sat., Sun. 10am–5pm

Geological and Mineralogical Exhibition (ETI)
Sonneggstrasse 5
Mon.–Fri. 10am–6pm, Sat. 10am–4pm, closed Sun.

Graphic Collection (ETI) (old and modern prints and drawings)
ETH Head Office, E 52, entrance in Künstlergasse
Mon.–Fri. 10am–5pm, Wed. to 8pm

Haller Atelier (sculptures by Hermann Halle, 1890–1950)
Corner of Höschgasse/Bellerivestrasse
June–Aug. Wed.–Sun. 1–6pm

Johann Jacob Museum (history of coffee)
Seefeldquai 17 (corner of Feldeggstrasse)
Fri., Sat. 2–5pm, Sun. 10am–5pm

Mühlerama
(museum of the history and technique of milling, in the historic Tiefenbrunnen mill, near Tiefenbrunnen railway station)
Tues.–Sat. 2–5pm, Sun. 1.30–6pm

Municipal Collections of Succulents
Mythenquai 88
Daily 9–11.30am, 1.30–4.30pm

Museum of Decorative Arts (Museum für Gestaltung)
Ausstellungsstrasse 60
Tues., Thur., Fri. 10am–6pm, Wed. 10am–9pm, Sat., Sun. 10am–5pm

Museum of the Indians
(1500 exhibits relating to the culture of the North American Indians)
Schulhaus, Feldstrasse 89
During school terms: Wed., Sat. 2–5pm, Sun. 10am–1pm

Museum of Masks
(some 250 traditional Swiss masks by Paul Strassmann)
Obere Waldstrasse (opposite No. 9)
May–Oct. 1st Sun. in the month 10am–noon and by prior arrangement;
tel. 7 34 10 55

Museum of the Swiss Hotel Business
Trittligasse 8
Wed., Fri. 2–5pm, Sat. 11am–5pm, Sun. 11am–1pm

Museum of Tin Figures
(dioramas with military and civilian themes; exhibition describing the
manufacture of lead and tin figures)
Obere Zäune 19
Sat. 2–4pm, Sun. 11am–3pm

Museum of Zurich Municipal Drainage
Near the Werdhölzli sewage plant, Bändlistrasse 108
Mon.–Fri. 9am–4pm, by appointment; tel. 4 35 51 11

Pestalozzi Memorial Rooms
(manuscripts, original editions, personal possessions)
Beckenhofstrasse 33
Tues.–Fri. 2–5pm

Rietburg Museum (non-European art and Swiss masks)
Villa Wesendonck, Gablerstrasse 15
Tues., Thur.–Sun. 10am–5pm, Wed. 10am–9pm

Shedhalle
Seestrasse 395
(special exhibitions of international and Swiss contemporary art)
Tues.–Fri. 2–8pm, Sat., Sun. 2–5pm

Johanna Spyri Foundation (manuscripts, book illustrations, etc.)
Zeitweg 13
Mon.–Fri. 9am–noon, 2–5pm

Swiss National Museum (Swiss culture, art and history)
Museumstrasse 2, behind the main railway station
Tues.–Sun. 10am–5pm

Thomas Mann Archives (ETH)
Schönberggasse 15 (near the University)
Wed., Sat. 2–4pm

Toy Museum of Zurich
(18th–20th c. toys from Germany, France and Switzerland)
Corner of Fortunagasse 15/Rennweg 26
Mon.–Fri. 2–5pm, Sat. 1–4pm

Tram Museum in Zürich-Höngg (old trams)
Limmattalstrasse 260
Wed. 7.30pm–9pm, Apr.–Oct. on 1st Sat.in month 2–5pm

Werner Coninx Foundation
(collection of works by the painter and mason Werner Coninx, 1911–60)
Near Klusplatz
Jan.–June: Tues., Thur. 2–5pm; Mon., Wed., Fri. by arrangement;
tel. 2 52 04 68
Oct.–Dec. Wed.–Sat. 2–5pm, Sun. 11–5pm

Zunfthaus zur Meisen Ceramic Collection
Münsterhof 20, near the Fraumünster church
Tues.–Fri. 10am–noon, 2–5pm, Sat., Sun. 10am–noon and 2–4pm

Zurich Altstetten Chueri-Studer-Huus Local Museum
(furnished churches, farmhouse rooms, shoe-maker's workshop, black-smith's forge, rural implements)
Dachslernstrasse 20, opposite the swimming baths
Jan.–June, Oct.–Dec. 1st Sun. in the month

University of
Zurich

Anthropological Museum
Winterthurstrasse 190 (Zürich-Irchel)
Re-opened from July 1995: Tues.–Fri. 9am–5pm, Sat., Sun. 10am–4pm

Archaeological Collection
Rämistrasse 73 (near the University)
Tues.–Fri. 1–6pm, Sat., Sun. 11am–5pm
(cast replica collection: Mon.–Fri. 9am–8pm)

Botanical Garden
Zollikerstrasse 107
Oct.–Feb. Mon.–Fri. 8am–6pm, Sat., Sun. 8am–5pm;
Mar.–Sept. Mon.–Fri. 7am–7pm, Sat., Sun. 8am–6pm

Ethnological Museum (Völkerkundemuseum)
(exhibits from Africa, Oceania, Indonesia, India, Sri Lanka, China, Japan,
America and from the Polar regions)
Pelikanstrasse 40, in "Zur Katz" Park
Tues.–Fri. 10am–1pm, 2–5pm, Sat. 2–5pm, Sun. 11am–5pm

Medical Museum
Rämistrasse 69
Tues.–Fri. 1–6pm, Sat., Sun. 11am–5pm

Palaeontology Museum
Künstlergasse 16
Tues.–Fri. 9am–5pm, Sat., Sun. 10am–4pm

Zoological Museum
(Swiss fauna from the Ice Age onwards, with multivision shows and micro-
scopic displays)
Künstlergasse 16
Tues.–Fri. 9am–5pm, Sat., Sun. 10am–4pm

Sightseeing in Zurich

Zurich is a town for sightseeing on foot, since the principal places of
interest are on both sides of the river Limmat and on the north shore of Lake
Zurich.

West of the Limmat

The pulsating activity of the city is focused on the Bahnhofstrasse, a street
1.2km/³⁄₄ mile long (most of it pedestrianised) which extends from the main
station to the lake (landing stages). The middle section of the street was
built in 1867 after the filling in of an old moat, the Fröschengraben; the
lower part, towards the lake, was built from 1877 onwards, the upper part
towards the station from 1885.

    Among the interesting buildings in the lower part, dating from the turn of
the century are the Weber business premises (Nr. 75), built in 1899 by R.
Kuder and A. Müller (re-built 1912–13 and 1928) and the Jelmoli department store (Seidengasse 1) a complex of buildings which has been reconstructed several times; it was originally designed in 1897 by H. A. Stadler
and J. E. Usteri with a skeleton in iron. The historic façade (1913–16) of the
Peterhof and Leuenhof premises was the work of the brothers O. and N.
Pfister.

★Bahnhof-
strasse

In the basement of Nr. 21 can be seen a comprehensive collection of
timepieces belonging to the Beyer watch and clock business. The exhibits
range from sun, oil and water-clocks to Swiss clocks with wooden wheels
and Nuremberg pendulum clocks. There are also automata, navigational
instruments and clocks from the Far East.

Beyer Museum
of the
Measurement of
Time

In the lower part of the Bahnhofstrasse lies the Paradeplatz, with the
palatial headquarters of the Schweizerischen Kreditanstalt (1876) and the
Hotel Savoy Baur en Ville, built in 1838 and reconstructed in 1978. In
the 18th c., there was a cattle market on the Paradeplatz and, later, as its
name suggests, it was used as a parade ground.

Paradeplatz

The Konditorei Sprüngli is the heart of a chocolate empire which has its
chief factory in Kilchberg. The Sprüngli firm, the largest confectionery
concern in Switzerland was divided about a century ago to form the chocolate factory Lindt and Sprüngli (Rudolf Sprüngli) and the Sprüngli Confectionery, now headed by Richard Sprüngli. As well as the main shop in
the Paradeplatz (renovated in 1985), there are seven other shops belonging

★Konditorei
Sprüngli

Pestalozzi Memorial

Federal College of Technology

to the firm. Well-known confectionery specialities are: mouth-watering gâteaux, the delicious "Luxemburgerli" and Sprüngli's chocolate cubes "number one".

Urania
Observatory
Pestalozzi
Gardens

Towards the upper end of the Bahnhofstrasse, on the corner of Urania-strasse, stands the Urania Observatory and, to the west, are the Pestalozzi Gardens with a bronze statue (1899) of the famous pedagogue Heinrich Pestalozzi (1746–1827).

To the west of the Bahnhofstrasse, extending to the Sihlporte, is a district containing many commercial offices and the Börse (Stock Exchange). To the east, towards the Limmat, is the "Kleine Stadt" ("Little Town"), the western half of the old town.

Main Railway
Station

The main railway station (Hauptbahnhof), built 1865–71 on the site of Zurich's old station, is still equal to present-day needs. On its south side is the Bahnhofplatz, now reserved exclusively for traffic. In the square can be seen a monument (1990) to the Swiss statesman Alfred Escher (died 1882) by R. Kissing. Beneath the square is a pedestrian concourse with a modern shopping area ("Shopville"). The west façade of the station is being given an artistic "facelift". On the north side of the station is the Air Terminal (buses to Zurich airport 20 minutes).

**Swiss
National
Museum**
(See plan
page 488)

Immediately north of the station is the Swiss National Museum (Schweizerisches Landesmuseum), a large castellated building with Gothic elements which was built 1893–98 to designs by Gustav Gull. It contains the most important collection of material on the history and culture of Switzerland. The main departments in this richly stocked museum are as follows: pre-history and the early historical period; weapons, flags and militaria; goldsmiths' and silversmiths' work; articles in non-ferrous metals and pewter; ceramics and glass; textiles, costume and jewellery; coins and medals; seals; stained glass; sculpture; furniture and domestic interiors;

Swiss National Museum . . .   *. . . cannon of 1678*

painting and graphic art; clocks, watches and scientific instruments; musical instruments; rural life; craft and industrial antiquities; library; special exhibitions. Of particular interest among the scientific instruments are the celestial globe by Jost Bürgi (1552–1632), the works of religious art and medieval wall paintings (including works by Hans Fries), the unique collection of old stained glass, the Armoury, with the celebrated murals by Hodler, a series of period rooms of the Gothic to Baroque periods, the most important antiquities in Switzerland of pre- and early history, and the largest collection of coins and medals in the country.

Behind the National Museum we find the Platzpromenade, a public garden on the triangular spit of land between the Limmat and its tributary the Sihl. To the north-west extends the city's large industrial zone.

Platzpromenade

North-west of the station on the left bank of the Sihl, at Ausstellungsstrasse 60, is the Museum of Decorative Arts (Museum für Gestaltung) which, from time to time, puts on special exhibitions of graphic art, design, architecture and applied art. The museum has drawings and prints from the 16th c. to the present day (including book-illustrations, commercial art, popular art) and a notable collection of posters with some 70,000 examples, including posters by Toulouse-Lautrec. The applied art collection is housed in the Bellerive Museum (see p. 493).

Museum of Decorative Arts

Old Town (west)

Between the Bahnhofstrasse and the left bank of the Limmat extends the western half of the old town. In this area is to be found the quiet tree-shaded Lindenhof, the site of a Roman fort and later of an Imperial stronghold and, today, a popular place for a short excursion. From the terrace there is a fine view of the old town.

Lindenhof

To the south, on a little hill, stands St Peter's Church, the oldest parish church in Zurich. It has an early 13th c. Romanesque choir under the tower

St Peter's Church

487

Swiss National Museum

Schweizerisches Landesmuseum Zürich

Musée National Suisse Zürich

Museo Nazionale Svizzero Zurigo

Museum Naziunal Svizzer Zürich

Ground Floor

First Floor

A Stairs up to 2nd and 3rd floors

© Baedeker

BASEMENT

10	Special exhibitions
11–13	Old trades and crafts
11a	Milling: wine-growing (19th c.)
11b	Coachbuilding and blacksmithing (19th c.)
11c	Part of a Zurich armoury (16th–17th c.)
11d	Casting of non-ferrous metals
11e	Bells (12th–18th c.); tower clocks (16th–17th c.)
12a	Comb-maker's workshop (19th c.)
12b	Cooper's workshop (19th–20th c.)
13	Shoemaker's workshop (19th c.)

GROUND FLOOR

1a–3	Carolingian and Ottonian art (9th–10th c.); Gothic art, religious and secular (13th–14th c.)
4–9	Heraldry and geneaolgy; Zurich Arms Roll, etc.; Swiss pewter (16th–19th c.)
14	Council chamber from Mellingen (1467)
15	Cloister (c. 1240)
16–18	Rooms from Fraumünster abbey, Zurich (c. 1500)
19, 21	Transition from Gothic to Renaissance: portraits, furniture (16th c.)
22	Pharmacy (18th c.)
77–80	Temporary exhibitions of pre-history and early history
81	Objects of the Bronze Age (1800–800 B.C.)
82–83	Neolithic material (4th millennium to c. 1800 B.C.); bust of Ferdinard Keller (1800–81), founder of Neolithic archaeology and the theory of pile-dwelling

FIRST FLOOR

23	Stained glass, in particular from Tänikon convent (1557–59); clocks (16th–17th c.); globe from St Gallen abbey (c. 1569); keyed instruments (17th–18th c.)
24	Small room from Valais (15th c.)
25	Drawings, in particular sketches for stained glass (16th c.); bas-relief carving from the Dominican nunnery of Oetenbach, Zurich (1521)

26	Room from Casa Pestalozzi, Chiavenna (1585)
27	Room from Rosenburg, Stans (1602)
28	"Winter room" (bedroom) from Schloss Wiggen, Rorschach (1582); coats of arms (c. 1600)
29	Room from Alter Seidenhof, Zurich (1620)
30	Stained-glass panels (16th c.); wool embroidery; furniture (16th–17th c.); portraits by Samuel Hofmann (1624–32)
31	Painting of the alliance between Louis XIV and the Confederates in 1663; stained glass from the cloisters of the Cistercian nunnery at Rathausen (1591–1623; coin collection from the monastery of Rheinau (1745)
32	Zurich interior (18th c.); Zurich stove (c. 17th c.)
42	Door surround from Zurich (17th c.); special exhibitions
43	"Summer room" from the Lochmann-Haus, Zurich (c. 1660); celestial globe by Jost Bülgi (1594)
44	Upper Chapel: special exhibitions
45	Secular silverware of the late medieval period (to about 1700); gilded drinking-bowls from the convent at Sarnen (14th–15th c.)
46	Stained glass from the cloisters of the former Cistercian nunnery of Rathausen (1591–1623); painted furniture (18th c.); views of Zurich by Conrad Meyer (c. 1656)
47	Special exhibitions of graphic art; tiled stoves (18th c.)
48	Winterthur china (17th c.) and stoves; portraits and stained-glass panels
49	Items of historical interest, canton of Zurich (17th c.); pair of globes by Vincenzo Coronelli (1688); coats of arms (17th c.)
50	Armoury: development of arms and armour in Switzerland from 800 to 1800; Burgundian war: diorama of the battle of Murten (22.6.1476) with about 6000 tin figures
51	Uniforma of the federal arms (1815–60)

and a Baroque nave (three-aisled, with galleries) of 1705. In 1538 the church acquired the largest clock dials in Europe, 8.7m/29ft in diameter. The great preacher and writer J. C. Lavater (1741–1801) was pastor here for 23 years; his former house was the Hans zur Armbrust (Nr. 6) on the square outside the church.

To the south is the Münsterhof, a pleasant square in the Old Town, with a long history. On the Münsterbrüche (1838) over the Limmat stands a bronze equestrian statue (by H. Haller, 1937) of Burgomaster Waldmann (beheaded in 1489), under whose rule Zurich reached the peak of its power in the 15th c. — Münsterhof

On the south side of the square is the Fraumünster (restored 1965), a three-aisled pillared basilica with a Gothic nave (13th–15th c.), an Early Gothic transept and a pointed spire. The Fraumünster was given by the Emperor Ludwig (Louis) the German to his daughter Hildegard in 853 and, from that time until the high Middle Ages, the head of the convent was also governor of the town. — **Fraumünster Kirche**

In the imposing Late Romanesque choir are five stained-glass windows by Marc Chagall (1970). The undercroft contains remains of the crypt of the abbey church founded by the Emperor Ludwig (Louis) the German in 853. The abbey itself was demolished in 1898 to make way for the Stadthaus, but the Romanesque and Gothic cloister survives, with paintings of old Zurich legends by P. Bodmer (1928). — ★ Stained glass

On the north side of the Münsterhof (No. 20) is the Zunfthaus zur Meisen, a magnificent Late Baroque guild-house (by D. Morf, 1752–57) in the style of a French hôtel (town mansion) with a cour d'honneur, which now houses the Swiss National Museum's ceramic collection of the 18th c., (including Zurich work from the porcelain factory in the Schooren) near Kilchberg and a court of honour. — ★ Zunfthaus zur Meisen / Ceramic collection

On the west side of the square is another old guild-house (No. 8), the Zunfthaus zur Waag (1636; restaurant) with a stately Baroque doorway and Late-Gothic window-frames in the guild-hall. — Zunfthaus zur Waag

Zurich

★Bürkliplatz
Quaibrücke

From here the Stadthausquai leads south past the Bauschänzli summer restaurant to Bürkliplatz and the Quaibrücke, which crosses the outflow of the Limmat to Bellevue Platz on the opposite bank. In Bürkliplatz is the landing stage for the lake steamers on which visitors can take delightful trips on the lake (see Lake Zürich). To the south, in good weather, there is a splendid view over the lake to the Glarus Alps.

Weinplatz

From the Weinplatz, with the Weinbauer fountain (1909), we cross the Limmat on the Rathausbrücke (1878), successor to a series of earlier bridges which for centuries provided the only crossing. Along the banks of the Limmat are well-preserved old Burghers' houses, such as the "Schipfe" housing complex on the west bank which dates from the 17th–18th c.

Old Town (east)

Rathaus

At the east end of the bridge, overhanging the river on the right, is the Rathaus (Town Hall, 1694–98), a massive Later Renaissance building, with rich sculptured decoration, in which the cantonal and communal councils meet in public. The tastefully furnished Baroque ceremonial hall is well worth seeing.

Limmatquai

Along the Limmatquai, a popular shopping street, are a number of elegant old guild-houses with richly appointed interiors reflecting the wealth of the guilds which governed the town until 1789: at No. 54 the Haus zur Saffran (1719–23), at No. 42 the Haus zur Rüden (1660) and at No. 40 the two-storeyed Haus zur Zimmerleuten (1709: extended 1783–85; with a beautiful oriel window), all now housing restaurants. No. 62 is the Haus der Museumsgesellschaft (1866–68; rebuilt in 1965).

Wasserkirche

On the south side of the Münsterbrücke stands the Late-Gothic single-aisled Wasserkirche ("water church"), once entirely surrounded by the Limmat. It was not connected to the land until 1839 when the Limmat quay was constructed. In front of the choir is a bronze statue of 1885 to Ulrich Zwingli (1484–1531) Zurich's great Reformer. Built on to the north side of the church is the Helmhaus (1794), with an open fountain hall, in which special exhibitions are put on by the municipal authorities.

Helmhaus

Grossmünster

On an open terrace above the river stands Zurich's principal church, the Grossmünster (Protestant), which dominates the city with its twin towers (domed tops added in 1782). Built between the 11th and the 13th c., it is a Romanesque three-aisled galleried basilica with an aisleless chancel over a crypt of about 1100. The upper levels of the towers date from 1487. On the upper part of the south tower, on the side facing the river, is a seated figure of Charlemagne (copy: original in the crypt), who is believed to have founded the house of secular canons to which the church originally belonged; on the north side of the north tower is a figure of the Reformer Heinrich Bullinger. notable features of the church are the two modern bronze doors (1935–36), the sculptured Romanesque capitals, remains of Gothic wall-paintings and the Late Romanesque cloister (c. 1200). In the choir are three vividly coloured stained-glass windows designed by Augusto Giacometti (1933) and in the crypt is the badly weathered statue of Charlemagne.

From 1519 until his death in the Battle of Kappel in 1531 the great Reformer Ulrich Zwingli was a secular priest in the Grossmünster. His residence was close by, at Kirchgasse 13. The Neo-Gothic Grossmünster chapel (1858–59) was designed by J. J. Breitinger, the minster terrace is by A. Negrelli.

★ Streets in the
Old Town
Napfgasse

A walk through the eastern part of the the old town is full of charm and interest, with many excellent antique shops adding to its attractions. Going north up Münstergasse, we come to the Napfgasse, with the Brunnenturm,

Grossmünster: statue of Charlemagne   *Kunsthaus (art gallery)*

headquarters of the Lombard money-changers in the 14th and 15th c. The most interesting house is No. 6, the Haus zum Napt, which has fine interior furnishings, including rooms in Renaissance and Regency styles.

In the Spiegelgasse is a house (No. 17) in which Lenin lived in 1917. In this street, too, was the cabaret in which Hans Arp and Tristan Tzara launched the Dadaist movement in 1916.

Spiegelgasse

The Spiegelgasse runs east into the Neumarkt in which are the Shoe-makers' Guildhouse (No. 5), now the Theater am Neumarkt. The Hans zum Rech (No. 4), which dates from the High Middle Ages, now houses the town archives. The 13th c. Grimmenturm, (No. 27, restored in the mid 60s) was originally a residence.

Neumarkt

Town archives

Set back from the street, this house was the birthplace of the great Swiss writer Gottfried Keller (commemorative plaque); he was the first Chief Clerk of the canton of Zurich. Close by, at Rindermarkt 12, is the Oepfel-chammer restaurant, a favourite haunt of his.

Keller Haus

The house in which he died is at Zeltweg 27, south-east of the Heimplatz. Also in the Zeltweg lived the young authoress Johanna Spyri for 15 years; some of her work can be seen at No. 13, where the Spyri foundation is housed.

Zeltweg

Spyri Foundation

To the north of Neumarkt stands the Predigerkirche (1611–14), the Prea-chers' (i.e. Dominicans') church, an Early Baroque building with a Neo-Gothic tower. In 1917 the Gothic choir, which was added in the 14th c., became the home of the cantonal archives. Adjoining the church is the Central Library, on the site of a Dominican monastery. The buildings are in process of extension (completion envisaged in 1995); the restored main house in the Zähringerplatz will house a special collection and the North American Library; there will also be a public wing with reading rooms

Predigerkirche

Town archives

Zentral-bibliothek

along the Mühlgasse, an administration block between the Seilergraben and the Chorgasse. The High-Gothic choir of the Predigerkirche will be freed from its present additions and once again will be revealed in its full splendour. Between the Chorgasse and the inner courtyard of the choir a new pedestrian precinct will be a welcome addition to the Old Town.

Hirschengraben
Haus zum
Rechberg

To the east of the Neumarkt is the Haus zum Rechberg, Hirschengraben 40 (at the corner of Künstlergasse), which was built by D. Morf for the guild master J. C. Werdmuller amid terraced gardens between 1759 and 1790. It is Zurich's finest Rococo building and the most important secular building of the 18th c. In 1799 the house was occupied by French and allied generals and, in 1815, by the Emperor Francis I of Austria. Also of interest is the Hans zum Neuberg (No. 59/60) which dates from 1733 but rebuilt in 1818; Alfred Escher, the Zurich statesman, was born here. On the upper floor of No. 42, the Haus zum Krönli, built in 1739 and restored in the 19th–20th c., can be seen fine panelling.

To the south-east is the Conservatory of Music.

Heimplatz
★ Kunsthaus

A short distance south of the Conservatoire is the Heimplatz, on the south-west side of which we find the Art gallery (Kunsthaus), with an important collection of pictures and sculpture from antiquity to the present day. To the right of the entrance can be seen a large piece of bronze sculpture, the "Porte de l'Enfer" ("Gate of Hell") by Auguste Rodin (1880–1917). The institution, run by the Zurich Society of Arts with the aid of a public subsidy, goes back to a society of artists, founded in 1787; the "Künstlergüetli" gallery was established in 1847. The buildings were extensively enlarged in 1925, in 1954–58 and in 1976.

In addition to Swiss painters of the 19th and 20th c., such as J. H. Füssli, F. Buchser, R. Koller, A Böcklin, F. Hodler, C. Amiet, A. and J. Giacometti, M. Gubler and M. Bill, there are important works by E. Munch, O. Kokoschka and M. Beckmann. Also to be seen are paintings by French Impressionists, including Manet, Monet and Cézanne, international avant-garde artists of the 20th c. such as Klee, Mondrian, Picasso, Chirico, Matisse, Chagall, and many exhibits in a Dadaist collection. The department of modern sculpture since the time of Rodin has works by Moore, Picasso, Barloch, Maillot, Rodin, Segal, Caler and Tinguely. The graphic collection has about 80,000 drawings and prints by J. H. Füssli, S. Gessner, F. Hodler, F. Hegi, L. Corinth, A. Dürer, Raffael and Rembrandt, P. Klee, F. Glarner, C. Amiet, M. Klinger and the Zurich "concrete" movement.

Schauspielhaus

Facing the Art Gallery, on the south-east side of the square, is the Haus zum Pfauen (House of the Peacock: built 1888–89, reconstructed 1976–78), with the Schauspielhaus (theatre), one of the most renowned of German-language theatres, completely remodelled in the recent rebuilding (see plan page 493).

Colleges

From 1642 to 1833 Zurich was surrounded by a ring of ramparts and bastions. After the demolition of these fortifications the moats were filled in, and the town was able to expand beyond its former limits. The monumental complexes of the University and the College of Technology are the result of this wave of building activity in the 19th and 20th centuries.

University

From the Heimplatz, the Rämistrasse, coming from the Bellevueplatz, continues up to a terrace on which stands the University (founded 1838, rebuilt 1911–14), with a 64m/210ft high tower. The University buildings contain a number of museums and collections. Extensive new university buildings on the Irschel, in the Unterstrasse district, were brought into use in 1978. Zurich is the largest Swiss university – in 1988 there were some 19,000 matriculated students.

Federal College
of Technology

Immediately north of the University is the Federal College of Technology (Eidgenössische Technische Hochschule), founded in 1855, which now has

Schauspielhaus, Zurich

GROUND-FLOOR PLAN

1 Entrance
2 Box office
3 Shops (books, etc.)
4 Smoking foyer
5 Entrance to basement
   stage
6 Cloakrooms
7 Stairs to gallery
8 Orchestra pit
9 Raised podium
10 Store
11 Workshops
12 Properties
13 Rest rooms (men)
14 Rest rooms (women)
15 Entrance for actors and
   staff
16 Entrance to restaurant

© Baedeker

some 11,000 students. The two-storeyed building with wings was constructed by Gottfried Semper in 1860–64 in the Historism style, and extended in 1915–25 by Gustav Gull. Semper was also responsible for the Federal Observatory (Sternwarte; Schmelzbergstrasse 25). In the main building of the College of Technology is a comprehensive collection of graphic art (exhibitions). Geological and mineralogical collections are housed at Sonneggstrasse 5. Extensions to the college were built on the Hönggerberg to the north-west of the town. From the north-west corner of the main complex a funicular decends to the Limmatquai.

To the south of the University, at Schönbergstrasse 15, is the Haus Zum oberen Schönenberg, built about 1665 and occupied from 1756–83 by Johann Jakob Bodmer (1697–1783), a leading Swiss representative of the Enlightenment, who entertained Goethe, Klopstock and Wieland here. Since 1960 it has housed the Thomas Mann Archives, containing all the papers left by the north-German novelist who died in 1955.

Haus zum oberen Schönenberg

Thomas Mann archives

At the junction of the Rämistrasse with the Utoquai is the spacious Bellevueplatz, from which a lakeside promenade offering extensive views runs south along the east side of Lake Zurich under the name of Utoquai and, farther on, Seefeldquai. To the left stands the Neo-Baroque Opera-House (Oper), designed by the Viennese architects Fellner and Helmer and built within the space of 20 months in 1890–91.

★Lake Zurich, east shore

Opera House

About 1½km/1 mile from the Bellevueplatz is the beautiful Zürichhorn Park (landing stage; restaurant).

Zürichhorn Park

At Höschgasse 3 is the Bellerive Museum, with temporary exhibitions of craftwork from the Zurich Museum of Arts and Crafts (textiles, glass, ceramics). Of particular interest are exhibits in Art-nouveau style, modern Swiss ceramics, and musical instruments from the Hug collection.

Höschgasse Bellerive Museum

Hochgasse 6 is the Centre Le Corbusier (1967; Heidi Weber Haus), which is now used as a forum for community action.

Le Corbusier Centre Pavilion

At the junction of Höschgasse and Bellerivestrasse we find the studio of the sculptor Hermann Haller (1880–1950), with a collection of his work and the urn containing his ashes.

Haller-Atelier

493

Zurich

Heureka	Near the Zürichhorn restaurant is a gigantic piece of mechanical sculpture by Jean Tinguely, "Heureka" (1964: operates in summer at 11 and 5).
★ E. G. Bührle Foundation	800m/½ mile east of Zürichhorn Park, at Zolliherstrasse 172, is the E. G. Bührle Foundation, founded in 1960. The villa houses one of the richest private collections of European art, mainly assembled by the industrialist Emil G. Bührle (died 1965) and notable particularly for its 19th and 20th c. French pictures, including the Impressionists, E. Delacroix, G. Courbet, C. Carot, E. Manet, C. Monet, E. Degas, A. Renoir, P. Bonnard, as well as medieval 15th c. wooden sculptures.
Botanical Garden	To the north (entrance at Zolliherstrasse 107) extends the new botanical garden, belonging to the university, it contains more than 1½ million plants.
Lake Zurich, west shore	The lakeside promenade, which follows the west shore of the lake from the Bürkliplatz, bears the names of General-Guisan Quai and, further south, Mythenquai. Near the landing-stage used by the lake steamers stands the
Kongresshaus Tonhalle	Congress hall (Kongresshaus), opened in 1939, which is built on to the older Tonhalle (1895) and is one of the major focal points of the social life of Zurich, with concerts, conferences and festive occasions of all kinds.
Belvoir Park	On the Mythenquai are the headquarters of a number of large insurance corporations, and above it lies Belvoir Park, with old trees, subtropical plants and a restaurant.
Rieter Park ★ Rietberg Museum	Above this again, beyond the Seestrasse, we find Rieter Park, at the north end of which, in the Gablerstrasse, is the Rietberg Museum, housed in a Neo-Classical villa modelled on the Villa Albani in Rome. It was built in 1857 for a German industrialist, Otto Wesendonck and is reputed to be an exact copy of the Roman Villa Albani. The villa originally served as a meeting place for the intellectual elite of Zurich, including Wagner and Conrad Ferdinand Meyer. In 1952 it was acquired by the city of Zurich and now contains the fine collection of Baron Eduard von der Heydt. The exhibits of non-European art include Indian sculpture, temple pictures and bronzes from Tibet, Chinese grave decorations, Buddhist steles, ceramics and jade, as well as carvings, masks and bronzes by African tribes, and craftwork from the Pacific, the Near East and North America.
Municipal Collection of Succulents	Farther along the Mythenquai at No. 88 is the Municipal Collection of Succulents.
Muraltengut	At Seestrasse 203, the Muraltengut has reception rooms which are used by the Zurich Town Coucil.
Rote Fabrik Cultural Centre	Seestrasse 409 houses the popular Rote Fabrik Cultural Centre; concerts by rock groups, salsa, Reggae and other modern musical movements take place here. In addition, there is a small palaeontological collection in the building.

Surroundings

Zürichberg	To the east of the city rises the Zürichberg (679m/2228ft), a wooded hill with houses reaching far up its slopes and a number of restaurants commanding extensive views. From the Central Station and the Paradeplatz there are
★ Zoological Garden	tram services (respectively Nos. 5 and 6) to the Zoo, one of the finest in Europe (opened 1929), with more than 2000 animals.
Fluntern Cemetery	Near here are various sports facilities and the Fluntern Cemetery, with the grave of the Irish writer James Joyce (1882–1949).
Dolder	From the Römerhofplatz a funicular 1328m/1453yd long serves the Waldhaus Dolder (548m/1798ft), an hotel from which it is possible to continue on

foot to the Dolder Grand Hotel, the golf course, the artificial ice rink and the
swimming pool with wave-making equipment.

From the Winterthurerstrasse another shorter funicular ascends to the
Rigiblick (586m/1923ft; view of the Rigi). **Rigiblick**

To the south-west of the city rises the Uetliberg (871m/2858ft) the most **★Uetliberg**
northerly summit in the Albis ridge. The Uetlibergbahn, a mountain rail- **Uetlibergbahn**
way, runs from Selnau station to the upper station at 816m/2677ft, from
which it is a ten-minute walk to the summit (restaurant). In clear weather
there is a superb view from the lookout tower over the Vallais, Bernese and
Glarus Alps, with the Black Forest to the north and the Säntis to the east.
From here there is an easy ridge walk of just over one hour to the Felsenegg
(790m/2592ft), from which a cableway descends to Adliswil (see Lake
Zurich). The return to Zurich is by the Sihltalbahn (Zürich-Selnau to **Sihltalbahn**
Sihlbrugg).

From the Stadelhofen station in Zurich another electric railway, the Forch- **Forchbahn**
bahn, runs south-east via Forch to Esslingen in the Zurich Oberland. There
are many marked trails in the countryside around Forch.

There are rewarding half-day and full-day motor-boat trips to be made on **★Lake Zurich**
Lake Zurich (see entry). For information contact the Zürichsee-Schiffahrt-
gesellschaft, Mythenquai; tel. 4 82 10 33.

11km/7 miles north of the city centre (reached by rail – holiday card valid – **★Zurich Airport**
or by bus from the Central Station), at Kloten (482m/1582ft) is Zurich (See plan
Airport, one of the ten largest airports in Europe. It is the headquarters of page 496)
Swissair, the Swiss National Airline.

The total area of the airport is some 800ha/1977 acres. Construction
began in 1945, and by 1948 two runways were ready for service. There were
major extensions in 1958, 1971 and 1980. There are now three runways in
service each 60m/197ft wide; the longest is the blind-landing runway
(3700m/4048yd). There are two terminals equipped with shops, restaurants
and service facilities: terminal A (with multi-storey car park A) for Swissair and its associated airlines Austrian, SAS, Delta Airlines, Singapore
Airlines and also by Crossair; terminal B (with multi-storey car park B) for
all other airlines and charter flights. On the second floor of car park B is a
large shopping area with a bank and a post office. Under the airport plaza
lies the railway station concourse and below this (18m/59ft below ground
level) four railway lines with 420m/1378ft of platforms. Adjoining car park B
is the bus station. On the radiating arm of terminal B is an observation deck,
and also the departure point for bus tours of the airport and sightseeing
flights. About 16,000 people are employed by the airport and on peak days
more than 50,000 passengers pass through it.

For flight information: tel. (01) 1 57 10 60.

South-east of Zurich Airport, on the Hegnau road, lies Dübendorf military **Dübendorf,**
airfield, with the museum of the Swiss Airforce. The exhibits include air- **Airforce**
craft, engines, power plants, photographs, documents, navigational in- **Museum**
struments and models illustrating the development of military aviation
since 1910 (open: Tues.–Fri. 1.30–5pm, Sat. 9am–5pm, Sun. 1–5pm).

West of Zurich, to the south of the Berne motorway are two small industrial **Schlieren,**
towns, now part of the city. 8km/5 miles west is Schlieren (pop. 12,500), **Dietikon**
with factories making trucks and elevators, and 12km/7 miles west is
Dietikon (pop. 25,000).

18km/11 miles north-west of Zurich, on an eastern spur of the Lägern hills **★Regensberg**
lies Regensberg (612m/2008ft; pop. 500), one of the best preserved medieval towns in the country which was founded about 1245 by the Barons of
Regensberg. The round tower (21m/69ft high) of the old 16th–17th castle
and the 57m/187ft-deep draw-well (the deepest in the country) in the upper

Zurich

Internationler Airport Zurich

Oberglatt

Ober-glatt

Bülach   Bülach   Bülach

N 1b

V.-Piste (3300 m)

Blindlandepiste (3700 m)

Westpiste (2500 m)

Private flying

Fracht

Terminal A

Observation Tower

Terminal B

Parkhäuser

Kloten

Rümlang

Workshops

SBB Railway line

Werft

Embrach Bassersdorf

Regensberg

Glatt

Oil tanks

Glatt-brugg

© Baedeker

Zürich   Zürich

ward date from the time of its building. The church, originally 13th c., was rebuilt in 1506. Among the carefully restored old burghers' houses the half-timbered "Rote Rose" house (1540), with the Rose Museum of the painter Lotte Günthard, is particularly notable.

The sleepy old town of Greifensee (437m/1434ft; pop. 5500) lies 15km/ 9 miles east of Zurich on the north-eastern shore of the lake of the same name (area 8.6sq.km/3sq.miles; depth 34m/112ft; nature reserve). The castle was once the seat of the provincial governor Salomon Landolt. The church (c. 1330), in High Gothic style, has an unusual triangular plan. Trips on the Greifensee can be made in the motor ship "Heimat" or in the steam ship "Greif" which was restored in the mid 1980s.

Greifensee

About 5km/3 miles south-east of Greifensee is the town of Uster (pop. 23,000).

Uster

Lake Zurich

M–O 4/5

Cantons: Zürich (ZH), St Gallen (SG) and Schwyz (SZ)

Lake Zurich (in German Zürichsee), which was gouged out by the Linth glacier during the last Ice Age, extends for a total length of 39km/24 miles in a beautiful pre-Alpine setting. With a maximum width of 4km/2 miles, it has an area of 88sq.km/34sq.miles (Unterer See 68sq.km/26sq.miles, Obersee 20sq.km/8sq.miles) and a depth of up to 143m/469ft. Its principal tributary, the Linth, rises in Glarus, flows through the Walensee and continues into Lake Zurich as a canal. The lake is drained at the north-west end by the Limmat which flows into the Aare. Although the lake lies in a densely populated region, with about a million inhabitants of the cantons of Zürich, St Gallen and Schwyz living on its shores, a third of its shoreline is still freely accessible.

★Situation and general

The passenger boat services on Lake Zurich (Mythenquai 33, CH-8038 Zürich; tel. (01) 4 82 10 33) are operated with modern motor vessels and also old steamships. They serve both shores as far as Rapperswill from Easter to October and, in the high season, also the Obersee.

Boat Services

North-east shore

The north-east shore of the lake, with an almost continuous succession of attractive towns and villages lying below vineyards and orchards and a whole string of beaches, is popularly known as the "Gold Coast" because of the many wealthy people who have houses here.

The first place beyond Zurich is Küsnacht (427m/1401ft; see Zurich), a town of 12,000 inhabitants, with a church first mentioned in the records in 1158. The present building dates from the 15th c. and has wall-paintings in the choir. Also of interest are the "Höchhus", a 15th c. tower house, and a former commandery of the Knights of St John, now a teachers' training college.

Küsnacht

3km/2 miles south-east lies Erlenbach (415m/1362ft), beautifully set at the foot of the vineyards belonging to the "Zur Schips" estate (sumptuous banqueting hall in the house) with Mariahalde, an elegant country house in Neo-Classical style (1770).

Erlenbach

5km/3 miles beyond this we come to the chief town of the district, Meilen (423m/1388ft; pop. 10,000). The Protestant church by the lake was given to Einsiedeln Abbey by the Emperor Otto the Great in 965; the choir in its present form dates from 1493–95.

Meilen

Old steamer on Lake Zurich

From Meilen a steep road (5km/3 miles) goes up to the Pfannenstiel (853m/2799ft), the highest peak on the north side of the lake, from which there are extensive views. There is a car ferry to Horgen on the south side of the lake.

Stäfa

About 7km/4 miles south-east is Stäfa (417m/1368ft; pop. 7000) the largest commune on the north side of the lake, taking in Uerikon, Oetikon and many small hamlets. The reformed church, restored in the 1980s, stands on a hill overlooking the village. The origins of the Classical parish church go back to the period before the end of the first millennium and show that the church, dedicated to St Verena, was owned by Einsiedeln Monastery. In Uerikon, on the lake, are two interesting old manor-houses and a 16th c. chapel.

Rapperswill

9km/6 miles east of Stäfa is Rapperswill (see entry), where the Winterthur road comes in on the left. From here a causeway (930m/1017yd long) crosses between the main part of Lake Zurich and the Obersee on the left to the peninsula of Hurden. Here there is a fishing village popular with summer visitors (chapel of 1497), and Pfäffikon, from which it is possible to return to Zurich either by the lakeside road or by the motorway.

Hurden
peninsula

North shore

Jona

From Rapperswill the route continues along the north shore of the Obersee into the canton of St Gallen, to the industrial district of Jona in the fertile area at the mouth of the river Jona. Here also are the former Cistercian nunnery of Wurmsbach (16th–17th c.), now occupied by a girls' boarding-school, and the 15th c. church of St Dionys, with wall-paintings of the same date. At the east end of the lake lies the village of Schmerikon (415m/1362ft).

Wurmsbach

Uznach

At the east end of the lake in the Linth plain we reach the neat little town of Uznach (414m/1358ft), with the Kreuzkirche (1494–1505) and a cemetery

chapel of 1679. Quite near the town stands the modern Benedictine missionary house of St Otmarsberg. From the road junction at Kaltbrun, to the
south-east, it is possible to continue either north via Ricken to Wattwil or
south via Näfels to Glarus (see entry).

South-west shore

From Zurich (see entry) road 3 follows the south-west shore of the lake past
a long string of old villages and modern villas surrounded by gardens, with   Kilchberg
many beaches. In 6km/4 miles it reaches Kilchberg (427m/1401ft) on the
hillside to the right of the road. This was the home of the Swiss writer
Conrad Ferdinard Meyer (1825–98) from 1875 onwards, and the German
novelist Thomas Mann (1875–1955) and his wife (d. 1980) spent the last
years of their lives here. Their graves are in the churchyard on the south
side of the little church.

The "Chocoladeforum" (open: Mon.–Thur. 9am–4pm, by prior arrangement; tel. (01) 7 16 22 33) provides interesting details on the story of
chocolate.

Beyond this is the village of Rüschlikon (435m/1427ft), with the well-known   Rüschlikon
IBM works near the Zurich–Sargans motorway. The research centre of the   IBM Research
International Business Machines Corporation is one of the leading labora-   Centre
tories of the American multi-national concern. In 1986 the two IBM
researchers G. Binnig and H. Rohrer received the Nobel prize for physics for
their raster-tunnel microscope which was developed in Rüschlikon, and
one year later two other physicists working in the laboratory, J. G. Bednorz
and K. A. Müller, won the Nobel prize for their super-conductor for electric
current.

In the local cemetery lies the Swiss industrialist G. Duttweiler (1888–
1962), who founded in 1925 the Migros food company.

3km/2 miles further on is Thalwil, a small town of 13,000 inhabitants with an   Thalwil
old-established silk industry.

5km/3 miles beyond Thalwil is Horgen (411m/1348ft; pop. 16,000) a long   Horgen
straggling industrial township with a Baroque church of 1782 containing
fine frescoes of 1875. In the local museum by the lake (Alte Sust, Bahnhofstrasse 27) can be seen prehistoric finds from the lakeside settlement of
Horgen as well as exhibits of local handicraft. There is a car ferry to Meilen
on the north shore of the lake.

The road then passes the village of Käphnach (415m/1362ft) on the right,   Au Peninsula
and the attractive Au Peninsula on the left. In the first house on the left past   Museum of
the bridge a museum of viticulture has been established, presenting   Viticulture
visually the work of vintners (care of vines, cellarage, bottling, marketing)
with the appropriate equipment and a complete cooper's workshop.

In another 5.5km/3 miles is Wädenswil (411m/1348ft), an industrial town of   Wädenswil
15,000 inhabitants. Above the town the Neues Schloss (1518) houses the
Federal Fruit-Growing Viticultural and Horticultural Research Station.

In Wädenswiler Grüntal the first Swiss fruit-liqueur museum (Mostorama)   Mostorama
was opened in 1988. Here the refining of local-grown fruit and the development of its use is explained from its inception up to the present.

From here a road branches off to the right over the Hirzel-Höhe (750m/
2461ft) to Sihlbrugg (18km/11 miles).

About 4km/2 miles further on is Richterswil (411m/1348ft), beautifully   Richterswil
situated in a cove of the lake. Above the village are two churches from the
terraces of which there are fine views.

A road on the right climbs 3km/2 miles south-east to Wollerau (507m/   Wollerau
1663ft) with a Neo-Classical church (1787), and then winds its way steeply
up, with fine views, for another 3km/2 miles to Schindellegi.

The road to Pfäffikon beyond Richterswil enters the canton of Schwyz and continues along the side of the lake which here attains its greatest width (4km/2 miles).

Freienbach

In 1.8km/1 mile it reaches Bäch beyond which is Freienbach (416m/1365ft) with a Baroque church. Then the islets of Ufenau and Lützelau come into view and straight ahead can be seen the peaks of the Tuggenburg range.

Pfäffikon

Then in 2km/1 mile the road reaches Pfäffikon (415m/1362ft; pop. 4000) at the southern end of the causeway across the lake, with the castle (13th c. tower) which belonged to Einsiedeln Abbey. At the northern end of the causeway is Rapperswil (see entry). The local museum on the Pfäffikersee is open on the 1st and 3rd Sun. in the month, and by arrangement; the typewriter museum is open by arrangement; tel. (01) 9 50 36 00.

South shore

The road continues along the south side of the lake, known beyond the causeway as the Oberer Zürichsee or Obersee (upper lake), passes the Etzelwerk power station and comes to Altendorf (430m/1411ft). 1.5km/1 mile beyond this off the road to the left is Lachen. On a hill to the right (505m/1657ft; road half-way up) stands the 15th c. St John's Chapel, which was built on the ruins of the old castle of Alt-Rapperswil (destroyed 1350).

Lachen

3km/2 miles further on is Lachen (420m/1378ft; bypass), attractively situated on the Obersee; it has a fine twin-towered Rococo church (1700–10), designed by the Thumb brothers of Vorarlberg.

North-east of Lachen at the east end of the lake is Uznach.

Alphorns ▶

Practical Information

Accommodation

Hotels	See entry
Holiday homes, Chalets	Details of terms for individual holiday homes and chalets can be obtained from local tourist offices in Switzerland (see Information) or from travel agencies at home.
Inexpensive accommodation	250 Swiss hotels and guest-houses have joined to form the "Leistungs-gemeinschaft Einfach und Gemütlich" (The Cheap and Cheerful Group). A list of addresses can be obtained from the Swiss National Tourist Office (see Information).
Holidays on the farm	Information about farmhouses providing holiday accommodation can be obtained from the Swiss National Tourist Office (see Information).
Student accommodation	The Swiss Student Travel Service offers inexpensive overnight accommo-dation in some Swiss towns. Informative brochures can be obtained from the Swiss National Tourist Office (see Information) or from SSR-Reisen (Hotel Dept., Postfach, CH-8026 Zürich; tel. (01) 2 97 11 11.
Group accommodation	The Swiss National Tourist Office (see Information) can provide lists of group accommodation. Accommodation for groups requiring full board, half-board or self-catering can be arranged without charge by: Kontakt Lupsingen, Gartenstr. 15, CH-4419 Lupsingen; tel. (061) 9 11 88 11.
Family holidays	The brochures "Hotels speziell für Familien" (Special Hotels for Families) and "Klub kinderfreundlicher Hotels" (The Child-friendly Hotels Club), issued by the Swiss National Tourist Office (see Information), provide details of accommodation suitable for children.
Accommodation in Castles	Visitors who have never before tried a holiday in a traditional historic setting should consult the information leaflet "Hotels und Restaurants in Schlössern" (Hotels and Restaurants in Castles) and "Hotels in histori-schen Bauten" (Hotels in Historic Buildings), available from the Swiss Tourist Office (see Information).
Camping	See entry
Accommodation for the Handicapped	See Help for the Handicapped
Youth Hostels	See entry

Air Lines

Swiss Air	Swissair (Schweizerische Luftverkehr AG) Zentralverwaltung Balsberg CH-8058 Zurich-Flughafen Tel. (01) 8 12 12 12

Agents at all Swiss airports
Crossair AG
CH-8058 Zürich-Flughafen
Tel. (01) 8 16 43 43

 Crossair

Agents in Basle (tel. (061) 3 25 36 40), Berne (tel. (031) 9 61 55 16), Geneva (tel. (022) 7 89 88 31), Lugano (tel. (091) 50 50 01)

Central Bahnplatz 3–4
CH-4000 Basle. Tel. (reservations) (061) 22 40 11

British Airways

13 rue de Chantepoulet
CH-1200 Geneva. Tel. (reservations) (022) 31 40 50

Bahnhofstrasse 100
CH-8000 Zürich. Tel. (reservations) (901) 2 11 40 90

Air Travel

Switzerland is linked to international air services through the airports of Zurich (Kloten) and Geneva (Cointrin). The airport Basle/Mulhouse is shared by France and Switzerland. There are excellent connections between Zurich (Kloten) airport (rail station directly beneath the airport) and Zurich main station. Geneva and Basle rail stations can be reached from the corresponding airports by a regular service of Swissair buses. Since 1987 there has also been a direct rail connection with Geneva (Cointrin) airport.

Airports

Since 1988 passengers travelling by Swissair and/or Swiss rail can effect all the customs formalities at the stations of Zurich, Geneva, Berne, Lausanne, Lugano, Lucerne, Neuchâtel and St Gallen.

Fly luggage

Geneva-Cointrin International Airport

Airlines

— Swissair
— Crossair

Air connections — Swissair not only flies international routes but also some internal stretches. The regional airline Crossair provides inland air connections and also flights into neighbouring countries. There are air services between the following towns in Switzerland:

Basle–Geneva, Basle–Zurich; Berne–Lugano; Geneva–Basle, Geneva–Lugano, Geneva–Zurich; Lugano–Berne, Lugano–Geneva, Lugano–Zurich; Zurich–Basle, Zurich–Geneva, Zurich–Lugano.

Regional airfields — The regional airfields of Berne-Belp, Birrfeld, Grenchen, La Chaux-de-Fonds/Le Locle, Lausanne-Blécherette, Lugano-Agno, Gstaad-Saanen, Samedan-St Moritz and Sion are only used by charter companies.

Pleasure flying — Information about pleasure flying can be obtained from the Aero-Club der Schweiz (AeCS), Lidostrasse 5, CH-6006 Lucerne; tel. (041) 31 21 21.

Banks

See Currency

Boat Excursions

General — There are boat services on the larger lakes and rivers. All ships have restaurants and provide full meals as well as evening round trips (often with dancing). The leaflet "Viel mehr aufs Schiff" and timetables both for special trips and trips on steamships can be obtained from the Swiss tourist bureaux (see information).

Inland Shipping Services — See map page 594. A selection of special excursions and trips operated by the various shipping companies (with addresses) are given below:

See The Rhine

Three-lake trip (Lake Bienne, Lake Neuchâtel and Lake Morat) at a special price with lunch; visit to St Peter's Island; trip on the River Aare from Bienne to Solothurn. Special features include breakfast or "brunch" and fondue trips.

Lake Bienne
(Bieler See)

Information:
Bieler-See-Schiffahrt-Gesellschaft (BSG)
Badhausstrasse 1
CH-2500 Biel/Bienne
Tel. (032) 22 33 22

Other excursions and further information see Lac de Neuchâtel (Neuen-berger See).

Excursions by the SBB ships of the "White Fleet", for example on the flagship "St Gallen", the motorship "M/S Thurgau", Zürich or "Säntis", to places on Lake Constance.

Lake Constance

Special attractions: In the high season on Tuesdays from Romanshorn whole day Folklore cruise on the "Schwäbischen Meer"; Trips on the car ferry Romanshorn–Friedrichshafen; Fondue (Sundays), Advent, and New Year trips.

Information:
Bodensee-Flotte SBB
Bahnhof-Romanshorn
CH-8590 Romanshorn
Tel. (071) 63 14 23.

Schweizerische Schiffahrtsgesellschaft on the Untersee and Rhine – see Rhine.

See Lake Thun and Lake Brienz.

Lake Brienz

The shipping company of Lake Geneva (CGN) has the largest paddle-wheel fleet in Western Europe, (four steam ships and four with diesel-electric motors).

Lake Geneva
(Lac Léman)

Special Attractions:
Whole day cruises, for example with a visit to Geneva, Lausanne, Montreux, Evian, Chillon Castle and Yvoire; midday cruises; firework cruises; cruises with special entertainment and a programme changing each year.

Information:
Compagnie Générale de Navigation sur le Lac Léman (CGN)
17 Avenue de Rhodaie
CH-1000 Lausanne 6
Tel. (021) 6 71 04 65

Geneva Office:
Jardin Anglais
CH-1204 Geneva
Tel. (022) 3 11 25 21

Round trips from Maur, Fällenden, Greifensee, Uster and Mönchaltdorf.

Greifensee

Information:
Schiffahrtgenossenschaft Greifensee (SGG)
Verwaltung
CH-8124 Maur
Tel. (019) 80 01 69

Boat Excursions

Hallwilersee

Cruises on the Hallwil Lake

Information:
Schiffahrtgesellschaft des Hallwiler Sees (SGH)
Delphinstrasse 224
CH-5616 Meisterschwanden. Tel. (057) 27 12 56

Lake Maggiore

Day trips, etc., from Locarno to Stresa and to the Italian markets of Luino, Cannobio and Verbania-Intra. Connections (also by hydrofoil) between the Swiss Brissago Islands and the Borromean Islands of Italy.

Information:
Navigazione Lego Maggiore
c/o Fart, CH-6600 Locarno. Tel. (093) 31 61 40

Lake Lugano

Cruises without break of journey; cruises with stops in Gandria, Campione, Morcote, Swiss in miniature (Melide).

Special attractions: Ticino evenings.

Lac de
Neuchâtel and
Lac de Morat

The shipping company of Lake Neuchâtel and Lake Morat operate principally on Lake Neuchâtel; numerous round trips are organised however, on Lake Morat and Lake Bienne.

Information:
Société de Navigation sur les Lacs de Neuchâtel et Morat SA
Case postale 1460
CH-2001 Neuchâtel. Tel. (038) 25 40 12

and Bieler-See-Schiffahrtgesellschaft (BSG).

The Rhine

The vessels of the Schweizerische Schiffahrtgesellschaft Untersee und Rhein ply between Konstanz–Stein am Rhein–Schaffhausen and vice versa. The river between Schaffhausen and Stein am Rhein is considered one of the most beautiful stretches of water in Europe.

Information:
Schweizerische Schiffahrtgesellschaft Untersee und Rhein
Freier Platz 7
CH-8202 Schaffhausen. Tel. (053) 25 42 82 and 25 80 56

Throughout the year the Basler Personen-Schiffahrts-Gesellschaft Kurs operates regular services and special trips. There are also day trips to Mulhouse and Breisach on the programme.

Particular attractions: Fondue-Ländler (dancing) and Spaghetti trips.

Information:
Basler Personen-Schiffahrts-Gesellschaft AG
Blumenrain 2
CH-4001 Basel. Tel. (061) 2 61 24 00

Lake Thun and
Lake Brienz

From Spring to Autumn there are regular trips on Lake Thun and Lake Brienz every day.

Special attractions: Midday round trips from Thun; evening round trips in summer; special trips for groups, firms, wedding parties; day tickets and season tickets on the lakes. All valid tickets issued both in Switzerland and abroad can be used on the regular ships.

Information:
Thuner See und Brienzer See
Schiffsbetrieb der Lötschbergbahn (BLS)
CH-3604 Thun. Tel. (033) 36 02 58

See the Rhine

The shipping company of the Lake of the Four Forest Cantons (Lake Lucerne) has a large fleet of nostalgic paddle-wheel steamers in which you can visit well known holiday spots and historic sites dating from the foundation time of the Swiss Federation around the lake.

Special attractions: Midday and evening trips with Folklore and dancing. Wilhelm Tell Express (See Railways): You travel by steamer from Lucerne to Flüelen; and here you change into the train (saloon cars) to Lugano/Locarno. The connection can be made daily in both directions from May to October.

Special attractions in winter: Every Friday at 7pm a fondue ship operates; New Year cruises with a gala dinner or a Spaghetti fiesta. During the winter season there are several regular services daily between Lucerne and Brunnen.

Information:
Schiffahrtgesellschaft des Vierwaldstätter Sees (SGV)
Werftestrasse 5
CH-6002 Luzern
Tel. (041) 40 45 40

The Lake Zug Shipping Company provides both breakfast trips (Schiffs-Zmorge) and an interesting evening circular programme from May to November; on Wednesdays and Fridays (at 8pm from Zug): Chinese Fondue, Risotto and Spaghetti Plausch, summer nights buffet, dance trips, raclette and fondue parties and the Lake Zug Metzgete.

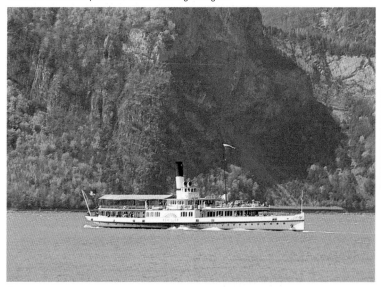

Steamer trip on Lake Lucerne

Information:
Schiffahrtgesellschaft für den Zuger See (SGZ)
ZVB-Haus an der Aa
CH-6304 Zug. Tel. (042) 26 25 25

Lake Zurich

There are regular services by steamship on Lake Zurich.
Further attractions: from May to October every Tuesday there are culinary evening trips (e.g. a "fondue cruise"); a cruise with dancing to a live orchestra from June to September, and many more.

Trips on the River Limmat: There are daily timetabled services from the Schweizerisches Landesmuseum (near the main station) to Zurichhorn–See–restaurant Enge and back to the Schweizerisches Landesmuseum.

Information for trips on Lake Zurich and on the River Limmat:
Zürichsee-Schifffahrtgesellschaft (ZSG)
Mythenquai 333
CH-8038 Zürich
Tel. (01) 4 82 10 33

A car ferry between Horgen and Meilen makes it easy to cross from the west to the east bank of the lake (or vice versa) in a few minutes.

Information for ferry services:
Zürichsee–Fähre Horgen–Meilen
Schulhausstrasse 7
CH-8706 Meilen. Tel. (019) 23 27 77

Business Hours

Banks

Banks in the larger towns are usually open from Monday to Friday from 8.30am to 4.30pm. They are closed on Saturday. Elsewhere banks have the same opening hours, but generally close from noon until 2pm. Some remain open until 5.30pm. In important business centres banks often remain open during lunch time.
  At airports and rail stations exchange offices may be open from 6am to 9pm and often until 11pm.

Offices

Offices of all kinds are normally open on Monday to Friday from 8am to noon and from 2 to 5 or 6pm.

Shops

Shops are usually open on Monday to Friday from 8 or 9am to 6.30pm. On Saturday they close at 4pm. Stores and some other shops in large towns are closed on Monday morning; once a week they remain open until 9pm.

Outside town centres and in smaller places shops and offices are generally closed for one or two hours at lunch time. In most holiday centres there are often exceptions to general business hours, and shops remain open longer in the evenings and for an hour or two on Sunday.

Post Offices

See Post

Public Holidays

See entry

Camping

Switzerland has at present over 500 camping sites, of which 90 remain open in winter. Most sites are administered by the Swiss Touring Club (see Information), the Swiss Camping and Caravan Association (SCCV), Habsburgerstrasse 35, CH-6000 Lucerne 4; tel. (041) 23 48 22 or by regional camping clubs.

The above can supply the "Swiss Camping and Caravan List"; this is also obtainable from the Swiss National Tourist Office (Schweizerische Verkehrszentrale – SVZ; see Information).

Information can also be obtained from the Verband Schweizer Campings (Sydefsdeli 40, CH-8037 Zurich 10; tel. (01) 44 57 13).

For motoring regulations for caravanners see Motoring.

Spending a night other than on an approved camping site, with the exception of a single night, in several cantons, is generally not allowed. It is best to contact the nearest police station for details of local regulations.

Car Rental

Basel   Avis
Basel-Mulhouse-Freiburg Airport; tel. (061) 3 25 28 40
Hotel Hilton, Aeschengraben 31; tel. (061) 2 71 22 62

Berne
Wabernstrasse 41; tel. (031) 3 72 13 13

Geneva
Geneva-Cointrin Airport; tel. (022) 7 98 23 00
Rue de Lausanne 44; tel. (022) 7 31 90 00

Lausanne
Avenue de la Gare 50; tel. (021) 3 20 66 81

Lugano
Hotel Albatro, Via Clemente Maraini 8; tel. (091) 22 62 56

Lucerne
Zurichstrasse 35; tel. (041) 51 32 51

Zurich
Zurich-Kloten Airport; tel. (01) 8 13 00 84
Gartenhofstrasse 17; tel. (01) 2 42 20 40

Basle   InterRent/
Basle-Mulhouse Airport; tel. (061) 3 25 29 03   Europcar
Hochstrasse 48; tel. (061) 3 61 66 60

Berne
Laupenstrasse 22; tel. (031) 3 81 75 55

Crans-Montana
Garage-Continental; tel. (027) 41 51 51

Geneva
Geneva-Cointrin Airport; tel. (022) 7 98 11 10
Rue de Zürich 36–38; tel. (022) 7 31 51 50

Lausanne
Place de la Ripone 12; tel. (021) 3 23 71 42

Locarno
Vaggio Verbano, Piazza Muraccio; tel. (093) 31 88 44

Lucerne
Garage Epper, Horwerstrasse 81; tel. (041) 41 14 33

Castles and Châteaux

Lugano
Via San Gottardo 101; tel. (091) 57 47 65

Zurich
Zurich-Kloten Airport; tel. (01) 8 13 20 44
Josefstrasse 53; tel. (01) 2 71 56 56

Hertz

Basle
Nauenstrasse 33; tel. (061) 2 71 58 22

Berne
Kochergasse 1; tel. (031) 3 11 33 13

Geneva
Rue de Berne 60; tel. (022) 7 31 12 00

Lausanne
Parking de Montbenon; tel. (021) 3 20 66 51

Lugano
Via San Gottardo 13; tel. (091) 23 46 75

Lucerne
Maihofstrasse 101; tel. (041) 36 02 77

Zurich
Zurich-Kloten Airport; tel. (01) 8 14 05 12

Castles and Châteaux

1 Coppet: Castle (17th c.)

2 Crans: Castle (18th c.)

3 Nyon: Castle (12th c./16th c.)

Castles and Châteaux in Switzerland

4 Prangins: Castle (18th c.)

5 Rolle: Castle (13th c.)

6 Morges: Castle (13th c./16th c.)

7 Vufflens-le-Château: Castle (14th c./15th c.)

8 Lausanne: Episcopal Castle (14th c./15th c.)

9 La Tour de Peilz: Castle (13th c.)

10 Montreux: Chillon Castle (11th c./13th c.)

11 Aigle: Castle (13th c.)

12 St-Maurice: Castle (15th c.)

13 La Sarraz: Castle (11th c./16th c.)

14 Oron-le-Châtel: Castle (13th c.)

15 Gruyères: Castle (13th c./15th c.)

16 Bulle: Castle (13th c.)

17 Romont: (13th c./16th c.)

18 Lucens: Castle (15th c./16th c.)

19 Yverdon: Castle (13th c.)

20 Grandson: Castle (13th c./15th c.)

21 Estavayer-le-Lac: Castle Chenaux (13th c./15th c.)

22 Murten/Morat: Castle (13th c.)

23 Gorgier: Castle (14th c./19th c.)

24 Boudry: Castle (16th c.)

25 Neuchâtel: Castle (12th c./15th c./17th c.)

26 Valangin: Castle (12th c./16th c.)

27 Erlach: Castle (13th c.)

28 Nidau: Castle (16th c./17th c.)

29 Porrentruy: Castle (13th c./14th c./16th c.)

30 Delémont: Castle (18th c.)

31 Rotberg: Castle (14th c.)

32 Erschwil: Thierstein ruined rastle (13th c.)

35 Dornach: Dorneck ruined castle (14th c.)

36 Prattein: Castle (14th c.)

37 Farnsburg: Ruined castle (14th c.)

38 Sissach: Ebenrain Castle (18th c.)

40 Balsthal: Ruined castle of Neu-Falkenstein (13th c.)

41 Oensingen: Bechburg Castle (14th c.)

42 Wangen an der Aare: Castle (17th c.)

43 Landshut: Castle (14th c.)

44 Hindelbank: Castle (18th c.)

45 Burgdorf: Castle (12th c./13th c.)

46 Jegensdorf: Castle (13th c.)

47 Worb: Castle (14th c.)

Castles and Châteaux

48 Oberdiessbach: Castle (17th c.)

49 Burgisten: Castle (16th c.)

50 Thun: Castle (12th c./15th c.)

51 Oberhofen: Castle (12th c./18th c.)

52 Spiez: Castle (12th c./16th c.)

53 Sion: Valère Castle (12th c.)

54 Sion: Tourbillon ruined castle (13th c.)

55 Interlaken: Castle (18th c.)

56 Brig: Alpine Castle (17th c.)

57 Hospental: Ruined castle (13th c.)

58 Attinghausen: Ruined castle (13th c.)

59 Altdorf: A Pro Castle (16th c.)

60 Schwanau: Ruined castle (13th c.)

61 Küssnacht: Gesslerburg ruins (12th c.)

62 Kriens: Schauensee Castle (13th c./16th c.)

63 Willisau: Castle (17th c.)

64 Gelfingen: Heidegg Castle (12th c.)

65 Hallwil: Castle (9th c./16th c.)

66 Horben: Castle (18th c.)

67 Aarburg: Castle (11th c.)

68 Aarau: Schlössli (13th c./15th c.)

69 Lenzburg: Castle (11th c./16th c.)

70 Wildegg: Castle (12th c./17th c.)

71 Bad Schinznach: Habsburg (11th c./13th c./16th c.)

72 Baden: Landvogteischloss (15th c.)

73 Baden: Stein ruined castle (13th c.)

74 Regensburg: Castle (16th c./17th c.)

75 Schaffhausen: Castle Munot (16th c.)

76 Walaltingen: Schwandegg Castle (14th c./17th c.)

77 Stein am Rhein: Burg Hohenklingen (12th c.)

78 Mammern: Liebenfels Castle (13th c./16th c.)

79 Steckborn: Turnhof Castle (14th c./17th c.)

80 Mannenbach: Arenenberg Castle (16th c.)

81 Märstetten: Altenklingen Castle (16th c./19th c.)

82 Frauenfeld: Castle (14th c./15th c.)

83 Winterthur: Hegi Castle (12th c./16th c.)

84 Sennhof: Kyburg (11th c.)

85 Hagenwil: Wasserburg (13th c.)

86 Arbon: Schloss (13th c.)

87 Nottwil: Schloss Wartensee (16th c.)

88 Gossau: Schloss Oberberg (13th c.)

89 Uster: Schloss (16th c.)

90 Rapperswil: Schloss (13th c.)

91 Näfels: Freulerpalast (17th c.)

92 Werdenberg: Schloss (13th c./16th c./17th c.)

93 Sargans: Schloss (12th c.)

94 Maienfeld: Schloss Salenegg (17th c./18th c.)

95 Haldenstein: Schloss (16th c.)

96 Klus: Burg Fragstein (ruined: 13th c.)

97 Zizers: Schloss Marschlins (13th c./17th c.)

98 Trimmis: Burg Liechtenstein (ruined: 14th c.)

99 Chur: Bishop's Palace (18th c.)

100 Rhäzüns: Schloss (13th c.)

101 Rothenbrunnen: Schloss Ortenstein (15th c.)

102 Rodels: Schloss Rietberg (12th c.)

103 Strada: Burg Jörgenberg (ruined: 12th c.)

104 Brigels: Burg Kropfenstein (ruined: 12th c.)

105 Zignau: Burg Riggenberg (ruined: 13th c.)

106 Mesocco: Ruined castle (11th c./12th c.)

107 Bellinzona: Castello Grande (13th c.)

108 Bellinzona: Castello di Montebello (13th c.)

109 Bellinzona: Castello di Sasso Corbaro (14th c.)

110 Locarno: Castello Visconti (15th c.)

111 Promontogno: Ruined castle (13th c.)

112 Sils: Burg Ehrenfels (ruined: 12th c.)

113 Thusis: Burg Hohen-Rhätien (ruined: 12th c.)

114 Mulegns: Burg Marmels (ruined: 11th c.)

115 Filisur: Burg Greifenstein (ruined: 13th c.)

116 Surava: Burg Belfort (ruined: 15th c.)

117 Zernez: Schloss Wildenberg (17th c./18th c.)

118 Ardez: Burg Steinsberg (ruined: 13th c.)

119 Tarasp: Schloss (16th c./18th c.)

For further details see entries in A–Z section.

Caves open to the public, Zoos and Alpine Gardens

○ **Caves open to the public (selection)**

1 Grotte de Milandre in Boncourt north-west of Porrentruy. Sinter formations, underground river.

2 Grotte de Réclère, near Réclère south-west of Porrentruy. Stalagtites.

3 Grotte de l'Orbe, near Vallorbe. Sinter formations, underground river.

4 Grotte aux Fees, near St-Maurice. Sinter formations, underground river.

Caves, Zoos and Alpine Gardens in Switzerland

5 Grotte de St-Léonard, in St-Léonard. Gypsum cave, underground river.

6 Beatus Caves, west of Interlaken. Sinter formations, underground river.

7 Sandstone Cave, near Göschenen. Mountain crystal cave with quartz, calcite and chloride strata.

8 Höllgrotten, north-east of Zug. Sinter formations.

9 Hölloch, near Muotathal, south-east of Schwyz. Sinter formations, fossils and an underground river.

10 Kristallhölle, near Oberriet. Limestone crystals, underground lake.

○ Zoological Gardens and Mini-Zoos (a selection)

11 Basle. Zoological Gardens. Animals from all over the world; terrarium, aquarium.

12 Basle. Tierpark, Lange Erlen. Deer, llamas, etc.

13 Reinach. Tierpark. Deer, birds.

14 Roggenhausen. Hirschpark. Red deer, wild pigs.

15 Zofingen. Hirschpark. Red deer.

16 Langenthal. Hirschpark. Red deer, wild pigs.

17 La Chaux-de-Fonds. Parc au Bois. Wild pigs, ibex, etc., vivarium.

18 Biel. Tierpark Bözingenberg. Ibex.

19 Studen. Tierpark Seeteufel (Zoo). Beasts of prey, aquarium, etc.

20 Berne. Tierpark Dählhölzi. European animals; aquarium, terrarium.

21 Le Vaud. Zoo la Garenne. European animals, birds of prey.

22 Lausanne. Vivarium (reptiles).

23 Lausanne. Sauvabelin Deer Park. Red deer, etc.

24 Servion. Zoo. Beasts of prey, red deer, etc.

25 Les Mareecottes. Reno Ranch. Mountain animals, wolves, bears.

26 Mitholz. Alpine Wildlife Park. Mountain animals.

27 Interlaken. Alpine Wildlife Park. Ibexes, marmots.

28 Brienz. Wildlife Park. Mountain animals.

29 Zurich. Zoological Gardens. Animals from all over the world, aquarium, terrarium.

30 Langnau am Albis. Langenberg Wildlife Park. Red deer, wild pigs, bears, etc.

31 Zug. Deer and Bird Park. Red deer, exotic birds.

32 Goldau. Nature and Animal Park. Red deer, wild pigs.

33 Hoch-Ybrig. Wildlife Park. Native animals.

34 Rapperswil. Children's Zoo. Mini-Zoo with dolphinarium. Deer Park near the castle.

35 Wald. Zoological Gardens. Kurhaus Tenne with a private Zoo.

36 Winterthur. Wildlife Park. Bruderhaus/Eschenberg.

37 Frauenfeld. Zoo plättli. Beasts of prey, monkeys, etc.

38 Oberglatt. Vivarium Python. Reptiles.

39 Gossau. Walter-Zoo. Beasts of prey, monkeys, etc.

40 St Gallen. Peter and Paul Wildlife Park. Native animals.

41 Piz Lagalb. Alpinarium. Alpine animals.

○ **Alpine Gardens**

42 Basle. University Botanical Gardens.

43 Weissenstein. Juragarten.

44 Aubonne. Arboretum.

45 Lausanne. Botanical Garden.

46 Geneva. Conservatoire et jardin botaniques.

47 Rochers de Naye. Jardin alpin Rambertia (Botanical Garden).

48 Pone-de-Nant. Jardin botanique alpin La Thomasia (Alpine Botanic Garden).

49 Champex. Jardin Alpine Floralpe (Alpine Garden).

50 Bourg-St-Pierre. Linnea Alpine Garden.

51 Riederalp. Aletschwald.

52 Neuchâtel. University Botanic Garden.

53 Fribourg. University Botanic Park.

54 Berne. University Botanic Garden.

55 Schynige Platte. Alpine Garden.

56 Grüningen. Botanic Garden and Arboretum.

57 St. Gallen. Botanic Garden.

58 Braunwald. Alpine Rose Garden.

59 Vaduz (Liechtenstein). Nature Park.

60 Davos. Alpine Garden.

61 Alp Grüm. Alpine Garden.

Congresses and Conferences

Congresses | Eighteen places in Switzerland have facilities for congresses. These are Basle, Berne, Biel/Bienne, Bürgenstock, Davos, Engelberg, Flims, Geneva, Grindelwald, Interlaken, Lausanne, Leysin, Lugano, Lucerne, Montreux, St Gallen, St Moritz and Zurich.

Details can be obtained by sending for the information brochure "Swiss Congress" of the Swiss Tourist Bureaux (see Information).

Trade Fairs | Dates of trade fairs open to the public are in the annual calendar "Messeplatz Schweiz" which can also be obtained from the Swiss Tourist Bureaux.

Currency

Currency | The unit of currency in Switzerland and Liechtenstein is the Swiss franc (German, Schweizer Franken; French, franc suisse; Italian, franco svizzero) of 100 rappen or centimes. There are banknotes for 10, 20, 50, 100, 500 and 1000 francs and coins in denominations of 5, 10, 20 and 50 rappen/centimes and 1, 2 and 5 francs.

Rates of Exchange | Rates of exchange frequently vary and can be found in national newspapers, at banks and at tourist bureaux.

Currency regulations | There are no restrictions on the import or export of either Swiss or foreign currency.

Eurocheques | It is advisable to take Eurocheques or travellers' cheques. Eurocheques can be made out up to an amount of 300 Swiss Francs. With a Eurocheque Card cash can be obtained from machines at banks.

Credit Cards | Banks, many hotels, restaurants, shops and car rental firms accept most international credit cards (Diners Club, American Express, Visa, Access, etc). The most widely used credit card in Switzerland is the Eurocard.

Customs Regulations

Visitors to Switzerland may take in duty-free personal effects such as clothing, toiletries, sports gear, cameras and amateur movie cameras with appropriate films, musical instruments and camping equipment, provisions for one day's requirements, other goods taken in as gifts up to a value of 100 Swiss francs (with the exception of meat and certain other foodstuffs), and (if over 17 years of age) 2 litres/3½ pints of alcoholic beverages up to 15%, 1 litre/1½ pints over 15% and 200 cigarettes or 50 cigars or 250 grammes/9 ozs of tobacco (double these quantities for visitors from outside Europe).

Diplomatic and Consular Offices in Switzerland

United Kingdom | *Embassy*

Thunstrasse 50,
CH-3000 Berne
Tel. (031) 44 50 21–26.

Consulates

37–39 rue de Vermont (6th floor),
CH-1211 Geneva. Tel. (022) 7 34 38 00.

Via Maraini 14A, Loreto,
CH-6900 Lugano. Tel. (091) 54 54 44.

15 Bourg Dessous,
CH-1814 La Tour-de-Peilz/Montreux
Tel. (021) 54 12 07.

Dufourstrasse 56,
CH-8008 Zurich. Tel. (01) 47 15 20–26.

Embassy

Jubiläumstrasse 93,
CH-3005 Berne. Tel. (031) 43 70 11.

United States of
America

Consulates

1–3 avenue de la Paix,
CH-1200 Geneva. Tel. (022) 7 33 55 37.

Zollikerstrasse 141,
CH-8008 Zurich. Tel. (01) 55 25 66.

Embassy

Kirchenfeldstrasse 88,
CH-3005 Berne. Tel. (031) 44 63 81.

Canada

Electricity

Current in Switzerland is supplied at 220 volts AC; 50 Cycles. Since English
plugs will not fit Swiss sockets an adaptor is necessary and can be obtained
from a suitable dealer.

Emergencies

There are emergency telephones on all Swiss motorways and on the more
important mountain roads.

Tel. 117

Police

Tel. 118

Fire Brigade

Tel. 144

Medical Service

Tel. 140

Breakdown

In urgent cases the Swiss radio transmitters will broadcast SOS calls.
Police and automobile clubs have details.

SOS on Radio

Zurich, tel. (01) 3 83 11 11

The Swiss Air
Rescue Service
(SRFW)

Geneva, tel. (022) 7 35 80 00

Alarm Head-
quarters (TCS)

Events

January	Many places: "Greiflet", "Dreikönigsplöder" (Three Kings Chatting) and "Dreikönigs-singen" (Three Kings Singing) – Fertility Rite January 6th. Basle: Vogel Gryff Hallwil: Bärzelitag (Bärzeli's Day). Kandersteg: Fur Market. Lausanne: Ballet Prize of Lausanne (international competition for late-developing artists). Lauterbrunnen: Inferno-Rennen (Ski-ing from the Schilthorn Summit). Meisterschwanden: Meitlisunntig. Mürren: Inferno ski-run (12km); Swiss Curling Championship. Pontresina, Samedan, St Moritz: Schlitteda. Schwanden: Bärzelitag (Bärzeli's Day). Solothurn: Film Festival. Umäsch: Silvesterkläuse (New Year Celebrations).
January/ February	Gstaad: International Ski Jumping.
February	Carnival and Lent: processions and masquerades (at many places). Altdorf: Cat Music in Lent. Ascona: Risotto eating on the Piazza of Ascona, Losone and Arcegno (this is Shrove Tuesday). Basle: Basle Carnival beginning on the Monday after Ash Wednesday at 4am with the "Morgenstraich" der "Cliquen", "Guggenmusiken" and "Schnitzelbänke" (parade through the old town by the Carnival Guilds accompanied by fifes and drums). Bellinzona: Carnival with risotto eating in the open air. Bienne/Biel: Carnival. Einsiedeln: Carnival with distribution of bread. Lugano: Carnelvale (Carnival) with risotto eating in the open air for everybody. Lucerne: Carnival with masquerades. Morat/Murten: Carnival with processions. Bad/Scuol/Schuls-Tarasp-Vulpera: Hom Strom (Chasing Winter away: first weekend in February). Solothurn: Carnival with processions.
Holy Week and Easter	Processions (at many places).
March	Basle: Trade Fair Geneva: Salon Internationale de l'Automobile (10 days) Glarus: Fridolinsfeuer (St Fridolin's Fire March 6th) Grisons: many places Chalandarmarz (Spring Festival March 1st) Lausanne: International Festival of Tourism.
March–July	Lugano: Primavera Concertistica di Lugano (Spring Concerts).
April	Appenzell: Landsgemeinde (Communal Assembly). Basle: Art and Antiques Fair; Clocks and Jewellery Fair; "Eiermarkt" (Egg Market) before Easter. Glarus Canton: Näfelserfahrt (Memorial Festival for the victory over the Austrians in 1388). Hundwil, Trogen; Landsgemeinde (Communal Assembly). Sarnen: Landsgemeinde (Communal Assembly). Stans: Landsgemeinde (Communal Assembly). Zurich: Sechseläuten (Six o'clock ringing).

"Basler Morgenstraich" – an annual festival

Processions (at many places).	**Corpus Christi**
Many places, May Day Celebrations (First Sunday).	**May**
Berne: International Jazz Festival; Geranium Market.	
Baden: Swiss Amateur Film Festival.	
Escholzmatt, Entlebuch, Schüpfheim: Wyberschiessen (Women's Shooting).	
Glarus: Landsgemeinde (Communal Assembly).	
Lausanne: International Opera Festival.	
Montreux: "Golden Rose" Music Festival.	
Zurich: Summer Festival.	
Lausanne: International Music weeks.	**May–June**
Wallis: Cow fights (at many places).	
Alpine processions (at many places).	**June**
Baar: Costume Festival.	
Basle: ART (International Arts Exhibition); Town Festival.	
Berne: Small Stage Festival.	
Bienne/Biel: 100km run from Biel (Braderie, Folk Festival).	
Geneva: Jazz Festival (summer jazz concerts in the "Jardin Anglais", 1 week).	
Locarno: Floral Parade.	
Lucerne: Nocturnal Festival with fireworks on the lakes.	
Morat/Murten: Battle Festival (Youth Festival with floral procession, June 22nd); Shooting Festival commemorating Battle of Mürten.	
Neuchâtel: Drum and Fife Festival of Western Switzerland.	
Wallis: Midsummer Eve Bonfire (at many places).	
Zurich: International Festival Weeks; Night Festival on the Lake.	
Dornach: Faust Pagen Play (every three to four years).	**June–July**
Lugano: New Orleans and Estival Jazz Festivals.	

Events

Montreux: Jazz Festival.
Mürren: International High Alpine Ballooning.
Spiez: Concert in the Castle.
Yverdon-les-Bains: Horse Racing.

June–September

Interlaken: William Tell Festival Play.

June–October

Fribourg: Triennial Photographic Exhibition (last 1994).
Interlaken: Folklore Evenings in the Kursaal.
Winterthur: Albani Festival (Traditional Club Festival of Music and Theatre; last weekend in June).

July

Aarau: Aarau Youth Festival (1st Friday in July).
Braunwald: Music week.
Davos: Swiss Alpine Marathon.
Dornach: Commemoration of Battle of Dornach (every 5 years).
Gstaad: International Tennis Championships of Switzerland.
Klosters: Summer Festival.
Kreuzlingen: Nocturnal Festival on the Lake.
Lausanne: Festival de la Cité (Old Town Festival).
Loèche-les-Bains/Leukerbad: Shepherds' Festival on the Gemmi (Folk Festival).
Lugano: Nocturnal Festival on the Lake with Fireworks.
Lucerne: Federal Rifleman's Festival.
Meiringen: International Festival Music Weeks.
Mürren: Inferno Berglauf (Mountain Run); Country Festival.
Sempach: Commemoration of the Battle of Sempach.
Vevey: Rhône Festival (Popular events on Lake Geneva).
Villars: Folklore Meeting.

July–August

Bienne/Biel: Bieler Braderie; Chess Festival.
Brig: Film performances in the castle courtyard, every Thursday Brig Mountain evenings in Ried-Brig.
Interlaken: Music Festival Weeks.
Lausanne: "Pour un Eté" (Concert, theatre and ballet performances).
Pontresina: Engadin Concert Weeks.
Rigi: Alpine Parade and Schwinger Festival (Wrestling).
Swiss Lakes: Evening trips on the Lakes.

July–September

Altdorf: William Tell Plays.
Ascona: New Orleans Music Fiesta; Street Concerts by Tessine Wind Band "Bandella".
Vevey: Marché folklorique (Market with wine tasting and local specialities every Saturday).

August

Everywhere: National Festival August 1st.
Many places: Herdsmen's and Alpine Farmers' Festival.
Assumption (August 15th): Processions at many places in the Catholic parts of the country.
Bienne/Biel: Old Town Chilbi.
Brunnen: Federal festival on the Rütli (August 1st).
Fribourg: International Folklore Meeting (end August); performances by yodellers, wrestlers and hornusser (propelling disks with a long club and catching them by the opposition).
Gstaad: Yehudi Menuhin Festival.
Klosters: Children's Festival.
Loèche-les-Bains: August 1st, Shepherds' Festival with illumination of the slopes of the Gemmi.
Mürren: Village Festival.
Rigi: August 1st, Federal Festival on the Rigi, with bonfires on the summit and folklore events.
Saignleégier: Horse Market.

"Hornussen"

Spiez: Castle Plays.
Vevey: International Festival Film Comedies.
Willisau: Jazz Festival.

Basle: Kleinbaslerfest. **August–**
Langenthal: Federal Hornuss Festival. **September**
Lucerne: International Music Festival.
Winterthur: Music Festival.

In many places: Hornuss matches. **August–**
Ascona: Summer-night concerts on the Island of Brissago; International **October**
Music Festival.

Aarau: Teenagers and Children's Lantern Procession (2nd Friday in **September**
September).
Basle: Reformation Feast and Folk Festival.
Berne: Mineral Exchange.
Brig: Castle Concerts, Theatrical Performances.
Oberwalliser: Applied Art Exhibition.
Einsiedeln: Blessing of the Angels (September 14th).
Geneva: Concours International d'Execution Musicale (2 weeks).
Gstaad: Alpine Gala (Theatre, Concerts).
Hasliberg: Chästeilet (Division of Cheese) and Popular Festival.
Lausanne: Comptoir Suisse (National Fair).
Locarno: Grape Festival.
Lucerne: Rowing Regatta; International horseracing.
Montreux: "Septembre".
Neuchâtel: Fête de Vendanges (Vintner Festival; last weekend in
September).
Zurich: Boys' shooting matches; Jazz Festival; Theatre Spectacular.

Many places: Wine Festivals. **September–**
Basle: Basle Altenfair, the oldest fair in Switzerland. **October**

October	Bienne/Biel: Grape-gathering Sunday on Lake Bienne; Onion Market. Châtel-St-Denis: Harvest Thanksgiving. Lausanne: Olympia Week (Various concerts). Locarno: Chestnut Festival. Lugano: Vine Growers' Festival Procession (1st Sunday in October). Morat/Murten: Commemorative run Morat–Fribourg.
October– November	Basle: Autumn Fair (October 24th to November 2nd). Berne: "Ziberle-Märit" (Onion Market, Folk festival; 4th Monday in November). Geneva: Foire International d'Inventions (Inventors' Fair). Lausanne: Salon des Antiquaires (Antique fair). Rütli: Rütli shooting. Sursee: Gansabhauet (Cutting down the Goose). Zurich: International Mineral Exchange.
December	Many places: Lichtkläuse (around December 6th); Masquerades, Silver-sterkläuse, etc. Geneva: Fête de l'Escalade (December 12th, anniversary of the abortive attack by the Savoyards).

Food and Drink

General

Swiss restaurants are noted for the excellence of their cuisine, which is as varied as the ethnic composition of the country. The cuisine of the various parts of Switzerland is strongly influenced by that of the neighbouring countries – in the German-speaking cantons by German cooking, in the French-speaking cantons by the "Cuisine Française", in the Italian-speaking cantons by the "Cucina Italiana". In addition, however, there are a number of specifically Swiss dishes, mostly using locally produced ingredients such as dairy produce and fish.

The midday meal is usually eaten about 12.30pm, called either "dîner" and followed in the evening (7pm onwards) by "souper", or "lunch" when the main meal is taken in the evening. Even quite small restaurants provide attentive service, using hot-plates (réchauds) to keep the food warm. The station buffets are usually excellent.

The cost of lunch or dinner will range between 10 and 20 francs in the more modest establishments to 20–50 francs in high-class restaurants. To eat à la carte is usually more expensive than to take the fixed price menu, which always provides a very satisfying meal. Many restaurants offer one-course meals which are very good value.

Swiss Menu

Meat

The Berner Platte is a very nourishing plate of ham and sausages with sauerkraut or beans. The Mittelland has another very substantial dish, Gnagi (slightly salted pigs' trotters), so tender that it is said to melt in the mouth. Favourite Geneva dishes are pied de porc au madère (pigs' trotters in madeira sauce) and gigot d'agneau (leg of lamb). Zurich has Gschnetzeltes (veal stewed with cream) and Leberspieler (calf's liver cooked on a spit, with bacon), Schwyz excellent Gegmsenbraten (roast chamois), the cantons on the Rhine Mistkratzerli or Güggeli (young chickens).

Sausages

Switzerland has a rich assortment of excellent sausages. Basle has Klöpfer (succulent cervelat sausages), St Gallen Schüblige and Bratwürste, Appenzell Pantli and Knackerli. Grisons has a particularly wide variety – Salsiz (a small salami), Beinwurst, Engadinerwurst, Leberwurst (liver sausage) and Tiges as well as Bündnerfleisch (air dried beef). The canton of Vaud also produces some excellent sausages, including boutefas, saucissons de Pay-erne, liver sausages and sausages made with vegetables. Then there are the longeoles of Geneva (pork sausages spiced with caraway and aniseed) and the Walliser Platte or "Valais dish" (cold meat including dried raw beef). The popular types of sausage in Ticino are coppa and zampone.

Fish dishes play a large part in the Swiss menu. The country's many lakes and rivers yield a variety of species: pike are found in Lake Constance, Lake Geneva, the Lac de Neuchâtel and the Lauerzer See, trout in the mountain streams around Arth-Goldau, in Lake Geneva, the Areuse and the moun-tain streams and lakes of southern Switzerland, barbel in Lake Zug, blue char in Lake Constance, dace, char and perch in Lake Geneva, bondelles and palées in the Lac de Neuchâtel. Further variety is added by various species of perch and barbel and by the eels of the mountain lakes. Blausee trout are regarded as a particular delicacy.

Fish Dishes

Among the favourite Swiss vegetables to accompany meat are Berner Rösti (sliced potatoes, lightly browned with bacon cubes), gratiné pota-toes, aubergines and artichokes. There are also a variety of attractively seasoned salads.

Vegetables

This is eaten mainly in northern Switzerland, where the influence of Ger-man cuisine makes itself felt. In addition to Spätzli or Knöpfli there is a Zurich speciality, the Zürcher Topf (macaroni with minced meat and tomato sauce, cooked in the oven). In southern Switzerland various forms of pasta are popular, including ravioli. Notable among the egg dishes are the chucheôles of Fribourg which are eaten with sweet mustard.

Pasta

The Swiss are particularly good at making cakes and sweets. Among the most tempting are Basler Leckerli (a kind of gingerbread), Schaffhauser Zungen (Schaffhausen "tongues"), Zuger Kirschtorte, Engadine nut-cakes, Argauer Rüblitorte the cream filled meringues (from Meiringen) of the Bernese Oberland, the bagnolet crème of the Jura (eaten with raspberries and aniseed biscuits), the délices (soda rolls), croissants, rissoles (pear tarts), nougat and pralines of Geneva and the zabaglione of Ticino. Vermi-celli, not the Italian pasta dish but a dessert made of chestnut mousse, is popular all over Switzerland.

Desserts

A Swiss speciality world renowned for its quality is chocolate, in a variety of flavourings.

Chocolate

Cheese

The excellent dairy products of Switzerland are famed world-wide, and the Swiss menu includes a variety of cheese dishes, varying from region to region. Cheese soups are particularly popular in central Switzerland; cheesecakes (gâteau or salée au fromage, ramequin) are found all over the country.

General

Appenzeller (Appenzell): A semi-hard cow's-milk cheese, treated with spiced white wine during the maturing process.

Types of Swiss Cheese

Bagnes (Valais): A hard cow's-milk cheese, used in the making of raclette (see below).

Brienzer Mutschli (Berne): a hard cow's-milk cheese, usually made on the mountain pastures in summer.

Chaschöl chevra (Grisons): a soft goat's-milk cheese.

Emmentaler (Central Switzerland): A hard cow's-milk cheese, used in raclette.

Swiss cheeses

Formaggelli (Ticino): A soft cheese made from ewe's or goat's-milk, usually eaten after several days' maturation.

Formaggini (Ticino): A small soft ewe's or goat's-milk cheese.

Goms (Valais): A semi-hard cow's-milk cheese, much used in the making of raclette.

Gruyère (Fribourg): A hard cow's-milk cheese, used in fondue.

Petit Suisse (Geneva): A fresh cow's-milk cheese.

Reblochon (Geneva): A soft cow's-milk cheese.

Saanen-Hobelkäse (Berne): A hard cow's-milk cheese, used in various cheese dishes or served by itself in thin slices.

Sbrinz (Central Switzerland): A hard cow's-milk cheese, mainly used in the preparation of various cheese dishes.

Schabzieger (Glarus): A hard cow's-milk cheese, with herbs.

Tête de Moine (Jura): A soft cow's-milk cheese.

Tilsiter (Thurgau): A semi-hard cow's-milk cheese.

Toggenburger Ploderkäse (Obertoggenburg): a soft cow's-milk cheese.

Tomme Vaudoise (Vaud): A fresh soft cow's-milk cheese.

Urserenkäse (Bernese Oberland): A mild soft cow's-milk cheese.

Vacherin Fribourgeois (Fribourg): A semi-hard cow's-milk cheese. There are two types, Vacherin à fondue and Vacherin à la main.

Vacherin Mont d'Or (Fribourg): A soft cow's-milk cheese, usually eaten after six weeks' maturation.

Vero Piora (Ticino): A semi-hard cow's-milk and goat's-milk cheese.

There are also a large number of regional varieties of cheese. Alpkäse is made on the mountain pastures in summer, and often toasted at an open fire (Bratkäsli). The process of cheese-making can be observed in the demonstration cheese dairy at Gruyère.

Two cheese dishes which are particularly popular in western Switzerland are fondue and raclette, both of them invariably accompanied by white wine.

Fondue (from French "fondre", to melt) is made by melting cheese and white wine, flavoured with kirsch and spices, in a special one-handled dish known as a caquelon. The dish is then set in the middle of the table over a flame to keep it hot, and each member of the party helps himself by dipping a piece of white bread on a special fork into the common bowl.

Fondue

In raclette (from French racler, to scrape), a large cheese is cut in half and heated until it melts, when the melted cheese is scraped off onto the plate and eaten with a potato in its jacket and various tasty accompaniments.

Raclette

Wine

Vines are grown in almost all the Swiss cantons, but particularly on the slopes above Lake Geneva and the lakes of the Jura and Ticino and in the wide valleys of the Rhône and the Rhine. Wine has been made in western and southern Switzerland since the 1st century B.C., in northern Switzerland only since the 7th or 8th c. A.D. Since the end of the 19th c. the area under vines has been considerably reduced. The present output of wine is about 1 million hectolitres, two-thirds of the total being white and the

Vine growing

Wine-producing Regions of Switzerland

White wines ☐
White and red wines ☐
Red wines ▨

Food and Drink

remaining third red (maximum strength 13% of alcohol by volume). Only small quantities of Swiss wine are exported, the imports of wine being significantly greater.

Varieties of wine   Lake Geneva, particularly in the Lavaux area (Vaud) between Lausanne and Montreux (from the Chasselas/Gutedel grape): Dézaley and St-Saphorin (the best), Pully, Lutry, Epesses; Aigle and Yvorne, from the Chablais area between Montreux and Martigny; and wines from the "Petite Côte" around Morges, the "Côte" from Rolle and the Mandement area (Geneva).

Valais: Fendant (from the Chasselas/Gutedel grape), in many different sorts; red Dôle (from a mixture of Pinot Noir/Blauburgunder and Gamay grapes); Johannisberg (known as "Rhin" or "petit Rhin", being made from Riesling/Sylvaner grapes); Ermitage, Amigne, Arvine, Humagne, Oeil de Perdrix (rosé); Muscat and Malvasier, two dessert wines made from the Pinot Gris grape ("Strohwein" or "straw wine"); and the very unusual Heidenwein, made from the highest vineyards (700–1200m/2297–3937ft) around Visperterminen; after maturing in the cellar for 10–20 years it yields the precious golden-brown Glacier.

Lac de Bienne and Lac de Neuchâtel: the slightly sparkling "Bernese lake wines" Schaffiser and Twanner; Cortaillod, Auvernier.

Ticino: Nostrano (red, from the Merlot grape); particularly good from Gordola.

Grisons: red wines - Veltliner (Vatellina), Malanser, Jeninser, Maienfelder, Fläscher (in the Bündner Herrschaft region).

Northern Switzerland: Meilener, Stäfener, Herrliberger from Lake Zurich; Neftenbacher, from the Töss Valley; Karthäuser (Ittinger), Steiner, Bachtobler from Thurgau; Bernecker, Melser, Wiler from St Gallen; Hallauer, Osterfinger, Rheinhalder from Schaffhausen; Villiger Schlossberger, Geissberger from Aargau; Riehener Schlipfen from Basle.

In Switzerland white wine is served in small tumblers. Soon after the wine harvest unfermented "must" (German "most", French "moût") appears in bars and restaurants. In Vaud there are numerous "wine trails".

Vineyards . . .   *. . . and the Aigle Museum of Wine*

Swiss fruit brandies are of excellent quality. Kirsch (the best of which comes from Zug), Enzian (from the roots of gentian), Birne (from pears), grappa and marc (from the skins of pressed grapes), Bätzi (from apples), etc. Alpenbitter, Kräuterlikör (Chrüter: a herb liqueur). **Spirits**

The two leading Swiss brands are Feldschlösschen (Rheinfelden) and Cardinal (Fribourg). Beer is often mixed with lemonade to produce shandy. Ex-bier is non-alcoholic. **Beer**

Passuger (Grisons), Henniez (Vaud), Elmer (Glarus), Eptinger (Basle-Land), Weissenburger (Berne). **Table waters**

See entry **Restaurants**

Getting to Switzerland

There are regular flights from major airports in Great Britain, USA and Canada to Zurich and Geneva. Swissair has international services between Switzerland and nearly 60 other countries. The Swiss National Tourist Office and other tourist bureaux provide information leaflets (and "Fly-Rail", "Welcome-pack" and "Fly-pack") as well as details of the facility for checking in at a rail station for flights by Swissair. **By air**

From London (Victoria) to Basle, via Calais, takes about fourteen hours, and from London (Liverpool Street) to Basle, via the Hook of Holland, about twenty hours. Travelling by train through the Channel Tunnel reduces this time. **By rail**

The distance from London to Basle is about 940km/585 miles. The journey can be made via the Channel Tunnel and then on motorways for most of the way. **By road**

Health Resorts

○ **Spas**

1 Rheinfelden (Alt. 280m/919ft)

2 Ramsach (Alt. 720m/2263ft)

3 Schwefelbergbad (Alt. 1400m/4595ft)

4 Lenk im Simmertal (Alt. 1105m/3636ft)

5 Saillon (Alt. 510m/1510ft)

6 Breiten (Alt. 900m/2954ft)

7 Andeer (Alt. 1000m/3282ft)

8 Serneus (Alt. 1031m/3384ft)

9 Bad Scuol and Bad-Tarasp-Vulpera (Alt. 1250m/4103ft)

10 St Moritz Bad (Alt. 1775m/5826ft)

11 Stabio (Alt. 347m/1139ft)

○ **Thermal baths**

12 Yverdon-les-Bains (Alt. 435m/1428ft)

13 Zurzach (Alt. 344m/1129ft)

14 Baden-Ennetbaden (Alt. 388m/1273ft)

Health Resorts and Spas in Switzerland

Health Resorts ○
Thermal Resorts ●
Mineral Springs ◐

15 Bad Schinznach (Alt. 350m/1149ft)

16 Lostorf (Alt. 525m/1725ft)

17 Lavey-les-Bains (Alt. 417m/1369ft)

18 Leukerbad/Loèche-les-Bains (Alt. 1411m/4631ft)

19 Vals (Alt. 1250m/4102ft)

20 Bad Ragaz (Alt. 525m/1723ft)/Valens (Alt. 915m/3003ft)

○ **Mineral springs**

21 Eptingen

22 Henniez

23 Weissenburg

24 Adelboden

25 Vals

26 Elm

27 Rietbad

28 Passugg

Help for the Disabled

The Schweizerische Invalidenbund (Froburgstrasse 4, CH-4601 Olten; tel. (062) 32 12 62), and Mobility International Schweiz (Hard 4, CH-8408 Winterthur; tel. (052) 2 22 68 25) issue a list of Swiss hotels suitable for the handicapped.

Town guides for the handicapped (Basle, Berne, Lausanne, Lucerne, St Gallen and Zurich) are obtainable from the offices of Mobility International Schweiz (address as above).

Hotels

The Swiss Hotel trade has a long and honourable tradition behind it. The general standard of quality is higher than in other European countries, and even in modest hotels the accommodation and service are usually among the best of their kind. Outside the larger towns such as Zurich and Geneva, the establishments are mostly of small and medium size.

Hotels and Inns

Further details, with prices, can be found in the free regional and local hotel lists and also in the "Schweizer Hotelführer" which can be obtained from travel bureaux and the Swiss Tourist Bureaux (see Information).

The official information office is the Schweizer Hotel-Verein (Swiss Hotel Association), Monbijoustrasse 130, CH-3001 Bern; tel. (031) 50 71 11, which however, will not undertake the booking of accommodation.

Official category	in this guide	Room rate per night in francs	
		one person	two persons
★★★★★	1	200–400	350–800
★★★★	2	150–300	180–450
★★★	3	100–220	150–250
★	4	90–150	120–200
★	5	40– 90	70–130

Categories

These are inclusive charges (i.e. with service and taxes). In purely tourist and holiday resorts the rates may be higher, particularly at the height of the season; and it is quite common in such places for hotels to let rooms only with half or full board.

A list of hotels and inns which provide good value can be found in the brochure "Check-in-1★-Hotels", "Preiswerte Unterkünfte in der Schweiz" and "Berggasthöfe in der Schweiz", published by the Swiss Tourist Bureau (see Information).

Reasonably Priced Hotels

2, Aarauerhof, 122 b.; tel. (064) 24 83 00
3, Zum Schützen, 12 b.; tel. (064) 23 01 24

Aarau

2, Beau-Site, 65 b.; tel. (033) 73 22 22
2, Parkhotel Bellevue, 95 b.; tel. (033) 73 16 21
3, Adler Sporthotel, 80 b.; tel. (033) 73 41 41
3, Huldi & Waldhaus, 80 b.; tel. (033) 73 15 31
4, Kreuz, 28 b.; tel. (033) 73 21 21

Adelboden

3, Schweizerhof, 50 b.; tel. (074) 5 18 88
4, Rössli, 34 b.; tel. (074) 5 24 60

Alt St Johann

3, Drei Könige & Post, 40 b.; tel. (044) 6 72 03
3, Krone, 85 b.; tel. (044) 6 72 06
4, Bergidyll, 37 b.; tel. (044) 6 74 55
4, Schweizerhof, 56 b.; tel. (044) 6 71 89
5, Zum Sternen, 9 b.; tel. (044) 6 71 30

Andermatt

3, Appenzell, 31 b.; tel. (071) 87 42 11
3, Romantik-Hotel Säntis, 60 b.; tel. (071) 87 87 22
4, Krone, 20 b.; tel. (071) 87 13 21
4, Adler, 41 b.; tel. (071) 87 13 89

Appenzell

2, Metropol, 70 b.; tel. (071) 46 33 37
3, Seegarten, 68 b.; tel. (071) 46 57 57
4, Rotes Kreuz, 30 b.; tel. (071) 46 19 14

Arbon on Lake Constance

Hotels

Arosa
1, Arosa Kulm Hotel, 230 b.; tel. (081) 31 01 31
1, Tschuggen Grand Hotel, 233 b.; tel. (081) 31 02 21
2, Bellavista, 130 b.; tel. (081) 31 24 21
2, Hohenfels, 90 b.; tel. (081) 31 01 01
3, Des Alpes, 70 b.; tel. (081) 31 18 51
3, Isla, 80 b.; tel. (081) 31 12 13
4, Hold, 30 b.; tel. (081) 31 14 08
4, Quellenhof, 35 b.; tel. (081) 31 17 18
5, Bündnerhof & Rössli, 38 b.; tel. (081) 31 25 57
5, Vetter, 40 b.; tel. (081) 31 17 02

Ascona
1, Castello del Sole, 150 b.; tel. (093) 35 02 02
1, Eden Roc, 100 b.; tel. (093) 35 01 71
2, Acapulco au Lac, 86 b.; tel. (093) 35 45 21
2, Castello-Seeschloss, 80 b.; tel. (093) 36 01 61
3, Carcani Mövenpick, 58 b.; tel. (093) 35 19 04
3, Romantik-Hotel Tamaro, 78 b.; tel. (093) 35 02 82
4, Al Faro, 20 b.; tel. (093) 35 85 15
4, Luna, 45 b.; tel. (093) 35 36 07
5, Antica Posta, 30 b.; tel. (093) 35 04 26
5, Villa Veratum, 19 b.; tel. (093) 35 35 77

Baden
2, Du Parc, 150 b.; tel. (056) 20 13 11
2, Linde, 85 b.; tel. (056) 22 53 85
3, Kappelerhof, 55 b.; tel. (056) 22 38 34
3, Zwyssighof, Wettingen, 45 b.; tel. (056) 26 86 22
4, Atrium-Hotel zur Blume, 45 b.; tel. (056) 22 55 69

Basle
1, Basel Hilton, 351 b.; tel. (061) 2 71 66 22
1, Euler Manz Privacy, 90 b.; tel. (061) 2 72 45 00
2, Basel, 108 b.; tel. (061) 2 64 68 00
2, Schweizerhof, 100 b.; tel. (061) 2 71 28 33
3, Alexander, 100 b.; tel. (061) 6 91 70 00
3, Helvetia, 34 b.; tel. (061) 2 72 06 88
4, Bristol, 55 b.; tel. (061) 2 71 38 22
4, Engel, 35 b.; tel. (061) 8 21 71 73
5, Hecht am Rhein, 53 b.; tel. (061) 6 91 22 20
5, Steinenschanze, 75 b.; tel. (061) 2 72 53 53

Beatenberg
3, Kurhaus Silberhorn, 45 b.; tel. (036) 41 12 12
3, Park-Kurhotel Mayolina, 71 b.; tel. (036) 41 14 74
4, Beau-Regard, 30 b.; tel. (036) 41 13 41
4, Gloria, 30 b.; tel. (036) 41 11 29
5, Beatus, 30 b.; tel. (036) 41 15 28

Beckenried
2, Sternen-Seehotel, 80 b.; tel. (041) 64 61 61
3, Nidwaldnerhof, 32 b.; tel. (041) 64 52 52
4, Edelweiss, 40 b.; tel. (041) 64 12 52
4, Rigli, 30 b.; tel. (041) 64 12 51

Bellinzona
3, Unione, 67 b.; tel. (092) 25 55 77
3, International, 39 b.; tel. (092) 25 43 43

Berne
1, Bellevue Palace, 230 b.; tel. (031) 3 20 45 45
1, Schweizerhof, 148 b.; tel. (031) 3 11 45 01
2, Bern, 170 b.; tel. (031) 3 12 10 21
2, Innere Enge, 52 b.; tel. (031) 3 09 61 11
3, Goldener Adler, 40 b.; tel. (031) 3 11 17 25
3, Kreuz, 180 b.; tel. (031) 3 11 11 62
4, National, 66 b.; tel. (031) 3 81 19 88
4, Jardin, 34 b.; tel. (031) 3 33 01 17
5, Glocke, 40 b.; tel. (031) 3 11 37 71
5, Regina Arabelle, 70 b.; tel. (031) 3 01 03 05

3, Waldhaus, 40 b.; tel. (028) 27 27 17   **Bettmeralp**
3, Bettmerhof, 45 b.; tel. (028) 27 17 41
4, Panorama, 23 b.; tel. (028) 27 13 75

2, Continental, 146 b.; tel. (032) 22 32 55   **Biel/Bienne**
2, Elite, 100 b.; tel. (032) 22 54 41
3, Dufour, 60 b.; tel. (032) 42 22 61
4, Atlantis, 92 b.; tel. (032) 42 44 11
4, Goya, 32 b.; tel. (032) 22 61 61

2, Seiler au Lac, 80 b.; tel. (036) 22 30 21   **Bönigen bei**
3, Seehotel Terrasse, 65 b.; tel. (036) 22 07 70   **Interlaken**

2, Märchenhotel Bellevue, 100 b.; tel. (058) 84 38 43   **Braunwald**
2, Niederschlacht, 75 b.; tel. (058) 84 36 84
3, Cristal, 40 b.; tel. (058) 84 10 45
3, Alpenblick, 100 b.; tel. (058) 84 15 44
4, Rübschen, 21 b.; tel. (058) 84 15 34
4, Tödiblick, 25 b.; tel. (058) 84 12 36

2, Salina Badehotel, 50 b.; tel. (028) 27 18 17   **Breiten ob Mörel**
3, Im Grünen, 90 b.; tel. (028) 27 26 62

3, Brienzerburli, 50 b.; tel. (036) 51 12 41   **Brienz**
3, Weisses Kreuz, 30 b.; tel. (036) 51 17 81
4, Seehotel Bären, 50 b.; tel. (036) 51 24 12
5, Löwen (Brienzerburli), 16 b.; tel. (036) 51 11 31

3, Simplon, 60 b.; tel. (028) 24 22 33   **Brig**
3, Central, 70 b.; tel. (028) 23 50 20
4, Ambassador, 48 b.; tel. (028) 24 20 20
5, Du Pont, 45 b.; tel. (028) 23 15 02

2, Villa Cäsar, 62 b.; tel. (093) 65 27 66   **Brissago**
3, Mirto au Lac, 45 b.; tel. (093) 65 13 28
4, Bellavista, 26 b.; tel. (093) 65 12 22
4, Eden al Lago, 45 b.; tel. (093) 65 12 55
5, Camelia, 50 b.; tel. (093) 65 12 41

1, Seehotel Waldstätterhof, 160 b.; tel. (043) 33 11 33   **Brunnen**
3, Bellevue au Lac, 90 b.; tel. (043) 31 13 18
3, Elite, 100 b.; tel. (043) 31 10 24
4, Brunnerhof, 90 b.; tel. (043) 31 17 57
4, Alpina, 40 b.; tel. (043) 31 18 13
5, Ochsen, 17 b.; tel. (043) 31 11 59

1, Palace Hotel, 142 b.; tel. (041) 63 25 50   **Bürgenstock**
1, Park Hotel, 116 b.; tel. (041) 63 25 45
3, Waldheim, 70 b.; tel. (041) 63 23 83

2, Cresta Palace, 160 b.; tel. (082) 3 92 29   **Celerina**
2, Cresta-Kulm, 76 b.; tel. (082) 3 33 73
3, Chesa Rosatsch, 40 b.; tel. (082) 3 06 44
3, Saluver, 36 b.; tel. (082) 3 13 14
Landgasthof Stüvetta Veglia, 20 b.; tel. (082) 3 80 08

2, Suisse, 80 b.; tel. (025) 79 18 81   **Champéry**
2, De Champéry, 138 b.; tel. (025) 79 10 71
3, Beau-Séjour, 40 b.; tel. (025) 79 17 01
4, National, 48 b.; tel. (025) 79 11 30
4, Rose des Alpes, 42 b.; tel. (025) 79 12 18
5, Buffet de la Gare, 18 b.; tel. (025) 78 13 29

Hotels

Château d'Oex	3, Résidence La Rocaille, 32 b.; tel. (029) 4 62 15
	3, Beau Séjour et Taverne, 70 b.; tel. (029) 4 74 23
	4, Bouquetins, 20 b.; tel. (029) 4 57 04
	4, Alpina-Rosat, MinOtels, 80 b.; tel. (029) 4 62 12
	5, Buffet de la Gare, 14 b.; tel. (029) 4 77 17
	5, La Printanière, 12 b.; tel. (029) 4 61 13
La Chaux-de-Fonds	2, Fleur-de-Lys, MinOtels, 62 b.; tel. (039) 23 37 31
	2, Moreau, 60 b.; tel. (039) 23 22 22
	3, Du Moulin, 34 b.; tel. (039) 26 42 26
	5, De la Balance, 22 b.; tel. (039) 28 26 21
Chiasso	3, Touring Mövenpick, 120 b.; tel. (091) 44 53 31
	3, Centro, 33 b.; tel. (091) 43 44 02
Chur	2, Duc de Rohan, 60 b.; tel. (081) 22 10 22
	3, Romantik Hotel Stern, 90 b.; tel. (081) 22 35 55
	3, Sommerau, 185 b.; tel. (081) 22 55 45
	4, Drei Könige, 60 b.; tel. (081) 22 17 25
	4, Zunfthaus zur Rebleuten, 20 b.; tel. (081) 21 50 21
Crans-sur-Sierre	1, Grand Hôtel du Golf, 120 b.; tel. (027) 41 42 42
	1, Lindner Hôtel Rhodania, 80 b.; tel. (027) 40 11 41
	2, Astor, 72 b.; tel. (027) 40 20 85
	2, De l'Etrier, 200 b.; tel. (027) 40 11 81
	3, Beau-Site, 50 b.; tel. (027) 41 33 12
	3, Eden, 70 b.; tel. (027) 40 11 71
	4, Crans-Belvédère, 45 b.; tel. (027) 41 13 91
	4, Centrale, 38 b.; tel. (027) 41 37 67
Davos	1, Flüela, 120 b.; tel. (081) 47 12 21
	1, Steigenberger Belvédère, 227 b.; tel. (081) 44 12 81
	2, Berghotel Schatzalb, 170 b.; tel. (081) 44 13 31
	2, Morosani Posthotel, 160 b.; tel. (081) 44 11 61
	3, Quisiana, 30 b.; tel. (081) 43 51 04
	3, Pischa, 130 b.; tel. (081) 43 55 13
	4, Elli, 22b.; tel. (081) 46 46 56
	4, Sporthotel Lohner, 60 b.; tel. (081) 46 44 45
Delémont	3, City, 30 b.; tel. (066) 22 94 44
	3, Le National Manotel, 54 b.; tel. (066) 22 96 22
	5, Au Gros Pré, 43 b.; tel. (066) 22 90 33
Les Diablerets	2, Ermitage, 150 b.; tel. (025) 53 15 51
	2, Eurotel, 220 b.; tel. (025) 53 17 21
	3, Hostellerie-Les-Sources, 100 b.; tel. (025) 53 21 26
	3, Le Chamois, 124 b.; tel. (025) 53 26 53
	4, Mon Abri, 45 b.; tel. (025) 53 14 81
	5, Diablotins, 190 b.; tel. (025) 53 16 33
Disentis/Mustèr	2, Cucagna, 90 b.; tel. (081) 9 47 59 54
	2, Parkhotel Bauer, 110 b.; tel. (081) 9 47 45 45
	3, Sporthotel Sax, 37 b.; tel. (081) 9 47 44 48
	4, Bellavista, 44 b.; tel. (081) 9 47 52 73
	4, Lukmanier, 11 b.; tel. (081) 9 47 51 07
Einsiedeln	2, Drei Könige, 100 b.; tel. (055) 53 24 41
	3, Bären Zunfthaus, 70 b.; tel. (055) 53 28 76
	3, Storchen, 60 b.; tel. (055) 53 37 60
	4, Rebstock, 54 b.; tel. (055) 53 18 95
	4, Sonne am Klosterplatz, 50 b.; tel. (055) 53 28 21
Engelberg	2, Hess, 84 b.; tel. (041) 94 13 66
	2, Treff-Hotel Teg. Titlis, 256 b.; tel. (041) 94 28 28

2, Waldegg vorm Ring, 130 b.; tel. (041) 94 18 22
3, Alpina, 30 b.; tel. (041) 94 13 40
3, Europe, Europäischer Hof, 120 b.; tel. (041) 94 00 94
4, Bellevue-Terminus, 112 b.; tel. (041) 94 12 13
4, Cathrin, 44 b.; tel. (041) 94 44 66

3, Christania-Silence, 44 b.; tel. (028) 71 21 12   **Fiesch**
3, Schmitta, 24 b.; tel. (028) 71 13 46
3, Kristall MinOtels, 50 b.; tel. (028) 71 17 17

In Flims Dorf: **Flims**
2, Crap Ner, 96 b.; tel. (081) 39 26 26
3, Vorab, 65 b.; tel. (081) 39 18 61
5, Berghotel Haldenhaus, 16 b.; tel. (081) 39 12 29

In Flims Waldhaus:
1, Park Hotels Waldhaus, 300 b.; tel. (081) 39 01 81
2, Adula, 180 b.; tel. (081) 39 01 61
3, Flimserhof, 40 b.; tel. (081) 39 17 31
4, Cresta, 80 b.; tel. (081) 39 35 35
5, Alpina (no restaurant), 19 b.; tel. (081) 39 01 61

3, Flüelerhof-Grill Rustico, 50 b.; tel. (044) 2 11 49   **Flüelen**
4, Weisses Kreuz, 60 b.; tel. (044) 2 17 17

2, Gauenpark, 68 b.; tel. (081) 7 33 31 31   **Flumserberg**
3, Alpina, 51 b.; tel. (081) 7 33 12 32
3, Gamperdon, 52 b.; tel. (081) 7 33 16 21
4, Mätzwiese, 28 b.; tel. (081) 7 33 11 28
4, Waldegg, 28 b.; tel. (081) 7 33 18 85

3, Falken (no restaurant), 27 b.; tel. (054) 21 27 25   **Frauenfeld**
4, Libelle, 30 b.; tel. (054) 7 20 43 43

2, Au Parc, 136 b.; tel. (037) 82 11 11   **Fribourg**
2, Duc Berthold, 60 b.; tel. (037) 81 11 21
3, De La Rose, MinOtels, 75 b.; tel. (037) 81 31 31
3, Elite, 68 b.; tel. (037) 22 38 36
Landgasthof Du Faucon, 48 b.; tel. (037) 22 13 17

On the Schwarzsee:
2, Primerose au Lac Sport, 160 b.; tel. (037) 32 16 32
3, Bad, 40 b.; tel. (037) 32 11 04

1, Les Armures, 52 b.; tel. (022) 3 10 91 72   **Geneva/Genève**
1, Beau-Rivage, 172 b.; tel. (022) 7 31 02 21
1, Metropole, 203 b.; tel. (022) 3 11 13 44
1, Le Richemond, 170 b.; tel. (022) 7 31 14 00
1, Noga-Hilton, 582 b.; tel. (022) 7 31 98 11
2, Ambassador, 126 b.; tel. (022) 7 31 72 00
2, Angleterre, 110 b.; tel. (022) 7 32 81 80
2, Carlton, 190 b.; tel. (022) 7 31 68 50
2, Le Warwick, 325 b.; tel. (022) 7 31 62 50
3, Cadett Mövenpick, 378 b.; tel. (022) 7 85 02 03
3, Savoy, 100 b.; tel. (022) 7 31 12 55
3, Edelweiss, 82 b.; tel. (022) 7 31 36 58
3, Suisse, 100 b.; tel. (022) 7 32 66 30
4, Bernina, 110 b.; tel. (022) 7 31 49 50
4, Pax, 70 b.; tel. (022) 7 35 44 40
4, Lido, 60 b.; tel. (022) 7 31 55 30
5, Luserne, 58 b.; tel. (022) 3 45 46 76
Landgasthof Auberge Port Gitana, 14 b.; tel. (022) 7 74 31 48

Hotels

Grächen
3, Grächerhof, MinOtels, 42 b.; tel. (028) 56 25 15
3, Gaedi, 50 b.; tel. (028) 56 18 28
4, Sonne, 24 b.; tel. (028) 56 11 07
4, Abendruh, 36 b.; tel. (028) 56 11 16
Landgasthaus La Collina, 120 b.; tel. (028) 56 20 16

Grindelwald
1, Grand Hôtel Regina, 180 b.; tel. (036) 54 54 55
2, Eigerblick, 125 b.; tel. (036) 54 54 14
2, Schweizerhof, 96 b.; tel. (036) 53 22 02
2, Silberhorn, 80 b.; tel. (036) 53 28 22
3, Alpenhof, 40 b.; tel. (036) 53 52 70
3, Fiescherblick, 50 b.; tel. (036) 53 44 53
4, Jungfrau + Crystal, 90 b.; tel. (036) 53 13 41
4, Lauberhorn, 50 b.; tel. (036) 53 10 82
5, Schweizerheim, 60 b.; tel. (036) 53 10 58
Landgasthof Alpenblick, 36 b.; tel. (036) 53 11 05

Gstaad
1, Gstaad Palace, 207 b.; tel. (030) 8 31 31
1, Grand Hotel Park, 180 b.; tel. (030) 8 33 77
2, Christiana, 40 b.; tel. (030) 4 51 21
2, Bernerhof, 93 b.; tel. (030) 8 33 66
3, Alphorn, 46 b.; tel. (030) 4 45 45
3, Gstaaderhof, 116 b.; tel. (030) 8 33 44
3, Sporthotel Rössli, 36 b.; tel. (030) 4 34 12

Heiden
2, Kurhotel Heiden, 98 b.; tel. (071) 91 91 112
3, Kurhaus Sunnenmatt, 60 b.; tel. (071) 91 55 51

Hergiswil am See
2, Seehotel Pilatus, 100 b.; tel. (041) 95 15 55
3, Seehotel Friedheim, 30 b.; tel. (041) 95 42 42
4, Roggerli, 26 b.; tel. (041) 95 11 33

Interlaken
1, Victoria-Jungfrau, 400 b.; tel. (036) 27 11 11
1, Beau-Rivage Grand Hôtel, 170 b.; tel. (036) 21 62 72
2, Métropole, 160 b.; tel. (036) 21 21 51
2, Krebs, 80 b.; tel. (036) 22 71 61
2, Park Mattenhof, 120 b.; tel. (036) 21 61 21
2, Royal-St-Georges, 170 b.; tel. (036) 22 75 75
3, Carlton, MinOtel, 80 b.; tel. (036) 22 38 21
3, Eden-Nova, 70 b.; tel. (036) 22 88 12
3, Chalet Swiss, 90 b.; tel. (036) 22 78 22
4, Alpina, 60 b.; tel. (036) 22 80 31
4, Harder-Minerva, 50 b.; tel. (036) 22 23 13
4, Lötschberg, 25 b.; tel. (036) 22 25 45
5, Waldhotel Unspunnen, 58 b.; tel. (036) 22 34 91
5, Rugenpark, 31 b.; tel. (036) 22 36 61

Kandersteg
1, Royal-Bellevue Résidence, 60 b.; tel. (033) 75 12 12
2, Schweizerhof, 60 b.; tel. (033) 75 19 19
2, Victoria & Ritter, 130 b.; tel. (033) 75 14 44
3, Adler, 44 b.; tel. (033) 75 11 22
3, Blümlisalp, 45 b.; tel. (033) 75 18 44
4, Alpenblick, 20 b.; tel. (033) 75 11 29
4, Alpina, 48 b.; tel. (033) 75 12 46

Klosters
1, Pardenn, 110 b.; tel. (081) 69 11 41
2, Albeina Sporthotel, 120 b.; tel. (081) 4 23 21 00
2, Aldiana Silvretta, 250 b.; tel. (081) 69 61 21; changes to 4 22 61 21 from April 16th 1996
3, Büel, 38 b.; tel. (081) 69 26 69; changes to 4 22 26 29 from April 16th 1996
3, Silencehotel Rätia, 42 b.; tel. (081) 69 47 47; changes to 4 22 47 47 from April 16th 1996
4, Wynegg, 30 b.; tel. (081) 69 13 40; changes to 4 22 13 40 from April 16th 1996

3, Du Lac-Seehof, 30 b.; tel. (041) 81 10 12   **Küssnacht am**
3, Hirschen, 65 b.; tel. (041) 81 10 27   **Rigi**

2, Laaxerhof, 250 b.; tel. (081) 9 21 71 01   **Laax**
2, Sporthotel Rancho Laax, 250 b.; tel. (081) 9 21 71 31
3, Arena Alva, 125 b.; tel. (081) 9 21 72 71
3, Sporthotel Larisch, 60 b.; tel. (081) 9 21 47 47
4, Ventira (no restaurant), 50 b.; tel. (081) 9 21 50 82
5, Crap Sogn Gion, 75 b.; tel. (081) 39 21 93

1, Beau-Rivage Palace, 320 b.; tel. (021) 6 13 33 33   **Lausanne**
1, Lausanne-Palace, 280 b.; tel. (021) 3 31 31 31
2, Château d'Ouchy, 80 b.; tel. (021) 6 16 74 51
2, Mövenpick Radisson, 470 b.; tel. (021) 6 17 21 21
2, Victoria, 100 b.; tel. (021) 3 20 57 71
2, Alpha, 240 b.; tel. (021) 3 23 01 31
3, AlaGare, MinOtels, 90 b.; tel. (021) 6 17 92 52
3, Bellerive, 70 b.; tel. (021) 6 16 96 33
3, City, 115 b.; tel. (021) 3 20 21 41
4, De la Forêt, 30 b.; tel. (021) 6 47 92 11
4, Angleterre, 55 b.; tel. (021) 6 17 21 11
5, Regina (no restaurant), 55 b.; tel. (021) 3 20 24 41
Landgasthof du Marché, 35 b.; tel. (021) 6 47 99 00

3, Jungfrau, 40 b.; tel. (036) 55 34 34   **Lauterbrunnen**
3, Oberland, 44 b.; tel. (036) 55 12 41
3, Silberhorn, 50 b.; tel. (036) 55 14 71

2, Kurhotel Lenkerhof, 135 b.; tel. (030) 6 31 31   **Lenk**
2, Parkhotel Bellevue, 70 b.; tel. (030) 3 17 61
2, Résidence, 44 b.; tel. (030) 3 25 44
3, Kreuz, 140 b.; tel. (030) 3 13 87
4, Mittaghorn, 20 b.; tel. (030) 3 13 66
4, Sternen, 23 b.; tel. (030) 3 15 09
5, Alpina, 20 b.; tel. (030) 3 10 57
Landgasthaus Berghaus Leiterli, 20 b.; tel. (030) 3 35 16

2, Grand Hotel Kurhaus Alpina, 130 b.; tel. (081) 34 11 36   **Lenzerheide**
2, Sunstar, 170 b.; tel. (081) 34 01 21
3, Sporthotel Dieschen, 84 b.; tel. (081) 34 12 22
3, Sporthotel La Riva, 50 b.; tel. (081) 34 01 34
4, Rätia, 22 b.; tel. (081) 34 11 46
4, Touring, 36 b.; tel. (081) 34 14 73
5, Danis, 47 b.; tel. (081) 34 11 17
Landgasthof Crest'Ota, 15 b.; tel. (081) 34 23 88

1, Valbella Inn, 100 b.; tel. (081) 34 36 36   Valbella
2, Post-Hotel Valbella, 160 b.; tel. (081) 34 12 12
3, Waldhaus am See, 73 b.; tel. (081) 34 11 09
4, Boffalora (no restaurant), 40 b.; tel. (081) 34 18 34
5, Kristall, 26 b.; tel. (081) 34 16 77

1, Les Sources des Alpes, 60 b.; tel. (027) 62 11 51   **Leukerbad/**
1, Badehotel Bristol, 150 b.; tel. (027) 61 18 33   **Loèche-les-Bains**
2, Bad Maison-Blanche, 75 b.; tel. (027) 62 11 61
2, Badehotel Regina Terme, 100 b.; tel. (027) 62 11 41
2, Astoria-Kurhotel, 75 b.; tel. (027) 61 14 15
3, Grichting + Badner-Hof, 75 b.; tel. (027) 61 12 27
3, Beau-Séjour, 38 b.; tel. (027) 61 12 38
3, Römerhof, 50 b.; tel. (027) 61 19 21
4, Walliserhof, 45 b.; tel. (027) 61 14 24
4, Alpina, 25 b.; tel. (027) 61 15 45
4, Derby, 50 b.; tel. (027) 61 17 27

Hotels

	4, Weisses Rössli (no restaurant), 36 b.; tel. (027) 61 33 77

4, Weisses Rössli (no restaurant), 36 b.; tel. (027) 61 33 77
5, Chamois, 11 b.; tel. (027) 61 13 57
Landesgasthaus Waldhaus-Grichting, 32 b.; tel. (027) 61 32 32

Leysin
2, Holiday Inn, 230 b.; tel. (025) 34 27 91
2, Leysin Parc, 100 b.; tel. (025) 34 20 34
3, Colina, MinOtels, 50 b.; tel. (025) 32 10 12
3, Le Grand Chalet, 60 b.; tel. (025) 34 16 14
4, Mont-Riant, 36 b.; tel. (025) 34 27 01

Liechtenstein-Vaduz
2, Park-Hotel Sonnenhof, 50 b.; tel. (075) 2 32 11 92
2, Schlössle Vaduz, 53 b.; tel. (075) 2 32 56 21
3, Engel, 30 b.; tel. (075) 2 32 03 13
3, Real, 17 b.; tel. (075) 2 32 22 22
Landgasthof Löwen, 13 b.; tel. (075) 2 32 00 66

Locarno
2, Arcadia al Lago, 89 b.; tel. (093) 31 02 82
2, Dellavalle, Brione, 85 b.; tel. (093) 33 01 21
2, Muralto, 150 b.; tel. (093) 33 01 81
2, Orselina, 140 b.; tel. (093) 33 02 32
3, Beau-Rivage, 90 b.; tel. (093) 33 13 55
3, Zurigo, 54 b.; tel. (093) 33 16 17
3, Dell'Angelo, 100 b.; tel. (093) 31 81 75
4, Villa Palmiera, 48 b.; tel. (093) 33 14 41
4, Schloss-Hotel, 61 b.; tel. (093) 31 23 61
5, Gottardo, 80 b.; tel. (093) 33 31 83
5, Mon Désir, Orselina, 49 b.; tel. (093) 33 48 42

Lucerne
1, Grand Hotel National, 144 b.; tel. (041) 50 11 11
1, Palace, 340 b.; tel. (041) 50 22 22
1, Schweizerhof, 214 b.; tel. (041) 50 22 11
2, Baslertor, MinOtels, 50 b.; tel. (041) 22 09 18
2, Europe Grand Hôtel, 350 b.; tel. (041) 30 11 11
2, Monopol & Métropole, 183 b.; tel. (041) 23 08 66
3, Alpina, 55 b.; tel. (041) 23 00 77
3, Chalet Seeburg, 93 b.; tel. (041) 31 19 22
3, De La Paix, 63 b.; tel. (041) 51 52 53
4, Derby, 30 b.; tel. (041) 51 26 62
4, Carlton Hotel Tivoli, 180 b.; tel. (041) 51 30 51
5, Pickwick (no restaurant), 23 b.; tel. (041) 51 51 08

Lugano
1, Grand Hotel Eden, 223 b.; tel. (091) 55 01 21
1, Montalbano Residence, 88 b.; tel. (091) 55 88 11
1, Principe Leopoldo, 48 b.; tel. (091) 55 88 55
2, Admiral, 145 b.; tel. (091) 54 23 24
2, Belmonte, 80 b.; tel. (091) 51 40 33
2, Du Lac, 90 b.; tel. (091) 54 19 21
3, Albatro, 80 b.; tel. (091) 55 05 05
3, Ceresio, 150 b.; tel. (091) 23 10 44
3, Calipso e Calipso Park, 276 b.; tel. (091) 54 33 41
4, Béha Lugano, 100 b.; tel. (091) 54 13 31
4, Albergo Pestalozzi, 85 b.; tel. (091) 22 95 95
4, Schmid, 62 b.; tel. (091) 54 91 21
5, Montarina, 40 b.; tel. (091) 56 72 72
5, Rosa (no restaurant), 57 b.; tel. (091) 22 92 86

Cassarate
3, Cassarate-Lago, 135 b.; tel. (091) 52 24 12
3, Diana, 67 b.; tel. (091) 51 41 41
4, Du Midi au Lac, 60 b.; tel. (091) 51 10 21

Castagnola
3, Aniro, 70 b.; tel. (091) 52 50 31
3, Carlton Villa Moritz, 100 b.; tel. (091) 51 38 12
4, Fischer's Seehotel, 36 b.; tel. (091) 51 55 71
5, Locanda Castagnola (no restaurant), 26 b.; tel. (091) 51 22 26

2, Porte d'Octodure, 110 b.; tel. (026) 22 71 21 **Martigny**
3, Forclaz-Touring, 120 b.; tel. (026) 22 27 01
3, De La Poste, 65 b.; tel. (026) 22 14 44
4, Relais du Grand Quai, 50 b.; tel. (026) 22 20 50
4, Du Vieux Stand, 58 b.; tel. (026) 22 15 06

2, Parkhotel du Sauvage, 140 b.; tel. (036) 71 41 41 **Meiringen**
2, Alpin Sherpa, 96 b.; tel. (036) 72 61 91
3, Baer, 28 b.; tel. (036) 71 46 46
4, Weisses Kreuz, 69 b.; tel. (036) 71 49 71
4, Victoria, 26 b.; tel. (036) 71 10 33
5, Adler, 24 b.; tel. (036) 71 10 32
5, Hirschen, 41 b.; tel. (036) 71 18 12

1, Crans-Ambassador, 135 b.; tel. (027) 41 52 22 **Montana**
2, Aida-Castel, 100 b.; tel. (027) 40 11 11
3, De La Forêt, 140 b.; tel. (027) 40 21 31
4, Cisalpin, 40 b.; tel. (027) 41 24 25
5, Monte Sano, 12 b.; tel. (027) 41 24 27

1, Le Montreux Palace, 500 b.; tel. (021) 9 63 53 37 **Montreux**
1, Grand Hotel Excelsior, 100 b.; tel. (021) 9 63 32 31
2, Suisse et Majestic, 250 b.; tel. (021) 9 63 51 81
2, Bonivard, 180 b.; tel. (021) 9 63 43 41
3, Golf-Hôtel René Capt, 100 b.; tel. (021) 9 63 46 31
3, Helvétie, 100 b.; tel. (021) 9 63 25 51
4, Hostellerie du Lac, 15 b.; tel. (021) 9 63 32 71
4, Bon Port (no restaurant), 59 b.; tel. (021) 9 63 34 31
5, Villa Germaine, 24 b.; tel. (021) 9 63 15 28

2, Fleur du Lac, 47 b.; tel. (021) 8 02 43 11 **Morges**
3, Du Mont Blanc au Lac, 80 b.; tel. (021) 8 02 30 72

2, Palace Mürren, 100 b.; tel. (036) 55 24 24 **Mürren**
3, Alpenruh, 60 b.; tel. (036) 55 10 55
4, Alpina, 50 b.; tel. (036) 55 13 61

3, Krone/Couronne, 65 b.; tel. 71 52 52 **Murten/Morat**
3, Weisses Kreuz, 52 b.; tel. 71 26 41

2, Beaulac, 92 b.; tel. (038) 25 88 22 **Neuchâtel/**
3, Touring au Lac, 80 b.; tel. (038) 25 55 01 **Neuenburg**
4, Des Beaux-Arts, 47 b.; tel. (038) 24 01 51

2, Beau-Rivage, 100 b.; tel. (022) 3 61 62 51 **Nyon**
3, Des Alpes, 70 b.; tel. (022) 3 61 49 31

2, Europe, 55 b.; tel. (062) 32 35 55 **Olten**
2, Olten, 63 b.; tel. (062) 26 30 30
3, Astoria, 55 b.; tel. (062) 32 12 12

4, De La Croix Blanche, 17 b.; tel. (037) 61 61 66 **Payerne**

1, Grand Hotel Kronenhof, 150 b.; tel. (082) 6 01 11 **Pontresina/**
2, Walther, 135 b.; tel. (082) 6 64 71 **Puntraschigna**
3, Atlas, 150 b.; tel. (082) 6 63 21
5, Bahnhof-Chesa Briotta, 31 b.; tel. (082) 6 62 42

1, Quellenhof, 187 b.; tel. (081) 3 03 20 20 **Bad Ragaz**
2, Grand Hotel Hof Ragaz, 187 b.; tel. (081) 3 02 30 30
3, Schloss Ragaz, 115 b.; tel. (081) 3 02 23 55
4, Poléra, 30 b.; tel. (081) 3 02 25 01

Hotels

Rapperswil
2, Hotel Schwanen AG, 37 b.; tel. (055) 21 91 81
5, Du Lac, 17 b.; tel. (055) 27 19 43

Rheinfelden
2, Eden Solbad, 65 b.; tel. (061) 8 31 54 04
3, Schiff am Rhein, MinOtels, 80 b.; tel. (061) 8 31 60 87
4, Ochsen, 14 b.; tel. (061) 8 31 51 01

Rigi
In Rigi-Kaltbad: 3, Bergsonne Silence Hotel, 40 b.; tel. (041) 83 11 47
4, Rigi First, 23 b.; tel. (041) 83 14 64

Rorschach
2, Parkhotel Waldau, 70 b.; tel. (071) 43 01 80
3, Mozart, 66 b.; tel. (071) 41 06 32
4, Jud, 48 b.; tel. (071) 41 76 44

Saas Almagell
3, Kristall-Saphir, 97 b.; tel. (028) 57 14 33
4, Portjengrat, 55 b.; tel. (028) 57 10 10
5, Edelweiss, 12 b.; tel. (028) 57 21 50

Saas Fee
2, Ferienart Walliserhof, 106 b.; tel. (028) 57 20 21
2, Saaserhof, 100 b.; tel. (028) 57 35 51
3, Alphubel, 70 b.; tel. (028) 57 11 12
3, Résidence Atlantic, 48 b.; tel. (028) 57 17 09
4, Rendez-Vous, 37 b.; tel. (028) 57 20 40
5, Mascotte, 18 b.; tel. (028) 57 27 24

Saas Grund
3, Monte Rosa, 45 b.; tel. (028) 57 35 25
2, Rodania, 60 b.; tel. (028) 57 24 23

Samedan
2, Bernina, 105 b.; tel. (082) 6 54 21
3, Golf-Hôtel des Alpes, 64 b.; tel. (082) 6 52 62
4, Terminus, 36 b.; tel. (082) 6 53 36

Samnaun
2, Post, 88 b.; tel. (081) 8 68 53 53
3, Samnaunerhof, 48 b.; tel. (081) 8 68 51 88

San Bernardino
2, Brocco & Posta, 60 b.; tel. (092) 94 11 05
3, Albarella, 130 b.; tel. (092) 94 01 01

St Gallen
2, Einstein, 117 b.; tel. (071) 20 00 33
2, Walhalla, 80 b.; tel. (071) 22 29 22
3, Gallo, 49 b.; tel. (071) 25 27 27
3, Sistar, 62 b.; tel. (071) 32 11 66
4, Sporting, 41 b.; tel. (071) 27 13 12

St Moritz
1, Badrutt's Palace Hotel, 380 b.; tel. (082) 2 11 01
1, Carlton Hotel, 180 b.; tel. (082) 2 11 41
1, Suvretta House, 350 b.; tel. (082) 2 11 21
2, Europa St Moritz, 200 b.; tel. (082) 2 11 75
2, Park-Hotel Kurhaus, 260 b.; tel. (082) 2 11 11
2, Schweizerhof, 150 b.; tel. (082) 2 27 71
3, Edelweiss, 100 b.; tel. (082) 3 55 33
3, Nolda, 70 b.; tel. (082) 3 05 75
3, Waldhaus am See, 72 b.; tel. (082) 3 76 76
4, Bellaval, 43 b.; tel. (082) 3 32 45
4, Bernina, 52 b.; tel. (082) 3 60 22
5, National, 40 b.; tel. (082) 3 32 74
5, Sonne (no restaurant), 150 b.; tel. (082) 3 03 62

Sarnen
2, Krone, 100 b.; tel. (041) 66 66 33
4, Obwaldnerhof, 15 b.; tel. (041) 66 18 17
5, Hirschen, 16 b.; tel. (041) 66 15 42

2, Cresta, 97 b.; tel. (081) 74 17 55	**Savognin**
3, Alpina, 100 b.; tel. (081) 74 14 26	
4, Pianta, MinOtels, 36 b.; tel. (081) 74 11 05	
2, Bahnhof, 100 b.; tel. (053) 25 19 24	**Schaffhausen**
3, Bellevue, 55 b.; tel. (053) 22 21 21	
3, Kronenhof, 61 b.; tel. (053) 25 66 31	
4, Matte-Eggli (no restaurant), 14 b.; tel. (053) 61 43 63	
5, Gasthof Maienburg, 11 b.; tel. (053) 61 34 03	
3, Schwägalp, 60 b.; tel. (071) 58 16 03	**Schwägalp**
4, Passhöhe, 6 b.; tel. (071) 58 12 43	
5, Säntisgipfel, 46 b.; tel. (071) 27 99 55	
2, Wysses Rössli, 46 b.; tel. (043) 21 19 22	**Schwyz**
5, Hirschen, 26 b.; tel. (043) 21 12 76	
2, Belvedere, 90 b.; tel. (081) 8 64 10 41	**Bad Scuol**
3, Bellaval, 50 b.; tel. (081) 8 64 14 81	
3, Romantik Guardaval, 80 b.; tel. (081) 8 64 13 21	
4, Crusch Alba ed Alveter, 40 b.; tel. (081) 8 64 14 05	
5, Quellenhof, 80 b.; tel. (081) 8 64 12 15	
3, Atlantic, 74 b.; tel. (027) 55 25 35	**Sierre/Siders**
4, Europe (no restaurant), 58 b.; tel. (027) 55 24 31	
5, Pension La Promenade, 20 b.; tel. (027) 56 34 04	
2, Margna, 110 b.; tel. (082) 4 53 06	**Sils Baselgia**
3, Sporthotel Grischa, 50 b.; tel. (082) 4 51 16	
1, Waldhaus, 220 b.; tel. (082) 4 53 31	**Sils Maria**
2, Edelweiss, 125 b.; tel. (082) 4 52 22	
3, Maria, 65 b.; tel. (082) 4 53 17	
4, Mira Margna, 34 b.; tel. (082) 4 52 40	
1, Chesa Guardelej, 210 b.; tel. (082) 2 31 21	**Silvaplana**
2, Albana, 60 b.; tel. (082) 4 92 92	
3, Julier-Chesa Arsa, 75 b.; tel. (082) 4 96 44	
4, Arlas, 24 b.; tel. (082) 4 81 48	
4, Engiadina, 90 b.; tel. (082) 4 81 15	
3, Du Rhône, 80 b.; tel. (027) 22 82 91	**Sion/Sitten**
4, Ibis, 150 b.; tel. (027) 33 11 91	
5, La Channe, 25 b.; tel. (027) 22 32 71	
2, Krone, 60 b.; tel. (065) 22 44 12	**Solothurn**
3, Astoria, 80 b.; tel. (065) 22 75 71	
2, Edenhotel, 80 b.; tel. (033) 54 11 54	**Spiez**
3, Des Alpes, 60 b.; tel. (033) 54 33 54	
4, Bellevue, 30 b.; tel. (033) 54 84 64	
2, Winkelried, 58 b.; tel. (041) 61 99 01	**Stansstad**
3, Seehotel Acheregg, 50 b.; tel. (041) 61 36 26	
2, Chlosterhof, 140 b.; tel. (054) 42 42 42	**Stein am Rhein**
3, Adler, 42 b.; tel. (054) 42 61 61	
4, Zur Rheingerbe, 16 b.; tel. (054) 41 29 91	
3, Walliserhof, 69 b.; tel. (028) 67 19 55	**Täsch**
3, Täscherhof-Bahnhof, 65 b.; tel. (028) 67 18 18	
3, Zur Linde, tel. (071) 33 28 22	**Teufen**
4, Säntis, 24 b.; tel. (071) 33 33 55	

Hotels

Thun	2, Freienhof, 98 b.; tel. (033) 21 55 11
	3, Seepark, 108 b.; tel. (033) 26 12 12
	3, Alpha, 60 b.; tel. (033) 36 93 93
Tiefenkastel	Albula, 85 b.; tel. (081) 71 11 21
Vaduz	See Liechenstein-Vaduz
Verbier	2, Rosalp, 50 b.; tel. (026) 31 63 23
	3, Le Mazot, 64 b.; tel. (026) 31 64 04
	3, Catogne, 40 b.; tel. (026) 31 62 72
	4, L'Auberge, 40 b.; tel. (026) 31 62 72
Vevey	1, Des Trois Couronnes, 109 b.; tel. (021) 9 21 30 05
	1, Le Mirador & Country Club, 137 b.; tel. (021) 9 21 30 05
	2, Du Lac, 100 b.; tel. (021) 9 21 10 41
	2, Du Parc, 130 b.; tel. (021) 9 21 23 22
	3, De Famille, MinOtels, 100 b.; tel. (021) 9 21 39 31
	3, Hotellerie de Châtonneyre, 35 b.; tel. (021) 9 21 47 81
	4, Bahyse, 25 b.; tel. (021) 9 43 48 10
	4, Des Négociants, 45 b.; tel. (021) 9 22 70 11
	5, De La Place, 16 b.; tel. (021) 9 21 12 87
Villars	1, Grand Hôtel du Parc, 110 b.; tel. (025) 35 21 21
	2, Bristol, 220 b.; tel. (025) 36 11 36
	3, Du Golf + Marie Louise, 138 b.; tel. (025) 35 24 77
Weggis	2, Posthotel, 100 b.; tel. (041) 93 23 23
	3, Central am See, 70 b.; tel. (041) 93 21 14
	Landgasthof Blaukreuz-Ferienzentrum, 35 b.; tel. (041) 93 27 81
Wengen	2, Beausite Park Hotel, 110 b.; tel. (036) 56 51 61
	2, Victoria-Lauberhorn, 120 b.; tel. (036) 56 51 51
	3, Belvédère, 120 b.; tel. (036) 55 24 12
	3, Falken, 80 b.; tel. (036) 56 51 21
	4, Schweizerheim + Chalet, 58 b.; tel. (036) 55 11 12
	4, Bären (no restaurant), 26 b.; tel. (036) 55 14 19
	5, Eden, 26 b.; tel. (036) 55 16 34
Winterthur	2, Garten-Hotel, 90 b.; tel. (052) 2 12 19 19
	3, Wartmann am Bahnhof, 120 b.; tel. (052) 2 12 84 21
	3, Motel Wüflingen, 72 b.; tel. (052) 2 22 67 21
	4, Römertor, 28 b.; tel. (052) 2 42 69 21
	Landgasthof Krone Winterthur, 66 b.; tel. (052) 2 13 25 21
Yverdon-Les-Bains	2, Grand Hôtel des Bains, 170 b.; tel. (024) 21 70 21
	3, Expo Hotel, 186 b.; tel. (024) 25 52 55
	4, La Maison Blanche, 37 b.; tel. (024) 21 26 42
Zermatt	1, Grand Hotel Zermatterhof, 145 b.; tel. (028) 66 11 00
	1, Mont Cervin, 263 b.; tel. (028) 66 88 88
	2, Alex, 140 b.; tel. (028) 67 17 26
	2, Ambassador, 220 b.; tel. (028) 66 11 11
	2, Parkhotel Beau Site, 120 b.; tel. (028) 67 12 71
	2, Walliserhof, 90 b.; tel. (028) 67 11 74
	2, La Ginabelle, 80 b.; tel. (028) 67 45 35
	3, Alpenroyal, 60 b.; tel. (028) 67 46 46
	3, Gornergrat, 100 b.; tel. (028) 67 10 27
	3, Hemizeus, 100 b.; tel. (028) 66 21 11
	3, Perren, 115 b.; tel. (028) 66 11 45
	3, Riffelberg ob Zermatt, 60 b.; tel. (028) 67 22 16
	3, Berghotel Riffelberg, 40 b.; tel. (028) 67 53 33

4, Kulmhotel Gornergrat, 40 b.; tel. (028) 67 22 19
4, Alphubel, 50 b.; tel. (028) 67 30 03
4, Rhodania, 42 b.; tel. (028) 67 28 63
4, Blauherd (no restaurant), 38 b.; tel. (028) 67 22 91
5, Schwarzsee, 12 b.; tel. (028) 67 22 63
5, Michabel, 55 b.; tel. (028) 67 11 31
5, Weisshorn (no restaurant), 30 b.; tel. (028) 67 11 12
Gadegg hut, 27 b.; tel. (077) 28 39 96

3, Bär-Post, 80 b.; tel. (082) 8 11 41   **Zernez**
4, Filli-Bäckerei, 40 b.; tel. (082) 8 10 72

2, Parkhotel Zug, 214 b.; tel. (042) 22 66 11   **Zug**
3, Rosenberg, 62 b.; tel. (042) 21 43 43
4, Löwen au Lac, 40 b.; tel. (042) 21 77 22

2, Posthotel Engiadina, 70 b.; tel. (082) 7 10 21   **Zuoz**
3, Belvair, 40 b.; tel. (082) 7 20 23
3, Sporthotel Wolf, 48 b.; tel. (082) 7 17 17

1, Baur au Lac, 210 b.; tel. (01) 2 20 50 20   **Zurich**
1, Dolder Grand Hotel, 300 b.; tel. (01) 2 51 62 31
1, Eden au Lac, 75 b.; tel. (01) 2 61 94 04
1, Savoy Baur en Ville, 150 b.; tel. (01) 2 11 53 60
1, Zürich, 350 b.; tel. (01) 3 63 63 63
1, Atlantis Sheraton, 310 b.; tel. (01) 4 54 54 54
1, La Résidence, 125 b.; tel. (01) 3 63 63 63
2, Swisshotel Zürich, 700 b.; tel. (01) 3 11 43 41
2, Dolder Waldhaus, 160 b.; tel. (01) 2 51 93 60
2, Tiefenau Zürich, 70 b.; tel. (01) 2 51 24 09
2, Zum Storchen, 115 b.; tel. (01) 2 11 55 10
2, Seiler Neues Schloss, 89 b.; tel. (01) 2 01 65 50
2, Rigihof, 110 b.; tel. (01) 3 61 16 85
2, Opera (no restaurant), 100 b.; tel. (01) 2 51 90 90
2, Wellenberg (no restaurant), 72 b.; tel. (01) 2 62 43 00
3, Atlantis Guesthouse (no restaurant), 126 b.; tel. (01) 4 54 54 54
3, Scheuble (no restaurant), 110 b.; tel. (01) 2 51 82 03
3, Montana, 150 b.; tel. (01) 2 71 69 00
3, Arc en Ville, 120 b.; tel. (01) 2 71 54 00
3, Florida, 150 b.; tel. (01) 3 83 68 30
3, Senator, 210 b.; tel. (01) 2 72 20 21
3, Limmat (Congress Centre), 106 b.; tel. (01) 2 71 51 40
3, Leoneck, 90 b.; tel. (01) 2 61 60 70
4, Limmathof, 100 b.; tel. (01) 2 61 42 20
4, Leonhard, 30 b.; tel. (01) 2 51 30 80
4, Goldener Brunnen, 40 b.; tel. (01) 4 62 67 33
4, Rothaus, 80 b.; tel. (01) 2 41 24 51
4, Alexander Guesthouse (no restaurant), 49 b.; tel. (01) 2 51 82 03
4, Splendid (no restaurant), 43 b.; tel. (01) 2 52 58 50
4, Rex (no restaurant), 80 b.; tel. (01) 3 61 96 46
5, Vorderer Sternen, 17 b.; tel. (01) 2 51 49 49

Re-opened in 1994 and not yet classified:
Zürichberg (no alcohol), 86 b.; tel. (01) 2 52 38 48

1, Zurich Airport Hilton, 550 b.; tel. (01) 8 10 31 31   Zurich airport
1, Zurich Renaissance Hotel, 408 b.; tel. (01) 8 10 85 00
2, Airport, 67 b.; tel. (01) 8 10 44 44
2, Mövenpick Hotel Airport, 570 b.; tel. (01) 8 10 11 11
3, Belair, 70 b.; tel. (01) 8 30 03 81
3, Novotel Zurich Airport, 550 b.; tel. (01) 8 10 31 11
3, Welcome Inn, 200 b.; tel. (01) 8 14 07 27

Information

Zurzach	2, Kurhotel Bad-Zurzach, 134 b.; tel. (056) 49 25 25
	2, Park-Hotel Bad Zurzach, 335 b.; tel. (056) 49 01 51
	3, Turmhotel and Turmpavillon, 154 b.; tel. (056) 49 24 40
	3, Zurzacherhof, 73 b.; tel. (056) 49 01 21
Zweisimmen	3, Post, 25 b.; tel. (030) 2 12 28
	3, Residence-Simmental, 40 b.; tel. (030) 2 17 15
	4, Krone, 50 b.; tel. (030) 2 26 26
	4, Sport Motel, 50 b.; tel. (030) 2 14 31
	5, Berghotel Sparenmoos, 24 b.; tel. (030) 2 22 34

Information

Swiss National Tourist Office (Schweizerische Verkehrszentrale – SVZ)

	Bellariastrasse 38
	CH-8027 Zürich
	Tel. (01) 2 88 11 11, fax (01) 2 88 12 05
In GB	Swiss National Tourist Office
	Swiss Centre, Swiss Court
	London, W1V 8EE
	Tel. (0171) 734 1921
USA	Swiss National Tourist Office
	Swiss Center, 608 Fifth Avenue
	New York, NY 10020
	Tel. (212) 757 5944
Canada	Swiss National Tourist Office
	926 The East Mall
	ETOBICOKE
	Ontario, M9B 6K1
	Tel. (416) 695 2090

Regional Tourist Offices

Grisons	Verkehrsverein, Alexanderstrasse 24, CH-7001 Chur, tel. (081) 22 13 60
East Switzerland and the Principality of Liechtenstein	Tourismusverband, Bahnhofplatz 1a, CH-9001, St Gallen, tel. (071) 22 62 62
Zurich	Verkehrsverein, Bahnhofbrücke 1, CH-8023 Zürich, tel. (01) 2 11 12 56
Central Switzerland	Verkehrsverband, Alpenstrasse 1, CH-6002 Lucerne, tel. (041) 51 18 91
North-west Switzerland	Verkehrsverein, Blumenrain 2, CH-4001 Basle, tel. (061) 2 61 50 50
Bernese Oberland	Verkehrsverband, Jungfraustrasse 38, CH-3800 Interlaken, tel. (036) 22 26 21
Bernese Mittelland	Verkehrsverband, (at the station), CH-3001 Berne, tel. (031) 3 11 12 12

Union Fribourgoise du Tourisme, 107, route de la Glâne, CH-1701 Fribourg, tel. (037) 24 56 44 — Fribourg

Fédération Neuchâteloise du Tourisme, Rue du Trésor 9, CH-2001 Neuchâtel, tel. (038) 25 17 89 — Neuchâtel

Fédération du Tourisme de la République et Canton du Jura, 8, rue de la Gare, CH-2726 Saignelégier, tel. (039) 51 26 26 — Jura

Office du Tourisme du Jura Bernois, 26, Avenue de la Liberté, CH-2740 Moutier, tel. (032) 93 64 66 — Berne Jura

Office du Tourisme du Canton de Vaud, 60, Avenue d'Ouchy, CH-1006 Lausanne, tel. (021) 6 17 72 02 — Lake Geneva District

Union Valaisanne du Tourisme, 6, rue Pré-Fleuri, CH-1950 Sion, tel. (027) 22 31 61 — Valais

Ente Ticinese per il turismo, Villa Turrita, CH-6501 Bellinzona, tel. (092) 25 70 56. — Ticino

Information Offices in Towns and Communities

Verkehrsbüro, Bahnhofstrasse 20, CH-5001 Aarau, tel. (064) 24 76 24 — **Aarau**

Kur- und Verkehrsverein, CH-3715 Adelboden, tel. (033) 73 22 52 — **Adelboden**

Office du Tourisme, 4, Avenue de la Gare, tel. (025) 26 12 12 — **Aigle**

Verkehrsbüro, Lehnplatz 16, CH-6460 Altdorf, tel. (044) 2 28 88 — **Altdorf**

Verkehrsverein, CH-8580 Amriswil, tel. (071) 67 13 31 — **Amriswil**

Verkehrsbüro, Bahnhofplatz, CH-6490 Andermatt, tel. (044) 6 74 54 — **Andermatt**

Verkehrsbüro, Hauptgasse 19, CH-9050 Appenzell (AI), tel. (071) 87 41 11 — **Appenzell**

Appenzell-Innerrhoden: see Appenzell (AI)
Appenzell-Ausserrhoden: Verkehrsbüro, CH-9100 Herisau (AR), tel. (071) 51 44 60 — **Apenzeller Land**

Verkehrsbüro, Bahnhofstrasse 40, CH-9320 Arbon, tel. (071) 46 33 37 — **Arbon**

Kur- und Verkehrsverein, opposite the Kursaal, CH-7050 Arosa, tel. (081) 31 51 51 — **Arosa**

Ente turistico di Ascona e Losone, Piazza San Pietro, Casa Serodine, CH-6612 Ascona, tel. (093) 35 00 90 — **Ascona**

See main name — **Bad**

Kur- und Verkehrsbüro, Bahnhofstrasse 50, CH-5400 Baden, tel. (056) 22 53 18 — **Baden**

Verkehrsverein, Schifflände 5, CH-4001 Basle, tel. (061) 2 72 19 55 — **Basle**

Central information offices:
Bahnhof SBB, CH-4051, Basle, tel. (061) 2 71 36 84

Kur- und Verkehrsverein, CH-3803 Beatenberg, tel. (036) 41 12 86 — **Beatenberg**

Verkehrsbüro, CH-6375 Beckenried, tel. (041) 64 31 70 — **Beckenried**

Ente Turistico di Bellinzona e Dintorni, Via Camminata 6, CH-6500 Bellinzona, tel. (092) 25 21 31 — **Bellinzona**

Verkehrsverein ''Pro Bregaglia'', CH-7605 Stampa, tel. (082) 4 15 55 — **Bergeli**

Information

Berne Verkehrs- und Kongressbüro (at the station), P.O.B. 2700, CH-3001 Berne, tel. (031) 3 11 66 11

Berner Oberland See Interlaken

Bernina See Pontresina

Bettmeralp Verkehrsbüro, CH-3981 Bettmeralp, tel. (028) 27 12 91

Biel/Bienne Verkehrsbüro, Zentralstrasse 60, CH-2500 Biel/Bienne, tel. (032) 22 75 75

Braunwald Kur- und Verkehrsverein, CH-8784 Braunwald, tel. (058) 84 11 08

Breiten ob Mörel Verkehrsbüro, CH-3983 Breiten ob Mörel, tel. (028) 27 13 45

Brienz am See Verkehrsbüro, CH-3855 Brienz, tel. (036) 51 32 42

Brig Verkehrsbüro, Bahnhofplatz, CH-3900 Brig, tel. (028) 23 19 01

Brissago Ente Turistico di Brissago e Ronco, CH-6614 Brissago, tel. (093) 65 11 70

Brunnen Kur- und Verkehrsverein, Bahnhofstrasse 32, CH-6440 Brunnen, tel. (043) 31 17 77

Bulle Office du Tourisme, CH-1630 Bulle, tel. (029) 2 80 22

Celerina Kur- und Verkehrsverein, CH-7505 Celerina, tel. (082) 3 39 66

Champéry Office du Tourisme, CH-1874 Champéry, tel. (025) 79 11 41

Château-d'Oex Office du Tourisme, La Place, CH-1837 Château d'Oex, tel. (029) 4 77 88

La Chaux-de-Fonds Office de Tourisme, 11, rue Neuve, CH-2300 La Chaux-de-Fonds, tel. (039) 28 13 13

Chexbres Office du Tourisme, CH-1605 Chexbres, tel. (021) 9 46 22 31

Chiasso See Mendrisio

Chur Verkehrsverein, Grabenstrasse 5, CH-7000 Chur, tel. (081) 22 18 18

Lake Constance Internationaler Bodensee-Verkehrsverein (IBV), Schützenstrasse 8, D-78462 Konstanz, tel. (075) 31 2 22 32

See Arbon

See Kreuzlingen

See Rorschach

Crans-Montana Office du Tourisme Crans-sur-Sierre, CH-3985 Crans, tel. (027) 41 21 32
Office du Tourisme, Montana-Vermala, Avenue de la Gare, CH-3962 Montana, tel. (027) 41 30 41

Davos Verkehrsverein, Promenade 67, CH-7270 Davos Platz, tel. (081) 45 21 21
Informationsbüro, Bahnhofstrasse 7, CH-7270 Davos Dorf

Delémont Office du Tourisme, 12, Place de la Gare, CH-2800 Delémont, tel. (066) 22 97 78

Les Diablerets Office du Tourisme, Bâtiment BCV, CH-1856 Les Diablerets, tel. (025) 53 13 58

Disentis/Mustér Kur- und Verkehrsverein, CH-7180 Disentis, tel. (086) 9 47 58 22

Verkehrsbüro, Hauptstrasse 85, CH-8840 Einsiedeln, tel. (055) 53 44 88 — **Einsiedeln**

Verkehrsverband Emmental, Mühlgässli 2,
CH-3350 Langnau im Emmental, tel. (035) 2 42 52 — **Emmental**

Oberengadiner Verkehrsverein, CH-7504 Pontresina,
tel. (082) 6 64 88; See Zernez — **Engadin/Engiadina**

Kur- und Verkehrsverein, Dorfstrasse 34, CH-6390 Engelberg,
tel. (041) 94 11 61 — **Engelberg**

Verkehrsverein Zentralschweiz, Pilatusstrasse 14, CH-6002 Lucerne,
tel. (041) 23 70 45 — **Entlebuch**

Verkehrsverein Fiesch-Fiescherthal, CH-3984 Fiesch, tel. (028) 71 14 66 — **Fiesch**

Kur- und Verkehrsverein Flims, CH-7018 Flims-Waldhaus, tel. (081) 39 10 22 — **Flims**

Verkehrsbüro, near the old church, CH-6454 Flüelen — **Flüelen**

Verkehrsbüro Tannenboden, CH-8898 Flumserberg-Tannenboden,
tel. (085) 73 33 32 32 — **Flumserberg**

Verkehrsbüro, Rathaus, CH-8500 Frauenfeld, tel. (054) 21 31 28 — **Frauenfeld**

Office du Tourisme, Square-des-Places 1, CH-1700 Fribourg,
tel. (037) 81 31 75 — **Fribourg/Freiburg**

Office du Tourisme, Rue de la Tour-de-l'Isle, CH-1201 Geneva,
tel. (022) 7 88 08 08 — **Geneva**

Office du Tourisme du Canton de Vaud (OTV), Avenue d'Ouchy 60,
CH-1000 Lausanne-Ouchy, tel. (021) 6 17 72 02 — **Lake Geneva**

See Chexebres

See Geneva

See Morges

Verkehrsverein Glarner Land und Walensee, Info-Stelle, Raststätte N3,
CH-8867 Niedermann, tel. (058) 21 21 25 — **Glarner Land**

Verkehrsbüro, Kirchweg 18, CH-8750 Glarus, tel. (058) 61 15 06 — **Glarus**

Kur- und Verkehrsverein, CH-3925 Grächen, tel. (028) 56 27 27 — **Grächen**

Verkehrsverein Graubünden (WGR), Alexanderstrasse 24,
CH-7000 Chur, tel. (081) 22 13 60 — **Graubünden**

Office du Tourisme, CH-1663 Gruyère, tel. (029) 6 10 30 — **Gruyère**

Office du Tourisme, CH-3961 Grimentz, tel. (027) 65 14 93 — **Grimentz**

Verkehrsbüro, CH-3818 Grindelwald, tel. (036) 53 12 12 — **Grindelwald**

Verkehrsbüro, CH-3780 Gstaad, tel. (030) 4 71 71 — **Gstaad**

Verkehrsbüro, Seeallee, CH-9410 Heiden, tel. (071) 91 10 96 — **Heiden**

Verkehrsbüro, Oberdorfstrasse 24, CH-9100 Herisau, tel. (071) 51 44 60 — **Herisau**

Verkehrsverein, Höheweg 37, CH-3800 Interlaken, tel. (036) 22 21 21 — **Interlaken**

Information

Jungfrau Region	See Interlaken
	Bahnen der Jungfrau Region, CH-3800 Interlaken, tel. (036) 22 52 52
Jura	Fédération du Tourisme de la République et Canton du Jura, 8, rue de la Gare, CH-2726 Saignelégier, tel. (039) 51 26 26
Kandersteg	Verkehrsbüro, CH-3718 Kandersteg, tel. (033) 75 22 33
Klosters	Kur- und Verkehrsverein, CH-7250 Klosters, tel. (081) 69 18 77
Kreuzlingen	Verkehrsbüro, Haupstrasse 39, CH-8280 Kreuzlingen, tel. (072) 72 38 40
Küssnacht am Rigi	Verkehrsbüro, CH-6403 Küssnacht, tel. (041) 81 33 30
Laax	Verkehrsverein, CH-7031 Laax, tel. (086) 9 21 43 43
Lake Maggiore	See Ascona
	See Grissago
	See Locarno
Lausanne	Office du Tourisme et des Congrès, Avenue de Rhodanie 2, CH-1000 Lausanne 6, tel. (021) 6 17 73 21.
	Branches: Hauptbahnhof (Zentralhalle, tel. (021) 6 17 14 27). Geneva Cointrin Airport (Auskunfthalle, tel. (022) 98 45 73). Palais de Beaulieu, Centre des Congrès et Expositions, Avenue des Bergières 10, CH-1000 Lausanne, tel. (021) 45 11 11. Office du Tourisme du Canton de Vaud, Avenue d'Ouchy 60, CH-1000 Lausanne, tel. (021) 6 17 72 02.
Lauterbrunnen	Verkehrsverein, CH-3822 Lauterbrunnen, tel. (036) 55 19 55
Lenk	Kur- und Verkehrsverein, CH-3775 Lenk im Simmental, tel. (030) 3 15 95
Lenzerheide-Valbella	Kur- und Verkehrsverein, CH-7078 Lenzerheide, Via Principale, tel. (081) 34 34 34
Leukerbad/ Loèche-les-Bains	Verkehrsverein, CH-3954 Leukerbad, tel. (027) 62 11 11
Leysin	Office du Tourisme, CH-1854 Leysin, tel. (025) 34 22 44
Liechtenstein	See Vaduz
Le Locle	Office du Tourisme, CH-2400 Le Locle, tel. (039) 31 43 30
Locarno	Ente Turistico di Locarno e Valli, Largo Zorzi, CH-6600 Locarno, tel. (093) 31 03 33
Lötschental	Verkehrsverein Lötschental, CH-3903 Kippel, tel. (028) 49 13 88
Lugano	Ente Turistico Lugano e Dintorni, Riva Albertolli 5, CH-6901 Lugano, tel. (091) 21 46 64
Lucerne	Verkehrsverein, Frankenstrasse 1, CH-6002 Lucerne, tel. (041) 51 71 71
Martigny	Office Régional du Tourisme, CH-1920 Martigny, tel. (026) 21 22 20
Meiringen	Verkehrsverein Meiringen-Haslital, CH-3860 Meiringen, tel. (036) 71 43 22

Ente Turistico del Mendrisiotto e Basso Ceresio, Via Zorzi, CH-6850 Mendrisio, tel. (091) 46 57 61 **Mendrisio**

Office du Tourisme, Rue du Theâtre 5, CH-1820 Montreux, tel. (021) 9 63 12 12 **Montreux**

Office du Tourisme, Place du Casino 1, CH-1110 Morges, tel. (021) 8 01 32 33 **Morges**

Office du Tourisme, CH-2740 Moutier, tel. (032) 93 64 66 **Moutier**

Kur- und Verkehrsverein, CH-3825 Mürren, tel. (036) 55 16 16 **Mürren**

Verkehrsbüro, Kirchgasse 6, CH-3280 Morat/Murten, tel. (037) 71 51 12 **Morat/Murten**

Office du Tourisme de Neuchâtel et environs, rue de la Place d'Armes 7, CH-2001 Neuchâtel, tel. (038) 25 42 42 **Neuchâtel**

Office du Tourisme, Avenue Viollier 7, CH-1260 Nyon, tel. (022) 61 62 61 **Nyon**

Verkehrsverein, CH-3981 Obergestein, tel. (028) 73 27 00 **Obergestein**

See Savognin **Oberhalbstein/ Sursée**

See Tiefencastel

Verkehrsbüro, CH-3653 Oberhofen am Thuner See, tel. (033) 43 14 19 **Oberhofen on Lake Thun**

Verkehrsbüro, CH-4600 Olten, tel. (062) 32 30 84 **Olten**

Kur- und Verkehrsverein, CH-7504 Pontresina, tel. (082) 6 64 88 **Pontresina**

Syndicat d'Initiative Régional d'Ajoie du Clos-du-Doubs (SIR), CH-2900 Porrentruy, tel. (066) 66 18 53 **Porrentruy**

Kur- und Verkehrsverein, Haus Schweizerhof, CH-7310 Bad Ragaz, tel. (085) 3 02 10 61 **Bad Ragaz**

Verkehrsbüro, Am Seequai, CH-8640 Rapperswil, tel. (055) 27 70 00 **Rapperswil**

See Aarau **Rhine**

See Basle

See Frauenfeld

See Graubünden

See St Gallen

See Schaffhausen

See Zürich

Verkehrsbüro, Industriestrasse 39, CH-8212 Neuhausen am Rheinfall, tel. (053) 2 74 55 **Rheinfall**

Kur- und Verkehrsverein, Marktgasse 61, CH-4310 Rheinfelden, tel. (061) 87 55 20 **Rheinfelden**

Union Valaisanne du Tourisme, 6, rue Pré-Fleuri, CH-1950 Sion, tel. (027) 22 31 61 **Rhône Valley/ Vallée du Rhône**
Office du Tourisme du Canton de Vaud, Avenue d'Ouchy 60, CH-1002 Lausanne, tel. (021) 6 17 72 02

Information

Riederalp	Verkehrsverein, CH-3981 Riederalp, tel. (028) 27 13 65
Rigi	Verkehrsbüro, CH-6356 Rigi-Kaltbad, tel. (041) 83 11 28
Rolle	Association des Intérêts du Cœur de la Côte et Office du Tourisme, Grand-Rue 6, CH-1180 Rolle, tel. (021) 8 25 15 35
Rorschach	Verkehrsbüro, Neugasse 2, CH-9400 Rorschach, tel. (071) 41 70 34
Saas Fee	Verkehrsverein, CH-3908 Saas Fee, tel. (028) 57 14 57
Saas Tal	See Saas Fee
San Bernardino	Ente Turistico, CH-6565 San Bernardino, tel. (092) 94 12 14
St Gallen	Verkehrsverein, Bahnhofplatz 1a, CH-9001 St Gallen, tel. (071) 22 62 62
St Gotthard	See Andermatt
St-Maurice	Office du Tourisme, Grand-Rue 48, CH-1890 St-Maurice, tel. (025) 65 27 77
St Moritz	Kur- und Verkehrsverein, Via Maistra 12, CH-7500 St Moritz, tel. (082) 3 31 47
Samedan	Verkehrsverein, CH-7503 Samedan, tel. (082) 6 54 32
Sarnen	Verkehrsverein, Hofstrasse 2, CH-6060 Sarnen, tel. (041) 66 40 55
Savognin	Kur- und Verkehrsverein, CH-7460 Savognin, tel. (081) 74 22 22
Schaffhausen	Verkehrsverein, Tronwagturm, CH-8202 Schaffhausen, tel. (053) 25 51 41
Schwägalp	Säntisbahn (Urnäsch), tel. (071) 58 19 21
Schweizer Nationalpark	Nationalparkhaus Zernez, CH-7530 Zernez, tel. (082) 8 13 78
Schwyz	Verkehrsbüro, Postplatz 9, CH-6430 Schwyz, tel. (043) 22 19 91
Bad Scuol	Kur- und Verkehrsverein, CH-7550 Bad Scuol, tel. (084) 8 64 94 94
Siders/Sierre	Office du Tourisme, Place de la Gare 10, CH-3960 Sierre, tel. (027) 55 85 35
Simmental	See Lenk
	See Zweisimmen
Sils Maria/ Segl Maria	Kur- und Verkehrsverein, CH-7514 Sils Maria, tel. (082) 4 52 37
Sion/Sitten	Office du Tourisme de Sion et Environs, Place de la Planta 3, CH-1950 Sion, tel. (027) 22 85 86
Solothurn/ Soleurs	Verkehrsbüro, Am Kronenplatz, CH-4500 Solothurn, tel. (065) 22 19 24
Spiez	Verkehrsverein, Bahnhofstrasse 12, CH-3700 Spiez, tel. (033) 54 21 38
Stans	Verkehrsbüro, Breitenhaus, CH-6370 Stans, tel. (041) 61 88 33

Verkehrsverein, Dorfplatz 13, CH-6362 Stansstad, tel. (041) 61 13 77   **Stansstad**

Verkehrsbüro, Seestrasse 97, CH-8266 Steckborn, tel. (054) 61 10 55   **Steckborn**

Verkehrsbüro, Oberstadt 10, CH-8260 Stein am Rhein, tel. (054) 41 28 35   **Stein am Rhein**

Ente Ticinese per il Turismo, Piazza Nosetto, CH-6501 Bellinzona,   **Ticino**
tel. (092) 25 70 56

See Bellinzona, Locarno, Lugano

Verkehrsverein, Bahnhof, CH-9053 Teufen, tel. (071) 33 38 73   **Teufen**

Verkehrsverein, Bahnhofplatz, CH-3600 Thun, tel. (033) 22 23 40   **Thun**

Verkehrsverband Thuner See, Thunstrasse 4, CH-3700 Spiez,   **Lake Thun**
tel. (033) 54 72 56

See also Brienz, Interlaken, Thun

See Amriswil   **Thurgau**

Verkehrsverein, Julierstrasse 42, CH-7450 Tiefencastel. tel. (081) 71 12 72   **Tiefencastel**

Liechtensteinische Fremdenvehrkehrschentrale, Städtle 37, FL-9490 Vaduz,   **Vaduz**
tel. (075) 2 32 14 43

Office du Tourisme, CH-1936 Verbier, tel. (026) 31 62 22   **Verbier**

Office du Tourisme, Grande Place 29,   **Vevey**
CH-1800 Vevey, tel. (021) 9 21 48 25

Office du Tourisme, CH-1884 Villars-sur-Ollon, tel. (025) 35 32 32   **Villars-sur-Ollon**

Verkehrsverein, La Poste-Platz 4, CH-3930 Visp, tel. (028) 46 61 61   **Visp**

Verkehrsbüro, CH-6354 Vitznau, tel. (041) 83 13 55   **Vitznau**

Verkehrsverband Zentralschweiz, Alpenstrasse 1, CH-6002 Lucerne,   **Vierwaldstätter**
tel. (041) 51 18 91   **See**

Kur- und Verkehrsverein, CH-7552 Vulpera, tel. (084) 9 09 44   **Vulpera**

See Walenstadt, Weesen.   **Walensee**

Verkehrsbüro, Seestrasse, CH-8880 Walenstadt, tel. (085) 7 35 15 45   **Walenstadt**

Union Valaisanne du Tourisme, rue de Lausanne 15, CH-1950 Sion,   **Wallis**
tel. (027) 22 31 61

Verkehrsverein, Kirchgasse, CH-8872 Weesen, tel. (058) 43 12 30   **Weesen**

Kur- und Verkehrsverein, CH-6353 Weggis, tel. (041) 93 11 55   **Weggis**

Verkehrsbüro, CH-3823 Wengen, tel. (036) 55 14 14   **Wengen**

Verkehrsbüro, Bahnhofplatz 12, CH-8400 Winterthur,   **Winterthur**
tel. (052) 2 12 00 88

Kur- und Verkehrsverein, Place Pestalozzi, CH-1400 Yverdon-les-Bains,   **Yverdon-les-**
tel. (024) 23 62 90   **Bains**

Insurance

Zermatt	Kur- und Verkehrsverein, Bahnhofplatz, CH-3920 Zermatt, tel. (028) 66 11 81
Zernez	Verkehrsbüro, CH-7530 Zernez, tel. (082) 8 13 00
Zofingen	Verkehrsbüro, Vordere Hauptgasse 33, CH-4800 Zofingen, tel. (062) 51 65 22
Zug	Verkehrsverband des Kantons Zug, Bahnhofstrasse 23, CH-6300 Zug, tel. (042) 21 00 78
Zürich	Schweizerische Verkehrszentrale, Bellariastrasse 38, CH-8023 Zürich, tel. (01) 2 02 37 37. Offizielles Verkehrsbüro (Auskunft, Zimmernachwies), Bahnhofplatz 15, Hauptbahnhof, CH-8023 Zürich, tel. (01) 2 11 40 00. Verkehrsverein Zürich, Direktion, Kongressbüro, Bahnhofbrücke 1, CH-8023 Zürich, tel. (01) 2 11 12 56
Zurzach	Kur- und Verkehrsverein, Quellenstrasse 1, CH-8437 Zurzach, tel. (056) 49 24 00
Zweisimmen	Verkehrsverein, Lenkstrasse, CH-3770 Zweisimmen, tel. (030) 2 11 33

Additional Useful Addresses

Automobile Clubs	See Breakdown Services
Embassies	See Diplomatic and Consular Information
Airlines	See entry
Swiss-German Chamber of Commerce	Handelskämmer Deutschland-Schweiz Talacker 14 CH-8001 Zürich Tel. (01) 2 21 37 02
Consulates	See Diplomatic and Consular Information
Emergencies	See entry
Swiss Cultural Information	Schweizer Kulturstiftung Pro Helvetia Hirschgraben 22, CH-8024 Zürich
SBB	See Railways, Schweizerische Bundesbahnen (SBB)
Telephone Services	Information Services for Switzerland: tel. 111
	Road Conditions: tel. 163
	Tourist Bulletin/snow forecast: tel. 120
	Avalanche Bulletin in winter, wind forecast in summer: tel. 187
	Weather Forecast: tel. 162.

Insurance

General	Since there is no national health service in Switzerland and medical treatment must be paid for, it is advisable to take out insurance cover against personal accident and sickness, as well as loss of, or damage to, luggage and personal effects. Special winter sports policies are obtainable.

Visitors to Switzerland who travel in their own vehicles should be in possession of an international insurance certificate ("Green Card") which can be obtained from the vehicles' normal insurers. The insurance effected in the United Kingdom normally only covers third party risks abroad and it is very desirable to have the fuller protection which the "Green Card" affords.

Motoring

Roadside Assistance

Headquarters:
Wasserwerkgasse 39
CH-3011 Berne
Tel. (031) 22 47 22

Branch offices in the larger Swiss towns.

Traffic information: tel. 163

Automobile Club of Switzerland (Automobil Club der Schweiz, Automobile Club de Suisse (ACS)

Headquarters:
Touring Club Suisse
9 rue Pierre-Fatio
CH-1211 Genève 3
Tel. (022) 7 37 12 12

Branch offices and information bureaux in the larger Swiss towns.

Emergency headquarters and traffic information: tel. (022) 7 35 80 00

Touring Club of Switzerland (TCS) (Touring-Club der Schweiz, Touring Club Suisse (TCS)

Touring Breakdown Service (24 hours a day): tel. 140.
  If you are in a rented vehicle (see entry) it is best to contact the firm from which the vehicle was rented.

Breakdown

See entry.

Emergencies

Accidents in Switzerland. What to do

However careful a driver you are an accident can always happen; even when you are very angry keep calm and be polite. Keep a cool head and take the following steps in order:

Immediate measures

1 Make the scene of the accident as safe as possible. Turn on your hazard lights, put out your warning triangle at a suitable distance.

Security

2 Take care of anyone who is injured, and send for an ambulance if necessary.

Injured

3 If there are any injured it is best to inform the police who will take charge of things for you.

Police

4 Make sure that you obtain a copy of a certificate from the police on which all possible information about the other driver or drivers is given. Make a note of the names and addresses of the other people concerned in the accident, take details of the number and make of the vehicles involved as well as the names and numbers of the insurance companies concerned. It is also important to make a note of the place and time of the accident and the address of the police station from which the officer concerned is stationed.

Information

5 Make sure you have all the evidence possible. Write down the names and addresses of, if possible, independent witnesses. Make sketches of the

Evidence

situation at the scene of the accident, or better still if you have a camera, take several snaps from various directions.

**Repairs to
damage.**
Accident Report

6 If possible fill in a European accident report (obtainable from your insurance company) and get it countersigned by any other driver involved. Do not sign any admission of guilt and especially do not sign any paper in a language which you do not understand.

Accident repairs

After an accident repairs should be undertaken as soon as possible. Note the following:

Claims against
you

1 If a claim is made against you inform your own insurance company. You can also get in touch with the Swiss insurance company whose name and address are on your Green Card.

Your own claim
for repair

2 Make your own claims for repair against the person who caused the accident and against his own insurance company. The Green Card is not much help here. To take care of the costs of your own claims a full comprehensive insurance is essential.

Traffic Regulations

An annual road tax of 40 Sfr is levied on all cars and motorcycles using Swiss motorways. An additional fee of 40 Sfr applies to trailers and caravans. The vignette (sticker) is valid between Dec. 1st of the year preceding and Jan. 31st of the one following the year printed on the vignette.

Driving on the
right

In Switzerland and Liechtenstein as in the rest of continental Europe vehicles travel on the right and overtake on the left.

General Traffic
regulations

Traffic signs correspond with the international norm. In built up areas trams and other vehicles on rails have priority at crossings and also at the junction of roads of equal status; otherwise traffic coming from the right has full priority. On mountain stretches, vehicles ascending have priority. In tunnels and rock galleries dipped headlights must be used. In the case of an accident on a main road the warning triangle must be set up at least 150m/165yd from the vehicle, and on other roads 50m/55yd away, after which the hazard lights must be switched off. Motorcyclists must have dipped headlights on while travelling and must wear a helmet.

Speed Limits

On motorways 120 kmph/75 mph, On main roads 80 kmph/50 mph, In built up areas 50 kmph/31 mph. Drivers are earnestly advised to keep strictly to speed limits as even minor infringements attract heavy fines.

Seat belts

Seat belts are compulsory in Switzerland; non-compliance leads to fines. Children under 12 years have to sit in the rear seats.

Drink-Driving

The maximum blood alcohol level permitted is 0.8 per cent.

Caravans

Caravans exceeding 2.1m/6.9ft in width and 6m/19.7ft in length must obtain a special permit at the frontier. With this they are allowed up to 2.2m/7.2ft wide and 7m/23ft long on normal roads but only up to a length of 6.5m/21.3ft on mountain roads. The speed limit for caravans is 80 kmph/50 mph.

Motor Caravans

There are various limits for motor caravans over 3.5 tonnes permitted weight. The regulations should be obtained before leaving for Switzerland. Information can be obtained from the Federal Customs Headquarters (Eidgenössische Oberzolldirektion: see Customs Regulations).

Winter

Snow chains are essential in winter in the mountainous areas of Switzerland and are compulsory on mountain roads. They are not allowed in long road tunnels.

Spikes

Private vehicles with spiked tyres are only permitted from the November 1st to March 31st (maximum speed 80 kmph/50 mph). With the exception

of the N2 between Göschenen and Airolo (The Gotthard Road Tunnel) and
the N13 between Thusis and Mesocco spiked tyres are not allowed on
motorways and main roads.

In the case of accidents where there are casualties the police must be   Accidents
called. If there is an accident causing damage the police need not be
informed but in many cases this is strongly recommended.

See also Emergencies.

See also Road Traffic.

Mountaineering

Switzerland is the classic country for mountaineering, which has become
increasingly popular as a sport since the middle of the 19th c., when it was
pioneered by British climbers at Zermatt. The Swiss Alpine Club, founded
in 1863, has built up a network of paths and huts to facilitate access to
the mountains; and the central Alps, with numerous peaks rising to over
4000m/13,124ft, offer the most magnificent glacier walks and climbs in the
whole of the Alps.

There is sometimes a tendency nowadays to underestimate the impor-   Equipment
tance of proper equipment; but this is essential for safe and enjoyable
climbing or mountain walking. It is important to have weather-proof (and
not too light) clothing, warm underwear, woollen socks, a light waterproof
windbreaker and good climbing boots, which must have treaded rubber
soles. The rucksack, which should have broad straps, should contain only
the most essential requirements (the guides are not required to carry more
than 7kg (15lb) in addition to their own equipment). A small reserve of food
(biscuits, chocolate, dried fruit, etc.) should always be carried. Other indis-

In the high Alps

pensable items are sun-glasses, sunburn cream (and for many people also a lip cream) and adhesive bandages.

Guides

The guides are subject to control by the Swiss Alpine Club and the cantonal authorities, who issue guides' licences only after testing their competence. The regulations on charges, food, carrying of luggage, etc., may vary from canton to canton, it is desirable, therefore, before engaging a guide to ask to see the list of charges and the local regulations and to check that the guide is insured.

Climbing without a guide is now very common; but it should be attempted only by climbers whose own competence on rock and ice, judgment and fitness are not much below those of the professional guides, or who are climbing with experienced Alpine mountaineers. Many accidents occur through a climber's ignorance of the hidden dangers in an apparently easy route, through losing the way when there is a sudden change in the weather or as a result of inadequate equipment. In the high mountains no one should climb alone; but it is also necessary to be wary of uninvited companions, who may give rise to grave difficulties or dangers. In the climbs mentioned in this Guide the need for a guide is indicated where appropriate.

Glaciers

Glaciers must be crossed early in the day, before the sun softens the snow covering the crevasses. Even experienced climbers should never tackle a glacier without a guide and a rope.

Mountain Sickness

At altitudes above 4000m/13,124ft or so, and for some people even below this, mountain sickness can be a problem. The symptoms are palpitations, dizziness, loss of consciousness and bleeding from the mouth and nose. The best remedies are rest, stimulants and, most effective of all, an immediate descent to a lower altitude.

Weather conditions

Weather conditions in the Alps, particularly on their north-western and northern slopes, are unreliable and full of potential danger for the climber. Two generally accepted indications of good weather are a fall in temperature in the evening, when the wind blows down into the valley after blowing up on to the mountains during the day, and a fresh fall of snow on the peaks. The "föhn" which makes the mountains appear nearer and dark blue in colour, often brings a long period of beautiful weather, though this may change suddenly at any time. Signs of bad weather are the appearance of cirrus clouds moving from W to E (even though they may disappear in the early afternoon), swirls of dust on the roads and driving snow on the ridges and peaks when the weather is otherwise good. In rainy weather there is increased danger of rock falls. In the event of a thunderstorm do not stand under isolated trees, haystacks, etc., in view of the danger of being struck by lightning; come down from the peaks and ridges at once, and keep away from running water.

Weather forecasts are posted up at stations and post offices and given daily on the radio. They can also be obtained by telephone (dial 162).

Alpenglow

Alpenglow (German Alpenglühen) is the reddish light cast by the setting sun on the rocky and snow-covered summits; in particular it is the afterglow of yellow, purple and violet hues which occurs 5–10 minutes after sunset when there is a slight build-up of clouds in the west and twilight has already fallen in the valleys.

Alpine Distress Signal

The international Alpine distress signal, for climbers who need help, is a series of six signals given at regular intervals within a minute by whatever means are available (blasts on a whistle, shouts, flashes of a torch, waves of some conspicuous article), followed by a minute's pause, a repetition of the signals, and so on until an answer is received. The answer takes the form of three signals at regular intervals within a minute.

The Swiss Alpine Club has established a large number of rescue stations and reporting posts to ensure that in the event of an accident help can be summoned quickly.

The Swiss Alpine Club, founded in 1863, maintains some 150 mountain huts, which are open to non-members as well as members of the club. In some of them there are limited facilities for obtaining food during the summer; in most of them, however, there is no warden, and it is therefore, necessary to inquire in the valley below about the means of gaining access, and sometimes to take the key with you. The charges for overnight accommodation are posted up in the huts.

The Swiss
Alpine Club
(SAC)

There are a number of excellently run climbing schools in Switzerland, providing instruction both for beginners and for those who want to learn specialised techniques. In most schools it is also possible to obtain guides. There are such schools, for example, at Wildhaus, Andermatt, Davos, Les Diablerets, Fiesch, La Fouly/Verbier, Grindelwald, Klosters, Pontresina, Meiringen, Kandersteg/Schwarenbach, Arolla and Villars-Chesières.

Climbing
Schools

Swiss Federation of Climbing Schools (Schweizerische Verband der Berg-steigerschulen)
c/o École Suisse d'Alpinisme
CH-1874 Champéry. Tel. (025) 79 14 30

Information

Mountain Railways, Cableways

These various forms of mountain transport are of great importance in Switzerland, and of particular value to tourists. Apart from the services they

Brienz–Rothorn railway

provide for winter sports enthusiasts they also enable the older or less strenuously inclined visitor to enjoy the experience of the mountain world. There are in all some 600 mountain railways and cableways. They are not only of use to winter-sports enthusiasts but make it possible for less active visitors and elderly people to reach the higher mountain areas. Some of the railways and cableways climb to heights of over 3000m/9843ft, such as those up the Kleines Matterhorn (3820m/12,533ft), Jungfrau (3457m/11,342ft), Gornergrat (3407m/11,178ft), Corvatsch (3298m/10,820ft), Piz Nair (3025m/9925ft) and Mont Gelé (3028m/9938ft).

There are the following types: Funicular (German Standseilbahn, French Funiculaire), in which the cars run on rails and are drawn by cable. Rack (Cog) Railway (Zahnradbahn, chemin de fer à crémaillère), with a middle rail fitted with a cog which engages with a pinion on the locomotive. Cableway (Seilschwebebahn or Luftseilbahn, téléférique or télécabine), with cabins for anything from 4 to 100 passengers suspended from a continuous cable. Chair-lift (Sesselbahn or Sessellift, télésiege), with open chairs (sometimes double) suspended from a continuous cable. Ski-lift (Skilift or Schlepplift, monte-pente), in which skiers are pulled uphill on their skis attached to a moving cable. Sledge-lift (Schlittenseilbahn, funiculaire à traîneaux), in which sledges are attached to a cable and drawn uphill. Many of these facilities operate for only part of the year.

Reductions   Price reductions such as regional season-tickets (e.g holiday or winter sports season tickets) of the various Swiss cable-car undertakings can be obtained.

Information   Schweizerische Verband der Seilbahnunternehmungen
Dählhölzliweg 12,
CH-3006 Berne. Tel. (031) 44 24 16

Museums

Visitors who like the unusual will certainly find a museum to their taste in Switzerland. A selection of the many specialised museums is indicated on the map on page 557. Detailed descriptions can be found under the corresponding heading in the A-Z section.

Opening times   Opening times vary; many close on Mondays. A number of museums in the smaller towns are closed between mid October and mid April.

○ Specialist Museums

1 Geneva. Car and Motorcycle Museum

2 Geneva. Museum on the History of Science

3 Geneva. Watch-making Museum

4 Geneva. Museum of Historic Musical Instruments

5 Geneva. Professor F. Peus' Flea Collection

6 Geneva. Swiss Mercenary's Museum

7 Geneva. Philatelic Museum of the United Nations

8 Nyon. Porcelain Museum

9 Morges. Alexis Forel Doll and Toy Museum

10 Morges. Vaudois Military Museum

11 Lausanne. Collection de l'Art Brut

12 Lausanne. Pipe Tobacco Museum

Speciality Museums in Switzerland

Selection of museums ●

Ballenberg Open-air Museum ●

13 Lausanne. Museum of the Olympic Games

14 Vevey. Food Museum

15 Vevey. Collection of Photographic Apparatus

16 La Tour de Peliz. Games Museum

17 Blonay. Railway Museum

18 Roche. Organ Museum

19 Aigle. Swiss Wine Museum

20 Bex. Le Bouillet Salt Mine with Museum

21 St-Maurice. Military Museum

22 Martigny. Car Museum of the Gianadda Foundation

23 Château d'Oex. Silhouette Museum

24 Rougemont. Fossils Museum

25 Gruyères. Cheese-making

26 Gruyères. Waxworks

27 Lucens. Sherlock Holmes Museum

28 La Sarraz. Horse Museum

29 Echallens. Corn and Bread Museum

30 Vallorbe. Gyger Railway Museum

31 L'Auberson. Baud Musical Automata

32 Ste-Croix. Musical Automata and Musical Instruments

33 Grandson. Vintage Cars

34 Yverdon. Science Fiction

35 Estavayer-le-Lac. Frogs

36 Avenches. Aircraft

Museums

37 Boudry. Wine production

38 Colombier. Military Museum

39 Neuchâtel. Automata

40 Le Locle. Clock and watches

41 Le Locle/Col des Roches. Milling Museum

42 La Chaux-de-Fonds. Rural Life and Crafts

43 La Chaux-de-Fonds. Watches and Clocks

44 Ligerz. Viticulture

45 Biel/Bienne. Buildings on Stilts

46 Biel/Bienne. Omega Watches and Clocks

47 Jerisberghof, Althus. Museum of Rural Life

48 Mühleberg. BKW Power-station

49 Fribourg. Marionettes, Sewing Machine Museum

50 Romont. Church Windows

51 Spiez. Regional and Vine Growing Museum

52 Interlaken. Model Railway (Large Layout)

53 Kiesen. National Milk-production

54 Toffen. Old-timer Museum

55 Berne. Swiss Alpine Museum

56 Berne. Swiss Postal Museum

57 Berne. Swiss Riflemen's Museum

58 Berne. Swiss Theatrical Collection

59 Utzenstorf. Swiss Hunting Museum

60 Solothurn. Artillery Museum

61 Solothurn. Kreuzen Mineral Museum

62 Mümliswil. Comb Museum

63 Porrentruy. Apothecary Museum

64 Seewen. Musical Automata

65 Basle. Architecture

66 Basle. The Transport Centre of Switzerland

67 Basle. Swiss Fire Service

68 Basle. Collection of Musical Instruments

69 Basle. Swiss Paper Mill

70 Basle. Museum of the History of Pharmacy

71 Basle. Sports

72 Basle. Collection of Caricatures and Cartoons

73 Basle/Weil am Rhein. Vitra Design Museum

74 Binningen. Automobile Collection

75 Münchenstein. Coaches and Sledges

76 Riehen. Toys

77 Riehen. Cats

78 Rheinfelden. Old-timer

79 Schönenwerd. Bally Shoe Museum

80 Zofingen. Ringier Printing Museum

81 Langenthal. Linen Museum

82 Oeschgen. Bicycle Museum/Dinosaur Museum

83 Alberswil. Farming Museum

84 Baden. Power Station Museum

85 Baden. Toys

86 Werdenberg. Castle Museum

87 Kölliken. Icon Museum

88 Wohlen. Straw Museum

89 Sursee. Swiss Capuchin Monks

90 Lucerne. Transport Museum

91 Lucerne. Glacier Garden Museum

92 Lucerne. Wagner Museum in Tribschen

93 Lucerne. Swiss Costume and European Harmonica Museum

94 Lucerne. Bourbaki Panorama

95 Guttannen. Wirzen Crystal Museum

96 Bürglen. William Tell Museum

97 Schwyz. Tower Museum (Weapons, etc.)

98 Goldau. Rockfall Museum

99 Zug. Fishing Museum

100 Affoltern. Model Railway and Cycle Museum

101 Wädenswil. Viticulture Museum

102 Freienbach. Printing Museum

103 Rüti. Fire Brigade Museum

104 Zimmerwald. Museum of Wind Instruments

105 Volketswil. Corkscrew Museum

106 Zurich. Criminal Museum

107 Zurich. Museum of Measurement of Time

108 Zurich. Sasha Morgenthaler Doll Museum

109 Zurich. Toy Museum

111 Zurich. City Drainage System

112 Zurich. Mask Museum

113 Zurich. Indian Museum

114 Zurich. Swiss Country Museum

115 Zurich. Palaeontology Museum

116 Zurich. Swiss Hotels

117 Zurich. Coffee Museum

118 Zurich. Tiefenbrunnen Mill Museum

119 Zurich. Medical History Collection

Museums

120 Zurich-Höngg. Tram Museum

121 Dübendorf. Museum of the Swiss Flying Troop

122 Winterthur. Kellenberg Watch and Clock Collection/Photograph Museum

123 Winterthur. Technorama

124 Winterthur. Coin Museum

125 Neftenbach. Museum of Viticulture

126 Eglisau. Fishing Museum

127 Schleitheim. Plaster Museum

128 Diessenhofen. Museum of Printed Materials

129 Stein am Rhein. Appenzell Cheese Factory (open to the public)

130 Stein am Rhein. Doll Museum

131 Steckborn. Bernina Sewing Machine Museum

132 Kreuzlingen. Fire Service Museum

133 Kreuzlingen. Radio and Communications Museum

134 Kreuzlingen/Schloss Girsberg. Doll Museum

135 Kradolf. Fire Service Museum

136 Amriswil. Collection of Coaches

137 St Gallen. Naïve Art

138 St Gallen. Textile Museum

139 St Gallen. Musical Box Museum

140 Teufen. Grubenmann Collections

141 Berneck. Radio Museum

142 Appenzell. Culture Centre

143 Appenzell. Brick Making

144 Gossau. Hilti Motorcycle Museum

145 Degersheim. Retonios Magic Museum

146 Lichensteig. Fredys Museum of Mechanical Music

147 Unterwasser. Alpine Dairy Museum

148 Sargans. Old-Timer Museum

149 Sargans. Gonzen Mining Museum

150 Pfäfers. Antique Bath Museum

151 Chur. Museum of Viticulture

152 Chur. Collection of Coaches

153 Davos. Silver Mining Museum

154 Lottigna. Military Museum

155 Melide. Swiss Miniatures

156 Meride. Fossil Museum

157 Gandria. Smugglers Museum

158 Bosco/Gurin. Walserhaus Museum

159 Riederalp. Alpine Museum

160 Zermatt. Alpine Museum

161 Leuk Stadt. Satellite Museum

162 Sierre. Tin Museum

Opening Times

See Business Hours

Passes and Tunnels

Switzerland has many roads leading over passes, some of them among the most fascinating mountain roads in Europe. The main N–S connections are magnificently engineered, but some of the minor pass roads are closed in winter.

Pass Roads

Information on the current road conditions and the opening times of Alpine passes can be obtained from the Automobil Club der Schweiz by telephoning 163.

See map below.

Passes in Switzerland

Alpine Road Tunnels

The tunnel through the Great St Bernard links Valais with the Valle D'Aosta (Italy). Toll charges for motorcycles, cars and caravans range from 27 to 56.5 Sfr, for coaches from 56.6 to 139 Sfr. If the return journey is made within 30 days a reduction of 30 or 20% is granted on the return toll. Season tickets are also available for multiple journeys.

Great St Bernard

A motorway vignette is required for driving through the 6.6km/4 miles long San Bernardino tunnel between Grisons and Ticino. No further toll charges are made.

San Bernardino

A motorway vignette is also required for driving through the 16.8km/10½ miles long St Gotthard road tunnel between Central Switzerland and Ticino. No further toll charges are made.

St Gotthard

○ **Mountain passes over 1000m/3282ft**

Altitude, maximum gradient/descent, and months when normally open are given after the name of the pass.

1 Col des Etroits. 1153m/3783ft. Ste-Croix to Pontarlier (France).
Maximum gradient 10%. Open all year

2 Col de Mollendruz. 1180m/3872ft. Morges to Vallorbe.
Maximum gradient 7%. Open all year

3 Col du Marchairuz. 1447m/4748ft. Nyon to Le Brassus.
Maximum gradient 15%. Open all year

4 Col de la Givrine. 1228m/4029ft. Nyon to Morez (France).
Maximum gradient 14%. Open all year

5 Pas de Morgins. 1333m/4492ft. Monthey to Evian-les-Bains (France).
Maximum gradient 14%. Open all year

Mountain Passes in Switzerland

Ω Tunnel

A	Gr.-St-Bernard Tunnel (Road)
B	Lötschbergtunnel (Rail)
C	Simplontunnel (Rail)
D	Furkatunnel (Rail)
E	St-Gotthard-Tunnel (Road)
F	Oberalptunnel (Rail)
G	San-Bernardino-Tunnel (Road)
H	Albulatunnel (Rail)

6 Col de la Forclaz. 1527m/5010ft. Martigny to Chamonix (France).
Maximum gradient 9%. Open all year

7 Grand St Bernard Pass. 2469m/8010ft. Martigny to Aosta (Italy).
Maximum gradient 11%. Open June to October. Road tunnel available

8 Col de la Croix. 1780m/5340ft. Villars to Les Diablerets.
Maximum gradient 13%. Open May to September

9 Col du Pillon. 1546m/5072ft. Gstaad to Aigle.
Maximum gradient 11%. Open all year

10 Col des Mosses. 1445m/4741ft. Château d'Oex to Aigle.
Maximum gradient 10%. Open all year

11 Jaun Pass. 1509m/4951ft. Bollingen to Bulle.
Maximum gradient 10%. Open all year

12 Selibühl Pass. 1587m/5207ft. Thun to Fribourg.
Maximum gradient 11%. Open all year

13 Brünig Pass. 1008m/3308ft. Lucerne to Brienz.
Maximum gradient 10%. Open all year

14 Simplon Pass. 2005m/6578ft. Brig to Domodóssola (Italy).
Maximum gradient 13%. Open all year

15 Susten Pass. 2224m/7297ft. Innertkirchen to Wassen.
Maximum gradient 9%. Open June to November

16 Grimsel Pass. 2165m/7103ft. Meiringen to Gletsch.
Maximum gradient 11%. Open June to November

17 Furka Pass. 2431m/7976ft. Gletsch to Andermatt.
Maximum gradient 14%. Open June to November

18 Nufenen (Novena) Pass. 2478m/8130ft. Ulrichen to Airolo.
Maximum gradient 10%. Open June to October

Wonderful Swiss scenery over the Nufenpass

19 St Gotthard Pass. 2108m/6916ft. Göschenen to Airolo.
Maximum gradient 10%. Open May to November

20 Oberalp Pass. 2044m/6706ft. Andermatt to Disentis.
Maximum gradient 10%. Open May to November

21 Klausen Pass. 1948m/6391ft. Altdorf to Linthal.
Maximum gradient 10%. Open May to November

22 Lukmanier (Lucomagno) Pass. 1978m/6492ft. Disentis to Biasca.
Maximum gradient 10%. Open May to November

23 San Bernardino Pass. 2066m/6779ft. Splügen to Bellinzona.
Maximum gradient 15%. Open May to October

24 Splügen (Spluga) Pass. 2113m/6933ft. Thusis to Chiavenna (Italy).
Maximum gradient 13%. Open May to November

25 Lenzerheide Pass. 1549m/5082ft. Chur to Tiefencastel.
Maximum gradient 10%. Open all year

26 Julier (Güglia) Pass. 2284m/7494ft. Tiefencastel to Silvaplana.
Maximum gradient 13%. Open all year

27 Maloja Pass. 1815m/5955ft. Silvaplana to Chiavenna (Italy).
Maximum gradient 13%. Open all year

28 Wolfgang Pass. 1633m/5358ft. Klosters to Davos.
Maximum gradient 10%. Open all year

29 Flüela Pass. 2383m/7819ft. Davos to Susch.
Maximum gradient 10%. Open April to November

30 Albula Pass. 2312m/7586ft. Tiefenkastel to La Punt-Chamues-ch.
Maximum gradient 12%. Open June to November.

31 Forcola di Livigno. 2315m/7596ft. Bernina Pass to Livigno (Italy).
Maximum gradient 12%. Open June to October

32 Bernina Pass. 2323m/7622ft. Pontresina to Tirano (Italy).
Maximum gradient 12%. Open all year

33 Ofen (Fuorn) Pass. 2149m/7051ft. Zernez to Santa Maria.
Maximum gradient 10%. Open all year

34 Umbrail Pass. 2501m/8206ft. Santa Maria to Bormio (Italy).
Maximum gradient 12%. Open May to November

Munt-la-Schera Tunnel The Munt-la-Schera Tunnel (3.5 km/2 miles; open 8 a.m.–8 p.m.) from Zernez to Livigno (Italy) is subject to toll. At present (1994) these are (for the single journey) 5 francs for cars plus 2 francs per person: for coaches, 15 francs plus 1 franc per person.

Loading of cars at alpine passes

Several alpine passes have rail tunnels. Sometimes it is possible to transport vehicles by rail.

Albula Loading stations: Thusis and Samedan
Duration: 1¼–1¾ hours. Up to 10 trips per day
Prior reservation at the loading stations recommended
Thusis, tel. (081) 81 11 13; Samedan, tel. (082) 6 54 04.

Lötschberg Loading stations: Kanderstag and Goppenstein/Brig
Duration: 15 minutes. Up to 31 trips per day.

Lötschberg–Simplon Loading stations: Kandersteg and Iselle di Trasquera (Italy)
Duration: about 1½ hours; change trains at Brig.

Simplon/Sempione Loading stations: Brig and Iselle di Trasquera (Italy)
Duration: 20 minutes.

Furka Loading stations: Oberwald and Realp
Duration: 15 minutes. Up to 16 trips per day.

Oberalp Loading stations: Andermatt and Sedrun
Duration: about 1 hour
Prior reservation at the loading stations recommended
Andermatt, tel. (044) 6 72 20; Sedrun, tel. (086) 9 49 11 37.

Post

Postal rates The rate charged depends on whether "A" class or "B" class is chosen.

"A" post As a rule, "A" class letters are delivered the next day to addresses in Switzerland, and abroad within three to five days. All letters must be marked by the sender with the letter "A" or have an "A-Prioritaire" sticker attached. Letters and postcards weighing up to 250g (up to 20mm thick) cost 0.80 Sfr within Switzerland. Those to Europe weighing up to 20g cost between 0.90 and 1 Sfr (airmail); up to 50g, 1.80 Sfr.

There is a surcharge for express letters and registered post.

Opening times Post Offices are open from Monday to Friday 8am–noon, 2–6pm and Saturday 8–11am.

Public Holidays

January 1st and 2nd
Good Friday
Easter Sunday and Easter Monday
May 1st, Labour Day
Ascension Day
Whit Sunday and Whit Monday
August 1st, National Festival
3rd Sunday in September, Federal Thanksgiving Day
December 25th/26th, Christmas

Public holidays
in the whole of
Switzerland

As far as opening times and timetables are concerned, the above days
count as Sundays. There are various other public holidays celebrated in the
various Cantons and regions. Information can be obtained from the local
Information Offices (see Information).

See Events

Local Festivals

Public Transport

The bus services run by the Swiss post office (PTT) play an important part in
the Swiss transport system, particularly in the mountainous regions with
more limited rail services. The postal buses serve even the highest Alpine
roads. Tickets are sold at all the larger post offices.

Buses

Reduced fares are available on the Swiss postbus holiday ticket which is
valid on all regular routes at present over a distance of 7500km/4660 miles.
There are also regional tickets.

See entry

Car Rental

Taxis are relatively expensive in Switzerland, prices varying from place to
place. Fixed prices for extras (e.g. luggage) are displayed in the vehicle.

Taxis

See entry

Railways

See entry

Air Travel

Passengers holding a rail ticket which is valid along Lake Geneva, Lac de
Neuchâtel, Lac de Bienne (including the river Aare), Lakes Thun, Brienz, the
Vierwaldstätter See and Lake Zurich as well as the Untersee and the Rhine
can use a ship even when this is not expressly stated on the ticket.

Ships

See entry

Boat excursions

Railways

The network of the Swiss Federal railways, which has been fully electrified
since 1960, comprises about 2900km/1800 miles. There are also many
private railways which complement the lines of the SBB so that the total
network is some 5000km/3100 miles. There are no ticket barriers; tickets
are inspected in the trains. No supplements are charged for express trains
except for TEE trains. Children travel free up to 6 years of age, between 6
and 16 they pay half fare.

Schweizerische
Bundesbahn/
Swiss Federal
Railways

(SBB/CFF/FFS)

Zentralverwaltung
Hochschulstrasse 6, CH-3030 Berne
Tel. (031) 60 11 11

Central
administration
of the SBB

565

Railways

Representation in Great Britain
In Great Britain the Swiss Railways have an agency at:

Swiss Centre
1 New Coventry Street
London W1V 8EE. Tel. (0171) 734 1921

In the USA:

Swiss Centre
608 Fifth Ave
New York NY 10020. Tel. (212) 757 5944

Canada
926 The East Mall
ETOBICOKE
Ontario, M9B 6K1
Tel. (416) 695 2090

Reduced Fares
There are reduced fares for families and parties, young people and pensioners. Especially advantageous is the half-price season ticket, the 6-day ticket at half-price, the Swiss Pass (a network ticket for rail, ship and post bus routes, as well as for the local transport facilities in 25 Swiss towns) and the Swiss Card (covers journeys to and from the border or airport to one's destination, and includes half-price tickets for rail, bus and post-bus). There are combined day tickets including a visit to a trade fair or an exhibition, tram/bus day tickets, the "Schweizer Städteplausch" (a weekend ticket in 15 Swiss cities and on the William Tell Express), "Schweizer Bummler" (an Alpine train/flight combination valid for one month) and regional holiday reductions.

Information can be obtained from the Swiss National Tourist Office (see Information).

Express Services

General
Before taking any of the following rail trips visitors should assure themselves about frontier crossings and customs regulations in the countries

Railways
—— Main lines
—— Branch lines

Basle main station

concerned. Information concerning timetables, reduced fares (children, students, groups, pensioners; Swiss Holiday Ticket) and reservations can be obtained from the Swiss Travel Office (see Information), from local travel bureaux and the Information Offices given below.

Route: Chur (Grisson)–Albula–St Moritz (Engadin)–Bernina–Poschiavo– **Bernina Express**
Tirano (Italy) or in the reverse direction. In summer a coach will take passengers on to Lake Como and Via Menaggion to Lugano.
Length: 145km/90 miles; duration 4½ hours.

Highlights:
The Bernina Express travels on Europe's highest mountain railway line in the Alps, built between 1894 and 1908. It begins with one of the most beautiful stretches (Chur–St Moritz) on the famous Glacier Express (see entry) and with a gradient of 7% is one of the steepest railways in the world operated without rack and pinion. All the zones of vegetation between the glaciers of Piz Bernina (4049m/13,289ft) and the palms of Tirano (429m/2695ft) in Italy are passed through on this journey.

Special features:
On fine summer days in July and August it is possible to travel on certain trains in an open panorama carriage ("Carozza panoramica").
    Trains with old-time dining cars operate between Chur and St Moritz.

The Bernina Express can be combined with the celebrated Glacier Express, see entry (St Moritz–Zermatt), the Engadin Express, see entry (St Moritz–Scuol–Landeck), or the Palm Express (St Moritz–Ascona).

Information:
A leaflet "Bernina Express" can be obtained from the Swiss National Tourist Office (see Information); further information from:

Railways

Rhätische Bahn (RhB)
Bahnhofstrasse 25
CH-7002 Chur. Tel. (081) 21 91 21

Centovalli Railway

Route: Domodóssola–Locarno.
Length: 52km/32 miles; duration 2½ hours.

Highlights:
This railway links the great European lines of the Simplon and the Gotthard on narrow gauge. It traverses the wildly romantic Centovalli past idyllic gorges and over numerous bridges with a maximum gradient of 6%.

Special features:
Visitors who have a complete day at their disposal should combine the Centovalli railway with a return trip (Zurich–St Gotthard–Centovalli-Simplon–Lötschberg–Brig–Zurich).
Information from the Swiss National Tourist Office (see Information).

Engadin Express

The Engadin Express links the Tirol with the Engadin, the Arlberg Railway with the Albula Railway; the Engadin Express Vienna–Salzburg–St Moritz runs throughout the year daily in each direction. The gap between Landeck and Bad Scuol is filled by Swiss or Austrian postal buses (PTT). The stretch between St Moritz and Landeck is 122km/76 miles long.

Highlights:
During the trip there are views of green alpine pasture, snow covered mountains, castles and the mighty fortress of Tarasp; in the background lie the woods and valleys of the Swiss National Park.

Features:
The Engadin Express also has connections with three other attractive trains – the Bernina Express, the Glacier Express and the Palm Express (see entries).

A leaflet "Engadin Express" can be obtained from Swiss Tourist Offices (see Information); further information is available at the tourist offices at St Moritz and Bad Scuol (See A to Z), also from:

Rhätische Bahn (RhB)
Bahnhofstrasse 25
CH-7002 Chur. Tel. (081) 21 91 21

Schweizer Reisepost
CH-7000 Chur. Tel. (081) 22 38 23

Glacier Express

Route: Zermatt–Brig–Andermatt–Chur–Davos/St Moritz or in reverse direction.
Length: 290km/180 miles; duration 7½ hours to St Moritz.

Highlights:
A trip on the Glacier Express – the "slowest express in the world" – is a memorable experience for every railway enthusiast. Using metre-gauge stretches of the Rhätische Bahn (RhB), the Furka–Oberalp Bahn (FO) and the Brig–Visp–Zermatt Bahn (BVZ), the express provides an east–west connection in the High Alps for tourists, and not only passes through magnificent mountain scenery but also makes use of real masterpieces of railway engineering. The train crosses 291 bridges and viaducts, goes through 91 tunnels including the longest metre-gauge tunnel in the world at the Oberalp pass (2033m/6672ft).

Features:
The Glacier Express carries first and second class coaches. Tickets for sections of the route only can also be obtained. Early reservation in all cases is necessary.

In connection with the centenary of the Rhätische Bahn a "Glacier Pullman Express" and a "Glacier Gourmet Express" were brought into service in 1989.

Information:
Information can be obtained from any railway station in Switzerland and from Swiss Tourist Offices (see Information) where a leaflet on the "Glacier Express" is also available. Most railway stations and travel agents in Switzerland and abroad can offer interesting package holidays which include travel on the "Glacier Express". Further information:

Rhätische Bahn (RhB)
Bahnhofstrasse 25
CH-7002 Chur. Tel. (081) 21 91 21

Furka–Oberalp Bahn (FO)
Box 256
CH-3900 Brig. Tel. (028) 23 66 66

The "Glacier Express"

Railways

Brig–Visp–Zermatt and Gornergrat Bahn (BVZ)
CH-3900 Brig
Tel. (028) 23 13 33

Since reservation for lunch in the dining car is compulsory, passengers should book in good time with the:

Schweizerische Speisewagen Gesellschaft
CH-7000 Chur
Tel. (081) 22 14 25

The Golden
Pass Route

Route: Lucerne–Interlaken–Zweisimmen–Montreux and vice versa.
Length: over 237km/147 miles; duration 5½ hours.

Highlights:
The Golden Pass route is one of the classic rail journeys in Switzerland. Passing through magnificent scenery, it runs from the banks of the Lake of the Four Forest Cantons (the Vierwaldstätter See) as far as the Swiss Riviera.

Special Points:
You first travel by the narrow gauge Brünig line to Interlaken, and then continue on the Lötschberg Railway (administration in Berne); previously belonging to the BLS; as far as Zweisimmen and then continuing on a narrow gauge railway of the Montreux–Oberland Railway (MOB) to Montreux. This last stretch is particularly enjoyable since panorama coaches (Panoramic and Super-panoramic Express) were introduced.

Information from the Swiss Travel Bureaux (see Information) and from Railways (see Railways).

Gornergrat
Railway

Route: Zermatt (1620m/5317ft)–Gornergrat (3089m/10,138ft).
Length: 9.34km/5¾ miles; duration: 45 minutes.

Highlights:
During the trip on the Gornergrat rack railway you will have magnificent views of the Gabelhorngruppe and the Matterhorn, which, especially in the morning, is beautifully mirrored in the waters of the Riffelsee; you will also see the Gorner Glacier (see A to Z "Surroundings of Zermatt"). Information from the Swiss Travel Bureaux (see Information) and from Railways (see Railways), and the:

Brig–Visp–Zermatt and Gornergrat-Bahn (BVZ)
CH-3900 Brig
Tel. (028) 23 13 33.

Gotthard
Railway

Route: Basle or Zurich–Gotthard Tunnel–Lugano or vice versa.
Length of route: Basle–Lugano about 300km/186 miles; Zurich–Lugano 216km/134 miles. Duration of journey: from Basle 4 hours and from Zurich 3 hours.

Highlights:
The Gotthard Railway (built between 1874 and 1882) gives the Swiss railways the quickest North–South connection over the Alps. The summit of the Gotthard Massif is pierced by a railway tunnel with a length of 15km/6 miles and a maximum height of 1154m/3,787ft. Since 1961 the Trans-Europa Express (TEE) "Gotthardo" has made the journey from Zurich to Lugano (First class with supplement) and this is the finest way of making this trip.

Special Points:
Sections of route can be booked using regional and express trains in second class.

Information from the Swiss Travel Bureaux (see Information) and from Railways (see Railways).

Route: This railway, which, with the Gornergrat Railway, is probably the best-known mountain stretch in Switzerland operates throughout the year from the Kleiner Scheidegg to the highest railway station in Europe, the Jungfraujoch (3454m/11,336ft). The maximum gradient is 1 in 4. The Jungfrau Railway (JB; rack-railway, metre gauge) was built between 1896 and 1912.

The Jungfrau Railway

Length of Route: 9.3km/5.8 miles (7.1km/almost 4½ miles are in tunnel); duration 50 minutes.

Highlights and Special Attractions:
See A–Z "Jungfrau Region".

Information from the Swiss Travel Bureaux (see Information) and from Railways (see Railways).

Head Office of the Jungfrau Railways is at:
Höheweg 37
CH-3800 Interlaken
Tel. (036) 22 52 52.

Route: St Moritz–Lugano–Locarno–Ascona (one night's accommodation)–Domodóssola–Brig–Visp–Zermatt or vice versa (at present only runs in summer).

Palm Express

Length of journey: about 300km/186 miles; total duration of journey 2 days (travel by postal bus from St Moritz to Ascona or vice versa about 5 hours).

Highlights:
This journey by the Palm Express which links the Engadin and Upper Valais with Ticino, or St Moritz and Zermatt with Ascona (overnight accommodation) and Locarno and Lugano, provides wonderful views of Swiss mountains and glaciers as well as sub-tropical lakeside scenery.

Special features:The Palm Express is a combination of postal bus and railway; the various stretches are operated by the Swiss Postal Bus Service, the "Ferrovie Autolinee Regionali Ticinese (Centovalli Railway, FART) and the Brig–Visp–Zermatt–Gornergrat Railway (BVZ).

Further information can be had from Swiss Travel Bureaux (see Information) where you can also obtain the leaflet "Palm Express"; the relevant authorities in Ascona, St Moritz and Zermatt (see A–Z) and Swiss Railways can also provide information.

Postautodienst
CH-3900 Brig
Tel. (028) 23 77 77

Postautodienst
CH-7500 St Moritz
Tel. (082) 3 30 72

Rhätische Bahn (RhB)
Bahnhofstrasse 25
CH-7002 Chur
Tel. (081) 21 91 21

Railways

Schweizer Reisepost
CH-7000 Chur
Tel. (081) 22 38 23

Pilatus Railway

Route: Alpnachstadt–Pilatus Summit and vice versa (at present only during summer).

Length of journey: 4.6km/3 miles; duration 30 minutes.

Highlights:
See A–Z "Surroundings of Lucerne".

Special Details:
With a gradient of almost 1 in 2 the stretch of the Pilatus rack railway (gauge 800mm) is the steepest in the world (in 1989 the Pilatus Railway celebrated it's centenary).

Information from the Swiss Travel Bureaux (see Information) and from Railways (see Railways).

Direction and Administration of the Pilatus Railway:
Inseliquai 8
CH-6002 Luzern
Tel. (041) 23 93 63

Rigi Express

Route: Konstanz–Wil–Arth-Goldau and vice versa (at present only during summer).

Length of route: 158km/98 miles; duration 2½ hours.

Special Details:
From Arth-Goldau Station there is a rack railway, opened in 1875 and electrified in 1906, up the Rigi. The maximum gradient is 1 in 5 (you are recommended to sit on the right); the journey of 9km/5.6 miles takes 35 minutes.

Information from the Swiss Travel Bureaux (see Information) and from Railways (see Railways).

Reisedienst der Schweizerische Bundesbahnen
Bahnhofstrasse
CH-5322 Koblenz
Tel. (056) 46 18 00

Sun Express:

Route: Ilanz–Disentis–Lukmanier Pass–Blenio Valley–Ascona along Lake Maggiore (from the beginning of July to the beginning of September every Tuesday; and in the high season also on Thursdays).

Return from Ascona–Gotthard Pass–Andermatt–Surselva.

Duration of journey: 10 hours.

Information from:

Postautodienst
CH-7130 Ilanz
Tel. (086) 2 16 50

Schweizer Reisepost
CH-7000 Chur
Tel. (081) 22 38 23

Information from the Swiss Travel Bureaux (see Information) and from Railways (see Railways).

Route: Lucerne–Flüelen–St Gotthard–Locarno–Lugano and vice versa.

Highlights:
The William Tell Express links two of the most attractive districts of the
country: Central Switzerland with Ticino. From May to September you can
travel by paddle-wheel steamer (out of season by a diesel motor boat) from
Lucerne on the Vierwaldstätter See to Flüelen (a three-course meal is
served in the ship's saloon); then follows a rail trip in a club car or panorama car of the SBB through the impressive Gotthard massif as far as the
towns of Locarno and Lugano.

Special Details:
During the boat trip the route is explained in several languages, and for the
rail section a written description is provided. The kernel of the trip is the
journey on the Gotthard Railway. The William Tell Express excursion can
be combined with several other trips and excursions. Because of limited
accommodation reservations and booking should be made in good time.

Information from the Swiss Travel Bureaux (see Information) and from
Railways (see Railways).

Schiffahrtsgesellschaft des Vierwaldstätter Sees (SGV)
Werftestrasse 5/Postfach 4265
CH-6002 Lucerne
Tel. (041) 40 45 40

An alternative to the railway is the postal coach of the Grand Canyon
Express.

Grand Canyon
Express (Postal
Coach)

Route: Chur–Laax and vice versa.

Highlights:
From June to October a postal coach runs daily from Chur through the
"Grand Canyon" of the Vorderrhein to Laax or vice versa. Between Bonaduz and Laax the road, which is little used, winds its way along the ravine to
the Vorderrhein Gorge. There are views of the white calcite pinnacles and
of the river glistening far below. The night is spent in the Sporthotel
"Rancho" in Laax (address, see below).

Special features:
There are four coaches at the disposal of visitors, each having room for
eight passengers and the driver. In good weather the roof is opened, but
even if it rains the coach is perfectly comfortable. In the price quoted for this
trip the rail journey from most Swiss stations to Chur or Laax (and return)
as well as the coach trip from Chur to Laax and vice versa and accommodation at the Sporthotel "Rancho" are included. For information and booking:

Sporthotel Rancho
CH-7031 Laax
Tel. (081) 9 27 11 11

Information concerning "Museum trains" with old-time steam engines,
old-time trams and other special trains (for example the Bernese Oberland
railway, the Rhätische Bahn) as well as the "Fitness Bahn" programme can
be obtained direct from Swiss Railways (see entry) or from Swiss Travel
Bureaux.

Museum trains
and "Fitness
Railway"

It is possible at most Swiss railway stations to rent bicycles ("Velo am
Bahnhof": 5 gear ordinary bicycles, mountain bikes, tandems, etc.). Hold-
ers of valid rail tickets receive a reduction. Information at all Swiss railway
stations.

Bicycle Rental

See Air Traffic.

Fly-Gepäck

Restaurants

There are many excellent restaurants in Switzerland, and only a selection can be given here. With few exceptions, hotel restaurants are not listed a second time (see Hotels). True gourmets can obtain more details from restaurant guides and specialist magazines; vegetarians can obtain an information leaflet "Vegetarische Restaurants" from the Swiss National Tourist Office (SVZ; see Information).

Aarau
Chez Jeanette, Vordere Vorstadt 17; tel. (064) 22 77 88
In Oberlinsbach: ★Hirschen; tel. (064) 34 22 22 (with 14 rooms)

Aarberg
Commerce, Stadtplatz; tel. (032) 82 45 45
Bahnhof, Bahnhofstrasse; tel. (032) 82 48 88

Abländschen
Le Mignon in the Hotel de la Croix Blanche; tel. (029) 7 85 50

Adelboden
Chez Romy in the Hotel Viktoria Eden; tel. (033) 73 46 73
Le Gourmet in the Hotel Beau-Site, Dorfstrasse; tel. (033) 73 22 22
Le Tartare in the Hotel Huldi ★ Waldhaus, Dorfstrasse; tel. (033) 73 15 31

Aesch
Nussbaumer, Klusstrasse 178; tel. (061) 7 51 16 85

Affoltern
La Fleur, Untere Bahnhofstrasse 33; tel. (01) 7 61 62 82

Agarone
Osteria Della Posta; tel. (092) 64 12 42
Grotto Romitaggio, in a beautiful garden among the vineyards; tel. (092) 64 12 42

Agno
La Perla, in the hotel of the same name; tel. (091) 59 39 21
Grotto Rusca; tel. (091) 59 29 76

Aigle
Restaurant de la Couronne, Yvorne; tel. (025) 26 24 58

Swiss cooking . . .   *. . . an old tradition*

Mühle, former 19th c. corn-mill, Mühlebachweg 41; tel. (061) 4 81 33 70   **Allschwil**

Seehotel Hecht, half-timbered house with rooms; tel. (055) 63 53 66   **Altendorf**

Im Schäfli, with accommodation, Kaffeegasse 1; tel. (072) 65 31 05   **Altenau**

Säntis, Landesgemeindeplatz; tel. (071) 87 87 22   **Appenzell**

★Auberge de la Couronne; tel. (021) 8 00 31 67   **Apples**

Gasthof Brauerei Frohsinn, former brewery, Romanshomerstrasse 15;   **Arbon**
  tel. (071) 46 10 46

Stueva-Cuolm, Italian cuisine; tel. (027) 31 01 31   **Arosa**
Central, with accommodation, Hubelstrasse 252; tel. (027) 31 02 52
Bajazzo; tel. (027) 31 21 15

★Ascolago, with a beautiful terrace above the lake and with accommoda-   **Ascona**
  tion, Via Albarelle; tel. (093) 35 20 55
★Giardino, in the hotel of the same name; tel. (093) 35 01 01
Elvezia, one of Ascona's oldest restaurants, where Stresemann (famous
  German ornithologist) and Briand (French Foreign Minister and Nobel
  Prize winner) met for discussions in 1925.
Al Porto, Piazza G. Motta; tel. (093) 35 13 21
Al Pontile, Piazza G. Motta; tel. (093) 35 46 04
In Losone: Grotto Broggini, Via San Materno; tel. (093) 35 15 67

Zunfthaus zum Paradies, Cordulaplatz 1; tel. (056) 21 50 58   **Baden**
Baden-Dättwil: Pinta, Sommerhaldenstrasse 20; tel. (056) 83 20 30
Ennetbaden: Hertenstein, restaurant with a view, Hertensteinstrasse 80;
  tel. (056) 21 10 20

See main names   **Bad**

★★Stucki, Bruderholzallee 42; tel. (061) 3 61 82 22   **Basle**
★Der Teufelhof, with accommodation decorated by contemporary artists,
  Leonhardsgraben 47; tel. (061) 2 61 10 10
★Les Quatre Saisons in the Hotel Europe, Clarastrasse 43;
  tel. (061) 6 91 80 80
Le Bourguignon, Bachlettenstrasse 1; tel. (061) 2 81 14 10
Chez Donati, St Johanns-Vorstadt 48; tel. (061) 3 22 09 09
St Alban-Eck, St Alban-Vorstadt 60; tel. (061) 2 71 03 20
Charon, Schützengraben 62; tel. (061) 2 61 99 80
Bahnhof-Buffet, SBB Railway Station; in the 2nd class buffet hang works by
  contemporary artists; Centralbahnstrasse 14; tel. (061) 2 71 53 33
Basler Keller, French cuisine in old vault, Münzgasse 12; tel. (061) 2 61 24 23
Café Gleich, vegetarian restaurant, Steinenvorstadt 23; tel. (061) 2 81 82 86
Château Lapin, friendly inn, Schneidergasse 20; tel. (061) 2 61 32 58
Fischerstube, in the smallest brewery in Switzerland, Rheingasse 45;
  tel. (061) 6 92 66 35
Kunsthalle, with outside tables during the summer, Steinenberg 7;
  tel. (061) 2 72 42 33
Rheinbrücke, good self-service establishment in the department store of
  the same name, Greifengasse 22; tel. (061) 6 95 95 11
Schlüssel-Zunft, historic 15th c. guild-hall serving Basle speciality dishes,
  Freie Strasse 25; tel. (061) 2 61 20 46
In Riefelden: Waldhaus, beautiful half-timbered house in a park on the
  bank of the Rhine; tel. (061) 3 13 00 11
In Binningen: Schloss Binningen, an old, stylishly furnished manor-house
  in a park, Schlossgasse 5; tel. (061) 4 21 20 55
In Bottmingen: Weiherschloss, renovated moated castle, Schlossgasse 9;
  tel. (061) 4 21 15 15

Restaurants

Bätterkinden ★Krone, Bahnhofstrasse 1; tel. (065) 45 34 34

Bellinzona Castelgrande, Salita al Castello; tel. (092) 26 23 53
Prisma da Charpie, Viale H. Guisan 5c; tel. (092) 26 34 46
Montebello, in the open in summer, Via alla Chiesa; tel. (092) 25 82 91
Grotto della Speranza, Via Pedemonte 12; tel. (092) 26 19 39

Berne Bellevue Grill, Hotel Bellevue Palace, Kochergasse 3; tel. (031) 3 20 45 45
Büner, Kasernenstrasse 31; tel. (031) 3 01 67 63
Schultenheissenstube in the Hotel Schweizerhof, Bahnhofplatz 11;
  tel. (031) 3 11 45 01
Du Théâtre, Theaterplatz 7; tel. (031) 3 11 71 77
Ermitage, wine-bar and restaurant, Marktgasse 15/Amthausgasse 10;
  tel. (031) 3 11 35 41
Kornhauskeller, former 18th c. corn-store and wine-cellar, Kornhausplatz
  18; tel. (031) 3 11 11 33
Menuetto, vegetarian restaurant, Münstergasse 47; tel. (031) 22 14 48
Äussere Enge, on the edge of town and offering a personal touch, Reichern-
  bachstrasse 2; tel. (031) 23 22 33
Jack's Brasserie in the Schweizerhof, Bahnhofplatz 11; tel. (031) 3 11 45 01
Brasserie Bärengraben, Muristalden 1; tel. (031) 3 31 42 18
Commerce, Gerechtigkeitsgasse 74; tel. (031) 3 11 11 61
Café Postgasse, small Old Town establishment, Postgasse 48;
  tel. (031) 22 60 44
Della Casa, Schauplatzgasse 16; tel. (031) 22 21 42
Klötzlikeller, wine-bar, Gerechtigkeitsgasse 62; tel. (031) 22 74 56
In Bollingen: Zum Sternen, Bolligenstrasse 126; tel. (031) 9 21 04 52

Biasca Della Posta, with 14 rooms, opposite the railway station;
  tel. (092) 72 21 21

Biel/Bienne Amphithryon, in the Hotel Elite, Bahnhofstrasse 14; tel. (032) 22 97 44
Paradisli, Seevorstadt 19; tel. (032) 22 28 60
Gottstatterhaus, situated by the lake 2km/1¼ miles south-west in the direc-
  tion of Neuchâtel; tel. (032) 22 40 52

Bottmingen Weiherschloss Bottmingen, Schlossgasse 9; tel. (061) 4 21 15 15

Brig Schlosskeller, Alte Simplonstrasse 26; tel. (028) 23 33 52
In Naters: Bumanns Kulinarium, Landstrasse 14; tel. (028) 23 63 64

Brigasso Mirafiori, with accommodation, with terrace above the lake;
  tel. (093) 65 12 34

Bulle La Fleur de Lys, Rue de Gruyères 31; tel. (029) 2 76 40
In La Tour-de-Trême: De La Tour; tel. (029) 2 74 70
In Broc: Auberge des Montagnards, Rue Montsalvens 6; tel. (029) 6 15 26

Burgdorf Emmenhof, Kirchbergstrasse 70; tel. (034) 22 22 75

Cavigliano Al Ponte dei Cavalli, accessible by the Centovalli railway from Locarno;
  tel. (093) 81 27 05

Celerina Stüvetta Veglia, with paintings by Swiss artists; tel. (082) 3 80 08

**La Chaux-de-
Fonds** Auberge des Rochettes, Route du Valanvron; tel. (039) 28 33 12
Au Cafignon, Croix-Fédérale 35; tel. (039) 29 48 47

Chiasso Corso, Via Valdani 1; tel. (091) 44 57 01
In Pedrinate: Al Ronco Grande di Pierre de Lusi; tel. (091) 43 43 33

Zunfthaus zur Reblauten (15th c. guild-hall with accommodation);   **Chur**
  tel. (081) 22 17 13
Bündner Stuben in the Hotel Stern, Reichgasse 11; tel. (081) 22 35 55
Basilic, Susenbühlstrasse 43; tel. (081) 22 35 05
Obelisco, Italian cuisine, Vazerolgasse 12; tel. (081) 22 58 58
Zum Kornplatz, Kornplatz 1; tel. (081) 22 27 59
In Malix: Belvedere, 5km/3 miles up from Chur on the road to Lenzerheide;
  tel. (081) 22 33 78

★Cerf, Rue du temple 10; tel. (021) 8 61 26 08   **Cossonay**

Crans-sur-Sierre: Rôtisserie de la Reine; tel. (027) 41 18 85   **Crans-Montana**
In Plans-Mayens: Le Mont-Blanc, with accommodation; tel. (027) 41 31 43
La Dent Blanche, Walliser Spezialitäten; tel. (027) 41 11 79
In Montana: Café de la Poste; tel. (027) 41 27 45
Au Gréni, Allée Katherine Mansfield; tel. (027) 41 24 43
In Vermala: Crevin, Schäferei; tel. (027) 41 21 80

★Auberge du Raisin, with accommodation, Place de l'Hôtel de Ville 1;   **Cully**
  tel. (021) 7 99 21 31

★Zum Kreuz, Stätlistrasse 3; tel. (041) 65 17 51   **Dallenwil**

In Davos Dorf: Bündnerstübli, Dischmastrasse 8; tel. (081) 46 33 93   **Davos**
In Davos Platz: Jenatschstube im Davoserhof, Am Postplatz;
  tel. (081) 43 68 17
Zauberberg, Chinese cuisine in the Hotel Europe, Promenade 63;
  tel. (081) 43 11 67
In Davos-Laret: Hubli's Landhaus, fish and meat dishes; tel. (081) 46 21 21

Du Midi, Place de la Gare 10; tel. (066) 22 17 77   **Delémont**

Les Lilas; tel. (025) 53 11 34   **Les Diablerets**
Café de la Couronne; tel. (025) 53 11 75

★Zur Sonne, Bahnhofstrasse 1; tel. 8 53 12 17   **Dielsdorf**

Plauen, Klosterplatz; tel. (055) 53 81 18   **Einsiedeln**

★Auberge du Château; tel. (037) 33 28 34   **Ependes**

Adler, historic inn with accommodation, Fruthwilerstrasse 2;   **Ermatingen**
  tel. (072) 64 11 33
Fischstube Seetal, with accommodation and garden terrace, Untere Seestrasse 60; tel. (072) 64 14 14

St Georges, 16th c. timbered house; tel. (028) 71 11 28   **Ernen**

La Gerbe d'Or, Rue du Camus 5; tel. (037) 63 11 81   **Estavayer-Le Lac**
Hôtel de Ville, Rue de l'Hôtel de Ville 16; tel. (037) 63 12 62
Hostellerie du Château, Rue des Granges 2; tel. (037) 63 10 49

★Bürgi's Burehof, Hauptstrasse; tel. (055) 53 24 17   **Euthal**

Faido, with accommodation; tel. (094) 38 15 55   **Faido**

Sternen; tel. (052) 42 13 13   **Flaach**
Ziegelhütte; tel. (052) 42 15 21

★Zur Mühle, in the Maienfeld direction; tel. (081) 3 02 61 64   **Fläsch**

Restaurants

The little medieval town of Ernen, a good place to eat

Flims	In Flims-Fidaz: Fidazerhof, with accommodation; tel. (081) 39 12 33
	In Flims-Waldhaus: National, with accommodation; tel. (081) 39 39 23 Conn, excursion restaurant near the Caumasee (lake), accessible only on foot (40 minutes) or by horse-drawn coach from Flims; local church; tel. (081) 39 12 31
Flüh	Martin, Hauptstrasse 94; tel. (061) 7 31 10 02 Wirtshaus zur Säge, Steinrain 5; tel. (061) 7 31 15 77
Fraubrunnen	Zum Brunnen, Bernstrasse 6; tel. (031) 7 67 72 16
Frauenfeld	Zum Goldenen Kreuz, with accommodation and 17th c. wood-panelling, Zürcherstrasse 144; tel. (054) 7 20 11 10 Roter Ochsen, Zürcherstrasse 224; tel. (054) 21 12 57 In Erzenholz: Zur Hoffnung, Schaffhausenerstrasse 266; tel. (054) 2 70 77 22
Fribourg	Auberge de Zaehringen, Rue de Zaehringen 13; tel. (037) 22 42 36 Fleur-de-Lys, Rue des Forgerons 18; tel. (037) 22 79 61 Raisin d'Or, Impasse des Eglantines; tel. (037) 28 26 73 Des Marechaux, Rue des Chanoines 9; tel. (037) 22 33 33 Buffet de la Gare DFF, French cuisine in the 1st floor, Place de la Gare 1; tel. (037) 22 28 16 Restaurant Français du Buffet de la Gare; tel. (037) 22 88 16 Auberge du Chasseur, Rue de Lausanne 10; tel. (037) 22 56 98
Ftan	★ Haus Paradies, in the hotel of the same name; tel. (081) 8 64 13 25
Gandria	Antico, with terrace; tel. (091) 51 48 71

★ Sihlhalde, 11km/7 miles from Zurich, Sihlhaldenstrasse 70;   **Gattikon**
  tel. (01) 7 20 09 27

★★ Le Chat Botté Hôtel Beau-Rivage, Quai du Mont-Blanc 13;   **Genf/Genève/**
  tel. (022) 7 31 65 32   **Geneva**
★★ Le Béarn, Quai de la Poste 4; tel. (022) 3 21 00 28
★★ Le Cygne, Hotel Noga Hilton, Quai du Mont-Blanc 19;
  tel. (022) 7 31 98 11
★★ Neptune. in the Hotel Du Rhône, Quai Turrettini 1; tel. (022) 7 31 98 31
★ Restaurant in the Hotel Intercontinental, Chemin du Petit-Saconnex 7–9;
  tel. (022) 7 34 60 91
★ Parc des Eaux-Vives, Quai G. Ador 82; tel. (022) 7 35 41 40
Le Gentilhomme, in the Hôtel Richemond, Jardin Brunswick;
  tel. (022) 7 31 14 00
Amphitryon, in the Hôtel les Bergues, Quai des Bergues 33;
  tel. (022) 7 31 50 50
Tsé Yang, Chinese cuisine. Quai du Mont-Blanc 19; tel. (022) 7 32 50 81
Auberge à la Mère Royaume, Rue des Corps Saints 9; tel. (022) 7 32 70 08
L'Arlequin in the Hotel Metropolis, Quai Général-Guisan;
  tel. (022) 3 11 13 44
Baron de la Mouette, Möwenpick, Rue du Rhône 40; tel. (022) 3 11 88 55
Roberto, Italian cuisine, Rue Pierre-Fatio 10; tel. (022) 3 11 80 33
La Coupole, Rue du Rhône 116; tel. (022) 7 35 65 44
Cavalier, Rue Cherbuliez 7; tel. (022) 7 35 09 56
Le Sénal, Rue E.-Yung 1; tel. (022) 3 46 58 10
Au Pied de Cochon, Place du Bourg-de-Four 4; tel. (022) 3 10 47 97
Brasserie Lipp, good plain French cooking, also in the garden in summer,
  Rue de la Confédération 8; tel. (022) 3 11 10 11
Café du Centre, near the Quai Général-Guisan; tel. (022) 3 11 85 86
Café de Paris, Rue des Gares 27; tel. (022) 7 32 84 50
Les Armures, Geneva's oldest café with the "best" cheese fondue in the
  city, Rue des Puits-St-Pierre; tel. (022) 3 10 91 72
Near the Palais des Nations: ★ Les Continents, in the Hotel Intercontinental,
  Chemin du Petit-Saconnex 7; tel. (022) 9 19 39 39
La Perle du Lac, in Mon Repos Park by the lake, Rue de Lausanne 128;
  tel. (022) 7 31 79 35
In Bellevue: Tse Fung, Hotel La Réserve, Route de Lausanne 301;
  tel. (022) 7 74 17 41
In Carouge: ★★ La Cassolette, Rue Jacques-Dalphin 31; tel. (022) 3 42 03 18
La Bourse, a "brasserie" with good, plain cooking, Le Jardin de la Bourse
  with a sophisticated dining-room and pizzeria, Les Caves de la Bourse
  with Italian cuisine, Place du Marché 7; tel. (022) 3 42 04 66
In Cologny: ★★ Auberge du Lion d'Or, Place Pierre-Gautier 5;
  tel. (022) 7 32 44 32
In Vandoeuvres: Cheval Blanc, Italian cuisine; tel. (022) 7 50 14 01
In Vésenaz: La Capite Chez Ermanno, à la Capite; tel. (022) 7 52 10 51
In Thonex: ★ Chez Cigalon, Route d'Ambily 39; tel. (022) 3 49 97 33
In Vessy: Alain Lavergnat, Route de Veyrier 130; tel. (022) 7 84 26 25
In Petit-Lancy: ★ Hostellerie de la Vendée, in the hotel of the same name,
  Chemin de la Vendée 28; tel. (022) 7 92 04 11

Ochsen, St-Galler-Strasse 31; tel. (071) 85 25 31   **Gossau**
Henessenmühle; tel. (071) 85 15 97

Restaurant in the Hotel Drachenburg, Am Schlosspark; tel. (072) 69 14 14   **Gottlieben**

Sakura, Japanese restaurant, Bahnhofstrasse; tel. 52 10 06   **Grenchen**

Hostellerie des Chevaliers, in the hotel of the same name;   **Gruyères**
  tel. (029) 6 19 33

Restaurants

Gstaad
Chesery, Lauenenstrasse; tel. (030) 4 24 51
La Bagatelle im Grand Chalet, Neueretstrasse; tel. (030) 0 32 52
Rialto, Italian cuisine, Haupstrasse; tel. (030) 4 34 74
Olden, with accommodation; tel. (030) 4 34 44

Guarda
Crusch Alba, in a beautiful Engadine house; tel. (081) 8 62 21 33

Gurtnellen
Gotthard, with accommodation; tel. (04) 6 51 10

Guttannen
Handeck, on the Grimsel pass road, with accommodation;
tel. (036) 73 11 31

Herisau
Bierquelle, Postrasse 39; tel. (071) 52 20 40
Marktplatz, Wiesental 1; tel. (071) 52 32 12

Interlaken
La Terrasse, in the Hotel Victoria-Jungfrau, Höheweg 41; tel. (036) 27 11 11
Hirschen, with accommodation; tel. (036) 22 15 45
In Wilderswil: Alpenblick, with rustic furnishings; tel. (036) 22 07 07
On the Jungfraujoch: by train from Interlaken, Wengen, Lauterbrunnen or
Grindelwald: Top of Europe (3454m/11,336ft); tel. (036) 55 22 91

Kandersteg
Au Gourmet, in the Waldhotel Doldenhorn; tel. (033) 75 18 19
Ruedihaus, old coaching inn with accommodation; tel. (033) 75 18 28

Klosters
★ Walserhof, with accommodation; tel. (081) 69 42 42. Number change
April 1996
Chesa Grischuna, Bahnhofstrasse 12; tel. (081) 69 22 22. Number change
April 1996

Kreuzlingen
Seegarten, with accommodation, Promenadenstrasse 40;
tel. (072) 75 26 77
Gasthaus Engel, Bachstrasse 11
Jakobshöhe, Bergstrasse 46

Küsnacht
★★ Petermann's Kunststube, Seestrasse 160; tel. (01) 9 10 07 15
★★ Ermitage, in the hotel of the same name; tel. (01) 9 10 52 22
Erle, Italian cuisine, Hörnlistrasse 16; tel. (01) 9 12 03 70
In Forch: Solitude, Schmalzgrueb 53; tel. (01) 9 18 01 20

Lambooing
Cheval-Blanc, Jura cuisine with cultural programme, Route de Diesse 8;
tel. (032) 95 12 43

Lauerz
Insel Schwanau, situated in the Lauerzersee (lake), ferry on request from
the Schwanau landing stage; tel. (043) 21 17 57

Lausanne
★★ La Grappe d'Or, Cheneau de Bourg 3; tel. (021) 6 34 05 05
La Rotonde, in the Hotel Beau-Rivage, Ouchy, Chemin Beau-Rivage;
tel. (021) 6 13 33 33
San Marino, Italian cuisine, Avenue de la Gare 20; tel. (021) 3 12 93 69
Café Beau Rivage, Ouchy, Place Général Guisan; tel. (021) 6 13 33 30
Auberge du Lac de Sauvabelin, by the lake; tel. (021) 6 47 39 29
Kwong Ming, Chinese cuisine, Avenue de Cour 74; tel. (021) 6 17 85 25
Maï-Thaï, Thai cuisine, Rue Caroline; tel. (021) 3 23 89 10
Le Pélican, Rue Centrale 9; tel. (021) 9 12 84 55
Le Chalet Suisse, Route du Signal 40; tel. (021) 3 12 23 12
In Pully: Palais Impérial, Avenue de la Tour Haldimand 5;
tel. (021) 7 28 25 93
In Crissier: ★ Girardet, Rue d'Yverdon 1; tel. (021) 6 34 05 05

Lenzerheide
Lenzerhorn, with accommodation; tel. (081) 34 11 05
In Sporz: ★ Guarda Val, old farmhouse; tel. (081) 34 22 14

La Malvoisie, in the Hotel Les Sources des Alpes; tel. (027) 62 11 51 **Leukerbad/**
Loèche-les-Bains

Le Leysin, cheese-making museum; tel. (025) 34 22 55 **Leysin**
La Berneuse Kuklos, panorama restaurant; tel. (025) 34 31 41

Neuhaus, Kasernenstrasse 3; tel. (061) 9 21 25 62 **Liestal**
Schützenstube, Rathausstrasse 14; tel. (061) 9 21 08 08

La Croisette, Rue du Marais 10; tel. (039) 31 35 30 **La Locle**
Chez Sandro, Italian cuisine, Rue de la Gare 4; tel. (039) 31 40 87

Cervo, Via Torretta 11; tel. (093) 31 41 31 **Locarno**
Antica Osteria, Via dei Pescatori 8; tel. (093) 33 87 94
In Orselina: Della Posta; tel. (093) 33 46 45
In Minusio: Navegna, on the bank of the lake, with accommodation;
  tel. (093) 33 22 22
In Muralto: ★★Centenario, Lungolago Motta 17; tel. (093) 33 82 22

★Thuri's Blumenau; tel. 38 35 70 **Lömmenschwil**

Bianchi, Via Pessina 3; tel. (091) 22 84 79 **Lugano**
★Al Portone, Viale Casserate 3; tel. (091) 23 59 95
Al Faro, Riva Paradiso 36; tel. (091) 54 51 41
Galleria, Via Vegezzi 4; tel. (091) 23 62 88
Parco Saroli, Viale Franscini 6; tel. (091) 23 53 14
Da Armando, Via Luigi Canonica 5; tel. (091) 23 37 66
Gambrinus, Piazza della Riforma; tel. (091) 23 19 55
Scala, Via Nassa 29; tel. (091) 22 09 58
Locanda del Boschetto, Via Boschetto 8; tel. (091) 54 24 93
In Sorengo: ★★Santabbondio, Via Fomelino 10; tel. (091) 54 85 35
In Massagno: Antica Osteria Gerso, Piazzetta Solaro 24; tel. (091) 56 19 15
Grotto della Salute, Via dei Sindacatori 4; tel. (091) 56 04 76

In Bernex: ★La Colombiere à Lully, Route de Soral 122; **Lully**
  tel. (022) 7 57 65 49

Trianon, in the Grand Hôtel National, Haldenstrasse 4; tel. (041) 50 11 11 **Lucerne**
Mignon, Hotel Palace, Haldenstrasse 10; tel. (041) 50 22 22
Arbalète, Hotel Monopol, Pilatusstrasse 1; tel. (041) 23 08 66
Au Premier, in Lucerne railway station; tel. (041) 23 57 77
Le Manoir, Bundesplatz 9; tel. (041) 23 23 48
La Vague, Hotel des Balances, Weinmarkt; tel. (041) 51 18 51
Old Swiss House, Löwenplatz 4; tel. (041) 51 61 71
Thai Garden, in the Hotel Astoria, Pilatusstrasse 29; tel. (041) 24 44 66
Zunfthaus zu Pfistern, Kornmarkt 4; tel. (041) 51 36 50
Wirtshaus Galliker, Schützenstrasse 1; tel. (041) 22 10 02
Zum Raben, Am Kornmarkt 5; tel. (041) 51 51 35
Schwanen, Le Bec Rouge, Schwanenplatz 4; tel. (041) 51 11 77
On Oberrüti: Waldhaus (forest establishment), beautifully situated with
  accommodation; tel. (041) 47 17 54

Hirschen, Hirschenplatz 2; tel. (032) 84 13 08 **Lyss**
Post, Bahnhofstrasse 17; tel. (032) 84 13 91

★Pöschtli, with accommodation, Maispracherstrasse 2; **Magden**
  tel. (061) 8 41 11 25

Weisskreuz, with accommodation; tel. (081) 51 81 61 **Malans**

★★Le Gourmet, in the Hotel Forum. Avenue du Grand St Bernard 72; **Martigny**
  tel. (026) 22 18 41
Trois Couronnes, Place du Boeuf 8; tel. (026) 23 21 14

Restaurants

Mels	★★ Schlüssel, Nidbergstube, Oberdorfstrasse 5; tel. (081) 7 23 12 38
Mendrisio	Stazione, with accommodation; tel. (091) 46 82 27
Misery	Auberge de Misery; tel. (037) 45 11 52
Montreux	Du Cygne, in the Palace Hotel, Grand Rue 100; tel. (021) 9 63 50 51 In Chamby-sur-Montreux: ★ Le Clos des Alpes; tel. (021) 9 64 46 18 In Clarens: ★ L'Ermitage, with accommodation, Rue du Lac 75; tel. (021) 9 64 44 11 Mai Thai. Rue du Lac 40; tel. (021) 9 64 25 36 In Brent: ★★ Le Pont-de-Brent; tel. (021) 9 64 55 30
Morcote	In Vico: Bellavista, with accommodation; tel. (091) 69 11 43
Morges	Le Petit Manoir, Avenue Paderewski 8; tel. (021) 8 02 42 43 Le Léman "Chez racheter", Rue Louis-de-Savoie 61; tel. (021) 8 01 21 88 Les Jardins Moghols, Indian cuisine, Rue Gare 8; tel. (021) 8 01 27 23
München-buchsee	Moospinte, Wiggiswil; tel. (031) 8 69 01 13 Bären, with accommodation, Bernstrasse 3; tel. (031) 8 69 02 99 Schützenhaus, Oberdorfstrasse 10; tel. (031) 8 69 39 81
Murten/Morat	Lord Nelson, in the Hotel Schiff, Ryf 53; tel. (037) 71 27 01 In Meyriez: Le Vieux Manoir, in the hotel of the same name, Rue de Lausanne; tel. (037) 71 12 83
Nebikon	★ Adler; tel. (062) 86 21 22
Neuchâtel	La Maison des Halles, Rue du Trésor 4; tel. (038) 24 31 41 Bistro de l'Arrosée, Rue Maladière 35; tel. (038) 23 03 20 Buffet de la Gare, Place de la Gare 1; tel. (038) 25 48 53 In St-Blaise: ★ Au Boccalino, Avenue Bacheln 11; tel. (038) 33 36 80 In Peseux: Grand Pin, Place de la Fontaine 2; tel. (038) 31 77 07
Le Noiremont	★ Gare, with accommodation; tel. (039) 53 11 10
Nürensdorf	★ Zum Bären, with accommodation, Alte Winterthurstrasse 45; tel. 8 36 42 12
Nyon	In Crans-près-Céligny: with accommodation, Rue Antoine Saladin 2; tel. 7 76 23 23
Olten	Felsenburg, Aarauerstrasse 157; tel. (062) 26 22 77 Zum Goldenen Ochsen, Ringstrasse 23; tel. (062) 32 19 35
Porrentruy	Buffet de la Gare, Place de la Gare 4; tel. (066) 66 21 35
Bad Ragaz	In Flappe: Paradies; tel. (081) 3 02 25 01 Löwen; tel. (081) 3 02 13 06
Rapperswil	Schloss, Lindenhügel; tel. (055) 27 18 28 Bellevue, with accommodation, Marktgasse 21; tel. (055) 27 66 30
Rheineck	Zur Alten Mühle, Töbelimülistrasse 15; tel. (071) 44 10 57
Rheinfelden	Drei Könige, Zürcherstrasse 9; tel. (061) 831 50 44
Rolle	Auberge de Bugnaux, Route du Vignoble; tel. (021) 8 25 16 82 In Bursins: ★ Auberge du Soleil; tel. (021) 8 24 13 44

Della Posta, with accommodation; tel. (093) 35 84 70
Ronco, with accommodation; tel. (093) 35 52 65

Ronco sopra Ascona

Pfeffermühle, Bellevuestrasse 1b; tel. (071) 41 16 58

Rorschach

Seefeld Le Gourmet, Rapperswilerstrasse 44; tel. (055) 31 16 73

Rüti

★Waldhotel Fletschhorn, with accommodation; tel. (028) 57 21 31
Alpen Landgasthof Hohnegg, with accommodation; tel. (028) 57 22 68

Saas Fee

Alt Guggeien, Kesslehaldenstrasse 85; tel. (071) 35 12 10
Neubad, Bankgasse 6; tel. (071) 22 86 83
Bel Etage, Engelgasse 12; tel. (071) 22 29 70
Am Gallusplatz: Gallusstrasse 24; tel. (071) 23 33 30
Schweizerhof by David, Fidelstrasse 2; tel. (071) 25 65 33
Peter und Paul, in the Wild Life Park (Wildpark); tel. (071) 25 56 25

St Gallen

Rôtisserie des Chevaliers, in the Hotel Kulm; tel. (082) 2 11 51
Grill Room Palace, in the Palace Hotel; tel. (082) 2 11 01
Chesa Veglia, Via Veglia 2; tel. (082) 3 35 96
Chasellas Suvretta, Via Suvretta 22; tel. (082) 3 38 54
In Champfer: ★★Jöhri's Talvo; tel. (082) 3 44 55

St Moritz

★Wirtschaft St Pelagius; tel. (071) 98 14 34

St Pelagiberg

In Peney-Dessus: ★★Domaine de Châteauvieux; tel. (022) 7 53 15 11

Satigny

★★Fischerzunft, with accommodation, Rheinquai 8; tel. (053) 25 32 85
Zum Frieden, Herrenacker 11; tel. (053) 25 47 15
Schützenhaus Birch, Birchweg 75; tel. (053) 25 13 56

Schaffhausen

Ratskeller, Strehlgasse 3; tel. (043) 21 10 87

Schwyz

Relais du Château de Villa, Rue Ste-Cathérine 4; tel. (027) 55 18 96
In Veyras: Noble Contrée, Route de Montana; tel. (027) 55 67 74
In Corin-de-la-Crète: ★La Côte; tel. (027) 55 13 51

Sierre

Restaurant in the Hotel Albana; tel. (082) 4 92 92
Chesa Arsa, in the Hotel Julier; tel. (082) 4 96 44

Silvaplana

Supersaxo, Passage Supersaxo; tel. (027) 23 23 10
La Planta, Avenue de la Gare 33; tel. (027) 22 60 34
Cheval Blanc, 23 Grand-Pont; tel. (027) 22 18 67

Sion/Sitten

Le Miroir d'Argentine, open from beginning of May to end of October;
   tel. (025) 68 14 46

Solalax-Près-Villars

Federal, Rue de la Gare 14; tel. (032) 97 10 34

Sonceboz

Zunfthaus zum Wirthen, Hauptgasse 41; tel. (065) 23 33 44
Tourelle, in the Hotel Tour Rouge, Hauptgasse 42; tel. (065) 22 96 21
Zum Alten Stephan, Gourmetnarrenstübli, Friedhofplatz 10;
   tel. (065) 22 11 09

Solothurn

★Belvédère, in the hotel of the same name, Schachenstrasse 39;
   tel. (033) 54 33 33

Spiez

Seehus, Seestrasse 4; tel. (01) 9 26 23 03
Im Kehlhof, Seestrasse 191; tel. (01) 9 26 11 55
Salzwaage, Malayan cuisine, Allenbergstrasse 47; tel. (01) 9 26 81 80

Stäfa

Zur Linde, with accommodation, Dorfplatz 7; tel. (041) 61 28 26
Zur Rosenburg, Alter Postplatz 3; tel. (041) 61 24 61

Stans

Restaurants

Stein am Rhein
(near Olten)
★ Sonne, Rathausplatz 127; tel. (054) 41 21 28

Steinen
Adelboden, Schlagstrasse; tel. (043) 41 12 42
Rössli, with accommodation, Dorfplatz 1; tel. (043) 41 13 20

Tägerwilen
Steinbock/Le Pavillon, Hauptstrasse 85; tel. (072) 69 11 72

Taverne
★ Motto dei Gallo, with accommodation; tel. (091) 93 28 71

Teufenthal
Zur Herberge, with accommodation; tel. (064) 46 12 20

Thörigen
★ Landgasthof Löwen; tel. (063) 61 21 07

Thun
Schloss Schadau, Seestrasse 45; tel. (033) 22 25 00
Krone, bistro and Chinese cuisine, with accommodation, Rathausplatz;
tel. (033) 22 82 82

Uetikon am See
★ Wirtschaft zum Wiesengrund, Kleindorfstrasse 61; tel. (01) 9 20 63 60

**Untereng-
stringen**
★★ Witsch's Restaurant, Zürcherstrasse 55; tel. (01) 7 50 44 60

Vaduz
★★ Au Premier, in the Hotel Real, Städtle 21; tel. (075) 2 32 22 22
Torkel, Hintergasse 9; tel. (075) 2 32 44 10

Verbier
★★ Pierroz, in the Hotel Rosalp, Route de Médran; tel. (026) 31 63 23
Le Relais des Semailles, Au Hameau; tel. (026) 31 45 80

Vevey
Le Raisin, Place du Marché 3; tel. (021) 9 21 10 28
Taverne du Château, Rue d'Italie 43; tel. (021) 9 21 12 10

**Vufflens-le-
Chateau**
★★ L'Ermitage de Bernard Ravet; tel. (021) 8 02 21 91

Wädenswil
Eder's Eichmühle, Neugutstrasse 933; tel. (01) 7 89 34 44

Weesen
Fischerstube, Marktgasse 9; tel. (058) 43 16 08

Weinfelden
Frohsinn, Wilerstrasse 12; tel. (072) 22 30 40

Weiningen
Winzerhaus, Haslernstrasse 28; tel. (01) 7 50 40 66

Weite-Wartau
Heuwiese; tel. (081) 7 83 10 55

Wettingen
Klosterstübli, Klosterstrasse 13; tel. (056) 26 06 88
Sternen, Spörri-Stube, Klosterstrasse 9; tel. (056) 27 14 61

Widen
Wirtschaft zum Stutz, Bremgartenstrasse 64; tel. (057) 33 13 14

Wigoltingen
★ Taverne zum Schäfli, Oberdorfstrasse 8; tel. (054) 63 11 72

Wilderswil
★ Hotel Alpenblick, Oberdorf; tel. (036) 22 07 07

Winterthur
Stube, in the Hotel Krone, Marktgasse 49; tel. (052) 2 13 25 21
Zum Trübli, Bosshardengässchen 2; tel. (052) 2 12 55 36
In Wülflingen: Restaurant-Schloss Wülflingen, Wülflingerstrasse 214;
tel. (052) 2 22 18 67
Wirtschaft und Weingut zum Taggenberg, Taggenbergstrasse 79;
tel. (052) 2 22 05 22

Yvorne
★ Auberge la Roseraie, Route de Lausanne; tel. (025) 26 53 67
Le Torrent; tel. (025) 26 19 28

Zell
Lindengarten, with accommodation; tel. (045) 88 22 55

Le Gourmet, in the Hotel Alpenhof; tel. (028) 66 11 75   **Zermatt**
Le Corbeau d'Or, in the Silence-Hotel Mirabeau; tel. (028) 67 17 72
Zum See; tel. (028) 67 20 45
Unter Rothorn; tel. (028) 67 26 75
In Findeln: Finderlhof; tel. (028) 67 25 88

Fédéral, Vordere Hauptgasse 57; tel. (062) 51 01 00   **Zofingen**

★Rathauskeller, Oberaltstadt 1; tel. (042) 21 00 58   **Zug**
Aklin, Am Zytturm, Kolinplatz 10; tel. (042) 21 18 66
Rosenberg, with accommodation, Rosenbergstrasse; tel. (042) 21 71 71
Hecht, Fischmarkt 2; tel. (042) 21 01 93

★Crusch Alva, with accommodation, Hauptstrasse 26; tel. (082) 7 13 19 or   **Zuoz**
   7 15 81

★★Tübli, Scheggengasse 8; tel. (01) 2 51 24 71   **Zurich**
★Scala, in the Hotel Zurich, Neumühlequai 42; tel. (01) 3 63 63 63
Wirtschaft Flühgass, Zollikerstrasse 214; tel. (01) 3 81 12 15
Il Giglio, Weberstrasse 14; tel. (01) 2 42 85 97
Baron de la Mouette, in the Mövenpick Dreikönighaus,
   Beethovenstrasse 32; tel. (01) 2 86 53 53
Zunfthaus zur Schmiden, Marktgasse 20; tel. (01) 2 51 52 87
Golden Dragon, Bernerstrasse Nord 224; tel. (01) 4 31 19 53
Accademia, Rowandstrasse 48; tel. (01) 2 41 42 02
Amberg, Hottingerstrasse 5; tel. (01) 2 51 26 26
Blaue Ente, in the Tiefenbrunnen mill, Seefeldstrasse 223;
   tel. (01) 4 22 77 06
Conti da Bianca, Dufourstrasse 1; tel. (01) 2 51 06 66
Königstühl, Stüssihofstatt 3; tel. (01) 2 61 76 18
Kronenhalle, with an impressive art collection, Rämistrasse 4;
   tel. (01) 2 51 66 69
Riesbächli, Zollikerstrasse 157; tel. (01) 4 22 23 24
Sala of Tokyo, Japanese cuisine, Limmatstrasse 29; tel. (01) 2 71 78 07
Haus zum Rüden, Limmatquai 42; tel. (01) 2 61 95 66
Nouvelle-Thai, Thai cuisine, Erlachstrasse 46; tel. (01) 4 62 66 22
Chesa da Seoul, Korean cuisine, Klingenstrasse 33; tel. (01) 2 72 21 21
Raja Bongo, Indian cuisine, Zwinglistrasse 3; tel. (01) 2 41 80 11
Real, Spanish cuisine, Rotwandstrasse 62; tel. (01) 2 42 66 06
Au Premier (station buffet), Main Station (Hauptbahnhof);
   tel. (01) 2 11 15 10
Castello, Italian cuisine, Kanonengasse 31; tel. (01) 2 41 11 80
Fribourg-Fondue-Stübli, Rotwandstrasse 38; tel. (01) 2 41 90 76
Hexagone Bistro, Kuttelgasse 15; tel. (01) 2 11 94 11
Idaburg Bistro, Gertrudstrasse 44; tel. (01) 4 51 18 42
Brasserie Lipp, Bar Jules Verne, Uraniastrasse 9; tel. (01) 2 11 11 55

In Glockhausen: Rosa Tschudi, Tobelhofstrasse 344; tel. (01) 8 21 03 95
In Kloten: Top-Air, in the airport; tel. (01) 8 14 33 00
In Zollikon: Wirtschaft zur Höhe, Höhestrasse 73; tel. (01) 3 91 59 59

Road Traffic

In the relatively heavily populated Swiss Alpine foreland the road network   Road Network
is exceedingly dense; roads through villages and small towns are often
narrow and require special care and attention. The mountainous regions
have a less closely meshed road network and the most important valleys
are easily accessible. The Swiss road network consists of motorways
(French – autoroutes; Italian – autostrade) which are subject to tolls, and
motorists need to display an annual vignette on their cars. There are official
national roads 1st class, national roads 2nd class which are equivalent to

Road Traffic

Schaffhausen
Basel
Aarau
Winterthur
Delémont
Olten
Zürich
St. Gallen
Biel/
Bienne
Solothurn
LIECHTEN-
STEIN
Zug
Neuchâtel
Luzern
BERN
Schwyz
Glarus
Fribourg
Altdorf
Chur
Davos
Thun
Interlaken
Lausanne
St. Moritz
Montreux
Brig
Genève
Sion
Locarno Bellinzona
Martigny
Zermatt
©*Baedeker*
Lugano

Trunk roads ━━

English main roads, and national roads 3rd class (important pass and valley roads), main roads and minor roads.

Road conditions

In general road conditions are excellent. Mountain stretches are, by their very nature, somewhat narrower and sometimes have steep descents and curves; in summer because of the considerable number of coaches on these roads extreme care is necessary.

Europa Routes

On the following stretches Europa Routes cross the territory of Switzerland:

E2: Vallorbe–Lausanne–Martigny–the Rhône Valley–Simplon Pass–Domodóssola (Italy).
E4: Basle–Berne–Lausanne–Geneva.
E9: Basle–Lucerne–Arth–Andermatt–St Gotthard–Bellinzona–Lugano.
E17: Basle–Zurich–Winterthur–St Gallen–St Margrethen.
E21A: Martigny–Great St Bernard–Aosta (Italy).
E60: Zug–Arth.
E61: St Margrethen–Chur–Splügen (village)–San Bernardino–Bellinzona.
E70: Bargen–Schaffhausen–Winterthur.

Since 1985 motorways and roads of motorways standard have been subject to toll and the signs on them are white and green. The motorway vignette which acts as a receipt for the toll can be obtained at frontiers, at post offices, filling stations and garages in Switzerland and from the Automobile Association in Great Britain. It costs 40 Swiss Francs (1995) and lasts for 14 months from December 1st to the January 31st of the following year.

Fuel (Petrol/ Gasoline/ Diesel)

As well as super and diesel, lead-free petrol is widely available in Switzerland, the cost varies considerably.

Outside business hours cars can obtain fuel at filling stations in towns and at automatic pumps on the motorways which take bank notes of 10 and 20 Swiss Francs and which are open 24 hours a day.

Distances in Switzerland (Kilometres)

	Zürich	Zug	Schaffhausen	St. Moritz	St. Gallen	Porrentruy	Olten	Montreux	Luzern	Lugano	Locarno	Lausanne	Kreuzlingen	Interlaken	Genève	Fribourg	Chur	Chiasso	Chaux-de-Fonds, La	Buchs/SG	Brig	Bern	Basel
Andermatt	117	78	170	162	155	204	125	200	75	111	102	234	164	93	296	186	92	135	220	133	78	154	169
Basel	85	113	93	291	166	68	41	182	94	267	258	198	139	147	264	127	196	291	98	188	236	91	
Bern	123	117	170	315	206	114	69	86	91	262	253	106	187	60	165	31	238	286	69	230	177		
Brig	195	156	247	240	228	306	190	123	153	146	113	153	242	117	215	180	170	170	244	211			
Buchs/SG	111	107	124	129	52	251	172	316	130	187	178	333	85	194	395	261	42	211	265				
Chaux-de-Fonds, La	158	164	206	360	239	62	101	122	160	316	307	98	225	129	142	68	273	340					
Chiasso	239	200	294	131	272	326	248	297	197	26	61	327	286	215	389	304	170						
Chur	119	115	171	77	94	257	180	324	138	146	137	341	125	185	403	266							
Fribourg	151	157	200	333	232	125	96	58	123	278	269	63	218	78	137								
Genève	288	295	334	424	366	204	234	93	262	361	324	62	352	215									
Interlaken	118	88	144	255	182	168	123	136	64	191	182	153	195										
Kreuzlingen	71	101	46	212	34	207	139	273	132	262	253	290											
Lausanne	226	232	272	378	304	157	172	26	200	299	262												
Locarno	206	167	258	163	252	293	215	246	164	37													
Lugano	215	176	267	126	261	302	224	283	173														
Luzern	55	25	107	237	118	130	52	183															
Montreux	189	215	255	363	287	183	155																
Olten	61	66	106	262	136	88																	
Porrentruy	144	150	158	346	222																		
St. Gallen	85	95	80	190																			
St. Moritz	206	202	258																				
Schaffhausen	53	82																					
Zug	30																						

Emergency fuel in cans can only be carried up to 25 litres/approximately 5 gallons.

See Motoring

Traffic regulations

Tel. 163.

Road conditions

Shopping and Souvenirs

The best known Swiss products are watches, clocks and jewellery. Also popular are lace and embroidery from St Gallen and the multi-bladed Swiss Army knives.

Souvenirs

There is a good selection of craft articles at the "Schweizer Heimatwerk" which has showrooms in Zurich and other large towns. Here mounted crystal, painted porcelain, wooden articles and vessels, musical boxes, dolls in traditional costume, carvings in wood, and other characteristic work of a particular district can be obtained.

Craftwork

Food of excellent quality can be bought. Among the most popular items are chocolate, cheese and spirits (cherry brandy from Zug and herbal liqueurs

Food

called "Chrüter") also wine, meat, and cherry bread. Mention must also be made of the famous Swiss confectionery products, such as those made by Sprüngli, Honold and Schober, and, finally, the Engadine nut gateaux and the Aargau "rüebli" gateaux. Coffee, conserves and ready-made dishes can be obtained in many varieties especially in chain stores such as Migros, Co-op, etc.

Sport

General
A good survey of the facilities for sport, accommodation, evening entertainment, etc., during the summer can be found in the leaflet "Die Schweiz – eine ganze Ferienwelt" which can be obtained from the Swiss Tourist Office or from Swiss Travel Bureaux (see information). Also the brochure "Sportferien à la Carte", with 14 selected week-long holidays for different (summer) sports, can be obtained from the above mentioned information bureaux on request. For information about winter sports in Switzerland see "Winter Sports" below.

Angling
Switzerland has some 135,000 hectares/334,000 acres of lakes in which angling is allowed. Since the regulations for fishing and the conditions for a fishing permit vary from canton to canton, anglers are recommended to obtain information from the police or from the fishing supervisory organisation in the place where they wish to stay, or from the cantonal fishing administration before their holiday begins.

A brochure giving details of the most important fishing areas and the place from which fishing permits are available in the various cantons can be obtained from the Swiss Tourist Bureaux (see Information).

Ballooning
On May 5th 1788 Jean-Pierre Blanchard made the first ascent in a balloon in the history of Swiss air travel only five years after the Montgolfier brothers. Today ballooning is not only a popular sport but is also a pleasurable pastime and holiday activity. Further information can be obtained from the Aeroclub der Schweiz in Lucerne (see flying below).

Mountaineering
See entry

Boat rental
See Water sports

Flying
Information about all kinds of flying is obtainable from the:

Aeroclub der Schweiz
Lidostrasse 5, CH-6006 Luzern
Tel. (041) 31 21 21

Special departments for gliding and parachuting.

The club also gives information about circular flights in Switzerland, the Alps, towns and other trips in aircraft. A leaflet about the most important aerosports and also details of schools for motor-boaters and parachutists and about organisations offering circular flights can be obtained from the Swiss Travel Bureaux (see Information).

Hang gliding and parasailing (for example in Engelberg) are becoming increasingly popular. Information from the:

Schweizerische Hängegleiterverband (SHV)
Postfach, CH-8620 Wetzikon
Tel. (01) 9 32 43 53

Golf
At present Switzerland has more than 40 golf courses and others are in course of construction or planned. Some of the golf clubs are near the

Swiss border, even on French or German territory. Details concerning registration formalities (proof of handicap, fees, etc.) can be obtained from the various golf clubs under the telephone numbers given. Information can also be obtained from the Swiss Travel Bureaux (see Information) and the Swiss Golf Union (ASG).

Association Suisse de Golf (ASG)
Place de la Croix-Blanche 19
CH-1066 Epalinges-Lausanne
Tel. (021) 7 84 35 31

The Swiss golf card "Golf in der Schweiz" can be obtained from the above address on payment.

Arosa Golf Club   **Arosa**
CH-7050 Arosa; tel. (081) 31 22 15
Alt. 1850m/6072ft: 9 holes

Patriziale Ascona Golf Club   **Ascona**
CH-6612 Ascona, Via al Lido 81; tel. (093) 35 21 32
Alt. 200m/656ft; 18 holes

Bad Ragaz Golf Club   **Bad Ragaz**
CH-7310 Bad Ragaz, Hans-Albrecht-Strasse; tel. (091) 3 03 37 17
Alt. 520m/1707ft; 18 holes

Basle Golf & Country Club (on French territory)   **Basle**
F-68220 Hagenthal-le-Bas; tel. (from Switzerland: 0033) 89 68 12 06
Alt. 368m/1208ft; 18 holes

Blumisberg Golf & Country Club   **Blumisberg**
CH-3184 Wünnewil; tel. (037) 36 34 38
Alt. 605m/1986ft; 18 holes

Club de Bonmont   **Bonmont**
CH-1261 Chéserex; tel. (022) 3 69 24 17
Alt. 590m/1936ft; 18 holes

Golf et County Club de Bossey (on French territory)   **Bossey**
F-74160 Bossey; tel. (from Switzerland: 0033) 50 43 75 25
Alt. 500m/1641ft; 18 holes

Breitenloo Golf Club (near Basserdorf)   **Breitenloo/**
Unter Zäune 9, CH-8001 Zurich; tel. (01) 2 61 99 02   **Zurich**
Alt. 560m/1838ft; 18 holes

Bürgenstock Golf Club   **Bürgenstock**
CH-6363 Bürgenstock; tel. (041) 61 24 34
Alt. 900m/2954ft; 9 holes

Case Postale 296, CH-3963 Crans-sur-Sierre; tel. (027) 41 21 68   **Crans-sur-Sierre**
Alt. 1500m/4923ft; 18 and 9 holes   **Golf Club**

Davos Golf Club   **Davos**
Postfach, CH-7260 Davos-Dorf; tel. (081) 46 56 34
Alt. 1560m/5120ft; 18 holes

Eastern Switzerland Golf Club   **Eastern**
CH-9246 Niederbüren; tel. (071) 81 18 58   **Switzerland**
Alt. 497m/1631ft; 18 holes   **Golf Club**

Sport

Echenevex
near Geneva
Maison Blanche (in French territory)
F-01170 Echenevex; tel. (from Switzerland: 0033) 50 42 44 42
Alt. 550m/1805ft; 18 and 9 holes

Engadine
Engadine Golf Club/Samedan Golf Club/St Moritz
CH-7503 Samedan; tel. (082) 6 52 26
Alt. 1738m/5704ft; 18 holes

Erlen
Erlen Golf & Country Club
Schlossgut Eppishausen, CH-8586 Erlen; tel. (072) 48 29 30
Alt. 450m/1477ft; 18 holes

Esery
D'Esery Golf Club (in French territory)
F-74930 Reignier; tel. (from Switzerland: 0033) 50 36 58 70

Geneva
Golf Club Genève
Route de la Capite 70
CH-1223 Cologny; tel. (022) 7 35 75 40
Alt. 400m/1313ft; 18 holes

Gland
Golf Club du Domaine Impérial
CH-1196 Gland; tel. (022) 3 64 45 45
Alt. 385m/1264ft; 18 holes

Hittnau-Zurich
Hittnau-Zurich Golf & Country Club
CH-8335 Hittnau-Zurich; tel. (01) 9 50 24 42
Alt. 800m/2626ft; 18 holes

Interlaken-
Untersee
Interlaken-Untersee Golf Club
Postfach 110, CH-3800 Interlaken; tel. (036) 22 60 22
Alt. 556m/1825ft; 18 holes

Lake Constance
Weissensberg
Golf Club
Bodensee Golf Club, Weissenberg (on German territory)
D-88138 Weissenberg; tel. (from Germany: 083 89) 8 91 90; from Swit-
zerland: 0049/83 89) 8 91 90
Alt. 500m/1641ft; 18 holes

La Largue
Golf de la Largue (in French territory)
Chemin de Largweg, F-68580 Mooslargue; tel. (from Switzerland: 0033)
89 25 71 11

Lausanne
Lausanne Golf Club
Route du Golf 3, CH-1000 Lausanne 25; tel. (021) 7 84 13 15
Alt. 853m/2800ft; 18 holes

Lenzerheide-
Valbella
Lenzerheide Golf Club
Postfach, CH-7078 Lenzerheide; tel. (081) 34 13 16
Alt. 1400m/4595ft; 18 holes

Lucerne
Lucerne Golf Club,
CH-6006 Dietschiberg-Lucerne; tel. (041) 36 97 87
Alt. 670m/2199ft; 18 holes

Lugano
Lugano Golf Club
CH-6983 Magliaso; tel. (091) 71 15 57 or 71 58 01
Alt. 290m/952ft; 18 holes

Mittelland
Golf Club
Mittelland Golf Club
CH-5036 Oberentfelden; tel. (064) 43 89 84 or 43 84 36

Montreux
Golf Club de Montreux
Route d'Evian 54, CH-1860 Aigle; tel. (025) 26 46 16
Alt. 395m/1296ft; 18 holes

Golf Club de Neuchâtel Voëns
CH-2072 Saint-Blaise; tel. (038) 33 55 50
Alt. 580m/1904ft; 18 holes

Obere Alp Golf Club (in German territory) **Obere Alp**
D-79780 Stühlingen; tel. (from Switzerland: 0049–7703) 71 02; from Germany: 07703) 71 02
Alt. 780m/2560ft; 9 and 18 holes

Golf Club de Pont-la-Ville **Pont-la-Ville**
CH-1649 Pont-la-Ville; tel. (037) 33 91 11
Alt. 730m/2396ft; 9 holes

Rheinblick Golf Club (in German territory) **Rheinblick**
Club address: Postfach CH-8455 Rüdlingen; tel. (073) 51 67 67 **Golf Club**
Situation: D-7891 Nack-Lottstetten; 18 holes

Riederalp Golf Club **Riederalp**
CH-3987 Riederalp; tel. (028) 27 29 32
Alt. 1950m/6400ft; 9 holes

Schinznach Bad Golf Club **Schinznach Bad**
CH-5116 Schinznach Bad; tel. (056) 43 12 26
Alt. 350m/1149ft; 9 holes

Schönenberg Golf & Country Club **Schönenberg**
CH-8824 Schönenberg; tel. (01) 7 88 16 24
Alt. 680m/2232ft; 18 holes

Golf Club de Sierre **Sierre**
CH-3962 Montana; tel. (027) 41 82 25
Alt. 540m/1772ft; 9 holes

Golf Club de Verbier **Verbier**
CH-1936 Verbier; tel. (026) 35 21 41
Alt. 1500m/4923; 18 holes

Villars Golf Club **Villars**
CH-1884 Villars; tel. (025) 35 42 14
Alt. 1600m/5251ft; 18 holes

Vulpera Golf Club **Vulpera**
CH-7552 Vulpera; tel. (081) 8 64 96 88; 9 holes

Wallenried Golf & Country Club **Wallenried**
CH-1784 Wallenried; tel. (037) 34 36 06
Alt. 545m/1789ft; 18 holes

Zurich Golf & Country Club **Zurich**
CH-8126 Zumikon; tel. (01) 9 18 00 50
Alt. 685m/2248ft; 18 holes

Dolder Golf Club
Kurhausstrasse 66, CH-8032 Zurich; tel. (01) 2 61 50 45; 9 holes

There are at present more than 80 mini golf courses in Switzerland.

Bicycles, whether private or rented can be carried by the railways and   Cycling
imported into Switzerland without any difficulty. Four types of bicycles can
be rented at about 200 stations of the Swiss Federal Railways (SBB-CFF-FFS) and a number of private railways:

Sport

Basic bicycles (Normal bicycles; with a child's seat provided free).
Children's bicycles
Mountain-bicycles
Tandems

Bicycles which are hired for a whole day or even by the week can normally be handed back at any station; however if you hire bicycles and tandems for only half a day then they must be returned to the station from which they were obtained. It is advisable to reserve a bicycle by telephone or personally at the appropriate SBB station, at the latest the evening before it is required.

In numerous places there are specially marked bicycle or mountain-bicycle tracks. The length of the total marked cycle network in Switzerland is over 5000km/1070 miles. Seven day individual cycle tours, for example from "Berne to Lucerne", "High Points of Central Switzerland" or "Around Lake Constance" with a special service for conveying luggage are ideal for those who would like to book an active cycling holiday. Information can be obtained from local travel offices, and an information leaflet about the most important cycle paths can be obtained from Swiss Travel Bureaux (see Information).

Riding

In Switzerland there are more than 100 riding centres where horses for riding either in the open-air or in covered riding schools can be rented. The riding centre of Haslital in the Bernese Oberland has offered riding holidays for more than 20 years; a week spent trekking on horseback is also very popular.

Information:
Pferdestall Wechselacher
Ejeltiweg 16, CH-3860 Meiringen
Tel. (077) 41 05 61

The Blatten-Belalp Tourist Union offers on weekends in summer three-day trekking on a mule in the Aletsch glacier region. The route is Natters–Blatten–Belalp–the Great Aletsch Glacier and Riederalp.

Information:
Verkehrsbüro
CH-3914 Blatten-Belalp
Tel. (028) 23 13 85

In many places there are riding courses for children; for example beginners can learn to ride in Einsiedeln. Riding holidays can also be combined with language courses.

The brochure "Reitferien in der Schweiz" can be obtained at Swiss Travel Bureaux (see Information). It is produced in association between the Swiss Tourist Office (SVZ) and the Swiss Horse Magazine.

Another attraction is a holiday in a horse-drawn wagon, for example through the Valais

Les Roulottes du Bonheur
CH-1349 Eclépens (19km/12 miles north of Lausanne)
Tel. (021) 8 66 77 50

Tennis and Squash

Tennis enthusiasts will find in Switzerland more than 700 tennis courts and more than 200 covered courts at their disposal; there are squash courts in many places.

Silvaplaner Lake   *Lake Geneva*

The brochure "Tennis Squash Guide Indoor and Tennis Holidays" as well as the information leaflet "Tennishallen in der Schweiz" (covered courts in Switzerland) can be ordered from Swiss Travel Bureaux.

See entry   Walking

There are over 1400 lakes and large rivers, including the Rhine, Rhône, Inn,   Water Sports
Ticino, Aare, Reuss and Limmat, which have excellent facilities for watersports enthusiasts.

Rowers and canoeists (even with collapsible canoes) can carry on their sport in most lakes and rivers. The finest water for rowing in the world is considered to be the Rot See (Red Lake) near Lucerne where international competitions take place every year.

Extended trips in canoes can be made for example on the Rhine, the Aare and the Reuss; canoeists are particularly fond of the Birs in the Jura and the Muota (Canton of Schwyz). Kayak trips can be made on the Inn, the Rhine, Reuss, Doubs, Broye, Venoge, Versoix, Ticino, Moesa and on Lake Lucerne. "River Rafting" (wild water canoeing) is possible on the Inn, Rhine, Simme, Saane, Aare and Rhône.

Visitors can swim from more than 170 bathing beaches on lakes and rivers, in more than 200 covered and public swimming pools, in over 380 open-air pools and in over 200 pools belonging to hotels.

Good wind conditions for sailors and wind surfers can often be found on lakes surrounded by mountains (Lake Geneva, Lac de Neuchâtel, Lac de Bienne, Lac de Morat, Lake Thun, Lago Maggiore, Lake Lucerne, Lake Uri, the Walensee, Lake Zurich and Lake Constance). Over 60 sailing and 100 wind surfing schools and 30 water-skiing schools provide instruction in these various forms of sport. Information and a list of schools can be obtained from the Swiss Tourist Office or from Swiss Travel Bureaux (see

Water Sports and Boating in Switzerland

Information) where the leaflet "Schweizer Wasserstimmen heiter" with notes for boat hire is to be obtained.

Water Sport Districts | See map above

Water Sports and Inland Boat Services

Boat Excursions: see entry

Regions for Water Sports

1 Lac de Joux (Alt. 900m/2953ft)
Sailing, wind-surfing, fishing

2. Lake Geneva/Lac Léman (Alt. 372m/1221ft)
Regular boat services between many places on the lake. Rental of sailing-boats and rowing-boats; water-skiing, fishing, sailing, wind-surfing and water-skiing lessons.

3. Lac de Neuchâtel/Neuenberger See (Alt. 432m/1417ft)
Regular boat services between many places on the lake. Rental of sailing-boats and rowing-boats; water-skiing, fishing. Sailing, wind-surfing and canoeing lessons.

4. Lac de Morat/Murtensee (Alt. 433m/1420ft)
Rental of sailing-boats and rowing-boats, wind-surfing, angling. Sailing and wind-surfing lessons.

5. Lac de Bienne/Bieler See (Alt. 432m/1417ft)
Regular boat services between many places on the shores. Rental of sailing-boats and rowing-boats; water-skiing, fishing. Sailing and wind-surfing lessons.

6. Lake Thun (Thuner See) (Alt. 560m/1837ft)
Regular boat sevices between many places on the lake. Rental of sailboats and rowboats; water-skiing, wind-surfing, fishing. Sailing and wind-surfing lessons.

7. Lake Brienz/Brienzer See (Alt. 567m/1860ft)
Regular boat services between many places on the lake. Rental of sailing-boats and rowing-boats; water-skiing, wind-surfing and fishing. Fishing lessons.

8. Sarner See (Alt. 473m/1552ft)
Regular boat services between most places on the lake. Rental of sailing-boats and rowing-boats; fishing, wind-surfing. Sailing and wind-surfing lessons.

9. Lake Lucerne/Vierwaldstätter See (Alt. 437m/1434ft)
Regular boat services between many places on the lake. Rental of sailing-boats and rowing-boats; wind-surfing. Sailing lessons.

10. Lake Uri/Urner See (Alt. 437m/1434ft)
Regular boat services between many places on the lake. Rental of sailing-boats and rowing-boats; wind-surfing.

11. Lake Zug/Zuger See (Alt. 437m/1434ft)
Regular boat services between Zug and Arth. Rental of sailing-boats and rowing-boats; wind-surfing.

12. Lake Zurich/Zürichsee (Alt. 410m/1345ft)
Regular boat services between many places on the lake. Rental of sailing-boats and rowing-boats; wind-surfing. Sailing and wind-surfing lessons.

13. Walensee (Alt. 423m/1388ft)
Regular boat services between Weesen and Walenstadt. Rental of sailing-boats and rowing-boats; fishing. Sailing and fishing lessons.

14. Lake Constance/Bodensee (Alt. 395m/1296ft)
Regular boat services between many places on the lake. Rental of sailing-boats and rowing-boats; wind-surfing and fishing. Sailing, wind-surfing and fishing lessons.

15. Heidsee (Alt. 1493m/4899ft)
Rental of sailing-boats; wind-surfing, fishing. Sailing, wind-surfing and fishing lessons.

16. St Moritzer See (Alt. 1771m/5811ft)
Rental of sailing-boats; wind-surfing, canoeing. Sailing, wind-surfing and fishing lessons.

17. Silser See and Silvaner See (Alt. 1795m/5889ft)
Regular boat services between certain places on the lake. Sailing, wind-surfing. Wind-surfing lessons.

18. Lake Maggiore/Lago Maggiore (Alt. 194m/637ft)
Regular boat services between many places on the lake.

19. Lake Lugano/Lago di Lugano (Alt. 274m/899ft)
Regular boat services between many places on the lake. Rental of sailing-boats and rowing-boats; wind-surfing, water-skiing. Sailing, wind-surfing and water-skiing lessons.

Tourists can bring their motor- or sailing-boats, provided they are registered in the country from which they come and are re-exported at the latest three months after their arrival, without particular customs formalities; there are no tolls for the boats. Kayaks, canoes, dinghies and surfboards are considered as tourist luggage and technically are not subject to duty.

The driver of a motor boat must be at least 14 years old. A foreign driving permit is required (it suffices for a temporary stay in Switzerland), when the motor of the boat exceeds 6kW or the sail area is more than 15sq.m. For both a compulsory insurance is required. The permit for a boat, which can be obtained from any cantonal authority, is valid for one month on all Swiss waters.

Sport

Winter sports areas	Altitude (m)	Max. altitude (m)	No. of cableway stations	Cross-country ski-runs (km)		Altitude (m)	Max. altitude (m)	No. of cableway stations	Cross-country ski-runs (km)
Acquarossa (TI)	538	2300	8	40	Disentis/Mustér (GR)	1150	3000	9	31
Adelboden (BE)	356	2350	29	40	Ebnat-Kappel (SG)	630	1300	5	13
Aeschi bei Spitz (BE)	859	1400	2	20	Einsiedeln (SZ)	900	1113	7	76
Airolo (T)	1442	2090	4	18	Eischoll (VS)	1230	2200	4	20
Alt St Johann (SG)	894	1620	5	40	Elm (GL)	962	2105	7	20
Amden (SG)	950	1700	5	10	Emmetten (NW)	762	1938	4	3
Andermatt (UR)	1436	2963	10	20	Engelberg (OW)	1000	3020	24	35
Anzère (VS)	1500	2462	12	15	Eriz (BE)	1005	1400	2	10
Appenzell (AI)	785	922	1	108	Ernen/Mühlebach (VS)	1196	2285	5	12
Arolla (VS)	2003	2889	5	18	Evolène (VS)	1378	2700	8	15
Arosa (GR)	1739	2653	16	25	Falera (GR)	1218	3018	32	60
Avers/Cresta (GR)	1963	2600	3	14	Fiesch (VS)	1062	2869	11	93
Axalp ob Brienz (BE)	1540	1960	3	5	Fleurier et Val-de-Travers (NE)	742	1450	–	120
Bad Ragaz (SG)	502	2222	5	27	Flims Waldhaus (GR)	1103	3018	13	60
Bad Tarasp-Vulpera (GR)	1268	2800	2	14	Flond/Surcuolm (GR)	1081	2280	18	30
Beatenberg (BE)	1121	1950	6	20	Flumserberg (SG)	1390	2222	18	20
Beckenried/Klewenalp (NW)	435	1937	8	–	Frutigen (BE)	779	2100	5	16
Bellwald (VS)	1600	2500	7	85	Giswil/Mörlialp (OW)	485	1850	5	4
Bergün (GR)	1373	2600	5	15	Grächen (VS)	1617	2920	11	16
Bettmeralp (VS)	1950	2709	14	10	Grimentz (VS)	1570	3000	11	22
Bever (GR)	1710	–	–	150	Grindelwald (BE)	1034	2468	30	35
Bivio (GR)	1769	2560	3	8	Grüsch (GR)	630	1800	5	11
Bourg-St-Pierre/St Bern. (VS)	1634	2800	3	25	Gstaad-Saanenland (BE)	1000	3000	–	140
Braunwald (GL)	1256	1900	8	8	Gyron (VD)	1131	2120	45	58
Breil/Brigel (GR)	1289	2400	10	25	Habkern (BE)	1067	1500	2	–
Briez (BE)	566	1960	5	15	Hasilberg (BE)	1230	2433	15	42
Brig/Simplon (VS)	684	2600	5	4	Haute-Nendaz (VS)	1255	3330	39	25
Bürchen (VS)	1500	2550	8	25	Hoch-Ybrig (SZ)	1048	1850	10	30
Celerina (GR)	1730	3030	9	150	Interlaken (BE)	567	–	2	12
Cernier et Val-de-Ruz (NE)	822	1435	–	66	Jaun (FR)	1020	1600	4	25
Châble, Le/Bruson (VS)	820	2220	7	30	Kandersteg (BE)	1176	2000	7	75
Champèry (VS)	1049	2300	13	7	Kiental (BE)	962	1411	4	6
Champex-Lac (VS)	1472	2200	4	30	Klosters (GR)	1191	2844	32	40
Chandolin (VS)	1936	2715	15	15	Laax (GR)	1023	2976	33	60
Charmey (FR)	89	1630	8	29	Lagnau i. E. and Emmental (BE)	673	1360	–	70
Château-d'Oex (VD)	968	1700	14	28	Lauterbrunnen (BE)	797	2971	–	17
Chaux-de-Fonds, La (NE)	994	1234	2	210	Lenk i. S. (BE)	1068	2098	17	42
Chur (GR)	595	2174	5	5	Lenzerheide-Valbella (GR)	1476	2865	38	50
Churwalden (GR)	1230	2865	11	50	Leukerbad (VS)	1411	2700	17	23
Collons, Les/Thyon (VS)	1802	2413	27	3	Leysin (VD)	1268	2300	2	39
Crans-Montana (VS)	1484	1500	40	52	Liddes et Val d'Entremont (VS)	1338	2200	2	20
Davos (GR)	1560	2844	39	75	Locarno/Cardada (TI)	205	1700	8	20
Diablerets, Les (VD)	1155	3000	38	60	Lungern/Schönbüel (OW)	752	2100	7	6

Winter sports areas	Altitude (m)	Max. altitude (m)	No. of cableway stations	Cross-country ski-runs (km)		Altitude (m)	Max. altitude (m)	No. of cableway stations	Cross-country ski-runs (km)
Malbun-Steg (FL)	1606	2000	7	19	Scuol (GR)	1244	2800	16	60
Maloja (GR)	1815	2159	1	150	Sedrun (GR)	1441	3000	13	60
Marbach (LU)	874	1500	4	32	Sentier, Le, et Vallée de Joux (VD)	1024	1476	–	140
Marécottes, Les/Salvan (VS)	1100	2300	5	20	Sigriswil (BE)	800	1400	2	18
Mayens-de-Riddes (VS)	1500	2354	12	4	Sils/Segl Maria (GR)	1815	3303	7	150
Meiringen/Haslital (BE)	595	2245	–	40	Silvaplana (GR)	1816	3303	9	150
Melchsee-Frutt (OW)	1920	2255	7	16	Sörenberg (LU)	1166	2350	19	27
Moléson-sur-Gruyères (FR)	1110	2002	6	2	Splügen/Rheinwald (GR)	1450	2215	8	40
Montreux (VD)	395	2000	8	12	St Moritz (GR)	1856	3030	24	150
Mörel-Breiten (VS)	759	2300	4	10	St Stephan (BE)	993	1989	4	48
Morgins (VS)	1320	2277	23	20	St-Imier et Vallon St-Imier (BE)	793	1460	4	80
Mosses, Les	1448	1900	12	60	St-Cerque (VD)	1047	1680	20	90
Moutier et environs (BE)	529	1250	–	15	St-Croix/Les Rasses (VD)	1066	1580	8	80
Münster (Obergoms) (VS)	1359	2180	1	85	St-Luc (VS)	1650	2580	15	15
Mürren (BE)	1650	2970	11	14	Stoos (SZ)	1256	2000	9	10
Müstair/Val Müstair (GR)	1248	2519	–	40	Tesserete e Valli di Lugano (TI)	517	1620	–	15
Naters/Blatten/Belalp (VS)	1322	3100	9	5	Torgon (VS)	1095	2000	9	6
Neuchâtel et environs (NE)	479	1087	2	30	Tramalan et environs (BE)	888	1220	2	35
Oberiberg (SZ)	1126	1856	5	30	Tschiertschen (GR)	1351	2400	4	6
Obersaxen (GR)	1281	2310	9	30	Ulrichen/Oberwald (VS)	1347	2080	8	80
Oey/Diemligtal (BE)	820	1850	17	36	Unterbäch (VS)	1228	2550	7	25
Ovronnaz (VS)	1350	2080	11	18	Unteriberg (SZ)	931	1856	–	30
Paccots, Les (FR)	1065	1300	9	13	Unterwasser (SG)	910	2262	6	40
Parpan (GR)	1511	2865	38	50	Urmein/Oberheinzerberg (GR)	1253	2183	3	14
Pontresina (GR)	1800	2978	11	150	Val d'Illiez (VS)	946	2300	16	–
Riederalp (VS)	1930	2335	11	6	Vals (GR)	1252	2500	4	5
Rigi-Kaltbad (LU)	1423	1800	9	14	Vella/Val Lumnezia (GR)	1244	2170	18	16
Roche, La/Berra (FR)	1750	1650	5	8	Verbier (VS)	1406	3330	99	40
Rougemont (VD)	992	2156	4	28	Vercorin (VS)	1341	2374	9	7
Saas Almagell (VS)	1672	3100	6	34	Vevey (VD)	396	1200	6	22
Saas Fee (VS)	1800	3600	26	26	Veysonnaz (VS)	1235	3300	27	10
Saas Grund (VS)	1560	3100	6	34	Villars-sur-Ollon (VD)	1253	2217	38	58
Saignelégier/Fr.-Montagnes (JU)	978	1260	–	75	Waltensburg/Andiast (GR)	1000	2400	7	4
Samedan (GR)	1720	2276	5	150	Wangs/Pizol (SG)	1275	2440	22	17
Samnaun (GR)	1846	2872	14	8	Wengen (BE)	1275	2440	22	17
San Bernardino-Villagio (GR)	1607	2525	8	18	Wilderswil (BE)	584	–	2	12
Samen/Langis (OW)	473	1500	1	30	Wildhaus (SG)	1098	2076	9	40
Sarn-/Heinzerberg (GR)	1150	2100	2	14	Wiler (Lötschental) (VS)	1421	2700	5	30
Savognin (GR)	1210	2700	17	40	Zermatt (VS)	1620	3820	–	22
Schwanden ob Sigriswil (BE)	1025	1500	3	12	Zernez (GR)	1471	–	–	150
Schwarzenburg/Gantrisch (BE)	792	1500	–	40	Zinal (VS)	1671	2900	9	12
Schwarzsee (FR)	1050	1750	10	10	Zuoz (GR)	1750	1750	4	150
Schwyz/Mythen region (SZ)	516	1570	14	45	Zweisimmen (BE)	1000	2000	5	80

Winter-sports enthusiasts in the Alps

Smaller lakes such as the Greifensee, Pfäffikersee, the Aargau lakes and the lakes of Grisson are not available for sailing boats.

Boats, etc., below 2.5m/8ft in length which are not subject to a permit can only be used in an area of 150m/164yd from a shore (exceptions are racing shells and surfboards). On all Swiss lakes there is a speed limit of 10km/6 miles per hour within an area 300m/328yd from the shore.

Winter Sports Switzerland is a paradise for winter sports with especially attractive skiing areas; these include the Jungfrau region with its mountain areas and the mighty Aletsch Glacier, the Engadine, where St Moritz is the best-known winter-sports resort in the world, and Zermatt, with the impressive rock pyramid of the Matterhorn in its unique valley.

Hundreds of prepared and marked pistes at heights between 1000m/3200ft and 3200m/10,500ft (Little Matterhorn) are at the disposal of skiers. For ascents there are more than 1600 ski-lifts, rack-railways, funiculars and cableways with an hourly capacity of 1.2 million persons.

About 4000 ski instructors, both male and female, give lessons in more than 200 Alpine skiing schools; and in addition there are more than 160 schools for cross-country skiing. There is a great deal of advertising material, for example a general survey ("Schweiz – (w)international") with details of tracks, activities, sports schools, as well as facilities for sport, entertainment and accommodation. Various information leaflets, such as "Snowboard" (including the snowboard camp in Wildhaus) and monoski; details of organisers of ski safaris, (white weeks, as in Villars), deep snow weeks, Langlauf weeks for pensioners (for example in Stalden), ice and "Schlittelplausch" for holiday makers, as well as ski kindergartens. Details can be obtained from any Swiss Travel Bureaux.

Various high-lying ski territories can guarantee snow throughout the year so that they can be used throughout summer.

Telephone and Telegraph

Telephone calls to places abroad can be made from public telephone boxes. First 00 must be dialled, then there will be a shrill whistle. To make a call to Great Britain dial 44 followed by the number without the first 0 of the area code; for Canada and America dial 1 followed by the number excluding the area code.

Telephone

From the United Kingdom to Switzerland and Liechtenstein dial 00 41 followed by the number required less the 0 in the code.

From the United States and Canada to Switzerland and Liechtenstein 011 41, etc.

Inland 111
International 191

Telephone
Information

See Information

Telephone
Service

Time

Switzerland and the principality of Liechtenstein observe Central European Time: i.e. one hour ahead of Greenwich Mean Time (six hours ahead of New York time). Swiss Summer Time, first introduced in 1981, is one hour ahead of Central European Time (two hours ahead of GMT, seven hours ahead of New York time).

Travel Documents

A valid passport is required. No visa is needed by holiday and business visitors from the United Kingdom (British subjects and British protected persons), Ireland, Commonwealth countries, the United States and many other countries.

Personal Papers

Visitors can take a private car, motor cycle or motor scooter into Switzerland for a temporary stay without customs documents, provided a valid national driving licence can be produced. An international insurance certificate ("green card") should be obtained from the vehicle's normal insurers: visitors from the United Kingdom and Ireland, as members of the EU, are not required to produce a green card, but since their own insurance covers only the minimum legal requirements it is very desirable to have the extra protection which the green card affords. Foreign cars must display an oval international distinguishing sign of the approved type and design. Failure to comply with this regulation is punishable by a heavy on-the-spot fine.

Vehicle
documents

Pets (dogs, cats) can be taken to Switzerland and Liechtenstein provided they have a rabies inoculation certificate from a veterinary surgeon. The inoculation must not have been shorter than 30 days and not longer than a year before the animal is imported. Of course, visitors from the United Kingdom would be foolish to take an animal with them since the animal would have to spend six months in quarantine on their return.

Pets

Walking

Switzerland is a veritable paradise for anyone who likes walking. There are approximately 50,000km/31,000 miles of marked footpaths and many other

General

tracks which can be explored individually. Destinations and the time taken to reach them are displayed on yellow signposts, not only for long walks but also for shorter ones. Suitable maps for walkers are available from the "Bundesamt für Landestopographie" on a scale of 1:25,000. Visitors who are particularly interested in flora and fauna will find beautiful walks through unspoilt countryside and protected areas, and there are many opportunities for guided walks. Food can be obtained either at simple kiosks or at country inns or mountain restaurants (see mountaineering). More than 160 huts and bivouacs of the Swiss Alpine Club (SAC; see Mountaineering) provide shelter and accommodation for those on mountain walks. Among the very many impressive upland walks are those through the sunny Ticino heights, across the Bergel, Prättigal or Schächental mountain paths, through the parched Saas Valley, the karst area of Leysin, or the Kiental with its abundant water. There are also classic paths across the Rigi, the Simplon or a walk at altitude over the Hörnli. Information brochures can be obtained from the Swiss Tourist Offices (see Information).

Hiking Passes Hiking passes, such as the Reka Pass of the Schweizer Reisekasse (Neuengasse 15, CH-3001 Berne, tel. (031) 22 66 33), include free trips on public transport and mountain railways as well as accommodation and breakfast in a hotel of your own choice.

Mountaineering See entry.

When to go

The best time to visit the pre-Alpine regions is from mid-May to the beginning of July; the best season for the mountains is during July, August and the first half of September, when all the passes are open. The summer resorts usually have a season beginning in May and ending about the end of September. The lakes in the south attract their greatest numbers of visitors in spring and autumn. Those who go to Switzerland in May can enjoy the contrast between the spring blossoms in the warmer pre-Alpine valleys and the wintry conditions still prevailing in the mountains. The winter-sports regions are at their busiest from the end of January to March; the season extends from December to the beginning or end of April, depending on altitude.

Climate See Facts and Figures.

Youth Hostels

Switzerland has some 120 youth hostels (German: Jungendherberge, French: Auberge de Jeunesse, Italian: alloggio per giovani) providing modestly priced accommodation, particularly for young people (with priority for those under 25). During the main holiday season it is advisable to book in advance; the maximum period of stay permitted in any one hostel will vary according to the demand for places. Youth hostellers must produce a membership card issued by their national youth hostel association.

Information Schweizerische Bund für Jugendherbergen
Postfach 265, Engestrasse 9
CH-3001 Berne. Tel. (031) 24 55 03

Zoos and Alpine Gardens

See Caves open to the public

Index

Index

Index

The Principal Sights at a Glance

Imprint

375 colour photographs, 33 town plans, 24 drawings, 22 general plans, 28 ground plans, 1 large map

Text: Dr Madeleine Reincke, Prof. Dr Wolfgang Hassenpflug, Hans Rathgeb, Christine Wessely, Vera Beck

Editorial work: Baedeker-Redaktion (Madeleine Cabos)

General management: Dr Peter Baumgarten, Baedeker Stuttgart

Cartography: Gert Oberländer, Munich; Christoph Gallus, Lahr; Hallwag AG, Bern (map of Lichtenstein); Mairs Geographischer Verlag, Ostfildern-Kemnat (large road map)

Source of illustrations: Anthony Verlag (3), Baedeker-Archiv (16), Baumgarten (5), Bodan AG (1), CERN (1), Fetzer (1), Swiss Tourist Boards (14), Globetrotter (1), HB-Verlags und Vertriebsgesellschaft mbH, Hamburg (8), Historia (9), Kröner (1), Lade Fotoagentur (4), Linde (2), de Morsier (1), Reetz (1), Reinke (231), Säntis Luftseilbahn Schwägalp (1), Sawade (1), Schliebitz/Schleicher (13), Schüster Bildagentur (3), Schweizerische Verkehrszentrale (52), Schweizerische Käseunion (1), Stetter (1), Storto (11), Ullstein (1)

Original English Translation: James Hogarth
Revised text: David Cocking, Julie Waller
Editorial work: Margaret Court

2nd English edition

© Baedeker Stuttgart
Original German edition